Policy Economics

A Textbook of Applied Economics on Developing Countries

Tony Killick

Overseas Development Institute, London

HEINEMANN
LONDON
NAIROBI · IBADAN

Heinemann Educational Books Ltd
22 Bedford Square, London WC1B 3HH
PMB 5205 Ibadan · PO Box 45314 Nairobi

EDINBURGH MELBOURNE AUCKLAND
HONG KONG SINGAPORE KUALA LUMPUR
NEW DELHI KINGSTON PORT OF SPAIN

Heinemann Educational Books Inc
4 Front Street, Exeter, New Hampshire, 03833, USA

To Inge

British Library Cataloguing in Publication Data

Killick, Tony
    Policy economics.
    1. Underdeveloped areas – Economic policy
    I. Title
    330.9'172'4   HC59.7

    ISBN 0–435–97373–8

Filmset in Great Britain by Willmer Brothers Limited, Birkenhead, Merseyside
Printed and bound by Spottiswoode Ballantyne, Colchester, Essex

Contents

PART 1: GENERAL PRINCIPLES

PART 2: POLICY APPLICATIONS

Preface

Development economics is coming of age. Although the subject has in the past been treated as a sub-discipline within economics, there is growing recognition that concern with development should permeate all teaching of economics in developing countries. There is hence beginning to emerge a body of literature, written for student use, which seeks to meet this need. There are now introductory texts written especially for students in developing countries, as well as books on public finance, econometric techniques, money and banking, and other subjects.

Many gaps remain, however. There is at present no textbook-type treatment of the principles of economic policy applied to developing countries, which goes beyond a purely introductory level. Various books have been written about development planning but these are strongly biased towards the exposition of techniques, to the neglect of substantive policy issues. Of course, there is a vast theoretical and empirical literature on the policy problems of developing countries but this is diffused and much of it is too specialized for student use.

This book is intended to meet the need for a textbook treatment of applied economics related to the problems of developing countries. It consists of three introductory chapters on the general principles of economic policy and planning, with the remaining eight chapters devoted to a carefully chosen selection of some key policy problems common to most developing countries. No attempt is made at a comprehensive coverage of the full range of policy issues because the number of problems is so great that a single book could offer only a superficial treatment.

I have chosen instead to attempt an in-depth examination of a more restricted range of issues, while also indicating general principles and approaches which could be applied to other problems. The specific policy issues covered in Chapters 4 to 11 have been selected by the criteria (1) that they are important and interesting; (2) that they are controversial, in the sense that there are disagreements about their diagnosis and solution; (3) that they require the analytical application of modern economic theory; and (4) that, taken together, they provide a reasonable balance between macro-economic and micro-economic issues.

A word about the general approach common to the whole book. First, it rejects a narrowly 'economic' approach. I have tried to go back to the merits of what used to be called 'political economy', in that all the problems are considered within a social and political context. I have tried throughout to be realistic about what can be expected of governments and to pay attention to the political feasibility of economic solutions. Chapters 1 and 2 are of particular importance in this context, laying a foundation for a realistic understanding of the nature of governments as economic agents upon which the rest of the book is built.

Secondly, I have rejected the fiction common in so much of the literature on developing countries that economic growth is the predominant goal of state policy. Short-term economic stability is another objective, badly neglected in the development literature, and I have tried to rectify this imbalance, especially in Chapters 7 and 8. Greater social justice and economic independence are other government objectives that receive attention here (see especially Chapters 5 and 6).

Thirdly, the discussion of alternative policy solutions has been based on the premise that most developing countries are mixed economies, neither purely capitalist nor purely socialist, and wish to remain so. In other words, most of the policies analysed are reformist rather than revolutionary, although Chapter 6 includes an explicit discussion of the merits of revolutionary solutions.

On the use of this book

The primary group for which this book is designed is second- and third-year undergraduates in developing countries who have already completed a basic introductory course in economic theory. It is also intended for other important categories of users:

(1) graduate students whose first degree gave them only limited exposure to applied and development economics;
(2) undergraduate and graduate students undertaking courses in development economics in industrial countries;
(3) practising economists working in the public sector and elsewhere who wish to bring themselves up to date, or obtain greater depth of understanding on specific issues.

The level of knowledge presupposed is that conveyed by standard introductory theory texts, such as the well-known works by Samuelson and Lipsey.

In addition to suggestions at the end of each chapter of questions for review work and class discussions, and of further readings, I have inserted 'boxes' in the main text which are intended as learning aids. These are of two types. There are 'key concept' boxes, drawing attention to, and defining, concepts of particular importance. And there are 'activity' boxes, suggesting exercises which the student might do as he proceeds through each chapter. Many of these activity boxes suggest applications of the general discussion in the text to the case of the student's own country. If time and other resources permit these to be undertaken, the student will learn a great deal about his own country, as well as the general subject-matter of the text. Industrial-country students using this book could choose some developing country, preferably a well-documented one, as their 'own', in order to carry out these exercises and obtain a better grasp of the circumstances of developing countries. India and Pakistan are probably the best documented of Asian developing countries; Egypt, Kenya and Nigeria are African countries with reasonably large literatures.*

So far as university instruction is concerned, this book can be used (1) as the basic text for a complete course or (2) as a supplementary input into other courses.

First, it can be used as the basic text in courses of development economics, applied economics and related subjects. For such purposes, a minimum approach would be to use it for a single-semester or one-year course (depending on the time students can devote to it), going through the text but being highly selective in undertaking the suggested exercises.

Alternatively, it can be used as the basis for an exploration of the problems of the local economy, taking up more of the suggested country-specific exercises. To do this thoroughly would require more time. It would also make greater demands on the instructor, who must give guidance on local data sources and indicate ways in which my general discussion might need modification when applied locally. However, I have always been dismayed by how little the typical student knows about the problems and policies of his country. The value of this book would be greatly enhanced if it were used as a base camp for an exploration of the local situation. I have used it in this way in Kenya and would urge instructors elsewhere to follow the same path. I would be very glad to learn of the reactions of those who make this use of it.

In either case, the first two chapters should be studied before the others. The problem-oriented chapters (4 to 11), on the other hand, are largely self-contained and their sequence could be varied with only minor inconvenience.

The second chief use is to employ the book to supplement courses in applied and theoretical economics. One problem of teaching economics in developing countries is that much of the literature has been written in, and for, industrial countries. Developing country students therefore often have difficulty in relating these writings to

* Students who would like to 'adopt' one of the east African countries may find my annotated bibliography, *The East African Economies* (Boston, Hall & Co., 1976) a useful guide to the literature on Kenya, Tanzania and Uganda.

their own situation. The fact that this book has been prepared explicitly for students in developing countries may ease this problem. It might provide useful supplementary reading for the following courses:

(1) *Economic theory*. On the theory of the firm and market structures (Chapter 10); the theory of technological change (Chapter 9); the theories of the balance of payments and of income determination in an open economy (Chapter 8); the theory of inflation (Chapter 7).
(2) *Development planning*. Chapters 1 to 3 provide a treatment of the theory and principles of policy and planning which is not available at a similar level elsewhere.
(3) *Specialized courses*, such as demography (Chapter 4); labour economics (Chapters 4, 5 and 6); industrial economics (Chapters 10 and 11); agricultural economics (Chapter 9); international economics (Chapter 8).

Finally, I have also had in mind the practising economist working for his government, or in parastatal bodies, or in private firms. Such professionals are typically using (or forgetting!) the economics they learnt some time ago. To keep abreast they need to refresh their knowledge from time to time. I hope that such practitioners will find that this book, and its suggested supplementary readings, provide such refreshment in a palatable form.

Tony Killick

Acknowledgements

This work grew out of courses I taught at the University of Nairobi and my greatest debt is to my students. Their bafflements over earlier drafts, and their helpful comments and suggestions, helped me greatly in preparing the final manuscript. I have also successfully prevailed on many fellow economists to comment on various parts of the manuscript. It is invidious to pick out particular names but a greater injustice would be done if I failed to mention my especial gratitude for helpful suggestions to Richard Anker, Edgar Edwards, John Gerhart, Herbert Grubel, William House, Faizullah Khilji, Robert Pozen, Peter Steiner and Peter Wyeth.

This book was written while I was employed by the Ford Foundation. Their excellence as employers and the encouragement of their Nairobi representative, David Smock, contributed substantially to what I was able to do. Mrs Mary Muthoni and Mrs Esther Mirie both put me in their debt for the quality and quantity of their typing of successive drafts. And to my wife, a deep-felt appreciation of her unfailing love, patience and support.

List of tables

List of figures

PART 1: GENERAL PRINCIPLES

1 Markets, governments and economic efficiency

'All government, indeed every human benefit and enjoyment, every virtue, and every prudent act, is founded on compromise and barter.' *Edmund Burke*

Contents

I. Introduction

The importance of public policy

By their actions and inactions governments can induce prosperity or suffering. They can raise the pace of modernization or brake the economy to a halt. They can bring hope or despair. There is scarcely an aspect of economic life which does not lie within the ambit of the state. Consider, for example, the budget.

Its tax proposals alter the living standards of the bulk of the population. They alter the distribution of welfare between groups of people. They alter the profitability of business, and the attractiveness of saving and investing. By changing relative prices, they alter the composition of demand, output and foreign trade.

The government spending proposed in the budget has equally wide ramifications. It directly affects the number of people the government will be able to

1

employ and the volume of investment in the economy. The services it provides will reach every major sector of economic activity – from agricultural extension services to the provision of industrial estates to the construction of roads, and the provision of education that supplies virtually every sector with skilled manpower. Upon these expenditures most people will depend not only for the education of their children, but for clinics and hospitals, and for protection from the lawless at home and hostile forces abroad.

Nor have we yet described the full effect of the budget. The size of the budget deficit and the ways in which it is financed are liable to have a major impact on the macro-economic balance: the level of activity, the rate of inflation, the balance of payments. It will affect monetary policies and thus impinge upon the whole financial system and the availability of credit. And tucked away in the minutiae of budget estimates will be items of little financial importance which nevertheless make a large difference to the impact of the state[1] on economic life: here a provision for inspectors to enforce price controls; there a subsidy to some state trading monopoly; and so on.

---

[1] With apologies to students of politics, I shall be using 'government' and 'the state' interchangeably in this book. Worse still, I shall use the convenience of referring to the state as if it is an entity, even though it is actually no more than a system of rules, procedures and coercive powers operated by individuals.

We can obtain a first idea of the impact of governments as economic agents by comparing the size of the budget with total activity, as measured by the national accounts. Table 1.1 does this for some of the most populous and important developing countries (although others are missing because of data problems).

> **Key concept.** This book will use the terms 'developing countries', 'LDCs' (less developed countries) and 'low income countries' interchangeably. This group of countries will also be referred to collectively as the 'Third World'.

Looking first at the 1974 figures, we can notice that government consumption is typically equivalent to about one-seventh of private consumption; that total state spending (including both current and capital items) is a slightly larger proportion of the gross domestic product (GDP), and that tax revenues average well over one-tenth of the GDP. These averages, however, conceal large differences between countries, as is clear from the table.

A second striking feature of the table is the way in which the proportions grew during 1960–74 – a statement true not only of the averages but also for almost all the country observations. Actually, this result is not unexpected because various empirical

Table 1.1
Indicators of Government Importance in Economies of Selected LDCs*

Country	Government consumption as % of private consumption		Total government expenditures as % of GDP		Tax revenues as % of GDP	
	c. 1960	c. 1974	c. 1960	c. 1974	c. 1960	c. 1974
Brazil	19	15	12	11	8	11
Colombia	8	9	7	11	7	10
Ethiopia	10	14	—	14	—	14
India	9	11	21	21	8	10
Malaysia	21	29	20	33	15	22
Morocco	18	21	—	23	—	31
Nigeria	7	15	15	20	8	17
Philippines	10	13	10	18	8	15
Thailand	14	16	12	16	11	13
Average (median) value of observations	14	15	12	16	8	14

Source: UN *Statistical Yearbooks* (various issues)
Note* Data relate to central governments except for India (includes state governments) and Nigeria (includes regional governments). Statistics labelled '*c.* 1960' refer in a few cases to 1959 or 1961; some of those labelled '*c.* 1974' refer to 1973 or 1975 and Malaysia's refer to 1971. A dash indicates data not available or not available in suitable form.

studies have indicated (1) that the size of the budget tends to increase relative to economic activity as economies grow; and (2) that there is a related but separable long-run tendency for the budget's share to increase over time, in rich and poor countries alike.

Activity. Look up your own country's statistics and make calculations comparable with those in Table 1.1. Those whose country is already listed should do a similar exercise for the most recent years available. Write a brief note on your results, comparing them with those in the table.

Large as the budget shares are, the table understates the full magnitude of state transactions in the economy, for it excludes local and regional government budgets and the numerous public corporations and other 'parastatal' agencies that exist in most countries. For example, Kenya's national accounts record that in 1977 the central government, narrowly defined, contributed under 9 per cent to the country's GDP but that the whole public sector (including public corporations, other state enterprises and local government) made up no less than 22 per cent of GDP – more than twice the share of the central government alone. If comparable figures were available for other countries they would probably tell a similar story. Finally, it is to be emphasized that this type of statistic is only an incomplete index of the economic importance of the state, scarcely recording the enormous influence of its legislative and regulatory powers.

It should be remembered, too, that governments can subtract from economic well-being as well as add to it. In the chapters that follow there will be numerous examples of policies which have had perverse effects or of avoidable problems being worsened by government refusals to take responsibility. For this reason also it is important to do all that is possible to help 'get policies right'.

A book like this that is concerned with governments and their policies is therefore dealing with a most important influence on the lives of the people (although because they are potent we should not fall into the error of thinking that governments are omnipotent). The objective of this volume, therefore, is to illuminate some especially important issues of policy but also, and more importantly, to show how the analytical methods and insights of economic theory can be applied to the everyday problems of public policy. If it succeeds, the reader will be in a position to extend the range of applications beyond the sample of issues treated here.

He will also have been stimulated to learn about his own economy and its problems, will have reinforced his understanding of some important aspects of economic theory, and will have been shown how even simple statistics can illuminate complex matters.

But policy-making implies politics and politics implies that problems – even what seem to be purely economic problems – will not exclusively be viewed as if through the eyes of the economist. A decision, let us say, to enter into a trade agreement with another country will be pondered by the government not only for its effects on imports, exports, government revenues and the like, but also for its repercussions on the country's foreign policies, its administrative feasibility, the possibility of retaliation by third countries, and so on. In making its decisions the government will be influenced by all these considerations, by its own philosophical inclinations, and the arguments and pressures of interested parties.

To be able to offer practical contributions to policy issues we have to be sensitive to the political context, and the non-economic factors that will contribute to a final decision. Too often economists fail to do this. In order for economists to make their own best professional contribution they need an understanding that extends beyond the conventional frontiers of their own discipline. It is for this reason that this chapter and the next two say quite a lot about the nature of politics and governmental decision processes, laying the ground for the specific problem chapters which follow.

The rest of this chapter is taken up with exploring such questions as, what can we learn from economics about the most appropriate balance between the private and public sectors? Can we draw any clear boundaries between ideology and the results of economic analysis? What characteristics should we attribute to the state as an active agent in economic life? Chapter 2 turns to consider the objectives of government policies, the instruments available to promote these, and the criteria by which the relative efficiencies of alternative instruments may be assessed, while Chapter 3 explores the role of development planning.

II. Economic Systems and their Ideologies

Market economies and planned economies

The first question to be taken up is whether there is much chance that politicians will listen to what economists say about the desirable balance between the state and the private sector. Isn't it likely that this is an issue which will be decided according to the philosophical convictions of those in power? Let us start the search for an answer by looking at the major types of economy and their associated ideologies.

Economies may be categorized according to several criteria.[2] The stage of development (or the level of per capita income) is the one in use when we refer to 'the developing countries' as class of economy. However, since we are primarily concerned now with the role of the state in economic life, it is more convenient for present purposes to classify economies according to the agents involved in making economic decisions. This criterion introduces a familiar distinction between market and planned economies, the differences between them being found in varying degrees of decentralization, and in differing roles for the state and private citizens.

Market economies

A market may be said to exist when there is a group of buyers and sellers for some commodity or service who are in sufficiently close touch with each other to be aware of, and affected by, the actions of the rest. The market price will be the outcome of the interacting preferences of buyers and sellers, who will respond to the positive and negative incentives offered them by prices. A market may also be viewed as a means of processing and disseminating very large amounts of information: processing the revealed preference of all the buyers and sellers; and disseminating signals in the forms of price incentives. It is on the basis of these signals that people decide what they want to buy and firms decide what they will produce. In the theory (or ideology) of the market economy, the consumer is sovereign. His decisions on what to buy and at what prices are supposed to determine what is produced (the reality is rather different, however!).

But a single market does not exist in isolation, for it will be strongly influenced by what is going on elsewhere. Thus, the market for cotton clothing will be influenced by the supply and demand for competing types of clothing and by the market conditions for labour. If demand for labour is high relative to supply, wages will rise and so increase the demand for clothing. But the clothing industry itself will likely be a major employer and so the state of the clothing market will influence the overall demand for labour, as well as other markets. Thus, there is an interdependent network of markets which between them govern a large part of economic life. *Such a network is called a price system, or a market economy.* Its distinguishing features are a high degree of decentralization of decision-making through the impersonal workings of a myriad of markets, in which persons and firms pursue their own interests by responding to the incentive signals of market prices, and in which the interactions between the markets can be thought of as a co-ordinating mechanism. The role of the state in a pure form of a market economy is the restricted one of providing the framework of law and order essential to the working of markets and of intervening to ensure that the system works as it ought to.

Planned economies

The *centrally planned economy* stands at the opposite end of the spectrum of economy types, for it is characterized by a high degree of centralization operated by a state planning authority. In this system, it is individuals who play the restricted role. The government's central planners take most important decisions and act as the instrument of co-ordination. For this reason, such an economy is sometimes called a *command economy*, for individuals are seen largely as responding to commands from the centre rather than to price incentives. In this case it is the planning authority which processes and disseminates information about all aspects of the economy, and co-ordination is attempted by the conscious exercise of forethought rather through the 'invisible hand' of the market. Individuals as consumers and workers still exercise considerable freedom of choice over what to buy and where to work but the range of alternatives open to them will be more the outcome of planning decisions than responses to individual preferences. In the market economy it is the consumer who is supposed to be sovereign; in the command economy the state plan is allegedly supreme.

In these descriptions economies were differentiated according to the agents involved in economic decisions. An alternative would be to classify economies by the ownership of the means of production. In principle, this is a quite different criterion, for control does not necessitate ownership, and ownership does not necessarily confer control. It is possible to imagine a society in which the means of production are publicly owned but run along the lines of a market economy;[3] it is also possible to imagine a planned economy with ownership in private hands (as in the case of Nazi Germany). In practice, though,

---

[2] Eckstein, 1971, offers a most interesting discussion of criteria for the comparison of economic systems.
[3] See Lerner, 1944, for the presentation of a model of pricing in a socialist economy.

market economies are associated with private ownership, or capitalism, and centrally planned economies are associated with public ownership, or socialism. So the market types just described are part of the great twentieth-century ideological divide, which engages developing countries scarcely less than the industrial ones. The market system to the ideologue of capitalism possesses some of the attributes of an end-in-itself, instead of being a mechanism whose existence is conditional on its efficiency in achieving other goals. Similarly with Marxists, planning is an object of faith, and suggestions that it be modified by the introduction of decentralized market incentives have been regarded as heretical.

Competing ideologies

The ideology of the market mechanism is expressed in terms of a liberal–democratic concern with the freedom of individuals to pursue their own interests limited only by a recognition of others' rights to do the same. As a famous advocate of competition and opponent of planning put it: 'Economic liberalism . . . regards competition as superior not only because it is in most circumstances the most efficient method known but *even more* because it is the only method by which our activities can be adjusted to each other without coercive or arbitrary intervention of authority.'[4] In the constitutional sphere, multi-party parliamentary democracy is seen as the best guarantee of individual liberties; in economic life the market mechanism is similarly viewed. Indeed, some writers have drawn an analogy between democracy and markets, with the exercise of purchasing power described as a casting of votes for the goods the consumer desires (although the analogy is not a very good one because income inequalities give some people more market 'votes' than others, thus breaching the democratic principle of 'one man, one vote'), and with economic decisions taken at the grass-roots level rather than being imposed from the top. Central planning is therefore seen as endangering personal freedom, and state economic activity is regarded with suspicion. To quote Hayek again: 'The authority directing all economic activity would control not merely the part of our lives which is concerned with inferior things . . . Economic control is not merely the control of a sector of human life which can be separated from the rest; it is the control of the means for all our ends.'

In the extreme case, a *laissez-faire* view is held, that the market mechanism will look after itself if left free to do so. A less extreme and more common view in the same tradition favours only those types of state intervention which maintain the social framework necessary for freely operating markets and private property, and which widen the range of opportunities between which individuals can choose.

The Marxian view is, of course, entirely different. Capitalism is regarded as both morally repugnant and unviable. It is repugnant because it is held to result in the exploitation of the many by the few; gross inequalities of income, opportunity and power; and the subordination of human wants to private greed. Its workings, in Marx's view, 'mutilate the labourer into a fragment of a man, degrade him to the level of an appendage of a machine, destroy every remnant of charm in his work and turn it into hated toil . . . drag his wife and child beneath the Juggernaut . . . [and bring] misery, agony of toil, slavery, ignorance, mental degradation . . .' Capitalism is also held to be unviable because of its own internal contradictions, 'the seeds of its own destruction'. Far from being a guarantor of human rights, the state in a capitalist society is seen as an instrument of the ruling class, 'a committee for the management of the common interests of the bourgeoisie' (Marx), whose highest purpose is the protection of private property (Engels).

That central planning is seen by Marxists as an essential part of the socialist alternative has been clearly expressed by Paul Sweezy: 'In a socialist society the theory of planning should hold the same basic position as the theory of value in the economics of a capitalist society. Value and planning are as much opposed, *and for the same reasons*, as capitalism and socialism'.[5]

Faced with such strongly opposed political philosophies of the proper economic role of the state, it is natural to wonder whether economic analysis has anything effective to contribute on this question. Is it not likely that the extent of state activity will be determined by the predispositions of the government of the day, rather than by the careful evaluation of costs and benefits that the economist would advocate? Only partly. First, we would be unnecessarily pessimistic to think that ideologies are so religious in character, and so rigid, that reason and evidence have no effect on them. As with religions so with ideologies, they have to adjust themselves to changing realities or die of irrelevance. Secondly, it is easy to get an exaggerated impression of the influence of ideology from the tendency of politicians – Left and Right – to use ideological language to rationalize pragmatic actions. It is easy to show, for example, that the leaders of the Soviet Union have trimmed their

---

[4] Hayek, 1944, p. 36 (my italics). The next quote is from pp. 91–2.
[5] Sweezy, 1942, p. 54 (my italics).

Marxian theory when it has appeared to conflict with the practical management of the affairs of state – almost as easy as it is to point to American presidents who have extended the scope of the state while praising the virtues of private enterprise.

It is for reasons such as these that some observers have written of a convergence of economic systems towards a common, middle, way. The powers and expenditures of the state become ever larger in even the most individualistic societies and, on the other side, there has been much discussion and some action towards a decentralization of planning and greater use of material incentives in the communist countries. However, the differences that remain are large and fundamental. More to the point, most economies, including developing economies, do not easily fit into one or other of the 'market' or 'centrally planned' categories. Instead they incorporate features of both systems and are therefore to be classified as 'mixed' economies.

The mixed economy

This title is looser than the other two because it covers wider variations in the organization of the economy. Nevertheless, in a typical mixed economy the ownership of productive assets remains largely in private hands, with a state sector which, however, tends to increase its share over time. Most decisions about the purchase and sale of consumer goods are still taken at the decentralized, market level, except that consumption by the state is a significant and growing part of the total (see the first two columns of Table 1.1). Most resources are still allocated through market forces which are, however, subject to much regulation by the central government. Especially in developing countries, there is likely to be a national plan through which the government tries to determine, or at least influence, the pace and forms of future economic development.

The mixed economy is not entirely without ideological underpinnings. It is essentially what is advocated by social democrats. Post-independence experiences suggest that African and Asian nationalism usually favours this type of economy. But the ideological commitments of the social democrat or nationalist are less extensive than those, say, of the Marxist, and he is thus more open to persuasion. Mixed economies, on the whole, are governed by pragmatists – men who evaluate actions according to their practical consequences and their bearing on human well-being, and are relatively uninterested in abstractions. The mixed economy is of particular interest to us because decisions about the economic activities of the state are more likely to result from

calculations of costs and benefits (as against philosophical preferences) – and because most developing countries are mixed economies anyway. China is a massive exception; Vietnam and Cuba are among other important centrally planned developing countries. But the great majority of LDCs are best classified as having mixed economies. *This book discusses economic policy primarily with mixed economies in mind* (although see the discussion of reform versus revolution in Chapter 6).

Key concepts. By a **market economy** is meant an interdependent network of markets for goods and services through which the forces of supply and demand determine the allocation of economic resources and many other aspects of economic life, and where the means of production are privately owned. A **centrally planned** or **command economy** is an economy in which most important economic decisions are embodied in directives from the government's central planning authorities, and where the means of production are publicly owned. In a **mixed economy** most means of production are privately owned but the state plays an active role in influencing the allocation of resources and other aspects of economic life.

This brings us to a question so far evaded. Even if economists *can* exert influence on the matter, does economics actually have much to say about the most efficient combination of public and private activities? The rest of this chapter is taken up with answering that but in order to do so we need to be clear about what sort of animal it is we have in mind when we talk about 'the government' or 'the state' as an economic agent, and we also need to define what we mean when we talk about the 'economic efficiency' of markets and the state. So the next section looks at the nature of governments and their decision-making processes, and this is followed by a discussion of the concept of economic efficiency.

Activity. Consider the locus of economic decision-making and ownership of assets in your own economy. How would you categorize it? It is probably a mixed economy, but does the mixture tend towards a market system or central planning? Is there a clear trend in either direction?

III. Governments and their Decision Processes

The welfare optimizing model

Economists, like schoolboys, delight in building models, meaning by 'model' an abstract set of relationships which tries to capture the essential elements of a real-world situation. In the individualistic tradition of western economics, theorists of public policy have developed a model of governments and how they make their decisions which will serve as a useful starting point. This can be described as a 'welfare optimizing' model and is closely related to the theory of consumer behaviour. Its main characteristics are:

(1) The task of government is taken to be the maximization of community, or social, welfare.
(2) Government action is argued to be necessary because of various defects of the market mechanism, with the extent of these 'market failures' defining the economic role of the government.
(3) The overall objective of maximizing social welfare is given more concrete expression in various subsidiary objectives, such as the elimination of unemployment, the maintenance of equilibrium on the balance of payments, optimization of the rate of investment, and so on.
(4) These subsidiary objectives are taken to be clearly defined, with potential conflicts between them removed by the application of a consistent set of priorities and weights.
(5) This set of preferences, established by the government as an expression of what the community wants, is called the social welfare function (SWF), called 'social' because it is taken to be an expression of community or national interests.
(6) With the SWF established, the task of a government faced with some specific policy problem (market failure) is to review all alternative lines of action and then to select that policy which will achieve the stated objectives with maximum efficiency.
(7) The result of this process is an optimum solution and if it is successfully applied to all problem areas the result will be a condition of what is known as 'Pareto optimality' in the whole economy, in which it is only possible to make one person better off by making someone else at least as much worse off.

The idea of market failure will be taken up later and

> **Key concept.** A social welfare function (SWF) is a ranking of society's preferences among alternatives. The preferences of the government are often taken as a proxy for the SWF.

the objectives and instruments of government policy will be subjected to closer scrutiny in the next chapter. But the essential nature of this model can be easily illustrated by using a type of analysis that is probably familiar to you in connection with the theory of consumer demand.

> **Activity.** I will be assuming some familiarity with indifference and transformation curve analysis. If necessary, you should quickly refresh your memories on this from an elementary theory textbook, e.g. Lipsey, 1975, appendix to ch. 15; or Samuelson, 1976, appendix to ch. 22.

We will take, as an illustration, a rather basic choice that has to be made in every society, between those consumption decisions which are made on an individual basis and those made by the state; in other words, the choice between the kinds of things we ordinarily spend our purchasing power on and items of 'collective consumption' such as education, the police and health services for which we pay taxes. Private consumption goods are drawn on the vertical axis of Figure 1.1 and public consumption goods on the horizontal. OT represents the amount of private consumption goods that would be attainable if all resources were devoted to their production; OT' shows the position with all resources devoted to public consumption goods; the curve TT' marks the boundary of feasible combinations of public and private consumption goods when varying proportions of resources are shared between these two items. This curve is drawn as concave to the origin on the grounds that available resources will not be equally well suited to the production of both types of consumption goods, so that to get a succession of *equal* increases in the output of one of them we have to give up *increasing* amounts of the other, under the influence of the law of diminishing returns.

The slope of the TT' curve at any point is known as the marginal rate of transformation and introduces a notion of fundamental importance to this book – the notion of a trade-off between competing goals. The slope of the straight line that has been drawn through the point A tells us the rate of transformation at that point: in order to get x more of public consumption y of private consumption would have to be sacrificed, or vice versa. One of the most fundamental difficulties

Figure 1.1 *The optimum combination of private and public consumption.*

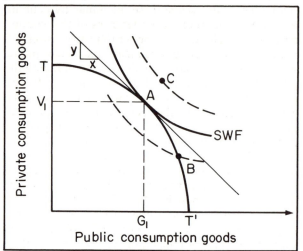

about economic policy-making is the need to confront trade-offs of this kind. It is sometimes only possible to achieve progress towards one goal at the cost of a retreat from another.

Faced with the boundary of feasible alternatives, TT', how is the best balance to be struck between the two types of consumption? We now superimpose a social welfare function, SWF, drawn in the familiar way of indifference curves. This represents combinations of private and public consumption goods each of which would provide the same social welfare, with a higher curve taken to imply greater welfare than a lower curve. The task then reduces itself to finding an SWF curve which is tangential to a point on the TT' curve, indicated by point A on the diagram. The formal condition for this type of equilibrium is that the marginal rate of substitution indicated by the slope of SWF should be equal to the marginal rate of transformation, indicated by the slope of the TT' curve. This condition is satisfied at A on the diagram. The optimal combination, therefore, is OV_1 private consumption and OG_1 public consumption. To settle, for instance, at B would not be optimal because society would not be on the

> **Key concepts.** When it is only possible to obtain more of one desired object at the sacrifice or some of another desired objective there exists a **trade-off** between them. Given sufficient information about alternative possibilities, the rate of trade-off (or **marginal rate of transformation**) is given by the slope at any point on a transformation curve like TT' in Figure 1.1.

highest attainable SWF curve. To settle at C is not a solution because this combination of goods cannot be produced by the economy. Thus, provided with the instruction that it should produce OG_1 of public consumption goods and permit OV_1 of private consumption goods, the task of the government is then to find that combination of taxes and expenditures which brings society to point A.

If at this point the reader is scratching his head and wondering what this model has to do with the real world he has my sympathy. All models are abstractions, assuming away some (preferably less important) aspects of reality in order to lay bare the logical nature of the remainder. But it can be asked whether this welfare optimizing model of government policy does not assume away too many essential features of the real world for it to be useful. To clarify this, we can ask what kind of social and political system would be necessary for the model to work, in the sense being an abstraction of feasible decision processes.

First, the model assumes the existence of a mechanism through which the government can translate community preferences into a social welfare function and that the government will adopt this as expressing its own policy objectives. In other words, governments are assumed always to know and act in the public interest.

Secondly, the model requires that society is broadly agreed in its objectives and priorities, for unless such a consensus exists it is not clear what could be meant by 'the social welfare function'. Thirdly, governments must have sufficient power to ensure that the public interest prevails over special interest groups within society. Fourthly, this power must be rather heavily concentrated at the centre, for if much of it is delegated to local governments and other public bodies the task of pursuing an internally consistent set of objectives by use of an optimal and co-ordinated set of policies becomes impossible.

Lastly, the model assumes a huge volume of information about the nature of the problems confronted, the possible ways of responding to these problems, and the consequences of adopting each of these alternatives. In other words, it assumes certainty, or at least the absence of chronic uncertainty, just as it also assumes that governments and civil service will be able to absorb and process all this information, and to consider alternative lines of action.

Some criticisms

To set out these implications of the model already casts doubt on its usefulness but before turning to examine alternative models we should note that there are theoretical as well as practical objections to the model. For one thing, it is not always made sufficiently clear that this is a *normative* model – showing how its advocates think government decisions *ought* to be made. It is dangerous to put forward a normative view of this kind and then to behave as if it had become fact. For it is rather obvious that the model, however good it may be as a prescription, has very little relationship to the way governments actually conduct their affairs.

> **Key concepts.** A **normative** model of decision-making is concerned with the question, how ought decisions to be made? A **positive** (or **behavioural**) model is addressed to the question, how are decisions actually arrived at?

The notion of the social welfare function also gives rise to many difficulties. It is supposed to represent the collective preferences of society – the public interest – but can the public interest be given any operational meaning? Is it supposed to be the sum of individual preferences? If so, how do we add them up? Is it wants that should be measured or only demands made effective by purchasing power? What should be done when there are major disagreements within society? And is the national interest the same thing as the majority interest, so that the wishes of minorities can be ignored? The social sciences have not yet found answers to these questions. It is common for two people or two political parties to hold completely opposite views about what is in the public interest. Neither in practice nor in principle can these disagreements be resolved by reference to factual information.

For reasons of this kind, most political scientists have abandoned concepts like 'the common good' or 'the national interest' as unhelpful, although economists continue to cling to the belief (or hope?) that the SWF is meaningful.

Even supposing that the SWF could in principle be given concrete meaning, by what mechanism could we discover its content? We could not do it through the market mechanism because for many public wants there is no possibility of an efficiently operating market. Presumably the SWF must be discovered through political processes such as voting, and most writers on this subject do indeed have western-style parliamentary democracies in mind. But even in this type of democracy it is not clear how voting would specify the SWF, for the electorate votes for people and parties and it is difficult to draw anything more than the most vague conclusions about policy

preferences from election results (to say nothing of the preferences of those who did not vote for the winning side). One could escape these dilemmas by defining the SWF as the revealed preferences of the winning party, but that is not much better than an evasion and requires us to view governments and their public servants as being exclusively devoted to pursuing the public interest, as distinct from personal, party and other sectional interests. Many would argue that the actual outcome of the economic and political mechanisms of capitalist societies is a neglect of public wants in favour of private gain.[6]

It is doubtful, therefore, whether the SWF is a useful concept, and the same doubt can be extended to the welfare maximizing model of government which depends upon it. One of the merits of this model, however, is that it does at least recognize the importance of taking a view of politics when examining issues of public policy. Policies and their implementation are expressions of political processes and the distribution of power. We are unlikely as economists to make much contribution to the well-being of society if we take the easy way out of disregarding the political context within which policies are formed. Every attempt is therefore made throughout this book to take account of political, as well as economic, realities.

But if it is important to consider political processes, and the welfare optimizing model is not helpful, what alternative can be offered? In trying to answer this question we first look at the nature of societies and their politics in developing countries and then examine the implications for the formation of public policy.

Political conditions in LDCs

It is, of course, dangerous, if not absurd, to talk of 'the developing countries' as if they form an homogeneous class of country. Nevertheless, some generalizations may be offered as applying to at least a large proportion of them (as well as to a good many of the 'developed' countries).[7]

(1) Society is marked by actually or potentially grave social conflicts, because of differences of religion, caste, tribe, language, regional origin, education, or inequalities of income.
(2) Partly because many LDCs have only rather recently achieved political independence after

[6] See Galbraith, 1962, for a persuasive statement of this view.
[7] For supporting evidence see Dahl, 1970, ch. 6 and the sources cited there: and the discussion of table 8.3 of Kuznets, 1966.

long periods of colonial rule, institutional and other capacities for giving expression to these differences, and for resolving them peacefully, are limited. Society is therefore prone to violent upheavals.

(3) Politics is less openly competitive than in the non-communist industrial countries, with multi-party parliamentary democracy the exception in Asia and Latin America, and almost extinct in Africa.

(4) Nevertheless, there is much political instability, with governments often changed by military coups and other unconstitutional means. Governments are therefore preoccupied with the tasks of maintaining their own popularity, authority and power.

(5) Partly because of the absence of openly competitive political systems and the strength of social divisions, governments are often not representative of the whole people.

(6) The seriousness of social divisions, the tendency to violent conflict, the newness of public institutions, and shortages of trained personnel combine to reduce the effective power of governments, however autocratic they seem to be. The 'arm of the law' does not stretch throughout society and there are often large differences between laws passed by the government and the actual conduct of civil affairs. There is hence a *de facto* dispersion of decision-making across society.

(7) For similar reasons, the quantity and reliability of information available to the government, and the ability of the public administration to process and act upon it, are severely limited. Decisions have to be made in the face of large uncertainties about the nature of the problems confronted, limited knowledge of the alternative lines of action available, and considerable ignorance about the consequences of a given line of action.[8]

> **Activity.** Go through these seven points examining the extent to which you think they apply to your own country.

Comparison of this list with the description of the welfare optimizing model suggests that the model bears little relation to political realities in many developing countries and that, if we are to have a usable model, it will have to abstract less dramatically from these realities.

One implication of the socio-political conditions just described is that governments often have to ponder their decisions within the context of a fragmented society, and cannot safely ignore the effects of their actions on these social divisions. Given a 'pluralistic' society made up of conflicting groups competing for influence over the allocation of resources, the state faces a choice between imposing a settlement with its coercive powers or negotiating a compromise acceptable to the main interests involved. When they take the path of conciliation (and most governments prefer that to the more risky alternative of coercion) governments will be preoccupied with the delicate task of maintaining social equilibrium, trying to maintain a balance between competing group pressures, balancing one group against another. There are many countries where the maintenance of social equilibrium has to be among the highest priorities of any government: in India, with its deep regional and linguistic divisions; in religiously divided Lebanon; in Malaysia, with its more numerous Malays and more prosperous Chinese; in Nigeria, which has already experienced a major tribal war; and in many others. The creation of Bangladesh out of the former East Pakistan is a reminder of the dangers of neglecting social equilibrium, just as racialist policies of white governments in southern Africa have undermined even the security of those they were intended to protect.

Thus, even if one believes there is a national interest which is something more than the net sum of group interests, it is evident that in one way or another group interests will have an important influence on government decisions. There will be other influences too, which have been neglected so far. Among these will be the capacities and predilections of the agencies involved in formulating policies and carrying them out. Governments are likely to have only imperfect control over these agencies, which will control the flow of information passing up to ministers and will resist decisions not to their own liking or which undermine the strength of the agencies themselves. Inertia and organizational interests will thus influence decisions; disregard of this has often resulted in a large gap between what the government decides should be done and what is actually carried out.

---

[8] Even in the industrial countries, where far more reliable information is available and can be processed by their public administrations, there are often large discrepancies between forecast changes and actual events – see, for example, Theil, 1961. A study of the US Federal Government similarly concluded that 'budget officials soon discover that . . . possible consequences of a single policy are too numerous to describe, and that knowledge of the chain of consequences for other policies is but dimly perceived for most conceivable alternatives' (Wildavsky, 1974).

Nor should we underrate the influence of individual participants in decision processes – ministers, civil servants, advisers. The abilities and personalities of each, the way they interact and the varying degrees of influence exerted by each will add a further dimension of complexity and unpredictability to decision-making.

On this view, then, we can repeat the quotation that begins this chapter: 'All government . . . is founded on compromise and barter'. Far from being a disinterested search among all available alternatives for optimal solutions, the decision process is characterized by bargaining between groups, organizations and individuals. Government action is often more a resultant of its attempts to manage this type of conflict than a consciously chosen outcome of systematic study.

An alternative model of government decisions

The world depicted in the last few paragraphs is a far less tidy one than that postulated in the welfare optimizing model. An alternative to that model, which incorporates the main features of this untidy world, should meet these specifications:

(1) It should not depend upon the concept of a SWF, nor on the notion that governments have clearly defined and ordered objectives.
(2) It should be able to accommodate the view of government actions as only partly controlled resultants of bargaining processes.
(3) It should accommodate the existence of large uncertainties about problems and policy outcomes.
(4) It should recognize the limited capacities of human institutions for considering large numbers of alternatives, and the often major informational and other costs of analysis.
(5) Partly as a consequance of (1) to (4), it should incorporate flexibility – room for the government to manoeuvre in, a margin for error.

Just as economists borrowed from the theory of consumer behaviour to develop the welfare maximizing model, so we may borrow from the modern theory of the firm for an alternative that at least partly meets the specifications just listed. This is known as the *satisficing* model of decision-making. It postulates that governments do not search for optima but for solutions that are 'good enough' – solutions which will command the necessary minimum of group, organization and individual support without provoking violent resistances from those who are opposed.

By way of clarification, this model can be illustrated in a manner directly comparable with the earlier discussion of Figure 1.1. We will remain with the example of the choice between public and private consumption goods, although the model could be applied to many other choice situations. By contrast with Figure 1.1, no use is made of a SWF; it is simply assumed that in its attempt to strike a compromise between the preferences of competing interests the government lays down minimum levels of public and private consumption. Any policy solution which meets these minimum requirements is acceptable as satisfactory.

Referring now to Figure 1.2, the government may specify that the consumption of publicly provided goods and services should be not less than G_1, because less than that would require drastic reductions in social and economic services and provoke much political dissatisfaction from those who benefit from them. It may similarly specify a minimum level of private consumption of V_1, because less than that would harm people's ability to satisfy their basic needs and would imply a politically very unpopular level of taxation. G_1 and V_1 can therefore be thought of as *targets* or *aspiration levels*, or as *constraints* within which the policy advisers must operate.

Figure 1.2 *The satisficing model of government decisions.*

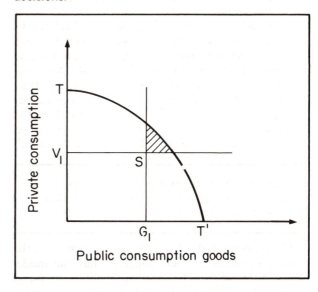

In this case, then, any set of policies that brings the economy to point S or to any part of the shaded area to its north-east will be acceptable to government. Once policies have been found that achieve this the search for better policies will cease. Note that I have drawn in a TT′ curve as in Figure 1.1, in order to make the two diagrams more readily compared, so any solution within the shaded area is not only satisfactory but also feasible. However, it would be more realistic to dispense with TT′ altogether because it presumes what is unlikely to be the case – that there will be full knowledge of the feasible alternatives that are available.

But, the alert reader will ask, if we do not have a TT′ boundary how can we know that S is attainable; how do we know that the government is not asking the impossible? This brings us to a more dynamic aspect of the satisficing model. The aspiration levels G_1 and V_1 are not immutable. Rather, the model requires governments to adjust their aspirations in the light of experience, responding to feedback information on results achieved from earlier decisions, altering their targets as the balance of power and influence changes. In this case, if aspirations are proved by experience to be unrealistic they will be scaled down. So if it proved impossible to find policies that would simultaneously achieve G_1 and V_1, these targets would have to be revised downwards until they became feasible. Similarly, if G_1 and V_1 proved very easy to achieve, this would tell the policy-makers that they had set their sights too low and should adjust them upwards.

To sum up, the satisficing model presents the choice of government policies as being the outcome of a set of targets or aspiration levels, arrived at as an outcome of conflicting pressures and adjusted in the light of feedback information on success or failure in meeting the targets. Any set of policies which meets the targets will be acceptable; the search for better policies will cease once the targets are met. The model is presented schematically in Figure 1.3.[9]

Figure 1.3 *Schematic presentation of the satisficing model.*

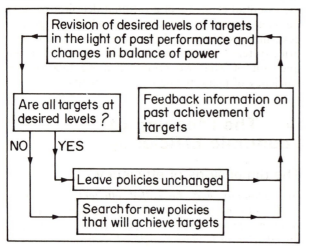

Comparing the two models

What can be said about the relative merits of the welfare optimizing and satisficing models? We have already criticized the welfare optimizing model for its unreality and by this test the satisficing model scores heavily. It assumes far less precision and consistency in government objectives, requiring only that minimum targets be set, dispensing with fine calculations of marginal rates of substitution and trade-offs, and eliminating the fiction of a SWF. It can accommodate the view of politics as being based on 'compromise and barter'. It also copes better with the existence of uncertainty and the need for flexibility, by permitting a wide range of acceptable outcomes. By the same token, it simplifies the decision process by allowing the search for solutions to stop as soon as a satisfactory one is found, instead of having to continue until the optimum is reached. It is more dynamic in that it has more to say about the processes from which government action ensues, and in more explicitly allowing for the adjustment of targets and policies over time.

Moreover, there is evidence that the satisficing model does conform more to how governments actually go about making policy decisions, whereas it would be difficult to find a real-word application of the welfare optimizing model. Two examples: a study of the selection of government agricultural projects in Kenya, Zambia and Tanzania found that these governments accepted any project which offered some rate of return on the capital invested; no concept of an optimal rate of return was employed.[10] There was, moreover, little consideration of alternatives; rather than evaluate the whole range of possible projects government officials stopped looking once they had found a project with some positive rate of return.

A second example is provided by a study of fiscal and monetary policies in Britain.[11] This found that these instruments of policy were not used actively so long as the 'target variables' of the unemployment rate and the balance of payments remained within a certain range of acceptable values. Fiscal and monetary policies were only activated when one or other of these 'target variables' took on unsatisfactory values (equivalent to being to the south-west of S in Figure 1.2) – when the unemployment rate became

[9] Adapted from Mosley, 1976, Fig. 1.
[10] Birgegard, 1975.
[11] Mosley, 1976.

intolerably high, or the balance of payments deficit too large. A search for better policies only commenced when the government's aspiration levels were not being achieved.

So if a *behavioural*, or descriptive, model is wanted the satisficing one is clearly preferable. However, that model has less to say if we ask the normative question of how ought governments to make their decisions? If that is the question to be answered the optimizing model should be taken more seriously, for we have already seen that it is a normative model. It is easy to show that in principle the optimizing process will result in superior decisions, as illustrated in Figure 1.4. This is simply an amalgamation of Figures 1.1 and 1.2. It can be seen from this that whereas the optimizing model produces the optimum solution, A, the satisficing model produces any solution in the shaded area SCD and that, unless it happens to settle at A, this solution will be sub-optimal (if it is accepted that A is the best). Solution S, for example, would be far within the possibilities boundary and thus would fail to maximize welfare.

Figure 1.4 *Optimizing and satisficing compared.*

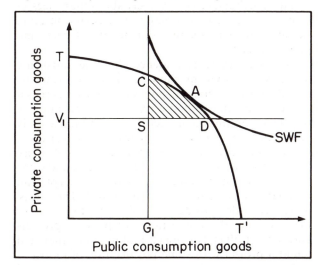

This conclusion should, however, be qualified in two important ways. First, by incorporating the notion of adjustable aspiration levels the satisficing model does provide a mechanism which should prevent the persistence of grossly sub-optimal solutions such as S; in this respect the two models are not as far apart as they may seem. Secondly, if the theoretical and practical difficulties of the optimizing model are so severe as to make it unusable then its 'optimum solution' cannot be given any practical meaning and therefore cannot be used as a standard by which to assess the results of alternative models.

But stripped of its pretensions the optimizing model still conveys a number of recommendations which we – and governments – should not disregard. These include (1) that if governments want to make efficient decisions they need to gather as much relevant information as is justified by the cost of doing so; (2) that efficient policies presuppose clear and consistent objectives (see Chapter 11 for an illustration of this); (3) that choice among alternatives is of the essence of decision and that refusals to make hard choices are an evasion of reality; (4) that the ultimate objective of government policies should be to meet the wishes of the people.

To sum up, we have been contrasting an essentially normative model with a behavioural one, i.e. models which are not strictly comparable. The normative optimizing model yields useful recommendations but is dangerous in the illusions it may create of what it is in the power of governments to do, and in the temptation to use it as if it has descriptive validity. The satisficing model is more realistic and thus provides more insights into actual decision processes, but provides fewer clues about how governments could improve their decisions.

Activity. To help form a judgement about the usefulness of the welfare optimizing and satisficing models write brief notes on the socio-political system of your own country, with respect to the identification and satisfaction of the national interest, the extent of unity within society, the concentration of power upon government, the capacities of the public administration and the information available to it.

Having sought to provide an understanding of the ways in which government actions are decided, and the essential elements of a rational decision process we can approach the question, what things are governments likely to do more efficiently than the price system? But this immediately raises the further question of what we mean when we talk of the efficiency of markets and of governments.

IV. The Meaning of Economic Efficiency

The dimensions of efficiency

Any economy may be called efficient when it is achieving a maximum output of preferred goods and services from available resources, when the distribution of income associated with that output is regarded as just, and when the economy is achieving an optimal expansion over time. What is desired, then, is that combination of private and public activities which would bring the economy as near as possible to this ideal efficiency, bearing in mind, however, that conflicts arise in trying to achieve these conditions simultaneously.

If you re-read the first sentence you will see that this ideal has three dimensions: (1) There is *static* efficiency, which means making the most of the resources currently available. (2) There is *distributional* efficiency, which is about how the benefits obtained from given resources are shared within society. (3) There is *dynamic* efficiency, which is concerned with stability and the way the economy expands over time. It is with static efficiency that conventional western economic theory has been largely preoccupied, but developing countries naturally have a greater interest in dynamic efficiency. The distributional dimension has tended to receive the least attention, although its great importance is now more fully recognized (and is the subject of Chapters 5 and 6). We will look at these three aspects in turn.

Static efficiency

Static efficiency has two aspects. Its first condition is maximum output from given amounts of labour, capital and other resources. This is illustrated in Figure 1.5. This is similar to Figure 1.1 except that it is concerned with all the goods and services it is possible to produce in the domestic economy, or obtain through foreign trade. This output has been classified into two 'goods', food and non-food, with the latter on the vertical axis. The transformation curve, PP′,

Figure 1.5 *Point B illustrates complete static efficiency.*

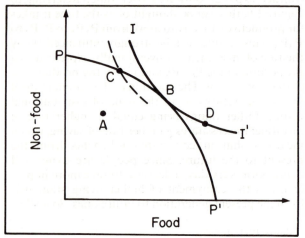

reveals the full range of *production possibilities* that is actually attainable in the economy, with OP′ measuring the amount of food that could be obtained if all resources were devoted to its output, and OP the comparable case for non-food.

The economy is therefore obtaining maximum output from existing resources when it is obtaining one of the combinations of food and non-food on the production possibility curve. Static efficiency requires that the economy be operating on the PP′ curve, rather than at some point within it, such as A. To satisfy this condition there must be *full employment* of labour and other resources.

But while being on the PP′ curve is a necessary condition of static efficiency it is not sufficient. Consider, for example, point P, i.e. that situation in which all resources are devoted to the production of 'non-food'. It satisfies the condition that resources are fully employed – but the people have nothing to eat! This brings us to the second aspect of static efficiency, that the goods produced must be a preferred combination, i.e. they should reflect not only the technical possibilities of production but also the wishes of the community.

These preferences are represented in Figure 1.5 by the familiar indifference curve, II′; by the same logic as that used for Figure 1.1, point B is the point of optimization. It is impossible to conceive of a community indifference curve which is tangential to point P because everyone needs to eat. Even the more plausible point C is shown not to be an optimal output because with that combination the community would not be on the highest feasible indifference curve and hence could increase its welfare by moving towards B. Point D would give equal welfare but is beyond the technical capacity of the economy, because it lies outside the PP′ boundary.

It could be objected that this conventional description of static efficiency is only relevant to a market economy because it sees production decisions as the joint outcome of the technical conditions of production and of consumer preferences, thus excluding central planning. This objection can be met, however, if we think of the II′ curve as representing the aggregated preferences of either (1) individual consumers, or (2) state planners, or (3) both groups combined.[12] Considered in this way the illustration has universal validity, although we have seen that the problems of relating this type of model to the real world are enormous.

---

[12] See Drewnowski, 1961, for an interesting discussion of the state preference function and its relationship to private consumers' preference functions.

> **Key concept. Static efficiency** is achieved in a fully employed economy operating on its production possibility frontier and producing a preferred mixture of goods and services.

Distributional efficiency

A weakness of the type of presentation in Figure 1.5 is that it is silent on the way in which the national income associated with static efficiency is shared among the population, which brings us to distributional efficiency. This concept is at once simpler and more complex than static efficiency. Its simplicity lies in its definition: an efficient distribution of income and wealth is one that is considered as just, or equitable. The complexity arises when we ask, what constitutes a just distribution? Complete equality, with all receiving the same? Or simply less inequality, in which case how much less? Or the eradication of poverty, in which case how should we measure poverty? And whose judgement are we referring to when we talk of a 'just' distribution? People disagree strongly about what justice means. A rich man may regard as fair a distribution that permits him to retain much of his income; a poor man will take an opposite view. Our idea of justice is subjective and self-interested. The only prospect, it seems, of investing distributional efficiency with any kind of *social* status is if there emerges from society a consensus, a broad agreement, on what a just distribution is (and if there are good reasons for thinking that what is claimed as a consensus really exists). An alternative is to accept what the government considers to be just, but that is open to many objections, not the least of which being that governments are often dominated by those who are doing well out of existing arrangements and who therefore have a vested interest in opposing radical change.

Economists have rather little to contribute to the definition of distributional efficiency, which belongs more to the realm of moral and political philosophy. One important philosophical contribution in this field has proposed the following 'principle of justice':[13]

> Social and economic inequalities are to be arranged so that they are both: (a) to the greatest benefit of the least advantaged ... and (b) attached to offices and positions open to all under conditions of fair equality of opportunity.

What economists are qualified to do, however, is to explore the ways in which the distributional aspect is related to the other dimensions of economic efficiency, and we return to this in a moment.

> **Key concept. Distributional efficiency** can be said to exist when there is a general consensus that the distribution of income and wealth is fair or just.

Dynamic efficiency

Dynamic efficiency may also be broken into different elements. One distinction is between the short run and the longer run. In the *short run* the problems are those of the *macro-economic balance* of the economy, and its management. The main problems arising under this heading are the avoidance of inflation (see Chapter 7) and balance of payments deficits (Chapter 8). Short-run dynamic efficiency may be said to be achieved when there is such a balance between aggregate demand and supply in the economy that (1) there is no deflationary underemployment resulting from insufficient total demand, (2) there is no inflation, and (3) there is equilibrium on the balance of payments. The meaning of these statements is elaborated in later chapters but it is worth adding here that while the governments of many of the industrialized market economies are often preoccupied with short-run economic management, the centrally planned and developing economies pay less attention to it. Whether developing countries are wise in this neglect is, however, debatable.

Longer-term dynamic efficiency is, of course, of great concern to LDCs because it relates to their success in achieving economic development. Here again, it is useful to recognize different components of this aspect of efficiency. Dynamic efficiency relates to the speed with which the production possibility frontier expands outwards over time. Referring to Figure 1.6, this can be thought of as the time it takes for productive capacity to move from P_1P_1 to P_2P_2 to P_3P_3. This, in turn, will be strongly influenced (1) by the rate of investment (conventionally expressed as a proportion of the GDP), and (2) by the productivity of that investment. The question of the optimal rate of investment returns us to the issue of distributional justice. Other things being equal, a higher rate of investment necessitates a higher rate of saving, which means a shift in consumption benefits from the present to the future. Since people are dying and being born every day, a decision to save more in part transfers the enjoyment of higher living standards from the present generation to future ones. So while a

---

[13] Rawls, 1971, p. 302.

main concern in developing countries has been to raise saving and investment rates, squeezing out the largest possible volume of saving is not necessarily the most desirable policy, especially when those squeezed are already close to the subsistence level. Governments have to balance the desire for better living standards in the future against the desire for the highest possible living standards now, and an optimal rate of growth is one that results from a socially acceptable balance between these competing claims.

Figure 1.6   *Dynamic efficiency illustrated.*

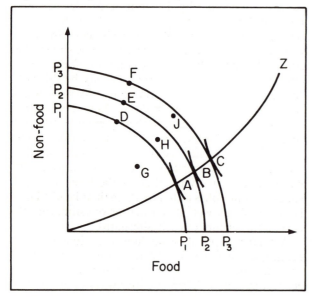

The productivity of capital has to do with its allocation among available possibilities; the availability of complementary resources like minerals, good land and skilled labour; and the technology it incorporates. The general principles are fairly obvious: (1) investible resources should be allocated to those outlets offering the highest returns to the economy, which, among other things, entails an efficient mechanism for making such allocations; (2) investments should incorporate the most productive technologies appropriate to the domestic economy (the meaning of an 'appropriate' technology is explored in Chapter 9).

As in the case of static efficiency, dynamic efficiency cannot be isolated from community preferences. In brief, productive *capacity* should expand at an optimal rate but the *actual* expansion of production should be along a desired growth path. This proposition is depicted in Figure 1.6, where points A, B and C are successive static equilibria established as productive capacity expands over time. The line OZ, which passes through these equilibria, indicates the growth path of the economy with respect to the

allocation of resources between food and non-food. Once again, the indifference curves may indicate only private preferences, or those of the government, or both. When state preferences are included, the OZ line will be influenced by the government's development strategy, for example as it affects priorities between agriculture and industry.

> **Key concept.** Long-run **dynamic efficiency** exists when the economy is expanding along a preferred growth path at a rate which reflects a socially accepted distribution of consumption between present and future generations.

> **Activity.** Why do you think the OZ line in Figure 1.6 is drawn as curving upward in a northerly direction? If you are familiar with 'Engel's law' you will know the answer.

Relationships between the three aspects of efficiency

Although it is analytically useful to distinguish the static, distributional and dynamic aspects of efficiency, you may already have realized that there are strong interconnections between them, so the distinctions are somewhat arbitrary. Static efficiency, for example, is a necessary precondition of dynamic efficiency, which is depicted in Figure 1.6 as movement from one point of static optimization to another (although the next chapter will show that in practice there are liable to be tensions between the pursuit of static efficiency and long-run economic development). Again, the short-term dynamic task of avoiding deflationary underemployment, also affects the economy's ability to operate on its production possibility frontier.

But perhaps the strongest connections are between the distributional aspect and the others. Look back at the case illustrated by Figure 1.5 and think about the two 'products', food and non-food. Since food features more prominently in the consumption of the poor and non-food makes up a larger proportion of the expenditures of the rich,[14] it is clear that community preferences, and the consequential allocation of resources, will be heavily influenced by the distribution of purchasing power. It is only possible to draw an indifference curve like that in Figure 1.5 on the basis of a *given* income distribution, so for each alternative distribution there will be a separate indifference curve.

---

[14] See Weiskoff in Chenery, 1971, ch. 14.

This is illustrated in Figure 1.7 where the curve XX' may be thought of as reflecting a rather unequal distribution of income, because it would result in a large allocation of resources to non-food relative to food. The second curve, YY', is drawn on the assumption of a more equal distribution, thus resulting in a larger allocation to food. Both points A and B satisfy the conditions of static efficiency but if the more equal distribution underlying YY' were regarded as fairer, then B would be superior to A.

Figure 1.7   *The influence of income distribution on community preferences.*

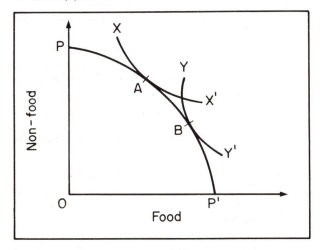

But this is not the end of the matter. This is clear if we think about the factor proportions required for the production of our two 'goods' and the implications of these proportions for income distribution. We can loosely identify food with agriculture and non-food with industry. Now, agriculture employs large numbers of manual workers relative to industry, which needs more capital and skilled labour. The unskilled can be identified with the poorer members of society while the owners of capital and skills are among the better-off. Now imagine that for some reason there is a shift in the pattern of demand towards a greater consumption of food. This will result in a larger derived demand for unskilled workers and a reduced demand for capital and skilled workers, raising the wages of unskilled workers relative to the returns obtained from capital and skill. In other words, the gap between rich and poor will be reduced. The opposite will be the case if demand changes in favour of non-food production. So, just as the structure of demand and production is a consequence of the distribution of income, the distribution of income is a consequence of the structure of demand and production.[15] Static and distributional efficiency are like a man and his bullock: each dependent on the other. Moreover, it would be easy to extend this analysis to show how an economy's dynamic growth path and its allocation of investible resources are also likely to have strong implications for the distribution of income, and so cannot be chosen in isolation from questions of social justice (see Chapter 6 on this).

The interrelatedness of static, distributional and dynamic efficiency throws up the further complication that conflicts may well exist between policies designed to achieve each of them. Chapter 6 suggests that securing distributional efficiency may be at a cost to economic growth: there may be a trade-off necessitating uncomfortable choices. Similarly, while in formal theoretical terms it can be shown that static efficiency is a necessary condition for dynamic efficiency, the real-world situation may be different. Monopolies, for example, undoubtedly contravene the idealized conditions of the perfectly competitive optimum but they may use their greater profits and security to undertake more investment than would occur in a highly competitive situation, thus increasing the longer-term growth of the economy (see Chapter 10). What, then, is the best policy: to shackle monopolies or to give them their head? There is no simple answer; it is a matter of estimating the costs and benefits of each alternative.

A final way of showing how the dimensions of economic efficiency are related to each other is to consider the ways in which it is possible to increase economic welfare. There are four ways of doing this:

(1) By moving from within a production possibility area on to the feasible boundary (e.g. from G to A in Figure 1.6).
(2) By moving along a production possibility frontier from an unwanted to a preferred position (e.g. from D to A in Figure 1.6).
(3) By moving from one equilibrium to another that is superior because it results from a fairer distribution of income (as illustrated by Figure 1.7).
(4) By moving up a preferred growth path (e.g. from A to B to C in Figure 1.6).

[15] One could therefore reject the type of analysis represented in Figures 1.5 and 1.6 on the grounds that one needs to define the indifference curve in order to establish what the optimal production mix would be, but that it is impossible to define the indifference curve without first knowing the production mix and the income distribution that results from it. To resolve this difficulty one would need a full general-equilibrium model of the economy, and the most that can be said for the diagrams is that they represent simplifications useful for illustrating some of the main aspects of the problem.

V. The Role of the State in a Mixed Economy

Having clarified the workings of governments as
economic agents and the meaning of economic
efficiency (and hence the criteria by which we may
judge the performance of markets and plans), the
scene is now set to address the question, what is the
most efficient balance between the private and public
sectors in a mixed economy?

The market failures approach rejected

Mention was made on page 7 that economists in the
individualistic tradition of western economic theory
have built into the welfare optimizing model of
government the view that the role of the government is
to correct the failings of an unregulated market
economy. The general principle adopted is that any
departure from complete efficiency constitutes a case
for the state to intervene in order to ensure optimality.
Thus, the existence of monopoly power, or
immobility of labour, or an unjust distribution of
income, or a low savings rate are market failures, seen
as requiring correction by government.

Although economists' discussions of the role of the
state are usually conducted along these lines, some
strong objections can be raised against this market
failures approach. On the one hand, it can be accused
of having a hidden anti-state bias by containing the
unstated value judgement that the state should do
only those things which the price mechanism does not
do well. On the other hand, it can be accused of a pro-
state bias, with its implicit assumption that when
markets fail the state will do better. Both objections
have substance, even though they pull in opposite
directions. Take the accusation of a pro-state bias
first.

Of the various arguments to be made here, the
strongest relates to what is known as *the problem of
the second best*. If you recall the earlier discussion of
static efficiency, the notion of 'Pareto optimality'
was introduced, referring to a condition in which it
was not possible to make someone better off without
making someone else at least as much worse off.
Theorists have established a variety of conditions for
the satisfaction of Pareto optimality. One of these was
stated in connection with Figure 1.1 – that the
marginal rate of transformation must equal to

the marginal rate of substitution, as at the point of
tangency, A, in the diagram.

The world in which we live is, unfortunately,
populated by obstacles to the attainment of Pareto
optimality. There are many constraints in the way of
achieving such a condition. Given these imperfections
we want some general principles to guide policies
designed to move the world in the direction of
optimality. It is tempting to think that we should
adopt policies for each sector of economic life that
would increase competition so that each would come
closer to perfect competition.

Unfortunately, things are more complicated than
that. The results of theoretical research indicate quite
the opposite: *if there are a number of constraints
preventing the satisfaction of optimality conditions it
will not generally be desirable to have these conditions
hold in the rest of the economy*. The conditions of
Pareto optimality only provide a basis for policy
recommendations if they are all satisfied everywhere
in the economy at the same time – a practical
impossibility. Theorists have not been able to put
forward a corresponding set of general rules for
second-best solutions in real-world situations.
Applying policies which would satisfy the conditions
of Pareto optimality in one part of the economy,
leaving sub-optimal conditions in other parts of the
economy, could quite easily lead to net reductions in
economic welfare.[16]

This 'theory of the second best' is of great
importance for practical economic policy-making, as
will be seen in later chapters, and you should be sure
of understanding it. It is not, however, easy to
demonstrate in a simple way, so I will offer three
illustrations.

For the first imagine an economy completely
efficient in all respects save that in one industry a
trade union is operating as a monopoly to raise the
wages of its members by restricting entry into their
profession. Since this is the only respect in which
optimality is violated we could be sure that
introducing policies to restore freedom of entry would
improve community welfare by bringing the economy
to optimum. But what if the union were acting in this
way as a countervailing power against a very large
employer? It would then be much more questionable
whether acting only against the union, leaving the
power of the employer untouched, would raise
community welfare.

For a second approach we return to the familiar
choice between food and non-food. Figure 1.8
reproduces the PP' curve presented in Figure 1.5 and

---

[16] For a fuller explanation see Lipsey and Lancaster, 1957, and also
Mishan, 1962.

the same point of optimization, B. But now assume the existence of constraints which prevent the economy from achieving the 'first-best' solution, B. The effect of these constraints is represented by the XX' line, showing that between points A and C it is not possible for the economy to operate at its production possibility frontier. Given these constraints, what is the second-best solution? Since we have established that for an economy to achieve static efficiency it must be on its PP' frontier, it is tempting to recommend that we should settle at either point A or C. But following this optimality rule in the face of the constraints does not, in fact, produce the second-best solution. The second-best solution is actually at D. Even though it is below the PP' curve, it gives that combination of food and non-food which is on the highest attainable indifference curve, I^2. Points A and C are inferior because they are on the lower indifference curve, I^3.

Figure 1.8 *An illustration of the second-best problem.*

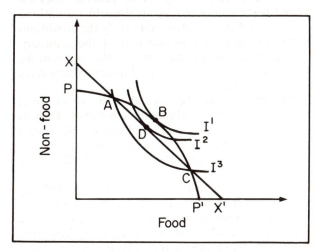

A third illustration is provided by Figure 1.9. Community welfare is measured up the vertical (this is done for convenience, not because it could actually be measured) and along the horizontal is given the number of government policy measures which together could maximize community welfare. OE is the hypothetical level of welfare that would be achieved if the economy were completely efficient, but it actually falls short of this by EA, so the economy is at A. Each of the dots represents a policy measure, introduced in sequence reading from left to right. Introduction of the complete set of measures, OP, would bring welfare to the maximum but there is no assurance that any single measure would improve welfare. If we knew a general principle that would give

Figure 1.9 *Policies derived from optimality rules can reduce welfare.*

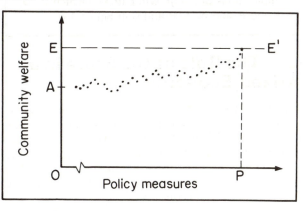

us the second-best solution at all times the row of dots would slope continuously upward to the right. But we lack such a general principle and so the diagram shows that some of the policy measures, while essential ingredients of OP, would move the economy further away from EE' (just as regulating the trade union while leaving the employer untouched could make things worse). In principle, we can only be assured of improving community welfare if the whole package, OP, is introduced, removing simultaneously all the constraints on the achievement of optimization. (Another, more down-to-earth, illustration of the second-best problem is provided in the discussion in Chapter 11 of the pricing policies of public enterprises – see page 295.)

The second-best argument has both theoretical and practical applications. Since we obviously live in a world where there are many constraints preventing complete efficiency, the second-best problem is always present. This means that one can rarely derive a theoretical case for some specific policy measure simply from the existence of a market imperfection. This is quite a blow to the market failures approach, although theoretical solutions are possible in some cases, given enough information about the constraints and policies in question (or a willingness to make assumptions in the absence of information!).

The problem of the second best arises because we lack the capacity to trace the enormously complicated effects of one change on the rest of the economy. If we had more information and better understanding we could work out second-best solutions. The practical implication, then, is that it is unwise to advocate any particular policy until the fullest possible study is undertaken of its likely effects. Each policy step must be carefully studied on its own merits, case by case, rather than being mechanically derived from some general rule.

> **Key concept.** The **theory of the second best** states that, given multiple constraints on the satisfaction of the conditions of Pareto optimality, it is not necessarily superior to meet more of these conditions than fewer of them. Given such constraints and imperfect understanding of all the consequences of any policy change, there is no general rule for the derivation of second-best solutions. Policies must be worked out from detailed investigations of particular cases.

The second-best problem draws attention to another point on which the market failures approach can be criticized. Economic efficiency, as defined in Part IV, is a highly idealized notion, incapable of full achievement in any possible real-world situation. In that case, it can be doubted whether this ideal provides a meaningful norm by which it is sensible to assess the workings of actual market economies. We need more realistic criteria. For this reason, some writers have developed the concept of 'workable' competition (see Chapter 10). Adopting this kind of pragmatic approach will result in less criticism of actual market performance and less advocacy of government intervention.

Moreover, one can object to the use of a market failure to justify state action because it is necessary to set the costs of intervention against the expected benefits. Government actions have costs of production just like any other outputs – a point explored in the next chapter. In the extreme case, a policy may be completely unsuccessful, resulting only in costs and no benefits. *It is not only markets which fail; there are government failures too.* Extraordinarily, it was left to Marxist economist Paul Baran to complain to his liberal colleagues that, 'In our time . . . faith in the manipulative omnipotence of the State has all but displaced analysis of its social structure and understanding of its political and economic functions . . .'[17]

That governments are far from omnipotent has been amply demonstrated in the recent history of many developing countries, of which examples are given later. That governments have failed to live up to the high standards set by economists of the welfare optimizing tradition is not at all surprising, and to point it out is not to betray an anti-state bias. Governments have to operate within many constraints and are often unable to achieve what they would like to do. On important matters they often cannot move far ahead of public opinion, and that is true of imposed governments as well as of elected ones. Indeed, because they lack a publicly accepted claim to a right to govern, imposed governments may be particularly nervous of public opinion; autocratic government is not necessarily strong government.

Quite apart from the general climate of opinion, governments are confined by the views of special interest groups which are powerful in society; quite a lot was said in Part III about the difficulties governments have in maintaining their own authority and securing social tranquility in pluralistic societies. Ministries and other public agencies, and the individuals who run them, will also be active participants in government decision processes, with their own interests, biases and preferences; filtering the information that is allowed up to ministers, restricting the alternatives presented to them, setting limits to what can actually be implemented. It is for reasons such as these that this chapter emphasizes government as proceeding by 'compromise and barter'.

Limitations of manpower and other resources are also important constraints, as is the absence in most civil services of incentives which adequately reward the efficient and penalize the incompetent. Uncertainty resulting from poor information has also been mentioned earlier: often governments cannot move effectively because they only dimly perceive the nature of the problems they are confronting, and have only the most approximate idea of the likely outcome of any particular policy.

It is the existence of constraints such as these that makes politics 'the art of the possible'. And we should not overlook the sad fact that some governments are unrepresentative, or unconcerned with the general welfare of the citizenry, or corrupt, or merely inept.

In ignoring state failures, then, the market failures approach is biased in favour of government intervention – a paradox since it was developed by liberal-minded economists generally convinced of the effectiveness of the price system. But those with more socialistic inclinations can point out an opposite bias, that the market failures approach takes an essentially negative view of state action: it is to remedy revealed defects in the market mechanism; in a real sense it is to 'make capitalism work'. When put in this way it becomes clear that the market failures approach is far from being ideologically neutral, and we may ask the question, why not follow the principle that the market mechanism should be used only in the face of failures of government planning? This is essentially what has been proposed by reformist Soviet economists who urge greater decentralization and use of price signals as an aid to central planning.

---

[17] Baran in Agarwala and Singh, 1958, p. 86.

A comparative efficiency approach

The practical conclusion to draw from the above is that there is no *a priori* presumption of the superiority of either markets or governments. Market failures are relative, not absolute, and the same is true of the deficiencies of state planning. Markets and plans both have strengths and weaknesses; benefits and costs. The economist's approach should be to compare these, advocating that markets be allowed to do those things in which they are the more efficient, and for the state to do those things in which it is the more efficient. What we seek is that combination of private and public activites which will maximize the net benefits obtained over time from available resources. *Our general principle, then, is let the private and public sectors each do those things in which they can produce better results than the other.*

How far can this principle take us in practical terms? It obviously cannot provide definitive answers for all economies at all times but there is enough evidence on the relative efficiencies of market and centrally planned economies for some generalizations to be made. I will set these out according to the three dimensions of economic efficiency described earlier.

Comparative static efficiency

> **Activity.** Readers may wish at this point to refresh their memories on the discussion of static efficiency, on pages 14–15.

An enormous amount of information is required to bring an economy anywhere near to the point of static efficiency: for each of hundreds of thousands of different goods and services complete information is needed on all the influences bearing upon supply; similarly complete information is required on the preferences of millions of purchasers. Unless this information is available and can be processed and communicated to those involved in making decisions, there is no possibility of fully utilizing all resources and of ensuring that the production mix is a preferred one.

It can be claimed for a well functioning market economy (the problem of markets that do not function well is discussed in a moment) that it handles this information problem well and at small cost. It does so through the medium of prices, which reflect both production costs and effective purchaser demand. If a market for a particular item is competitive on both the supply and demand sides the resulting price will, at least approximately, equate at the margin the resource costs of production with the

value placed upon it by purchasers. It will also create incentives for maximizing output from the resources at hand.

Decentralization is the secret of the market's handling of the information problem. This can be compared with the situation of the central planner confronted with the same informational requirements. For his plan to result in static efficiency he needs the same amount of accurate information which he must then process, interpret and communicate to those involved in taking and implementing decisions. In principle, centrally planned economies could solve these problems by trial and error but in practice such economies have found them intractable, despite modern developments in communications, mathematical programming techniques, and computer technology. The flow of data is inadequate but it is impossible, even so, to process more than part of what is available. Even more fundamental, the system creates incentives for the provision of misinformation – public enterprise managers tend to exaggerate their material, labour and capital requirements so as to ensure ample supplies; they also have an incentive to provide 'information' that will minimize the production targets they are set each year (see Chapter 11). In such situations it is impossible to ensure that a central plan will result even approximately in static efficiency. Improved performance is likely to require decentralization, and economists in Europe's centrally planned economies have been searching for ways of achieving this without relinquishing the essential features of central control.[18]

So far as static efficiency is concerned, therefore, there is a general case in a mixed economy for allowing resources to be allocated through the decentralized instrumentality of the market mechanism, rather than by central direction.

Generalization 1

A well functioning market mechanism is more likely to achieve static efficiency in the allocation of resources than is state regulation. In general, therefore, microeconomic production and consumption decisions are better left in private hands.

Now, it is immediately necessary to qualify this in a number of important respects. First, even a well

[18] Manove, 1971, presents a most interesting discussion of Soviet-type planning and suggests ways of achieving substantial decentralization within a central planning framework. The most he claims, however, is that his system produces plans that are internally consistent, which is not at all the same thing as static efficiency. A consistent plan can be hopelessly sub-optimal.

functioning price mechanism will fail in the face of external economies and diseconomies, with the consequence that there will be a neglect of public wants. Secondly, in any modern economy there are liable to be at work strong forces limiting competition and creating other market 'imperfections'.

Take first *the neglect of public wants*. It is a necessary condition for static efficiency in a market economy that prices should fully reflect the costs of production and purchasers' valuations of the benefits to be derived. Roughly defined, real costs and benefits not included in market valuations are called externalities, and these can be positive (external economies) or negative (diseconomies).[19] Industrial pollution of the air is an external diseconomy because it represents a cost to society that is only to a very limited extent borne by the polluters. The enjoyment by firm B of the services of skilled workers trained by firm A is an external economy to B because the training has cost it nothing.

> **Key concept. Externalities** are costs or benefits which are not reflected in market prices. If the net balance of these costs and benefits is positive there is an external economy: a negative net balance indicates an external diseconomy.

A good many of the goods and services provided by the state result from the failure of the price mechanism to deal with the problems posed by externalities. Take, for instance, the provision of national defence. Always assuming that there is some genuine external threat to security, all citizens benefit from the provision of defence. Yet it is difficult to imagine an effective market for this service, valuable though it is, because so long as it exists every citizen benefits from it whether or not he contributes towards its cost. In other words, it is practically impossible to exclude those who do not choose to pay – the 'free riders' – from enjoyment of the benefits and thus there is no incentive for any individual to pay. There are a number of such cases, for which it is very difficult to imagine the existence of satisfactory private markets. Other examples include justice, law and order, and broadcasting.

There is an additional, broader, category of items for which private markets could function but not well, or in ways that would be regarded as socially undesirable. For example, commercial competition for the provision of piped water to a community would involve a wasteful duplication of investment. And leaving the provision of health facilities in private hands for those who could afford to pay would be

generally regarded as socially unjust. Other items of these types include sewerage, postal services, education, roads, and telecommunications. Agricultural research is an example explored in Chapter 9. Although there are countries which leave these services primarily to the private sector, in most their provision is regarded as primarily a responsibility of the state. What is needed is a reasonable balance between private consumption and items of collective consumption like those just mentioned, but critics of capitalism point out that the provision of public consumption often gets left behind: 'public squalor in the midst of private affluence'.

Generalization 2

It is a responsibility of the state to provide socially desirable services which the price mechanism either would not produce at all or would only do so at greater cost or with smaller social benefits.

Take next the existence of monopoly power and other impediments to the competitiveness of markets. These make for an inefficient allocation of resources, in that prices will not accurately convey the cost of the inputs they utilize. For example, Chapter 10 surveys the effects of monopoly power in product markets and reaches the conclusion that, on balance, it is likely to have harmful effects, by causing a misallocation of productive resources and managerial slackness resulting in avoidably high costs of production.

This problem of market imperfections goes beyond the question of monopoly power: dualistic, or fragmented, markets are a special problem undermining the efficiency of the price mechanism in developing countries; poor information flows (including misinformation in advertising) and the existence of a variety of conditions reducing the mobility of factors of production are among other weaknesses that deserve the attention of the state – provided always that the costs of state action are exceeded by the benefits resulting from it.

Generalization 3

The achievement of static efficiency will require state action to eliminate the ill-effects of monopoly power and other impediments to the competitiveness of private markets.

---

[19] See Scitovsky, 1970, ch. 14 for a fuller treatment of the concept of externalities.

Comparative distributional efficiency

As regards distributional efficiency, we should recall first the warning given earlier that distributional questions cannot realistically be divorced from the pursuit of static or dynamic efficiency: the allocation of resources and the chosen growth path will have strong implications for income distribution. That is the case, for example, with Generalization 1, that the market mechanism is more likely to achieve static efficiency than state regulation. The market mechanism may also produce socially unacceptable inequalities, and there may thus be a tension between efficiency in the allocation of resources and social justice.

The incidence and nature of income inequalities are examined in depth in Chapter 5. It is shown there that there are generally much greater inequalities in capitalist industrial countries and LDCs than in centrally planned economies. It is also shown that strong forces are usually at work to perpetuate the inequalities (or slow down attempts to achieve greater equality) and that the growth paths followed by many 'mixed economy' developing countries have failed to bring an equitable share of benefits to the poor.

But while it is generally true that a market economy is likely to give rise to large inequalities this is not enough to constitute a blanket case for state intervention as such. One way in which inequality perpetuates itself is that the rich can use their wealth to command disproportionate political power. Some governments *result from* inequality and are not in the least interested in redistribution. In other words, state action can be an obstacle to justice. So inequality does not create a general case for state action; rather it creates a particular case for what can loosely be called *socialistic* action. Inequalities in the countries of eastern Europe are smaller than those in western Europe not because the former are centrally planned but because they are socialist.

Lastly, we should remember that policies to reduce inequalities may impose costs on the economy – in reduced growth and distorted prices – so that (1) it is important to search for the least-cost policies to achieve a given equalization, and (2) it is necessary to weigh the expected distributional gains of a measure against its costs before arriving at a final decision.

Generalization 4

The market mechanism will result in self-reinforcing inequalities which are likely to be judged socially unjust. This indicates a need for socialistic intervention by the state, provided that the resulting improvements are regarded as outweighing the costs of achieving them.

Comparative dynamic efficiency

> **Activity**. Before proceeding, the reader may refresh his memory on the description of dynamic efficiency on pages 15–16.

We will dispose of the issue of short-run dynamic efficiency quickly, proceeding rapidly to longer-run developmental considerations. There is today little disagreement that an unregulated market economy tends to be unstable – to experience unwanted fluctuations in output, employment and prices. There is equally little disagreement that it is a responsibility of the state to correct this defect by manipulation of macro-economic variables, as set out in Chapters 7 and 8.

Generalization 5

An unregulated market economy is inherently unstable: the state should so manage the macro-economic variables of the economy as to neutralize this instability.

Turning now to the *longer run*, the position is more obscure. On the one hand, a powerful theoretical case can be made out for extensive state participation in the development process; on the other hand, it is not clear that such participation has actually achieved many improvements.

Take first the theoretical case against leaving development to be determined by the price system. Economists have put forward various arguments to the effect that growth and development will be retarded by market forces. One of the most powerful of these argues the existence of 'vicious circles' or 'a low-level equilibrium trap' in which national poverty is self-perpetuating. This argument postulates that saving as a fraction of national income is a rising function of per capita income (at least among poor countries), so that low-income countries have low saving rates. Being poor, they will also have small internal markets, reducing returns to investment and thus their ability to attract foreign capital. Exports might seem to offer an escape from the limitations of the domestic market but developing countries depend largely on primary product exports, the markets for which (so it is argued) expand only slowly. To this gloomy picture it only remains to add a demographic dimension – the fact that most LDCs are experiencing historically rapid population growth, making it all the more difficult to raise per capita incomes.

The 'poverty trap' is illustrated in Figure 1.10. Rates of growth of total national income and population are measured on the vertical; the horizontal measures per capita income. The YY' line indicates the relationship between the *growth* of national income and the *level* of per capita income. It shows that, over the relevant range, the rate of growth will increase as per capita income increases, because expansion of the domestic market will make investment more attractive and a rising savings rate will make more investible resources available. The PP' curve shows the relationship between per capita income and the rate of population growth, showing that this rate of growth will also go up as per capita incomes grow until it reaches the biological limit to the growth of a human population. The two curves show zero growth at a subsistence level of per capita income, marked S on the horizontal. At all levels of income between S and T the population growth curve is above the income growth curve; the reverse is true at income levels to the right of T.

Figure 1.10   *The poverty trap.*

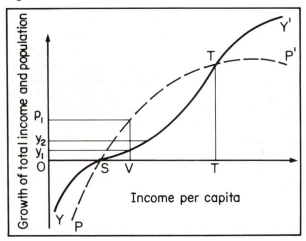

To illustrate how the poverty trap works, take some point on the horizontal between S and T, say V. Imagine that by a favourable turn of events, perhaps a bumper harvest, the economy is able to raise its living standards above the bare subsistence, S, to V. In consequence, net saving and investment will become positive and the economy will begin to grow, at the rate OY_1. After a time-lag, however, the population will also begin to grow, at OP_1, which is faster than the initial growth of total national income because the PP' curve lies above the YY' curve at V. Even if during the time-lag the economy increases its growth rate further, say to Y_2, this will still be outstripped by population, so that per capita incomes are pushed back down, returning eventually to the subsistence equilibrium at S. However, if the economy can somehow get itself to the right of T, growth becomes self-sustaining, with national income expanding more rapidly than the population. T therefore represents

the point of 'take off' into self-sustaining growth.

The policy conclusion drawn from this model is that, left to itself, the economy will remain caught in a poverty trap. What is needed is a massive mobilization of resources, which only the state can undertake, so that a 'critical minimum effort' (or a 'big push') can get the economy to the point of take-off. This, then, is an argument for an active state role in development.

There is a second cluster of arguments which, taken by itself, is less gloomy than the trap theory, although it does not reject the existence of such a trap and can be thought of as reinforcing the trap hypothesis. These arguments are concerned with the failure of the price system to provide an adequate basis for making decisions about the future.

The general point can be put simply. Market prices reflect today's conditions of supply and demand, and markets usually exist only for currently available goods and services. The price system may be an efficient mechanism for arriving at decisions about the disposition of resources for current use but today's prices will be a poor basis for saving and investment decisions – decisions which concern allocations for the *future*. For example, we have already seen that the demand for non-food consumption goods is likely to grow more rapidly than the demand for foodstuffs (see page 17). But today's prices reflect today's pattern of demand, so a would-be investor studying the current situation may well receive signals that exaggerate the future potential of investment in food. Ideally, what is needed is a system of markets that includes 'future food' as well as 'present food' and so on for all other items. Investors and savers would then have a firmer foundation upon which to make decisions. The idea of markets for future goods is not a far-fetched one. There are, for example, 'futures' markets for many important commodities in international trade and also for major currencies. However, actual futures markets only cover a small fraction of possible transactions. In the absence of such markets, people are faced with large uncertainties which may discourage them and hamper future growth. Such uncertainties also increase the risk that some investments will be wasteful because by the time they come to fruition there may not be an adequate demand for the goods that they produce, or anyway that higher returns could have been obtained from different investments.

An uncertainty on which economists have placed special weight arises from the fact that a decentralized market system leaves each investor to make his own decisions in ignorance of the investment decisions being considered by others. One consequence of this may be that there will be over-investment in some lines and not enough in others. More serious, perhaps, will be a systematic bias towards uncertainty and pessimism about future demand and profits. For if each investor ignores or underestimates the expansionary effect on future markets of investments other than his own, he will be less inclined to invest than if the economic system gave him full information about the totality of investment plans. Each investor would then realize that many investments were likely in other industries, and that these would expand the demand for his own product.[20] Being decentralized, the market system does not provide this information.

A final, related, criticism of the dynamic deficiencies of the market is that, while it may be quite efficient in allocating resources at the margin – expanding an industry here, contracting one there – it is much less good at effecting large, discontinuous changes in the economic structure. But (the argument continues) development is essentially a process of structural change, resulting in radical transformations in patterns of demand and output, and in the physical and institutional framework.

Taken as group, then, these arguments are a powerful case for development planning and for active government involvement in economic decision-making. By pooling information about likely future trends and intentions, and by adopting a conscious strategy towards the structural pattern of development, the planners could provide a superior set of signals to reduce uncertainty, encourage larger saving and investment rates, and steer the economy along a chosen growth path.

However, not all these criticisms of the dynamic deficiencies of the price system should be taken at face value. For instance, the poverty trap's prediction that

developing countries will be unable to sustain rising per capita incomes has not been borne out by experiences in the 1960s and 1970s. Table 1.2 assembles some relevant data, although you should bear in mind that these estimates are subject to large error margins, especially for developing countries.

Column (1) of the table shows that it is generally true that savings rates rise with per capita incomes. The western and centrally planned industrial countries have significantly higher savings rates than the developing countries and within the developing countries the savings ratios emerge as a rising function of per capita income (with the oil producers as a special case!). The poorest LDCs do indeed have low savings, just as the poverty trap model predicts.

But even the poorest countries have been able to achieve economic growth. Column (2) refers to the growth of total GDP and you can see from the top three lines of the table that developing countries achieved appreciably faster growth than the industrial countries in 1965–73. Column (3) shows that this advantage was neutralized by more rapid population growth in developing countries, so that the expansion of per capita income was much the same for each of the three major country groupings. Among developing countries, growth was fastest in those with the higher incomes (as predicted by the model) but even the poorest managed some increase in per capita income (contrary to the model). A growth rate of only 0·9 per cent a year (always assuming the data are reliable enough for this figure to have meaning) is very slow but at least does not show these countries to be slipping backwards.

----

[20] See Scitovsky, 1954, for a lucid statement of this argument.

Table 1.2
Savings and Growth Rates by Stage of Development

	Gross domestic savings ratio, 1972[a] (1)	Growth rate in 1965–73 of:	
		Total GDP[b] (2)	GDP per capita[b] (3)
Industrialized market economies	23·5	4·6	3·6
Centrally planned economies	29·0	4·8	3·2
Developing countries	20·7	6·0	3·5
Developing Countries by Per Capita Income:			
Higher income ($375)	19·6	6·6	4·1
Middle income ($201–375)	18·7	5·7	3·2
Lower income ($200 or less)	13·2	3·3	0·9
Oil producers	36·3	8·1	5·4

Source: World Bank, 1976.
Notes: (a) Gross domestic investment less net import of capital from rest of the world, expressed as a percentage of GDP.
(b) Annual percentage rate of growth.

Furthermore, the notions of the 'big push' and 'take-off' have fallen into disrepute. While it is true that Soviet-type economies have achieved high rates of investment – typically 25 to 30 per cent of gross domestic product – and the governments of some developing countries have also been quite successful in raising the investment rate, economists have come to realize that there is far more to the achievement of growth than merely maximizing the quantity of investment. Misused, a large volume of investment can be accompanied by stagnation while more modest resources can generate quite rapid growth when well employed.[21] Similarly, governments, like their individual citizens, often consume a large proportion of additions to their receipts, so that the resources they mobilize will often be used for purposes other than long-run development.

Lastly, the argument to the effect that the market cannot achieve necessary structural transformations can be rejected as historically blind: most of the now industrial countries of the west experienced enormous structural changes during the course of their development, and did so within what was essentially a market framework.[22]

Notwithstanding these objections, there undoubtedly remains a strong theoretical case for development planning and substantial government participation in development. But this brings us to a second difficulty – that there is often a large gap between the theoretical case for state action and what governments actually do. Chapter 3, for example, records a disillusionment with planning and a good deal of evidence showing that the actual practice of development planning falls a long way short of its theoretical advantages. Much of that chapter is devoted to exploring the reasons for this and ways of improving plan implementation. It finds no simple solutions, however, and few grounds for expecting dramatic improvements in the future. More generally, it is not at all clear that the development experience of those LDCs with very active government policies has been superior to those in which more decisions have remained in the private sector.[23]

So the outcome of this discussion of comparative dynamic efficiency is ambiguous and yields only a weak conclusion.

Generalization 6

A market economy is likely to fall well short of full long-run dynamic efficiency but it has yet to be demonstrated that governments achieve generally better results. There is thus little scope for generalized recommendations; the likely costs and benefits of market and state alternatives should be assessed against their specific contexts before deciding a line of action.

Markets, governments and the stage of development

There are two further points to dispose of before concluding this section. We should note arguments to the effect that the special characteristics of developing countries make a stronger case for state intervention than has been made in the last few pages. The argument here is that there exists a particularly severe degree of market imperfection in LDCs: fragmented and dualistic markets for labour and capital; poor transportation and information flows; much monopoly in the industrial sector; important externalities which are not reflected in market signals. Thus, the efficiency of the market in each of its dimensions will tend to be less in LDCs, strengthening the case for public intervention.

However, an exactly opposite argument can be mounted, to the effect that it is a further characteristic of LDCs that their governments and administrations are also likely to be particularly inefficient. Parliaments are less likely to be effective; civil services will be under-manned at the senior levels; less information will be available to decision-makers; laws and other decisions are less likely to be implemented. It seems, after all, that there is a case for leaving decisions in the private sector.

With these two arguments neutralizing each other, it is not possible to derive from the fact of underdevelopment any generalization about the best balance between the public and private sectors. This brings us to another conclusion, which is that we should not take a static view of what this balance should be. As an economy progresses changes will

---

[21] In Ghana, for example, the government was successful in achieving large increases in investment during the first half of the 1960s but this was accompanied by falling rates of economic growth, due to mis-allocations of these resources and declining utilization of existing capital: see Killick, 1978, ch. 4.

[22] See Deane, 1965, for an excellent study of British economic development.

[23] This conclusion emerges from Myint's (1972) survey of the record of south-east Asian countries.

occur in the efficiencies of markets and of governments. Hopefully, both will improve over time, so we cannot make any firm predictions about long-term trends in their comparative efficiencies. What these longer-term considerations do mean, however, is that a fluctuating balance of advantage between markets and planners is likely so that today's judgement about what is desirable will not necessarily be valid five years hence.

Generalization 7

The desirable balance between state and private activity will fluctuate over time and should thus be subjected to continuous re-examination.

> **Activity.** Write down ways of improving the efficiency of your economy by altering the balance of responsibilities between the public and private sectors. Consider how application of the seven generalizations presented above would alter the balance in your country.

The limitations of an economic analysis

Early in this chapter the question was asked whether economics has much to contribute to a definition of the best balance between the private and state sectors. We are now in a better position to answer that question, by saying that economics does have something to offer but falls well short of providing a complete definition. The seven generalizations presented above are not vacuous, even though they are very general and sometimes rather inconclusive. The analysis has drawn attention to the likely limitations of both markets and the state, insisting that an efficient balance between the realms of private and public decision-making can only be hoped for if it is chosen on the basis of the comparative efficiencies and costs of the two sectors. This principle is rarely applied and its application could be fruitful in many situations.

Nevertheless, we would be fooling ourselves if we thought that economics alone could define the role of the state. Ideology, history, the social and cultural framework, and a host of other factors will enter into the debate. To a large extent, therefore, we have no realistic alternative than simply to accept the existence of the state as an economic agent with, in some sense, an independent existence of its own. It is not, in general, helpful to regard the state as a passive instrument for realizing a social welfare function; governments and their administrations will have their own priorities and, not infrequently, these will involve

a denial of individual preferences, as when they discourage the consumption of cigarettes or alcohol on social grounds. In many areas governments have to take the initiative – in the provision of roads, for example – because there is simply no practical alternative and something has to be done.

Implications for the economist as a policy adviser

To some extent, then, the economist is required to live with state preferences, just as he has long been used to accommodating the preferences of individuals. To make life more difficult, he has to do so knowing that preferences will be unclearly defined, will probably be somewhat contradictory, and will be subject to constant change. It is a tricky environment to work in, but not an impossible one so long as he is conscious of the need to keep his feet on the ground and avoid Fairyland models that abstract fatally from political realities.

If politics is the art of the possible, economists who aspire to exert influence on policy choices are obliged to judge what 'the possible' is in any given problem area – and to measure the expected benefits from what is possible against the costs of achieving it. One consequence is that it is often much easier to achieve small improvements to existing policies than to effect major new departures, although this is not to say that they should never make radical proposals!

Unfortunately, the training received by an economics graduate will often do little to prepare him for the complexities of the tasks just mentioned. There has grown up in North America and elsewhere a narrowly 'scientific' view which is a far cry from the concern of earlier generations with questions of political economy. The universities of developing countries are by no means immune from this type of bias. In consequence, modern economics is largely silent on the nature of the state as an economic agent. To the extent that we have earlier in this chapter identified the model of government implicit in economists' normative theories of economic policy, we have seen it to abstract in a very high degree from observed political realities. The economics graduate may therefore find himself 'all dressed up with nowhere to go' – brimming with knowledge of refined economic theory and sophisticated econometric techniques, but innocent of ideas on how to translate this knowledge into improved policies.

In modern economics the standard view of the role of the economist as a policy adviser is *positivist*. On this view, the economic adviser takes the economic objectives handed down to him by the government, dispassionately reviews the evidence, sets out the alternative lines of action available, describes (in neutral language) the advantages and disadvantages of each of these, and then leaves it to the politicians to make their choice. There are powerful objections to this view. For one thing, it is impossible for an economist to give advice which is not influenced by his own values and preferences. For another, government objectives are rarely specified with the accuracy and consistency implied by the positivist approach. But, above all, the positivist model is a recipe for ineffectiveness. Political decisions are the resultants of highly complex interplays of pressures, points of view, special interests, bureaucratic distortions and personal prejudices. Any important change of policy is the outcome of committed advocacy, of the exercise of personal influence, of bargaining, of the distribution of administrative and political power. The economist who prefers his professional virginity to getting involved in such transactions greatly reduces his prospects of improving economic policies.

To urge that economists be willing to get their hands dirty, to take sides, to 'compromise and barter' is not to completely reject the positivist view. We would be failing as professionals if we did not constantly aspire to objectivity in our handling and presentation of evidence, if we did not strive always to induce decision-makers to greater precision in the definition of their objectives, and to undertake the widest practicable review of available alternatives. To work within the going system is not to accept it as ideal, and among economists' most important tasks is to reduce the uncertainties and other constraints that stand in the way of more rational and consistent decisions. The next chapter is intended to include some practical guidance along these lines.

Suggestions for Revision and Group Discussions

1 Review your understanding of the following:
  (a) Planned, market and mixed economies.
  (b) A social welfare function.
  (c) A marginal rate of transformation.
  (d) The difference between normative and positive models.
  (e) Satisficing.
  (f) The theory of the second best.
  (g) Externalities.
  (h) The poverty trap.
  (i) Static, distributional and dynamic efficiency.
2 What sources of information could you use in order to compile a list of the principal ways in which the government affects economic life in your country?
3 What do you understand to be the principal functions of an economic system?
4 What is the economic rationale for drawing the TT' curve in Figure 1.1 as concave to the origin?
5 'Criticisms of the welfare optimizing model to the effect that it is unrealistic are misplaced because it is a normative not a behavioural model.' Do you think it is legitimate to draw such a sharp distinction between what is and what should be?
6 It has often been argued that governments of LDCs should concentrate on achieving the maximum rate of economic growth, if necessary at the expense of static efficiency and short-term economic stability. Consider the welfare implications of this and the circumstances in which it would *not* be sound advice. In pondering your answer consider the four ways of raising welfare summarized on page 17. Reference to Figure 1.6 may also be helpful.
7 Page 11 sets out a list of specifications for a realistic model of government decision-making. Write a note assessing the extent to which the satisficing model meets these specifications.
8 Compare the welfare properties of the growth path passing through A, B and C in Figure 1.6 with the paths passing through D, E and F, and through G, H and J.
9 Use the developing country data in Table 1.2 to plot YY and PP curves in a diagram using the same axes as Figure 1.10. What are the implications of the results for the validity of the poverty-trap model? (Note: rates of population growth can be obtained by subtracting column (3) growth rates from column (2) in Table 1.2.)
10 Study the following passage contrasting political and non-political rationality. Use it as a basis for a discussion of the positivist view of the role of the economist, summarized on the last pages of this chapter.

Political rationality is the fundamental kind of reason, because it deals with the preservation and improvement of decision structures, and decision structures are the source of all decisions. Unless a decision structure exists, no reasoning and no decisions are possible ... There can be no conflict between political rationality and ... technical, legal, social, or economic rationality, because the solution of political problems makes possible an attack on any other problem, while a serious political deficiency can prevent or undo all other problem solving ... Non-political decisions are reached by considering a problem in its own terms, and by evaluating proposals according to how well they solve the problem. The best available proposal should be accepted regardless of who makes it or who opposes it, and a faulty proposal should be rejected or improved no matter who makes it. Compromise is always irrational; the rational procedure is to determine which proposal is the best, and to accept it. In a political decision on the other hand, action never is based on the merits of a proposal but always on who makes it and who opposes it. Action should be designed to avoid complete identification with any proposal and any point of view, no matter how good or how popular it might be. The best available proposal should never be accepted just because it is best; it should be deferred, objected to, discussed, until major opposition disappears. Compromise is always a rational procedure, even when the compromise is between a good and a bad proposal.

From Paul Diesing's *Reason in Society* (1962)
quoted by Wildavsky, 1974, pp. 189–90.

Suggestions for Further Reading

(Full publication details of the recommendations given in the 'Suggestions for further reading' at the end of each chapter can be found in the bibliography at the end of the book.)

The subject-matter of this chapter has not been dealt with very systematically in economics, especially in relation to developing countries, so it is impossible to recommend any single work. The following should be useful references on particular topics, although few of them relate specifically to LDCs.

Grossman, 1974, provides an excellent introduction to the study of comparative economic systems and to the subject-matter of Part II of the chapter. It includes a selected reading list.

The literature relating to Part III – on governments and their decision processes – is especially weak but the first four chapters of Bauer and Gergen, 1968, are recommended. Read the second of these (by Zeckhauser and Shaefer) first for an orthodox expression of the economic theorist's view and then ch. 1, 3 and 4 for other viewpoints. See also Lindblom, 1968, for a political science introduction to policy-making. Tinbergen, 1967(B), is a classic study of the principles of economic policy but seriously marred, in my view, by political naivety. Chapters 14 and 15 of Simon, 1957, contain much that is relevant, including an exposition of the satisficing model of decision-making. Mosley, 1976, also presents the satisficing model and then applies it to fiscal and monetary policies in Britain. Chapters 4 and 5 of Hirschman, 1963, contain an interesting discussion of policy-formation in Latin America.

The concepts of economic efficiency discussed in Part IV are discussed and applied extensively in Scitovsky, 1970, although his main emphasis is on static efficiency.

Further clarification is provided by Assar Lindbeck's admirable essay in Kaser and Portes, 1971. His essay has strongly influenced Part V of the chapter, even though it does not have much to say directly about developing countries. Chapter 7 of Myint, 1967, contains a clear statement and critique of the poverty trap and other criticisms of the dynamic efficiency of a market economy.

The distinction between normative and positive economics, which crops up several times in the chapter, is dealt with more fully in Lipsey, 1975, ch. 1; and in ch. 2 of the American version, Lipsey and Steiner, 1975. James O'Connor ably presents a Marxian viewpoint in an essay in Hunt and Schwartz, 1972. Fairly demanding but admirable surveys concerning several of the topics of this chapter are to be found in ch. 1–5 of Burkhead and Miner, 1971; and in Steiner's contribution to Blinder, *et al.*, 1974.

See also the additional references given in the notes to this chapter.

2 Objectives, instruments and implementation

'Wisdom denotes the pursuing of the best ends by the best means.' *Francis Hutcheson*

Contents

I. The Three Dimensions of the Policy Problem

An exchange of memoranda

To set the scene, consider the following imaginary exchange of memoranda:

From: Minister of Industries

To: Chairman, State Industrial Development Corporation (SIDC)

Subject: The failure of the corporation to promote government objectives

1. As you know, the SIDC was set up by government to promote the industrial development of our country by supplementing the inadequate level of private investment and investing directly in manufacturing enterprises. It was expected that in this way the rate of industrialization would be accelerated, employment would be created, and scarce foreign exchange would be saved. After its initial capitalization, it was anticipated that SIDC would be self-financing, using profits earned on past investments to fund new projects.

2. For some time past the government and the party have been receiving complaints about the failure of SIDC to live up to these expectations. Far from being self-financing, the corporation regularly makes large losses which have to be met by government subsidies. This poor financial record has meant that no money has been available for new investment, so that SIDC has contributed little to industrialization for some time. It is also found that the corporation has largely invested in industries processing imported raw materials so that, when allowance is made for the cost of imported capital equipment, it has actually been a net burden on the balance of payments. Finally, there have been numerous allegations that the managements of several of your enterprises are incompetent.

3. I invite your response to these complaints.

From: Chairman, State Industrial Development Corporation

To: Minister of Industries

Subject: The failure of government to allow SIDC to succeed

1. I have read your memorandum with interest and am grateful for the opportunity to reply to the complaints you have received.

2. It is, of course, true that SIDC has not been profitable in the past and has therefore needed the financial support of the government. It must also be admitted that SIDC has undertaken little new investment in the last few years because government has not been willing to vote us more funds than are needed to cover current losses on our existing operations. I share with you disappointment with this state of affairs but attribute it not to the shortcomings of the corporation but to the government's own lack of realism and clarity, and to its interference in the internal affairs of the corporation.

3. As you know, a great deal of political pressure has been brought to bear on the corporation's management to provide jobs for numerous individuals and groups, and I have more than once complained to you that as a result our factories are seriously over-manned. These pressures to create jobs obviously undermine the possibility of making profits. You will also remember that the corporation was instructed to make a large investment in a steel mill on the grounds that it would save foreign exchange, even though we pointed out that there were no prospects that such an investment would be profitable. It was, in any case, unrealistic for the government to expect that SIDC could quickly become profitable because we have concentrated on projects that were not sufficiently promising to attract private capital and because it takes time before an enterprise overcomes its teething troubles and starts to make money.

4. As regards the calibre of management of our enterprises, in this matter too we have not had a free hand. For example, I am sure it is not necessary to remind you that the corporation was required to appoint your predecessor as managing director of one of our largest subsidiaries to ease the political difficulties of dropping him from the government.

5. I trust you will find these comments to your satisfaction.

Clearly, these gentlemen have only just begun what promises to be a lengthy and irate correspondence but we will leave them there in order to disentangle the various elements of the dispute (Chapter 11 is about the economics of public enterprise and you will see there that the situation portrayed above is not fanciful).

On examination, the argument can be seen as being conducted at three different levels. First, there is disagreement about the *objectives* of policy (criticized by the chairman as 'unclear and unrealistic'); secondly, there is criticism of the appropriateness of the policy *instruments* chosen by the corporation (especially its choice of projects depending on imported raw materials); thirdly, there are complaints about poor *implementation* of policies ('inefficient managements', 'government interference').

The chairman was surely justified in drawing attention to the difficulties created by the government's stated objectives for the corporation, set out in the first paragraph of the minister's memo, because of the strong potential conflict between using SIDC as a means of creating jobs in industries not promising enough to attract private investors and the expectation that it should be commercially profitable. This is a classical dimension of the policy problem: the pursuit of multiple and potentially conflicting objectives.

Complaints about SIDC's policies also appear justified. Told to create jobs, save foreign exchange and promote industrialization, it makes little sense to invest in projects depending on imported materials rather than locally produced inputs. This raises questions about the appropriateness, or efficiency, of SIDC's chosen policies – another oft-recurring dimension of economic policy issues. No less common is the implementation aspect, exemplified in this case by poor enterprise managements and counter-productive government interference in the corporation's work. Objectives may be clearly defined and efficient policies chosen but the risk of failure is still large because of the danger that policies will not be carried out in the intended manner or not enforced at all.

This chapter is about these three dimensions of the policy problem, about the relationships between objectives, policy instruments, and implementation.

> **Activity.** Take any major policy controversy that
> has received public discussion in your country
> and see if it becomes clearer when you analyse it
> into the objectives–instruments–implementation
> categories set out above.

II.   Objectives and Instrument of Economic Policy

Multiple and hierarchical objectives

> **Activity.** It will be assumed in the following that
> you have already studied Chapter 1.

It is very easy to write down a list of objectives of
economic policy to which practically all
governments – from neo-fascist through liberal-
democratic to communist – publicly subscribe, for all
governments are on the side of the angels, are they
not?[1] Rapid economic growth, a just distribution of
incomes, price stability: this kind of list has in
common with the universal declaration of human
rights the fact that all governments say they favour it.
The difficulty, of course, is to penetrate the rhetoric of
public pronouncements to find out the government's
real objectives and priorities, and this is largely a task
of observing the preferences that are revealed by what
the government actually does, as distinct from what it
says it is going to do. Indeed, one of its actual
objectives may be to conceal from the public what its
true objectives are!

Even when governments are sincere in saying that
their policies are such and such our difficulties are far
from being over. There is first a point touched on in
Chapter 1 that, in practice, decision-making power
will inevitably be delegated and diffused within
society. The various agencies and persons who share
this power will have their own objectives, not
necessarily the same as, or consistent with, those of
the central government. In other words, when we are
told, say, that it is a government objective to raise the
level of saving in the economy we need to ask, how
wide is the consensus on the desirability of this among
those who effectively wield power and influence? The
Minister of Finance may be in favour, but is the Prime
Minister and the Governor of the Central Bank?

Second and of crucial importance, there is the
question of the priorities or weights that are attached
to the various goals. That was the problem of the
chairman of SIDC: how much weight should he place
upon the creation of jobs, the saving of foreign

exchange, the generation of profits? Had he known
the answer he would have been in a better position to
devise optimal policies for his organization.
Governments are notoriously reluctant, or unable, to
be precise about their priorities, about how much of
one objective they are willing to give up in order to get
more of another. We return to this shortly.

Yet another difficulty is that objectives and
priorities change over time, as circumstances alter.
This gives rise to policies which are inconsistent with
each other or no longer appropriate because some
were designed to achieve goals which have become
redundant. For example, the educational system may
currently have too many teachers' training colleges
and not enough primary schools, reflecting an earlier
period when top priority was given to increasing the
number of qualified teachers, even though the priority
may since have been shifted to universal primary
education.

Among the points to emerge from these
paragraphs are the notions that a government is likely
to pursue a multiplicity of objectives but that these
will not command equal importance. No doubt one
could say that there is only one final objective of
economic policy – to maximize the welfare of society.
But this does not help very much so let us turn now to
look in more detail at the most commonly occurring
goals of economic policy in LDCs, at their relative
importance, and at the conflicts that may arise
between them.

Table 2.1 attempts to do this, building upon the
concept of economic efficiency introduced in the last
chapter and distinguishing major objectives (those
which are prefixed by a letter) from what are called
subsidiary objectives (those which are numbered).
(Ignore the right-hand column for the time being.)
Maximizing the inflow of capital from the rest of the
world, for example, is called a subsidiary objective
because it is likely to be adopted not for its own sake
but because of the contribution it may make to the
larger objective of developing the economy.

Table 2.1 is just one man's attempt at classification
and there is plenty of scope for argument about the
items that have been included or left out, and about
the status they have been given. But it does have the
merit of showing the potentially large number of
policy objectives and of conveying the idea that not all
deserve equal status. It also shows that some

---

[1] Thus, of the eighteen governments, covering a very wide political
spectrum, which replied to a questionnaire on their objectives
virtually all asserted their pursuit of: increased national income; an
improved employment situation; price stability; a more equal
distribution of income between individuals; balanced regional
economic development. Compare Tinbergen, 1964, pp. 118–19.

subsidiary objectives (price stability, reduced inequality, reduced population growth) are particularly attractive because they may promote more than one major objective (see asterisked items in Table 2.1).

Activity. A class discussion is suggested to explore why asterisks have been placed after some of the subsidiary objectives in Table 2.1, i.e. how they might promote more than one major objective.

The possibility of conflict between objectives

However, the main interest of Table 2.1 lies in the right-hand column, marked 'potential conflict areas'. This shows for each of the subsidiary objectives which other objectives they may conflict with. For example, no. 1 ('satisfaction of private consumption wants') is marked 'D, 2, 3, 4'. This is meant to indicate that the satisfaction of private consumption wants is liable to conflict with major objective D – economic development (because it will compete resources away

from investment) – and with subsidiary objectives 2, 3 and 4 – the satisfaction of public wants (also because they will be competing with each other for available resources), balance of payments equilibrium (because high consumption will increase the demand for imports), and price stability (because of the danger that private purchasing power will exceed available supplies and thus tend to bid prices up).

It would be tiresome to go through every entry in this way but your attention is particularly drawn to the following points:

(1) A great deal of potential conflict is noted between the major objectives of static efficiency and social justice, on the one hand, and long-run development on the other. This is because the satisfaction of both private and public wants will tend to conflict with the developmental goals of high saving and investment, and because policies to ensure price stability could similarly result in reduced investment. Social justice is likewise seen as carrying the threat of retarding the pace of development because increased employment can be pursued by means which retard economic growth, as in the example given at the beginning

Table 2.1
Major and Subsidiary Objectives of Economic Policy and Potential Conflicts†

Policy objectives	Potential conflict areas
A *Static Efficiency (short run)*	
1. Satisfaction of private consumption wants	D, 2, 3, 4
2. Satisfaction of public wants*	D, 3, 4
3. Balance of payments equilibrium*	4
4. Price stability*	D
5. Removal of market imperfections* (see also no. 6)	
B *Social Justice*	
6. Increased employment*	D, 3, 4
7. Reduced inter-personal income inequalities*	D
8. Reduced inter-regional income inequalities* (see also nos. 2, 4, 5 and 14)	D
C *National Cohesion*	
9. Economic independence	A, D
10. Provision of economic symbols of nationhood (see also nos. 2, 6 and 7)	A
D *Economic Development (long run)*	
11. High saving	A
12. Maximum capital inflows from rest of world	C
13. Structural change (modernization)	A, C
14. Reduced population growth* (see also nos. 2, 3 and 5)	

Note: †Major objectives are prefixed by a letter and set in italic type; subsidiary objectives are numbered and in ordinary type. An asterisk (*) denotes a subsidiary objective that tends to promote more than one major objective.

of this chapter (over-manning in the public sector); greater inter-personal and inter-regional equality can also be sought by means which retard development, for example if they weaken incentives or place resources in low-productivity uses.

(2) Rather strong potential friction is also seen to exist between the major objectives of static efficiency and national cohesion. The main point here is that the pursuit of economic independence and the provision of 'the economic symbols of nationhood' (a splendid capital city, a prestigious national airline, an extensive network of overseas embassies) are likely to represent an inefficient use of resources, in the static sense of maximum output from given resources. It is a kind of 'collective consumption' which competes for resources with other objectives. This does not, however, necessarily argue against economic independence or the symbols of nationhood. There is no logical way of choosing between static efficiency and national cohesion, although economists do often write as if it is self-evident that static efficiency is the more meritorious.

(3) A considerable degree of potential conflict is indicated between the subsidiary objectives coming under the 'static efficiency' heading. Several of these have already been mentioned; one other that deserves attention is the possible conflict between the pursuit of balance of payments equilibrium and price stability. This arises because improving the balance of payments will generally require increased exports and/or fewer imports, reducing the availability of goods on the domestic market and creating the danger of an inflationary excess of demand over supply. This topic is taken up in Chapters 7 and 8.

(4) The removal of market imperfections and reduced population growth are the only subsidiary objectives which do not threaten to conflict with others. They therefore gain in attractiveness on this account, especially because they are both asterisked as contributing to more than one major objective.

(5) Using the same criteria, the satisfaction of private consumption wants and economic independence suffer from the disadvantages of only promoting one major objective while potentially conflicting with various other major or subsidiary objectives.

Activity. Why do you think the removal of market imperfections is marked as contributing to more than one major objective? Which others might it promote?

The reconciliation of competing objectives

The reader will probably have noticed from Table 2.1 and the text that they have all along referred to 'potential' conflicts between objectives. This is intended to indicate that while the danger of conflict is there it is not impossible to avoid. How, then, can these potential conflicts be averted?

Trade-offs

One approach involves reintroducing the notion of *trade-offs* made familiar in the previous chapter. In the welfare-optimizing tradition, we can seek to quantify the trade-offs that exist between any two objectives, confront these with the marginal rates of substitution of the policy-makers and thus settle on an optimal combination of the type illustrated in Figure 1.1 on page 8. To provide a more specific example, take the well-known 'Phillips curve' which is in most theory textbooks. A Phillips curve of the type portrayed in Figure 2.1 postulates a trade-off between price stability and the level of employment in the economy. As unemployment is reduced the power and pushfulness of the trade unions may increase and they will tend to force money wages up at rates exceeding the growth of labour productivity. This will raise unit labour costs and these cost increases will be passed on to the consumer in the form of higher prices, thus increasing the rate of inflation. Reductions in the inflation rate may necessitate government actions to curb purchasing power and investment, tending to increase unemployment, reduce the bargaining power of the unions, and so on.

Figure 2.1 has been drawn to show that the choice between points a and b on the curve is between a 4 per cent change in the rate of inflation and a 2 per cent change in unemployment. If the economy starts at

Figure 2.1 *The trade-off between price stability and employment.*

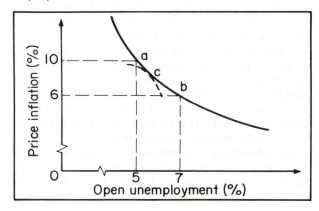

point a, with inflation at 10 per cent a year and open unemployment at 5 per cent, it can bring inflation down to 6 per cent only at the cost of increasing unemployment to 7 per cent (at point b). Or if we start at point b, we can get unemployment down to 5 per cent but only at the cost of pushing inflation up to 10 per cent.

What should be done? In theoretical terms, this is an easy problem: we confront the government with this evidence and ask it to specify its own preference function (the dotted schedule in Figure 2.1). We then settle on that part of the Phillips curve at which the marginal rate of substitution is equal to the marginal rate of transformation (point c). But for reasons explored in Chapter 1 this approach has severe practical limitations. It is unlikely that a government will provide the type of information needed for the specification of a preference function, even less likely that it will adhere to it consistently. We might alternatively try a satisficing approach, asking the government to specify the maximum tolerable rates of inflation and unemployment and then seeking a solution that satisfies these constraints.

> **Activity.** If the last paragraph is not clear to you, review Part III of Chapter 1. If it is clear, try (1) to explain why the dotted preference schedule in Figure 2.1 is concave instead of having the convexity of most indifference curves; and (2) redraw Figure 2.1 to illustrate a satisficing solution.

Shadow prices

A different line of approach that can be used in some cases of goal conflict is the application of *shadow prices*. The theoretical derivation of shadow prices, like the trade-off approach, stems from the welfare optimizing model and has some of its disadvantages, the most characteristic of these being the great difficulty of bridging the gap between the theory of shadow prices and their real-world calculation. Nevertheless, it has been found possible in many countries to estimate some key shadow prices and to apply these to cost-benefit evaluations of public sector investments. It is thus an approach which has at least some degree of practicality.

A shadow price is to be compared with the market price for the same item and the need for it arises from the market failures discussed in Chapter 1. Because of externalities, market distortions, government

regulations and other reasons, prices often do not reflect the social value (or cost) of the item in question. For example, it is widely believed that wage rates of urban unskilled workers over-value this type of labour in LDCs because its opportunity cost, in terms of output foregone, is lower than the money wage. Similarly, the tendency of governments to resort to import and exchange controls to shore-up an over-valued currency means that official exchange rates often understate the scarcity value of foreign exchange. Shadow prices are intended to correct for these discrepancies between actual and social valuations. The appendix to this chapter elaborates further on the meaning and estimation of shadow prices, and their use in cost-benefit analysis.

> **Key concept.** A **shadow price** attempts to measure the total utility value to society of an output or the scarcity value to society of an input. They are used when it is believed that actual prices do not faithfully indicate these values and are usually estimated as adjustments to market prices.

I will give two examples of how they can be used to reconcile potential conflicts between policy objectives. Referring back to Table 2.1, you will see that it indicated the possibility of a conflict between the objectives of increased employment and long-run economic development. It is not uncommon for the process of development to fail to absorb increases in the labour force and for governments to react to the resulting increases in unemployment with employment-creating measures which are harmful to development (as in the SIDC case in Part I). However, a possible reason why the development process fails to absorb increases in the supply of labour is that wages are too high (i.e. the market price of labour is greater than the social value), causing investors to choose capital-intensive production techniques which use little labour.

However, if a shadow wage were substituted for the actual wage in the appraisal of investment projects this tendency would be weakened. Labour would now show up as a smaller cost item relative to capital and there would be less incentive for the selection of capital-intensive techniques. In this way the use of the shadow wage would help to reconcile the objectives of employment creation and long-run development.

The second example involves the tensions noted earlier between the objectives of satisfying consumption wants with the objective of long-run economic development. At this point we must introduce a new type of shadow price, the social rate of discount – a concept which receives fuller treatment in the appendix. The social rate of discount, which is expressed as an annual interest rate, can be thought of as a reflection of society's (or the government's) time preferences. For example, if we are told that the social rate of discount is 10 per cent this tells us that to be compensated for foregoing $100 of consumption now society will have to be offered at least $110 in a year's time, otherwise the postponement of consumption will not be regarded as worthwhile.

By deflating future streams of benefits by the social rate of discount it is possible to convert them into 'present values', so that in the example given in the previous paragraph the present value of $110 in a year's time, discounted at 10 per cent, is $100. This then provides us with a technique for making rational decisions about the competing claims of the present and the future. The present satisfaction of private and public consumption wants can be directly compared with the present value of the (larger) future consumption possibilities resulting from economic development. All future benefits (and costs) can be converted into present values and the policy-making task is to maximize the present value of current and future net benefits.

At present the applicability of shadow prices as a technique for reconciling tensions between objectives is limited. This type of analysis is largely confined to the evaluation of large public-sector projects and there remain many difficulties in the way of translating the theory into practice. Nevertheless, cost-benefit analysis is a technique of growing importance and is likely to receive wider application in the future.

Multiple policy instruments

In the face of multiple and conflicting objectives the most common reconciliation technique, however, is the use of *multiple policy instruments* designed to achieve simultaneously more than one goal. This point will be elaborated in Part III so we will simply consider an illustration at this point. Mention was made earlier of the possibility of conflict between the objectives of equilibrium on the balance of payments and price stability. Getting rid of a payments deficit will likely require cutting down on imports and expanding exports, both measures tending to reduce the availability of goods to the domestic economy. Price stability, on the other hand, will require that total domestic demand and supply should be kept in line with each other. So a policy of improving the balance of payments, say by imposing import

restrictions, will tend to spill over into domestic inflation, by reducing supplies relative to demand. Conversely, one way of combating domestic inflation is to increase imports, increasing supply relative to demand – but only at a cost to the balance of payments. It is, however, possible to reconcile these by employing a co-ordinated package of policy measures, essential to which would be policies to reduce domestic demand, like tax increases, reduced government spending and credit restrictions. The careful choice of multiple policy instruments can go a large distance towards the reconciliation of potentially conflicting objectives.

Not necessarily all the way, however. Economists have no magic wand with which to miraculously marry the incompatible. Sometimes governments foolishly, or out of some political necessity, pursue objectives which are flatly opposed to each other. Hopefully, the contradictions arising in these cases will eventually lead to a re-evaluation by the government. No less frequently, the theoretical means of reconciliation are known but the relevant policy instruments are not strong enough, or acceptable enough, to stand the burden placed upon them (an example is the enormous difficulties almost all governments have in achieving both low inflation and low unemployment). Or the capacity of the public administration to implement the chosen policies may be insufficient to achieve the desired results.

In these cases of unresolved conflict the only recourse is to change one or more of the dimensions of policy: revise objectives; improve policies; strengthen implementation.

Activity. Using your country's development plan or some other apparently comprehensive statement of government objectives, draw up a table similar to Table 2.1. This may then be used as a basis for class discussion, exploring questions such as: Are objectives clearly defined? Is there a clear hierarchy among them? Are there any significant omissions? What are the most important actual or potential conflicts between them?

Clarity, realism and target-setting

You may remember from the beginning of the chapter that the chairman accused the government of a lack of clarity and realism in its objectives for SIDC but not much has been said about these issues so far. Look back at Table 2.1 and ask yourself about the precision of the objectives listed there. What, for example, is actually meant by economic development? Is it to be taken, as it often has been, as synonymous with economic growth? Or should it, as many now argue, also refer to the distribution of the gains from growth and the elimination of poverty?[2] The notions of 'social justice' and 'national cohesion' are even more vague.

The subsidiary objectives, being narrower, should at least be reasonably precise but again there are many ambiguities. Note the imprecision of 'increased employment'. Note too the ambiguity of references to the satisfaction of 'wants'. Does this refer to needs or to demand made effective by purchasing power? Is price stability denoted by a complete absence of any price increases? By how much do we want to reduce interpersonal inequalities – until there is complete equality, or merely an absence of poverty, or what?

In moving from objectives to policies it can be extremely important to remove this type of ambiguity, otherwise the fuzziness will affect the policies as well as the goals. One way of doing this is to set quantitative targets – a certain maximum percentage level of unemployment, a maximum value to the size of the balance of payments deficit, a specific savings ratio, and so on. Armed with these the economist is better able to make specific suggestions about policies, as will be shown shortly. Moreover, when objectives are translated into targets it is much easier to form a judgement about their feasibility and thus about any need to adjust them to the realities of the situation.

A caution is, however, due against the proliferation of targets. The impression of accuracy they convey may be quite spurious; they may be arbitrary numbers reflecting no more than aspirations, rather than being carefully considered priorities formed after meticulous study of feasible policy alternatives.

The instruments of economic policy

You have already come across numerous references to 'policy instruments' in this book; it is high time that the meaning of this term was made clear. A policy instrument may be defined as a means controlled by the government of changing the behaviour of the economy. Table 2.2 sets out some of the chief instruments of economic policy and illustrates the type of use to which each can be put. It is worth spending a little time studying this table. After doing so the rather abstract definition just offered should take on more meaning. Thus, the table lists the government's powers of taxation and spending as among the instruments available to it. Its legislative powers also feature prominently: its ability to impose direct controls; to establish and vary the legal framework of economic activity. All the items listed in the left-hand side of the table are under the direct control of the government and the right-hand side records some of the numerous ways these instruments can be used to change economic behaviour in pursuit of government objectives.

We can at this point mention a few analytical distinctions which are useful when thinking about economic policy instruments. The first concerns their *mode of operation* and draws attention to the important difference between instruments that affect the economy in a direct way and those which exert a largely indirect influence. Instruments which operate directly include government expenditures (which produce some service or a physical asset such as a new road), direct controls (which regulate the quantity of imports or place legal limits on prices and rents) and other legislative provisions, for example to nationalize an industry, or to reform the law on land tenure.

Most of the indirect instruments are designed to achieve their desired results by altering the price signals generated by the market system. Examples include attempts to discourage certain types of consumption through taxation, to encourage saving by raising interest rates, and to encourage exports by depreciating the exchange rate. By contrast, direct measures bypass the market mechanism and are often alternatives to it. All governments use both direct and indirect means but the balance which is struck between them has an important bearing upon the system of resource allocation which prevails in an economy.

A different distinction arises from thinking about the *type of impact* which the various instruments can have, the main difference here being between instruments that are general or specific in their impact. Use of the overall budgetary balance, variations in interest rates, or in the rate of exchange, are examples of instruments having a general impact on the macro-economic balance of the economy. By contrast, a tax on a commodity, the award of a subsidy to an industry, and the imposition of a price control are examples of instruments which are specific in their incidence. Obviously, choices between these two types will depend on the objectives being pursued.

Yet another useful distinction is between an instrument and a change in value of an instrument. For example, a decision to impose a tax on imported cloth where no tax formerly existed brings a new policy instrument into use, whereas a decision to change the rate of tax on cloth would represent a variation in the use of that instrument. This distinction is particularly relevant when one is

---

[2] For a discussion of this important issue see Baster, 1974.

Table 2.2
Chief Instruments of Economic Policy and Their Use

Policy instruments	Typical uses
1. *Fiscal Policy*	
(a) Direct taxes on income and profits	To reduce income inequalities; to regulate aggregate demand.
(b) Import duties	Protection of domestic producers.
(c) Other indirect taxes (purchase, sales and turnover taxes)	To discourage luxury consumption.
(d) Social security levies	To finance pensions; compulsory saving.
(e) Transfer payments (unemployment, sickness and retirement benefits; subsidies)	To reduce income inequalities and poverty.
(f) Government current expenditures	Provision of services (justice, education, agricultural extension, family planning).
(g) Government capital expenditures	Provision of infrastructure (roads, communications, water).
(h) The budgetary balance (extent of government borrowing)	To adjust the balance between aggregate domestic demand and supply.
2. *Financial and Monetary Policy*	
(a) Promotion/support of financial intermediaries	To improve credit and saving facilities.
(b) Variation of interest rates	To regulate the macro-economic balance of the economy.
(c) Credit controls	
3. *Direct Controls*	
(a) Exchange controls	To protect the balance of payments.
(b) The exchange rate	
(c) Price and rent controls	To counter inflation.
(d) Wage controls	To set minimum standards; to prevent inflationary wage increases; to encourage employment creation.
(e) Immigration quotas	To promote training of indigenous personnel.
(f) Industrial licensing	To achieve a planned pattern of industrialization.
4. *Miscellaneous*	
(a) Exhortation for voluntary action	'Buy local goods', 'work harder', 'pay your taxes'.
(b) Creation of parastatal organizations	Marketing boards; provision of public utilities; research institutions; agricultural production boards.
(c) Nationalization	To promote economic independence.
(d) Investment incentives (tax holidays, accelerated depreciation)	To encourage investment, especially from abroad.
(e) Other legislative provisions	Company and anti-monopoly legislation; patent laws; land reform.
(f) Requests for official foreign aid	To encourage investment and protect balance of payments.

employing formal quantitative models for policy purposes (which we turn to in Part III). In the same context, it can be convenient to differentiate between policies which are used to bring about small changes in the economy and policies which alter the structure of the economy and of society. This convenience arises because the former type of instrument can be plugged into a behavioural model of the economy to see what effects it will have, whereas the latter will call for a new model, having altered the structural relationships upon which the old model was based. For most purposes, however, we can dispense with this distinction. It is, in any case, a difficult one to draw in practical circumstances.

> **Key concept.** A **policy instrument** is a means controlled by the government of changing the behaviour of the economy. It may achieve its effect directly, or indirectly through the alteration of price incentives. Its impact may be widely felt throughout the economy or be specific to some particular economic variable.

Having surveyed both the objectives and instruments of economic policy, the next task is to explore the relationships between them.

> **Activity.** You should go through the left-hand side of Table 2.2 and identify the main instruments which are employed in your own country. Are any important ones omitted from the table? Can you identify the main uses to which they have been put? What sort of balance has been maintained in your country between direct and indirect instruments?

III. Economic Policy and Mathematical Models

Mention was made earlier of the possibility of using multiple policy instruments to reconcile conflicting objectives and this provides a convenient starting point for an exploration of the relationships between objectives and instruments.

An informal statement

To do this properly we will have to go into some formal, but simple, mathematical reasoning. The essential points can, however, be presented in an intuitive manner. Imagine a government with only one objective, to increase the amount of employment. Just deciding the objective will not change anything; it will have to use at least one policy instrument in order to get results. It may, for example, undertake a government investment programme. But that programme will require imports of capital equipment and will therefore tend to create a deficit on the balance of payments.

Faced with the situation we assume the government formulates a second objective, to reduce the payments deficit. The two objectives are now liable to conflict because more employment will mean more spending power which will mean a greater demand for imports and exportables. It is easy to see that this conflict is unlikely to be resolved so long as the government relies exclusively on its investment programme. It

stands a much better chance if it brings one or more additional policies into use. For example, it could impose taxes on imports in order to reduce demand for these goods, or it could devalue the currency, which would raise the domestic price of imports and make exporting more profitable.

This example illustrates the general point that *the more objectives the government wishes to pursue the more instruments it will need to use*. This is only a rule of thumb, not a rigid principle. It is possible that a devaluation by itself would be enough to spark an export-led expansion of employment as well as keeping the balance of payments in a healthy condition, and that the government investment programme would not be needed. This possibility of using one instrument to achieve more than one objective is greatest when the objectives are specified in an imprecise form ('increase' employment; 'reduce' the balance of payments deficit). It is much smaller when the objectives are translated into specific targets ('increase employment by 4 per cent'; 'reduce the balance of payments deficit to zero'). Only by good luck would one instrument, say a devaluation, bring both employment and the balance of payments simultaneously to exactly the targeted levels.

In general, then, the ability of governments to achieve multiple objectives is a function of the *number* of policy instruments it employs for these purposes. Equally important, it is a function of the *efficiency* of the chosen instruments – their appropriateness to achieve the desired results. Thus, the effectiveness of devaluation in our example would depend critically on the responsiveness of the export industries to the new incentives and of consumers to the higher import prices. The larger the responses, the more powerful the devaluation in effecting the desired changes.

What is meant by the efficiency of an instrument will be explored later. For the time being we concentrate on a more formal statement of the general rule presented two paragraphs ago. This principle, and the model underlying it, is most closely associated with the name of the eminent Dutch economist Jan Tinbergen and the next step is to provide a simplified statement of his system.

The Tinbergen system

On the basis of certain simplifying assumptions, to be stated shortly, Tinbergen places all relevant economic variables into two categories. First, there are *target variables* (called t-variables). These relate to such items as the level of employment, the rate of inflation, the growth of output, the distribution of income – variables the government is likely to be interested in but which it does not directly control. What the government can, and is assumed to, do is to set target values for these, which is why they are called target variables. Mathematically speaking, the values of these targets are exogenously determined by the government.

Policy instruments are the second type of variable, and they are called *instrument variables* or policy variables (p-variables). These refer to the type of instrument listed down the left-hand side of Table 2.2: taxes, direct controls, government services and so forth. Mathematically, the values of these are determined within the system – they are endogenous variables, or unknowns, because what values are placed upon them will depend upon the values of the target variables. For instance, we cannot decide what the exchange rate should be until we know what targets have been set for imports and exports.

So we have:

(1) target variables (t-variables) whose values are known and determined exogenously by government;
(2) instrument variables (p-variables), whose values are unknown and endogenously determined by the targets set by the government.

We can now write out a system of linear equations to represent the behaviour of the economy, like this:

$$t_a = f_a (p_1 \ldots \ldots p_z)$$
$$\cdot$$
$$\cdot$$
$$\cdot \qquad\qquad\qquad (1)$$
$$t_y = f_y (p_1 \ldots \ldots p_z)$$

where f is a constant expressing the relationships between the target variable, t, and instrument variables, $p_1 \ldots \ldots p_z$.

We now have a set, y in number, of simultaneous linear equations and the problem is to know whether or not we can solve it. In mathematics the general rule for the solution of a system of this type is that there should be as many dependent variables (variables of unknown magnitude, the p-variables in our case) as there are equations. If there are fewer dependent variables than equations the system will be 'incompatible' or over-determined and no solution will be possible. If the number of dependent variables is greater than the number of equations there are said to be 'degrees of freedom' in the system equal in number to the excess number of unknowns, and there will generally be an infinite number of possible solutions. To solve the system uniquely the degrees of freedom must be eliminated, e.g. by placing values on some of the p-variables, thus transforming them from unknown into exogenous variables. Only when the

number of unknowns is equal to the number of equations will there be a unique solution.

Returning to system (1) above, we see there is one equation for each target variable, making y equations in all, and that there are a total of z instrument variables. So for the system to be soluble, the number of instrument variables must be at least equal to the number of target variables, i.e. $z \geqslant y$. For there to be one unique solution then $z = y$. If $z < y$ it will be impossible to satisfy all the targets, given the number of instruments; a solution would then involve abandoning some targets, or bringing more policy instruments into use, or both.

The key conclusion of the simplified Tinbergen system presented above, is, therefore, that *for a government to achieve multiple policy objectives it must use at least as many policy instruments as the number of its objectives.* However, so simple and general a system can scarcely advance our knowledge very far. The next few paragraphs therefore present a practical application of this approach.

An illustrative application

We will go back to the problem introduced earlier, of the possible conflict between the objectives of employment creation and a healthy balance of payments. This can be illustrated by use of the following simple model of the economy, where

Y = gross domestic product
I = private investment
G = government expenditure
X = exports
E = the volume of wage employment (in thousands)
D = the size of the balance of payments deficit

a, b and c are constants

The behaviour of economy is described by the following equations:

$$Y = a(I + G + X) \qquad (2)$$
$$E = bY \qquad\qquad\qquad (3)$$
$$D = cY - X \qquad\qquad (4)$$

These tell us, first, that the gross domestic produce (Y) is a function of the levels of private investment, government spending and export earnings. The functional relationship, a, between the sum of these three is a multiplier. Secondly, the volume of wage employment is shown as a function of Y, i.e. that the numbers employed will vary with output. In this case the coefficient b is the reciprocal of average value-added per worker. Thirdly, the size of the balance of payments deficit is shown also to be a function of Y, less the value of exports. The coefficient, c, in this case represents society's average propensity to import.

There are a number of ways in which we can use this set of equations. What we want to do here is to explore the possibilities of achieving certain policy targets in this system, concentrating on employment and the balance of payments as objects of government targets. In this case we can simplify the equations (2), (3) and (4) into two others, by substituting equation (2) into both (3) and (4). We can then write:

$$E = ab(I + G + X) \qquad (5)$$

$$D = ac(I + G + X) - X \qquad (6)$$

We assume the government sets a target level of 700 on the volume of employment, allowing the balance of payments to find its own level. We now have two simultaneous linear equations containing:

(1) three exogenous variables: I (which is assumed to be determined independently at $150 million), X (assumed independently determined by conditions in world markets at $200 million) and E (fixed by government decision at a target level of 700);

(2) three constants: a, b and c, with the following assumed values: a = 2·5; b = 0·7; c = 0·3;

(3) two unknowns, D and G.

G is the only instrument variable, so there is one instrument (G) and one target (E).

Substituting the assumed values in equations (5) and (6) we can write:

$$700 = 2·5 \times 0·7 (150 + 200 + G) \qquad (7)$$

$$D = 2·5 \times 0·3 (150 + 200 + G) - 200 \qquad (8)$$

From (7) we can calculate that G = 50 and substituting this value in (8) gives D = 100.

So in order that employment should be at 700, government spending should be set at $50 million. However, this level of spending, in conjunction with the other variables, leaves a balance of payments deficit (D) of $100 million. This may not be a viable situation so the government might, therefore, decide that the deficit must be eliminated, i.e. they may set a second target of D = 0. If we substitute a zero value for D in equations (5) and (6) the system can no longer be solved. With D = 0 the necessary value of G in equation (7) would still be 50 but in equation (8) it would have to be approximately minus 83. The two equations are therefore incompatible. There is now one instrument variable (G) asked simultaneously to meet two targets and, except by coincidence, it cannot do it. At least one additional instrument is now required.

This could take the form of a tax on imports, where T = the average rate of tax. A more complex equation for D, the balance of payments deficit, is now needed incorporating the negative effect of the tax on the demand for imports. Equation (6) could, for example, be rewritten:

$$D = \frac{ac(I + G + X)}{1 + T} - X \qquad (6a)$$

Mathematically, the term $1 + T$ offers a simple way of adjusting import demand downward in response to taxation. Leaving all other values as in the previous solution (except that D = 0), it can be calculated from equations (5) and (6a) that the necessary value of T is 0·5, or 50 per cent. (Try solving the problem yourself to see if you get the same result.)

Activity. Returning to equations (5) and (6), let I = 200, X = 275, a = 2·0, b = 0·8, c = 0·25. Assume the government sets the target D = 0 and allows E to find its own level. What level of government spending (G) will be required? How much employment will be created? Why do you think more employment is created in this case than in the case solved in the text?

An evaluation of the system

Having provided a demonstration of the principle that governments need at least one instrument for each target and having illustrated the use of a Tinbergen-type system, how much further has it taken us and what are its limitations? The limitations are, in fact, rather severe.

All economic models are abstractions. They seek to simplify the real world, concentrating upon its essentials, discarding the irrelevant and in this way reducing problems to manageable proportions. Models should not, therefore, be criticized because they simplify; the appropriate question is rather whether they simplify successfully. Do they only discard factors which are irrelevant to a problem or of secondary importance, or do they throw the baby out with the bathwater by failing to incorporate essential aspects of the problem? In a word, do they over-simplify?

To answer this question for the Tinbergen system it is illuminating to set out the assumptions on which the model is based, and to discuss their realism.

(1) The simplified Tinbergen system assumes that the operation of the economy can be expressed in the form of linear equations and that there are no

time-lags. It therefore assumes away the existence of random factors and non-quantifiable elements. But quite a lot of objectives (economic independence, improvements in the quality of life, the satisfaction of public wants) and instruments (industrial licensing, land reform legislation, nationalization) are difficult, if not impossible, to reduce to numbers. In any case, governments are rarely precise about their objectives, for reasons mentioned in Chapter 1. Moreover, complex (non-linear) relationships and time delays are major aspects of the real world.

(2) The system assumes that changes in policies introduced to achieve targets will be marginal, in the sense that they will not alter the structural relationships in the economy, represented by the coefficients (f). If the values of the fs were altered by the values of the ps the system could not be solved. But it is especially likely in countries at an early stage of development that policies will change structural relationships. Indeed, structural change is needed if development is to proceed.

(3) It assumes that we have perfect, or near-perfect, knowledge of relationships between variables (the values of the fs), i.e. we know how the economy works and what the consequences will be of a given policy change. In practice, however, economists are hazy about the workings of the economy and have only the most approximate idea of the impact of any specific policy action.

(4) The system implicitly assumes that government action (and the information needed to decide what do to do) is costless. So long as a given policy instrument is shown to result in the achievement of a target it is taken for granted that it should be employed. But Chapter 1 was at pains to point out that most government actions impose costs, so that rational policy decisions involve a comparison of the costs with expected benefits.

(5) The system makes a sharp distinction between objectives (targets) and policy instruments. But reality is more complex. If there is a hierarchy of objectives, as suggested in Part II, many of what were there called secondary objectives can also be thought of as means. In Table 2.1, for instance, 'high saving' is listed as secondary to the major objective of economic development: is high saving to be thought of as an end or a means in this case? Or employment creation: is that a means to the reduction of social injustice or an end in itself? Similarly with nationalization: some would view it as a means for protecting consumers or of achieving greater economic

independence; for the Marxist, on the other hand, the nationalization of private property is an essential part of his concept of socialism and is therefore advocated as if for its own sake.

Clearly, then, the model does involve some drastic simplifications. Moreover, we should not be lured by mathematics into abandoning our own common-sense – as a matter of logic it is simply not the case that it is impossible, except by coincidence, to use one instrument to achieve more than one target. It is perfectly sensible, for example, to give import licensing authorities instructions like, 'reduce the total value of imports by x per cent and also raise the proportion of raw materials in total imports by y per cent'. There may be implementation problems but there is no logical flaw in such an instruction.

It would be wrong to finish on a negative note, however, because the case in favour of the quantitative approach has not yet been fully stated. If this approach has limitations, it has considerable strengths as well.

First, it reveals the advantages of being precise and consistent in one's objectives and leads economists and adminstrators to ask politicians the types of question that make for greater precision. Secondly, the development of a model of the economy makes it easier to assess the range of feasible outcomes and thus better equips the economist to tell the government whether its targets and policies are realistic or not. For example, we can tell from the equations on page 41 that a target for E of, say, 1500 would not be possible without an enormous increase in government spending, which itself is unlikely to be feasible.

Thirdly, the quantitative approach encourages precision about the effects of a change in an instrument variable. Referring again to page 41, we can calculate that raising G from 50 to 60 will have the effect of increasing E by 17·5 and D by $7·5 million. Precision of this type is especially to be sought after in the task of maintaining short-run dynamic efficiency in the economy. Fourthly, the approach creates a demand for better information. If this information is forthcoming it is easier to make a rational choice among policy alternatives and to recommend changes large enough (but no larger) to obtain the desired results. We are also better able to make sure that the government's various policies are consistent with each other. Fifthly, and as has already been shown, the Tinbergen method provides an additional approach to the difficult task of reconciling conflicts between objectives, by the use of carefully selected multiple policy instruments.

Faced with these lists of advantages and

disadvantages, what conclusions can we derive about the merits of the quantitative approach? Controversy on this issue still rages among economists and it can scarcely be settled here, but there are one or two inferences to be drawn.

In listing the ways in which the Tinbergen system over-simplifies we were implicitly asking whether it is possible for mathematical models to catch enough of the complexity of real economic life to yield usable results. The simple model presented in this chapter excluded a great deal of the complexity; more sophisticated versions are available which can handle more of it. The basic model can be modified to handle time-lags and at least some forms of non-linear relationships. It can be modified to require a less rigid boundary between targets and instruments. It is possible to make provision for the existence of uncertainty.[3] But these increases in sophistication are achieved only at a cost. The models are far more complex, require more information and expertise, are more difficult to use and less easy to explain to those who finally make the decisions. And the more sophisticated the model, the greater the danger that it will take on a life and justification of its own, diverting the economist's attention away from the less glamorous, but crucial, task of getting down to the practical details of policy specifics.

There is, then, a fundamental dilemma: *the easy models over-simplify, the complex models are often costly and impractical.* The alternative is scarcely more satisfactory, however. At its best, the alternative is policies based on the considered judgement of people who have come to acquire a sensitive 'feel' for the way the economy works. At its worst, the alternative is the 'use of slogans, shibboleths, and unanalysed preconceptions ... which are not quantified and tested against data'.[4] The result in this case will be a hit-or-miss collection of policies and of possibly large costs imposed upon the economy because of the pursuit of inconsistent ends by inappropriate means.

It boils down to an issue bearing a strong family likeness to the discussion in Chapter 1 of the competing claims of the welfare-optimizing and satisficing models of decision-making. This is no coincidence because the Tinbergen approach is strongly in the welfare-optimizing tradition. The conclusion here is similar to that of Chapter 1, that the quantitative approach is strong in indicating ways in which decision-making should be improved but is subject at present to rather severe practical limitations. Of necessity, many important decisions will continue to be made without the aid of formal models and it would be a large mistake to neglect these. But as economists we ought always to be looking for opportunities to improve the rationality of decision-making. In circumstances where quantitative techniques would promote this end they should be employed.

> **Activity.** Review this section and make a list of the circumstances that would be favourable to the successful introduction of quantitative techniques. To what extent do you think these circumstances obtain in your own country?

IV. Assessing the Efficiency of Policy Instruments

Seven efficiency criteria

In the words of the quotation at the beginning of this chapter, 'Wisdom denotes the pursuing of the best ends by the best means'. There have been various references in this chapter to 'appropriate' or 'efficient' policy instruments but the meaning of this has gone undefined, so the question to be taken up in this section is how we can tell whether we are indeed using the 'best means'.

The quantitative approach to policy planning gives us a first lead into this issue because the coefficient (f), expressing the relationship between an instrument variable and a target variable, is a measure of the power of a given change in the instrument to effect a consequential change in the target variable. Take the following simple equation stating the determinants of the amount of saving (S) in an economy, with R = the rate of interest, expressed as a percentage:

$$S = 500 + 9(R) \qquad (8)$$

This tells us that with a zero interest rate the amount of saving would be 500 and that an additional 9 of saving will occur for every percentage point of interest offered. With interest of 5 per cent, total saving would amount to 545, and so on. The coefficient 9 gives some measure of the power, or efficiency, of the manipulation of interest rates as a means of regulating the level of saving. If the target amount of saving is 600, interest rates must be raised to about 11 per cent to get this result. On the other hand, the

---

[3] However, when uncertainty is introduced it is no longer formally the case that a solution will be reached when there are as many instruments as targets. See essay by L. Johansen in Bos, *et al.*, 1973.
[4] Fox, *et al.*, 1973, p. 18.

coefficient clearly gives us only some of the information we would like. Raising interest rates to 11 per cent may have unwanted effects on the volume of investment; it may take a long time before this action has the desired results on saving. Its success may depend on complementary measures, for example to control inflation; and it may spur powerful pressure groups into political agitation. Assessing the efficiency of policy measures is a far more complex task than the mere examination of numerical coefficients. At least the following questions need to be asked about a policy in evaluating its likely efficiency:

(1) How large will the response of the target variable be to a given change in the instrument variable?
(2) How probable is it that the expected results will actually be achieved, and how quickly will they be achieved?
(3) Does the policy act upon the causes of the problem it is directed at?
(4) What are the resource costs of this policy?
(5) Is this policy selective in its application, and flexible over time?
(6) What indirect economic effects will the policy have; will they be positive or negative?
(7) What will be the socio-political effects of the policy?

We will examine each of these questions in turn.

The magnitude of response

This is the test illustrated by the saving example. Other things being equal, the general rule should be to *choose the more powerful instruments*, the ones with the largest coefficients. The acceptability of a policy change to the politicians and to society as a whole will be related to the extent to which it is a break with the past. A proposal for a small change (for example, raising interest rates from 5 to 6 per cent) stands a much better chance of acceptance than for a large, discontinuous change (a tripling of interest rates) in the pluralistic mixed economies of most LDCs. One therefore wants to choose powerful instruments that will need only modest manipulation to achieve desired results.

The speed and probability of results

Of the two dimensions of this criterion, probability is the one that requires most explaining. The point about the *speed* of results is that all policies require some time to achieve their ends but some are quicker

than others. For example, a government may seek to promote industrialization by creating a favourable 'climate' for private investment but this may take a long time to achieve results. Direct state investment in industry would be speedier. In general, the faster-acting policies are to be preferred over the slow, if only because the longer the delay the greater the uncertainty about the outcome (although there may be circumstances in which delay is desirable).

The *probability* of achieving desired results will be affected by a number of considerations. The most important is the ease with which a measure can be implemented. In fact, this subject of implementation is so important that Part V of this chapter is devoted to it. The content of Part V will not be repeated here except to stress two points: (1) the ease of implementation crucially affects the probability that a measure will have the desired results – the more difficult the implementation the smaller the probability of success; (2) the ease with which a measure can be carried out is one of the factors to consider when deciding whether or not to go ahead with the measure – implementation is not something to think about after the crucial decision has been taken.

A second and more obvious influence on the probability of achieving desired results has to do with the state of knowledge: we may merely be guessing that a measure will have such-and-such results, we may be advocating a plunge in the dark. And greater ignorance will surround some instruments than others. If, for example, the task is to raise a given amount of revenue for the budget we may be fairly confident from past experience that one way to do it is to raise the rate of income taxation by a certain percentage, whereas we may be far less confident about the effect, say, of imposing a new capital gains tax for the same purpose.

In brief, the general rule is to *prefer those instruments most likely to achieve their intended results, and to do so quickly.*

Action upon causes

Most policy measures are responses to felt problems, and hence we can ask of a policy, does it act directly upon the causes of the problem? Or does it merely suppress the symptoms or compensate for them? The general rule is obvious: other things being equal, *to prefer measures which act upon causes* to those which do not. But there are exceptions. In some cases it will not be desirable to remove the causes of the problem; in others it will not be practicable. For example, a firm may command monopoly power, which the government wants to act against, because it operates in an industry subject to economies of scale. Its monopoly powers spring from its ability to achieve scale economies and, in this case, it is likely to be in the public interest to devise policies which allow the firm to continue to operate on a large scale (the 'cause of the problem') but which provide safeguards against the firm's abuse of its monopoly power.

In some cases, it may be simply unfeasible for a government to act on the causes of a problem. This is so with drought and famine which result when the rains fail. Despite advances in our control over the environment, it is not yet reasonable to expect governments to guarantee the arrival of the rains; their problem is rather one of devising measures to protect the community against the adverse consequences of unfavourable weather – irrigation, adequate food reserves, and so on.

Resource costs

All policies cost something and one test of efficiency, therefore, is to measure, and compare, how much they cost. The general rule, of course, is *to adopt the least-cost way of achieving a desired result*. This can be called the 'cost-effectiveness' rule.

A natural first approach to the measurement of cost is to inquire about its claim on government revenues. This is how officials of the Ministry of Finance will approach it but is imperfect for the purposes of economic analysis. Think, for example, of the provision of subsidies on essential foods.

The cost of the subsidies to the budget may be large but this does not give a good measure of the resources consumed by this policy because subsidies are essentially transfer payments, from the general body of taxpayers to those who benefit from the subsidies. The direct resource costs in this case are limited to the costs of administering the scheme. More generally, budgetary data may not be reliable indicators of real resource costs for a reason already explored – that the wages of civil servants and the prices of other elements in the budget may not be an accurate measure of their social costs. They may overstate or understate and we would then want to correct the budget figures by the use of shadow prices along the lines discussed in the appendix to this chapter.

In any case, budgetary data are confined to direct costs but there may also be indirect costs. Two examples: (1) An income tax which is deducted at source shifts much of its administrative burden to private employers, who are legally responsible for ensuring that the correct tax is deducted from the wages of their workers. This means extra records and the employment of additional clerks to do the work. It

is a cost to the economy but not to the budget. (2) Use of immigration quotas to limit the inflow of foreign workers is likely to involve limited administrative resources; the larger real cost to the economy is in any loss of output because foreigners are not free to enter as they are needed.

Selectivity and flexibility

To ask about the *selectivity* of an instrument is to ask whether its effects are confined to the furtherance of whatever objective it is intended to promote. For example, among possible ways of promoting the expansion of an export industry we might include devaluation or the subsidization of that industry. We would tend to reject devaluation as the less efficient of the alternatives because it would have many other effects on the economy besides the one intended. The subsidy, on the other hand, would be confined to the target industry and would be the more selective.

The quality of *flexibility* relates to the ease with which an instrument can be discontinued or varied over time, and the extent to which its use forecloses future options. Nationalization is an example of an inflexible instrument: it tends to be irreversible because once an industry has been nationalized it will be very difficult to persuade private investors to buy it back again, and it forecloses future options by tying up large government funds in compensation payments (assuming compensation to be paid) which otherwise could be put to other uses.

The general rules from these considerations are, therefore: don't take a shot-gun to kill a mosquito; *choose instruments which hit their targets in a selective manner; prefer flexible over inflexible instruments*.

Indirect economic effects

The extent to which a policy is liable to have effects on the economy other than those intended is obviously related to the question of selectivity just discussed. The complexity of economic systems is, however, such that virtually all measures have ramifications that were not their chief purpose. The important thing, then, is to be as conscious as possible before a policy decision is taken of what these indirect effects will be, and whether they will be positive or negative. A positive indirect effect is one that promotes some policy objective additional to the one that is the chief motive for introducing the measure. A negative effect is one which conflicts with other policy objectives. One of the most substantial benefits that can result from the quantification of policy problems, as discussed in Part III, is that use of a model helps us to trace and measure the indirect effects of policy alternatives.

To go back to our earlier example of the impact of an increase in interest rates to encourage saving, the indirect economic effects of this measure may include: (1) a fall in the volume of investment, tending to slow down economic growth; (2) a rise in the price of capital relative to labour, tending to promote employment creation; (3) an inflow of short-term capital from the rest of the world (or a reduced outflow); (4) a contraction of the construction industry as a result of reduced investment . . . and so on. Some of these results are favourable, others not. The general rule is clear: *choose instruments to maximize the excess (or minimize the shortfall) of favourable over unfavourable indirect economic effects.*

Socio-political effects

Many policies are chosen or rejected on non-economic grounds, and quite reasonably so since governments have many things to worry about besides economic problems. In fact, the sharp distinction made here between economic and non-economic effects is arbitrary and tends to break down in practice, although it is a convenient simplification for present purposes. It was already urged in Chapter 1 that economists should not ignore these non-economic effects if they wish to influence policies. Indeed, there is some irresponsibility in an economist who refuses to get involved in such matters. One certainly stands a better chance of being listened to by policy-makers if one shows sensitivity to *all* the factors that go into a final decision.

Precisely what type of consideration should be taken into account under this heading will depend upon the circumstances of the case and upon the nature of the government. Among the most general we can include the following:

(1) The expected popularity, or otherwise, of the measure with the general public (affecting the likelihood that the government will adopt it and also the likelihood that it will be sufficiently tolerated to be successfully implemented).
(2) Its effect, if any, on the country's relationships with the rest of the world (the export subsidy mentioned earlier is likely, for example, to be resented by competing countries, who may retaliate).
(3) Its effect on personal liberty: in those societies which place much value on individual liberty this

is an important consideration and is sometimes invoked as an argument against the use of direct controls, as compared with policies that operate through the market and leave individuals free to make up their own minds about how they will dispose of their incomes.

The general rule, of course, is *to select those instruments which will bring the maximum socio-political benefits or minimum socio-political costs,* all judged in terms of the values of society and the objectives of the government.

To sum up, the following general rules have been suggested when choosing among alternative policies for achieving a given objective:

(1) Choose the more powerful instrument.
(2) Choose the instrument most likely to achieve the intended result, and to do so quickly.
(3) Choose the measure which acts upon the causes of the problem.
(4) Adopt the least-cost way of achieving the desired result.
(5) Choose the instrument which is most selective in its effects and most flexible over time.
(6) Choose the instrument which will maximize the excess (or minimize the shortfall) of favourable over unfavourable indirect economic effects.
(7) Choose the instrument which will bring maximum socio-political benefits (or minimum socio-political costs).

Activity. The text has suggested various exceptions and qualifications to these rules. Review these and see if you can think of any others.

The reader will probably have realized that, in any particular application, it is most unlikely that each criterion will point towards the same choice. He will also have seen that each test is not necessarily of equal importance. In the typical case a policy measure will score heavily by some of the tests and poorly by others. In order to arrive at an overall conclusion we therefore need to place weights on each of the tests, reflecting their relative importance, and these weights will depend upon the issue in question. Some criteria may be considered irrelevant to the case in hand; others may be of overriding importance.

To make matters even more complicated, the boundaries between the criteria are not sharply defined. For example, the indirect economic effects will often shade into the socio-political effects. The criteria will assist us to take a decision about the relative merits of policy alternatives on the basis of a fairly systematic review of the relevant considerations but they are not a substitute for judgement.

One further limitation is that the general methodology adopted in this section may encourage a policy-by-policy or problem-by-problem approach, to the neglect of viewing economic policies as a co-ordinated whole. It does not necessarily follow that by selecting what appears to be the most efficient policy response to each separate problem the government will end up with an efficient package of policies, viewed overall. For the individual instruments will not necessarily reinforce each other nor will they always add up to a consistent approach to economic issues. In fact, it may be desirable to adopt some apparently inferior solutions to particular problems in the interests of coherence and co-ordination among economic policies. A problem-by-problem approach may also lead to a proliferation of many policy instruments which, taken together, are beyond the capability of the public service to administer effectively.

The task of taking an overall view and of securing co-ordination is especially a responsibility of planning agencies and the next chapter has much to say about the role of planning in this context. Before going on, however, it may be helpful to provide an illustration of the use of the criteria just discussed.

Illustration: alternative investment incentives

Many governments seek to raise the level of investment in their countries by offering incentives to private foreign investors. A variety of incentives are in use in different parts of the world and in this illustration we will examine the relative merits of three of the most common of them.

The context

We will take the typical situation of an LDC, suffering from shortages of investible resources and foreign exchange, and a serious unemployment problem. We assume this country to be largely dependent on imports of capital goods, except for some locally produced construction materials, and that it is seeking to build up its industry from a rather small base. The government decides in principle to offer special incentives to foreign investors, with the primary objective of increasing industrial investment.

By attracting more foreign capital, the government also hopes to expand employment opportunities, reduce pressure on the balance of payments and stimulate further investments from domestic sources.

The government's economists are told to examine the relative merits of three incentives and to recommend the one which will best satisfy these objectives, while at the same time safeguarding against the creation of grossly inefficient industries. The instruments to be examined are:

(1) *Exemption from profit taxation* for a period of years (we will take the rate of profits tax to be 50 per cent).
(2) *Duty relief*, i.e. refunds of duties paid by the company on its imported equipment and raw materials.
(3) *Cheap credit*, i.e. the provision of a special low-interest loan by a government-owned investment bank.

The relevant criteria

Not all the seven criteria set out on the last few pages are relevant to this case and we must eliminate those which are not. First, the criterion of speed and probability can be dropped. There is no evidence that the three policy instruments would differ significantly from each other in this respect, nor are there any obvious logical grounds for expressing a preference. Since the object of the exercise is to make comparisons between the instruments, we can drop this criterion because by this test there is no reason for preferring one over the others.

We can also discard the test of whether the instruments act upon the causes of the problem. The cause of the problem in this case is that the level of profits (without incentives) is lower in the domstic economy than it is in the home countries of the potential investors, or in alternative places of investment. The general level of industrial profits in a country is the outcome of a highly complex set of circumstances – the stage of development, the size of the economy and the availability of natural resources being among them – and it is beyond the power of the instruments under examination to make much impact on these causes.

Finally, we need not concern ourselves in this case with the socio-political effects of the instruments, on the grounds that in each case they are not likely to be significant. The basic decision to encourage foreign capital, which has been handed down, may well have large socio-political consequences but the choice as between the three instruments is unlikely to make much difference to these.

A qualitative evaluation

We are thus left with four relevant criteria, namely:

(1) the magnitude of response;
(2) the resource costs of the alternatives;
(3) their selectivity and flexibility;
(4) their indirect economic effects.

How do the alternative instruments fare by these tests?

As regards the *magnitude of response*, each instrument is likely to bring some positive results by way of attracting more foreign investment. It is fairly easy to see, though, that the option of cheap credit is the least promising in this respect. It will be attractive only to those foreign investors who are interested in finding local sources of finance; and the credit provided may substitute for funds which otherwise would have been raised abroad, thus undermining the principal objective of the incentive. As between the other two instruments, we should prefer exemption from profits tax on the grounds that its attractiveness is the more general of the two. All private investors are in business to make profits and will thus be keenly interested in a concession which has the effect of doubling the profits available for distribution to shareholders (it is doubled because the rate of profits tax is 50 per cent), but not all investors will have in mind projects which will use many imported materials and so be able to benefit much from the duty relief concession. It is also possible that the increase in available profits resulting from profits tax exemption would result in more reinvestment, further promoting the primary objective.

The magnitude of response is therefore likely to be greatest in the case of profits tax exemptions.

Now to the *resource costs* of the alternative instruments. The two principal cost items here are (1) financial cost to the budget in terms of revenue foregone or used up, and (2) administrative costs. By this test the *cheap credit* alternative looks the least-cost instrument. We can realistically assume that the general structure of interest rates is artificially low in our country, for reasons touched on earlier, so the amount of subsidization (the difference between the commercial rate and the concessionary rate) necessary to provide the credit may be quite small. The administrative burden is also likely to be slight. By comparison, both the other measures are likely to result in substantial losses of revenue (to judge from the actual experiences of many LDCs). Because of its general appeal, this loss is liable to be greatest in the profits tax case. The administrative burden, on the

other hand, is likely to be heaviest with duty relief, because of the considerable paperwork involved in scrutinizing and approving claims for duty rebates, safeguarding against abuses, and so on. Some of the administrative burden may be shifted to the investors themselves but only by reducing the attractiveness of the concession.

Cheap credit is therefore the least-cost alternative, with nothing much to choose between the other two.

The *selectivity and flexibility* criterion points to yet another conclusion. Each can be regarded as selective in that the concessions would only be offered to the 'target group' of foreign investors but each is not equally flexible over time. Both cheap credit and duty relief score poorly by this criterion. A loan, once provided, is not normally recallable, nor is it normally possible to vary the agreed terms. Duty relief is more flexible, because the future rate of relief can be varied or it can be dropped altogether once the initial agreement has expired. But in practical terms, and like other forms of protection, the beneficiary may come to depend upon this relief, arguing that there are no local sources of supply and that the cost of duty increases would therefore have to be passed on to the consumer, with inflationary consequences. The profits tax exemption is the most flexible over time because it can be wholly or partly withdrawn after the initial agreed period without the same threat to the future viability of the industry.

So while the instruments score equally in terms of selectivity, it is the profits tax holiday which offers the greater flexibility over time.

The indirect economic effects are particularly important here, and in two cases are likely to be rather strongly adverse. Take first the case of cheap credit. The effect of this concession will be to reduce the cost to the investor of capital relative to labour. He will thus have an incentive to build a capital-intensive process into his project which will (1) reduce the number of new jobs created and (2) reduce any beneficial effects to the balance of payments by encouraging larger imports of capital goods (remember that the economy produces few capital goods). Moreover, if the credit were to substitute for imported capital – a possibility mentioned when discussing the magnitude of response – this would further reduce the balance of payments benefits of the investment.

The indirect effects of duty relief are similarly likely to be adverse to the balance of payments, for they have the effect of reducing the price of imports relative to the cost of local sources of supply. They will thus tend to encourage permanent use of imported supplies and discourage the development of domestic sources. This will be bad for domestic development and job creation, as well as for the balance of payments.

By contrast, exemption from profits taxation does not carry the same dangers of introducing price distortions. The concession is neutral both with respect to factor proportions and to the use of domestic and imported supplies. It is neutral because a firm maximizes its profits by choosing a minimum-cost combination of inputs; exempting it from profits taxation will not affect the nature of this combination. More positively, the concession contains safeguards against the encouragement of very inefficient enterprises, for it will only be attractive to firms which expect to make some profits and, because less of their profits will be taxed away, it gives them an incentive to keep their costs down and enjoy the benefits in the form of untaxed profits.

The indirect economic effects thus point strongly in favour of the profits tax concession.

To sum up, by three of the four criteria the profits tax concession appears the most efficient of the instruments and can therefore be recommended to the government in preference to cheap credit and duty relief.

It so happens that this illustration has yielded a clear-cut recommendation but the balance of advantages and disadvantages could have been more even. As a further aid, and as a further exploration of the possibilities of this approach, we can also try to quantify the judgements contained in the preceding paragraphs and to place numerical weights on the four criteria.

A quantification

The criteria will be weighted out of a total of 100. The magnitude of response is judged to be the most important test in this context, with the selectivity and flexibility of the instruments as of the least significance. The other two are of intermediate importance. These judgements are reflected in the weights displayed in the first column of Table 2.3.

The numbers in the other columns record the score of each concession in relation to each criterion and are intended to reflect the discussion in the text. Beneficial effects have positive numbers and are scored up to a maximum of 10. Costs and undesired effects are scored in negative numbers up to a maximum (the worst possible score) of -10. When we multiply the scores of each concession by the weights in the first column we arrive at weighted totals, recorded in the bottom line of the table. These totals present a quantification of the relative merits of the three instruments.

Table 2.3
Quantifying the Merits of Alternative Investment Incentives

Criterion	Weight	Profits tax exemption	Cheap credit	Duty relief
Magnitude of response	35	8	3	5
Resource costs	25	−4	−1	−4
Selectivity and flexibility	15	5	1	2
Indirect effects	25	2	−8	−4
Weighted Totals* (100)		305	−105	5

Note: * These totals are obtained by multiplying the scores of the concessions by the respective weight of each criterion. Readers uncertain about the methodology of weighted totals should look at an introductory text of applied statistics, probably in a chapter dealing with index numbers.

The results provide clear confirmation of the earlier qualitative conclusion on the superiority of the profits tax exemption. They also provide an indication, that would have been less easy to derive from the text, that cheap credit is substantially the worst of the three instruments considered. This results, as you can see, from the especially large negative indirect effects associated with this option.[5]

Activity. The scores in Table 2.3 are based only on my subjective judgement. Review the qualitative evaluation in the text and try putting in your own scores. Do you arrive at the same general recommendations?

There is a risk here of pushing the logic of the method too far. Most dangerously, the results have a spuriously objective look about them, as statistics usually do, and obscure the subjective way in which they were established. Nevertheless, the results are not entirely indefensible and are of some interest.

Part V of Chapter 8 makes more detailed use of the efficiency criteria outlined above, in comparing the merits of currency depreciations and exchange controls as instruments for managing the balance of payments.

[5] Readers interested in pursuing the issue of investment incentives should see Levy and Sarnat, 1975.

V. Implementation

Rules for improving implementation

It was convenient at the commencement of this chapter to distinguish policy instruments and implementation as separate dimensions of a policy problem. Convenient but dangerous. It is convenient because, by and large, officials operating at different levels are responsible for decision-making and for putting the decisions into effect. It is usually the minister and his most senior officials who are responsible for choosing policies; the task of implementing them falls largely on less senior levels of the bureaucracy.

But a sharp distinction between policy-making and implementation is dangerous because we can only make decisions about the best policy to achieve a certain objective after we have considered whether it is capable of being administered to achieve the desired results. If in other respects the pros and cons of two alternative policies are evenly matched but one will impose much larger administrative burdens and provoke more bureaucratic resistances, such knowledge is obviously crucial to any rational choice between them. Moreover, although the choice of a particular instrument – take the example of profits tax exemption as an investment incentive – may be the 'big' decision, the administration of the exemption will involve detailed, lower-level decisions which may alter the inducement offered and modify the results achieved. This is particularly likely to happen if the high-ups have not thought seriously about implementation aspects and hence fail to give meaningful guidance to the lower-downs on how to put the measure into effect.

It is therefore a key principle of policy-making that *implementation aspects should be explicitly included in deliberations leading to the choice of policy instrument.* To leave implementation as something to be thought about afterwards is to court the choice of policies which are difficult, even impossible, to fulfil.

> **Key concept. Implementation** consists of the ability to achieve specified ends by chosen means.

It is possible to go beyond this principle to suggest general rules favourable to successful implement-ation. A policy instrument is most likely to be effective if it meets the following conditions:

(1) The objective it is intended to achieve should be clearly and precisely specified. The notion of implementation presupposes an agreed yardstick against which we can measure actual results.

(2) The chosen instrument should be as simple as possible. By simplicity we refer to the number of agencies, offices and individuals involved in the implementation task: the larger the number the greater the risk of delay and distortion. Co-ordinating the activities of a number of agencies is especially difficult, so the use of multiple agencies should be avoided whenever possible. A 'simple' policy instrument will aim directly at its target and will involve a minimum number of lower-level decisions concerning its form and implementation.

(3) It should be possible to administer the policy within the already-existing institutional and bureaucractic framework. If this is not possible, explicit provision should be made for the creation of whatever special administrative capacity the instrument needs. Obviously, it should not call for additional resources which are not available.

(4) The decision-makers should specify clearly where the responsibility lies for carrying the policy into effect. This is important because, as Williams has pointed out, 'Responsibility for implementation tends to slip between the cracks. Almost everyone assumes that specification and implementation are somebody else's task'.

(5) The decision-makers should be sensitive to the interests and motives of those who will be involved in implementation. A policy stands a better chance of effective fulfilment if those involved have a personal interest in seeing it succeed or, at least, do not have an incentive to subvert it. Example: a policy of decentralizing planning which would shift spending powers from the centre to regional bodies will be viewed as a loss of power by the centre and is thus likely to be resisted there. This does not mean that decentralization should not occur but those who plan the decentralization should design it so as to minimize effective resistance from officials at the centre.

This disarmingly common-sense list of general rules is often disregarded during policy-making and, in consequence, many policies fail completely or produce results at variance with those intended. In practice, implementation is sufficiently uncertain that key ministries might set up special units charged with the task of monitoring and improving imple-mentation. However, a sceptic might react to this idea by saying that creating an 'office of implementation' simply adds to bureaucratic complexity and creates yet another point at which things may go wrong.

Whether or not an 'office of implementation' is the most appropriate response, there is abundant evidence that the implementation problem is a major one. This is especially the case with development planning. The next chapter therefore examines the role of development planning in the policy process and pays special attention to the question of implementation.

Activity. A brief class discussion could throw up lists of policies announced by government which (1) failed to produce any significant results at all, or (2) produced different results from the announced intentions. Can you identify reasons for these failures, for example by reference to the general rules above?

Suggestions for Revision and Group Discussions

1 Review your understanding of the following:
   (a) The three dimensions of the policy problem.
   (b) A shadow price.
   (c) A policy instrument.
   (d) The differences between aspirations, objectives and targets.
   (e) The distinction between direct and indirect policy instruments.
   (f) Target variables and instrument variables.
   (g) The Tinbergen system.
   (h) The seven criteria of instrument efficiency.
   (i) Implementation.
2 In the light of the discussion in Part II, write a note on ways in which the government's objectives for SIDC described on page 30 could have been reconciled with each other.
3 Restate in your own words how the social rate of discount may be used to reconcile the desire for high current consumption standards with rapid economic growth. If necessary, consult the appendix to this chapter before answering.
4 What is the significance of the distinction between marginal policies and those which alter the socio-economic structure?
5 In what circumstances is it true that the number of policy instruments in use must equal the number of targets?
6 Use equations (5) and (6) to plot a graph of the trade-off between employment and the balance of payments, using alternative amounts of government spending.

7 In the problem solution on page 41, suppose that all government expenditure was for capital formation and that this increased availability of capital raised average value-added per worker by 10 per cent. How would this affect equation (3) and what complications would it produce for the use of the model in equations (5) and (6)?
8 The seven criteria of instrument efficiency in Part IV are of basic importance to this book. Preferably with an instructor's guidance but otherwise as an individual exercise, readers should undertake an application of these criteria comparable with the illustration on pages 48–9. They might, for example, be applied to alternative instruments for changing industrial location, or to a case selected from local issues.

Suggestions for Further Reading

Most of the literature on the subject-matter of this chapter is written at a more advanced level than is appropriate here. Johansen, 1971, is a textbook which adopts the Tinbergen approach to the relationships between targets and instruments. The first two chapters provide a useful introduction and later chapters apply the techniques to various issues of public finance in industrial countries. It does, however, require some mathematical expertise. Tinbergen, 1955 and 1967(B), are his own main presentations but are quite demanding works. Fox, *et al.*, 1973, is valuable but advanced; ch. 1, 2 and 13 are especially recommended. Fleming, 1968, offers a non-technical critique of the Tinbergen approach. Implementation is a topic seriously neglected by researchers. Most of the little work that has been published relates to welfare policies in the USA and has limited relevance to developing countries. Interested students should nevertheless see the Summer 1975 issue of the journal *Policy Analysis.* See also Pressman and Wildavsky's *Implementation,* 1973. The sub-title of this book reads, 'How Great Expectations in Washington are Dashed in Oakland; or, Why It's Amazing that Federal Programs Work at all, This Being the Saga of the Economic Development Administration as Told by Two Sympathetic Observers Who Seek to Build Morals on a Foundation of Ruined Hopes'.

See also the additional references given in the notes to Chapter 3.

Appendix: A Primer of Cost-Benefit Analysis and Shadow Pricing

Reference was made in this chapter to the use of shadow prices to reconcile conflicting policy objectives, for example in making decisions about the competing claims of present and future consumption. The use of shadow prices as aids to policy decisions usually arises in the context of investment decisions, made by means of *cost-benefit analysis*. The techniques of cost-benefit analysis (CBA) are widely employed by private firms and in the public sector to assist decisions about the acceptance and timing of new investments. Governments also use CBA to provide guidance on whether it is in the public interest to agree to requests by private investors for tax relief or other favours.

Later chapters make further reference to the use of this technique. The use of CBA in the investment policies of public enterprises is discussed briefly in Chapter 11; and Chapter 4 provides a numerical application in order to estimate the 'present value of a life'. This appendix is therefore designed to give a brief first introduction to the basic principles of CBA. Students already familiar with it need not waste their time here; those who want a less superficial treatment should consult the references at the end of this appendix.

Basic principles

Profit maximization is the basic decision criterion of this methodology and CBA is essentially a technique for measuring profits or losses. In the case of *social* CBA, however, it is the profitability, or net income, to society that we are trying to measure, and it is possible to adjust the calculations so that they provide some reflection of the government's income distribution and employment-creation objectives, as well as the simple maximization of net income.

The starting point of a cost-benefit evaluation is the construction of a cash flow which records, year by year, the expected value of all costs and all benefits. For convenience, the years are usually numbered from zero to the end of the project's life (0, 1, 2 . . . n), rather than labelling them 1980, 1981 and so on. To see how a cash flow can be constructed we will take the highly simplified case of a possible investment in a public enterprise with the following project details:

Initial fixed capital cost (year 0)	$30 000
Start-up costs (working capital) (year 0)	10 000
Annual operating costs, excluding interest (starting year 1)	2 000
Annual revenues: year 1	4 500
from year 2	9 000
Residual (salvage) value	5 000
	plus working capital

Project life: ten years of operation.

This information can be presented in the form of an annual cash flow, as in Table 2.4.

Before going further, there are a few points to note about this cash flow. First, observe that the salvage value of the project plus the recovered working capital is added in as a revenue item at the end of the project's life. Secondly, note that interest payments are excluded from operating costs, and also that there is no provision for depreciation or the repayment of any loans. Briefly, the reason for these latter exclusions is that the CBA technique automatically makes provision for full recovery of capital invested. It shows

---

Table 2.4
Summary Cash Flow

						Year					
	0	1	2	3	4	5	6	7	8	9	10
Expenditures ($'000)											
1. Fixed capital investment	30										
2. Working capital	10										
3. Operating costs		2	2	2	2	2	2	2	2	2	2
4. Total expenditures	40	2	2	2	2	2	2	2	2	2	2
Receipts ($'000)											
5. Sales revenues		4·5	9	9	9	9	9	9	9	9	9
6. Residual value											15
7. Total receipts		4·5	9	9	9	9	9	9	9	9	24
8. Net cash flow (line 7 minus line 4)	−40	2·5	7	7	7	7	7	7	7	7	22

us by how much the value of benefits will exceed the costs, including the initial investment costs. So to include loan amortizations and depreciation in the cash flow would involve double-counting. Similarly, the result of a cost-benefit calculation can generally be expressed as a rate of return on the investment. This rate may then be compared with the interest rate that would have to be paid on a loan taken out to finance the project to see whether the profits would more than cover the cost of borrowing. So to include interest payments as one of the cost elements would be inappropriate.

If you add up the amounts in line 8 of Table 2.4 you will find that there is a net surplus of \$40 500 (net receipts in year 1 to 10 amount to \$80 500 against the year 0 investment of \$40 000). It therefore seems a profitable project which should be accepted. However, this would be much too crude a basis upon which to make a decision because it ignores the crucial aspect of the timing of costs and receipts.

If you were offered a certain sum of money now or the same sum of money in twelve months' time which would you accept? You would take the money now, and for good reasons. For one thing, the money could be invested in an interest-bearing bank deposit. If you allowed the interest to accrue, you would be able to withdraw a larger sum of money in twelve months than you are being offered now, how much larger depending on the interest rate being paid.

Another way of putting the same point is to say that in order to be induced to forego some income now you would have to be offered some larger amount in the future. Say that you are being asked to forego \$100 now, which you would be able to place in a bank account earning 10 per cent interest a year. In this case you would have to be offered at least \$110 in a year's time to forego the \$100 now because the \$100 would have compounded to \$110 in a year's time. We can stand this on its head and say that the *present value* of \$110 in a year's time is \$100 because we are discounting the \$110 in a year's time at 10 per cent per annum:

$$\frac{110}{(1+0\cdot10)} = 100$$

In brief, there is a sense in which a sum of money at some time in the future is worth less than the same sum now, even if there is no inflation. The rate at which our valuation of the worth of a given sum of money diminishes over time is called the *rate of discount*.

In the numerical example just given the discount rate was 10 per cent. We can extend the example to cover a two-year period. At the same discount rate, \$100 now would have compounded to \$121 in two

years' time, so the present value of \$121 in two years' time is again \$100:

$$\frac{121}{(1+0\cdot10)^2} = 100$$

From these examples we can generalize a formula for calculating the present value (PV) of some future net benefit, as follows:

$$PV = \frac{B_t - C_t}{(1+r)^t}$$

Where B = the nominal value of benefits; C = costs; t refers to a given year and r = the rate of discount. From a formula of this type a table can be constructed showing the present value of \$1 for a series of years at different discount rates. This type of table is to be found in any of the standard texts on CBA, referred to at the end of this appendix. An extract from one of them is provided shortly.

> **Key concepts.** A **cash flow** is a year-by-year statement of the expected costs and benefits of a project. The **discount rate** is the rate at which our valuation of the worth of a fixed amount of money diminishes over time. The **present value** (PV) of an amount accruing in the future is the value of that sum when deflated by the discount rate according to the formula for PV given in the text.

Going back to our illustrative public enterprise project, it is now clear that it would be wrong simply to add up the entries in line 8 in order to assess profitability. Looking at the cash flow you see that the largest expense occurs in year 0 (the initial investment) and the largest net revenue occurs in year 10 (because of the inclusion of the residual value of \$15 000). We need to use discounting techniques in order to reduce the project's net cash flow to present values, as set out in Table 2.5 below. Column (b), headed 'discount factor', is taken from a table showing the present (year 0) value of \$1 for years 0 to 10 when discounted at 10 per cent.

Comparing the net totals of columns (a) and (c) shows that the effect of discounting is to reduce the value of profits from \$40 500 to \$4710. The biggest impact of this procedure is in year 10, when the present value of the net receipt of \$22 000 is only \$8490. This illustrates a general point: *the longer we postpone the receipt of some net benefit the smaller is its present value* – a point which is also shown by the diminishing present values in column (c) of the constant net cash flows of \$7000 in years 2 to 9.

Table 2.5
The Present Value of a Cash Flow Discounted at 10 Per Cent

Year	Net cash flow ($'000) (a)	Discount factor at 10% (b)	Present value ($'000) ((a)×(b)) (c)
0	−40	1·000	−40·00
1	2·5	0·909	2·27
2	7	0·826	5·78
3	7	0·751	5·26
4	7	0·683	4·78
5	7	0·621	4·35
6	7	0·564	3·95
7	7	0·513	3·59
8	7	0·467	3·27
9	7	0·424	2·97
10	22	0·386	8·49
Total	+40·5		+4·71

The rates of return referred to in Chapters 9 and 11 are 'social' rates, so the next step is to clarify the difference between commercial and social CBA.

The use of shadow prices

There are two chief differences between commercial and social uses of CBA. First, social evaluation employs shadow prices when appropriate. Secondly, an attempt is made to incorporate into the evaluation of a project its income distribution effects, the externalities it may generate and other socially significant indirect effects. Commercial evaluation, on the other hand, uses market prices and generally ignores indirect effects. We will concentrate here on the use of shadow prices (see the definition of a shadow price on page 35).

As already mentioned in the main body of Chapter 2, shadow prices are required for social evaluations whenever market prices do not accurately express the value or cost to society of some item. Discrepancies arise between market and social values as a result of market imperfections, externalities, the impact of taxation and other government actions. The basic principles of shadow pricing can be summarized as follows:

(1) Resources employed in a project should generally be valued in terms of their *opportunity costs*, i.e. the value of the output that must be foregone in allocating resources to the project.
(2) Outputs should generally be valued in terms of the *utility* that will be derived from them. As a

practical solution, this is usually taken as being represented by purchasers' *willingness to pay*. However, when a project output is replacing an alternative supply (as in the case of import substitution) it should be priced at the *value of the resources released* by this substitution (the value of the foreign exchange savings, in the case of import substitution).

Shadow prices can be applied to a large number of different items, of which only three of the most important will be mentioned here: the shadow wage of unskilled labour; the shadow rate of exchange; and the social rate of discount. The next few paragraphs briefly mention some of the chief considerations entering into the calculation of these social prices. One point common to all three, however, is that the shadow price is usually derived as an adjustment to a market price.

To derive the *shadow wage for unskilled labour* we apply the principle of opportunity cost. We therefore have to inquire into the value of output foregone by employing workers in the project we are considering, and this is usually done by making the simplifying 'neo-classical' assumption that the marginal product of a worker is equal to his wage. His wage is therefore used as a proxy for the value of a worker's output. If a project's workers were formerly employed elsewhere in the modern sector of the economy this might seem a simple matter of pricing them at the wages they were receiving in their former employment. However, the case is not so simple because it is most likely that their former employers will be able to replace them with new recruits so that the ultimate source of our project's workforce may be quite different from its proximate source. The approach taken by most economists to this question is to treat the rural economy as the 'employer of last resort' and assume, therefore, that the ultimate source of new modern sector unskilled employment is traditional agriculture. In this case, the opportunity cost is represented by the marginal product of labour in traditional agriculture and it is usually possible to obtain some indicators of the value of this.

To this basic opportunity cost certain adjustments may be necessary. First, it is possible that every new job created by our project will attract more than one immigrant from traditional agriculture (see Chapter 5, page 127). Perhaps there will be two immigrants for every new job, in which case the shadow wage should be *twice* the marginal value product of labour in traditional agriculture. On the other hand, it is possible that, if there is a great deal of urban unemployment and the project is a small one, our project's labour will be derived from unemployed workers already seeking jobs in the modern sector and will induce no new immigration at all. Since the marginal product of an unemployed worker is zero, the shadow wage should in this case also be zero. However, the case of induced immigration is more likely than a net reduction in unemployment equal to the number of jobs created, so it is rarely correct to use a zero shadow wage.

It is often also necessary to adjust upwards the marginal productivity of labour in traditional agriculture to reflect (1) the inducement premium that may be necessary to attract people from the rural areas – to cover their transport and removal costs and the psychic costs of transferring into an alien, often unhealthy and dangerous, urban environment; (2) the generally lower cost of living in rural areas; and (3) the additional infrastructural costs (water, sewerage and so forth) that will probably have to be incurred by the government as a result of additional modern sector employment. On the other hand, it may also be decided to make an adjustment downward if the government regards employment-creation as a desirable objective in its own right and if it would not be satisfied with the number of new jobs that would result from application of the opportunity cost principle.

Evidently, the real-world estimation of a shadow wage is no easy matter!

There are two basic reasons why we might want to employ a *shadow rate of exchange* in social CBA. One is that all governments impose taxes on imports and quite a lot also tax exports. The effect of this taxation is to drive a wedge between the official rate of exchange and the prices that importers pay and exporters receive for their goods. In being willing to pay duties, importers show they place a value on foreign exchange in excess of the official rate. The second reason is that governments often maintain official exchange rates which overvalue the domestic currency. They therefore constantly experience balance of payments crises or only avoid them by maintaining exchange controls of the type discussed in Chapter 8. This over-valuation means there is an excess of demand over supply for foreign exchange even after taking the effect of taxation into account. A scarcity premium is placed on foreign exchange, the most common symptom of which is a black market in foreign currencies, and traders are able to earn abnormal profits on the imports they sell. The existence of such a scarcity premium drives a further wedge between the official rate of exchange and the price which people pay for foreign goods.

For both these reasons, the 'effective' rates which the public pays or receives for imports or exports are liable to differ markedly from the official rate. In order that the foreign exchange costs and benefits of projects can be valued at a rate which truly reflects the social valuation placed upon foreign exchange, we need a shadow exchange rate which will take these effects of taxation and over-valuation into account.

It is fairly easy to accommodate the effects of taxation because the data are usually available to compute the average tax rates on imports and exports. The scarcity premium resulting from over-valuation is more difficult to estimate. Three possible solutions can be suggested, which ought to yield similar results:

(1) By estimating the average 'excess' profits accruing to importers because of over-valuation. This can be taken as the difference between after-tax import prices and the final prices paid by consumers, less an allowance for distribution costs and 'normal' profits.

(2) Where imports are controlled by licences, the government could sell these by public auction to the highest bidders. The amount by which the auction price exceeded the face value of the licences would give us a guide to the size of the scarcity premium – besides having the additional advantage that most of the excess profits would accrue to government rather than to private importers.

(3) To undertake balance of payments projections designed to answer the question, by how much would it be necessary to devalue the currency (with tax rates held constant) in order to restore equilibrium to the balance of payments and get rid of controls?

Having somehow estimated the size of the scarcity premium and calculated average taxes on imports and exports, the shadow exchange rate is then derived as a weighted average of the effective rates faced by importers and exporters.

We turn finally to the *social rate of discount* (SRD). This is arguably the most important of all shadow prices because we have already seen that the results of CBA are highly sensitive to the chosen rate of discount. Whether our illustrative project was discounted at 10 or 15 per cent made all the difference between its showing a profit or loss.

There are two alternative bases on which we might estimate the SRD. The first of these was foreshadowed in the main body of Chapter 2, where (page 36) it was suggested that we can use the SRD to balance the competing claims of the present generation and future generations – of present consumption against future consumption. Viewed in this way, the SRD is an expression of society's *time preferences* – the rate at which our valuation of the worth of some given amount of consumption diminishes over time.

An alternative approach is to invoke the opportunity cost principle, which makes the SRD an expression of the *social marginal productivity of capital*. If at the margin the application of public investment funds is expected to yield, say, 12 per cent then we should only undertake projects which yield at least this rate of return (ignoring externalities and other indirect effects).

The difficulty is that these two approaches do not normally yield the same results. There is nothing in the real-world workings of the market mechanism in LDCs to bring these two rates into equality and although, in theory, government fiscal and monetary policies could be manipulated to bring them into line, he would be an optimist who believed that actual policies usually achieve this result.

Economists differ in the solutions they propose in the face of this dilemma but probably the most widely adopted approach is to make the assumption that fiscal policies will bring social time preferences into line with the social marginal productivity of capital and hence to estimate the SRD on the basis of marginal productivity. But this in itself is no simple solution. In a world of freely functioning capital markets, interest rates would give us a reasonable approximation of the marginal product of capital, but

the capital markets of most developing countries are highly imperfect. The problem is compounded by the fact that even efficient capital markets would only indicate the private marginal product of capital, whereas we need the social marginal product.

Here too, then, we are forced to the conclusion that the actual estimation of the SRD is at most an approximate exercise: a matter of taking market interest rates and adjusting them with such information as can be obtained on the social marginal product of capital. In practice, the SRD is often chosen rather arbitrarily – a fact which weakens the case for using social CBA.

Note on further reading

The exposition in this appendix has been modelled on Roemer and Stern, 1975, which is strongly recommended to the reader who wishes to pursue this matter at a practical level. Bierman and Smidt, 1971, is recommended as a thorough introduction to the commercial applications of CBA. Little and Mirrlees, 1974, and UNIDO, 1972, provide well-known and influential presentations, although there are substantial differences between them. Squire and Tak, 1975, are strong on shadow pricing; Layard, 1972, provides a valuable collection of readings.

3 Planning, policy-making and implementation

'It is a bad plan that admits of no modification.' *Publius Syrus*

Contents

Development planning has become so widespread that 'having a plan' is almost a defining characteristic of LDCs, with both national governments and international agencies viewing the existence of a plan as a symbol of commitment to long-run development. No book on economic policies in developing countries would be complete, therefore, without a coverage of planning and its role in policy-making. We commence by examining the principles of development planning, turn to look at planning in practice and finally consider the future of planning, given the difficulties it has encountered.

I. Principles of Development Planning

A plan as a super-instrument

All economic agents – consumers, workers, companies, governments – undertake planning in one form or another. These plans are not usually written but they exist because people have certain goals and

spend some of their time scheming how most easily to secure these. Such is the trade mark of planning: a deliberate effort to work out the best ways of securing chosen goals. As a general definition, then, planning could be described as the exercise of forethought in an attempt to select the best means of securing specified ends.

Viewed in this way, planning can be regarded as an attempt to raise the rationality of decision-making: carefully specifying objectives and systematically sifting alternative policy instruments, so as to find the optimal means of achieving the objectives. This conception of planning clearly has affinities with the welfare-optimizing model of decision-making outlined in Part III of Chapter 1 and we will see later that it throws up similar problems.

Development planning is, therefore, a member of a larger family of plans. As its name implies, its main distinguishing characteristic is that it is oriented to the general objective of developing the national economy. Another characteristic of development planning, by contrast with the usually shorter duration of the plans of individuals and firms, is that it is medium term, typically covering five years. We will add further to this list of characteristics as the chapter proceeds but can already suggest the following general definition of development planning.

> **Key concept. Development planning** is the exercise of forethought in an attempt to select the best policies, to be implemented over a medium-term period, for the development of the national economy.

The question arises how development planning fits into the classification of objectives and instruments presented in Chapter 2. Should we group it with objectives or with instruments? In so far as it fits into either category, it makes more sense to think of development planning as a type of instrument rather than as an objective. True, some governments behave as if the possession of a plan is something desirable in itself – to fill the political shop window or to impress aid donors – but those who are serious try to use planning as a means of achieving chosen ends, rather than as an end in itself.

However, if planning is an instrument it obviously is not just an ordinary instrument, like the income tax or the health service. One way in which a development plan differs from an ordinary instrument is that it takes a view over a longer period, whereas the use of ordinary policy instruments is more likely to be a short-term response to immediate needs. This is not a distinction to push too far, but a military analogy may be appropriate, in which the plan is seen as concerned with strategy, and specific policy acts are seen as defining the tactics which execute the strategy.

Now, a strategy takes an overall view. So writing a plan involves looking at economic policy as a totality, at the interconnections between various policy instruments and the web of reactions they set up. In other words, preparing a plan can be viewed as a way of arriving at a set of decisions which is internally consistent and reinforcing. Viewed in this way, *a plan is a super-instrument*: it is policy seen as a whole.

Since we have defined planning as the exercise of forethought to select optimal ways of securing chosen ends, it might seem natural to take the desirability of planning for granted. Who could object to such a rational procedure? It is, however, a mistake to take the desirability of planning for granted because there are costs to set against the benefits it may bring. What planner could object to the principle that his work should bring greater benefits to society than the costs it involved?

We therefore need to examine the arguments in favour of development planning, the way it works out in practice and the costs it involves before we can form a rounded judgement. So we proceed now to look at the arguments in favour.

The case for development planning

We can start by taking up the point made a moment ago, about planning as a super-instrument, a procedure for determining an internally consistent package of policy measures. The emphasis here is on planning as a means securing co-ordination among the numerous policy instruments the government will employ at any given time. You may remember in this context the warning given in Chapter 2 against the dangers of an *ad hoc* approach to policy, where matters are tackled on a problem-by-problem basis (see page 47). The danger of this approach is that, although each separate decision may seem sensible in itself, when taken as a whole the policies will conflict with one another. There will be inconsistencies and tensions between them.

The desirability of co-ordination, of seeing economic policy as a system, is all the stronger because developing countries have come increasingly to take a multi-dimensional view of what 'development' consists of. The period when development was measured simply in terms of the growth of total or per capita income is past. Governments are now more likely to include the reduction of unemployment, poverty and inequality in their definition of economic development. The increased complexity of this objective necessitates more varied policies to promote development. Many separate instruments will be needed, with numerous agencies involved in their implementation. So the need for co-ordination is stronger today than in earlier times, when goals had fewer dimensions and a smaller number of policy instruments could suffice.

Besides its co-ordinating role, planning has the special characteristic of introducing time into the mechanisms of policy formation (Elliot, 1958, p. 67):

> Planning injects the time factor and the problem of process into the centre of economic analysis. The essence of economic planning is that it is futuristic: it is forward-looking; it involves systematic thought and preparation *ex ante*; it involves 'pre-time' thinking . . .

A decision to undertake development planning thus requires policy-makers to look beyond the immediate future and decision-making processes that encourage them to do so. Policy-makers are thus stimulated to try to understand the future implications of their present actions. They are encouraged to trace all the ramifications of the policies they introduce – and policies often have different results from those intended. Possibly most important of all, they have an incentive to anticipate – and forestall – the future emergence of new problems.

In short, a serious commitment to development planning is a commitment to lengthen policy-makers' time horizons, raising important questions about the internal consistency of economic policy and about their impact over time. In the absence of medium-term planning, these aspects are liable to be neglected under the everyday pressures of economic management.

Most of the points made so far are arguments in favour of planning generally, whose validity is not confined to the particular circumstances of developing countries. There is, however, an additional group of arguments, already outlined in Chapter 1, which is more specific to LDCs.

> **Activity.** It would be useful at this point for you to refresh your memory on the discussion of Chapter 1, pages 23–6.

In the discussion there of the dynamic limitations of the market mechanism, a simple model was outlined of the 'poverty trap' theory, in which developing countries are viewed as stuck in a vicious circle of low incomes, low investment and static per capita incomes. The policy inference drawn from that model, you may remember, was that a 'big push' was necessary in order to break out of the vicious circle. It is a short stride from there to arrive at the conclusion that development planning is the obvious vehicle for such a push. If resources have to be mobilized on an unprecedented scale, if saving and investment have to be raised dramatically, and if these resources have to be utilized for development, then it is only the central power of the state that can hope to achieve these things. Development planning is a tailor-made mechanism for attempting them.

This argument, we saw, has been supplemented by another, to the effect that, while the market mechanism may be good at allocating resources at the margin, it is much less well equipped to achieve the structural changes which are part of development. Here too the inference is drawn that planning is needed to achieve necessary changes in the basic structure of the economy: accelerated industrialization; and major investments in power, transport, communications and distribution.

For reasons given in Chapter 1, this group of arguments has not withstood the test of time very well. Very poor countries certainly stand at a major disadvantage in their efforts to raise living standards but there is little in the experience of the last decades to suggest that they are actually caught in a trap. Average incomes have risen in even the poorest group of developing countries, although only slowly. It might be replied that this is because of the results of planning and therefore is not a counter-argument to the poverty trap theory. But reasons will be given later for doubting whether this is a generally valid reply.

One of the other dynamic deficiencies of the market outlined in Chapter 1 was its failure to provide a good basis for making decisions about the future. The price signals given by the market mechanism, since they reflect today's conditions of supply and demand, are not necessarily a good guide to investment decisions which concern the future. What is worse, this defect is liable to discourage investment and retard development. So development planning can be seen as a vehicle for providing a better information base upon which to make investment decisions – reducing uncertainties about the future by the exchange, aggregation and synthesis of information about current and expected future economic conditions. The type of activity which would provide this superior data base has come to be known as 'indicative' planning and has been described as 'a kind of spiritual illumination: because men understand more they behave better' (Shonfield, 1969, p. 145). We will return to this case shortly.[1]

These various arguments in favour of planning carry implications for the content of development plans, so our next step is to take a brief look at the main characteristics of such plans.

> **Activity.** Do you think any important arguments have been neglected in this review of the case for planning? If so, what others would you add?

What's in a good plan?

The preceding discussion has established that a well-devised plan will present a superior array of information on which to make decisions about the future; will contain a co-ordinated, mutually-reinforcing set of economic policies; will incorporate at least a medium-term time horizon; and will set out the types of structural change through which it is intended to develop the economy. But these considerations tell us only a limited amount about the contents of a 'good' plan and the following

---

[1] For a highly sophisticated statement of this type of argument see Meade, 1970, although this does not relate specifically to LDCs.

paragraphs offer a more systematic account of what is in a well-prepared plan.

(1) It will be *comprehensive* in the sense of including the private sector and parastatal organizations, as well as the central government. This is desirable, partly because it is impossible to take a sensible view of the government's own future revenues and investments in the absence of expectations about what will happen in the rest of the economy. Not only that but in a mixed economy, where most production is in private hands, there may not be any meaningful sense in which one could talk about planning the future development of the economy unless that planning in some way included private activities.

(2) Since present problems do not exist in a historical vacuum, a well-prepared plan will include a *review of the past performance of the economy* as well as an *identification of the most serious current problems*. There is not much chance of improving future performance unless we understand the forces that have held us back in the past, and unless we have a rather precise conception of the nature of the problems to be overcome.

(3) Much stress was placed in Chapter 2 on the desirability of *defining the government's economic objectives* with as much precision as possible, and of establishing *priorities* between them. It is only when that is done that we can hope to choose the best policies with which to achieve the objectives. The extent to which a plan specifies objectives and priorities is one of the criteria by which we may judge its quality, although it must be confessed that few would score high marks by this test.

(4) Having determined the objectives, and having preferably translated these into specific *targets*, the task is then to present a *strategy* through which they can be achieved. Economists have borrowed the notion of a strategy from military writers to refer to a package of specific policies, directed at large issues and at major economic variables, and intended to operate over a relatively long time-span. (An example of a development strategy is analysed in the discussion in Chapter 6 of 'redistribution through growth'.)

(5) The strategy will, in turn, be translated into *policy specifics*. The earlier discussion has already emphasized the importance of using the plan to ensure *co-ordination*, safeguarding against the dangers of inconsistency resulting from a problem-by-problem approach to policy-making.

(6) Even though the plan will be comprehensive, what it has to say about the government's own spending intentions will be particularly important. Thus, the well-prepared plan will set out *programmes of government capital spending* for the plan period, which should also be broken down into specific *projects*. The programmes should obviously reflect the priorities and strategy announced in the plan. And a good number of the projects should have been evaluated by the social cost-benefit methods introduced in the appendix to Chapter 2.

(7) In order to fulfil its function as a superior information base for decisions about the future, the plan should supplement its specific policy targets with a fuller range of *projections or forecasts* about the behaviour of the economy over the plan period (and perhaps beyond). These can be obtained from econometric models designed both to ensure that optimal policies have been selected to achieve chosen goals, and to make sure that the targets and forecasts are consistent with one another. Input-output analysis is often employed as a check on consistency.[2]

(8) Although the plan is likely to be medium term, it may incorporate a *perspective plan* which places the medium-term intentions into the context of a statement about the desired pattern of economic development over the next twenty to thirty years. It may also be supplemented by *annual plans*, as is shown later.

The points listed above would be misleading if they conveyed the impression that what constitutes a well-designed development plan is the same for all economies. The period it should cover, the level of sophistication in its preparation, the emphasis as between the elaboration of policies, programmes and projects, the manner in which the private sector is included – these and other decisions will be moulded by the circumstances of the national economy. If the economy is an open one, vulnerable to disturbances created by changing world conditions, a flexible type of planning will be needed. If the economy is a fairly complex one, with a substantial industrial sector,

---

[2] A number of the books mentioned at the end of this chapter contain introductions to quantitative techniques for development planning. The reader who wants to go into this subject in more depth should consult Spulber and Horowitz, 1976. O'Connor and Henry, 1975, provide a valuable introduction to the uses of input-output analysis; Blitzer, *et al.*, 1975, is good on the uses of econometric models.

more elaborate planning methods will be needed than in an economy still dominated by primary production. And the kind of planning undertaken will likely be constrained by the availability of qualified economists and other planning personnel.

Especially as regards the private sector and parastatal organizations, one basic choice is the extent to which the planners decide to achieve their aims by exerting influence over these sectors or by imposing legislative controls. Plans which depend largely on influence are often called *indicative* plans; plans that operate through controls may be described as *directive* plans. The best-known example of indicative planning is the type employed in France, where the planning process has been classified into the following stages:

Select the growth rate
of the economy

↓

Clarify the implications of
this for future development

↓

Specify how the public sector
will contribute

↓

Indicate the developments expected
in the private sector

↓

Influence the private sector in
the desired directions

The last stage of 'exerting influence' is accomplished partly by the data base provided in the plan, partly by involving the private sector in the plan preparation process, and partly by meetings in which government officials seek to persuade private executives to act in conformity with plan intentions.

Although the French case has been held up as a success story, there are others who doubt its achievements and whether it can be successfully transplanted in LDCs. Planners may become impatient with the compromises and disappointments inherent in the use of persuasion and turn to the more coercive use of directives. But controls create their own problems: they do not necessarily bring about intended results; they create distortions; and they may discourage the very expansion of the private sector upon which the development of a mixed economy depends. Chapter 8's discussion of import controls includes examples of this kind, although not in the context of development planning.

> **Activity.** Study the last few pages to draw up a list of criteria which you can apply to evaluate the strengths and weaknesses of your own country's development plan.

We know from our own lives that we are not as good as we would like to be. So it is with development planning. The next section therefore moves from the general principles of planning to examine how it has worked out in practice.

II. The Practice of Development Planning

The disillusionment with planning

Although many observers are critical of the way development planning has worked out in practice, it has unquestionably brought improvements too. By comparison with what would be expected in the absence of a planning effort, the new procedures have forced officials and others to ask, and try to answer, important questions about the future. Planning has provided a vehicle for advisers to press for more careful economic evaluations of proposed actions; by doing so they have increased the understanding of the problems and have improved the quality of policy choices. The planning framework has been used to achieve a more orderly build-up of power, transport and other infrastructural capital; it has helped to raise the, often terrible, methods of project selection in the public sector.

But despite these achievements, there is today a rather widespread disillusionment among economists, perhaps among governments, with the utility of development planning. Although it is not a matter that can be reduced to any simple demonstration, there would be general agreement today that the practice of planning has generally failed to bring many of the benefits expected from it. Waterstone's (1966) major study of past experiences concluded that 'there have been many more failures than successes in the implementation of development plans'.[3] The keynote paper for an important conference on 'The Crisis in Planning' was entitled 'The prevalence of pseudo-planning'. And a survey of trends in development economics claimed that the results 'have been sadly disillusioning for those who believed that planning was the only way'. Another

---

[3] The following two paragraphs are based on p. 163 of Killick, 1976. The specific sources referred to are detailed in the notes to that article.

work on planning and budgeting in LDCs argues that 'Planning is not the solution – it's part of the problem'.

The disillusionment seems to have spread to most parts of the Third World. A major study of Asia by Myrdal, 1968, stated that 'planning can be considered a going concern only in India and Pakistan ...'; and events have since seen the disintegration of Pakistan as it then was and the publication in India of a fifth five-year plan widely regarded as unrealistic. The Organization of American States has reported that 'it was repeatedly discovered that long-term plans were either not put into effect, or they were implemented officially for only a fraction of their time, or they were simply ignored at the moment of governmental decisions'. In a study of the plans of twenty-two tropical African countries to be quoted again, Shen formed the opinion that, 'The numbers exercise which now marks the course of macro-planning in Africa appears to be futile'; the Economic Commission for Africa similarly stated that development plans 'had little, if any, impact on the overall development of [West African] countries and can at best be taken as an expression of the desires of governments or the hopes of small groups of experts'. (Note the 'at best' – what might be the worst?)

> **Activity.** Is there a disillusionment with planning in your own country? If so, for what reasons?

The disillusionment may well have swung too far but we clearly need to investigate why it has occurred. Some general answers can be suggested but we will start with case materials on planning experiences in Nigeria and Kenya.

Planning experiences in Nigeria and Kenya

In a major study, Dean (1972) examined the implementation of the first four years of Nigeria's development plan for 1962–8. In 1966 the plan became a dead letter because of a military take-over and escalating turmoil in the country, culminating in the civil war of 1967–9. In examining his results we should bear in mind two important factors. First, Nigeria is a federal state and important economic powers were then held by the various regional governments. That inevitably made central planning more difficult than in a unitary political system where all major powers are concentrated at the centre. Secondly, the 1962–8 plan was the first to be prepared after the attainment of political independence from Britain in 1960. The data base was weak, there was an

acute shortage of planning personnel and there was little past experience with comprehensive development planning.

Nigeria at that time was therefore bound to have considerable problems with plan implementation. All the greater weight should thus be attached to successes recorded by Dean. He finds, for example, that the plan probably resulted in a set of projects with higher economic returns than those that would have been executed without the plan, 'though the process through which this occurred was indirect and unexpected'. He cites road transport as a case in point (although goes on to add that the plan's railway policy was not implemented). The plan succeeded in raising investments in the sectors with the highest priorities, although not to the extent intended. He also finds that the avoidance of inflation and balance of payments crises were related to the planning processes.

Nevertheless, Dean's overall conclusion was that plan implementation in 1962–6 'was largely unsatisfactory'. He based this conclusion largely on the government's spending record. Total spending (current and capital; federal and regional) in the plan's first four years was only 43 per cent of the planned total, with particularly large shortfalls in the priority sectors of primary production and industry. The record on capital spending alone was much worse: although there were increases during the four years, even in 1965–6 capital spending was less than one-sixth of the planned amount. In the same year the utilization of external aid was only one-ninth of the planned level. These failures, he suggests, were the inevitable result of unrealistically inflated targets for capital spending and aid receipts.

From the viewpoint of this chapter, an inability by planners to influence economic policy formation was even more significant:

> The plan did not play a central role in any other realm of national life. It played a peripheral role in the government's decision-making processes; the satisfactory growth of the economy prior to 1966 was due more to the private sector than to direct action under the plan ... and the plan played almost no role at all in dealing with those pressing social and political problems which led finally to the political-military crisis of 1966 ... (pp. 236–7)

It was, he argues, the dynamism of the private sector, rather than the plan, which induced the fairly rapid economic development of that period, although he adds that the plan was at least part of a total policy orientation which favoured expansion in the private sector and could thus claim a share of the credit.

A study of the implementation of Kenya's third five-year plan, for 1974–8, applied somewhat different tests to the implementation record.[4] Focusing on the key agricultural and roads sectors, it tested the extent to which government projects detailed in the plan had actually been implemented in subsequent government budgets, and the extent to which the plan's specific policy proposals were carried into effect. The results were not encouraging.

Project execution was tested by the calculation of 'implementation ratios' expressing actual expenditures on each project during the plan period as ratios of the expenditures set out in the plan. The results are summarized in Table 3.1 below. You will see from this that a substantial proportion of projects included in the plan was never started at all (line A of the table). A much larger proportion had actual expenditures (after adjusting for inflation) of less than 40 per cent of those set out in the plan (line B). And only about one-twentieth of projects had actual expenditures that were within plus or minus 10 per cent of plan estimates (line D). Taking all projects together, the average implementation ratio was 0·56; only a little over half of the planned capital formation actually occurred.

Table 3.1
Project Implementation in Kenya's Third Development Plan (Percentages of Total Value of Projects in Each Sector)

Implementation ratio	Agriculture	Roads
A. No expenditures	9	17
B. Up to 0·39	54	29
C. 0·40–0·89	22	42
D. 0·90–1·10	4	6
E. Above 1·10	11	6
F. Total	100	100

Source: See footnote 4.

Clearly, the extent of implementation revealed in this analysis was unimpressive, to put it mildly.

The record with respect to the specific policies announced in the plan was more mixed. Some important achievements were secured, for example in shifting the pattern of government capital formation in desired directions. Other policy intentions were only partially fulfilled and some were not acted upon at all. Overall, then, the Kenyan record was similar to the Nigerian: there were some achievements but the overall performance left much to be desired.

Scanning the possible reasons for the generally poor record of Nigerian plan implementation, Dean focused especially on 'inadequate executive capacity' and on the influence of the political system. He elaborated inadequate executive capacity to include:

(1) poor co-ordination among agencies or different levels of government;
(2) failures to produce new information or to use information already available;
(3) the failure of agencies to make decisions or take actions at the times required.

In turn he attributed these failures to shortages of trained and experienced personnel, and to the 'framework' in which the personnel worked, by which he meant the motivations, distribution of tasks and systems of incentives in the public service.

He provides illustrations of failings under each of the three aspects of executive capacity. Poor co-ordination was indicated by the fact that the plan's control mechanism had to be worked out during the first year of implementation. 'Officials in a ministry sometimes refused to consult with officials in another ministry; occasionally this occurred even when consultation was formally obligatory.' Information failures were indicated by shortages of essential data on projects and by ignorance of the activities of regional organizations. Failures of co-ordination and information then led to the third category – failures to make decisions or take actions when they were needed. The Kenyan study similarly drew attention to inadequate executive capacity as a source of implementation weakness.

The 'unfortunate effects of the political system on plan control' was identified as the second principal cause of poor implementation in Nigeria:

> Politicians took actions which increased the costs of the plan and reduced the flow of funds; political criteria and irregular financial practices influenced the choice of projects in ways which reduced the returns to investment; and staff policies [e.g. tribal favouritism] reduced employee incentives ... The cost of executing the plan rose 26 per cent in the first three years of the plan period; political factors played roles in adding about 8 of these 26 percentage points. Further, it cannot be argued that these and other lapses from effective planning represented the economic price that had to be paid for a stable political framework ... [The two military coups] of 1966 showed that the political system was not stable. (Dean, pp. 234–5)

The plan, he says, was an input into the political system rather than one of its outputs and, in practice,

---

[4] The following paragraphs are based on the essay by Killick and Kinyua in Killick, 1980.

the priorities of the politicians were contrary to those of the plan.

> **Activity.** A primary test of plan implementation employed in the Nigerian and Kenyan studies was to compare planned and actual government spending. Can you think of any ways in which this criterion might be criticized?

These, then, are the findings of two of the few country studies of development plan implementation that exist.[5] We can next compare these generally negative results with the conclusions of another researcher who has bravely attempted inter-country comparisons.

A multi-country implementation study

Two articles by Shen (1975 and 1977) make impressively ingenious use of published statistics in order to test plan implementation in a large number of tropical African countries, and to identify possible causes of failure. His method consists essentially of comparing plan targets with actual outcomes and of examining whether non-plan factors provide a stronger explanation of actual behaviour.

His first step is to test for the existence of significant statistical correlations between plan targets and actual results. If the two were closely correlated this is taken to indicate successful implementation. He does this for a variety of macro-economic variables such as the growth of GDP, exports, imports, consumption, and investment. He also undertakes a similar test for the growth rates of selected sectors of production, such as agriculture, manufacturing and transport. He obtains weak correlations, indicating low plan success rates. At the macro-economic level, he obtained significant correlations between planned and actual magnitudes for only two of the five variables and no significant correlation for the most important of these – the overall growth of GDP. At the sectoral level, the results were even weaker. Only for manufacturing was a significant correlation obtained between planned and actual growth. In agriculture there was actually a negative correlation – the higher the plan target, the slower actual growth!

He concludes from these tests that implementation records have been dismal and then searches for alternative variables which might provide a stronger statistical 'explanation' of actual performance. In the case of the primary target variable of GDP growth, he finds that the growth rates achieved in the period before the plans were launched provide a much

stronger explanation: to a large extent LDC economies grow at historically determined rates and plans appear powerless to exert much influence. In his analysis of sectoral performance, Shen tested whether the sectoral growth rates that could be predicted from the normal operation of market forces gave a stronger explanation than the efforts of the planners. With the exception of the health sector, his answer was a resounding yes. The behaviour of the major sectors of production was similar to what would have been predicted in the absence of planning.

Another point of interest is his finding that planners have a tendency to over-optimism. In his sample of twenty-one African countries he found, for example, that the actual growth of the economy exceeded plan targets in seven countries but fell short of the targets in the other fourteen. Some countries' plans have unrealistically high growth targets.

This fact and the findings that historical and market forces offer a better basis for predicting actual performance are very damaging to the argument in favour of planning summarized on page 59, that plans can promote development by providing a superior data base upon which to make decisions about the future. On the contrary, plans frequently offer misleading guidance as to likely future developments. It would often have been more sensible for private investors to base their decisions upon past trends and current economic conditions than on the aspirations of planners.

> **Activity.** Discuss ways in which comparisons of planned and actual growth rates might give a misleading measure of plan effectiveness.

So, although it would be wrong to suggest that development planning has achieved nothing, there does seem to be enough evidence of poor implementation to justify some of the disillusionment mentioned a few pages ago. The question now poses itself, what are the reasons for the poor implementation record?

Reasons for poor implementation

Observers have offered a wide variety of explanations of why there is often a large gap between plans and actualities. Some point to deficiencies in the plans themselves; others to inadequate planning resources;

---

[5] Islam, 1977, provides a study of planning in Bangladesh by an eminent Bangalee economist. This would surely repay careful study but was not available when this chapter was written.

some to changes in economic conditions beyond the control of the planners; others to institutional weakness and the failings of the civil service; some to the malign influence of politicians. We go through these point by point in the following paragraphs.

Deficiencies in the plans

If a plan is not well conceived it can hardly be expected to succeed. For example, a plan may contain targets which are unrealistically ambitious – unrealistic because they do not take adequate account of the financial, manpower and institutional obstacles to rapid economic development. A plan may be technically deficient, in that it is based on a poorly constructed econometric model, or because its various targets have not been made consistent with one another.

A plan may not succeed in raising economic performance because it fails to identify the most serious economic problems. It may fail to translate targets into precise policy recommendations, or choose inferior policies. A plan may not be implemented because the planners did not interest themselves in the creation of an administrative machinery for carrying the plan into fulfillment, for example to co-ordinate the plan with the budget. The plan may lack flexibility and may be difficult to adjust in the face of changing circumstances.

Inadequate planning resources

Especially at early stages of development there may not be enough of the resources needed for successful development planning. There will be shortages of reliable and up-to-date statistics upon which to build the plan and with which to monitor its progress. There will be shortages of qualified and experienced economists, statisticians, engineers and other specialized personnel. The qualified planning personnel who are available may be concentrated in the Ministry of Planning, leaving the executing ministries, such as agriculture, transport and education, with especially acute skill shortages. One resource that is particularly likely to be lacking is the capacity for co-ordination within and between agencies. Effective co-ordination requires not only adequate staff and information but also a rather clearly defined hierarchy of authority, but in practice the boundaries of authority are liable to be fuzzy.

Exogenous shocks

In the typical developing country, several key economic variables will be highly sensitive to conditions beyond the reach of government policy. The heavy dependence of many LDCs on external trade, for example, makes their economies – especially their balance of payments – highly vulnerable to the effects of changes in the world economy. A recession in the USA or Japan or West Germany can send the prices of LDCs' export commodities plummeting (but remember the other side of the coin: a boom in those countries can send commodity prices soaring). Inflation in the industrial world can have a serious effect on the prices paid by the Third World for its industrial imports. These fluctuations in the prices of imports and exports (the 'terms of trade') are outside the control of any one developing country. They are exceedingly difficult to forecast and can play havoc not only with the balance of payments, but with the government budget (because much revenue is derived from taxes on trade) and the state of domestic demand. These are 'exogenous shocks' which can throw an economy far off the course charted in the plan.

Nearer to home, many LDCs, having still predominantly agricultural economies, are open to ravages caused by abnormal weather. If the rains fail, as they do so often in major parts of Africa and Asia, the crops will die and the livestock will starve. The same will happen if the rains are too plentiful and cause widespread flooding! In the medium term, the planners can hope that the good years will cancel out the bad and work on the assumption of 'average' weather. But there can be a succession of bad years. Or adverse weather can cause lasting damage, as with the sudden frost in August 1975 which destroyed three-quarters of Brazil's main export crop, coffee.

It is tempting also to include political instability under this heading of exogenous shocks. Military take-overs, civilian unrest, even democratic elections can result in radical changes in the national leadership. These may render the current development plan redundant, since a plan has large political implications. Many a plan has been abandoned before the end of its intended life because of a change in government. From the point of view of the planners, such change is exogenous, beyond their control. Rather obviously the frequent changes of government common in some countries is an obstacle to effective medium-term planning.

Bureaucratic weaknesses

Writers have identified a number of ills under this heading. In some countries, planning failures have been attributed to the location of the planning agency in an inappropriate part of the machinery of government. It is common, for instance, for the planning responsibility to be tacked on to the traditional budgetary functions to form a combined Ministry of Finance and Planning. On paper, there is much to be said for this but in practice what often happens is that the 'finance' section of the ministry, because it controls the purse-strings, has more power than the 'planning' section. So what should be a happy co-ordination of the plan and the budget turns out to be a tug-of-war, with all the heavyweights on one side. Sometimes a separate Ministry of Planning is created but this is far from a guaranteed solution because the ministry may be regarded as unimportant and lacking in political 'clout'. It has often been argued that the planning agency should have an authority which enables it to override the preferences of other ministries and, therefore, that it should logically come directly under the authority of the chief executive (the Prime Minister or the President). One difficulty about this proposal is that the chief executive will have many other responsibilities and may not be willing or able to devote much time to planning tasks. Paradoxically, the agency could find itself in a weaker position than if it had a full-time Cabinet minister at its head, even though he be less powerful than the chief executive.

Another type of bureaucratic weakness often blamed for the non-implementation of plans is poor co-ordination between the many agencies involved in plan preparation and execution. This, in fact, is a problem intrinsic to national planning. Planning calls for a great deal of co-ordination but, as already mentioned, the capacity for co-ordination within the public administration is severely limited.

Civil servants themselves have often been criticized as lacking in dedication to the task of development. Complaints of slowness, red tape, exessive caution and lack of flexibility are commonplace. So are allegations of corruption and other instances in which officials place personal interests above those of the nation. We should also remember the aspect mentioned by Dean in his notion of 'inadequate executive capacity': that morale in the civil service may be too low to get as much out of scarce manpower as could be done. If promotion is based almost exclusively on seniority, or perhaps on favouritism, there is little incentive for planning officers to make more than a routine effort.

Politicians as spoilers

The anti-planning influence of political system and politicians is, of all the factors listed, the most frequent complaint. This was already mentioned in connection with the Nigerian case but many other instances could be cited. Waterstone's (1966, p. 340)

study of experiences with development planning concluded that 'lack of government support for the plans is the prime reason why most are never carried out successfully'. Seers has argued that political forces encourage the production of 'pseudo-plans' – paper plans with no serious effort at implementation. The reasons he gives include:[6]

(1) Politicians are too busy to involve themselves much in the planning process.
(2) Politicians do not think in the terms required for planning. They tend to be pragmatists, often not at ease with economic problems; and the qualities required for success in politics are not generally the qualities that make good planners.
(3) Politicians' true objectives often differ from their public pronouncements; so plans are used for public relations purposes and may not reflect the true priorities of the rulers.

There appears to be a consensus among economists that the malign influence of politics is the chief explanation why plans are often poorly implemented. But there is a puzzle in this explanation. There is much evidence that economic performance is the chief influence on how the public judges its government. This being so, politicians have a strong vested interest to safeguard their own popularity by securing economic prosperity. Since plans are intended to improve policies and raise economic performance, we would expect the ruling party (or group) to give strong support to the plan. Why should the politicians be spoilers when they stand to benefit from successful implementation? It is, perhaps, too self-justifying for economists to shift responsibility for plan failure on to the shoulders of another group. More recently, therefore, another viewpoint has suggested that the fault may lie not in the wilful wrong-headedness of politicians but in the basic idea that a medium-term plan is compatible with workable political decision-making processes.

Planning and decision-making

You may remember that Chapter 1 offered some generalizations about the nature of politics in developing countries and explored the implications of these for the way we should view governmental decision-making in such societies.

> **Activity.** You are advised to refresh your memory on the discussion in Chapter 1, pages 9–10, before proceeding further.

---

[6] See the essay by Seers in Vol. 1 of Faber and Seers, 1972.

The generalizations offered there suggest some rather strong inferences about the nature of decision-making and about the feasibility of medium-term planning. Emphasis is placed on the existence of social divisions and conflicting interest-groups. Government decision-making in these circumstances becomes a balancing act, a process of conflict-resolution in which the avoidance of social unrest and the maintenance of its own power become the government's chief objectives, rather than the maximization of the rate of economic development.

Because competing groups within society, and the manner in which the state deals with them, interact with each other, the balance of power and the mixture of policies which is viewed as the most desirable will constantly change. An economic decision can therefore only be understood in the context of the conditions that exist at that particular time. Decision-making is a continuous and interactive process. It has its own logic even though, when viewed over time, it seems inconsistent.

Because of the complex ways in which social forces interact and in which government policies affect society, there will be large uncertainties about the consequences of any new policy. These uncertainties will be made all the greater by the frequent unavailability of information about what is going on. Because of uncertainty, because of inertia and because of the greater riskiness of radical changes, policy moves will tend to be 'incremental'. That is, they will be designed to produce only small, gradual changes in the socio-economic system.[7]

Uncertainties, shifts in the balance of political power, changes in the world economic environment, variations in the composition of the Cabinet and in the responsibilities of its ministers – these changes will leave government goals and priorities in a constant state of flux, sometimes to such an extent that it is impossible to say anything precise about government objectives.

The picture we have, then, is of policy-making as a continuous outcome of bargaining and compromise, undertaken in ever-changing circumstances, in the face of much uncertainty and shifting priorities. The question arises, how might medium-term development planning play a role in such a process?

The answer appears to be that, as generally practised, development planning fits ill with the realities of politics. *Inflexibility* is its main fault. It requires that government objectives can be precisely defined and will remain stable in the medium term, but this is often unfeasible. It also tacitly assumes that economic development is the top priority, although the actions of many governments show that is not the case. It assumes a manageably small degree of

uncertainty, so that it makes sense to make decisions now about what should be done in four or five years' time, when uncertainties are in fact very great. It encourages the view of major economic policy-making as a once-every-five-years effort rather than a continuous, interactive process. It tacitly assumes that political time-horizons are long enough for medium-term planning to be realistic, despite much evidence to the contrary.

According to this line of explanation, then, the frequent non-implementation of plans is because they – and the economists who prepare them – are politically naive. Plans, according to this view, do not work because they cannot work; because 'politics isn't like that'; because they are too inflexible to accommodate the dynamics of social change and continuous policy-formation; because uncertainties shorten time-horizons and undo the best of plans.

> **Activity.** This would be a convenient point at which to review the various explanations for plan implementation failures set out on the last few pages. Is it possible to say anything firm about the relevance of any of these to planning in your own country?

III. The Future of Development Planning

We have been through a formidable list of factors that may prevent the theoretical advantages of planning from being achieved in practice. Of course, only some will be applicable to any particular case. And how much weight should be attached to each is a matter for the reader's own judgement. But clearly it is not a list which can be intelligently shrugged off, dismissed as unimportant. We can be quite sure that at all times in all countries there will be forces at work to drive a wedge between what is planned and what is achieved. This being so, intellectual honesty requires us to ask the question, is development planning worth the effort?

Does development planning have a favourable cost-benefit ratio?

Cost-benefit analysis has become a popular tool of economic planning. Its decision criterion is that one should compare the benefits of an action with its costs and should undertake those actions which promise

---

[7] For a description and espousal of incremental decision-making consult Braybrooke and Lindblom, 1963.

the largest net benefits. But planners ought to be willing to apply to their own activities the tests they apply to others. Planning, we have shown, has benefits to offer; but we have also implied that it has costs. What are these costs and how do they balance out against the benefits?

Development planning involves some obvious direct costs. It requires the creation of a ministry which has to be housed, staffed, fed with paper and in other ways serviced. Relative to the government's total budget, the financial cost is small. But the opportunity cost may be greater. If plans are poorly implemented, it is very possible that the scarce economists and other specialists whose energies are consumed in planning could be better employed in other tasks where they would achieve more results.

Remember also the information costs mentioned in Chapter 1. A well prepared plan has a large thirst for economic statistics and other information. Much of this has to be obtained specially for the planners and obtaining it can require large resources. The larger the uncertainties, the greater the need for information and the cost of obtaining it.

There may also be substantial indirect costs. Planning may actually be a substitute for desirable policy changes. Not a few plans are announced with a great flourish of publicity to give the impression that the government is doing a lot when in fact it is doing little. Most plans, of course, do not fall under this description but, by inserting additional layers of authority into the machinery of government, they may slow decisions down. And they provide a lazy or conservative official with a good excuse for deferring a decision – 'we must wait for the plan', or 'it's not in the plan'.

It is similarly possible that, if it were taken seriously as a blueprint for economic policy, the plan could reduce the government's room for manoeuvre in adjusting to changing economic circumstances (Caiden and Wildavsky, 1974, p. 308):

> What approach to government decision-making would be appropriate for a society best characterised as poor, unstable and uncertain? . . . Poor countries cannot and should not attempt at all costs to follow a fixed path. Just the opposite. They should enhance their ability to change course at short notice. They cannot avoid error but they might be able to reduce the cost of making mistakes.

More specifically, preoccupation with medium-term development planning may divert attention away from the need for active short-run economic management to deal with recession, inflation and foreign exchange crises (see Chapters 7 and 8). Many LDCs have experienced grave inflationary and

balance of payments pressures but far fewer have devoted much priority to the active use of stabilization policies.

There is lastly a point referred to earlier: that some plans have provided misleading signals concerning likely future trends in the economy. If investment decisions were made on the basis of these signals (and one of the arguments in favour of planning is that it should provide a basis for decisions about the future), it is probable that they caused investment mistakes. Resources were likely wasted, through over-investment in some areas and under-investment in others.[8] To the extent that this waste would have been avoided in the absence of a (misleading) plan, it is a cost of planning.

No decision about the desirability of medium-term planning would be complete unless it gave due weight to the various costs detailed above. Against them we have to set the benefits – the improvements in economic performance and policies that would not have occurred without planning. As in the Nigerian example, there are undoubtedly things to enter on the credit side of the ledger. The planning process has had an educational effect on politicians, civil servants and others raising their understanding of economic problems and their ability to respond with well-chosen policies. Planning agencies have been able to improve public sector project selection.

Notice also that much of the theoretical case for planning is unaffected by the practical defects described earlier. However difficult it may be, there remains an obvious need for taking an overall view of economic policy, for studying the interactions between policy instruments and for co-ordinating them. It is still desirable to try to anticipate problems and thus defuse them; to try to understand the future implications of present actions. And planning is an activity which gives economists an opportunity to insert their professional expertise into government decision-making, even if that advice is often unheeded. Later chapters provide specific examples of problem areas in which planning is of crucial importance. This is true of population policy, explored in Chapter 4, to give an example. Similarly, Chapters 5 and 6, on poverty, inequality and unemployment, suggest the need for a complex package of policies (a strategy) which would be difficult to entertain in the absence of planning.

But just because there are benefits we cannot simply take it for granted that in all cases planning

---

[8] In Killick, 1978, pp. 198–9, I suggest that excessive optimism in Ghana's 1963–9 plan caused over-investment in industry, resulting in excess capacity, high costs and a waste of investible resources.

has a favourable cost-benefit ratio. There are cases where planning has clearly brought net benefits; others where the costs have outweighed the benefits; and a lot more where it would be impossible to give even an intelligent guess without much research.

Besides requiring us to think about debits as well as credits, a cost-benefit approach to planning has the further advantage of posing the question, what might be done to improve the cost-benefit ratio? What suggestions can we make to strengthen the results obtained from planning and to minimize its costs? Various proposals have been made in this area, so we conclude by reviewing some ideas for improving plan performance.

> **Activity.** Is it possible to say anything specific about the costs and benefits of planning in your own country? Can you provide examples of improvements which are unlikely to have occurred had there been no plan? Is there any evidence on the types of indirect cost mentioned above?

Towards greater flexibility

The most serious defects of most development plans is their *rigidity*. They cannot easily cope with the impact of changes in the world economic situation and other exogenous shocks. They assume stable governments and stable objectives when instability is often the rule. They require enough confidence about the future for it to make sense to plan several years ahead, when chronic uncertainty often prevails. They assume governmental time-horizons are sufficiently distant for a five-year plan to be realistic, when in fact ministers are often preoccupied with the present (aptly illustrated by a well-known remark by former British premier Harold Wilson that 'a week is a long time in politics'). They encourage the view of policy-making as a once-every-five-years effort, while in reality it is continuous.

A large stride would have been taken towards more effective planning if it could be made sufficiently flexible to cope with the realities just mentioned. How might this be achieved?

Rolling plans

One possible way of raising plan flexibility is through what are known as rolling plans. A rolling plan can be defined as a medium-term plan which is rewritten every year. Let us say a plan is published for 1980–4. The idea is to roll that plan forward a year at a time, so

the next plan would be for 1981–5, then 1982–6, and so on. The advantages of such a system are evident. If between 1980 and 1981 there is a major change in the terms of trade, or a new president is elected, or improved information throws light on a previously neglected problem; or experience shows that parts of the 1980–4 plan were unrealistic, then the 1981–5 plan can be adjusted to accommodate these facts. The government would have introduced flexibility without scrapping the framework of medium-term planning. Moreover, planning would become continuous instead of a five-year recurrence. It would therefore be much better adapted to the idea of policy-making as continuous. It would probably have a stronger educational spin-off, in building up a cadre of experienced planners and of ministers familiar with the ways planning affects their responsibilities.

The idea of rolling plans is not a new one but few governments have tried it. The objection usually raised is the amount of work involved. Officials with vivid experiences of the enormous effort required to produce a single five-year plan shudder at the thought of doing it every year. To put it more in the language of the economist, rolling plans require large inputs of planning resources: they may raise the benefits from planning but they also raise its costs. Because there is so little experience with rolling plans, it is not easy to say how much substance there is in this objection. It would require greater planning resources – more specialized personnel, more data. But it would be wrong to think that a government would need five times the resources needed to produce one plan every five years. There are economies of scale in the planning industry. Once the procedures become institutionalized and those concerned gain experience, the needed extra resources might not prove too great.

Annual plans

Another device for providing greater flexibility in planning involves the production of annual plans. One possibility here is to prepare a conventional medium-term plan, say for 1980–4, and then to supplement it in each year after the first with annual plans for 1981, 1982 and so on. These annual plans could perform a number of functions. First, they could spell out in detail precisely what part of the 1980–4 plan was to be implemented in the next twelve months. Secondly, they could be co-ordinated with the government's annual budget, hence reducing the danger that the budget will neglect the plan (as often happens). Thirdly, the annual plan could modify the medium-term plan in the light of changing circumstances, new information and shifting priorities.

This, too, is an attractive idea and a number of countries have adopted it. Of course, it also requires additional planning resources and places a heavier burden on the planning ministry. More seriously, it is doubtful whether annual plans can introduce sufficient flexibility. If the basic medium-term plan is to retain any operational status, the annual plans cannot make more than marginal modifications, otherwise an entirely new five-year plan is needed and we are back to the case for rolling plans.

Some observers take the view that the difficulties of comprehensive medium-term planning are so great that no workable solution can be found. So one proposal is that the annual plan should become the centre-piece of the planning effort. Waterstone, for instance, has suggested a planning process consisting of the following elements:[9]

1. The preparation of annual plans on which the two basic items were: (a) an inventory of current public investment, rationalized by the application of general economic and other criteria and made consistent with available financial resources, and (b) policies for stimulating private investment along appropriate lines.
2. The improvement of budgetary organization, administration and procedures for (a) linking annual plans with budgets, (b) relating investment and recurrent budgets, (c) controlling expenditures and (d) reporting on the progress of projects and programs.
3. The preparation of multi-annual sector programs which concentrate on the identification of a shelf of potentially viable projects in each sector.

The annual plan, dovetailed with the budget, would be on the centre of the stage under this scheme, with medium-term planning confined to particular sectors of production, such as agriculture and manufacturing. It would be easy to think of variants on this basic idea. There are some policy areas which by their very nature virtually demand a longer-term perspective. Population policy is one. Manpower planning is another. Waterstone's scheme could therefore be modified to incorporate longer-term plans in these areas.

It is also fairly easy to think of snags. There would be enhanced flexibility but a loss of a time perspective. There would also be many problems with time-lags. Actions under a plan in any one year are liable to make their main impact only in subsequent years, just as projects need more than a year to be completed and to yield their benefits. To put it another way, what happens to the economy this year is largely predetermined by things that happened last year and earlier. The cause-and-effect relationships would be difficult to identify with annual planning. But though there would be snags, the type of procedures

advocated by Waterstone might, on balance, be an improvement.

A few writers have gone even further in their quest for flexibility and in their abandonment of medium-term planning. Caiden and Wildavsky (1974) have argued strongly that even annual budgets will not work in the conditions of most LDCs: even twelve months is too long a time-span for forward planning. There is, they argue, often an air of unreality about the annual budget, because it is predicated on conditions and forecasts that differ markedly from the actual course of events. They therefore advocate moving away from annual budgeting in favour of what they call 'continuous budgeting'. This might, for example, take the form in any year of giving each ministry the same budget it had in the previous year (adjusted, no doubt for changing prices) but then allowing ministries to present arguments in favour of additional amounts at any time during the year. It would be preferable, they argue, to concentrate on reforms of this kind, rather than to keep trying with what they regard as mistaken attempts at medium-term planning.

Theirs is a rather extreme view, open to many objections, but they do address themselves to a real problem. There often are large deviations between the revenues and expenditures presented in the annual budget, and the eventual outcome. Moreover, these deviations are typically not random. There are systematic biases: a general tendency to underestimate current spending, to overestimate revenues and aid receipts. If we are not willing to go so far as to abandon one-year planning, we should at least recognize that even in this short time there can still be many gaps between what is intended and what occurs.

> **Activity.** See the assignment suggested in Chapter 7, page 182. You might prefer to undertake it now, as a test of the government's ability to predict twelve months forward.

To sum up, there is no shortage of ideas about what might be done to increase the flexibility of planning and improve its effectiveness as a vehicle for improved economic policies. It is not the purpose of this chapter to advocate any particular solution. Our main concern has been to analyse the difficulties encountered in the practice of planning, and to point out the direction in which reforms should be pushed.

The difficulty lies in striking a balance between the need for flexibility and the desirability of employing a

---

[9] From Faber and Seers, 1972, Vol. 1, p. 94.

time horizon which extends beyond the immediate. Caiden and Wildavsky do not strengthen their own case when they gleefully point out that (p. 270):

> When planning is placed in the context of continuous adjustment, it becomes hard to distinguish it from any other process of decision. By making planning reasonable we have made it indistinguishable from the processes of decision it was designed to supplant.

That is precisely the danger. You may recall the distinction drawn in Chapter 1 between behavioural and normative decision models. The behavioural point of view may lead us into thinking that what is easiest is best. If we take this view, and planning becomes similar to 'any other process of decision', we are neglecting the normative task of trying to *improve* decision-making. Unless it can be shown that the costs outweigh the benefits, we should not abandon planning just because it is difficult.

But if we design plans as if they exist in some ideally rational and predictable world, we condemn them to futility because they will not be implemented. There is a saying in England that 'the best is sometimes the enemy of the good'. A compromise is needed between what is desirable and what is workable.

Suggestions for Revision and Group Discussions

1 Review your understanding of the following:
  (a) The distinction between 'indicative' and 'directive' development plans.
  (b) Perspective plans.
  (c) Rolling plans.
  (d) Planning resources.
  (e) Implementation.
  (f) Exogenous shocks.
2 State your understanding of the description of a development plan as a 'super-instrument'.
3 What connection do you see between the 'poverty trap' hypothesis presented in Chapter 1 (pages 23–4) and the desirability of development planning?
4 The following is a list of elements in a decision-making process. Arrange these in what you would consider a logical sequence. Discuss the

consequences for this sequence of a lack of clarity about objectives.
  Formulation of a strategy.
  Selection of projects.
  Establishment of priorities.
  Selection of policy instruments.
  Definition of objectives.
  Target-setting.
5 Discuss ways in which uncertainties affect the case for, and modalities of, planning. Compare the examples of a stable and a very unstable economy.
6 What do you understand by the 'opportunity costs' of planning?
7 The book by Caiden and Wildavsky (1974) presents a highly critical view of conventional approaches to development planning. Write a review of this book in which you also consider objections to their arguments.

Suggestions for Further Reading

There are a number of general textbooks dealing with the principles of development planning. W. A. Lewis, 1966, is long established and popular. Tinbergen is a renowned authority; see his *Central Planning* (1964) and *Development Planning* (1967A). Griffin and Enos, 1970, offer a rather more recent treatment. On the quantitative aspects of planning techniques, see the references suggested in note 2.

A wide range of materials is available on the practice of development planning. Waterstone, 1966, remains an authoritative study of the lessons of experience. Valuable papers are presented in Faber and Seers, 1972, in two volumes. See especially the essays by Seers, Leys and Waterstone in Vol. 1. Caiden and Wildavsky, 1974, offer a well written and highly provocative viewpoint. Much of the substance of this chapter (and some of Chapter 1) has been drawn from my article on the possibilities of development planning (Killick, 1976); a reading of it might reinforce your understanding of this chapter.

The implementation studies referred to in the text are by Dean on Nigeria, 1972; Killick and Kinyua in Killick, 1980, on Kenya; and Shen, 1975 and 1977, for inter-country comparisons. Stolper, 1966, also concerns planning in Nigeria and is a useful supplement to Dean's work.

PART 2: POLICY APPLICATIONS

4 The population issue

'Of all the things in the world, people are the most precious . . . We believe that revolution can change everything, and that before long there will arise a new China with a big population and a great wealth of products, where life will be abundant and culture will flourish. All pessimistic views are utterly groundless.' *Chairman Mao Tse-tung, September 1949*

'We have this big population. It is a good thing, but of course it also has its difficulties . . . Steps must therefore be taken to keep our population for a long time at a stable level, say, of 600 million. A wide campaign of explanation and proper help must be undertaken to achieve this aim.' *Chairman Mao Tse-tung, February 1957*

Contents

I. Population: Problem or Resource?

Alternative perceptions of the population issue

Most of the remaining chapters of this book ask 'here is a problem; what should be done about it?'. But this is an approach we cannot adopt here because there is still controversy about whether population growth is a problem and whether there is any call for government action in this area. In the absence of a consensus, a good deal of this chapter is devoted to an examination of the chief arguments that surround this controversy; only later can we turn to look at the policy implications.

Much of the difficulty arises because the issue offers different perceptions depending upon the viewpoint it is seen from. Western demographers and conservationists, for instance, look at it from a *global* viewpoint and are alarmed by the explosion in the number of people in the world that has occurred during the last century. Developing country governments, on the other hand, are more likely to take a *national* viewpoint and to ask, is it in the national interest that we should adopt a population policy? For the great bulk of the population, however, the issue is seen as a *marital* one: how many children do we want to have and, what can be done to avoid exceeding the desired number?

The issue is further complicated because those seeking answers to these questions may adopt differing criteria. Many see the issue of family size and family planning as an ethical or religious one; others see it as relating primarily to the health of the family and the nation; yet others perceive it primarily as an economic issue. This chapter naturally gives most weight to economic considerations but it is as well to be clear now that a purely economic approach is not enough and that national policy-makers also have to take other considerations into account.

The resulting opinions are wide-ranging. Many think of children as an asset: a source of joy in the family; a future source of labour, security and inventiveness; a source of military strength and national prestige. For others high fertility threatens to worsen poverty by outstripping the world's capacity to grow food, by denuding the planet of its mineral wealth, by frustrating economic development. We have already had a foretaste of this last point of view, in Chapter one's discussion of the poverty trap theory of underdevelopment, a discussion that concluded on a hopeful note (see page 25).

In approaching the population issue we first set out the facts of the present-day population situation and place it in historical perspective. Then we go through various arguments that have been made against or for population growth. Finally, we will examine the policy implications of the analysis.

II. The Population Situation

What's different about LDCs?

Countries are usually classified as 'developed' or 'developing' according to differences in per capita incomes. But it would scarcely be an exaggeration to say that if they were instead classified according to the pace at which their populations were increasing very similar groupings of countries would result. One of the outstanding facts of the contemporary world is that the populations of most LDCs are expanding much more rapidly than the populations of most industrial countries, with a growth rate of above 2·5 per cent a year for LDCs taken as whole and below 1·0 per cent for industrial countries. To put the point another way, at current growth rates, it will take LDC populations twenty-five to thirty years to double in size but seventy to eighty years for a doubling of industrial country populations.

If we ignore the effects of international migration, the growth of a population is given simply by the difference between the rates at which people are dying and are being born. These are normally expressed as crude death rates and crude birth rates, which measure the annual number of deaths or births per thousand of the population. Thus, if a country has a crude death rate of 15 this means that in any one year an average of 15 people will die out of every thousand people. A crude birth rate of 35 means an average of 35 live births annually for every thousand people. With 15 dying and 35 being born, there is a net addition to the population of 20 per thousand, or 2 per cent, and this is called the rate of natural increase. If there is significant net international migration, in or out of the country, the actual growth of the population will differ from the natural rate, but this is not a significant factor in most LDCs.

> **Key concepts. Crude death and birth rates**
> measure the average number of deaths and births
> in a year per thousand members of the
> population. The **rate of natural increase** is
> obtained by subtracting the crude death rate from
> the crude birth rate and is generally expressed in
> percentage terms. The simplest of several
> measures of fertility is the **general fertility rate**
> which measures the annual number of live births
> per thousand women aged 15 to 44.

Table 4.1 sets out crude death and birth rates, and the resulting rates of natural increase, by world region. These figures emphasize the differences between poor and rich countries, with an overall rate of population growth more than three times higher in the developing regions than in industrial regions (compare column 4, lines 5 and 10). Both birth and death rates are higher in the developing countries but the contrasts in death rates are substantially smaller (15 against 9) than the contrasts in birth rates (42 against 17). Indeed, Latin America and east Asia have managed to get their death rates down to industrial country levels, but in all developing regions birth rates are much larger than in any of the industrial regions.

> **Activity.** Compare the statistics for your own
> country with those given in Table 4.1. How does
> your country's record compare with other LDCs?

Regarded historically, the faster expansion of population in the developing regions is a relatively new development. So far as can be judged, it was the other way round for the first two or three decades of the twentieth century, with population growth rates in what we now call the developing regions generally below 1 per cent a year. How are these trends to be explained? Population experts have developed a useful model of a 'demographic transition' to answer this question and we turn now to look at this.

The demographic transition

Stated very simply, the demographic transition model states that during the process of modernization there occurs first a fall in mortality and later a fall in fertility

Table 4.1
Population Statistics by World Region

	Population 1976 (m.) (1)	Crude birth rate 1965–76 (2)	Crude death rate, 1965–76 (3)	Rate of natural increase, 1965–76[a] (4)	Density 1976[b] (5)	Density on agricultural land, 1970 (6)
Developing Regions						
Africa	412	46	20	2·6	14	174
Latin America	333	38	10	3·8	16	95
East Asia[c]	57	33	9	2·4	32	370
South Asia	1 283	42	17	2·5	81	226
All developing regions[d]	2 085	42	15	2·7	56	203
Industrial Regions						
North America	239	17	9	0·8	11	4·5
Europe	476	16	10	0·6	96	62
USSR	258	18	8	1·0	11	33
Japan	112	18	7	1·1	302	387
All industrial regions[d]	1 085	17	9	0·8	88	38
World[e]	4 044	32	13	1·9	30	155

Sources: UN Demographic Yearbook, 1976; World Bank, 1974, Annex Table 15 (for column 6).
Notes: (a) The difference between columns (2) and (3) but expressed as a percentage growth rate.
    (b) Persons per square kilometre.
    (c) Excludes China whose population data can only be roughly estimated. The UN estimates the Chinese data as follows:
        Total population: 852 m., Birth rate: 27, Death rate: 10
        Rate of natural increase: 1·7, Density: 89.
       Japan is also excluded from this line – see industrial regions.
    (d) China and Oceana excluded. Averages are weighted by 1973 populations.
    (e) Includes China and Oceana.

and that during the intervening period a large increase in population occurs. Four phases can be isolated in this model:

(1) *Pre-modern.* In this phase both death and birth rates are generally high and approximately in balance, although death rates fluctuate rather with variations in natural conditions. Modern scientific knowledge has not yet been applied to the eradication of disease, nor to the planning of family size. The total population is growing only very slowly. This phase relates to the whole world before the seventeenth century and to LDCs until much more recently.

(2) *Early transition.* The application of scientific advances, improved living standards and modernization produces sharp falls in death rates in this phase. Birth rates remain generally stable but may rise a little in response to improved health and a retreat from traditional methods of limiting family size. Rapid population growth therefore occurs; this is the phase when the 'population explosion' begins. It applies to eighteenth-century Europe and most of today's LDCs.

(3) *Late transition.* Changing socio-economic conditions and attitudes, and the spread of contraception and other modern techniques of fertility control bring sharp reductions in birth rates, while the decline in mortality slows down. There is therefore a deceleration of growth and the population explosion subsides. In Europe this phase began in the nineteenth century and became more marked in the first half of the twentieth century. Japan has been through this phase since the end of the Second World War; Mauritius, South Korea and Barbados are among developing countries which have entered this phase.

(4) *Modern.* Both mortality and fertility have fallen to general low levels (although birth rates are rather erratic) and the rate of natural increase is down to less than 1 per cent a year. Most of Europe, the USA, USSR, Japan and other industrial nations have entered this phase, but virtually no developing countries.

This model is illustrated in Figure 4.1, where the vertical distance between the death and birth rate curves gives the rate of natural increase and the shaded area therefore provides a visual impression of population growth over time.

We see there the widening gap between birth and death rates in the early transition phase, leading to rapid population growth, and then the narrowing of that gap in the late transition, as birth rates also begin to fall rapidly. At the beginning and end of the process birth rates are only a little above death rates and population grows only slowly.

This model is given a more concrete, but still only schematic, form in Figure 4.2, which provides a graphical presentation of the recent demographic histories of western Europe and developing countries. We see there that, starting around 1800, the demographic transition was completed in the European countries in periods ranging from 75 to 150 years, with birth and death rates now fairly stabilized at the levels presented in Table 4.1. The position of most developing countries is as portrayed in the right-hand diagram, with death rates having fallen dramatically during the middle two decades of the twentieth century, after hundreds of years of high mortality, and with birth rates beginning to fall but still at high levels. The consequence, of course, is the explosive population growth already revealed in Table 4.1.

> **Key concept.** The **demographic transition model** concerns the relationships between socio-economic development and demographic trends. It postulates that, as development occurs, there is first a fall in mortality and later a fall in fertility and that during the intervening transition there is a large increase in population. The model subdivides the process into pre-modern, early transition, late transition and modern phases.

Underlying these movements in crude death and birth rates are a number of other important social and

Figure 4.1   *The demographic transition model.*

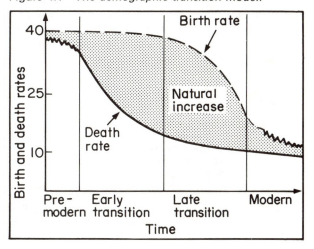

demographic changes.[1] As populations enter the demographic transition their age structures change: starting with 35 to 40 per cent of the population aged under 15, this proportion rises to a peak of around 45 per cent during the transition, falling to 25 to 30 per cent when the modern phase is reached. Since children are generally only minor contributors to output, the rise in the proportion of children during the transition entails more economic dependants relative to the adult labour force.

Contrasting age distributions can be illustrated by what are known as *age pyramids*. Age is measured on the vertical scale of these diagrams, usually by five-year classes: percentages of the total population are measured on the horizontal, with the left-hand side relating to males and the right-hand side relating to females. Figure 4.3 reproduces age pyramids for Sweden, as illustrative of a European country with an only slowly-growing population (the 1960–70 growth rate was 0·7 per cent annum), and for Thailand, representing the LDC case with rapid population growth (3·2 per cent per annum).

Large differences between the two cases are immediately apparent, with high proportions in the young age groups in Thailand and small proportions of elderly people. The Swedish diagram is not a pyramid at all, being approximately rectangular until it reaches the 60–64 age group. The shaded areas of the diagrams show the economically active members of the population, i.e. those working or seeking work.

The youthful age structure of a rapidly growing population has an important consequence, known as 'population momentum'. This refers to the fact that *rapid population growth tends to sustain itself*, so that even the most determined efforts to reduce the growth rate are likely to yield only slow results.

A youthful age structure imparts momentum to a growing population because a large proportion of adult women are of child-bearing age and because a large proportion of the population consists of girls who, in turn, will grow into women and have babies. Going back to the Swedish and Thai cases, compare the following figures:[2]

	Sweden	*Thailand*
Females under 15 as % of total population	10	22
Females aged 20–34 (the most fertile age range) as % of total adult female population	26	46

Population momentum is one of the most powerful forces working against a rapid fall in birth rates in developing countries.

During the late transition phase, however, complex social and economic forces come into play to reduce birth rates. Changed attitudes towards the desirable size of the family and an associated spread of family planning is, of course, a most important factor. So too is the fact that, as health standards rise, deaths among infants and young children decline sharply so that it is no longer necessary for a couple to have as many children in order for a given number of them to survive. The number of children born to married women in the pre-modern and early transition phases averages between five and six but the number of *surviving* children rises from an average of between two-and-a-half and three in the earlier phases to between four-and-a-half and five as countries enter the later transition.

Another important change that occurs is that the age at which women marry rises. Thus, the average age of women at marriage in developing countries today is under 20 years, whereas in Europe it is about 26 years. Similarly, the proportion of women who never marry tends to be very low during the early transition but to grow thereafter. Hence, the proportion of women aged 45–49 who have never married tends to be below 3 per cent in LDCs as compared with about 16 per cent in contemporary Europe. These two factors also contribute substantially to reduced birth rates.

Another important feature is that there has been a marked acceleration in the transition during this century. Today birth and death rates can fall much more rapidly than was the case during the early industrial revolutions. Figure 4.2 has already indicated the speedy fall in LDC death rates in 1940–60; birth rates are also capable of rapid declines, as in Japan, where the crude birth rate halved from 33·5 in 1948 to 17·0 in 1957. In consequence of this quickening of the pace, the demographic transition can now be completed in half or less of the seventy-five years or more that was necessary in Europe.

Essentially, then, the demographic transition model postulates a close connection between the processes of socio-economic modernization and the demographic changes just described. It provides a reasonably good fit with the historical experiences of most of today's industrial nations. Can it therefore be used in order to make confident predictions about future movements in countries which have only

---

[1] The factual statements in this and the next few paragraphs are based on Table 3 of Philip M. Hauser's essay in the US National Academy of Sciences, 1971; and World Bank, 1974, Tables 5 and 6.
[2] Computed from data in the 1973 UN *Demographic Year Book*. Thai figures relate to 1970: Swedish figures to 1965.

Figure 4.2   *Recent demographic histories of (a) western Europe and (b) developing countries.*

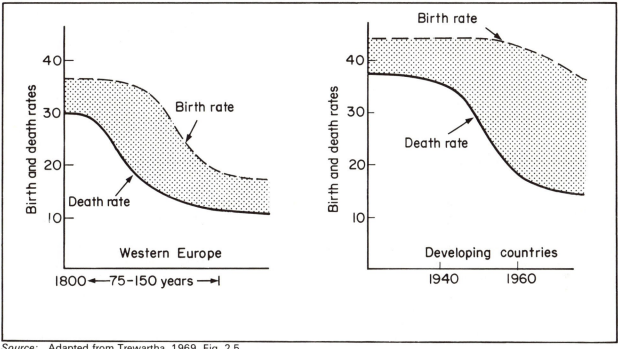

Source: Adapted from Trewartha, 1969, Fig. 2.5.

Figure 4.3   *Age pyramids for Thailand and Sweden.*

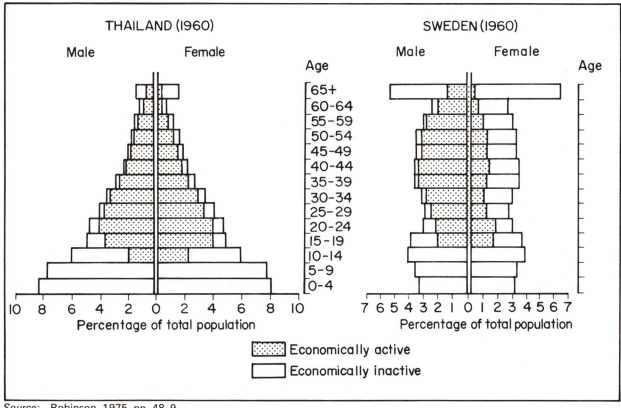

Source: Robinson, 1975, pp. 48–9.

recently begun to modernize? It is always sensible to be cautious about extrapolating historical tendencies into the future.

A highly complex interplay of socio-economic changes generated the demographic transitions of western countries; most LDCs start with quite different social systems and values, and there is thus no assurance that these cultures will even approximately reproduce the patterns of the west. The cultures of Africa and Asia may prove more persistently 'high fertility' cultures. On the other hand, while the demographic transitions of the west occurred essentially in a *laissez-faire* framework, on the basis of spontaneous changes in individual motivations, in many of today's LDCs there are official population policies seeking to reduce the birth rate. This is a potentially important new element encouraging a completion of the transition. Moreover, there are now Asian examples which suggest that the model may well be valid there, although none, as yet, from tropical Africa. Japan is the chief example, but it is now possible to cite South Korea, Taiwan, Singapore and a few other countries which show signs of following the same cycle.

Activity. On the basis of national statistics, can you fit your country into the demographic transition model? If so, how far along the road has it got? Has the birth rate begun to decline?

An historical perspective

It was stated earlier that most LDCs can be placed in the early transition phase of the demographic cycle. It is during this phase that population growth becomes most rapid and it was shown at the beginning of this chapter that population growth is generally much more rapid in LDCs than in industrial countries. Since LDCs contribute about 70 per cent of total world population, expansion in these countries has a strong influence on total world population. Indeed, it is only when we look at today's trends in the context of population history that the abnormality of the current situation can be grasped.

Figure 4.4 illustrates the historical context, with each bar giving a visual indication of estimates of how long it took to add each successive billion (thousand million) to the world's population. Thus, it took from the beginning of the human species until around AD 1810 for world population to reach one billion; the next billion was added between 1810 and 1925; the third billion took only from 1925 to 1960; and the fourth billion took a mere fifteen years, to 1975.

Figure 4.4   *Years taken to add one billion to world population.*

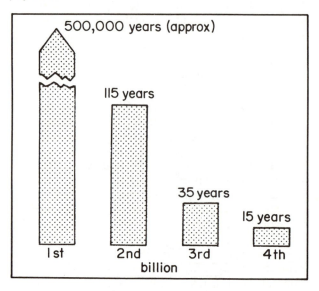

The uniqueness of what is happening at the present time is further indicated by estimates of the annual growth rate of world population during the last two centuries:[3]

	Annual % growth of world population
1750–1800	0·43
1800–1850	0·51
1850–1900	0·63
1900–1950	0·89
1950–1976	1·84

You can see from these figures a gradual speeding-up during the nineteenth and into the twentieth centuries and then an extraordinary acceleration since 1950, with an expansion rate during the last quarter century more than twice as fast as in the first half of the twentieth century. It was during the eighteenth and nineteenth centuries that the industrial countries experienced their demographic transitions but the LDCs were still in the pre-modern phase, with high death rates nearly offsetting high birth rates. The explosion during the last quarter century, on the other hand, has been entirely attributable to the developing regions of the world.

Although the rate of world population growth may now be gradually declining, experts predict that rapid expansion will continue for some time. Population projections are admittedly fraught with uncertainties,

---

[3] Calculated from Kuznets, 1966, Table 2.2 and recent UN *Demographic Year Books*.

especially if they are made far into the future. In particular, it is extremely difficult to predict what will happen to LDC birth rates in the next few decades – how fast and far birth control techniques will spread – and assumptions about this variable make a great difference to the results of long-term projections. Table 4.2 therefore reproduces projections of world population on three alternative fertility assumptions.

The projections in columns (2) and (3) assume only slow reductions in fertility during the remainder of the twentieth century; the projections in columns (6) and (7) assume very rapid fertility reductions in 1970–85; and figures in columns (4) and (5) reflect an intermediate assumption.

We see from this table that even the lowest projections, in columns (6) and (7), show an increase in world population of 1·5 billion people in 1970–2000. It is already clear, though, that these figures are too small to be achievable. The 'moderate' projection is probably more realistic, showing a world population of nearly 5 billion in 1985 and nearly 6 billion by 2000.

A second point to note from the table is that the 1985 projections are not very sensitive to the choice of assumption, varying for the world as a whole between a high of 5 and a low of 4·4 billion. By the year 2000, on the other hand, the choice of assumption makes a greater difference: the projections in this case vary between 5·1 and 6·7 billion. What happens to fertility could by the end of this century make a difference of 1·5 billion people, or nearly half the 1970 population! Thirdly, note that overwhelmingly the largest part of the population expansion will come from LDCs, no matter which projection we take. The LDC share in world population will rise to between 75 and 80 per cent by 2000.

Historically, then, it is reasonable to talk about the existence of a 'population explosion'. But while these figures may startle us, should they also scare us? The answer to this question should not be pre-judged because many other socio-economic variables have also 'exploded' in the twentieth century – output, education, communications – but we do not think of them as problems. Nothing said so far has been intended to imply a judgement on the desirability of the population explosion, so we next examine various economic arguments that have been presented on this issue. In setting out on this journey, however, we should again remind ourselves that a purely economic approach is inadequate, and non-economic considerations will be introduced later.

III. A First Approach to the Question

A naive presentation

The essence of the viewpoint that sees rapid population growth as retarding economic development can be stated quite simply. The trend in average per capita income is an important indicator of the pace of development. This statistic is arrived at by dividing total national income (or a similar national accounting aggregate) by the size of the population. With rapid population growth, therefore, the denominator is larger than would be the case with more moderate growth, hence average per capita incomes are smaller. Income has to be shared between a larger number of people.

An illustration of this argument is provided if we compare the growth of the industrial and developing countries in 1960–74, as summarized below (per cent per annum):[4]

	Industrial countries	Developing countries
Growth of total GNP	4·9	5·6
Growth of population	0·8	2·7
Growth of per capita GNP	4·1	2·9

[4] GNP figures from International Monetary Fund, 1975, Table 1; population growth from Table 4.1.

Table 4.2
World Population Projections on Alternative Assumptions (in Billions of People)

	1970	FERTILITY ASSUMPTION					
		Slow reduction		Moderate reduction		Rapid reduction	
		1985	2000	1985	2000	1985	2000
	(1)	(2)	(3)	(4)	(5)	(6)	(7)
Developed countries	1·1	1·3	1·4	1·3	1·4	1·2	1·3
Developing countries	2·5	3·7	5·3	3·5	4·5	3·2	3·8
World	3·6	5·0	6·7	4·8	5·9	4·4	5·1

Source: Frejka, 1973. I have used his projections 5, 3 and 2 respectively for the slow, moderate and rapid fertility reduction projections in Table 4.2.

In this period total output grew more rapidly in developing countries but the gap between *per capita* output in the rich and poor nations continued to widen. Many conclude from these statistics that the widening gap between rich and poor countries is due solely to faster population growth and, therefore, that developing countries should adopt policies to limit this expansion.

This is a strong case but, as presented, the argument is an over-simplification. It rests on the unstated premise that the growth of total GNP is independent of the growth in population. But that is to pre-judge the issue, for there are others who see population growth as a stimulant to the expansion of output.

To resolve the issue, then, a careful exploration is needed of the interactions between demographic and economic change.

The cost-benefit curve

An alternative line of approach to this question, confining ourselves simply to economic considerations, is to examine the costs and benefits of an addition to the population. Most people are both consumers and producers during their lifetimes; they impose costs on the national economy but they also contribute to the benefits it generates. This suggests a general principle: *if over his or her lifetime the benefits produced by an additional member of the population exceed the additional costs to the economy, then the birth of this person is economically desirable; but if the person imposes net costs on the economy, society would be better off if the birth had not occurred.*

What is suggested here, then, is an application of cost-benefit techniques to the issue of population policy. You may feel a repugnance against employing this materialistic calculus of profit and loss to such a basic human question as family size. But it is a fact that demographic trends have an important bearing on economic well-being; an economist thus has responsibility to apply his skills to this issue no less than to other, less emotive, questions. We therefore proceed.

In cost-benefit terms we identify *three stages of a person's life*. First, there is infancy and childhood. During this time the person is a consumer – of food, clothing, shelter and, hopefully, of educational and health services – but an insignificant producer. He may help on the family farm, or on the market, or in the house but the value of these activities will not compensate for the cost of his consumption. In this phase, then, he is a consumer, a net cost to the economy.

The second stage is his working life. He leaves school, finds a job or goes to work on the farm. He will probably marry and have children so his income will have to sustain his family as well as himself. If he is an employee, it is likely that his productivity will be greater than his wage, the difference accruing as profit to his employer. He will pay taxes to the government. During this stage, then, he is a net benefit to the economy, whose productivity substantially exceeds his own personal consumption. Finally, he retires or becomes too old to do much work. His productivity becomes slight, diminishing in old age to zero. He is once again a net cost to the economy.

The cycle just described is summarized in Figure 4.5. Time is measured on the horizontal axis and net costs and benefits on the vertical. Point O represents the time of birth and the period OC is the expectation of life at birth. The cost-benefit curve, XX', indicates for any point in his lifetime whether he is producing net benefits or net costs. The time span OA corresponds to the first stage described above; AB is the second stage, his working life; BC is the retirement stage.

> **Activity.** Can you think of reasons why the cost-benefit curve shows the person to result in net costs for a while even before he is born?

Having quantified both the costs and benefits it is now a relatively simple matter to decide whether, over his lifetime, this person is a net benefit or net cost to the economy. If the latter, then the economic welfare of the rest of the population would have been greater had he not been born. As explained in the appendix to Chapter 2 (see page 53), the technique of discounting should be employed when adding up benefits and costs occurring over time. The test, therefore, is

Figure 4.5 *The cost-benefit curve.*

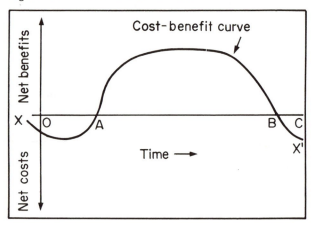

whether the discounted value of his costs and benefits is positive or negative. A quantification of this approach is provided later (see pages 91–3).

So long as we confine ourselves to the purely economic facets of the controversy, much of the debate on the population issue is concerned with the question whether additions to the population will bring (discounted) net benefits or net costs to society, so it will be useful to hold the model summarized in Figure 4.5 in your mind when you go through the various arguments, which we will now proceed to do. We begin by examining arguments against rapid population growth.

Activity. Draw a diagram similar to Figure 4.5 with two cost-benefit curves, (1) for someone who receives no education and (2) for someone who obtains a university degree.

IV. Arguments Against Rapid Population Growth

The problem of economic dependants

Look back at Figure 4.3 (page 77). You will see there that one of the main differences between the Swedish and Thai populations is the much larger proportion of children in Thailand. In that country 44 per cent of the population is below 15 years old, whereas the comparable figure for Sweden is 21 per cent. That contrast is typical of developed and developing countries. LDCs have younger populations and therefore larger proportions of children.

Now, children are net consumers. They are therefore *economic dependants* because they depend for their sustenance on the output of others. Here, then, is one of the chief reasons for believing that rapid population growth has a retarding effect on economic development: *LDC economies have to carry a large burden of young dependants.* Typically, 34 to 45 per cent of total LDC populations are child dependants, as against 20 to 25 per cent in most industrial countries. The output of the active labour force has to feed a much larger number of young mouths in developing countries. Reducing the number of births is thus likely to have an approximately fifteen-year beneficial effect on the welfare of the rest of the population, by reducing the number of dependants while probably having little or no detrimental effect on total output.

Key concept. Dependency is usually defined as relating to children aged below 15 and adults aged 65 and over. The number of dependants is sometimes expressed as a ratio either of the total population or of the population aged 15 to 64.

This is one of the most powerful arguments against rapid population growth but the counter-point has often been made that at the other end of the age structure LDCs are in a favourable position relative to industrial countries. Looking again at Figure 4.3, you can see that the proportion of *aged dependants*, (those aged 65 or more) is much lower in Thailand than in Sweden. In this case the proportions are about 11 per cent for Sweden and only 3 per cent for Thailand. Again the comparison is typical. This contrast is partly the statistical result of the large numbers of young people in LDCs, but is also because larger proportions survive to old age in the industrial countries, giving more people going through the retirement stage of life.

So if we add together both young and old dependants the comparison is less to the disadvantage of LDCs than by simply comparing child dependency. However, this counter-argument is not entirely convincing. The smaller proportions of aged in LDCs only partly compensate for greater child dependency. If we add both together, the total dependant proportion of an LDC population is typically 45 to 50 per cent, against 35 to 40 per cent in industrial countries. The International Labour Office estimated that in 1970 there were 1·2 dependants per active member of the labour force in developed countries, against an average of 1·7 in LDCs.[5] This is an important reason why average living standards are lower in developing countries.

So the conclusion is that *the dependency argument is a valid and strong reason for wishing to avoid rapid population growth.*

Employment and income distribution effects

While it is obviously correct to call children economic dependants, they are also future workers. If their productivity in adulthood is great enough this will more than compensate for their childhood years as net consumers. But is this likely to be the case?

One of the key variables in an answer to this question is the ability of the person in question to find productive employment, but it is often argued that rapid population growth reduces employment

---

[5] Calculated from ILO data in Jolly, *et al.*, 1973, p. 77.

Figure 4.6 *The effects of unemployment on the cost-benefit curve.*

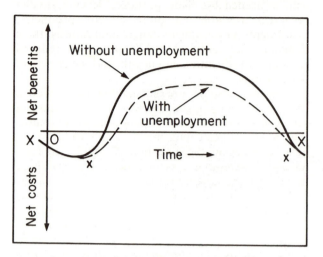

prospects. This is a topic explored more fully in the next chapter but the main point is simple. After a notional fifteen-year time-lag, an increase in population induces a rise in the size of the labour force. This rise is a national asset if the labour can be productively employed; it is a problem if employment opportunities are expanding less rapidly, resulting in more unemployment and under-employment. Figure 4.6 illustrates the effects of worsened unemployment on the cost-benefit curve introduced earlier.

The diagram assumes that a general worsening in the employment situation will affect a person in two ways: (1) it will delay the time when he gets his first job and (2) it will reduce the average number of days of employment in each year thereafter. It is easy to think of alternative ways in which a deteriorating employment situation could affect him but the case just described keeps the illustration simple. What it does is to shift the curve downward towards the broken curve XX′ – an adverse shift which reduces the chance that this man will be a net producer over his lifetime. In the extreme case (not illustrated) he will never find enough productive employment to cover his own consumption (i.e. he will always have to rely on the incomes of others) and his cost-benefit curve will lie below the horizontal axis throughout his life.

The crucial question, whether rapid population growth is likely to be associated with a worsening unemployment problem, is examined in the next chapter. It concludes (page 126) in the affirmative: LDC labour forces are growing so fast as to make it very difficult to absorb the increasing numbers in productive employment, and nine-tenths of the increases result from population growth. Employment-creating policies of the type outlined in

Chapter 6 can alleviate the problem, but rapid population growth makes it a more difficult one to solve.

It can also be said that rapid population growth worsens income inequalities and poverty. This too is a topic explored more fully in the next chapter but, to refer forward, it is shown there (page 124) that poverty is associated with large families and that the interaction of these factors helps to perpetuate poverty and inequality.[6] It also points out that the population-related growth in the supply of labour tends to depress wages, thus providing a further obstacle to reduced inequalities. It is not surprising, therefore, that a World Bank study found inequality and population growth to be positively correlated with each other, with an increase of 1 per cent in the rate of population growth associated with a 1·6 per cent fall in the income share of the poorest 40 per cent of the population.[7] Policies to restrain population growth may therefore help reduce inequality.

The conclusion is, that *the employment and income distribution arguments provide sound additional reasons for wishing to avoid rapid population growth.*

Besides the availability of employment, the shape and height of the cost-benefit curve will be critically influenced by the amounts of 'co-operant factors', such as capital and land, that are available per worker. An abundant supply will result in high labour productivity and will raise the curve; shortages will have the contrary effect. There is a group of arguments to the effect that rapid population growth reduces the availability per worker of these co-operant factors, so we next examine these.

Saving, investment and budgetary effects

The first of these argues that population growth in LDCs has an adverse effect on aggregate *saving* and, hence, on investment. Both personal and government saving may be affected. At the personal level, it is argued that the costs of large numbers of children prevent people from saving as much as they would otherwise do. Against this, we should set the facts that incomes are too low in many LDCs for any but the most prosperous to do much saving, and also that it is the poor who have the largest families. So, in relation to total saving the effect of population growth on personal saving may not be large.

---

[6] Kuznets, 1976, also found a strong negative correlation between per capita income and household size – the largest households have the smallest average incomes.
[7] Chenery, *et al.*, 1974, p. 17.

The impact on government saving may be larger. The large numbers of children associated with rapid population growth create a powerful demand for government provision of education and health services. As an illustration, it has been projected for Chile that the total cost of education and health by the year 2000 would be 70 per cent higher if fertility remains high than with low fertility assumptions.[8] Since education and health already make large claims on government revenues, additional needs arising from population expansion will make it more difficult for the government to save, to set aside some of its current revenues for capital formation.

Little research has yet been published to settle this question. A study by Leff did indicate significant negative correlation between child dependency and aggregate saving in developing countries, but the result was not a strong one, the statistics were not reliable, and his methods have been criticized.[9] It is probably wise, therefore, not to place much weight on the alleged connection between population and saving, pending more evidence.

However, if for other reasons population growth inhibits the expansion of per capita incomes, it will also hold back saving, because there is much evidence that saving is strongly correlated with per capita income.[10]

A related point is that a more rapidly growing labour force means that available capital assets have to be spread over a larger number of workers than would otherwise be the case. More precisely, an increased expansion of the labour force will result either in more unemployment (which is the point made on page 82) or in *less capital per employed worker*. In the latter case, the cost-benefit curve will also be lowered, as illustrated in Figure 4.6, because the amount of capital per worker is a prime determinant of labour productivity.

Another way of illustrating essentially the same point is to calculate how much investment is needed simply to maintain existing levels of per capita income for a growing population. Illustrative estimates suggest that this 'demographic investment' may absorb as much as two-thirds of total investment in LDCs, leaving only one-third to be devoted to raising per capita incomes.[11]

As already implied, rapid population growth will affect the composition of investment, especially as between directly productive and other forms of investment. Not only will larger investments be needed in education and health, but the rapid urbanization associated with growing populations will necessitate expensive investments in city infrastructures – in housing, transport, water and sewerage. Much of this burden will again fall on government budgets. Greater state capital formation will be needed for these purposes, leaving smaller resources available for more directly productive investments. Governments can, of course, resist these demands but only at the expense of reduced standards of education and health, and the growth of urban slums.

There may also be some squeeze on the *tax* side of the government budget. On this, as in the case of saving, if for other reasons population growth retards the growth of per capita incomes, this will have an adverse effect on the government's ability to raise adequate tax revenues, because the tax base is a rising function of per capita income.

The conclusions here are that *rapid population growth will reduce the amount of capital available per employed worker and thus productivities. It is also likely to change the composition of current government spending and of capital formation in directions which will slow down economic growth. If for other reasons population growth holds back per capita incomes, it will have adverse effects on saving and tax capacity. Taken together, these arguments considerably strengthen the case for reducing population growth.*

Activity. Turn to budget statistics of your own country. Which have been the fastest growing items of current and capital spending? What has been the trend in government saving on current account? Is it possible to relate these developments to population growth?

The pressure on mineral assets

The final major group of arguments against rapid population growth is concerned with its effect on the world's natural resources – minerals and land. Take first the case of mineral resources.

The crucial characteristic of these is that they are non-replaceable. They can be mined and once they are used that is the end of·them, except for some recycling. It is an undoubted fact that the world is using up known deposits of minerals at an historically phenomenal rate and there are many – unflatteringly called the 'doomsday school' – who believe that it will not be long before the world begins to run out of minerals of crucial economic importance, including petroleum.

---

[8] See essay by B. H. Herrick in Keeley, 1976.
[9] See Leff, 1969, and the discussion of his results in the June 1971 issue of the same journal. See also Kelley, 1976, who found an ambiguous relationship between family size and saving.
[10] See Mikesell and Zinser, 1973, pp. 3–7.
[11] World Bank, 1974, Table 12.

But what has population growth got to do with this? The doomsday school sees a close connection. The demand for these raw materials, they argue, is rising rapidly, partly because of population growth. So if the world is to avoid catastrophic shortages of essential minerals it must reduce the expansion of population.

The validity of this argument is dubious. In common with some of the pro-population arguments discussed shortly, it makes the mistake of equating people with demand. An addition to the number of people is not the same thing as an addition to effective demand, least of all in developing countries. Demand is made 'effective' by the exercise of purchasing power but when a couple has a new baby this does nothing for their purchasing power. In fact, the argument is a boomerang to be turned against those who use it. The enormous growth in demand for the goods which have a high mineral component–chiefly manufactured goods – has been concentrated in the industrial countries in a period when they have experienced only slow population growth. The demand for manufactures rises rapidly with income – they have high income elasticities of demand – so to the extent that rapid population growth reduces the expansion of per capita incomes it also reduces total demand for the world's mineral resources.

This is not necessarily to deny that the world may face serious shortages of some minerals; it is merely denied that this is a valid argument for reduced population growth.

There is a second, more firmly founded, line of argument, based on diminishing returns. Economic minerals are among the co-operant factors which influence labour productivity and hence the height of the cost-benefit curve. A larger labour force means smaller mineral deposits per worker than would otherwise be the case, and thus lower productivities. So long as we assume a fixed quantity of economic minerals this is unanswerable but Kuznets has argued strongly that we should not make that assumption:[12]

The scarcity of natural resources in the underdeveloped countries is primarily a function of under-development; underdevelopment is not a function of scarce natural resources ... It seems legitimate to assume that the supply of natural resources relative to population in most underdeveloped countries is sufficient for technologically feasible advanced methods to provide a larger population with higher per capita product ...

He is surely right in suggesting that there are many deposits of economic minerals awaiting discovery. Even so, population growth will do nothing to make their discovery easier and will mean that, when found, the deposits will have to be shared among more people.

Therefore, *the argument that rapid population growth is a major reason for the depletion of the world's mineral resources is untenable. The argument from diminishing returns has validity but there are likely to be valuable mineral deposits as yet undiscovered. These arguments do not provide a strong case for limiting population growth.*

Activity. Possible topic for a group project. Investigate, with information from geologists, the extent and intensity with which your country has been geologically explored. What minerals are believed the most promising prospects for future discovery?

Pressure on the land

The first economist to take a major interest in the economics of population was Thomas Malthus. In his *Essay on Population* (1789) he argued that, whereas the production of food and other necessities grows in arithmetical progression (1, 2, 3, 4 ...), population expands in geometrical progression (1, 2, 4, 8 ...), so that the number of people will outgrow our capacity to feed them. In the absence of 'moral restraints' on family size, he predicted that starvation and disease would result from over-population, thus providing the harshest remedy of all to the population problem.

A modern version of the Malthusian view can be put as follows. In many parts of the world there is already much malnutrition, sometimes outright starvation, and high densities of population on fertile land. Traditional systems of shifting cultivation and land rotation depend for their viability on allowing the land to revert periodically to lengthy periods of fallow, when the natural vegetation grows back and restores the fertility of the soil. But, except in the few countries which still have unpopulated areas of good land, growing population pressures shorten fallow periods. This diminishes the fertility of the soil, causes the land to be subdivided into ever smaller, less viable, plots and causes soil erosion. Since increasing amounts of labour are being applied to an essentially fixed area of land, diminishing returns set in, lowering productivities and the cost-benefit curve. It is thus increasingly difficult to maintain dietary standards and malnutrition worsens.

---

[12] Kuznets, 1974, pp. 8–9.

The weakness of this argument is that it discounts the application of modern scientific knowledge to improved cultivation techniques, higher-yielding seed varieties and other forms of technical progress. Malthus was wrong in his dire predictions not because of a logical flaw in his argument but because he did not foresee the enormous improvements that would be achieved in agricultural yields and productivities – improvements which also increased the area of land considered to be cultivable. If we look at the world as a whole, these have allowed a vastly larger population to be better fed than when he was writing.

This point is illustrated in Figure 4.7, where the number of workers is measured on the horizontal and output per worker is measured on the vertical. The Malthusian argument is that in most parts of the world we are on the declining part of the (unbroken) average productivity curve, i.e. to the right of A, because there are more and more people trying to support themselves on a given area of land. Productivity diminishes and hence the availability of food per person. But this 'law of diminishing returns' takes technology as unchanging. Once we introduce technical progress, the effect is to achieve successive rises in the productivity curve. Better tools, improved seeds, the application of fertilizers mean greater yields per hectare and output per man. So, what has been happening in the world can be thought of as a movement from point 1 to points 2, 3, etc., on the diagram. The law of diminishing returns is still valid. We may be moving down the curve, but these downward movements have been more than offset by the impact of improved techniques, so that productivity has risen from P_1 to P_4.

Figure 4.7 *Diminishing returns and technical progress.*

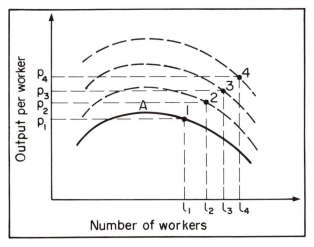

However, the global distribution of these benefits has been very uneven. While Europeans and North Americans have rich and varied diets, so that heart failures due to overweight have become a major health hazard, enormous numbers of people in Asia and Africa sustain themselves on low quality diets that have improved little over those of their forefathers. Malthus was wrong about Europe but might he be right about today's developing countries?

Developing countries are finding it difficult to improve the diets of their peoples. While LDCs as a group were virtually self-sufficient in food in the 1950s, by 1970 they were importing 15 to 20 million tonnes of major staple foods. There have been widely-publicized famines on the Indian subcontinent and in the Sahelian zone of Africa, on the southern fringe of the Sahara desert. While some countries have been successful in developing their agriculture others have lagged behind. In Bangladesh, for example, food production has failed to keep pace with demand, average food consumption has gone down and malnutrition among the poor has probably worsened.[13] Overall, there has been only the slowest progress towards improving nutritional standards, as indicated by the following estimates of the annual percentage growth of per capita food production:[14]

	1950–60	1960–70
Developed countries	1·80%	1·53%
Developing countries	1·02%	0·19%

It appears there was negligible progress in the 1960s, despite the 'green revolution' discussed in Chapter 9. For millions, malnutrition and the danger of starvation remain everyday facts of life.

Crop yields remain generally low in LDCs and, without doubt, it is technically possible for the world to adequately feed populations much larger than today's. The difficulty, is to convert the technical potential into actual and economical practice. To quote Kuznets again:[15]

> The technological-economic potentials can be realised in many parts of the world . . . *only* if the political, social and economic institutions are changed with consequent changes in the scales of values and priorities guiding the population.

Ways of improving agricultural productivities are explored further in Chapter 9, which points out numerous measures that could be taken but draws

[13] Chen and Chaudhury, 1975.
[14] World Bank, 1974, Table 16.
[15] Kuznets, 1974, p. 91.

attention also to the complexities of the task. While the large potential for improvement is undoubted, there is no assurance that all countries will achieve satisfactory results in harnessing modern knowledge to agriculture, which leaves the danger of major food shortages in particular countries. Nor is there adequate assurance that the world distributive system will protect the problem areas against inadequate food supplies.

Malthusian considerations do not provide a strong case for reducing population growth if we are willing to assume that developing countries will successfully raise agricultural productivities nearer to their technical potentials. But there is no assurance that they will be sufficiently successful. Reduced population growth would give them more time to make the necessary adaptations, and reduce pressures on food supplies.

> **Activity.** Can you find any data on dietary standards and per capita food production for your own country? If so, do the trends strengthen the case for reduced population growth?

Having gone over the chief arguments against rapid population growth, it is time to look at the major viewpoints that see this growth in more favourable light.

V.   Arguments Favourable to Population Growth

The historical precedent

The first of these draws upon the historical experiences of the now industrialized countries. These countries also experienced abnormally rapid population growth when they were going through their industrial revolution: there were large falls in death rates which were matched by reduced fertility only after a long time-lag. As a minimum, it can be said that the growth in the numbers of people did not prevent development; there is a strong school of thought which believes that it positively assisted industrialization.

Accelerated population growth meant a fast-expanding labour force which could meet the labour needs of the new industries. This enlarged volume of employment meant, in turn, that there was an expansion of markets, permitting the fuller utilization of economies of scale, creating an environment favourable to innovation and high investment. Associated with the declining death rates, there were

improvements in general health standards, which helped to improve labour productivities and, perhaps, inventiveness. So far as nineteenth-century Europe is concerned, historians therefore tend to see the population explosion as beneficial. Indeed, the fact that it had a relatively stagnant population in this period is often given as a reason why France got left behind in Europe's industrial revolution.

It is natural to ask, if population growth was favourable to economic development in Europe, is it not also likely to be favourable to the Third World? There are, unfortunately, a number of reasons for approaching this historical argument with caution, because the economic circumstances of the LDCs differ markedly from those of Europe at the beginning of the nineteenth century.

First, declines in European death rates were a *consequence* of rising economic prosperity, so that the population explosion did not occur until the industrial revolution was already under way. In many LDCs, on the other hand, the decline in death rates has *preceded* economic modernization and so the population explosion has occurred earlier. In consequence, to quote Kuznets again:[16]

> While in the earlier period [1750–1930] population grew most rapidly in those countries and areas in which economic performance, on a per capita basis, was high and rising, in the recent decades population growth was most rapid in the countries and areas in which economic performance was relatively low.

Secondly, the rate of population growth in Europe was much below the rates currently experienced in most LDCs. At all times during 1750 to 1930 population growth in Europe as a whole was well below 1 per cent a year and hardly any individual country experienced growth faster than 1·5 per cent.[17] One consequence was that child dependency rates were never as high as they are in today's LDCs. Large-scale migrations from Europe to the Americas and Oceana was an important factor, providing a safety valve to prevent population pressures from becoming too acute. International migration is, however, not an option available to today's developing countries, apart from a few special cases.[18]

Thirdly, there was already, at the outset of Europe's industrial revolution, a large availability of resources for investment and entrepreneurial talent. There was

---

[16] Kuznets, 1966, p. 40.

[17] ibid, Table 2.2, p. 38.

[18] Large-scale migrations of workers from Pakistan to Arabian countries, and similar movements of Malawian workers to South Africa are among the exceptions.

little by way of a foreign exchange constraint, because of colonial exploitation and Europe's head-start advantage in manufacturing exports. It was therefore possible to absorb the growing labour force into productive employment: the 'co-operant factors' were available. This, of course, is a major contrast with the LDCs, faced with serious and often growing problems of unemployment and other forms of labour under-utilization, discussed in the next chapter. As an eminent economic historian has written of the British industrial revolution:[19]

> The fact was that the new technology was introduced into a country which had labour, land and capital resources in reserve . . . without some slack in other resources – in land and capital – the growth of population might have come up rapidly against an output ceiling. *With* this additional slack it provided a positive incentive to economic change and growth.

There are a few developing countries which may possess such a slack – perhaps some of the oil-producing countries – but that is not the general situation today. Therefore, *the circumstances of the Third World differ too much from those of nineteenth-century Europe for the historical argument to provide a sound case in favour of population growth.*

Necessity as the mother of invention

The name of Albert Hirschman has long featured among the most important and stimulating writers on economic development. He presents a challenge-and-response model of development, in which the emergence (or creation) of bottle-necks and other disequilibria are seen as providing the challenge necessary to call forth the decision-making and innovative forces essential to development. He sees population growth as providing such a challenge.[20]

In his view, the threat posed by population pressures to living standards will lead to counter-developments to maintain existing consumption standards. These counter-measures result in an increase in the people's ability to control their environment, to organize themselves for development, and enhances their 'ability to invest'. This would have the effect of raising the cost-benefit curve in Figure 4.5.

These propositions are too general to yield empirically testable predictions. Another writer has, however, given this viewpoint a more concrete form. Drawing especially on Asian experiences, Boserup (1965) suggests that the increasing unviability of traditional systems of cultivation, resulting from rising population densities, forces the population to

modify production techniques so as to cultivate the soil more intensively without depleting its fertility – necessity as the mother of invention. Traditional agriculture with low population densities, she argues, is a leisurely way of life, often lived in small communities with little contact with the outside world. Population growth transforms this, inducing harder, more regular, work and greater contact with the outside world. She therefore concludes that:[21]

> Primitive communities with sustained population growth have a better chance to get into a process of genuine economic development than primitive communities with stagnant or declining populations, provided, of course, that the necessary agricultural investments are undertaken.

How is this argument to be evaluated? First note that Boserup claims only a limited applicability for her thesis, relating it only to 'primitive' societies with low population densities. In fact, she follows the quotation above with the sentence, 'This condition may not be fulfilled in densely peopled communities if rates of population growth are high'. She also expects that the processes of agricultural adaptation will result in declining labour productivity so that it 'can hardly be described as economic growth'. Nevertheless if population growth does provide a spur to agricultural innovations, the long-run benefits of this could be large. (The growth of 'informal' activities in the towns as a response to fast growing urban labour forces may provide an urban equivalent of Boserup's agricultural case.)

Two further questions may be asked. Is agricultural innovativeness positively correlated with population pressures? Is population pressure the most efficient means of stimulating rural change? On this second question, Hirschman is in no doubt: 'Among the inducement mechanisms we have studied . . . population pressure must rank as the least attractive one'. It is, he says, a 'clumsy and cruel' stimulant, with which most LDCs are already abundantly supplied.[22] This also goes some way towards answering the first question: there is already hardship enough in the rural economy to provide incentives for self-improvement; adding the demographic factor may not make much

---

[19] Deane, 1965, pp. 34–5. Chapter 2 of this book provides a valuable examination of the complex interrelationships between demographic and economic factors during the British industrial revolution.
[20] See Hirschman, 1958, especially pp. 176–82.
[21] Boserup, 1965, p. 118.
[22] Hirschman, 1958, pp. 179, 182.

difference. In the absence of firm empirical evidence, it is difficult to go beyond that.[23]

So here the conclusion is that *the challenge-and-response argument applies mainly to early-stage, low-density LDCs. In these, population growth might stimulate innovation but does not provide an efficient or humane inducement mechanism.*

Activity. Do you think agricultural progress and population pressures have been positively correlated in your own country? Can you identify specific improvements that were introduced in response to population growth?

Economies of scale

The existence of major economies of scale is a central feature of modern economic systems. They occur in most forms of industrial activity (see Chapter 10), in the provision of infrastructural facilities and to some extent in agriculture. Some writers, Boserup among them, have developed from this fact another pro-population argument: a larger population broadens the market, permitting economies of scale, lower unit costs, higher productivities and hence a higher cost-benefit curve.

If 'the market' in this context is thought of in terms of monetary demand, e.g. for manufactured consumer goods, then this argument can be criticized on the same grounds that we criticized the 'doomsday school' on page 84. People are not effective demand. As Kalecki put it, 'An increase in the number of paupers does not broaden the market'. The critical question is whether the increasing numbers will be able to find high-productivity employment. If they cannot, and for other reasons discussed on earlier pages, they will tend to depress per capita incomes and thus actually limit the size of the market. As it relates to market demand for manufactured consumer goods, if for other reasons population growth holds back the expansion of per capita incomes it will hinder rather than assist the enjoyment of scale economies.

The demand for social infrastructure – schools, health clinics, roads – is not, however, essentially a market demand; in this case the argument from economies of scale should be taken more seriously. To give an example, the cost per farmer of providing agricultural extension services for a scattered population is likely to be well above the cost for more concentrated communities. The same is true of education, health, water and so forth. Population growth occurring in sparsely populated areas can thus permit scale economies. Unfortunately, it is not possible to quantify the magnitude of the benefits that may result from these economies. In any case, this is not so much an argument for population growth as for population concentration. The Tanzanian government, for example, pursues a policy of 'villagization' intended precisely to collect formerly scattered peoples into villages so that basic services can be made available to them at reasonable cost. This policy does not depend upon population growth.

As it related to effective market demand, the argument from economies of scale is invalid. In sparsely populated areas, increasing numbers may permit scale economies. in the provision of social infrastructure and services, although policies to achieve greater concentrations of existing populations may be a more efficient alternative.

Empty lands

This argument has a family relationship to the one just considered, because it also relates to sparsely populated areas. The argument here is exactly the reverse of the neo-Malthusian case considered on pages 84–5, namely that with small populations on cultivable land we may still be on the rising portion of the productivity curve in Figure 4.7. In the extreme case, good land may be entirely unpopulated – a failure to utilize a valuable productive resource. Moreover, low population densities characterize many developing countries, as shown by the figures in column (5) of Table 4.1 (page 74). In Africa and Latin America average densities are only 14 and 16 people per square kilometre – about half the world average and far below Europe or Japan. Is it not likely, therefore, that increasing returns may be important in many LDCs?

One difficulty with this argument is that aggregated statistics on densities are unhelpful for present purposes. They are simple averages which typically conceal large variations between the various countries in a region, and also within countries. Take the African average of 14 persons. Even if we confine ourselves to the larger countries of Africa, we find Nigeria with a density of 61, Uganda with 53, Ghana with 37 and so on. And within each of these there are also larger variations. In Ghana, for example, the central region has a density more than ten times that of the large northern region.

For the purposes of the empty lands argument it is more relevant to consult statistics of densities of rural populations on *agricultural* land, such as those presented in column (6) of Table 4.1. This provides a very different picture.

---

[23] Levi, 1976, examines the Sierra Leone case and finds the evidence there is consistent with Boserup's theory, although he is cautious about the interpretation of the data.

From column (6) we see that agricultural densities in the major developing regions greatly exceed those of the industrialized regions (with the exception of Japan). In both Africa and east Asia average densities on agricultural land are more than ten times the overall population densities given in column (5); the Latin American multiple is about six; the south Asian multiple approaches three. Here too, of course, there are large variations within the regions and within the countries which comprise them.

Taking all the developing regions together, density on agricultural land is shown as nearly four times as large as the overall density in column (5) of the table. The reason, of course, is that there are large areas of arid or semi-arid land, of swampland and of mountains with little or no cultivation and few people. These lands are empty for good reasons: the land is unyielding and the life extremely hard.

The mere existence of low aggregate densities and of empty lands does not, therefore, constitute a sound argument in favour of population growth. It is necessary to show that unpopulated or under-populated land is potentially productive and that accretions to the population would actually move into these areas, rather than concentrate in existing population centres. There may be countries which can satisfy these conditions. The hinterlands of Liberia and Brazil come to mind as largely undeveloped and potentially high-yielding. But such a situation is not typical of many developing countries.

To conclude: *the empty lands argument is valid for sparsely populated areas of good cultivable soil but in the typical case good land already supports substantial populations.*

Activity. Evaluate this argument in relation to the situation in your own country. Is inadequate population a serious constraint on the development of any large areas of cultivable land?

Developed country over-consumption

The next argument is to the effect that the chief problem in the world is not population growth but international inequality. There is an enormous gap between living standards in the industrial countries and LDCs, with level of consumption in the former far in excess of any objective criteria of basic needs. With a more equitable distribution of world income, the LDCs could support larger populations at higher living standards. Policy-makers should therefore concentrate on reducing world inequalities rather than on population policies.

The factual validity of this argument is not in doubt. The western and communist industrial countries between them have about 30 per cent of world population but generate about 80 per cent of total world income. Per capita income and consumption levels reflect this discrepancy. But do these facts provide helpful guidance to LDC policy-makers? For many years developed countries have been paying lip service to the objective of raising their aid programmes to LDCs to just 0.7 per cent of GNP! With few exceptions, they have failed to do so, despite pressures from numerous international gatherings. In fact, in 1977 net official aid flows to developing countries were equivalent to less than a third of 1 per cent of industrial country GNPs.[24]

Developing country policy-makers therefore have to live with the brute fact that there is not about to be any major redistribution of world income, however immoral that may be. The peoples of the USA, the Soviet Union, the European Community will not sacrifice their affluence for the benefit of the poor of Africa, Asia and Latin America. If the governments of the rich tried to impose such a sacrifice they would likely be overthrown, for aid has few friends in the industrial world. The LDCs should, of course, continue to exert maximum pressure for greater aid and other resource transfers, but it would be foolish to base national policies on the assumption that a major redistribution will occur.

In any case, it is not clear why policies to improve the world distribution of income are seen as competing with population policies. If for other reasons it is believed desirable to limit population growth, the adoption of policies to achieve this should in no way weaken LDC efforts to improve world income distribution. On the contrary, the industrial countries may be just a little less unwilling to provide assistance if they see LDCs willing to tackle their own problems and if they have some assurance that the aid will not merely be swallowed up by ever-growing numbers.

Thus, we conclude, *the argument from developed country over-consumption is irrefutable but unhelpful. It does not provide a sensible reason for abstaining from population policies.*

A missing correlation

The final argument to be considered states that if population growth were as harmful to economic development as some argue, there should be a negative statistical correlation between rates of

---

[24] World Bank, 1978A, p. 35.

growth of population and per capita incomes. The countries with the most rapid expansion of population should have the slowest increase in average incomes per head. *But no such negative correlation can be observed.* Kuznets examined this and concluded that there was no uniform or significant relationship between these two variables[25] and other investigators have come to similar conclusions.

It is helpful in evaluating this point to recall the demographic transition model outlined earlier. This can be interpreted to predict that as countries begin to develop and enter the early transition phase there will be an acceleration of population growth because of falling death rates. In this phase, then, there can be a *positive* correlation between economic and population growth rates; only in the late transition phase, when birth rates are also falling, does the model predict a negative correlation.

The model moreover stresses the *interaction* of demographic and economic forces, rather than positing a one-way relationship:[26]

> What is contained in the data being correlated is the influence both of population on the economy and of the economy on population ... Unless we have some belief about the relative strength of each direction of causation, and their resultant combined force, we cannot have any expectation about the sign of the correlation coefficient.

Many variables will influence economic and demographic trends; too much is left out of correlations of GNP and population growth for them to provide much test of whether population growth helps or hampers economic development. The most we can infer is that population growth is not a *dominant* influence on economic performance; it warns us against taking an alarmist view of the gravity of the population problem.

Remember also the earlier reference to the relationship between poverty and family size, and to the fact that the most rapid population growth occurs among the poorest members of society. As you will see from the next chapter, there are typically harsh degrees of income inequality in developing countries, with the poorest 40 per cent of the population receiving only around an eighth of total incomes. With population growth especially occurring among the poor but a high proportion of the benefits of economic growth accruing to the relatively well-to-do, this will weaken any statistical relationship between the expansion of per capita income and population.

So *the absence of a negative correlation between the growth of population and per capita income is a good* *reason for not taking an extreme view of the population problem. But it fails to demonstrate that no problem exists because the interactions between demographic and economic variables are too complex to be tested in this way.*

VI.   A Summary, an Illustration and a Caution

A summary of conclusions

We have now been through a large number of arguments for and against population growth and you may by now be feeling a little confused. The conclusions arrived at on each of the arguments reviewed are summarized below.

Arguments against rapid population growth

(1) The high child *dependency ratios* associated with rapid population growth imposes heavy burdens on poor economies and is a valid and strong reason for wishing to limit population growth.

(2) Rapid population growth is likely to be associated with *poverty and income inequalities*, and a source of worsening *unemployment*. These are sound additional reasons for limiting the expansion of population.

(3) Rapid population growth will reduce the amount of *capital* per employed worker and thus productivity. It is also likely to change the composition of government spending in directions which will slow down economic growth. It is liable to have adverse effects on *saving* and *tax capacity*. Taken together, this group of arguments considerably strengthens the case for reducing population growth.

(4) The argument that rapid population growth is a major reason for the rapid depletion of the world's *mineral assets* is untenable. The argument from diminishing returns, in this connection, has validity but there are likely to be valuable deposits as yet undiscovered. These arguments do not provide a strong case for limiting population growth.

(5) *Malthusian considerations* do not provide a strong case for reducing population growth if we

---

[25] Kuznets, 1974 – see table on p. 43 and related text. His coefficient of correlation between growths of per capita income and population actually has a positive sign but is not statistically significant.
[26] Cassen, 1976, p. 806.

are willing to assume the successful application of modern knowledge to agriculture in LDCs. But there is no assurance of success. Reduced population growth would leave more time for the necessary improvements and would reduce pressures on food supplies.

Arguments favourable to population growth

(1) The circumstances of the developing countries differ too much from those of nineteenth-century Europe for the *historical argument* to provide a sound case in favour of population growth.

(2) The *challenge-and-response* argument applies mainly to early-stage, low-density LDCs. In these, population growth may stimulate innovation but does not provide an efficient or humane inducement mechanism.

(3) As it relates to effective market demand, the argument from *economies of scale* is invalid. In thinly populated areas, however, increasing numbers may permit scale economies in the provision of social infrastructure and services, although policies to achieve greater concentrations of existing populations may be a more efficient alternative.

(4) The *empty lands* argument is valid for sparsely populated areas of good cultivable soil but in the typical country good land already supports substantial populations.

(5) The argument from developed country over-consumption is irrefutable but unhelpful. It does not provide national policy-makers with a sensible reason for abstaining from population policies.

(6) The *absence of a negative correlation* between the growth rates of population and per capita income provides a good reason for not taking an extreme view of the gravity of the population problem. But interactions between economic and demographic variables are too complex for this type of correlation analysis to be a good test of the impact of population on development.

> **Activity.** Please study the above summary before proceeding further and make sure that you understand it. Also make sure that you are clear about any respects in which you disagree with the conclusions summarized there.

In my view and in the view of a large majority of economists who have concerned themselves with the issue, *the balance of the arguments summarized above decisively indicates that rapid population growth is likely to impede economic development.* The first three arguments – on dependency effects, on employment and income distribution effects, and on investment and budgetary effects – are particularly persuasive. Several of the pro-population arguments have only limited applicability and are relevant mainly to thinly populated areas. They also tend to be essentially defensive, in that they are rarely used to actually advocate faster population growth but merely to oppose attempts to reduce it.

If the conclusion is accepted that, on balance, rapid population growth is likely to impede development, it remains to give some indication of the *relative seriousness* of this problem. We are already warned against taking an alarmist view. The population problem does not face developing countries with imminent catastrophe. Events have invalidated the gloomy 'poverty trap' theories of underdevelopment. Even the poorest LDCs have been able to achieve some growth in per capita incomes, despite the population explosion.

But the truth remains that rapid population growth makes development more difficult, makes it harder to feed and raise the standards of the poor, worsens the problem of finding them productive employment. The precise seriousness of these factors will be especially influenced by the density of population on cultivable land. Some countries are still blessed with low densities on good land but they are the exception; high densities and diminishing returns are more common. To risk a sweeping generalization, *population growth probably ranks among the two or three most fundamental problems to the Third World.*

A cost-benefit illustration

In this chapter's 'first approach' to the economics of population growth the idea of the cost-benefit curve was introduced. It was suggested that an economic test of the desirability of increasing the population can be made by adding up the discounted values of the net consumption costs and production benefits that can be expected from an additional person over his lifetime. If there are net benefits, it will raise the general welfare of the community for him to be born; if there are net costs, the rest of the community would be economically better off without him.

> **Activity.** You may want to refresh your memory on this by referring again to pages 80–1.

The conclusion reached in the previous section was that, on balance, the effects of population growth are negative. That is to say, the social costs of an additional person are likely to be greater than the social benefits. Table 4.3 provides a numerical illustration of this, using Indian data.

One conclusion reached earlier was that rapid population growth worsens unemployment and often leads to diminishing returns. This is reflected in column (3) of the table which sets out coefficients that are applied to the average productivity of an Indian worker. These coefficients have zero values at early ages and extreme old age because in these periods the person's productive contribution will be negligible. They then rise, to achieve a maximum value of 0·8 at ages 25 to 54. It is assumed, in other words, that the additional worker's productivity will only be 80 per cent of the average, either because he will be more prone to unemployment, or will only be able to find low-productivity employment, or some combination of the two. Applying these coefficients to the average productivity figures in column (2), his annual productivity can be calculated, as in column (4). From his production we subtract his estimated consumption in column (5), to get his net contribution, in column (6). You can see from this that he will be a net consumer for the first fourteen years of his life and for the last decade; between times he is a net producer.

However, the column (6) results have to be adjusted for the possibility that he may die prematurely. Coefficients indicating the probability of his survival are given in column (7), based on Indian mortality data. These are applied to the column (6) results to give his adjusted net annual production in column (8). Note from column (7) that there is a 25 per cent chance that he will die before reaching the age at which he would become a net producer, i.e. 25 out of every 100 males will die before they are 15 years old. These unfortunate 25 are all cost and no benefit so far as the economic welfare of rest of the community is concerned. This makes a great deal of difference to the results of Table 4.3. The final column (10) gives the present (year 0) value of total net consumption or production in each of the age classes, utilizing the principles outlined in the appendix to Chapter 2.

Adding up all the figures in column (10), the net result indicates the net present value of this person's life to be minus $65; *the rest of the community would be better off by a total of $65 in present values had this person not been born.* From which it is tempting to draw the conclusion that it would have been in the general interest for the government to have spent up to $65 on population policies that would have avoided his birth.

Of course, not too much weight should be put on the results of this exercise. They are highly sensitive to the chosen assumptions, and the rate of discount, although I have tried to keep them realistic. It also omits the many important non-economic considerations that ought to be reckoned with.[27]

Nevertheless, economic factors are important too and should no more be neglected than non-economic ones. After all, India's population is growing at the rate of about 12 million people a year. If each of these were to have a net present cost to society of minus $65 that would total nearly $800 million – not a sum to be lightly disregarded!

Activity. Use the results in column (10) of Table 4.3 to draw a graph similar to Figure 4.5 (page 80), measuring the present value of costs and benefits on the vertical.

Limitations of a purely economic approach

But it is time now to broach the non-economic aspects of this topic. Enough has already been said to show that the interactions between economic and demographic factors are complex and move in both directions. Precisely how they interact with each other, and the specific consequences of these interactions will vary according to social and cultural conditions. We can attempt to quantify, as in Table 4.3, but only if we remember that the results present just part of the story.

The assumption implicit in the discussion of Table 4.3 is that the goal of society is the maximization of income or 'economic welfare'. But society has non-economic goals too and when we introduce these the conclusions of the economist do not necessarily remain valid. Specifically, *children are valued for their own sake,* even though they may be an economic burden. They are a source of joy and enrichment in the family; and in many societies a large family is still a source of prestige and a demonstration of virility. Negatively, the practice of contraception may be frowned upon by religious and other leaders. These, too, are factors which should be considered by the government when it formulates its policies with respect to population growth.

It would, however, be a major mistake to think that all non-economic considerations conflict with the economist's advocacy of slower population growth. There are strong social considerations which point to the same conclusion. First, reduced family size is

---

[27] See Blandy, 1974, for a critical examination of the application of cost-benefit calculations to the economics of family size.

Table 4.3
The Net Present Value of a Life (Based on Indian Data)
(All monetary values have been converted into US $)

Age class (1)	Average productivity p.a.(a) ($) (2)	Adjustment factor(b) (3)	Actual productivity ($) (2×3) (4)	Consumption p.a.(c) ($) (5)	Net production/consumption (4−5) (6)	Adjusted probability of survival(d) (7)	Adjusted net production ($) (6×7) (8)	No. of years in period (9)	Net present value in period at 10%(e) ($) (10)
0	280	0	0	10	−10	0.92	−9	1	−8
1–4	288	0	0	21	−21	0.79	−17	4	−54
5–9	302	0	0	54	−54	0.76	−41	5	−106
10–14	318	0.1	32	79	−47	0.75	−35	5	−56
15–24	344	0.5	172	122	+50	0.73	+37	10	+60
25–34	378	0.8	302	149	+153	0.68	+104	10	+65
35–44	417	0.8	334	164	+170	0.60	+102	10	+24
45–54	465	0.8	372	182	+190	0.48	+91	10	+8
55–64	510	0.6	306	164	+142	0.32	+45	10	+2
65–74	566	0.4	226	141	+85	0.17	+14	10	(f)
75–85	622	0	0	111	−111	0.06	−7	10	(f)
TOTAL NET PRESENT VALUE									−65

Notes:

(a) According to Indian statistics, average value-added per worker in 1971 was $277, and had been growing at about 1 per cent a year. $280 has therefore been used as a base figure and has been increased at 1 per cent per annum.

(b) Notional values intended to reflect the probability of unemployment or of employment with below-average productivity.

(c) Average consumption per member of the Indian population was equal to $76 in 1971. A reasonable time contour of consumption was constructed, showing maximum consumption during active adult life, and a 1 per cent per annum growth rate was applied to this.

(d) Taken from a table of survivors at specific ages for males in India, 1951–60 in UN *Demographic Yearbook*, 1966, Table 23. The figures in column (7) give the probability of survival at the mid-point of the age class.

(e) Discounted at 10 per cent by methods described in the appendix to Chapter 2. The figures are totals for each sub-period; they are not annual amounts.

(f) Negligible.

intimately connected with the status of women in society. The spread of family planning in western societies was closely associated with the emancipation of women – a recognition that frequent child-bearing not only impairs the health and vitality of the mother but effectively prevents her from playing a full role in society. In many countries womenfolk still suffer an inferior status in society – in terms of work, participation in decision-making and social life. A strong argument could be made that reduced family size is a necessary condition for any radical improvement in the status of the feminine half of the population.

Health considerations are also important. Numbers of women still die in childbirth; far more suffer from poor health because of frequent pregnancies. Even more serious are the medical consequences of illegally performed abortions. Because of inadequate family planning facilities and anti-abortion laws, illegal abortions are still common in the Third World. The risks of death from these operations are considerable; the risks of persisting injury or ill-health are even larger. The children of large but poor families are also liable to suffer and are especially prone to malnutrition and ill-health. Fear that they will not be able to look after their children properly is one of commonest reasons why couples adopt family planning.

Some weight was placed earlier in the chapter on the argument that rapid population growth worsens unemployment, especially in the towns. If this is accepted, it too has major social implications. For unemployment tends to be most severe among young adults in the towns and with this go prostitution, crime and other anti-social activities. Even without the unemployment problem, the abnormal pace of urbanization associated with rapid population growth creates major social problems of overcrowded and insanitary living conditions.

So: *Decisions about population policy should not be based on purely economic considerations. However, a number of social factors reinforce the economic case for restraining the growth of population.*

Growing numbers of developing countries agree with the conclusion just set out. The problems associated with population growth have made themselves felt and, as exemplified by the quotations from Chairman Mao at the beginning of this chapter, leaders have increasingly responded to these by adopting policies designed to reduce population growth. This has been especially the case in Asia and the Caribbean, but the trend is also observable in Africa and Latin America. In 1974, for example, fifty-three LDCs had adopted, or were supporting, family planning programmes, against only four in 1960.

About half of these had taken action on health grounds alone; the others were explicitly seeking to reduce population growth.

The next step, then, is to look at the policy implications of the foregoing analysis. From here on we adopt the premise that it is desirable to avoid rapid population growth and will explore the best ways of achieving this result.

Activity. This would be a suitable point at which to review your understanding of, and attitude towards, what has been written so far. Do you agree with the premise that it is desirable to avoid rapid population growth, so far as your own country is concerned?

VII. Policy Implications: Is a *Laissez-Faire* Solution Feasible?

Will development bring its own solution?

The progress of the now industrial countries through the demographic transition occurred without active government help. It occurred because there emerged a spontaneous desire on the part of married couples to limit the number of their children. But this was not just a coincidence. Economic development sets up forces which raise the costs of children to their parents, creating incentives to avoid large families. When these incentives are coupled with the availability and knowledge of family planning techniques, couples can put their preferences into practice and reduced birth rates result. As the demographic transition model suggests, development itself reduces the growth of population. This is not merely a crude extrapolation of western historical experience but is a factor which can be observed in the contemporary world. For example, all Asian countries with per capita incomes above $200 have experienced declining birth rates, with the exception of the predominantly Catholic Philippines.

Why should this be the case? Why is economic modernization associated with declining fertility? The answer to this is only imperfectly understood but studies of fertility have produced sufficiently strong and consistent results that at least a partial answer can be offered.[28] Research results show the following to be important influences on the number of children:

---

[28] See Cassen, 1976, pp. 788–99, and Birdsall, 1977, pp. 85–90 for surveys of the relevant literature.

(1) *Infant mortality.* There is near unanimity in finding a strong positive correlation between infant mortality (defined as death within twelve months of birth) and fertility – as mortality goes down so does fertility. Part of the causation runs from fertility to mortality – the offspring of women who have a long succession of frequent pregnancies are more likely to be sickly and under-nourished. But the causality runs the other way too – as improved medical and other conditions reduce the incidence of infant deaths it is no longer necessary for a couple to have so many children in order to achieve a desired number of survivors.

(2) *Female education.* Virtually all studies find this a strong explanatory variable: the better educated the mother the smaller the number of children she is likely to have. This is partly because education postpones the age of marriage. However, it also widens the mother's horizons, so that she is likely to develop interests that go beyond the confines of the family, interests she may be unable to fulfil if she has a large family of young children to tend. An educated woman is also more likely to be aware of modern family planning methods.

(3) *Female employment and status.* These are closely related to education, but there is evidence that modern sector employment exerts some independent influence in reducing fertility, as does the associated emancipation of the status of women in society. Recall a point made earlier, that the spread of family planning in industrial nations was closely related to improvements in the status of women.

(4) *Urbanization.* This is another factor closely related to (2) and (3) but which seems to exert an additional influence of its own. Other things being equal, urban families are smaller than rural ones, perhaps because bringing up children in the towns is more costly and hazardous.

(5) *Family planning.* Knowledge of, and access to, modern family planning methods also exerts a downward influence on fertility, again holding other variables constant. Presumably the explanation of this is that there are a good many 'unwanted births' that occur because couples are unable to limit their families to the size they desire.

The important thing in the present context is that socio-economic modernization is likely *automatically* to bring these forces into play. Infant mortality rates will go down. More girls will receive better education. More women will find work in the modern sector; hopefully their status will rise at the same time. The population will be increasingly urbanized. Knowledge and use of modern family planning methods will spread.

Granted, then, that economic development will reduce birth rates, the question we now have to explore is whether the reduced population growth will be sufficient. Is it likely that private decisions by couples to limit the size of their families will produce a *socially optimal* result? To answer this we need to explore the incentives which will influence couples' decisions.

Who bears the costs and who enjoys the benefits?

The essence of the *laissez-faire* case, in favour of leaving it to parents to make decisions about family size free from any pressure or inducement from the state, is that it is the parents who bear the costs of having children and that they can therefore be left to settle for themselves the best family size. But is it the case that the parents bear the costs of their children? Only in part.

In having a child a couple will incur the following types of cost:

(1) The opportunity costs of the mother, i.e. the output or income foregone by the mother during pregnancy and subsequently when nursing and looking after the child.

(2) The monetary and subsistence costs of the pregnancy and of rearing the child, e.g. of feeding and clothing it.

(3) The costs of educating the child, if it is sent to school. These are of two types: (a) monetary costs, for school fees, books, uniforms and the like, and (b) opportunity costs, or the value of the output foregone by sending him to school rather than have him more available to contribute to family labour.

(4) Health costs: doctors' fees, medicines and so on.

Against these considerations the parents can set the economic and non-economic benefits derived from having another child. There will be two major potential economic benefits: (1) the contribution of the child to family labour (the size of which will depend critically upon whether the child goes to school), and (2) later material support from the child to the parents, especially during their old age.

Reading down this list of costs and benefits, it is easy to see why economic development makes large families less attractive to parents. The opportunity cost of the mother's time will increase, as women are brought increasingly into employment and as their educational standards improve. Educational costs will become more burdensome as schooling is made compulsory and as less use is made of child labour. The prospect of financial support in old age will also diminish in importance to the extent (1) that the state becomes able to provide pensions for the aged, and (2) to the extent that customary obligations on children to support their parents weaken because of urbanization and the replacement of old values by new.

However, children involve some major costs to society which are not borne by parents. The largest direct costs are for education and health services, which are always subsidized by the state, often very heavily. There are also the less obvious indirect costs to society created by the increased pressure of numbers upon available land and capital; and possible negative saving, employment and income distribution effects, discussed earlier. Because some of the costs are 'external' to the parents, *the incentive to limit family size will be larger for society at large than for the parents.* They bear only part of the costs.

This notion is illustrated in Figure 4.8. The net benefits or costs to the family of an additional child are measured on the vertical and the number of children in the family on the horizontal. The XX′ curve shows the relationship between the marginal benefits or costs of a child and family size, reflecting only the 'internal' costs, i.e. those borne by the family. The curve slopes down on the grounds that, as the number of children increases, each successive one pushes harder against the limited resources of the family, imposing larger costs to offset the psychological and other benefits it may confer. As the family grows it will become increasingly difficult to feed, clothe and educate all its members. Health and psychological pressures on the parents are also likely to increase and this may reduce the non-material pleasures derived from having another child.

The diagram is drawn so that the family will have an incentive to limit the number of children to five; the sixth and subsequent children will impose net costs.

However, the XX′ curve reflects only the internal costs, i.e. it takes no heed of the educational and other expenses borne by society at large. The YY′ curve shows the position as it would be if parents were responsible for the total costs of their children, including the externalities. The amount of these externalities is indicated by the vertical distance AB. You can see that if the parents had to bear these total costs the family would have an incentive to limit the number of children to three; more than that would involve them in net additional costs.

How important is this factor likely to be in practice? Attempts to quantify the external costs usually limit themselves to the direct educational and health costs and ignore the indirect externalities. Even so, the estimates typically show the direct external costs to be a large proportion of the total. An estimate for the USA, for example, put these at 40 to 50 per cent of the total costs of rearing a child; a study of Barbados put the proportion at 30 per cent.[29] The indirect externalities are obviously difficult to quantify but could nonetheless be significant.

Many conclude from this type of analysis that it provides a case for the adoption of government policies to reduce population growth. But the *laissez-faire* economist still has an arrow in his bow. Granted that there will be external costs, he may say, the solution to this is to *internalize* them, i.e. make the parents fully responsible for all the costs of their children. This would involve requiring education and health to be fully paid for, and some form of taxation on children to compensate for the indirect externalities. But as a practical policy recommendation this cannot be taken seriously: it is politically absurd and contradicts the objective of social justice. It is precisely through educational and health programmes that the state can assist the poor (see Chapter 6), and it is the poor who would suffer most from a withdrawal of government subsidies and a tax on children.

We are thus led to the policy conclusion that, because society at large bears some of the costs of additional children, there is a case for government

---

[29] See Friedman, 1972, for the US estimate; and Balakrishnan, 1973, for Barbados.

Figure 4.8 *The economics of family size.*

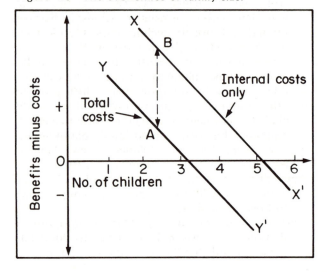

programmes to reduce population growth. In principle, these should utilize public resources up to the point where the cost of preventing one more birth is equal to the social benefits of preventing it. Any amount spent per-birth-prevented less than AB in Figure 4.8 will result in a net gain to society.

> **Activity.** To what extent does the state subsidize education and health in your own country? Can you identify any other external costs which are relevant to your case?

Additional reasons for public intervention

Even if we leave externalities to one side, there are additional arguments in favour of the official adoption of a population policy. First, the *laissez-faire* argument rests on the tacit assumptions (1) that couples will make rational choices about the number of children they want and (2) that they will be able to effectively implement their decisions. Assumption (1) is probably questionable but we can let it go. Assumption (2) amounts to a presumption that couples will have adequate knowledge of, and access to, modern methods of family planning. Such an assumption is not too wide off the mark for industrial societies; it is absurd when applied to many developing countries. For a variety of reasons, large numbers of people living in LDCs do not know about contraception and other family planning techniques, and/or do not have ready access to family planning clinics. For example, the World Bank has estimated that only about 12 per cent of women of fertile age living in LDCs are practising contraception.[30]

There are, it is true, traditional methods of birth control of varying degrees of effectiveness. In general, though, they reflect the usual relationship between traditional and modern technologies: the old ways are much less efficient than the new. So economic development will create incentives for smaller families but people will be unable to respond to these as they would like to. In this situation, there is little prospect that the resulting population growth will be socially optimal. Governments ought, therefore, to actively disseminate information about family planning and improve couples' access to clinics so that they can achieve their own preferred family size. By doing so they will be promoting the interests of society as a whole but they will also be increasing couples' own control over their lives.

A second additional reason for the adoption of population policies is simply put: there are good *non-economic* grounds for doing so, as was outlined on pages 92 and 94. Population policies are especially likely to have beneficial effects on the health of mothers and children, and you will recall that about half the developing countries who by 1974 'had adopted population programmes had done so for health reasons.

There are thus various reasons for concluding that a laissez-faire *approach to the population issue is socially undesirable: governments should adopt policies to reduce population growth.*

It is possible to test this conclusion by asking whether resources devoted by governments to population control policies offer social rates of return which are at least as good as rates of return from alternative types of expenditure. If the conclusion is soundly based it should be found that rates of return from population measures are satisfactorily high. A large number of cost-benefit studies have been undertaken of population programmes over the world and, although the measurement problems are formidable, they virtually all show high rates of return. In fact, the rates of return are generally far in excess of what would normally be expected from more conventional investments. This is so even with population programmes which are not regarded as highly successful. Population policy in India, for instance, has not been very successful, yet cost-benefit studies have found high rates of return even there.[31] The Barbados study already mentioned is fairly typical in finding a cost-benefit ratio of 1:5 from that country's family planning programme.[32]

There is one last point to make before turning to the specifics of government intervention. *Population policies are never to be thought of as a substitute for positive efforts to develop the domestic economy.* This may seem obvious but is necessary to state because one of the less honest arguments sometimes used against population policies is to the effect that 'we should get on with developing the economy instead of worrying about the number of people'. Of course the economy should be developed but a development effort and population measures are complementary not competitive. This chapter has already given strong reasons for thinking that rapid population growth will impede economic development. It has also shown that development itself will help reduce the pace of population expansion. It is thus essential to set population policies into a developmental context and nothing said in the remainder of this chapter should be read as implying the contrary. *The*

---

[30] World Bank, 1974, Table 28 (China excluded).
[31] See result by G. B. Simmonds cited by Nortman, 1972, p. 12.
[32] Balakrishnan, 1973.

adoption of population policies is part of the development effort.

VIII.   Policy Implications: Objectives, Strategies and Instruments

Objectives and targets

Chapter 2 has taught you the desirability of defining policy objectives with as much precision as possible. So as we turn now to examine the specifics of population policies we should clarify what we are trying to achieve.

In principle, it is possible to define the economically optimal rate of population growth as that rate at which the last addition to the population imposes zero net costs on society. If we take into account the costs of population policies, it is that rate at which the net social costs of an extra person are equal to the costs of preventing his birth. But this definition is impractical because we have little idea how to translate it into specific numbers. We have neither the information nor the understanding of the economic effects of marginal additions to a population. So what to do? We might be tempted to set the target at a zero growth rate. But that would be questionable logic. The fact that *rapid* population growth (say, 2·5 per cent a year or more) impedes development does not necessarily imply that *slow* growth would also have negative effects. We frankly do not know and, in any case, the outcome would vary with country circumstances.

But if a precise definition of objectives is not attainable, there is one type of common confusion which the economist can warn against. This is a confusion that arises when governments fail to clarify the motives for their population policies – whether they have adopted them purely to improve health standards or for economic reasons as well. Such a lack of clarity is to be avoided because (1) economic considerations indicate a larger reduction in population growth than would be justified on purely health grounds, and (2) each motive indicates use of different policy instruments. Health-oriented programmes will normally be incorporated into the state's health services; the emphasis will be on the passive provision of family planning services so that couples may have whatever number of children they prefer; measures such as the liberal provision of legal abortion facilities will be resisted. Indeed, a health-oriented programme does not need population

targets. Population growth will simply be the incidental outcome of parental choice, *which can be quite consistent with rapid population growth.*

Economically oriented programmes, by contrast, seek deliberately to avoid rapid population growth; play more active roles in promoting family planning; provide inducements for couples to avoid large families; bring more policy measures into use; and may well go beyond the confines of the health service to administer their policies. They will, of course, also promote improved health but will go beyond what is necessary for that purpose. If it is agreed that economically oriented policies are socially desirable, *the objective of policy is to be defined in terms of reduced growth.*

Activity. Has your own government adopted a population policy? If so, has it been justified mainly on health grounds or in terms of the desirability of reducing population growth? Is the government clear about its objectives?

It is difficult to be more concrete than that. Being unable to measure the socially optimal growth rate, one is left with the intuitively plausible suggestion that a target of reducing population growth to about 1·0 per cent a year would be 'safe', because it would avoid the worst consequences of rapid growth without creating the problems that can arise from a stationary population. But to refer to a target of 1·0 per cent brings out the essential point: most LDCs have growth so far in excess of this figure that the only realistic goal is the vague one of reducing growth 'as much as possible'. Even successful policies will still leave growth well above the 'safe' 1·0 per cent for two or more decades. There is thus much to be said for avoiding arbitrary numerical targets in favour simply of maximum effort.

Target variables and constraints

It is common but rather misleading to equate reduced population growth with reduced *marital fertility*, or smaller family size. That is the most important target variable but there is a second important one which can be loosely called the *incidence of marriage*. This label is used to refer both to the proportion of women who marry and the age at which they marry.

Recall here what was said on page 76, that, by comparison with the industrial nations, the proportion of women who do not marry is low in LDCs and the average age of marriage is considerably younger. Even if marital fertility were the same in both groups of countries, population growth would still be substantially faster in developing countries because of the higher incidence of marriage. Population policies must therefore be concerned with this as well as with the task of reducing marital fertility. On the other hand, fertility is a less difficult variable to influence than the incidence of marriage.

Policies need also to be designed so as to (1) weaken existing constraints on effective policies and (2) maximize the results given these constraints. The desired family size is likely to be the most formidable obstacle. There is much evidence from around the Third World that couples desire more children than is consistent with government objectives for reducing population growth. It is easy to understand why if we return to Figure 4.8 on page 96. According to that illustration, the socially desirable number of children is three but the couple will choose to have five. Because part of the costs of children are borne by society at large, it is *rational* for couples to prefer more than the socially optimal number of children. For reasons already given, economic development will raise the cost of children, shifting the XX′ curve to the left, but not fast enough.

Couples may also be deterred from family planning because of fears of health hazards arising from the use of contraceptives. (There are indeed health dangers arising from the use of most contraceptives, although they are often greatly exaggerated. In any case, these dangers should be compared with the dangers of pregnancy or of the illegal abortions which are so often resorted to in the absence of contraception. Such comparisons are rarely made but the evidence is that the danger of death resulting from pregnancies and abortions are much greater than those arising from contraception.)[33]

The demand for family planning facilities is thus likely to fall short of the level the government would wish, and this resistance may be reinforced by opposition to family planning from communal, religious and political leaders. The state can, however, try to hasten the leftward move of the XX′ curve by propaganda and by providing material incentives. In doing so, however, it must also bear in mind its own capacity for delivering family planning services. This may well be limited by shortages of trained personnel.

We return to these points shortly but the essential feature is that policies need to take cognizance of the constraints, for example by incorporating measures to convince couples of the desirability of family planning; and to train additional manpower; and by avoiding actions likely to provoke social resistances (such as the attempts to coerce Indian men into being sterilized that helped defeat Mrs Ghandi's government in 1977).

Influencing the incidence of marriage

The proportion of people who get married and the age at which they marry will be determined by a complex of cultural, legal, sociological and economic factors, many of which the government will be unable to influence. Nevertheless, later marriages can make a large difference to the birth rate, as they have in Malaysia, Sri Lanka and Tunisia. Governments are not entirely without powers in this area. In societies where women traditionally suffer low status, governments can do various things to improve the women's rights, through legal reforms, educational policies, and their own employment policies. As women's educational and employment opportunities increase, more will remain unmarried (because some marry only because they cannot earn incomes with which to support themselves) and those who marry will do so at a later age. Governments can also raise the legal minimum age of marriage, as the Indian government did when it raised the minimum age of marriage for girls from 14 to 18 years. However, this kind of legislative change is unlikely to be effective in most circumstances; in many countries it would be widely disregarded and unenforceable (as proved the case in India).

If they are sufficiently determined, governments can go further by exerting pressures on young people not to marry (or have children) at an early age. This can be done through government and party propaganda, in the allocation of public housing and other government services. This approach is employed in the People's Republic of China, where there is not only much propaganda in favour of later marriage but also, according to one authority:[34]

> A young person will not be able to go to school if married and is not likely to become a cadre or party member, or reach any position of authority if he or she has more than three children . . .

However, this type of pressure may provoke hostility and thus reduce the general acceptability of official population policies.

> **Activity.** Can you find any data on the age of marriage in your country? If so, is there any clear trend? Is the government doing anything to influence it?

[33] World Bank, 1974, p. 207.
[34] Orleans, 1975, p. 525.

Influencing marital fertility: strategy

Governments have more options when it comes to influencing marital fertility and the main thrust of population policies is likely to be directed at this variable. We therefore examine it in more detail.

In putting together its policies a government will have a number of decisions to make: on the best strategy to adopt; on the amount of resources to be devoted to its programmes; on the instrumentalities to employ; and on the organizational framework. Naturally, these are not independent of each other but it is convenient to take them in that order.

It is especially appropriate to talk about the *strategy* of fertility policies because a strategy can only be pursued over an extensive period and the impact of population measures has to be measured in terms of decades, rather than single years or five-year planning periods. It is, in other words, essential for population policy to be cast into a rather long-term perspective, for it is aimed at accelerating the demographic transition – a transition that took European countries 75 to 150 years.

One major strategic decision is about *the extent of government involvement*. There is here a continuum of possibilities, ranging from the provision of official support to voluntary family planning organizations, through the provision of government family planning clinics, all the way to highly activist policies in which paramedical personnel go into private homes to promote family planning methods, in which sex education is provided in the schools, in which legal abortions are made easily available, and in which policies are backed up with financial inducements and/or compulsion. As implied earlier, a key decision here is whether policies are for health purposes or to reduce fertility in the interests of society at large.

Assuming the government decides to take a fairly active role it then has to select the *target group* to concentrate on because, at least in the earlier stages, it will not be practicable to provide equal coverage to all couples. Should publicity be aimed at men or women? Which age group to concentrate on? Should the towns or the rural areas receive priority? Which socio-economic groups should receive most attention?

Most experts are agreed that in countries just beginning to implement a population policy, educated women living in the towns are the best target group. Women should be the focus rather than men because the most effective contraceptives are for use by women. They should be educated because this will make them more receptive to family planning ideas, will increase the likelihood that they are in paid employment (giving them larger financial incentives to avoid pregnancy), and because they will have a higher social status (so others may copy them). They should be living in towns because this too will give them stronger incentives to avoid large families and because they are easier to reach.

There is some dispute about what the best age range is. Some argue in favour of concentrating on young (20 to 30) women because that is when they are most fertile and because their youth may make them more receptive to new ideas. Others have found older (30 to 40) women more receptive. They may already have had as many children as they want and see family planning as a way of ending child-bearing, instead of just spacing it out. And, while fertility is lower in this age group, the fact is that 40 per cent of all births in LDCs are to mothers (mostly in their 30s and 40s) who already have four or more children; this factor alone accounts for well over half of fertility differences between industrial and developing countries.[35]

As population measures develop and the coverage of the initial target group becomes fairly complete, the focus can be extended in a number of directions, either simultaneously or in some sequence – into the rural areas, towards the less well educated, and towards younger or older women.

Decisions about the target group will also influence the *line of publicity* that is chosen. What arguments will be most persuasive? Experience suggests that publicity related to the welfare of the family is more effective than appeals to the national interest. And in countries – such as much of tropical Africa – where there is still a high fertility ethos, publicity needs to be directed to opinion on what is a desirable family size. It then tends to be most effective when it emphasizes the spacing of children over time, rather than reducing the total number – even though the end result is likely to be a smaller number of children!

Strategy-related decisions are also needed on how much revenue and other resources the government will allocate to its population policies. Decisions about this are obviously related to prior decisions about the extent of state involvement; they will also depend upon the specific instrumentalities chosen, discussed in the next section. It is worth emphasizing two points at this stage, however. First, finance is unlikely to be the binding constraint, because the cost of population policies relative to total government spending is generally small. The Indian government spends more per capita on its family planning programme than most LDC governments but its budget allocation is only about half of 1 per cent of total government spending. Perhaps India should spend much more but it is clear that the programme could be increased several times over without

[35] Kuznets, 1975, p. 389.

seriously eating into government revenues. It is a matter of priorities.

Secondly, there are economies of scale in family planning programmes. The 'costs per acceptor' in countries with only small programmes are higher than in those with large programmes.[36] It is a false economy to run a small programme.

Influencing marital fertility: instrumentalities

There are four important ways of reducing marital fertility: (1) contraception; (2) sterilization; (3) abortion; (4) financial inducements and penalties. We will look at each in that order.

Contraception

Assuming the government will set up family planning clinics to dispense contraceptives, decisions have to be made about the types of contraceptive to supply. There are many different types but the two chief ones are the oral contraceptive ('the Pill') and the intrauterine device (the IUD or 'the loop'). The IUD is a simple device inserted into the uterus and has been found to have large advantages for use in mass programmes. It does not reduce the sexual pleasure of either partner; once fitted, it requires no attention and remains effective as long as the woman wishes to keep it; it is cheap; once fitted, women usually keep it in for long periods. Family planning clinics therefore frequently push the use of this device.

It has snags, however. The chief of these is that, for physiological reasons, it is unsuitable for a substantial minority of women. It also requires trained personnel to fit it and there are occasional medical complications. The Pill is a popular alternative, and is the most commonly used contraceptive in industrial societies. But it is more expensive, depends for its effectiveness on being taken with complete regularity and is probably not so well suited for use by the illiterate or poorly educated. It may also create more medical complications than the IUD.

Sterilization

Male or female sterilization is, of course, the most certain method of preventing conception but it is also the most drastic. Male sterilization has nevertheless become a widely practised method of family planning in the USA and it has also received attention in some developing countries. India provides the best-known example. In the early 1970s so-called 'vasectomy camps' were set up, offering $12 to $15 to men willing to be sterilized (a vasectomy is a method of male sterilization). From 1971 to 1973 more than 5 million men and women were sterilized in India, although the campaign fell into disrepute later when the government began to coerce people into being sterilized.

Personal repugnance to the idea of being sterilized and the fact that once the operation is performed it is usually irreversible are likely to limit the spread of this method, although the American and Indian experiences show that it does have potential.

Abortion

Of the alternatives so far considered, the legalized provision of abortion facilities under medically controlled conditions is arguably the most effective method of limiting family size. It is estimated that about two-thirds of the dramatic reduction that occurred in Japanese birth rates after the Second World War was attributable to legalized abortion and this remains an important factor in that country even today. However, few developing countries have moved decisively in favour of legalized abortion. China, Bangladesh and Tunisia are partial exceptions, but this is generally an unpopular option. However, in Africa and Latin America illegal abortions are a frequent last resort for desperate women, even though often carried out by unqualified people in unhygienic conditions.

The problem with legalized abortion as an instrument of population policy is that it runs up against the constraints identified on page 99. It requires the attention of qualified doctors working in properly equipped clinics and thus makes heavy demands on scarce resources. It is also likely to aggravate social resistances to population policies, for there are strong religious and humanitarian objections to abortion. Indeed, most people would agree that abortion is a last resort and an admission of failure – a failure to make it easy for unwanted pregnancies to be avoided by contraception or other methods. Nevertheless, such failures will undoubtedly continue on a large scale and, if opinion will stand it, the provision of properly supervised abortions deserves to be considered as part of a population policy. The alternative is not that unwanted pregnancies will be avoided but rather that they will be terminated illegally and dangerously by the unqualified.

---

[36] World Bank, 1974, p. 122.

Financial inducements

There are both negative and positive inducements to be considered under this heading. Negatively, there is the idea (to quote Bangladesh's 1973–8 development plan) that there should be 'progressively increasing punitive measures against additional children after the second child on all couples'.[37] This might take the form of a tax on families above some specified maximum size. This was a suggestion dismissed earlier, because it creates a severe conflict with the objective of distributional justice, to say nothing about its political and administrative feasibility.

A positive approach, in which the state would provide financial rewards to those who limit their families, is more attractive and could have desirable redistributive effects as well. One example was already mentioned, of the payments made by the Indian government to men who have vasectomy operations. This type of scheme is straightforward because there is no doubt that someone who has been sterilized will not have any more children.

An alternative is to reward couples who agree to use family planning methods to limit the number of their children to some agreed maximum. This may be attractive to a large number of people but poses formidable administrative problems of how to check that couples have not had more children than they report. Possibly the most interesting inducements that have been suggested involve deferred interest-bearing payments, for example the provision of scholarship vouchers which can be used later to help pay for schooling (a version of this has been tried in Taiwan), and a lump-sum deposit in a savings account which the parents can use in their old age (a version of this was introduced in southern India).

The administrative difficulties of most of these schemes are, however, formidable and the budgetary cost potentially large. They have not, therefore, been widely adopted. As a minimum, however, the state ought to stop subsidizing large families except when this is justifiable on distributional grounds. It is quite common, for example, for income tax laws to provide tax allowances for children. Since it is the relatively rich who pay income tax, this has the effect of positively encouraging the well-to-do to have large families. Such allowances could be abolished without contravening the desire for greater equality. The same is true of the often generous provisions for maternity leave for women civil servants. Again, many of these come from the richest 10 or 20 per cent families to whom less generosity would be more consistent with national objectives.

The organizational framework

In addition to the choices already mentioned, governments have to make decisions about the organizational structure for the execution of population policies. The structure will have a variety of tasks:[38]

(1) providing the services the government has decided upon (sterilization, contraceptives, etc.);
(2) publicizing the availability and desirability of these;
(3) supervising their grass-roots provision;
(4) monitoring them, providing feedback information and evaluating results in order to make improvements;
(5) training personnel;
(6) providing or promoting back-up research.

In most cases governments link population measures to the national health service, with the responsible agency coming under the Ministry of Health. There are advantages in such an arrangement. It utilizes a physical and administrative structure which is already in place; it economizes on the use of medical expertise; it allows family planning services to be directly related to other aspects of health care; it probably encourages the population to have confidence in the services offered.

But using the national health service has disadvantages too. The leadership of the health ministry is not necessarily convinced of the desirability of an active population policy; it will already have more than enough to do and may be unwilling to divert resources away from more conventional health work; it is liable to adopt conservative views on the medical qualifications of family planning personnel and to resist the idea of paramedical staff with specialized training only in this area; it is not likely to be interested in, or good at, publicity; it will be hospital- and clinic-based, so that the people will have to come to it instead of family planning workers going out to the homes and workplaces of the people.

The ultimate choice depends on the prior question of the extent of state involvement. For low-profile, health-oriented and not very active policies, using the health service is probably the best solution. But successful activist policies will almost certainly have to break loose from the health service – using it, of

---

[37] Quoted by Stamper, 1977, p. 64.
[38] See the essay by M. Freymann in Berelson, *et al.*, 1966, for a stimulating discussion of the organizational issues.

course, but not being confined to it. The policy will need greater political influence than could be wielded by any department of a health ministry; it will require aggressive publicity campaigns, specially trained paramedical personnel, specialized research, and so on.

> **Activity.** Use the discussion of Part VIII to work out criteria by which population policies may be assessed. If your country has a population policy, employ the criteria to evaluate this.

IX. Conclusions: Conditions for Success

The leadership lag

The decision whether or not to adopt an official population policy and how active it should be is, of course, a matter for the country's political leadership. There are many countries which have yet to opt for an active policy and a few which positively encourage population growth, e.g. by banning the sale of contraceptives. Even among those countries which have nominally adopted policies to reduce growth, there are large differences in the extensiveness of their commitment and the success of their programmes. Perhaps the single most important explanation of these differences lies in the degree of support for the programmes given by political leaders.

Although organized political opposition to population measures is rare and there is little evidence that this issue affects the way people vote, it is quite common for individual politicians to express opposition. These are often joined by religious leaders. Of all the major churches in the world, only the Catholics have strong doctrinal objections to the use of modern family planning methods (that is an important exception, however, for the Catholics are dominant in most of Latin America and strong in other LDCs) but other religious leaders are often also suspicious of it. They tend to associate such innovations with an erosion of the traditional values they advocate, and with a loosening of sexual morality.

In countries where there is a delicate balance between rival ethnic groups, there may also be communal complications, with each community fearing that it will lose power if its birth rate is cut while its rival's remains high. This has been a factor in countries such as Sri Lanka, Malaysia and Guyana. Were they to adopt active population policies, this could easily become a sensitive issue in some of the ethnically divided nations of Africa, such as Nigeria and Zimbabwe.

Therefore, there may be pressures, on national leaders to avoid taking a strong stand in favour of population control. It is also the case that in many developing countries demographic data are still poor, so that there is limited awareness of the dimensions of the population problem. There is also the matter of time horizons. The population problem makes itself felt only gradually and policies to deal with it produce results only over the long term. Politicians, on the other hand, tend to be preoccupied with the short term and to give little weight to policies whose results have to be measured over decades.

It is therefore not too surprising that there is often a leadership lag, with governments reluctant to take a strong public stand on the issue. But leadership from the highest national levels is most important. With it the constraints are not so difficult to overcome: the resources can be found; the publicity machinery of the state and the ruling party can be pressed into service; sex education can be introduced in the schools; religious and communal leaders can be reassured. Without a lead from the top, a population programme can be reduced to a mere facade, providing the appearance of action without the reality.

> **Activity.** Has your country's political leadership taken up a clear position on the population issue? If so, on what side has it come down?

Other favourable factors

Political leadership may not be sufficient, however. Recall in this context the earlier finding (page 95) that infant mortality rates and female education have been found the strongest determinants of fertility. Improvements in these variables can thus have a strong influence on the success of a population policy.

Infant mortality, remember, is positively correlated with fertility – the two go down together. But despite the progress that developing countries have made, infant mortality remains far higher than in industrial nations, as indicated by the following estimates for 1975 (deaths within twelve months of birth, per thousand births):[39]

Low-income countries	122
Middle-income countries	46
Industrialized countries	15

[39] World Bank, 1978B, Annex, Table 17.

The incidence of infant mortality in the poorer LDCs is eight times as great as in the industrial countries. There are similar contrasts for deaths among children aged 1 to 5. So there is still much scope for reducing infant mortality and this would also help to reduce fertility. A similar argument holds for female education and its influence on the employment and status of women. Improved educational facilities for girls are twice blessed: they raise the availability of modern skills and they reduce fertility.

A third and less obvious influence will be exerted by the development of a political and administrative framework throughout the country. This provides a communication network, grass-roots leadership and the physical facilities through which population policies can be publicized and executed. The highly developed nature of its party and administrative network is a prime reason why China has what is believed to be one of the most effective population policies in the world.

The possibilities of success

Because of the large size of the problem and the difficulties of mounting a successful programme in a poor country, there is a temptation to be pessimistic about the prospects for success. It is fitting to end, therefore, by pointing out (1) that few population policies have been in existence for more than a decade, so that it is too early to judge them, but (2) that several developing countries have begun to obtain real results from their efforts. The best-known examples – Taiwan, South Korea, Hong Kong – are admittedly rather atypical, having achieved a more advanced stage of development than most LDCs. China is a low-income country believed to have a very successful policy, although the Chinese are too casual about demographic statistics for reliable estimates of the effects of their policies. In any case, that too is not a typical developing country because of its unique socio-political system.

Countries like India, Egypt and Mauritius are more representative and each has made undoubted progress. In Egypt, for example, the crude birth rate was reduced from 44 to 35 in 1960–75; in Mauritius the birth rate was reduced by $2\frac{1}{2}$ points even in the first four years of its population programme. Even in India, often given as an example of a country that has achieved little from its population policies, very substantially reduced birth rates have been achieved in areas where the population campaign has been strongly focused. The chief Indian problem is that there are still enormous numbers of people who are not effectively covered by family planning services at all but even so its national birth rate declined from 44

to 36 in 1960–75. Tropical Africa admittedly fails to provide us with any success stories because few African states have yet adopted active population policies and there is little political commitment to those that do exist.

So the lessons of experience are not necessarily discouraging. Given strong leadership, well chosen policies set in the context of an overall programme of economic and social development can bring large reductions in the growth of population.

Suggestions for Revision and Group Discussions

1 Review your understanding of the following:
   (a) Crude birth and death rates.
   (b) The rate of natural increase.
   (c) Total fertility rate.
   (d) Infant mortality rates.
   (e) Density of population.
   (f) The four phases of the demographic transition.
   (g) The cost-benefit curve.
   (h) Dependency ratios.
   (i) The external costs of children.
   (j) The incidence of marriage.
   (k) Population momentum.
2 Write a note describing what happens to (a) child and (b) aged dependency ratios during the phases of the demographic transition.
3 Explain the statement in the text that rapid population growth tends to perpetuate itself.
4 Discuss the following statement: 'Economic growth in my country has been proceeding at 4 per cent a year but population has been expanding at 3 per cent a year. If we could reduce population growth by one percentage point the rate of expansion of per capita incomes would be doubled'.
5 Write down what you think are the main influences on the height and shape of the cost-benefit curve.
6 Briefly restate in your own words the chief arguments favourable and unfavourable to population growth. Relate each of these to the circumstances of your own country.
7 Review your understanding of Table 4.3 (page 93) and its significance.
8 Describe the information that can be obtained from an age pyramid.
9 Discuss the most appropriate objectives, strategies and instrumentalities for population policies in your own country.

Suggestions for Further Reading

There is no wholly satisfactory general treatment of the subject-matter of this chapter. The World Bank, 1974, contains a wealth of information and is strong on policy aspects. Cassen, 1976, (especially) and Birdsall, 1977, provide excellent reviews of the literature on the relationships between population and development; Cassen (p. 786) offers a guide to further reading, as well as 268 separate references! Gray and Tangri, 1970, provide a well chosen selection of readings. The US National Academy of Sciences, 1971, and Keeley, 1976, also contain useful collections of research papers.

On the historical aspects of the subject see Kuznets, 1966 ch. 2, and 1974 pp. 1–120. Friedman, 1972, is a brilliantly argued and provocative advocacy of a *laissez-faire* solution, although mainly related to the US situation. Kingsley Davis's essay in Nash, 1977, provides a trenchant critique of economic and family planning theories of reproduction. On the state of population policies in LDCs see Nortman, 1972.

There are two journals that the interested reader should particularly consult. The *Population and Development Review*, as its title implies, is largely devoted to articles dealing with the subject-matter of this chapter. *Population Studies* is another journal that publishes many relevant contributions.

Readers interested in the Chinese case should consult articles by Chen, 1970, and Orleans, 1975. Tien, 1973, provides a detailed study of demographic decisions in the People's Republic in 1949–69.

See also the additional references given in the notes to this chapter.

5 Poverty, inequality and unemployment: diagnoses

'He never wants anything but what's right and fair; only when you come to settle what's right and fair, it's everything that he wants and nothing that you want.' *Thomas Hughes*

Contents

I. New Faces of an Old Problem

Does development trickle down?

We start with three facts.

(1) The distribution of income in most developing countries is highly unequal, more so than in either the centrally planned or market industrial countries. Typically, the poorest two-fifths of the population receive only one-eighth of total incomes, and the richest one-fifth receive more than a half of the total.

(2) The incomes of many people in LDCs are so small that they live in conditions of permanent poverty. For example, it has been estimated that in the mid-1960s 840 million people in developing countries were seriously under-nourished.

(3) Most LDCs are marked by much unemployment and underemployment of labour, with perhaps 30 or 40 per cent of the labour force under-utilized in some degree.

Inequality, poverty and unemployment can scarcely be described as new problems; they have been recognized as major blemishes in developing country economies ever since economists began to take an interest in the Third World. What is new is the degree of concern being expressed about these problems and the amount of attention being paid to ways of alleviating them.

If you look at one of the textbooks on economic development published in the 1950s or 1960s you will find little attention paid to income distribution and poverty. This was due not to insensitivity on the part of their authors but rather to the view that these aspects of economic life were best thought of as *symptoms* of underdevelopment and colonialism, symptoms which would therefore diminish as independence was achieved and development gained momentum. As regards the market for labour, major writers were concerned with the problem of how to secure an 'adequate supply of labour for industrialization, rather than with the problem we now see around us of how to find work for all the unemployed in the cities.

We are now two decades wiser. Since the Second World War the evidence indicates that the LDCs have grown more rapidly than they have ever done before and more rapidly than today's industrial countries did at the equivalent stage of their own development. Moreover, progress has not just been in terms of the growth of output. There has also been structural change, modernization, the creation of new institutions and of greater infrastructual capacity. But there are many who believe that poverty, inequality and unemployment are worsening instead of improving. What is now rejected is the casual assumption of earlier writers that all would benefit in reasonable measure from the fruits of economic development – the so-called 'trickle down' theory of development. The predominant belief today is that although there has been substantial growth and development this has made little or no difference to the lives of large numbers of the poorest members of the population. Some writers have gone so far as to suggest that hundreds of millions of poor people have been hurt rather than helped by 'economic development'.

> **Key concept.** The **trickle-down theory of economic development** urged governments to concentrate on maximizing the rate of growth of output in the economy on the assumption that this growth would benefit all major groups in society.

If we cannot rely on the conventional processes of growth to solve poverty, inequality and unemployment, governments must take a more positive view, devising policies to grapple with these problems while also maintaining the momentum of growth. The old view that the growth of GDP was synonymous with economic development has now given way to an insistence that 'development' is a wider concept which requires that economic expansion raise the living standards of the mass of the population. On this view, economic growth which predominantly benefits only those who are already well-to-do would not be counted as 'development' at all.

Poverty, inequality and unemployment are all aspects of social injustice. But when we bracket these three together are we, in fact, referring to three facets of the same problem or to three different, though related, problems, each requiring its own remedy?

One problem? Or two? Or three?

Although this chapter and the next take this trio of problems together, you will find as you go along that they are frequently distinguished from one another. There are important ways in which they differ.

Take first the question of unemployment. Would its elimination solve the other two problems? It would not. It is common for people to have work but for them and their families still to be living in poverty. Thus, a study of poverty in Rawalpindi, Pakistan revealed that only 2·3 per cent of those classified as living in poverty had no work.[1] If a person has no skill to offer, nor other assets, and has a large family dependent upon him, his earnings may simply be insufficient for their needs. Many of the poor are farmers trying to scratch a living from a tiny plot of land, or from labouring, or from trade. Low productivity, rather than lack of work, is their problem.

For similar reasons, employment creation may not make a big impact on the distribution of income. One of the chief reasons for unequal incomes is that the ownership of wealth – valuable assets that can generate income – is usually highly concentrated. The creation of employment would help to equalize earnings from employment but would not do much to equalize the distribution of wealth.

It can also be argued, in the opposite direction, that improving the poverty and inequality situation could be achieved by means that would leave unemployment largely unaltered. The chief ways of redistributing income in the industrial market economies are through taxation and welfare benefits. These measures do not necessarily do anything to create employment; they could even have the opposite effect, by discouraging investment.

So while there obviously are important connections between unemployment and inequality, they are not synonymous. As one writer has put it, 'participation in the *distribution* of the benefits of growth does not necessarily mean participation in the *production* of those benefits'.[2] Indeed, it is possible that governments may see employment-creation measures as a soft option reducing the pressure for, and diverting attention away from, effective measures to improve the distribution of income.

This leaves the question whether poverty and inequality can be treated as referring to essentially the same problem. The relationships between them are clearly very close but again we should be discriminating. It is possible, for example, to redistribute income from rich to middle-income

---

[1] Calculated from Wasay, 1977.
[2] Edwards, 1974, p. 8.

families without altering the position of the poor. Such a change would show statistically as a reduction in inequality but it would leave poverty undiminished. Similarly, it would be possible to improve the lot of the poor by taxing the middle class, leaving the rich untouched: poverty would be reduced but the effect on the overall distribution of income would be ambiguous.

The selection of specific policy instruments can, in fact, be strongly influenced by whether the purpose is to improve the overall distribution or to reduce poverty. In the latter case the focus is upon helping specific groups identified as poor; in the former case greater attention will be paid to reducing the disproportionate share of the rich. Income inequalities tend to be greatest in the urban areas while most poverty is found in the rural economy. Poverty-oriented policies are thus likely to pay special attention to raising standards in the rural areas; income distribution policies may concentrate on improving the situation in the towns.

What follows is therefore careful to distinguish between the inequality, poverty and unemployment problems whenever it seems necessary. The remainder of this chapter examines the measurement, extent and causes of these problems. Chapter 6 takes up the question of what governments can do to counter these evils.

Activity. Do you think that many of the people who live in poverty in your own country do so for reasons other than lack of paid employment? What other reasons?

II.   Definition, Measurement and Evidence

I have been using the terms unemployment, inequality and poverty rather glibly as if their meanings are understood by all. That, however, is far from being the case. These concepts are difficult to define and measure accurately. The purpose of this section is to clarify the problems and briefly survey the evidence, as it relates to developing countries. We start with inequality.

Measuring inequality

To talk of 'the' distribution of income is misleading. One can arrange data on income distribution in several ways. One way is to present a *functional* distribution, in which total income is classified by factor of production or type of income, e.g. into wages, rent, interest and profits. The most common presentation, however, is to classify the data according to the amount of income, known as the *size* distribution of income. Discussions of inequality are generally based on size distributions, which is the basis used in this chapter. There are, however, important connections between these two concepts. Broadly speaking, a country in which a large part of the national income goes to labour (including the incomes of the self-employed) is likely to have a more equal size distribution of income than a country in which much of national income is in the form of profits and other property incomes. The poor derive most of their income from the use or sale of their own labour.

Key concept. A **functional distribution of income** classifies national income data according to its allocation between factors of production. A **size distribution of income** arrays incomes according to their magnitude, irrespective of how they were earned.

An imaginary and simplified size distribution is presented in Table 5.1, where a sample of 250 families are grouped, according to their pre-tax incomes, into four classes. The income classes are in column (1) and the number of families falling into each income range is shown in column (2). The numbers in column (2) are then converted into percentages of the total of 250 families, in column (3), from which we can see, for example, that 10 per cent of the total sample of families have incomes of less than $100 and that a further 50 per cent have incomes of between $100 and $199.

From a distribution of this type we can also estimate the total value of incomes received and how it is allocated between the income classes. The simplest (but not necessarily the best) way of doing this is to assume that the average value of incomes received in each class is given by the middle value of the class and these mid-points are shown in column (5) (see the footnote to the table concerning the highest income class, which has no mid-point). By multiplying these assumed means by the number of families in each class we obtain estimates of total income, as shown in column (6). The grand total arrived at is $60 000 (which, dividing by 250, gives us a mean income per family of $240). It is then a simple step to express this information as percentages of the $60 000, as is done in column (7).

A comparison of column (3) with column (7) tells us quite a lot. We can see that the poorest 10 per cent of

Table 5.1
A Size Distribution of Income

Income range before tax ($) (1)	Number of families (2)	% of families (3)	Cumulative percentage (4)	Income mid-point ($) (5)	Total income ($) (6)	% of total income (7)	Cumulative percentage (8)
0–99	25	10	10	50	1 250	2·1	2·1
100–199	125	50	60	150	18 750	31·2	33·3
200–399	75	30	90	300	22 500	37·5	70·8
400 and above	25	10	100	700*	17 500	29·2	100·0
Totals	250	100			60 000	100·0	

Note: * Since the final income class of '$400 and above' has no upper limit there is no mid-point. In the table it is assumed that the mean value of the incomes of families falling into this class is $700.

Table 5.2
The Size Distribution of Income Among Families in Brazil

Monthly income (before tax) (NCr$) (1)	Percentage of population (2)	Percentage of total income (3)
None	1·7	0·0
0–2·0	5·4	0·7
2·1–3·2	12·5	2·9
3·3–4·4	12·1	4·4
4·5–5·9	14·6	7·1
6·0–9·9	22·3	16·0
10·0–19·9	20·4	26·7
20·0–50·0	8·9	25·3
Over 50·0	2·1	16·8

Source: Fishlow, 1972, p. 392.

We can take the measurements further by presenting size distributions graphically in what is known as a *Lorenz curve*. The first step is to convert the percentage distributions into cumulative figures, as is done in columns (4) and (8) of Table 5.1. We can then plot a graph measuring percentages of total income on the vertical and percentages of the relevant population on the horizontal, as is done in Figure 5.1. Now, if there were complete equality of income the relationship between the two axes would be described by a straight line drawn at an angle of 45° from the origin – indicating that 10 per cent of the population receive 10 per cent of incomes, that 50 per cent receive 50 per cent, and so on. This 45° line is called the *line of equality*. We can now plot the cumulative percentages from Table 5.1 on this graph, and trace a continuous

the families receive only just over 2 per cent of total incomes and that the richest 10 per cent receive almost 30 per cent of the total – a substantial but by no means far-fetched degree of inequality. For example, compare the results from the imaginary data in Table 5.1 with the figures in Table 5.2 on the Brazilian size distribution of income in 1960.

The figures show that the poorest 20 per cent of Brazilian families receive less than 4 per cent of total income, and the top 10 per cent receive about 40 per cent of the total. The statistics of many developing countries show even larger extremes of inequality.

Note, in this connection, that our discussion is in terms of the *proportionate shares* of various income classes, not with the absolute monetary values of the differences between them. Although it is perfectly possible to gauge inequality according to the absolute sizes of the differences, most discussions of inequality use relative shares as a better measure, as is done here.

Figure 5.1 *A Lorenz curve.*

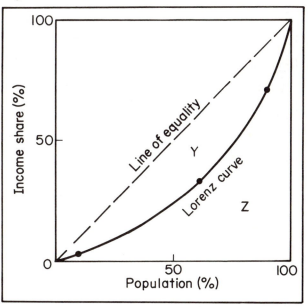

curve through them. This is the Lorenz curve; it gives us a visual picture of the extent of inequality, indicated by the extent to which the curve falls below the line of equality.

> **Activity.** Use the data in Table 5.2 to draw a Lorenz curve for the distribution of income in Brazil.

Always provided we have comparable and reliable figures, we can use this technique (1) to compare income distributions between countries and (2) to study trends in a country over time. Thus, Figure 5.2 below reproduces Lorenz curves for India and Sri Lanka, on the one hand, and the USA and UK, on the other. This indicates a generally more unequal distribution in India/Sri Lanka, although the result is a little ambiguous, as will be shown shortly.

The usefulness of the size distribution statistics has not yet been exhausted, for it is possible to go beyond the visual presentation of a Lorenz curve to calculate a numerical measure of the extent of inequality or income concentration. Statisticians have developed a number of measures of concentration and that most commonly used in income distribution studies is the *Gini coefficient*. This coefficient ranges in value between 0 (perfect equality) and 1 (perfect inequality, in which only one member of the population receives all the income). It measures the area between the line of equality and the Lorenz curve as a fraction of the

total area beneath the line of equality. The area between the equality line and the Lorenz curve in Figure 5.1 is marked Y and the area below the Lorenz curve is marked Z. The formula for the Gini coefficient (G) is, therefore:

$$G = \frac{Y}{Y + Z}$$

The value of G associated with the data in Table 5.2, for example, is 0·5: exactly halfway between the two possible extremes. The values of G obtained from income distribution studies in mixed economies generally lie in the range of 0·35 to 0·65 (the upper values, of course, indicate very extreme inequalities). Gini coefficients for the centrally planned socialist countries are smaller: typically 0·2 to 0·25.

Gini coefficients, like Lorenz curves, can be used both to make comparisons between countries, and between points in time within a single country. To use the Brazilian case again, Fishlow calculated (on the basis of different figures from those given in Table 5.2) that G rose from 0·59 to 0·63 between 1969 and 1970, indicating a trend towards greater inequality.

> **Key concepts.** The area between the 45° **line of equality** and the **Lorenz curve** gives a visual indication of the extent of inequality. The **Gini coefficient** is a measure of this area expressed as a fraction of the total area beneath the line of equality.

There are, however, difficulties about Lorenz curves and Gini coefficients for comparative purposes, in that they only yield unambiguous results when one Lorenz curve lies wholly below another (to say nothing of the difficulties of obtaining statistics which are both accurate and comparable). When the curves intersect, as in Figure 5.2, the results can be ambiguous. Although it is a reasonable interpretation of Figure 5.2 to say that there is greater inequality in India/Sri Lanka than in USA/UK, careful observation shows that the poorest 20 per cent of the population actually receive a larger share of total income in India/Sri Lanka. Interpretation of the values of G for this case would be similarly ambiguous.

Because of these difficulties, a commonly used alternative to these attempts to measure the *overall* size distribution of income is to resort to *partial* measures which concentrate on the shares going to preselected segments of the population. In these cases interest is usually focused on the income shares of 'the poor' (who might be defined as the bottom 10, 20 or even 50 per cent of the population) and of 'the rich'

Figure 5.2   *A comparison of Lorenz curves.*

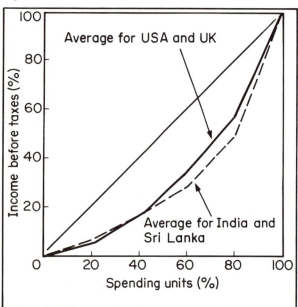

Source: Myrdal, 1968, p. 564.

(usually the top 10, 5 or 2 per cent of the population). This calls for some modification of size distribution tables, so that figures are arranged by decile or quintile, or whatever grouping of the population is being used (a decile is a tenth, or ten percentage points; a quintile is a fifth, or twenty percentage points). The data in Table 5.1 already enable us to compare the income shares of the top and bottom deciles, with the latter getting 2·1 per cent of total income and the former receiving 29·2 per cent.

Some complications

The accurate measurement of income distribution and trends over time is a complex task and there is little good quality data available. There are, to start with, questions about the *population unit* whose income one is trying to measure. It is of no use, for example, trying to do it for every individual because that would leave children, housewives and other dependants seemingly without any means of support and would attribute all incomes exclusively to those who receive them. A far better solution is to collect data on a family basis, for the family is a natural income unit. Even here there are complications. For one thing, the number of children in families varies with income, so it is desirable to correct data for differences in family size. Second, this type of study usually refers to the western-type 'nuclear' family, but this fails to catch the effects of the 'extended' family rights and responsibilities common in many LDCs. Extended family practices can, in fact, be a potent mechanism for reducing income inequalities, obligating the well-to-do to share their receipts with less prosperous relatives. If we want an accurate picture we should record these income transfers.

In some countries differences between races, tribes, castes, or other social groups may be a serious aspect of inequality. This is true, for instance, in Malaysia, where a person of Malay origin is three times as likely to be living in poverty as a person of Chinese origin; or southern Africa, where the median incomes of the white populations are vastly greater than of Africans; or in Liberia, with its enormous differences between the standards of the historically dominant Americo-Liberian community and the subsistence economy of the hinterland tribes. Income distribution studies which concentrate on individuals or families may fail to catch the group dimensions.

Besides these issues, there are other problems associated with the *definition of income*. For one thing, it is important to include the value of subsistence production (foods and other items produced for consumption within the family); to fail to do so would give a misleading idea of the position

of the poor, much of whose consumption is often of subsistence goods. A bias in the opposite direction results from the fact that capital gains (increases in the value of assets) are usually excluded from the definition of income, even though they can add substantially to the ability of recipients to satisfy their material wants. Exclusion of this item biases results in the direction of equality because it is the wealthy who own most assets and are thus most likely to enjoy capital gains.

The *timing* of income distribution studies can also bias results if in the period studied some important groups are doing better or worse than usual. In principle, one wants to measure 'permanent' income, i.e. the average income that each family can be expected to obtain over the long run, but in practice this is scarcely possible. It is also important to try to take account of the effects of taxation and the receipt of benefits from government. If the fiscal system is progressive it will tax the rich and transfer to the poor; exclusion of these effects can thus overstate inequality.

There are other obstacles to the collection of high quality data. Income distribution is usually studied on the basis of sample surveys which try to collect in-depth information on a limited sample of families over a period of time. But it is notoriously difficult to obtain reliable information on income – from the rich and the not-so-rich alike. It is also difficult to be sure that the sample is sufficiently large and representative, partly because of insufficient knowledge of the characteristics of the population at large – what statisticians call the 'sample frame' – and because of the heavy cost of mounting a large survey.

The statistical indicators used to measure inequality may also impart a bias. In fact, it is impossible to find a measure which is completely neutral. The Gini coefficient, for example, attaches more weight to changes affecting middle-income groups than it does to changes affecting the rich or the poor.

Finally, there are difficulties about the meaning of inequality. Does inequality exist whenever the Lorenz curve deviates from the 45° line? Most people believe that complete equality is impracticable. On this view inequality is a relative, not an absolute, condition but then what criterion are we to use in forming our judgements? One suggestion is that we should apply the standards set by the centrally planned socialist countries of eastern Europe, in which the bottom 40 per cent of families typically receive about 25 per cent of total income. But some would argue that this does not go far enough while others would argue that such a degree of equality is incompatible with a market or mixed economy.

> **Activity.** If an income distribution study has been published for your own country, study it and write a note on the adequacy of the population unit, the definition of income, and the sample it employed.

Evidence on inequality

The measurement problems surveyed above should have prepared the reader for the news that we have only poor information on past trends and on the current income distribution situation. We are nevertheless not completely at a loss and the next few paragraphs try to summarize such information as is available.

Table 5.3 summarizes the results of work by the World Bank and others. The upper part of the table presents mean values for sixty-four countries, classified by the US dollar value of incomes per head, and shows the shares of total income accruing to the poorest 40 per cent, the 'middle' 40 per cent, and the top 20 per cent. The lower part of the table presents similar information for nine selected LDCs and mean

Table 5.3
International Statistics on the Size Distribution of Income

	Share in total income of:		
	Lowest 40% (1)	Middle 40% (2)	Top 20% (3)
By Level of Per Capita Income *			
1. Up to $150 (9)	15·7	33·8	50·4
2. $150–300 (15)	11·5	30·3	58·3
3. $300–750 (12)	13·3	32·3	54·4
4. Above $750 (19)	16·9	38·9	44·1
For Selected Developing Countries			
5. Brazil (1970)	10·0	28·4	61·5
6. Colombia (1970)	9·0	30·0	61·0
7. India (1964)	16·0	32·0	52·0
8. Ivory Coast (1970)	10·8	32·1	57·1
9. Kenya (1969)	10·0	22·0	68·0
10. Malaysia (1970)	11·6	32·4	56·0
11. Philippines (1971)	11·6	34·6	53·8
12. Thailand (1970)	17·0	37·5	45·5
13. Zambia (1959)	14·5	28·5	57·0
14. Mean of lines 5–13	12·3	30·8	56·9

Source: Chenery, *et al.*, 1974, Table I-1.
Note: * The figures in lines 1–4 are mean values for countries grouped according to per capita income. The numbers in brackets indicate the number of countries in each sample. The figures relate to incomes before tax.

values for these nine. The individual country figures bring out an important aspect which is obscured in the upper part – that country situations differ widely, so that there is a wide dispersion about the means. Thus, the income share of the poorest 40 per cent varies between 9 per cent (Colombia) and 17 per cent (Thailand), and of the richest 20 per cent between 45·5 per cent (Thailand) and 68 per cent (Kenya). The share of the middle group is rather more stable.

These country differences, plus the dubious reliability of the statistics, make generalization hazardous. Nonetheless, the averages in the table are interesting. Comparing the figures in line 14 with line 4, we can see that inequality tends to be most severe in LDCs, with the rich receiving a larger share, and the poor a smaller share, of total incomes than in countries with per capita incomes of more than $750. The means in line 14 show the poorest 40 per cent receive only about 12 per cent of incomes, while the richest 20 per cent get about 57 per cent.

However, the averages in lines 1 to 4, reveal a more complex pattern. These still show inequalities to be smallest in the richest countries but the very poor countries (with per capita incomes of up to $150) rank second by this criterion. What the figures suggest is that inequality is only moderate at very early stages of development, that it worsens as average incomes begin to rise (observe the way in which inequality increases from line 1 to 2) but then after a while it gradually diminishes again. More sophisticated analysis of this type of data provides support for this generalization.[3]

This is admittedly a rather fragile hypothesis to build upon a foundation of incomplete and unreliable cross-section figures but is consistent with what we know about historical trends in the size distribution of income in western industrial coutries. Studies by Kuznets of long-run trends in the USA, England, Germany and other western industrial countries tentatively indicate a tendency for pre-tax inequalities to diminish over time, especially during the last fifty to sixty years. For example, Department of Commerce estimates for the US show the share of the richest 5 per cent to fall consistently from 30 per cent of total incomes in 1929 to 20 per cent in 1973. This tendency towards greater equality may be more strongly marked if the figures were adjusted for the impact of taxation and government spending. This is illustrated in Figure 5.3. The income share of the poorest 40 per cent of the population is measured on the vertical axis and per capita income on the horizontal. The two curves portray relationships between these two

---

[3] See Ahluwalia, 1976, but also Beckerman, 1977, who is sceptical of this finding.

variables. That marked 'A' is derived from a regression analysis using data from a large sample of countries, including industrial countries. The curve marked 'B' is based on a regression which was confined to a sample of developing countries only.

Although the slopes of the two curves differ, they both have the same property of showing a sharp decline in the income share of the poor as average incomes begin to rise from the lowest levels, followed by a slower improvement beyond a certain turning-point. Statistical analysis revealed a turning point of $470 for curve 'A' and of $370 for curve 'B'.

The reasons for the type of relationship portrayed by the curves will be clarified in the later discussion of the dynamics of inequality. But it is important to add here that the relationship should not be interpreted in a deterministic way, as if there is no escape from worsening inequality in the early stages of development. Figure 5.3 simply shows the outcome of past experiences: if countries pursue different growth paths and if their governments make a stronger effort to avoid a deterioration, then the record of the future could be different from the facts of the past. It is the *character* of the growth process that is crucial. Chapter 6 is largely devoted to exploring ways in which governments can try to improve income distribution.

Figure 5.3 *The relationship between inequality and the stage of development.*

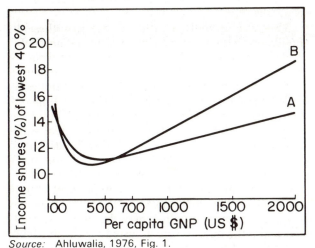

Source: Ahluwalia, 1976, Fig. 1.

The meaning and measurement of poverty

Unless we are willing to use absolute equality as our yardstick, inequality is relative – relative to some other point in time, to some other country, or to some target for income shares. But to clothe these relative statements with human meaning we need also to know what they imply for living standards. Figure 5.2, for instance, shows that the poorest 20 per cent of the people in India and Sri Lanka receive a larger share of total income than their counterparts in the USA and the UK – which sounds quite encouraging until we realize that the poorest 20 per cent in the USA have average family incomes of over $7000 a year – vastly more than their Indian counterparts, whose poverty is among the severest in the world. In comparisons of this kind the absolute values matter more than the relativities.

A possible reaction to the US–Indian comparison is to say that while there is inequality in both countries, poverty is a serious problem only in India, because it is only in India that people have to struggle merely to keep themselves alive. At the back of such a judgement is the view that, while inequality is a relative concept, poverty is an absolute condition. In this vein, it would be possible to define poverty as *that minimum of income necessary for survival and physical efficiency.* The task then becomes one of defining the minimum – in terms of calorific intake, square metres of shelter per person, so much clothing per person, and so on. Having done so, a 'poverty line' can be drawn, below which people do not have this necessary minimum.

Although the development of such a definition is an attractive goal, considerable researches have produced little or no agreement about where to draw the poverty line. For example, the number of calories consumed per person is a popular indicator but its interpretation is greatly complicated by the fact that human calorific requirements vary with age, sex, climate, adequacy of housing and type of work. Moreover, one cannot assess the adequacy of a diet simply by measuring the number of calories it contains: it is also important to take in enough protein, vitamins and minerals. So defining a minimum diet is a complex matter; defining agreed minima of shelter and clothing is even harder. And what actually is meant by 'physical efficiency' in the definition just offered? No illness? But the rich get sick too!

There is also the influence of culture and convention. Religious beliefs, superstitions, a preference for the familiar, a wish to conform, and a desire for dignity, all affect the consumption standards of even the poorest people. It will be unhelpful to define minimum standards without taking these factors into account. But to do so is to take a large step away from an 'objective' definition of poverty, for their effects cannot be quantified, their impact will vary from one social group to another, and they will change over time. In other words, we must then stop thinking of poverty as an absolute condition and view it as one that can only be understood in the social setting in which it occurs.

There are many who prefer this view and see poverty as *deprivation relative to the norm in society*. Relative poverty, then, is about people's ability to furnish themselves with a *socially acceptable* minimum standard of living. Marx, for example, defined subsistence to include that which was 'socially necessary' to sustain the proletariat. But the definition of poverty as relative deprivation also has problems. It implies that poverty will be found in practically all countries, no matter how rich. Thus, more than 12 per cent of all people in the USA were officially classified as living below the poverty line in 1975; the poverty line for a family of four was $5500 per annum. It implies also that poverty will always be with us, because there will always be some who are relatively deprived, no matter how affluent they seem by absolute standards. This may breed a feeling of hopelessness about the possibility of ever removing poverty. It requires us to describe as poor groups whose living standards are above the wildest dreams of others in different societies. We may agree that an unemployed American living in a squalid, dangerous and over-crowded ghetto is socially deprived but we may hesitate to bracket him with the Malian nomad whose last cattle are starving or with the Bangalee beggar who sleeps in the streets of Dacca. The notion of relative poverty obscures the qualitative difference between these cases.

Activity. A class discussion is suggested on the ways in which social conventions, religious beliefs and moral values affect what is considered to be a minimum acceptable standard of living in your own country.

Relative deprivation also suffers from the disadvantage of being essentially subjective – difficult, if not impossible, to quantify. It thus rules out meaningful comparisons between nations, or even between social groups within nations. For concrete discussions of the extent of relative poverty writers are invariably forced to use measurable standards which are no less arbitrary than measures of absolute poverty. One such arbitrary suggestion, for example, is that relative poverty should be defined as referring to families whose incomes are below one-half of the median value of family income in the country in question.

Key concepts. Absolute poverty refers to people receiving incomes below the minimum income considered necessary for survival and physical efficiency. **Relative poverty** refers to people with living standards below what is generally regarded as a socially acceptable minimum.

Evidence on poverty

As is apparent from the above discussion, absolute poverty is the more relevant concept if one wants to measure the extent of poverty on an international basis. The most commonly applied approach is to place a value on the minimum income essential for survival and physical efficiency and then to estimate the number of people living below this poverty line. The statistics presented in Table 5.4 draw the line at an annual income (in 1969) of fifty US dollars per person and provide estimates of the proportions of the population in each region and country with per capita incomes of less than this minimum. Enough has already been said about the statistical and conceptual difficulties that no further caution should be necessary about the limitations of this type of presentation. Still, the $50 line can scarcely be criticized for being over-generous and yet we see that *about one-third of LDC populations have incomes of less than $50 per head*. In absolute numbers, nearly 370 million people in Asia, Africa and Latin America are living below this poverty line.

The country figures in Table 5.4 are arranged in ascending order of national per capita income and it is clear at a glance that the proportions below the poverty line are inversely related to average incomes, which is what we would expect. The poorest countries experience the most poverty. Nevertheless, some do better than others. Pakistan comes out relatively well, with a proportion below the poverty line about the average for all LDCs but with a per capita income well below the LDC average. Thailand and the Ivory Coast also have below-average poverty relative to per capita income, whereas Tunisia, Brazil and Colombia fall into the opposite category.

The chief conclusion suggested by this study, however, is that poverty is a major problem throughout the Third World. The source on which Table 5.4 is based shows that 29 out of 39 countries with average incomes of less than $700 had more than 10 per cent of their populations living below the $50 poverty line. In only 4 out of the 39 were less than 10 per cent of the people living below a poverty line of $75.

This type of result is open to the objection that, in

addition to all the other problems associated with the notion of absolute poverty, it is especially difficult to make international comparisons in monetary terms. There is, in fact, something absurd about talking of people living on incomes of less than fifty US dollars a year. It would be totally impossible for an American to survive on $50 (in 1975 the poverty line for an individual American was drawn at $2800!) and most economists agree that this type of comparison overstates the gap between developing and developed countries.

This objection can, however, be overcome by estimates based on non-monetary comparisons, such as dietary standards. Reutlinger and Selowsky (1976), for instance, made careful estimates of the numbers of people whose diets provided fewer than a minimum desirable number of calories. Their precise results depended on the assumptions made but they came to the general conclusion that in the mid-1960s 840 million people in developing countries – or 56 per cent of their total populations – were receiving diets that fell short of the desirable minimum by more than 250 calories a day. Another 290 million people (19 per cent of LDC populations) had calorie deficits of less than 250. Only a quarter of the total population enjoyed diets giving them more than the minimum

Table 5.4
Proportions of LDC Populations Below $50 Poverty Line, by Region and for Selected Countries

	1969 GNP per capita ($)	% of population below $50
Asia	132	36·7
Africa	168	33·6
Latin America	437	13·4
All above	187	32·5
Burma	72	54
Tanzania	92	58
India	100	45
Pakistan*	100	32
Thailand	173	27
Philippines	233	13
Ivory Coast	237	7
Tunisia	241	22
Malaysia	323	11
Zambia	340	6
Brazil	347	14
Colombia	347	15

Source: Chenery, 1974, Table I.2. Figures have been adjusted to exclude countries with per capita incomes in excess of $700.
Note: *Includes Bangladesh.

calorie standard. Malnutrition is believed to be particularly widespread among young children.

Accepting, then, that poverty is widespread in developing countries, is this problem getting better or worse over time? Widely differing answers are given to this question. The earlier discussion of Figure 5.3 (see page 113) suggested that the income share of the poor diminishes during the early phases of development. However, a declining *share* is consistent with rising *absolute values* of income: all that is necessarily implied is that the incomes of the rich are rising more rapidly than those of the poor. One influential study has gone further, however, to suggest that the low income groups lose absolutely as well as relatively, so that economic growth further impoverishes the poor:[4]

> Inflation, population growth, technological change, the commercialisation of the traditional sector, and urbanisation all combine to reduce the real incomes of the poorest 40 per cent of the population in very low income countries in the before-takeoff stage of development.

Other research results conflict with this conclusion, however. In the study cited earlier, Ahluwalia (1976) finds that while the share of the poorest 40 per cent goes down, their incomes rise in value.[5] A similar finding can be deduced from a study by the International Labour Office (ILO). In line with the results shown in Table 5.4 above, they show a widespread incidence of poverty throughout the Third World, with 39 per cent of total population classed as 'destitute' and another 28 per cent 'seriously poor' but not destitute.[6] They also estimate that the number of people in both categories went up in 1963–72. However, their statistics also yield the calculation that the *proportion* of the population classified as destitute declined from 44 to 39 per cent in 1963–72. Were the real incomes of the poor actually going down this would presumably show up in an increasing incidence of destitution.

Given all the conceptual and statistical problems, it would be naive to place much weight on any of the results summarized in the last few paragraphs. We should also be wary of attempts to generalize for large groups of countries; experiences differ markedly between nations, depending upon their circumstances and their policies. The question whether early-stage growth actually impoverishes the poor is best regarded as an unsettled one, but the balance of what

[4] Adelman and Morris, 1973. The quote is from p. 183.
[5] Ahluwalia, 1976, pp. 332–5.
[6] International Labour Office, 1976, pp. 20–3. The declining proportion of destitutes is calculated from data in their Tables 2 and 3.

evidence we have indicates that it does not. What is beyond doubt is that poverty is a scourge of the gravest magnitude in virtually all developing countries. And, if it is not actually getting worse, it is certainly not diminishing fast enough.

We are luckily on rather firmer statistical ground in offering some generalizations about the *characteristics of the poor*, for this topic has been more conclusively researched. Table 5.5 presents comparative information on the characteristics of families classified as living in poverty and those with living standards above the poverty line, for Malaysia and Brazil. These two economies are, of course, very different from each other: Brazil has travelled a long way down the development path, while Malaysia is a good deal further back. However, the table shows that their poor have very similar characteristics which are consistent with what we know about poverty in other countries too.

The statistics in the table (and the results of other poverty studies) suggest the following generalizations:

(1) *The incidence of poverty is especially high in rural areas.* In both countries the majority of poor families were in rural communities, while a significantly smaller proportion of the non-poverty families were rural. Poverty is, therefore, particularly likely to occur in agriculture: in Malaysia 75 per cent of all the heads of poverty households derived their incomes from agriculture, against only 36 per cent of the non-poverty households.

(2) *The poor are more likely to be unemployed.* This is most strikingly the case in Brazil, as can be seen from line 2(c) of the table. There is only a small difference in Malaysia but the difference is probably larger in most LDCs. We can note also a tendency for a high proportion of the poor to be self-employed (especially as smallholders); whereas the more affluent non-poverty cases are more likely to be employees, working for a settled wage.

(3) *The poor have little education.* The figures for both countries show that having no education roughly doubles the probability of living in poverty; hardly any of the poor have secondary or other post-primary education.

(4) *The poor have more children.* Line 4(c) of Table 5.5 shows the incidence of poverty to be much

Table 5.5
Poverty Profiles for Malaysia and Brazil
(Percentages of the Total Number of Households in Each Category)

		MALAYSIA (1970)		BRAZIL (1960)	
		Poverty households (1)	Non-poverty households (2)	Poverty households (3)	Non-poverty households (4)
(1)	Living in rural areas	88	62	60	46
(2)	Employment status of head of households				
	(a) employee	38	59	33	43
	(b) self-employed	55	30	42	41
	(c) unemployed	3·9	3·5	17	8
	(d) other	3·1	7·5	8	8
Total		100	100	100	100
(3)	Education of head of household				
	(a) none	43	26	64	35
	(b) some primary	54	53	35	55
	(c) some post-primary	3	21	1	9
Total		100	100	100	100
(4)	Number of children				
	(a) 0 to 2	43	65	44	74
	(b) 3 or 4	31	22	29	19
	(c) 5 or more	26	13	27	7
Total		100	100	100	100

Sources: Fishlow, 1972, Table 2; Anand, 1977, pp. 13–14.

greater in families with five or more children, and much smaller in families with up to two children.

The figures in Table 5.5 present only a selection of the more important characteristics of the poor. Other aspects cannot be generalized across countries. In Malaysia, for instance, the incidence of poverty is much higher among Malays than among Chinese; it is also higher in the northern parts of the country. In Brazil people who stay put in their home villages are more likely to be poverty-striken than those who migrate. Each country has its own special conditions and we should beware the danger of over-generalizing.

> **Activity.** Do the poor in your own country have the characteristics shown in Table 5.5? Can you add to the list? Are there any studies of poverty which provide evidence?

Defining the employment problem

I have already referred several times to 'the unemployment problem' without offering any definition of what is meant by that. It is high time to remedy this omission but that is easier said than done, for the concept is a slippery one, especially when applied to LDCs.

The conventional definition of an unemployed person is someone who has no work, is willing to work at existing wage rates and is actively looking for a job. The number of such unemployed people is then usually expressed as a percentage of the total labour force, where the labour force is defined as all those with work plus the unemployed. Thus, if there are 10 million unemployed and 90 million with jobs, the unemployment rate is 10 per cent:

$$\frac{10}{90+10} = 0 \cdot 1 \text{ or } 10\%$$

Most of the hard statistics we have on the unemployment problem are of the type just described but on closer inspection the apparent simplicity of this measure melts away.

> **Key concepts.** A person who is **unemployed** is usually defined as someone having no work and actively looking for it. The **unemployment rate** is the number of unemployed as a percentage of the total **labour force**, where the labour force is given by the number with jobs plus the unemployed. This type of unemployment is often called 'open' unemployment.

A key aspect of the unemployment rate is that it tries to measure unemployment which is *involuntary*. It would not make sense to describe as unemployed someone who does not want a job, say an elderly farmer who is content for his sons to look after the family farm. But the involuntary character of unemployment is elusive. There exist in all countries 'discouraged workers' – people who would like to have a job but who become so disheartened about their prospects of finding one that they have stopped looking. Shouldn't we count them as unemployed and, therefore, as belonging to the labour force? On any reasonable view we should because if job opportunities improve some of these people will be encouraged to start seeking a job again, so that the recorded number of 'involuntary' unemployed will not go down to the same extent as the number of new jobs.

What this implies is that the number who would be recorded as unemployed (and the size of the labour force) will vary according to the rate of expansion of work opportunities. As has been aptly observed, 'the number of people for whom work is needed depends partly on the number for whom it is provided'[7] The expansion of employment opportunities will, in turn, depend upon the growth of the economy, the factor proportions employed and the policies pursued by the government. Strictly speaking, therefore, we can only measure the involuntary unemployment rate with given growth rates, policies, etc., but that is not very helpful because they will be changing all the time.

There are other difficulties too. For one thing, the above concept of involuntary unemployment is difficult to apply to the traditional sector, where there is no sharp distinction between workers and dependants. At the busy harvesting and planting times, virtually everyone in a farming household will be helping out in the fields, even young children. But in the slack season the demand for labour will be far less. How, then, do we define the agricultural labour force and measure the unemployment rate? Do we include the young, the old, the womenfolk who work only during the peak periods?

Even in urban areas, where the concept seems more relevant, there are severe measurement problems. A country's labour statistics normally only relate to modern sector activities. Those working in the 'informal' sector – in very small businesses, or doing odd jobs, or peddling shoe-laces in the streets, or living off crime – are rarely caught in the statistical net.[8] But the lower-paying informal activities do at

---

[7] Mouly and Costa, 1974, p. 31.
[8] See Hart, 1973, for a fascinating and pioneering study of informal employment.

least offer some kind of living until a modern sector job comes along. Those who are desperate, those with families to feed, have to find some source of income and cannot afford to spend all their time looking for a modern sector job. They will thus not be counted as unemployed when a labour census is undertaken, even though their informal activities take up only part of their time or yield them only the smallest incomes.

There is a sense, then, in which being unemployed is a luxury only some can afford! This explains why unemployment statistics show very large proportions of young people and women: they can fall back on their families to feed and shelter them while they seek work. A much smaller proportion of those recorded as unemployed are heads of households: their families depend upon them, and their time must be spent scraping together a living somehow. Only if they have reason to expect success will they take time off from the informal sector to chase a modern sector job. Here again, we find a situation in which the size of the modern sector labour force will vary according to people's expectations about their prospects of finding a job.

For reasons such as those given above, the earlier definition of the unemployment rate does not give at all an adequate measure of the employment problem. Nor does it behave as would be considered normal in industrial countries. There, when the number of jobs goes up the unemployment rate is expected to go down. In developing countries, recorded unemployment may go up when the number of modern sector jobs goes up, as discouraged workers are attracted back on to the labour market, as more migrants are attracted from the villages, and as people shift out of the informal sector in search of the new jobs.[9]

> **Activity**. Topic for class discussion: do the above observations on the difficulties of defining unemployment apply to your own country? Available unemployment statistics should be studied as a basis for this discussion.

What is apparent is that the under-utilization of labour takes a number of forms, so that no one statistic is likely to give us an adequate measure. The following is a brief summary of the chief types of under-utilization.

(1) *Open unemployment*. As discussed above, a concept mainly relevant to the urban modern sector and made up predominantly of young people and women.

(2) *Hidden unemployment*. There are a number of different forms of this:

(a) There are the 'discouraged workers' mentioned earlier. They are unemployed in the sense that they would like to have a job if only they thought they could find one; but their unemployment is hidden because they would not fall under the standard definition of open unemployed.

(b) There are people who nominally have jobs, for which they are paid, but in fact do nothing. The civil service and public corporations are often pressurized to hire more people than they need, in order to find 'jobs' for relatives, tribesmen, girlfriends, supporters and others who attach themselves to senior officials and politicians. Or overemployment may occur in the public sector simply out of a general government decsion to create more employment. Foreign-owned firms may come under similar pressures and hire more workers than they need, for public relations reasons. The labour of those who have jobs but nothing to do is unemployed in that it contributes nothing to the national product, but it does not get recorded in official unemployment statistics.

(c) Economists used to think there was another important category, similar to (b), in the rural economy, consisting of people who could be withdrawn out of agriculture without reducing output, either because their efforts actually contributed nothing to output (zero marginal product) or because others already engaged in agriculture would increase their own productivities to compensate if some workers migrated to other sectors of the economy. However, modern researchers doubt whether this is a common situation.

(3) *Seasonal unemployment*. The demand for labour in agriculture is often highly seasonal, especially in regions dominated by a single crop which yields only one harvest a year. During the peak seasons every able-bodied person will be needed; between times only a proportion of available labour will have work.

(4) *Underemployment*. The waste of labour resources is by no means confined to people who are unemployed and therefore contributing nothing

---

[9] In Ghana, for instance, analysis showed that the number of recorded unemployed went up by 833 for every 1000 people placed in new jobs, implying that for every successful job placement nearly two additional people were induced to register as officially unemployed, cf. Killick, 1972.

to output. 'Underemployment' is another form of wastage of major importance in developing countries. Several types of underemployment can be noticed:

(a) The visibly underemployed. This refers to people who have work which occupies them for less than some 'normal' or desired number of hours per week. These may be occasional workers or workers with regular but only part-time employment.

(b) Self-employed workers, the demand for whose services does not regularly require their full-time effort. Petty traders, porters, shoeshine boys, lottery ticket sellers and many others could be put into this category.

(c) The so-called 'urban surplus' of workers who have migrated from rural areas in search of modern sector jobs but who have had to settle for low productivity urban informal work. These can be described as under-employed if their urban work has a lower productivity than they had in the rural economy. In this case, national product would be raised if they went back to the villages and the difference between their rural and urban productivities could be used as a measure of the extent of their under-employment.

> **Key concept. Underemployment** refers generally to workers who are neither unemployed nor fully employed.

There are, then, many different forms of labour under-utilization, and it is evident that some of these forms are virtually impossible to measure with any degree of accuracy. For this reason there is no single country for which there is a reliable estimate of the total amount of under-utilization.

Faced with this unsatisfactory state of affairs, some economists have sought a short-cut:[10]

One might try to cut through conceptual difficulties by thinking in terms of not so much of under-employment as of low-productivity or low-income employment, and regarding the number of those whose work brings in an (arbitrarily defined) unduly low income, together with the unemployed, as reflecting the numbers for whom work or more work needs to be provided.

This 'poverty approach' to the employment problem has been widely employed, especially under the influence of the International Labour Office (ILO). However, it really offers no solution because poverty and labour under-utilization are conceptually

different conditions. Referring back to Table 5.5 (page 116), for example, we saw that only a minor proportion of the heads of households living in poverty were unemployed. Most were employees or self-employed. If we were to estimate all those with inadequate incomes and call them underemployed we would in most LDCs end up with an enormous figure which, however, would include people whose poverty was not related to the types of underemployment described earlier.

It is preferable, therefore, to maintain the distinction between poverty and labour under-utilization, even though it leaves us without a solution to the measurement of under-utilization.

Evidence on labour under-utilization

Having made it clear already that there are no satisfactory estimates of the total extent of labour under-utilization, all that is possible here is to summarize such fragmentary evidence as does exist in order to obtain at least an idea of the relative gravity of the problem.

Open unemployment

Reverting to the types of under-utilization set out on the previous pages, *open unemployment* is the easiest to measure, especially in the towns, so we start with some estimates of that. These are summarized in Tables 5.6 and 5.7.

Table 5.6
Open Unemployment in LDCs, by Region, 1975

Region	Total Nos. (millions)	Total Rates (%)	Urban only Nos. (millions)	Urban only Rates (%)
Asia*	18	3·9	6	6·9
Africa	10	7·1	3	10·8
Latin America	5	5·1	5	6·5
All regions	33	4·7	14	8·0

Source: ILO, 1976, Table 1.
Note: *Excluding China and other Asian centrally planned economies.

According to the approximate estimates in Table 5.6, there were about 33 million people openly unemployed in the three main regions of the Third World in 1975, representing a little under 5 per cent of their labour forces. More than half of the unemployed were in Asia but the highest incidence, expressed as a

[10] Mouly and Costa, 1974, p. 32.

proportion of the labour force, was in Africa, while Asia had the lowest unemployment rate. The rates in the urban areas were a good deal higher in all regions, with Africa again having the worst record.

From the differences between the total and urban rates, it is apparent that the incidence of open unemployment is lower in the rural areas. This is corroborated by figures in Table 5.7, which also provides other details of the unemployment situation.

The averages in Table 5.7 are roughly consistent with those in Table 5.6. Table 5.7 shows an urban unemployment rate (in the 1960s) of around 10 per cent, against 8 per cent (for 1975) in Table 5.6. It also provides a more precise comparison of urban and rural unemployment, showing the urban unemployment rate to be more than twice as high as the rural rate. Table 5.7 also reveals particularly large unemployment rates in the 15–24 age group. The alarmingly high rate of 18 per cent for this group should, however, be read in the context of the earlier comment that it is the young who can 'afford' to be openly unemployed because they can generally fall

back on their families to maintain them until they eventually find work.

The relative youth of many of those recorded as unemployed helps to explain another feature illustrated in Table 5.7, namely the difference in the incidence of unemployment among illiterates and those with secondary schooling. It is the younger generation which is the better educated so this result is not too unexpected. However, it should be linked with another consideration: school leavers sometimes start with unrealistic expectations about what kind of job their education will bring them. They are likely to aspire to white-collar jobs and it takes time before the unsuccessful adjust their expectations downwards and start looking for jobs they regard as second best. Unemployment among university graduates (not shown in the table) is, however, quite low. Most graduates are still able to find acceptable jobs fairly quickly, although there are exceptions, especially in India and Sri Lanka.

Hidden unemployment

On this there is only the most scattered information. Sabot has published an interesting study relating to urban Tanzania in 1971, comparing open unemployment to an alternative measure which includes 'discouraged workers'. His results are summarized in Table 5.8.

Table 5.7
Estimates of Open Unemployment in Developing Countries
(Percentages of Labour Force; Median Values of Country Estimates)[a]

	Unemployment rate
Urban open unemployment	
(a) All ages	10·3
(b) Aged 15–24	18·2
Comparison of urban and rural open unemployment	
(a) Urban	10·1
(b) Rural	4·4
Urban unemployment by sex and age	
(a) Male, all ages	9·3
(b) Female, all ages	7·9
(c) Male, 15–24	16·4
(d) Female, 15–24	15·3
Unemployment and education (both sexes)	
(a) No education	4·3
(b) Secondary education[b]	10·2

Source: Turnham, 1971, Tables III.2; III.3; III.7.
Notes: (a) Based on data collected in various years during the 1960s.
   (b) The precise definitions in this category varied from one country to the next.

Table 5.8
Alternative Measures of Unemployment Rates in Urban Tanzania, 1971

	(Percentages)		
	Males	Females	All workers
Open unemployment	4·5	20·9	8·0
Open unemployment plus discouraged workers*	5·8	32·5	12·0

Source: From Sabot, 1977, Table I.
Note: *Includes in both the numbers of unemployed and the labour force people without money income 'passively' seeking paid employment.

If his results are at all representative of towns in other developing countries, they indicate that the number of 'discouraged workers' is large. In the Tanzanian case they raised the overall unemployment rate by half and there was a particularly high incidence among women. An estimate for Colombia supports the view of this as a major source of underutilization, showing that in 1967 about one-tenth of the urban male labour force could be described as 'persons without work who would probably seek it if [open] unemployment were much lower'.[11]

Two other categories of hidden unemployment were listed earlier. There were those who apparently had a job but in fact did nothing. There are no estimates for the number of such people! And there was the 'rural surplus'—those who could migrate out of agriculture without any reduction in output. Attempts have been made to estimate the extent of this in various countries with results that invariably show it to be small. One careful estimate for India in 1961 (a country with high population densities where, therefore, this problem might be expected to be large) concluded that only 0·63 per cent of the agricultural labour force could be *permanently* withdrawn without any loss of agricultural output.[12] The explanation of results such as this is simply that at the peak seasons everyone is needed, has a positive productivity and could only be withdrawn at the loss of some output. This is, of course, quite consistent with the existence of much seasonal unemployment.

Seasonal unemployment

This type of unemployment is very widespread in agriculture. Table 5.9 summarizes the findings of a number of studies of the seasonal utilization of agricultural labour in LDCs and it can be observed from column (4) of this that typically, and taking the year as a whole, not much more than half of available labour is utilized. Only China achieves a high year-round utilization. In all except one case, however, virtually all available labour (90 per cent or more) is used for at least two months (see column 1), which further supports the idea that there is little surplus labour which could be permanently withdrawn without loss of output. In many months, though,

there are severe degrees of under-utilization, as shown in columns (2) and (3).

The figures in Table 5.9 may exaggerate the degree of seasonal unemployment because people may find non-agricultural work to do during the slack months. Also, the amount of seasonal under-utilization will be strongly influenced by the extent of diversification of the crops grown and how many harvests they yield each year. But despite these qualifications, there is no doubt that this is a major—quite possibly the largest—source of labour under-utilization in agrarian developing countries.

Underemployment

We turn next to examine evidence on the various forms of *underemployment*. As regards 'visible underemployment', Turnham has collected the results of a number of urban surveys showing considerable variations from one country to the next but that typically about one-tenth of the urban employed labour force work less than thirty hours per week.[13] He also shows that women are particularly likely to be victims of short-time working.

It is harder to find reliable evidence of visible underemployment in rural areas (partly because it is strongly affected by seasonal factors), but an Indian study estimated that in 1964–5 about 3 per cent of the rural labour force were working less than twenty-eight hours per week, with another 3 per cent working twenty-eight to forty-two hours.[14]

Kritz and Ramos (1976) undertook a study in three major Latin American cities and similarly found a

[11] International Labour Office, 1970, Table 1.
[12] Lal, 1976, Table 4.
[13] Turnham, 1971, Table III. 8.
[14] Krishna, 1976, Table 7.

Table 5.9
Utilization of Labour in Agriculture

Country/region		Utilization as a % of available labour supply:			
		No. of months with 90%+ utilization (1)	Months with below 60% utilization (2)	Months with below 30% utilization (3)	Average % utilization for whole year (4)
China		8	1	0	86
India	(a) Madhya Pradesh	4	6	2	65
	(b) Maharashtra	2	6	—	59
Ghana	(cocoa)	2	8	2	52
Iraq	(a) Middle Tigris	—	9	4	45
	(b) Diyala	2	8	3	52

Source: Adapted from Clark and Haswell, 1964, Table XXV.

widespread incidence of underemployment. There were large numbers of people doing only occasional work which often occupied only part of their working week. Among the self-employed there were large variations in the demand for the output of these workers, so that typically they were producing only about 60 per cent of what they could produce in peak periods. They concluded from this type of evidence that urban underemployment affects more people than open unemployment and may be at least as serious. They added the interesting observation that in developing countries changes in the employment situation 'may take the form of variations in the extent and intensity of underemployment, and only secondarily, if at all, in the rate of open unemployment' (p. 127).

The so-called 'urban surplus labour' was another form of underemployment described earlier, defined as workers with urban productivities below what they would be in rural areas. Sabot estimated the 1971 incidence of this in Tanzania, concluding that about one-tenth of the total urban labour force could be placed in this category (the incidence was twice as great among the urban self-employed).[15]

At the end of this survey of evidence we are unable to offer even the most approximate generalization about the total extent of labour under-utilization in developing countries. But though the evidence is fragmentary and unsystematic, it leaves no room for doubting that the extent of under-utilization is large. It constitutes a serious waste of resources as well as a major source of human deprivation. It is, therefore, of grave concern to economic policy-makers.

> **Activity.** It is quite likely that the literature on your own economy includes studies of aspects of labour under-utilization. Compare the results with the evidence surveyed above in order to gauge its relative importance in your country.

We have now completed our survey of the evidence on the poverty, inequality and employment problems. The last task of this chapter, before looking at possible policy solutions in Chapter 6, is to examine the causes of these three problems.

III.   The Causes of the Problems

The origins of poverty in LDCs

When we come to look at the causes of the problems of inequality, poverty, and unemployment we come closer to an understanding of the relationships

between them. Take first the case of poverty. Looking again at the figures in Table 5.4 (page 115), what stands out is that the proportions below the poverty line are strongly correlated with the stage of development (as represented by average per capita income) but that the incidence of poverty is also modified, for good or bad, by the distribution of income.

For example, Thailand (per capita income $173) has an estimated 27 per cent of its population living below the $50 line whereas Colombia (per capita income $347) has 15 per cent below the poverty line. The main influence on this contrast is the more advanced stage of development of Colombia, although it was noted in the discussion of Table 5.4 that Thailand has less poverty and Colombia more poverty than we would predict simply on the basis of average incomes. Turning back to Table 5.3 (page 112) you can see that the reason for these deviations from trend is that Thailand has a relatively equal income distribution whereas Colombia has one of the most unequal distributions in the world.

Underdevelopment is the chief cause of poverty in developing countries, often aggravated by severe degrees of inequality. This is in contrast with wealthy countries, which already have the means to ensure adequate living standards for all. In these countries poverty results from a failure of distribution; in LDCs it is the generally poor living standard of almost everyone which is the brute fact, and redistributive policies can only hope to ameliorate the worst effects of this.

To understand the causes of poverty, then, we need both to understand the causes of inequality and of underdevelopment. The causes of inequality are examined on the next few pages but a thorough study of the causes of underdevelopment is beyond the scope of this chapter. Many factors contribute to underdevelopment: shortages of capital, skill, entrepreneurial and managerial ability; unequal relationships between rich and poor countries in the international economy; dualistic economic structures inherited from colonialism; ill-chosen government policies; political exploitation of the many by the few . . . to present only an incomplete list. Hopefully the reader will obtain a better understanding of many of these factors but it cannot be claimed that this book provides a systematic exposition of the roots of underdevelopment. To some extent, therefore, only a partial analysis is offered of the causes of poverty Fortunately, a more complete treatment is possible in the cases of inequality and the under-utilization of labour.

---

[15] Sabot, 1977, Table VII.

The causes of inequality

The distribution of income in an economy is broadly determined by the ownership and use of income-earning assets, of market and political power, and of what can be called the distribution of dependence.

Ownership and use of income-earning assets

The ownership of assets can be subdivided into material and non-material assets. Take first the case of *material assets*, or *wealth*. One of the chief causes of income inequality in the non-communist world is that material assets are subject to particularly severe degrees of inequality. It is a safe assumption that asset distribution in almost any society is more unequal than income distribution, although there are virtually no LDC statistics to support this statement. Take the example of the UK. By the standards of most western industrial countries, income concentration in the UK is moderate, but the distribution of wealth, i.e. income-earning assets, is heavily skewed. Compare the following figures of the distributions of income and wealth:[16]

	% share of total income	% share of total wealth
Richest 1%	7	43
Richest 5%	19	68
Richest 10%	28	79
Gini coefficient	0·33	0·87

The point about wealth, of course, is that it generates income – both directly as dividends, rent and interest, and indirectly through the ability to realize capital gains. So the very skewed distribution of wealth is liable to have a major impact on the overall distribution of income.

Agricultural land is the most important type of wealth in developing countries so the ways in which its ownership is spread or concentrated will have a major bearing on overall income distribution. Where the ownership of land is heavily skewed – as it is in Colombia, for example – inequality will result and with it the existence of large numers of rural people either with no land at all or with plots too small even to provide for subsistence needs. But it is difficult to generalize about land ownership in developing countries. In much of tropical Africa traditional collective systems of land tenure have prevented the worst inequalities. In many Asian and Latin American countries, and in southern Africa, however, much of the land is in the hands of a small group, and there is a tremendous hunger for land among the peasantry. In India, for instance, about 15 per cent of all rural households classified as living in poverty have

no land at all and another 10 per cent have plots so small that their owners remain largely dependent on casual wage labour as their chief source of income.

The most important of the *non-material* assets is education. A person's education has a powerful influence on the type of work he can get so if access to good education is confined to a small elite this will make for large inequalities. Other examples of the influence of non-material assets are the extent to which natural ability in modern skills is concentrated in particular groups in society; and the extent to which tribal or personal 'connections' can be used to bestow privileges on a fortunate few.

Income-earning assets also influence the distribution of income through their impact on *labour productivity*. In a rough and ready way, labour incomes reflect the productivity of workers. This productivity will, in turn, be powerfully affected by the access of workers to capital equipment, training and other resources. An almost universal feature of LDC economies is that labour productivities in agriculture are much lower than in the modern sectors of the economy, due especially to the much smaller availability of capital, training and modern know-how to the rural worker (see Chapter 9). Thus, large inequalities are created between the towns and villages. This helps to explain the fact noted earlier that the incidence of poverty is particularly severe in rural areas.

Market and political power

Access to *market power* is another important consideration. This too is a type of asset – determining the ability of people to enhance their incomes through the exercise of monopoly power. Chapter 10 examines the case of industrial monopoly in some detail and shows that monopoly is associated with larger profits and that these are a transfer from consumers to monopoly-capitalists, thus worsening inequalities. Workers may use trade unions in a similar way, restricting entry into an occupation or industry, thereby raising wages above competitive levels. Such increases in wages would be at the expense of employment and hence would accentuate income differences within the labour force. It is difficult to say how important this kind of union activity is in developing countries but it probably does contribute to large urban-rural differences in some countries.

Market power is frequently converted into *political power* which can also be used to reinforce inequalities.

---

[16] Figures quoted by Sharp, 1973, ch. 8. Income shares are before tax.

The state exerts a major impact on the distribution of the national income through its taxation, spending and other policy-making powers.

The use of these powers is explored more fully in the next chapter. The chief points at issue are whether the fiscal system is 'progressive' or not (i.e. whether the tax burden and the allocation of government services and investments are decided according to the criterion of need) and whether other aspects of policy are biased in favour of the rich or poor. Too often taxes on commodities fall heavily on the poor, while government services are concentrated in the (relatively well-to-do) cities. It is also a common complaint that taxation, failures to control inflation, pricing policies and industrial protection worsen the 'terms of trade' of rural dwellers – raising the prices they have to pay to meet their needs relative to the prices they receive for their output.

However, the way in which political power can be used to influence income distribution is not confined to the topics mentioned in the last paragraph. It extends to the entire political framework of a country. That the general orientation of politics can have a most potent influence on inequality is demonstrated by the universal finding that the centrally planned socialist countries (industrial and developing alike) have far less inequality than other political systems.

> **Activity.** Consider the distribution and use of assets, of market and political power, and of dependence in your own country and discuss whether each favours large or small income inequalities. Is it possible to say anything about trends over time?

Distribution of dependence

The final source of inequality mentioned earlier was called the *distribution of dependence*. Two different aspects can be placed under this heading. First, there is the impact of unemployment. An unemployed person is, of course, an economic dependant, forced to rely on the income of others in order to survive. Rather obviously, widespread unemployment (open and hidden) worsens inequalities, especially in the cities. Secondly, there is the influence of family size. Young children are also economic dependants – mouths to feed and bodies to clothe – amongst whom the family's income must be shared. But recall from Table 5.5 that the number of children is not randomly distributed among families: it is the poor who have the largest families. As the saying goes, 'the rich get richer and the poor get children'. So this demographic factor also accentuates inequalities – a point to which we will return shortly.

The dynamics of inequality

The discussion of Figure 5.3 suggested tentatively that there is a roughly U-shaped relationship between the income share of the poorer members of society and the stage of economic development. The income share of the poorest 40 per cent was predicted to first fall sharply and later to rise gradually. How might such a process be explained?

There are a number of forces at work in the early stages of development pushing in the direction of greater inequality. First, urbanization commences, with a migration of young men from the countryside to the factories, offices and shops of the towns. With urban wages typically three times the value of average incomes in the rural areas, this creates a dualistic economic structure. Secondly, industrialization and the spread of other modern activities is associated with the introduction of western technologies which require large inputs of capital and human skills but create little employment for unskilled migrants.[17] There is thus created a movement towards especially large inequalities in the growing urban sector. These are, thirdly, further accentuated by a concentration of ownership of the newly-created industries in a relatively small number of (often foreign) hands.

Fourthly, even within the rural economy, the initial situation of relative equality is liable to give way to a more skewed distribution, as agriculture becomes commercialized. A minority of farmers will take advantage of this, specializing in export and other cash crops and introducing more modern cultivation methods. But many smallholders will be left behind and remain essentially subsistence farmers eking out a bare existence by traditional methods (see Chapter 9). Finally, before or during the changes just outlined, population growth will go up, for reasons explained in the previous chapter, and there is strong evidence that links accelerating population growth with worsening inequalities. This is not just because of the larger size of poor families but also because a rapidly-growing population leads to a labour force that is probably expanding faster than the demand for labour. This tendency for over-supply in the unskilled labour market depresses wages and thus the incomes of labour relative to capital.[18]

Of course, this is a grossly overgeneralized description of the development process, to which

---

[17] Tinbergen, 1975, has especially stressed the inegalitarian effects of technological progress in the histories of the western industrial countries.
[18] Ahluwalia, 1976, p. 326, for example, found that an accelerating population growth enhances the income share of the richest 20 per cent of the population and reduces it for the rest.

many exceptions could be found.[19] Nevertheless, it offers a plausible account for many countries and provides at least a partial rationale of the downward-sloping segment of the U-curve in Figure 5.3.

> **Activity.** Does this description of early-stage economic development fit the history of your own country?

From this generalization we can pass to another: *once established, inequality tends to perpetuate itself.* Having achieved an advantage, the rich can manipulate the socio-economic system to enhance their privileges.

The most obvious factor making for the self-perpetuation of inequality stems from the interaction of the distributions of wealth and income. Remember that the distribution of wealth is generally more skewed than incomes; the rich own a disproportionately large share of material assets. These assets yield incomes, which reinforces income inequalities. Because saving is a rising function of income, the rich save proportionately more than the less well-to-do and can thus acquire more land and other assets, which further worsens the skewed distribution of wealth and incomes. A vicious circle is at work.

This is by no means the end of the matter. Wealth is often translated into political power, in which case the rich may come to dominate the political system. They can then consolidate their domination by closing the political processes against democratizing forces which would undermine their position. And having achieved domination they can manipulate the power of the state to serve their own ends.

The interactions between wealth and education may constitute another vicious circle. It was noted earlier that educational qualifications enhance earning power, so that those with good educations are generally among the more affluent members of society and the uneducated are generally poor. But the causality can work in the opposite direction: the rich can afford to buy superior educations for their children so that this advantage is passed from this generation to the next. The well-to-do also offer living conditions and a domestic environment which make it easier for the children to do well in their studies, so that the provision of schooling for the children of poor families will not necessarily break the advantages of the rich (as has been discovered in the USA).

There is also the demographic factor once again. The fact that the poor have more children than the affluent also helps to perpetuate inequality. The poor are unable to save and to afford good education for their children, not only because their family incomes are small but also because they have so many mouths to feed. In rural areas, large families also intensify pressure on the land and may cause the fragmentation of land holdings into ever smaller, increasingly unviable, plots. And because the poor see children as providing them with security in their old age, and are worse educated than the rest of the population, they are, as was seen in Chapter 4, less responsive to the idea of family planning, so that this demographic factor also tends to persist over time. Moreover, a continuing expansion of the labour force will worsen unemployment and hence weaken any tendency for wages to rise.

Some view the relationship between the distribution of income and the structure of consumer demand as providing another mechanism of self-perpetuating inequality. The effect of a highly unequal distribution of income is to create a structure of demand in favour of items largely consumed by the rich, for they are the ones with the most purchasing power. This will create a relatively large market for sophisticated manufactured goods and, with the assistance of protection, an industrial sector will grow up on the basis of this pattern of demand. But these types of goods are often produced by relatively capital-intensive techniques which create little employment; and inequalities tend to be largest in the industrial sector. Thus, it is claimed, the productive structure created in response to inequality will itself tend to generate more inequality. On this view, local production using advanced technology tends to generate the unequal income distribution required to provide the market for the goods it produces.

This argument is an intuitively plausible one but it overlooks that the rich also have a relatively large demand for labour-intensive services. The employment of domestic servants is only the most obvious example of this. It is perhaps for this reason that empirical tests of the hypothesis set out in the previous paragraph have failed to provide strong supporting evidence. At most, the quantitative effect of a shift in demand on the distribution of employment and income has been found small;[20] one test using Colombian data failed to find any supporting evidence at all.[21]

Even if we disregard this latter hypothesis, however, we are still left with powerful forces making for the

---

[19] This description accords fairly well with the pattern of structural change established by Kuznets's (1966) studies of the growth histories of the now industrial countries.
[20] See Morawetz, 1974, pp. 503–7, for a general survey of the literature relating to this.
[21] Ballentine and Soligo, 1978.

perpetuation of inequality. At least four interlocking vicious circles are in operation, depicted schematically in Figure 5.4.

It can be seen, therefore, that powerful economic and social forces are at work both worsening and perpetuating inequalities in developing countries. But these forces should not mislead the reader into believing that we are dealing with an insoluble problem. There are a variety of things that governments can do. And we should not lose sight of the fact that the curves in Figure 5.3 show gradually diminishing inequalities once per capita incomes rise above certain critical levels. Apparently, the vicious circles are not so invincible that the trend towards worsening inequities cannot be reversed.

Before going further into these matters, however, we will complete this chapter by investigating the causes of the under-utilization of labour.

Figure 5.4   *The vicious circles of inequality.*

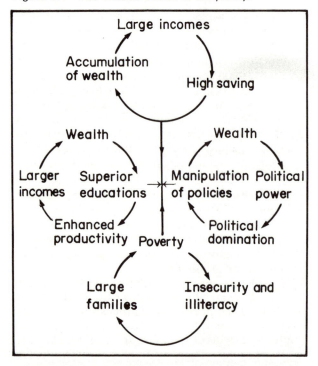

> **Activity.** The idea of interlocking vicious circles of inequality is open to some criticisms which will be mentioned in Chapter 6. Can you anticipate ways in which it can be criticized?

Why is labour wasted?

It should be apparent from the earlier outline of the numerous types of labour under-utilization that no

simple statement of one or two determinants can explain the origins of this problem. There are actually a large number of contributory factors, of which only the most important are singled out in the next few paragraphs. In approaching this matter it is helpful to organize the discussion around influences on the supply of and demand for labour, commencing with supply.

Supply of labour

One of the most potent forces making for the under-utilization of labour is the rapid growth of LDC labour forces. The actual growth in 1960–70 and projections for 1970–90 are presented in Table 5.10; the figures make sombre reading. We can note that total LDC labour forces grew by 175 million people in 1960–70 and are expected to go up by another 500 million in 1970–90. Translated into annual growth rates, this means that the labour force is growing at well over 2 per cent a year, compared with only about 1 per cent in the industrial countries. The regional breakdown in the table shows, moreover, that all major groups of developing countries are going through similar experiences.

The main cause of the more rapid growth of labour forces in LDCs is, of course, the faster increases in population revealed in Chapter 4 (see Table 4.1). According to the ILO, about nine-tenths of the total growth in LDC labour forces is attributable to expanding populations; the other one-tenth is explained by rising proportions of adults with work or seeking it. In some Moslem and other countries, where religion and tradition have not favoured women working outside the home, the participation rate is rising quite rapidly with the erosion of old attitudes and the gradual emancipation of women. Nevertheless, it is the demographic factor which is of predominant importance.

The fast growth of the labour force places a great strain on the ability of the economy to generate new work opportunities on a sufficient scale to absorb the rising numbers. This is especially true in the towns and cities because the migration of people from rural areas means that urban populations grow even faster than the total. To illustrate, it is estimated that in 1950–70 the rural populations in developing countries grew at 1·62 per cent a year, while their urban populations expanded at an annual rate of 4·58 per cent – nearly three times as fast.[22] It is likely that the urban labour force grew even faster than total urban population because a particularly large

---

[22] World Bank, 1974, Annex Table 6.

Table 5.10
The Growth of the Labour Force

| | TOTAL LABOUR FORCE (MILLIONS) | | LABOUR FORCE GROWTH RATES (% P.A.) | | | | | |
	Industrial countries	Developing countries	Industrial countries	South Asia	East Asia	Africa	Latin America	All developing countries
1960	439	837	1·1	—	—	—	—	2·2
1970	488	1012	1·0	—	—	—	—	1·9
1980	542	1239	1·1	2·3	1·6	2·2	2·8	2·1
1990	593	1547	0·9	2·6	2·1	2·5	3·0	2·4

Sources: ILO data presented in World Bank, 1974, Annex Table 10; and in Todaro, 1977, Tables 13.2 and 13.3.

proportion of the rural-to-urban migrants are young men in search of work. If the urban labour force is growing at, say, 5 per cent annually it will double every fourteen years, but there are few urban economies which can expand the number of jobs at that rate.

This helps to explain why open unemployment is particularly severe in the towns. But if there is much unemployment in the towns, why do the migrants still pour in from the villages? To answer this question we have to refer again to the generally far higher wages that can be earned in modern urban jobs than in farming and other rural work. Two conflicting economic considerations will influence the young man wondering whether to leave his village and try his luck in town. On the one side, there is the possibility of obtaining a much better living than he can hope for at home; on the other side, there is the danger that he will be unsuccessful in his search for a job in town and will remain unemployed. So he will set the urban-rural income differential against the chances of finding a job. To put it in an admittedly over-simplified way, if the expected urban income, defined as the urban wage times the probability of finding an urban job, is greater than the expected value of his income in rural work then he will have an economic incentive to move to the town.[23] Whether he will actually make the move will also be affected by other, non-economic, considerations ('the lure of the bright lights') but empirical investigations have found that economic variables provide quite strong statistical explanations of the rate of migration.

An implication of this view of migration is that large urban-rural income differentials (sustained by economic dualism) are among the most important explanations of the under-utilization of labour in the urban economy (although we should not lose sight of the other side of the coin: the outflow of people from the villages probably reduces the degree of rural under-utilization to some extent).

Activity. Search for data on urban-rural income differentials in your own country. Consider the implications of these for the incidence of migration. Does what you can discover about rural-urban migration in your country fit with the economic explanation offered above?

The educational system also contributes to urban unemployment. The size of the educated labour force is likely to be growing more rapidly even than the total urban labour force, making it especially difficult to absorb these young people into productive employment (recall from Table 5.7 that open unemployment is especially common among those with secondary schooling). Moreover, the fact that they are educated will both increase their dissatisfaction with the rural way of life and raise their expectations of finding a job in town. It may also encourage them to hold unrealistic views about the type of job they can expect to obtain. So the educated will be especially likely to join the throng of migrants seeking work in the towns.

The picture, then, is of rapidly expanding supplies of labour, especially in the towns and of educated workers. What of the *demand* for labour?

Demand for labour

The implication of large-scale under-utilization of labour, of course, is that demand has failed to keep pace with supply. There are a number of reasons why this is often the case. The rate of expansion of work opportunities will largely be a function of two key variables: (1) the speed with which the national economy is expanding and (2) the factor proportions

[23] The argument of this paragraph summarizes what is called the 'Todaro model' of migration. For an introduction to this model see Todaro, 1977, ch. 14; a more sophisticated presentation is in Todaro, 1969.

utilized in the growth process. Take first the speed with which the economy is growing. This varies widely from one economy to the next, depending on the severity of the constraints upon expansion. The key limiting factors – the 'binding constraints' – also differ between countries.

Shortages of saving and investment are probably the most pervasive constraint on the growth of LDC economies, even though economists no longer place as much weight on the role of investment as an engine of growth as they used to. Nevertheless, the contrast between investible resources in industrial and developing countries is so large that it cannot fail to be a potent force preventing LDC economies from growing fast enough to absorb large increments to the labour force:[24]

> Although their labour force is often growing twice as fast, investment per worker in developing countries is often less than a tenth of that in developed countries. Their investible resources per new member of the labour force may be only 5 per cent or less of those in developed countries. Since alternatives to the technology employed in developed countries, especially in manufacturing, may be very limited, it is not surprising that the growth rates of the labour force offer a challenge that few policymakers have so far successfully met.

However, there may be other variables which prevent countries from making good use of even the limited investible resources they do possess. There may not be the institutional framework (including a tolerably efficient capital market) to permit resources to be properly allocated. Or shortages of entrepreneurial, managerial or other skills may depress the productivity of capital. In countries with severe balance of payments problems, inadequate import capacity may be the binding constraint. Some countries are held back because they have few natural resources: poor soil and no economic minerals. The land constraint may be aggravated by inefficient land tenure systems.

Whichever is the binding constraint in any particular case, few LDCs have demonstrated an ability to sustain economic growth fast enough to fully utilize their expanding labour resources. This brings us to the second main influence on the demand for labour: the *factor proportions* utilized in the process of economic growth. Many developing countries have failed to utilize as much of their labour as they could have done because of the development strategies they have pursued and the technologies they have adopted.

Throughout the 1960s and into the 1970s, many LDCs put their faith in a strategy based upon import-substituting industrialization. Industrialization was seen as the key ingredient of economic modernization and import-substitution (behind high protective barriers) the easiest way of achieving it. But industry, especially industry which copies the consumer-good manufactures of the industrial west, demands large inputs of capital, management and skill while creating only a limited number of jobs for the unskilled:[25]

> The expansion of industrial manufacturing alone cannot be expected to solve the unemployment and under-employment problem in most developing countries. A manufacturing sector employing 20 per cent of the labour force would need to increase employment by 15 per cent per year merely to absorb the increment in a total work force growing at an annual rate of 3 per cent. The required rate of increase of manufacturing output is even greater than 15 per cent if increases in labour productivity are taken into account. In the light of these orders of magnitude, the contribution of the industrial sector to employment growth over the last decade has been disappointing ... in a number of countries in Latin America and Africa, despite significant investments in manufacturing, employment in the sector grew less rapidly than population, and in some cases even declined in absolute terms.

Even countries which have achieved rapid industrialization, such as Venezuela and Brazil, still suffer a great deal of open unemployment in the towns.

Quite apart from the pursuit of capital-intensive strategies of industrialization, the techniques of production selected by firms have also often had a bias against the large-scale employment of unskilled and semi-skilled workers. A variety of factors have contributed to this bias.

In industry and other modern activities the best-known methods are those developed in the labour-scarce, capital-rich western countries. There has been little effort to adapt these methods to the quite different resource endowments of LDCs, or to develop new, more appropriate, techniques for local application. (The notion of an appropriate technology is explored in Chapter 9.) Because they only know much about western techniques, managers and engineers sometimes automatically adopt them without inquiring about the availability elsewhere of more labour-using methods.

This 'engineering bias' is often reinforced by prices for labour and capital which positively encourage capital-intensity. Minimum wage laws, government salary structures, the influence of trade unions, the pay policies of multinational corporations all help to

[24] World Bank, 1974, pp. 34–5.
[25] Morawetz, 1974, p. 496.

raise urban, modern-sector wages well above competitive, market-clearing levels. Laws and conventions holding down interest rates, over-valued exchange rates (Chapter 8) and tax concessions for foreign investors similarly hold the price of capital well below levels which would reflect their scarcity in the economy. So the investor is faced with a distorted set of factor prices which offer him greater profitability if he uses much (artificially cheap) capital and economizes on (artificially expensive) labour.

Activity. Discuss the extent to which the markets for capital and unskilled labour in your own country result in prices which accurately reflect their relative scarcities.

Even though a number of other contributory factors have been neglected here, we can see that there are a variety of demographic and economic forces at work causing the supply of labour to outstrip the demand for it. To summarize: rapid population growth (supplemented by increasing participation rates among adults) cause the total labour force to grow rapidly. This problem is aggravated in the towns by big urban-rural income differentials which cause large-scale migration from the rural areas, especially by the educated. On the side of demand, many LDCs face acute constraints in seeking to accelerate their development; these constraints limit the ability of the economy to absorb the growing labour supply into productive employment and this limitation is often aggravated by the choice of capital-intensive development strategies and production methods.

Having now studied the nature and causes of the poverty, inequality and employment problems, the scene has been set for an examination of the policies which governments might pursue to remedy these evils. The next chapter evaluates the policy alternatives which are available.

Suggestions for Revision and Group Discussions

1 Review your understanding of the following:
  (a) The trickle-down theory of development.
  (b) Wealth and capital gains.
  (c) Functional and size distributions of income.
  (d) Lorenz curves and Gini coefficients.
  (e) The distinction between absolute and relative poverty.
  (f) The unemployment rate.
  (g) The distinction between open and hidden unemployment.
  (h) Underemployment.
  (i) The vicious circles of inequality.
2 Discuss the advantages and limitations of using the rate of growth of per capita GDP as an indicator of the pace of economic development.
3 Do you think the distinctions between the problems of poverty, inequality and unemployment have practical significance for your own country?
4 In what ways is the functional distribution of income likely to affect the size distribution of income? Would it be possible to change the latter without changing the former?
5 Do the following figures show an increase or decrease in inequality?

	Period 1	Period 2
Average income of richest 50%	$1000	$1500
Average income of poorest 50%	$100	$300

6 Discuss the statement in the text that, 'being unemployed is a luxury only some can afford.' What difficulties does it imply for the measurement of unemployment?
7 How would you explain the statistics in Table 5.7 showing lower unemployment rates for women? Is this likely to be because of 'reverse discrimination' against men?
8 A deeper study of the Todaro model of rural-to-urban migration is recommended, starting with the references given in note 23.
9 Write a note outlining that part of standard micro-economic theory which underlies the view that distorted factor prices contribute to the under-utilization of labour.
10 Revise your understanding of the statement that: 'The distribution of income in an economy is broadly determined by the ownership and use of income-earning assets, of market and political power and of the distribution of dependence'.

Suggestions for Further Reading

There are three good collections of readings dealing generally with the subject-matter of this chapter: Chenery, *et al.* (1974); Edwards (1974) and Jolly, *et al.* (1973). A careful study of each of these is a 'must' for the student who wants to go into this subject in greater depth. Ahluwalia (1976) provides a useful supplement to the Chenery volume. Meier (1976) pt. I and IV also offers useful readings, and Lipton (1977) offers a thorough analysis of the urban bias in economic growth.

The serious measurement problems reviewed in this chapter are dealt with in greater depth in various sources. On poverty, Anand (1977) gives a useful general discussion as well as interesting case materials on Malaysia. See also the first two chapters of Townsend (1970). Yotopoulos and Nugent (1976), ch. 12 and 14, survey the measurement of inequality and unemployment, and provide econometric applications.

Chapter 3 of Atkinson (1976) offers an authoritative but straightforward introduction to the measurement of inequality. Turnham (1971) is strongly recommended both for its treatment of the difficulties of measuring the under-utilization of labour and for the wealth of evidence it provides.

Morawetz, (1974) provides a clear and authoritative discussion of the employment implications of industrialization. Kuznets (1965 and 1966) presents pioneering historical studies of long-run income distribution trends. The March 1978 issue of *World Development* is on the theme of poverty and inequality and should be consulted. It includes discussion of the oft-cited cases of Korea and Taiwan. Country materials and other empirical work can be found in the references given in the chapter's notes. Readers should also consult the suggestions at the end of Chapter 6.

6 Poverty, inequality and unemployment: solutions

'Anyone concerned with the welfare of the world's underprivileged people must recognise that business cannot continue as usual in the development community.' *Adelman and Morris*

Contents

I. Objectives, Revolutions and Reforms

The case for policy action

> **Activity**. Be sure to read Chapter 5 before commencing this one.

By itself, the existence of poverty, inequality and unemployment is not sufficient to establish a case for action by the government. You may recall that distributive efficiency was defined in Chapter 1 as an income distribution which is considered as just. Unless every family receives exactly the same income there will always be some disparities and the difficult task is to define a *socially acceptable* degree of inequality. Only when the concentration of incomes is greater than this socially acceptable level can we say that distributional inefficiency exists and that 'something ought to be done about it'.

However, Chapter 1 suggested that 'the market mechanism will result in self-reinforcing inequalities which are likely to be judged socially unjust. This indicates a need for socialistic intervention by the state, provided that the resulting improvements are regarded as outweighing the costs of achieving them' (page 23). The evidence just presented in Chapter 5 has provided ample support for this conclusion. Poverty has been shown to be widespread; inequalities are especially severe in developing countries; there is much unemployment and other forms of under-utilization of labour. In many of these countries there are, moreover, forces at work to perpetuate, often to worsen, these conditions.

It would be escapism to maintain a neutral moral position in the face of these facts. This chapter (and the remainder of this book) therefore begins from the premise that *there exist socially unacceptable levels of poverty, inequality and unemployment in many developing countries*. A case is therefore assumed for remedial action by the state. This case is further reinforced by the fact that poverty and its associated evils would take a great deal of time to be eliminated in the absence of policy interventions designed specifically for this purpose:[1]

> ... in many countries minimum incomes and standards of living for the poor cannot be achieved, even by the year 2000, without some acceleration of present average rates of growth, accompanied by a number of measures aiming to change the pattern of growth and use of productive resources by the various income groups ...

We can therefore proceed to discuss policy alternatives but, in doing so, it is important to remember that the situation varies greatly from one country to another, so that the case for action is not the same in all countries.

Activity. Do you think distributional efficiency prevails in your own country? If not, do you think the injustices are severe or only moderate?

Defining objectives

The first two chapters stressed the importance of defining policy objectives and priorities as precisely as possible. The case under discussion now is a good illustration of this point. It is all too easy for governments to profess their commitment to 'greater equality' or 'full employment', as most of them do. But what does 'greater equality' mean? Complete equality? The elimination of poverty? Greater taxation of the rich? Equality of opportunity? A commitment to 'greater equality' is no commitment at all, for it implies no clearly agreed meaning and offers no yardstick by which to assess the adequacy of government efforts to achieve this 'objective'. Even when the government is entirely sincere in stating this as a goal, the lack of precision is likely to have adverse consequences, among them the danger that policies which started out with redistributive intent will come to serve other purposes. There is much LDC evidence which fits with the following judgement on policies in the USA:[2]

> The distributional consequences of our equity programs often turn out to be perverse. We seem to manage these programs without much continuing thought to their equity objectives. Equity objectives or standards are

rarely spelled out in the legislation. Once enacted equity concerns seem to recede.

The study just quoted thus emphasizes the importance of being explicit about what it is intended to achieve and of collecting the data necessary to test whether the results match up to the intentions. Much the same is true of the 'full employment' objective. Does that mean the total absence of any form of labour under-utilization? Or just open unemployment? Or some unspecified irreducible minimum? Here too greater precision is necessary before the employment objective can take on concrete meaning and before we can evaluate the success of policy measures.

In setting about this task there are a number of alternative goals that can be considered. The government might concentrate on reducing the problem of poverty: establishing some minimum level of living for all people. Or it could concentrate on income shares: setting some target for the share in total income of, say, the poorest 40 per cent of the population and/or for the reduction of the incomes of, say, the richest 5 per cent. Another approach could focus on minimizing the adverse consequences of inequality: reducing the disadvantages of the poor in terms of access of education, health services and the like, and democratizing political processes. Or the main thrust of policies could be upon the reduction of regional or urban/rural differences. Again, a government may choose to give priority to solving the employment problem, in the faith that by doing so it would also make a major contribution to the reduction of poverty and inequality.

It is not a question of one of these approaches being right and the rest wrong; it is a matter of the precise nature of the problems confronted by a particular country, and of the government's philosophy. What is clear is that these alternative goals are not necessarily consistent with each other and, therefore, that choices have to be made among them. As was pointed out in Chapter 5, the choice of an anti-poverty programme would lead to the adoption of different policies from those appropriate for the equalization of income shares. Chapter 5 similarly established the considerable difference between the poverty and unemployment problems: those living in poverty are not necessarily (or even usually) unemployed; the unemployed are not necessarily living in poverty.

For the purposes of this chapter I propose a hierarchy of objectives which is hopefully appropriate for many developing countries, and ethically

---

[1] From ILO, 1976, p. 43.
[2] From an essay by Bonnen in Haveman and Margolis, 1970, p. 253.

acceptable to the reader. It is proposed to assume that the government gives top priority to the alleviation of poverty but that it wishes to achieve this by means that will also improve income distribution by placing much of the burden on the rich, and which will reduce the employment problem by putting the economy on a labour-intensive growth path. We might sum this up as a 'progressive, employment-creating anti-poverty' objective.

An objective of this type could be made specific by setting targets, for instance of the minimum number of people with incomes below a defined poverty line; for the consequential reduction in the income share of the richest 5 per cent of the population; and the number of new productive jobs entailed. The important thing is that a priority is established, so if anti-poverty and employment-creating policies compete for the same resources it is clearly established that anti-poverty takes precedence. There will be a good deal more to say about the importance of precise objectives later in the chapter. A further point of terminology: it will be convenient shorthand if the objectives of reducing the incidence of poverty, inequality and labour under-utilization are referred to collectively as 'equity objectives'.

Reform or revolution, the basic choice

We have established the likelihood that in many developing countries unacceptably extreme degrees of inequality will exist and tend to perpetuate themselves, and the desirability of policy measures to counteract this distributional inefficiency. But many governments are not interested in egalitarian measures – measures to reduce income in-equalities – and the question arises whether it will be feasible to achieve adequate improvements through existing political and economic structures. The structures themselves can be part of the problem, in which case radical transformation rather than marginal reform may be needed. In other words, the problem of poverty poses the classical choice between reform and revolution. What light can we as economists throw on the choice that ought to be made?

The key to this question lies in the view we take of the strength of the interlocking vicious circles portrayed in Figure 5.4 (page 126). If we regard these as a very powerful mechanism for the perpetuation of poverty and inequality we are also likely to be sceptical of the prospects for securing adequate improvements through reform. Of especial importance in this connection is the vicious circle which goes from wealth to political power to political domination to the manipulation of policy in favour of the dominant group and hence back to wealth again. If we believe that a dominant group will never peaceably relinquish its privileges we are likely to advocate a revolutionary solution, in which the elite is forcibly overthrown and the socio-economic system radically transformed in an egalitarian direction.

Remember, though, that Figure 5.3 (page 113) showed that the tendency for increasing inequality went into reverse as the economy became more developed, with the income share of the poorest 40 per cent of the population gradually increasing. This suggests that the forces of self-perpetuating inequality are not as intractable as might be supposed and the next few paragraphs look at possible reasons for this.

Let's start by looking at the connection between wealth and political power. Three reasons can be offered why the rich may not be able to permanently protect their privileges by dominating the political system. First, the rich are not necessarily a unified class sharing identical interests and attitudes. The 'upper class' may consist of a motley collection of conservative aristocrats whose wealth is based upon inheritance, of newly-risen entrepreneurs and business executives whose wealth is based upon industrial expansion and the application of modernizing attitudes, and of highly educated senior public servants commanding large salaries and 'perks' but suspicious alike of aristocrats and businessmen. At most, these three groups may form an uneasy alliance but the factors which divide them may be stronger than the privileges which unite them, so that they may not operate effectively as a cohesive group.

They may, secondly, differ in their perception of their own class interests. In this group which we are calling 'the rich' there will be some who understand that there is today a reduced public toleration of extreme inequalities and who will be sensitive to the need to accommodate some reforms so as to avert a revolutionary situation in which they will stand to lose all. But this view of 'enlightened self-interest' is likely to be opposed by others, more cut off from social realities and determined to make no concessions. Thus a division may appear among the rich in which the 'enlightened' see it as in their own interests to ally themselves with moderate reformist movements.

The third force weakening the ability of the rich to dominate the political system is the fact that while wealth is a political resource it is not the only one. The sheer size of the poor as a group, as compared with the small number of very rich, is itself a resource, even when the poor do not have votes or cannot use them in a meaningful way. The ability to organize into trade unions, co-operatives and peasant movements can, of course, greatly increase the political strength of these large numbers. And the processes of economic modernization and urbanization make it easier to create mass organizations, more difficult for an elite to control social forces.

Considerations such as these help to explain why domination by a rich elite is not necessarily immutable and can change into a more democratic system without the necessity for revolution. Peru provides an interesting illustration of how an unquestioned domination by a wealthy few was not sufficient to guarantee the perpetuation of their privileges. Starting with political relationships of dominance, much poverty and a small number of large fortunes, the elite was forced by social pressures (especially the emergence of a substantial middle class and the increasingly organized power of the underprivileged Indian population) into gradual retreat, later accelerated by a military coup in 1968.[3] The political systems of many of today's industrial countries have similar histories, of movement from oligarchies to openly competitive political systems which are more difficult for small groups to control.

What of the other vicious circles identified in Figure 5.4? Have there also been important forces at work to weaken their power? We will deal with these more briefly but the following factors are particularly important.

(1) The vicious circle that runs from income to wealth and back has in the western industrial nations been mitigated by a long-term trend for property incomes to decline relative to wages, so that a highly skewed distribution of wealth has only limited impact on the distribution of income. The figures given on page 123 of the much greater concentration of wealth than of income in the UK themselves suggest the limited impact of the former on the latter; in fact, property incomes accounted for only about 11 per cent total UK personal incomes in 1970. Historically, this has partly been due to a growing demand for labour relative to supply as the economy develops, bidding up wages relative to other factor rewards. With much under-utilization of labour and rapidly growing labour forces, today's developing countries are, unfortunately, a long way from that situation.

(2) The circle which runs from income to education and back is not very strong. Access to education has become widely diffused in the industrial countries, diminishing the privileges of the rich, raising general levels of skill, productivity and earnings, and narrowing occupational differentials. The same forces are at work in LDCs too, where access to education is much

wider than was the case when the industrial countries were at a comparably early stage of development (although this is far from denying that the rich still have large educational advantages).

(3) The circle which runs from poverty to large families and back is likely to be modified by the increasing economic pressures on poor families to limit the number of children, for reasons given in Chapter 4. There is often a strong demand for family planning services in LDCs and, while the population problem remains extraordinarily acute, we may expect the connection between poverty and very large families to diminish over time.

(4) Differences between earnings in the rural and urban sectors are at the heart of the problems of poverty, inequality and the under-utilization of labour, but here again long-term forces are likely to reduce these. As labour and other resources migrate from the rural economy into towns this should raise marginal productivities in agriculture relative to those in urban work, thus diminishing sectoral inequalities. This type of process has occurred in the industrial countries, although here too population growth may hamper it in today's LDCs.

> **Activity.** Political variables are of decisive importance in determining the feasibility of a 'progressive, employment-creating anti-poverty' campaign. Discuss the feasibility of such a campaign in your own country, using the analytical framework employed above.

Nothing has been said so far about the nature of the alternative strategies which can be adopted in pursuit of 'progressive, employment-creating anti-poverty'. We must now begin to do so because the choice between reform and revolution cannot be decided in abstraction from the political feasibility of the policies that may be pursued. Even the decision to give priority to the anti-poverty objective is not politically neutral, for it may be that it is poverty which most threatens law, political stability and private property, so that anti-poverty measures may command wider support among the well-to-do than an alternative priority on reducing the income share of the rich.

It is useful to distinguish two different lines of approach to anti-poverty policy:

[3] See the essay by Shane Hunt in Ranis, 1971, and also the comments on it by Schydlowsky.

(1) An approach which emphasizes the redistribution of existing wealth and income in favour of the poor. This can be called static redistribution.

(2) An approach which emphasizes an improved distribution of future additions to income and wealth, so that most of the benefits of growth henceforth accrue to the poor. This can be called dynamic redistribution, or redistribution through growth.

> **Key concepts. Static redistribution** refers to the use of taxation and state spending to transfer existing income and wealth from the rich to the poor. **Redistribution through growth** refers to policies designed to ensure that future increments to income and wealth accrue mainly to the poor, thus reducing inequalities over time.

The static approach would use the state's powers of taxation, spending and legislation in order to ensure the absence of extreme income disparities. To achieve major results, it would involve large reductions in the incomes of the rich through high income tax rates, the taxation and/or nationalization of property and the reallocation of government services in favour of the most needy. Obviously, this is a strategy likely to provoke strong resistances from the privileged, who would see they had little to lose from opposition.

The alternative, incremental, approach offers a greater prospect of a non-revolutionary solution. Because it would be sought largely through the improved distribution of the benefits of future growth, rather than through the redistribution of existing resources, it would have an attraction to the 'enlightened' members of the wealthy class. It would provoke less opposition and thus have a better chance of gaining enough political support to put it into action within the framework of the existing political system. This point can be restated in terms of games theory, as deployed in Chapter 2. The static redistribution case is a 'zero sum' game because the gains of the poor must be at the expense of rich – a situation the rich will oppose. The dynamic approach is a 'positive sum' game in which all can win incremental additions to income, although the gains are greater for the poor: an easier situation for the rich to live with.

There is little scope for a general answer to the question, reform or revolution? There are strong forces at work to perpetuate inequality but there are also tendencies in the opposite direction. The possibilities of achieving non-revolutionary improvements from an existing socio-economic

system will depend upon the relative strengths of these opposing tendencies. These will differ from one country to the next and will be influenced by the choice between static redistribution and redistribution through growth. The only general prescription is to repeat the advice that economists ought always to be offering: weigh the costs and benefits of the alternatives before deciding what to do.

Consideration of the costs of the alternatives points away from revolutionary solutions. Revolutions can be relied upon to impose heavy costs, in terms of economic disruption as well as human suffering. It is also generally the case that revolutionaries are much clearer about what they want to destroy than what they want to put in its place. Marx once said that 'Anyone who makes plans for after the revolution is a reactionary'. A revolution based upon that premise is unlikely to yield cost-effective solutions to the problems of this chapter.

But it would indeed be reactionary to deny that sometimes revolution offers the only way out. The 'openness' of the political system is likely to be among the most crucial variables, determining the extent to which it will provide legitimate opportunities for the use of political resources other than wealth, and hence its sensitivity to mass grievances. The time factor will also be crucial. The historical forces at work weakening the vicious circles of inequality are long-term, just as the incrementalist approach to income redistribution can only bring gradual improvements. Where the problems are urgent and there is great pressure to achieve quick results there will be little scope for peaceful, evolutionary and moderate solutions.

The question of *land ownership* may provide the key in countries where this is highly concentrated and there are not large areas of fertile land awaiting settlement. In these circumstances land reform is likely to be an essential ingredient of a successful 'progressive employment-creating anti-poverty' campaign. There will be intense popular pressure for reform but the landowners are liable to be among the most conservative, least enlightened groups in the country. And there will be no question of an incremental approach – existing assets will have to be redistributed, although perhaps gradually. How the interested parties react to this issue may reveal whether poverty can be tackled by reform.

Finally, a choice between reform and revolution will involve many factors other than those just mentioned. Revolutions are advocated for reasons other than poverty and inequality: the absence of personal freedom or security; unpopular foreign and military policies; racial oppression. On the other hand, many hesitate to support revolution because of the death, destruction and misery it may bring – and for fear that a revolt will overthrow one oppressor only to spawn another. Normally, only a small minority actually wants a revolution; most will turn to it only as a last resort, when it is obvious that grievances cannot be remedied through peaceful reform.

Given this general aversion to violent solutions, we turn now to examine in more detail some of the policy options available in the reformist wardrobe, concentrating on the alternatives of static redistribution and redistribution through growth already mentioned.

II.   The Potentials of Static Redistribution

Using both sides of the budget

Past discussions of the use of fiscal means to redistribute incomes traditionally focused on questions of taxation, especially direct taxes. This, however, was a case of mistaken emphasis. All that taxes can do is to take income away – to 'level down' – and it is only through the spending side of budget that the state can positively assist the poor – to 'level up'. There is, moreover, much evidence showing that the tax system is a rather weak redistribution device and that government spending can have a greater impact. In order to discover the effect of the government's budget on the distribution of income it is therefore important to study the incidence not only of taxation but also of government outlays.[4]

> **Key concepts.** The **incidence** of a tax or a state expenditure is its 'final resting place'. This should not be confused with who is legally responsible for paying a tax or with the initial recipient of an expenditure. Taxes on products (e.g. on cigarettes) are often **shifted** to final consumers; and the ultimate beneficiaries of a government service may be quite different from those who are supposed to gain.

Establishing the incidence of taxation and expenditures is, unfortunately, a difficult task, especially on the expenditure side, and few reliable estimates exist for developing countries. Relatively good information is available on the UK, however, and this is an interesting case because it is generally regarded as having progressive direct taxes and a well-developed system of 'welfare state' services.

> **Key concepts. A progressive tax system** is one which taxes an increasing share of income as income rises. **A progressive expenditure pattern** is similarly one whose benefits are inversely related to income, with the poor receiving proportionately more than the well-to-do.

Table 6.1 presents British data relating to a family of two adults and two children, and shows the impact of the tax system and of total welfare benefits by size of original income.

Table 6.1
The Incidence of Taxation and Government Spending in the UK, 1972[a]

Original income[b] (£ p.a.)	Total taxes as % of adjusted income[c] (1)	Total benefits as % of adjusted income[c] (2)	Net balance (2–1) (3)
557–815	25	81	56
816–1193	29	50	21
1194–1748	33	25	−8
1749–2560	33	19	−14
2561–3749	33	14	−19
3750 and above	32	8	−24
Averages	32	18	−14

Source: Economic Trends, November 1973, Table D and E (London, HMSO).
Notes: (a)   The figures in this table relate to a family of two adults and two children. They are derived from a family expenditure survey. The tax estimates relate to all major taxes, direct and indirect. The benefit estimates relate to the incidence of health and education services, housing subsidies and welfare payments (e.g. pensions, unemployment pay, family allowances).
(b)   Income before taxation and before receipt of benefits.
(c)   Income before taxation but after receipt of cash benefits.

The inferences to be drawn from this table are quite typical of what we know about other countries: that the tax system is not strongly redistributive but the distribution of benefits can be quite a powerful weapon. In this specific case, the incidence of taxation is roughly proportional over a wide range of incomes;

---

[4] See Burkhead and Miner, 1971, pp. 327–7, for a brief discussion of the many difficulties involved in determining the incidence of taxes and expenditures.

all those with an original income of £1194 or more were paying roughly a third of this in taxes. Only at the bottom end of the income scale (relating only to about 7 per cent of the total sample of this category of family) was there any progressivity, but even the poorest class were paying a quarter of their incomes in taxes (bear in mind that these figures relate to total taxes, including taxes on commodities).

The provision of government services and welfare benefits had a more potent impact, as can be seen from column (2). For the poorest families, benefits made up no less than 81 per cent of their total incomes (which implies that many in this category were wholly dependent on benefits), with the percentage remaining as high as 50 per cent for those with original income of £816 to £1193; at the other end of the scale, benefits comprised only 8 per cent for those with original incomes of £3750 and above. The net effect of taxes and benefits is given in column (3), which shows a consistently progressive trend (due largely to the progressivity of benefits) but that only the small number of families in the lowest two income classes received benefits greater than the taxes they paid.[5]

It is against this background that we now look separately at the taxation and spending sides of the government budget.

Using the tax system

The chances of effectively using the tax system as a redistributive device depend upon the successful implementation of a structure of taxes in which the actual tax burden falls largely on the relatively rich. This sentence should be read so that the stress falls upon 'implementation' and 'actual burden' and the reason for this is that it is easy to pass an income tax law which is highly progressive on paper but which is largely evaded by upper-income groups. In terms of actual revenue receipts, income taxes are often of secondary importance in developing countries, which generally rely rather heavily upon indirect taxes – taxes on commodities or transactions. This is in contrast to industrial countries where income taxes are mass taxes and often the most important single source of government revenue. The income tax cannot touch the majority of people in any but the most prosperous LDCs because most of people's incomes are too small for it to be either desirable or feasible to tax them at all heavily.

This greater dependence on indirect taxes can be a major obstacle towards the construction of a progressive tax structure because indirect taxes are often regressive, i.e. fall most heavily on the poor. If a tax is levied on a consumption good the amount of tax to be paid is the same for rich and poor purchasers alike. Thus, the reason why the UK tax structure is shown in Table 6.1 as being roughly proportional over the greater part of the income range is that the progressive effects of the income tax are offset by the regressive effects of various indirect taxes.

Indirect taxes are not inevitably regressive, however. Tanzania is a developing country which has a progressive set of indirect taxes.[6] If they are confined to 'luxury' goods and services they will bear most heavily upon the well-to-do and leave the poor largely unaffected. Import duties on consumer goods, for example, are generally progressive because the poor can afford few imported goods while the rich spend a lot on them. But while it is possible to construct a progressive system of indirect taxes, it is difficult in practice. Since the income base for direct taxes is narrow in low-income countries, thus limiting revenues from these sources, the government has little option but to look to indirect taxes to yield the bulk of its revenue requirements. But if indirect taxes are to produce much revenue they must cast their net wide and cannot simply be restricted to items of high-income consumption. So it remains broadly true that systems of indirect taxation tend to be regressive.

If the tax system is to be progressive overall it is mainly upon income taxes that we must pin our hopes. Some income tax structures are indeed highly progressive, with marginal rates of taxation (that proportion of an increment in income payable in tax) rising to 80 per cent or more. There are, however, some severe limitations on what can be achieved by highly progressive structures in LDC conditions. First, the number of people whose incomes are really large is likely to be small relative to the total population; the incomes of the 'middle class' are likely to be too small to bear more than moderate taxation. So a progressive income tax may only much affect a small group relative to the total population and thus can have only a limited impact on overall income distribution.

Secondly, the wealthy are in a strong position to take advantage of tax loopholes (sometimes deliberately inserted for that purpose) or to evade paying the taxes

[5] The table shows that the average family had a *net* tax bill after benefits of 14 per cent of adjusted income. This is due largely to the fact that several major types of government expenditure could not be allocated by recipient in column (2), such as defence and administration. The tax surplus was required to pay for them.
[6] See Huang, 1976, especially Table 3.

they are legally due to pay. They can afford to hire tax specialists to advise them on these matters; they may well be in a position to shift some of their incomes into non-taxable forms, such as company cars and housing, entertainment allowances and capital gains. They may also enjoy enough political protection to keep them out of trouble with the law, or be able to afford the bribes necessary for this purpose. (The payment of a bribe also represents a redistribution of income but it is rare for bribe money to find its way into the pockets of the poor.) Even when they are not corrupt, tax administrations are likely to be undermanned. What is more, the more progressive the tax scale the stronger the likelihood that those most affected will take measures to evade their legal responsibilities, so that introducing an apparently highly progressive tax scale can be self-defeating. This has been the case in India, where the marginal rate of income tax rose to a maximum of nearly 96 per cent but was widely evaded.[7]

Thirdly, highly progressive income and profits taxes can have disincentive effects on saving and investment strong enough to retard the development of the economy. This is because a part of the personal incomes taxed away may otherwise have been saved and made available for productive investment; and because much company investment is self-financed out of retained (after-tax) profits, so the more that is taken by the profits tax the less will be available for direct investment. Although it is difficult to generalize on this matter and much depends on the taxes employed, there is some evidence that taxation does have substantial effects on private-sector saving. A study of twenty African countries, for instance, showed that a $1 increase in tax revenues was associated with an $0·80 reduction in private saving; other studies show the same general tendency.[8] This need not reduce aggregate saving and investment if the government uses the extra resources for capital formation. But the case we are considering here is where the resources would be directly redistributed to the poor, rather than being invested, so the adverse consequences for economic growth could be significant.

These rather pessimistic remarks about the redistributive potential of direct taxation are, unfortunately, borne out by empirical studies of tax incidence. Recall from Table 6.1 that the tax incidence is shown to be roughly proportional for all but the poorest in the UK – a country noted for the progressivity of its income tax. Even the figures in the table probably provide too favourable a picture because of the superior ability of the rich to obtain income in non- or lightly-taxable forms. An American study has shown, for example, that when allowance is made for capital gains and other types of untaxed income the effective rate of income tax is much less on very large incomes than when the rate is computed solely from taxable income. For example,

those with a gross income of $1 million or more were in 1966 paying at an average rate of just over 55 per cent on taxable income but at only 28 per cent when all other forms of income were included.[9] It is not so surprising, then, that another study should have concluded that, overall, the US tax system is essentially proportional for the vast majority of families and thus has little effect on the size distribution of income.[10]

LDC studies point in the same direction. A study of Peru concluded that taxation was roughly proportional to income;[11] the same conclusion was arrived at in respect of Colombia, where progressive direct taxes were offset by regressive indirect taxes.[12] The widespread evasion of the income tax in India has already been mentioned. An African illustration is provided by Kenya, where it was found that, after allowance for evasion, the tax system was probably regressive over a wide range of incomes and that the income tax was paid by only a third of 1 per cent of the total population.[13]

In brief, then, the revealed power of taxation as a redistributive instrument is small. This is not, of course, to say that we should abandon its use; in some countries it is ineffective because there is little political will to give it teeth. One promising type of taxation that has not been mentioned at all is the taxation of land and other forms of wealth; in principle this could be a potent egalitarian device because the accumulation and inheritance of wealth is one of the mechanisms tending to perpetuate inequalities. But here too there are large problems of administration, evasion and political will, and few countries have developed wealth taxes. The general conclusion to draw from these considerations is, therefore, that taxation does have some redistributive potential but it would be naive to expect taxes to make large differences to the distribution of income. Even countries which have tried quite hard to use taxation for this purpose have had limited success.

[7] The 'Wanchoo Report' of the Direct Taxes Committee of Enquiry, India, March 1972, gave high tax rates as 'the first and foremost reason for tax evasion' and recommended reductions.
[8] See Mikesell and Zinser, 1973, pp. 15–17 and the sources quoted there.
[9] Fromm and Taubman, 1973, Table 9.1.
[10] Pechman and Okner, 1975.
[11] Hunt, op. cit.
[12] ILO, 1970.
[13] Westlake, 1973.

Activity. It has been argued in this section that indirect taxes tend to be regressive and that LDCs are rather dependent on revenues from indirect taxes. LDCs with per capita incomes of $100 to $300 derive an average of about 65 per cent of total tax receipts from indirect taxes.[14] Look up the latest figures for your own country and for ten years earlier; then (1) calculate the present share of indirect taxes, (2) compare it with the LDC average just given, (3) look at the trends in the share over the ten-year period, (4) write a brief note on the implications of your results for income distribution.

Using government expenditure powers

The expenditure side of the budget can be approached more optimistically because Table 6.1 has already shown that, in the UK at least, government spending has a rather potent effect on the distribution of purchasing power.

To approach this topic it is useful to distinguish three types of government spending: (1) the provision of goods and services, such as education and health, which raise people's effective living standards in ways which can be measured; (2) the provision of cash benefits, or *transfer payments*, such as pensions and unemployment pay; and (3) other forms of spending which may raise living standards but do so in ways which cannot be allocated among different income groups. Examples of this last category would include defence, justice and general administration – services which are best thought of as being available to all and hence broadly neutral with respect to the distribution of income.

Categories (1) and (2) are the ones to concentrate on here, and it is interesting for these cases to go back to the source of Table 6.1 to gauge their relative importance. Table 6.2 shows the value of major types of allocable expenditures for the average two-adult, two-child British family.

Subsidized educational and health services emerge as the most important items and this is particularly significant because education especially and health to a lesser extent raise worker productivities, thus also promoting the objective of economic growth. However, fuller discussion of the redistributive use of government services is deferred until later.

Although transfer payments are shown to be of secondary importance, they none the less do have significant redistributive potential, not least because they can be geared to identified poverty groups, such as the aged and disabled (through pensions), the unemployed, and those with large families (through family allowances and free school meals). This type of payment is important both in socialist countries and the 'welfare state' systems of western industrial

Table 6.2
Value to a Family of Various Government Payments and Services, 1972

	£ per year	As % of original income
(1) Original income	2 388	100·0
(2) Transfer payments		
(a) family allowances	46	1·9
(b) pensions	7	0·3
(c) others *	79	3·3
(d) Sub-total	132	5·5
(3) Government services		
(a) health service	111	4·6
(b) education	205	8·5
(c) Sub-total	316	13·2
(4) Total all benefits	448	18·8

Source: As for Table 6.1.
Note: *Includes national assistance, unemployment benefits, welfare foods and housing subsidies.

countries. Transfer payments are much less important in LDCs, however, as can be seen in Table 6.3 below. As percentages of both government spending

Table 6.3
The Composition of Government Spending: Selected Regions, 1967

	Africa	Latin America	Asia	Europe and North America
Expenditures as Percentages of GNP:				
Education	3·1	3·2	3·2	4·0
Health	1·4	1·3	1·2	2·8
Defence	1·6	2·3	5·0	3·3
Transfers	3·6	4·1	3·2	16·4
Other	13·0	11·4	7·2	10·7
Total	22·7	22·3	19·8	37·2
As Percentages of Total Expenditures:				
Education	13·7	14·3	16·2	10·8
Health	6·2	5·8	6·1	7·5
Defence	7·0	10·3	25·3	8·9
Transfers	15·9	18·4	16·2	44·1
Other *	57·3	51·1	36·4	28·8
Total	100·0	100·0	100·0	100·0

Source: From an unpublished study by G. S. Sahota quoted by Musgrave and Musgrave, 1976, p. 759.
Note: *Difference between itemized expenditures and total tax revenues.

[14] Chelliah, 1971, Table 6.

and of GNP, transfer payments in Africa, Asia and Latin America are much smaller than in the western industrial nations.

It is easy to understand why. As already mentioned, because they are poor countries, the tax base in LDCs is narrow and there are thus severe constraints on the amount of revenue that can be raised. This explains why total government spending relative to GNP is shown in the upper part of Table 6.3 as only little more than half in the Third World what it is in the industrial countries. Given these constraints and the desire for economic development, only limited resources can be made available for welfare benefits.

Add to this the fact that the potential numbers who might have a claim to such benefits in LDCs is very large relative to the total population, because of widespread poverty, and the great strains that welfare state provisions would place upon public administrations, and it is clear why this type of provision plays only a minor role in the fiscal systems of LDCs. The essential point was well expresssed by the late Kwame Nkrumah:[15]

> The Welfare State is the climax of a highly developed industrialism. To assure its benefits in a less developed country is to promise merely a division of poverty. Undoubtedly there must be an investment of a proportion of the capital reserves in the establishment of minimum wage levels to assure proper diet, as well as minimum health and housing facilities. But poverty is progressively reduced only as productivity progresses and part of its surplus can be made available in increased wages, better housing and generally improved social conditions.

We will return to this point in a moment but before doing so should also mention that even in the countries of western Europe welfare state provisions have not always been very efficient, nor have they succeeded in removing absolute poverty. They have been inefficient because, first, they lack the merit of selectivity described in Chapter 2: they tend to be blanket provisions, often available without regard to need, and so require expenditures far larger than a needs criterion would justify. Secondly, however, it has been found that these provisions often fail to catch those most in need of assistance despite various attempts to reach them.

So far as this kind of expenditure is concerned, then, we are forced to the conclusion that *welfare transfer payments are unlikely to make more than a minor contribution to the reduction of poverty in developing countries.*

Activity. Use your country's fiscal statistics to list the main types of transfer payment made by the government. To what extent are these aimed at poverty groups? Are they likely to make much difference to the distribution of income?

The potential and limitations of static redistribution

For the most part, we have looked at fiscal policy as a way of achieving static redistribution. That is to say, we have concentrated on the potential of taxation for reducing the existing incomes of the rich and of state spending powers to augment the existing incomes of the poor. But recall Chapter 5's conclusion on the sources of poverty, that 'underdevelopment is the chief cause of poverty in developing countries, often aggravated by severe degrees of inequality'. What we have been doing, in other words, is to examine the possible impact of fiscal measures that would affect the secondary source of poverty (unequal income distributions) but would leave the primary cause (underdevelopment) no better than before.

If underdevelopment is the chief reason for poverty this suggests that policies of static redistribution, whether by fiscal or other means, will be only partially effective. The question is, how much of a contribution can we hope that static redistribution will make towards the 'progressive, employment-creating anti-poverty' goal? To explore this we need a specific numerical example. Brazil is one of the few LDCs for which there are tolerably good income statistics but it is too far along the road to development (its average per capita income is over $450) to be a good example for present purposes. India is more important and representative but its income statistics are much weaker. We will therefore take an imaginary LDC which has the population and net national product of India and the income distribution of Brazil. This country is naturally called Brazindia and the results of combining the two sets of data are summarized in Table 6.4.

The object is to explore for this very poor country with a skewed distribution of income the potential benefits of static redistribution. It is now assumed:

(1) That policy measures are taken which reduce the average income of the richest 2 per cent of the population from $741 to $500, or by about a third. This is an optimistic assumption about the power of redistributive measures to effectively reduce the incomes of the rich.
(2) That policy measures are also taken to reduce the average incomes of the next-richest 8 per cent from $252 to $200, or by about a fifth – again optimistic, given the modest income level they start with.
(3) That the revenue gathered in this way is redistributed to the poor in the proportions, three-quarters to the poorest 30 per cent and one-quarter to the next-poorest 30 per cent of the population.

---

[15] Nkrumah, 1972, pp. 105–6.

Table 6.4
Distribution of Income in Brazindia

Segment of population (1)	Numbers (million) (2)	Share of total income (%) (3)	Aggregate income ($ million)* (4)	Per capita income ($) (5)
Poorest 30%	141	8	3 336	24
Next 30%	141	18	7 506	53
Next 30%	141	35	14 595	103
Next 8%	38	23	9 591	252
Richest 2%	9	16	6 672	741
Totals/averages	470	100	41 700	89

Sources: Population and total income figures are based on Indian statistics; the income shares are adapted from Fishlow's Brazilian study (1972), as presented in Table 5.2, page 109.
Note: *Net national product in US dollars.

This again is optimistic in its presumption that government programmes will effectively ensure that the money actually goes to those who need it rather than finding its way back into the pockets of the relatively prosperous, as so often happens.

The results of this exercise are set out in Table 6.5, which compares income shares and per capita incomes before and after redistribution.

The results are instructive. Note first that the redistribution virtually doubles the income share and average incomes of the poorest 30 per cent, whose per capita incomes go up from $24 to $46. Secondly, a more minor improvement is recorded for the next poorest 30 per cent. Thirdly, the income share of the richest 2 per cent is much reduced, with a lesser reduction for the next richest 8 per cent. So static redistribution can effect improvements. *But the poverty problem remains enormous.* The poorest 30 per cent still have an average income below a $50 poverty line and well over 60 per cent have incomes of less than $100. The basic point, of course, is that this is a very poor country, with an average per capita income of below $90, so that what we have been showing is what Nkrumah meant by 'the division of poverty'. Even though income is unequally distributed the richest 2 per cent are not very rich, with an average income before redistribution of $741. This is the truth of the statement that the tax base in LDCs is narrow.

Of course, if we were to start with a less unequal income distribution the potential for static redistribution would be less. For example, assume that the share of the richest 2 per cent of the population is 'only' 12 per cent of total income, and that the next richest 8 per cent receive 18 per cent of incomes. Then, applying the other assumptions as before, there is a much smaller revenue available for redistribution which would only raise the incomes of the poorest 30 per cent by $2·70 and of the next poorest by $0·90.

Table 6.5
Effects of Redistribution in Brazindia*

Segment population	Share of total income (%) Before (1)	After (2)	Per capita income ($) Before (3)	After (4)
Poorest 30%	8	15	24	46
Next 30%	18	20	53	61
Next 30%	35	35	103	103
Next 8%	23	18	252	200
Richest 2%	16	11	741	500
Totals/averages	100	100	89	89

Note: * The 'after redistribution' figures are calculated on the assumptions that taxation will reduce average incomes of the richest 2 per cent to $500 (i.e. by about a third) and of the next richest 8 per cent to an average of $200. The income thus released is assumed to be allocated 75 per cent to the poorest 30 per cent and 25 per cent to the next-poorest 30 percent.

> **Activity.** To test your understanding of this exercise, apply your own set of assumptions to the data in Table 6.4 and substitute your results in the columns of Table 6.5. Consider the implications of your results.

The main conclusion, then, is that *in low-income countries policies of static redistribution cannot solve the problem of poverty. They can, nevertheless, make a valuable contribution to its alleviation, depending on the extent of the initial inequalities and on the effective implementation of progressive fiscal measures.* Note also that this discussion of the uses of fiscal policy has been silent on reducing the amount of labour under-utilization, which is also one of our concerns. Progressive taxation and spending programmes are unlikely, in themselves, to do much to alleviate the employment problem, although there are specific fiscal measures which can contribute, to be discussed shortly.

In countries with low per capita incomes economic growth offers the only fundamental chance of eradicating absolute poverty and the under-utilization of labour. But not just any pattern of economic growth. It has to be a labour-intensive growth path whose benefits are shared in an equitable manner. This brings us to the second approach mentioned earlier, of 'redistribution through growth'.

III. Redistribution Through Growth

A summary statement

The concept of redistribution through growth is more comprehensive than static redistribution because it is a complete strategy of economic development. As such, it is a long-term approach. It seeks to tackle poverty, inequality and unemployment by accelerating (or at least maintaining) the growth of the economy in ways which ensure that increments to assets and output are more equitably distributed, especially to those living in poverty, and which generates as much new productive employment as possible.

What is involved in redistribution through growth? A brief summary is given below, followed by an elaboration of some of its chief features, and some of the difficulties associated with this strategy. The main components of this strategy are as follows:

(1) *Sectoral priorities* which particularly favour the development of smallholder agriculture and the 'informal sector' (which can be roughly defined as consisting of small-scale non-farming activities in the towns and rural areas). As was shown in Chapter 5, most poverty is found among smallholders and the landless in rural areas. It is also common among the underemployed and unemployed of the towns. Smallholder agriculture and the informal sector are labour-intensive, so their development will both generate more employment and raise the productivities (and hence incomes) of those already working in them. Negatively, an only second-order priority is indicated for the expansion of the modern industrial sector (although it is likely to remain important) and for large-scale, plantation-type agricultural ventures.

(2) *Rural development* is a related aspect of the strategy, aimed especially at raising standards in rural communities. It goes beyond the higher priority for smallholder agriculture mentioned in the previous paragraph by approaching the development of the rural economy in an integrated way – seeking to raise output but also the availability of social services and amenities. This involves the co-ordination of programmes for the improvement of agriculture, water, transport and so forth. It is often associated with the *decentralization* of development planning activities. In some countries, *land reform* is an essential ingredient. The basic intention of this thrust of the strategy is to reduce the large urban-rural disparities which were seen in Chapter 5 to be fundamental to the problems of poverty and unemployment.

(3) *Factoral priorities* which favour labour-intensity and employment creation, and economize on the use of capital and foreign exchange. Employment creation programmes are likely to be crucial in assisting rural poverty groups without enough land, and the urban unemployed or underemployed. They are thus likely to be central to any successful attack on the poverty and employment problems. The adoption of more appropriate technologies is crucial to this aspect of the strategy (and is a topic treated in some detail in Chapter 9).

(4) *Population restraint* (discussed in Chapter 4) is another important aspect in countries with rapidly expanding populations, because of the connections between poverty and family size, and between the growth of population and un-employment.

(5) *Poverty groups*. The strategy is selective in that it concentrates on measures to raise the living conditions of precisely identified poverty groups. Poverty is by no means a uniform condition. Its nature differs between town and village and

between different groups within each type of community. Thus, subsistence farmers can be differentiated from the rural landless, with the open urban unemployed and the urban 'working poor' as other separately identifiable groups. The incidence and nature of poverty is also likely to be affected by differing regional conditions. And these groups will differ in the degree of their integration into the national economy and in their links with more well-to-do groups in society. Because of these varying circumstances, a given policy measure will affect poverty groups in differing ways, so precise knowledge of the nature of these groups is essential before we can accurately devise policies to help them.

(6) *Improved access.* Implicit in the above is an aspect that should be made explicit: the strategy emphasizes improved access of poverty groups to goods, services and capital assets provided by the state. Especial emphasis is placed on ensuring that poverty groups obtain better access to good education, health services, piped water and power; and that government capital formation in roads, housing, irrigation, etc., should be designed to reach the poor. Education is seen as of special importance in this context, as will be seen later.

> **Key concept.** A **poverty group** is a group of poor people homogeneous with respect to the effect on them of a given policy measure.

It is evident from this description that redistribution through growth involves state action over a very wide front and the use of many policy instruments. For example, it has far-reaching implications for the design of government service and investments: in on-going

> **Activity.** Which do you think are the main poverty groups in your own society? In what ways might different policies be needed to meet their varying needs?

programmes of education, health, agricultural extension and so on, and in capital expenditures on road, schools, clinics, etc., the activities have to be redesigned so as to focus specifically on the needs of the poor. To go into all the ramifications of this strategy would require a book of its own, so the following pages simply pick out some of its key aspects for fuller treatment. Since they are dealt with in other chapters, the issues of population control and technology policy – both key elements of the strategy – will be neglected in what follows.

Sectoral priorities

The rationale for concentrating development efforts on smallholder agriculture and the informal sector should by now be familiar to you. These are the sectors in which there is the highest incidence of poverty. They are also labour-intensive. There are similarly straightforward reasons for demoting modern industry and large-scale farming down the list of sectoral priorities. Relative to small-scale farming and 'informal' manufacturing, these are capital-intensive sectors, associated with large inequalities. An emphasis on modern industrialization (such as that pursued by many developing countries in the 1960s and into the 1970s) will likely worsen income disparities, divert resources away from the rural poor and increase open unemployment in the towns through the migratory processes analysed by the 'Todaro model' summarized in the last chapter (page 127).

This set of sectoral priorities is often justified by reference to 'employment elasticities' of the type set out in column (3) of Table 6.6 below, which measure the relationship between the growth of output and of employment in the main types of economic activity.

As can be seen from the bottom line, the ratio of total employment growth to total output growth was 0·6. That is to say, about six-tenths of output growth could be attributed to the employment of more labour, with the other four-tenths attributable to higher productivity per worker. However, column (3) shows some striking variations between sectors.

The relative sluggishness of manufacturing as a source of new employment is confirmed by its employment elasticity of only 0·4; more than half the increase in manufacturing output resulted from rising productivities. This, in turn, was most likely a consequence of the capital-intensive methods used in this sector because the amount of capital per worker is the chief influence on labour productivity. More surprisingly, agriculture is also shown as having an elasticity of only 0·4. Agriculture typically employs far more workers per unit of capital than industry but the figures in Table 6.6 suggest that the development of Latin American agriculture followed a strongly capital-intensive path in the 1960s, thus preventing this sector from making a maximum contribution to the solution of the employment problem (or the alleviation of poverty). It is the service activities, in the lower half of the table, which show the largest elasticities. This is consistent with much other evidence showing services to be labour-intensive.

However, care is needed in drawing policy inferences from the type of data presented in Table 6.6. The high elasticity for services, for instance, may be misleading because here there is likely to be a great deal of

Table 6.6
Annual Growth Rates in Employment and Output, by Sector in Latin America, 1960–9 (% p.a.)

	Employment (1)	Output (2)	Elasticity of employment (1) ÷ (2) (3)
Agriculture	1·5	4·0	0·4
Mining	2·2	4·2	0·5
Manufacturing	2·3	5·9	0·4
Construction	4·0	5·0	0·8
Transport and public utilities	3·4	5·4	0·6
Commerce and finance	4·1	5·1	0·8
Miscellaneous services	4·0	3·9	1·0
Unspecified (services)	8·2	7·3	1·1
Aggregate employment and output	2·8	4·8	0·6

Source: Economic Survey of Latin America 1968 (New York, United Nations, 1970), Tables 1-22 and 1-23. Reproduced from Edwards, 1974, Table 3.

underemployment. To some extent, the service industries are 'employers of last resort' – industries into which people drift if they cannot find satisfactory work elsewhere. A policy inference from the high elasticities to the effect that service industries should be encouraged would be dangerous if the figures were strongly influenced by the existence of underemployment.

Care should also be taken in drawing negative conclusions about the employment potential of manufacturing. The figures presented in Table 6.6 only measure the 'impact' effects of the various sectors. The elasticities are simply ratios of employment growth to output growth in each sector. As such, they fail to reflect the linkages between sectors, or the indirect effects. Manufacturing has particularly strong linkages with the rest of the economy so that, while industrialization may have only a limited direct impact on employment, it may sufficiently stimulate the growth of other sectors as to have major indirect effects on the total availability of work. Input-output analysis is a planning technique used to measure the indirect as well as direct effects of changes in any one sector; quite often the total effects differ substantially from the impact effects.[16]

So while there is no reason to disagree with the main sectoral thrust of redistribution through growth, there are grounds for being careful about drawing policy inferences from unsophisticated indicators like those in column (3) of Table 6.6 and for drawing excessively negative conclusions about the potentials of industrialization.

Once the priorities have been determined, there is the selection of policy instruments to implement these priorities. A variety of instruments are available for governments wishing to influence sectoral growth rates, some of which are described more fully below

under the heading of rural development. The government can use its own spending powers to exert influence, especially in the provision of extension and other economic services, and in its decisions about the provision of power, water, roads and other infrastructural investments.

In its decisions about taxation, the provision of protection against overseas investment, its control of agricultural and industrial prices, its provision of subsidies, and its wage policies, the government can exert a large influence on the structure of costs and final prices in the economy and hence on the system of incentives to investors. As a negative example of the ways in which a government can influence the growth of a sector, Chapter 9 (pages 241–2) elaborates a variety of ways in which policies have often discriminated against agriculture.

Rural development and land reform

Rural development programmes feature as an essential ingredient of redistribution through growth. It is intended to create new productive employment and also raise the productivity of the labour that is already employed in agriculture. Both are necessary. Greater labour absorption is necessary for the solution of the employment problem; improved productivities (and hence incomes) from those already engaged are essential in order to tackle the chief source of rural poverty. For both purposes, measures to reduce the often extreme seasonality in the demand for agricultural labour are essential.

[16] See Hirschman, 1958, for an advocacy of industrialization because of its superior linkages. O'Connor and Henry, 1975, offer a good introduction to the uses of input-output analysis.

As mentioned earlier, however, rural development is not synonymous with attempts to raise agricultural output. It looks beyond the productive system and concerns itself also with the infrastructure and amenities available in rural areas. The objective, therefore, is to effect a simultaneous improvement in farm incomes and in rural amenities, to raise rural living standards and reduce the worst contrasts between town and country.

At their most ambitious, rural development policies offer comprehensive, integrated programmes throughout the entire rural economy. But more limited (and therefore more practicable) versions are available. The government can choose to offer a comprehensive package of measures to some selected region or settlement scheme. Or it can offer a 'minimum package' of government services and investments, either nationally or regionally, in the hope that this will lead to a self-sustaining growth process. Or again the government can concentrate on programmes aimed to meet some more narrowly defined need, such as the provision of training, or credit or irrigation.

Rural development obviously depends on the development of agriculture. A good deal is said about how to do this in Chapter 9 and will not be repeated here. But in its most characteristic forms rural development programmes contain large non-agricultural components as well. These may include provision for improvements in transportation and marketing facilities; the encouragement of rural industries based on the processing of local produce; provision of piped domestic water supplies and electricity; improved housing and so forth. Public works projects may be a particularly important component. These would employ under-utilized labour for the construction of feeder roads, irrigation works, village schools and clinics, and other labour-intensive investments in rural infrastructure. The special merit of this type of public works project is that it can (in principle) be timed for the slack agricultural periods, when there is little demand for labour on the farms. Valuable assets can be created by means that utilize seasonal labour surpluses and minimize the expenditure of investible funds and foreign exchange. The employment so created should be particularly valuable to the landless and other rural poverty groups, who should be given priority in the allocation of such jobs.

Attempts to raise economic standards in rural communities may, however, be frustrated by prevailing social conditions. Systems of land ownership and tenure are often of critical importance. There is little scope for effective rural development in societies still based on semi-feudal landlord-tenant relationships, in which tenant-farmers are exploited by their landlords,

for example by being forced to hand over a large proportion of their output as rent. Nor will the situation be much better where there is a high concentration of land ownership in a small number of hands, with these large farms cultivated by mechanized methods which create few employment opportunities and which give rise to a large class of landless and underemployed farm labourers.

Land reforms which break up large farms into smaller units and which improve the rights of tenant-farmers are twice-blessed: they increase the demand for labour via a shift to more intensive, labour-using cultivation and they redistribute assets to the rural poor. Both the poverty and underemployment problems are alleviated. To be effective, however, land reforms need to be carefully designed if they are to provide maximum benefit to poverty groups:[17]

> Equity-oriented land reform should be so programmed that (i) the effective ceiling on size of holding is low; (ii) the beneficiaries belong to the poorest group; (iii) the extension and (non-land) input distribution system favours the beneficiaries; and (iv) owned and self-operated land, as well as leased land, is redistributed.

Moreover, land reform must be accompanied by the provision of extension advice, credit, marketing facilities and other inputs into the agricultural system if it is to be effective and if it is not to result in large losses of output.

What has just been said of land reform applies generally to rural development programmes: they have to be specifically designed to reach the poverty groups for whom they are intended. Unless that is done, there is the ever-present danger that the already well-to-do and influential members of rural society will be able to appropriate many of the benefits for themselves. A decentralization of planning is commonly advocated as a means of safeguarding against this:[18]

> Ideally, the planning and implementation of rural development programmes involve adequate regional planning, strong central coordination, effective local level organisation and the participation of the rural people in the planning and implementation process.

Decentralized planning is not only seen as likely to be more sensitive to the needs of the poor but also because the conception of integrated rural development cuts across departmental boundaries – agriculture, transport, health, education – and a non-departmental agency is therefore needed to coordinate these varied activities at the local level.

[17] World Bank, 1975, p. 200.
[18] Ibid, p. 6.

Factor proportions and prices

The last pages of Chapter 5 referred to the existence of distortions in the prices of labour and capital which encouraged the use of capital-intensive methods and thus deepened the employment problem. Redistribution through growth, on the other hand, is designed as a labour-intensive development strategy. Partly the labour intensity is to be achieved by placing priority on the expansion of the more labour-using sectors of production, as already discussed. But partly it is to be achieved through a shift within industries to production methods which make greater use of unskilled and semi-skilled labour.

The development and adoption of more 'appropriate technologies' is central to this part of the strategy and is a subject dealt with at length in Chapter 9. But many economists would argue that the pursuit of labour-intensity is futile while factor prices remain artificially biased *against* the use of labour. Policy changes are therefore urged which would at least get rid of the distortions and which might go further to introduce a 'reverse distortion' in favour of the employment of unskilled labour, in the interests of reducing the unemployment and poverty problems.

> **Activity.** You may wish to refresh your memory at this point on the description of factor price distortions on page 128–9.

Examples of the type of policy change commonly advocated in this connection are:

(1) Depreciating the rate at which the national currency exchanges for foreign currencies. This raises the domestic price of imported capital equipment – an important consideration since most developing countries import a large proportion of their capital goods.
(2) Financial reforms which would raise interest rates and improve the efficiency of the capital market. The underlying belief here is that the cost of capital in the organized part of the capital market is too low to reflect its true scarcity value in the economy, so this too encourages the use of capital-intensive methods.
(3) Incomes policies designed to prevent formal-sector wage levels from being raised by institutional factors to levels well above the true economic value of unskilled labour. This involves attention to the government's own pay policies, its policies towards the trade unions, towards multinational corporations and towards minimum wage legislation.

(4) The provision of a government subsidy on the employment of labour, or levying a penal tax on the employment of capital.

The theoretical justification for these attempts to affect the volume of employment by altering relative factor prices is derived from standard neo-classical production theory. This rests on the assumption that a firm is faced with a range of alternative methods for producing a given output and that it will choose a production technique that incorporates a profit-maximizing mix of the factors of production. Reducing the price of labour relative to capital will, therefore, induce a shift towards production techniques which use more labour, thus generating more employment. The point is illustrated in Figure 6.1 below.

Figure 6.1 *The influence of factor prices on employment.*

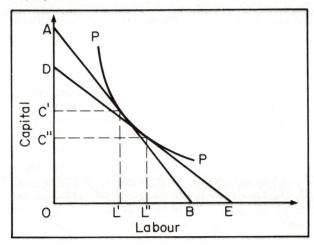

Figure 6.1 introduces what is known as an isoquant map, with which you are likely to be already familiar. This simplified presentation assumes only two factors of production, capital and labour, quantities of which are measured along the axes. The curve PP – called an isoquant – describes the production function of a producer by showing all the possible combinations of labour and capital which he can use in order to achieve a given level of output. The diagonal line AB – called an isocost curve – tells us the relative prices of labour and capital, showing how much labour or capital can be purchased for a given total expenditure. For a given expenditure, it would be possible to hire OA of capital and no labour, or OB of labour and no capital, or any combination of labour and capital between these extremes, reading off the diagonal.

The producer is assumed to run his business so as to maximize his profits. He will therefore choose that combination of factors which minimizes the cost of producing his chosen level of output. Geometrically, this state is achieved at the point of tangency between the price line and the isoquant. In Figure 6.1 profits are maximized, given the relative factor prices of line AB, with the employment of OC′ of capital and OL′ of labour.

Assume now that the government acts to raise the price of capital and lower wages. A new price line is needed to reflect this change in relativities. This is portrayed by the line DE. It is now possible to hire less capital but more labour with a given expenditure than was the case with the AB line. With the DE line profits are maximized with a different combination of labour and capital, specifically with OC″ capital and OL″ labour. New employment has been created; there has been a shift away from the use of capital. The magnitude of this change in factor proportions in response to a change in factor price relativities is called the 'elasticity of substitution'. Geometrically, it is given by the slope at any given point of the PP curve.

> **Key concept.** The **elasticity of substitution** measures the proportionate change in the capital-labour ratio in response to a given change in the ratio of the price of labour to the price of capital.

The most favourable case is when the elasticity of substitution is 'large', e.g. greater than 1·0, because then a given lowering in the relative cost of labour will induce a large proportionate creation of new jobs. This condition is most likely to be met when there is a wide range of known alternative methods of production for producers to choose between.

Not all economists are persuaded by the neo-classical school, however. Some have suggested that there may be only a single known technique of production, rather than the smooth continuum of possibilities implied by the PP isoquant. If there is only one method of production the factor proportions will be technically determined and altering factor prices will have no influence on employment. In other words, there is a zero elasticity of substitution.

This is a rather extreme possibility, however, because it is unlikely that the entire production process, from beginning to end, will be technically determined. Even if there is only one known core technique there are still likely to be choices available, for example, in the rate at which the capital equipment is utilized and in the handling of materials

and products. In fact, a very unlikely set of conditions has to be assumed for factor prices to exert no influence on factor proportions.[19]

A more defensible – and more commonly adopted – position, therefore, rests upon 'elasticity pessimism'. The argument here is that, although the elasticity of substitution is likely to have some positive value, it may none the less have only a small value. If this were the case, it would take a large relative reduction in wages to achieve a small increase in employment. This, in turn, would be liable to worsen the distribution of income. Because the proportionate fall in wages would be larger than the proportionate increase in employment, there would be a net reduction in total wage payments; the share of wages in the national income would go down, with a corresponding increase in the share of property incomes. For reasons given in Chapter 5 (page 108), this change in the functional distribution of income is likely to worsen the size distribution of income.

The 'elasticity pessimist' school of thought stresses that, even if there is a range of known alternative techniques, changes in factor prices can only be expected to have a large impact on factor proportions employed in new investment. There is bound to be only limited scope for changing factor proportions in plant which is already installed, producing an already specified product. Nevertheless, there will be some scope, depending on how the plant is run. For example, the ratio of workers to fixed capital can be roughly doubled by changing from single-shift to two-shift operation (always assuming there is a market for the additional output). There is also likely to be scope for the substitution of labour for equipment in ancillary operations such as materials handling (fork-lift trucks versus manual handling) and packaging (machine versus hand packaging). It may also be possible to alter the intensity with which equipment is utilized by varying the number of workers per machine.

The dispute between the pessimists and the optimists is about a factual matter: the size of elasticities of substitution in developing countries. Since this is a measurable concept, it ought to be possible to settle the dispute by simple reference to the facts. Unfortunately, however, different investigators come up with markedly different results. One study of nineteen different manufacturing industries in three LDCs arrived at pessimistic results, with an overall average elasticity of 0·77 and with no industry having an elasticity of greater than 1·0.[20] A Brazilian study, on the other hand, obtained elasticity values for

---

[19] See Winston, 1974.
[20] Chetty quoted in Kelley, *et al.*, 1972, Table 6.12.

manufacturing varying between 0·44 and 2·67, with an overall average of exactly 1·0, and estimated that the elimination of factor price distortions would raise the total employment of unskilled workers in manufacturing by 24 per cent.[21] Yet another study, of six industries in ten countries (five of them LDCs), concluded that there was considerable scope for factor substitution in all but one of the industries, with an overall average elasticity of 1·7.[22]

There is, of course, every reason to believe that elasticities will vary between industries, because the available range of technical alternatives will differ according to the product. But the problem goes deeper. Although the elasticity of substitution is measurable in principle, there are formidable practical obstacles in the way of obtaining accurate, unbiased results. The magnitudes of results are as likely to be determined by the methodology employed as by the technical data of the industry under study; even slight variations in concepts employed, or in the period over which measurement is attempted, produce markedly different conclusions.[23] Note also that practically all empirical researches in developing countries have been confined to manufacturing; we know little about factor substitutability in agriculture and the various service industries. So an appeal to the facts does not settle the dispute between pessimists and optimists.

What policy inferences can be drawn from this inconclusive discussion? Three are suggested: (1) Factor prices do matter, do influence production methods. (2) Some additional employment can be created by holding down (or subsidizing) wages, raising the cost of capital, or some combination of the two. (3) But a policy of holding the cost of labour down relative to capital, could worsen the size distribution of income (by reducing the share of wages in national income), depending on the magnitudes of substitution elasticities. If elasticities are generally small there may, therefore, be a trade-off between employment creation and reduced inequality. This is an area of policy in which caution is needed. A wage subsidy financed by progressive taxation could, in principle, minimize this trade-off because it would not require any reduction in wages paid and the burden would fall mainly on the well-to-do. But in reality the large revenue burden imposed by a wage subsidy is likely to rule it out as a practical matter.

> **Activity**. Is it possible to specify your own government's policy towards relative factor prices? If so, do you think these are conducive to the solution of the employment and inequality problems?

Some other aspects

One of the most venerable debates in development economics has centred round the question whether countries are best advised to follow inward-looking policies which emphasize self-sufficiency and import substitution or outward-looking policies designed to maximize gains from world trade and payments, especially by encouraging exports. No clear position has been taken in this debate by the advocates of redistribution through growth but evidence is accumulating that the outward-looking alternative, based on the exportation of labour-intensive goods, is more harmonious with the strategy.

Countries often cited as having successfully combined rapid and equitable growth – Taiwan and Korea – have certainly pursued an export-led growth path and have achieved remarkable rates of expansion in export industries which provide employment to many unskilled and semi-skilled workers. The results of a variety of empirical studies of the employment-creating potentials of alternative industrial policies have clearly suggested that an export-oriented strategy is to be preferred by this criterion.[24] The policy task here, then, is to devise measures to help domestic producers to be competitive on world markets, which is among the subjects taken up in Chapter 8.

Other chapters contain policy recommendations which also harmonize with redistribution through growth. Chapter 7 suggests, for example, that inflation is more likely than not to worsen income inequalities. Effective anti-inflation policies, discussed in that chapter, could thus be viewed as being a desirable component of redistribution through growth. Similarly, Chapter 10 shows that concentrations of monopoly power in the industrial sector worsen inequalities, so that the anti-monopoly measures outlined there could also be seen as reinforcing the pursuit of greater social justice.

Another point that needs clarification is the relationship between policies of static redistribution, reviewed in Part II of this chapter, and dynamic redistribution, or redistribution through growth. They have been presented as alternative approaches but this over-draws the choice to be made. A better appreciation can be obtained if we ask the question, from whom are the resources to come to launch the large development effort implied by redistribution through growth? So far as domestic resources are

[21] Tyler, 1974.
[22] Pack, 1974. See also Pack, 1976.
[23] Morawetz, 1974, pp. 515–16.
[24] Morawetz, 1974, pp. 309–10 summarizes the findings of some of these studies.

concerned, the answer must be that, if the main objectives are to reduce poverty and improve distribution, it is the well-to-do who must bear the main burden. In other words, a progressive system of taxation is needed, just as it is in the case of static redistribution. The main difference concerns the way in which the revenue raised from this system is employed. With static redistribution more emphasis is placed on direct transfers to the poor through welfare services; in the dynamic version the main thrust is on using the resources to promote economic growth, but of a type that will primarily benefit the poor.

The impossibility of drawing a sharp dividing line between the static and dynamic versions is quite clear when we consider the use of land reform. It was stated earlier that land reform is an essential ingredient of redistribution through growth in countries with large concentrations of land ownership or exploitative landlord-tenant relationships. But land reform is a classic instrument of *static* redistribution: it takes assets from the wealthy and redistributes them to the poor.

It would be quite wrong, therefore, to interpret Part II as suggesting that static measures have nothing to contribute: they are essential ingredients . . . but unlikely to be sufficient by themselves.

A final point to be made about the policies discussed above is that they are a package of measures, designed to reinforce one another. This is why we have been describing redistribution through growth as a strategy. A strategy was defined in Chapter 3 as 'a package of specific policies, directed at large issues and at major economic variables, and intended to operate over a relatively long time-span' (page 60). The impact of the various measures taken together is likely to be greater than the impact of each of the measures taken singly – the whole is greater than the sum of the parts. Indeed, implementing just parts of it while neglecting the rest may actually worsen the problems rather than improve them. However, this 'strategic' quality of redistribution through growth also creates some difficulties, to which we will return shortly.

A note on the 'basic needs' approach

It is quite likely that you have seen or heard reference to a 'basic needs' strategy of development and are wondering how this relates to redistribution through growth. The quick answer is that it is very similar but that there are a few differences between the two.

One such difference is the emphasis placed on a definition of absolute poverty which is related to the satisfaction of a minimum core of basic needs.

Proponents of the basic needs approach tend to be more confident than most others that it is possible to measure basic needs in a satisfactory and agreed way, and that these measurements can then be used as a basis for setting targets for the alleviation of poverty. These basic needs refer both to private consumption levels and the provision of public services. The conception of these needs, however, is sometimes pushed beyond the confines that economists generally work within, to include non-material aspects, such as the quality of life and the observance of human rights.

A second difference from the redistribution through growth approach is the degree of emphasis placed on the participation of the mass of the people in decisions and actions which affect their welfare. It calls for the creation of institutions which facilitate popular participation in development, in order to ensure a continuing national commitment to the alleviation of poverty; it suggests that the poverty groups themselves should contribute to decisions about what their basic needs are. In many countries, this thrust of the strategy is towards greater democracy.

Aside from these aspects, the basic needs approach pursues similar objectives as redistribution through growth and by similar means.[25] The reader will not go far astray if he treats the two as identical for most purposes.

IV. Some Difficulties

Redistribution through growth is a seductive concept. It appears to offer rather painless solutions to very painful problems. It seems to suggest that we can pursue effective measures to tackle the poverty, inequality and employment problems while still maintaining the momentum of economic growth. Indeed, sustained growth is essential to the success of the strategy. But in this, as in other areas of life, we should be wary about allowing ourselves to be seduced. There is a danger that the attractions of the seducer will blind us to some blemishes. In particular, there is a danger that we may fail to see some potential inner contradictions in the strategy.

One of these has already been mentioned, in the warning (page 147) of the possibility that the manipulation of factor prices to promote employment could actually worsen the distribution of income. Now take another instance in which the

---

[25] The most authoritative statement of the basic needs approach is in the ILO, 1976. To satisfy yourself about the similarity of the two approaches, see their summary on p. 68.

employment and distributional objectives may conflict with one another, this time relating to the provision of education.

Should education be expanded?

A number of distinguished and concerned writers have noted the rapid expansion of education in many developing countries during the past two or three decades and have advised against a continuation of this trend. This is partly because education is swallowing up an increasingly large proportion of government revenues and competing heavily with other desirable resource uses. A more specific argument for restraint, however, is that educational expansion contributes to the unemployment problem:[26]

> Indiscriminate and costly education expansion will lead to further migration and unemployment ... From the viewpoint of educational policy, it is safe to predict that as job opportunities become scarce in relation to the number of applicants, students will experience increasing pressure to proceed further up the educational ladder. The private demand for education, which in many ways is a 'derived demand' for urban jobs, will continue to exert tremendous pressure on governments to invest in post-primary school facilities. But for many of these students the spectre of joining the ranks of the 'educated unemployed' becomes more of a reality with each passing year. Government over-investment in post-primary educational facilities often turns out to be an investment in idle human resources. This is not only bad economics: in the long run it is also likely to be bad politics ...

In similar vein, another writer, studying the problem of educated unemployed in India, has urged that there is an 'overwhelming' case for cutting back on the growth of secondary and university education in that country.[27]

Against this school of thought, which is largely concerned with the impact of education on unemployment, we must set the findings of other researchers who have found a strong connection between the spread of education and the reduction of income inequalities.[28] Indeed, this is one of the main explanations of why the U-curve of Figure 5.3 (page 113) begins to rise as development proceeds.

Education raises productivities. It thus makes it easier for the poor to raise their living standards, for example by raising their understanding of, and receptivity to, improved cultivation techniques. Recall, in this context, the finding in Chapter 5 that the incidence of poverty is strongly correlated with illiteracy. Moreover, if more and more educated manpower comes on to the labour market, exceeding

the demand for this labour at existing wage levels, this will erode the often very large pay differentials between professional, skilled and unskilled workers. The highly trained will no longer command such a scarcity premium, the gap between their pay and the pay of the unskilled will narrow and inequalities within the wage labour force will diminish. The diffusion of education is also likely to have a more general democratizing effect, reducing the monopoly of an elite in its access to advanced training and making it more difficult, therefore, for the elite to maintain its dominance. Considerations of this type led one major study to conclude that the provision of education is one of the two most effective policies for improving the distribution of income in LDCs:[29]

> Of the variables of greatest significance in this analysis, the most reliable for increasing the quality of income distribution appear to be the rate of improvement in human resources and direct government economic activity. Increased access to the acquisition of middle-level skills and professional training appears, from our results, to be quite predictable in equalising effects on the income distribution.

So here we have two starkly opposed points of view, one derived from a primary concern with unemployment, the other from a concern with inequality. Each point of view is perfectly reasonable given the standpoint from which it is offered. What is implied is a necessity to choose between less unemployment and less inequality. This is why it is important to have clearly defined priorities between the objectives of reducing poverty, inequality and unemployment. The general standpoint of this chapter is to give priority to reduced poverty, which suggests that education should continue to expand within the limits of available resources.

Activity. A class discussion, or essay, is suggested on the desirability of rapid educational expansion in your own country.

Does redistribution conflict with growth?

This chapter and the last have placed stress on the importance of economic growth as the only possible long-term solution to the problems of absolute

[26] From Todaro, 1977, p. 223.
[27] Mark Blaug in Jolly, et al., 1973, p. 210.
[28] Researchers who have come to this conclusion include Ahluwalia, 1976; Tinbergen, 1975; Adelman and Morris, 1973.
[29] Adelman and Morris, 1973, p. 184.

poverty and labour under-utilization. One of the greatest merits of the redistribution through growth strategy is that it is built on a recognition of this fact. But the question poses itself, won't the shift of relative incomes and resources in favour of the poor slow down the rate of growth? On this subject too there is much disagreement.

The unease of those who suspect that there may be a trade-off between equity and growth stems from a suspicion that if a government were choosing policies that would maximize the growth of the economy it would end up with substantially different instruments than if its primary concern was to select policies for the alleviation of poverty. Serious possibilities of conflict between the objective of equity and the growth that is seen as an essential means of equity arise in two areas: (1) relating to the quantity of saving and investment, and (2) relating to the productivity of the factors of the production.

The quantity of saving and investment

The main body of economic theory, as well as our own common sense, tells us that the rich are likely to save more, relative to their incomes, than the poor. Redistribution through growth, however, seeks to reduce the share of the rich in national income, both through a fairer distribution of the benefits of economic expansion and also through progressive taxation that places the main burden of financing the development effort on the wealthy. Relative to national income and absolutely because of progressive taxes, the rich will have smaller after-tax incomes out of which to do their saving. Hence it is feared that there will be an adverse effect on the total amount of domestic saving. Other things being equal, this will also reduce the amount of investment and the economy's rate of expansion.

The opposing school of thought is inclined to reject the validity of western economic theory in this context, and believes that in LDCs the rich are not particularly high savers. They are accused rather of indulging in 'conspicuous consumption'; the effect of extended family obligations may also reduce their propensity to save. Even if the rich in LDCs do save more, some of this saving is likely to be sent abroad into unnumbered Swiss bank accounts and the like (and is therefore not available to finance domestic investment) or is invested in unproductive forms, such as gold, jewellery and urban housing.

This is another of those disputes which it ought to be possible to settle by reference to evidence (although there is no reason for expecting to get the same answer for all developing countries – the rich are less spendthrift in some societies than others), but on which there is no conclusive evidence. There is evidence that the amount of saving goes up with income but it is not clear whether this is also true of the proportion of income saved.[30] Data on household income and saving are too weak for any strong conclusions to be drawn at this stage. The possibility of a trade-off is certain but we cannot yet say anything general about its probability.

Domestic saving is not the only source of investible funds. In most developing countries there is also a net inflow of funds from the rest of the world, in the forms of government-to-government aid and from foreign private investors. Inflows of foreign private capital may also pose a problem within the redistribution through growth strategy. The existence of large investments by multinational corporations in LDC economies may itself be a source of inequality, for a number of reasons. First, the LDC subsidiaries of these corporations are likely to possess considerable monopoly powers which increase inequalities (see Chapter 10). Secondly, the expatriates brought in to run these enterprises will receive large salaries and fringe benefits to attract them to work abroad; their incomes will be enormously greater than the incomes of all but a small number of indigenous people. Thirdly, in some countries an informal alliance exists between the managements of multinational subsidiaries and a local ruling elite. The multinationals depend on the ruling elite for tax concessions, licences, protection against foreign competition, labour permits for foreign personnel and so forth. Ministers, senior officials and their friends will, in turn, look to the multinationals for directorships, jobs, bribes or other favours. So even if we are only concerned with income distribution among the indigenous population, the existence of multinational investments may buttress an unjust system.

The dilemma posed here is that foreign private investments raise total capital formation and thus contribute to economic growth, even though they are also liable to be associated with inequality. Counter-measures to avoid the inequities associated with foreign investment may also frighten this capital away and reduce economic growth.

The productivity of the factors

There are a number of ways in which redistribution through growth could reduce the productivity of the factors of production, the volume of output and the rate of economic expansion. Take first the productivity of *capital*. There is a general presumption that redistribution through growth

---

[30] See Mikesell and Zinser, 1973.

should raise the productivity of capital by shifting resources into labour-intensive activities (where the productivity of capital is generally high). But there will be other forces pulling in the opposite direction. This strategy requires that investment resources be redirected in favour of poverty groups. This means increased allocations to assist smallholder farmers, to the urban and rural informal sector and to backward regions. Such a reallocation of resources is obviously desirable from the equity point of view but it is liable to impose an economic cost.

Smallholder farmers, because of their large numbers and their relative 'backwardness', are difficult to reach effectively with education, roads, water, extension services and so on. As contrasted with a strategy that concentrates on the larger, more 'progressive' farmers, the more prosperous regions, and the better organized formal sector, a redirection of resources in favour of the poor is likely to produce lower rates of return, at least in the medium term. Take the case of the urban informal sector. Not very much is yet known about its nature, problems and potential, nor about how best to help it. Many are doubtful whether this is a sector with much potential for development. But the strategy calls for a much larger allocation of resources to this type of activity. Since they are bound to be somewhat experimental, attempts to help this sector will inevitably result in some failures and the overall productivity of resources devoted to the development of this sector may be low.

Then there is the productivity of *land*. A shift of emphasis in favour of smallholders can achieve large results. Many of them presently use only traditional methods so there are large gains to be achieved from the application of modern knowledge to their cultivation techniques. But to successfully improve their techniques, especially by means that will not reduce the rural demand for labour, is no simple matter, as is shown in Chapter 9. In this area too a substantial proportion of failures must be expected in the medium term.

The introduction of land reforms provides an even stronger example. A land reform, being a change in the whole mode of production, injects a major disruption into the agricultural economy. However desirable it may be on equity grounds, it must generally be expected to result in an initial fall in output. There are contrary examples of reforms which have stimulated output immediately but they are the exceptions. Realistically, most land reforms must be expected to result in a medium-term loss of output and thus in reduced economic growth.

Finally, there is the productivity of *labour*. Going back to the discussion of Table 6.6 (page 143), one of the major thrusts of the strategy is to give priority to the sectors with the larger employment elasticities. But the opposite side of that coin, as was shown, is that the sectors with the largest employment elasticities are the sectors with the weakest record on improving labour productivity. A sector with an elasticity of, say, 0·9 is a sector in which productivity growth contributes only one-tenth of total output growth.

Historically, however, much of modern economic growth has resulted from rising productivities. It is even possible that by concentrating on the sectors with the lower productivity growth we will hamper the long-run expansion of employment. The demand for labour within an industry is strongly influenced by trends in the productivity of labour. When productivity rises relative to the wage rate it pays a firm to employ more; one of the findings of industrial economics is that firms which are most successful in raising productivities are also the ones with the more rapidly expanding labour forces. So by concentrating on the sectors with the highest employment elasticities we could be hampering the expansion of total output and even the long-run growth of employment itself. Against this danger, however, we must set the gains in labour productivity that will be achieved if the strategy is successful in reducing the under-utilization of labour.

This outline of the various ways in which equity objectives may conflict with a desire for rapid economic growth has been deliberately one-sided. To redress the balance, we should note also that redistribution through growth is liable to improve the balance of payments, because the poor spend a smaller proportion of their incomes on imports than the rich. For countries which are held back by foreign exchange shortages, this may result in an increase in growth. Or if we begin to improve the health, nutrition and education of the under-privileged we are likely also to raise their productivities. The under-utilization of labour has been viewed here as a problem but it can also be viewed as an opportunity – a valuable resource capable of contributing more to the national product than it actually does.

Note also that several of the potential trade-offs described above tend to disappear with time. This is true of land reform, for instance, where there is likely to be a substantial long-run increase in output to set against the initial disruption in production.

Again, it would be wrong to form a judgement without considering the policy framework of redistribution through growth. The merit of warning of the possibility of contradictions within redistribution through growth is that it may stimulate governments and their advisers to take care to select policies which minimize the risk of trade-offs. For example, progressive taxation will tend to discourage private saving. But some types of taxes have stronger disincentive effects than others. Indirect taxes and some taxes on wealth have weaker disincentive effects than income taxes, for example.[31] So a carefully designed tax system can reduce the danger that redistribution will reduce the amount of saving and investment. Similarly with the shift in favour of smallholder agriculture and land reform: careful planning can safeguard against the dangers of output losses. It is in *poorly conceived* rural development and land reform where equity and growth are most strongly in conflict.

Technology policy offers especial promise as an instrument for the avoidance of equity-growth conflicts. The development of more appropriate technologies would increase the possibilities of effectively aiding the small farmers and the informal sector without the productivity losses referred to earlier. The availability and knowledge of more labour-intensive techniques of industrial production could increase the elasticities of substitution and so minimize the risk that manipulating factor prices to encourage employment would worsen the distribution of income.

So while there are *potential* conflicts between the desire for greater equity and for economic growth, such conflicts are not *inevitable*. If the danger is recognized policy measures can be selected to avert it. There is no strong evidence one way or the other on whether developing countries with improving equity situations experience difficulties in maintaining satisfactory growth rates. There are certainly specific examples of countries which have been successful in combining improvements in income distribution with rapid growth, as with the oft-cited cases of Taiwan and Korea.

Even if some slowing of economic growth were an inevitable result of the pursuit of equity objectives, it would be open for us to say that some reduction in growth is a price we are willing to pay. The pace at which the incomes of the poor go up is arguably more important than the rate of growth of average per capita income, which average is strongly influenced by what happens to the incomes of the richest 20 per cent.[32]

Problems of adequacy and implementation

Assuming it is possible to devise an internally consistent strategy of redistribution through growth which resolves the problems referred to in the last few pages, this does not dispose of all the difficulties associated with this strategy. There remain questions about the speed with which it can produce results, the adequacy of its policy instruments, and its administrative feasibility.

Can the strategy work fast enough?

Attempts to improve the poverty, inequality and employment problems are hemmed in by severe limiting factors which can only be expected to change slowly within the reformist context adopted in this chapter: the rate of population growth; the physical and technical characteristics of production; institutional and manpower capabilities; the ownership and management of resources; the international environment; the internal structure of economic and political power. In the face of these constraints, it should at least not be taken for granted that the strategy will produce results rapidly enough to satisfy local opinion. It is an incremental strategy, achieving its results principally by an improved distribution of the benefits of future growth. Even if growth is reasonably rapid it may take many years before absolute poverty is eliminated.

The preceding discussion has drawn attention to a variety of ways in which major results can only be expected in the longer run: in getting more appropriate technologies into place; in learning how most effectively to assist the small farmers and the informal sector; in obtaining the full benefits of land reform. The point can be summed up in the thought that redistribution through growth is a development strategy and since development is a long-term process the resulting redistribution will be similarly long term. But if it is too slow the feasibility of an acceptable reformist solution will be thrown into doubt and support for a revolution will grow.

Activity. Are there good reasons for believing that the pursuit of equity objectives would slow down the growth of your own economy? If so, what might the government do to minimize this danger?

---

[31] See Musgrave and Musgrave, 1976, pp. 488–92 for a concise discussion of the effect of various taxes on saving.
[32] Another way of putting this is to say, that an equity–growth trade-off may disappear if we attach 'poverty weights' to the growth of the incomes of various income classes, or if we adjust GDP growth for a factor expressing some inequality aversion: on this see Chenery, *et al.*, 1974, pp. 38–42 and Beckerman, 1977.

Are the policy instruments adequate?

A related issue is whether the policy instruments employed in the strategy are likely to be effective, given the gravity of the problems and constraints. Part II, for instance, drew attention to the difficulties of devising a genuinely progressive tax structure in the conditions of the Third World. Attention has also been drawn to the key importance for the strategy of appropriate technologies. To solve the employment problem these would need to incorporate factor proportions drastically different from the production methods of the west:[33]

> An appropriate technology to employ only the extra workers entering the labour market each year would have to be such that the investible resources per worker would be only one-sixtieth of what they are in developed countries. Even allowing for some substitution between labour and capital ... this is a large hole in the production function to fill.

But technology is a difficult area for governments to work in effectively and few in developing countries have yet adopted sufficiently radical departures from past research efforts to convince that they will be able to develop the technologies on which the strategy depends.

Or take the importance in the strategy of shifting the economy's growth path in favour of smallholder agriculture, the informal sector and other activities with large employment elasticities. Just how great is the power of governments to influence sectoral growth rates? We should recall here the results of Shen's (1975) researches into the effectiveness of sectoral planning, summarized in Chapter 3 (page 64). You may recall that he found that planned rates were very weak predictors of actual sectoral growth rates and that sectors grew in much the same way as they would have done had there been no planning at all. One reason for this is that the pattern of domestic demand, as modified by international trade, sets rather severe limits on the freedom to manipulate sectoral rates of expansion. It can be replied to Shen's results that more would have been achieved had planning been taken more seriously. That is no doubt true and Chapter 3 offers some suggestions for strengthening planning. But it would be unwise to take dramatic improvements for granted.

This book is about the domestic policies of LDCs. Matters requiring international action are deliberately neglected here, not because they are unimportant but because they are beyond the power of any LDC government to enforce (except, perhaps, Saudi Arabia!). However, one of the limitations of redistribution through growth is that it does depend on international action to be fully effective.[34] Mention was made earlier of the superiority of pursuing outward-looking policies based on the expansion of labour-intensive export industries. But this presumes that the industrial countries will not erect trade barriers against these goods, which compete with their own industries. The industrial countries have a bad record on this score, although this has not prevented some LDCs from achieving major increases in manufactured exports. The need for reciprocal action by the rich nations to support equity-oriented strategies in LDCs is great and undoubted, but United Nations conferences and the like have meagre results to show for all their discussions of these issues.

In brief, then, there are certain key areas in which available policies may be inadequate to produce the desired results.

Can the strategy be implemented?

Redistribution through growth is a strategy; a mutually reinforcing package of many different policy instruments. The fact that it is mutually reinforcing, that it does take an overall view of economic policy, rather than approaching matters in a piecemeal fashion, is a strength. But it is a weakness too. As was explored in Chapter 3, the administrative capacity of public administrations to implement effectively policies and projects is severely limited. It may be simply unfeasible to carry out all the measures needed for redistribution through growth within a short time-span. Actually, this is not so much a shortcoming of redistribution through growth as such, but of any development strategy which requires the implementation of a large number of policies and projects.

In the face of this implementation constraint, the *phasing* of the measures is of great importance. Even though it may only be possible to introduce the strategy bit by bit this may not be too harmful if the sequencing of the various measures is carefully thought out. It is, however, difficult to generalize about an optimal sequencing; that is a matter that would have to be worked out for the particular country in which the strategy was being applied.

---

[33] Stewart and Streeten, 1976, p. 401.
[34] See Richard Jolly's essay on this in Chenery, *et al.*, 1974, ch. VIII.

Conclusion: mobilizing the political system

The reader may by now be thinking that redistribution through growth is beset by so many difficulties that it is a non-starter. The difficulties are genuine enough but remember that the strategy has strengths as well. It offers a politically more practical (positive-sum) course than an exclusive concentration on (zero-sum) static redistribution. It does not make the mistake of equating development with growth, but it does not make the opposite mistake of neglecting the enormous benefits that economic growth can bring to the poor and unemployed.

Nor should the list of unresolved difficulties in the strategy create excessive pessimism about its feasibility. At least some countries have pursued policies in the tradition of redistribution through growth and have achieved major successes. Many of the difficulties can be resolved if there is the political will to do so. The element of political will and organization is likely to be decisive. What has been said about land reform can be written larger to refer to the whole pursuit of social justice:[35]

> Experience with land reform in the past points to the overriding importance of the political factor in securing meaningful change ... Ambitious programs of land reform will seldom be implemented unless there are shifts in political sentiment and power. Many countries have legislated land reform, but only a few can be said to have implemented it ... [In some countries] a community of interests between landowners and officials, combined with an absence of organised pressure from the beneficiaries, largely nullified positive land reform efforts. The land reform experience in much of Asia and Latin America suggests that some form of rural organisation, especially involving local representation, may be a critical condition for successful land reform.

The way in which a country's political system operates – the manner in which political resources are distributed and used – is critical in many areas of economic policy-making but especially so in this area of reducing poverty and inequality. A prior or simultaneous reordering of social relations and political power is likely to be essential for the successful implementation of redistributive policies. For this to occur and persist the mass of the poor, who are so often weakly organized and politically oppressed, must learn to mobilize the political system in their own interests.

We conclude, then, on a political note. But there is no need to apologize for that in a textbook of applied economics: any sharp distinction between economics and politics is not only artificial, it is harmful.

> **Activity.** Try to identify, with as much precision as you can, specific ways in which the distribution of political resources in your own country affects the feasibility of reducing poverty and inequality.

Suggestions for Revision and Group Discussions

1 Review your understanding of the following:
   (a) Progressive taxation and progressive government expenditures.
   (b) The distinction between direct and indirect taxes.
   (c) The incidence of taxation and government spending.
   (d) A poverty group.
   (e) An employment elasticity.
   (f) The elasticity of substitution.
2 Use the statistics in Table 6.5 to draw pre- and post-redistribution Lorenz curves for Brazindia. Write a brief comment on your results.
3 Write down your own understanding of the meaning of redistribution through growth and the ways in which it differs from static redistribution.
4 Do you think that an industry's elasticity of substitution is a variable which can be influenced by government policy?
5 Discuss the significance for redistribution through growth of the savings behaviour of the rich.
6 One way of resolving apparent conflicts between the pursuit of greater income equality and economic growth is to use a set of 'poverty weights' or a numerical expression of 'inequality aversion'. It is suggested that you pursue this by using the references given in note 32. Perhaps try an application of one of these techniques to actual or imaginary data on your own country.
7 Summarize the main positive and negative influences that redistribution through growth can be expected to have on the productivities of the factors of production.
8 What do you think are the chief difficulties of implementing a system of progressive taxation in developing countries?
9 Discuss the point of view that the under-utilization of labour 'reflects the attitudes and institutions of a backward society and can therefore not be treated as a source for its transformation' (Streeten).

---

[35] World Bank, 1975, pp. 197–8.

Suggestions for Further Reading

Many of the suggestions made at the end of Chapter 5 are also relevant to this chapter. This is especially true of Chenery, *et al.* (1974), which provides the most definitive treatment of redistribution through growth, Edwards (1974) and Jolly, *et al.* (1973). The International Labour Office (ILO) (1976) also offers a useful account of the type of policy approach emphasized in this chapter.

Stewart and Streeton (1976) offer a valuable discussion of redistribution through growth and some of its difficulties. Mouly and Costa (1974) contains a wealth of policy suggestions for improving the employment situation. The World Bank (1975) provides valuable coverage of rural development, land reform and other relevant policy areas.

See also the additional references given in the notes to this chapter.

7 Inflation

'Inflation is unjust and deflation
is inexpedient.' *J. M. Keynes*

Contents

I. Introduction

Inflation is universal, continuous and irreversible. It
affects all economies, with varying degrees of severity,
and the literature on it is large. But these writings have
not resulted in any consensus about the causes and
consequences of rising prices. Sharply differing views
are held about the origins of inflation. There are also
disagreements about whether it constitutes a problem
calling for corrective action by the state.

In tackling this topic, we are therefore walking into
a minefield of unsettled controversies. Much of this
chapter is taken up with surveying alternative
viewpoints on the causes and consequences of
inflation, before turning to the matter of policy
correctives. We start, however, by defining our terms
and by surveying the evidence on inflation in
developing countries.

Definitions and measurements

We can define inflation as a persistent rise in the
general level of prices. Note this definition carefully
because it implies (1) that an increase in some
particular price is not inflationary if compensated by
falls in other prices and (2) that a once-for-all rise in
prices due, say, to a poor harvest, is not best described
as inflationary unless accompanied by responses that
turn it into a process continuing over time. A rise in
the general price level means, of course, that a given
sum of money will buy a smaller quantity of goods
than was formerly the case. This suggests an
alternative way of defining inflation, as a persistent
fall in the purchasing power of money: the higher the
price level, the lesser is the value of money.

The most frequently employed measure of inflation
is a rate of increase in a consumer price index, often
called a 'cost-of-living index'. Such an index is based

on observations of the prices of a 'basket of goods' selected as representative of the spending patterns of consumers within some specified range of incomes. The items in the basket are given weights according to their relative importance in total consumption and the price data are reduced to index series. A country with a well developed statistical service will have a number of consumer price indices – for different income levels and also for different regions of the country. It is thus arbitrary to talk about 'the' rate of inflation because trends in the various 'indices are liable to differ one from another.

Identification of 'the' inflation rate is further complicated by the fact that there are other types of price indices which also offer measures of inflation. At one remove from the consumer index of retail prices, is the wholesale price index. This often has the merit of giving earlier warning of an upsurge in prices than a retail index, because it takes time for a rise to work its way through to the shops and markets. Another index deserving mention is the 'GNP deflator', which is derived from comparisons of GNP estimates in current prices and in constant prices. This reflects not only consumption but also the prices of capital goods and exports. From whatever index is chosen it is possible also to compute an index of the value of money, from the reciprocal of the price index.

There are some severe conceptual and practical problems associated with the measurement of prices, particularly when there is much inflation. Figures of inflation presented below must, therefore, be treated as approximations only. On the other hand, there is no reason to think that they give a seriously misleading impression and it is thus not essential to explore the measurement problems here.[1]

> **Key concept. Inflation** is a persistent rise in the general level of prices, or a persistent fall in the purchasing power of money.

. . . universal, continuous, irreversible

An examination of world price trends supports the earlier contention that inflation has become universal, continuous and irreversible. Take first the statistics presented in Table 7.1.

We see from these figures that there have been positive and significant rates of inflation in each of the country groupings over the whole decade, substantially more rapid in the second half of the decade than in the first. Taken together, we also see that the developing countries have experienced more inflation than the industrial countries – a generalization that will be qualified in a moment, however.

Table 7.1
World Trends in Consumer Prices

	(Average annual percentage increases) 1967–72	1972–7
1. Industrial countries	5	9
2. Non-oil developing countries of which:	10	25
(a) Africa	5	16
(b) Asia	5	11
(c) Western hemisphere*	16	36
3. Oil-exporting countries	8	14

Source: As for Figure 7.1.
Note: * Chiefly Latin American and Carribean countries.

Figure 7.1 provides further analysis of inflationary trends in the 1970s. As can be seen, the most rapid acceleration occurred between 1972 and 1974. It affected all the major groupings but especially the non-oil exporting LDCs, whose average inflation rate rose to 33 per cent in 1976, dropping only slightly in 1977.

Inflation, then, is footloose: it spreads from one country to another through the mechanisms of international trade and finance. Thus, the rapid world inflation in 1974 and 1975 was partly a result of the $4\frac{1}{2}$-fold rise in crude oil prices between 1973 and 1974, and ensuing rises in industrial production costs. A rapid expansion of world money supplies also contributed to the accelerated inflation of the 1970s, as will be mentioned later. In principle, if all countries had completely flexible exchange rates the worldwide propagation of inflation could be avoided – another point to be taken up later – but in practice most countries maintain rather inflexible exchange rates for their national currencies. So inflation is worldwide.

There is, however, an important exception to this generalization. Price indices for the centrally planned economies of eastern Europe and elsewhere scarcely display any increase at all (although even these countries were unable to avoid the world inflation of the later 1970s). It is said, for example, that the fares charged on the Moscow underground railway are today still at the levels set when it was opened in 1935. In these countries most prices are determined administratively, not by conditions of supply and demand, and the planners have been able to achieve a high degree of price stability.

---

[1] Students interested in pursuing the measurement aspects of this topic should consult the chapter dealing with index numbers in a textbook of applied statistics, e.g. Yamane, 1967, ch. 11.

Figure 7.1 *(a) World trends in consumer prices; (b) trends among non-oil exporting LDCs.*

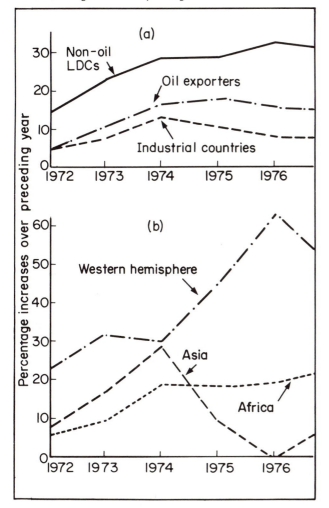

Source: IMF International Financial Statistics, May and August 1978.

This does not mean that demand never exceeds supply in these countries, simply that such conditions do not bid up prices. Instead there are shortages, sometimes accompanied by rationing or by long queues of people trying to buy before supplies run out. It is also common for the state to keep the prices of certain essentials down by providing subsidies. This set of circumstances can be called *repressed inflation*, denoting the presence of an excess of demand relative to supply which is prevented by state controls from spilling over into price increases. To some extent, therefore, the apparent absence of inflation in the centrally planned economies is misleading, especially so because they sometimes conceal price increases in the guise of 'new' products, and also because those prices which are freely

determined by supply and demand (mainly horticultural products) are excluded from official price indices.[2]

If the centrally planned countries are a special case, so also are the countries of Latin America. It was shown earlier that LDCs, taken together, have had far more inflation than the western industrial countries. However, looking at Table 7.1 and Figure 7.1 it is obvious that the LDC average is strongly influenced by the abnormal inflation of the western hemisphere, which is dominated by Latin America. In 1967–72 inflation in Africa and Asia was no greater than in the industrial countries and even in 1972–7 inflation on these two continents was far below the level of the western hemisphere LDCs. Most of the countries that have experienced severe inflation have belonged to this region (although Indonesia is an Asian country which has gone through a period of extremely rapid price rises, or *hyperinflation* as it is called, where the consumer price index went up from 100 to 71 797 between 1963 and 1971). In fact, even among the Latin American countries the regional average is much distorted by the abnormal records of a small group of hyperinflation countries, as indicated by the following figures of annual increases in consumer prices:

	Western hemisphere	*Western hemisphere excluding Argentina, Chile and Uruguay*
1975	45%	20%
1976	63%	18%
1977	50%	22%

The geographical concentration of hyperinflation is reflected in research on the subject, most of which relates to a few Latin American countries – countries generally at a more advanced stage of development than most members of the Third World.

At the beginning of this survey of world trends inflation was described as 'irreversible' – a strong statement that must now be substantiated. See now Table 7.2, which is based on a study of the consumer price experiences of a sample of seventy developing countries and twenty-four industrial countries in 1964–74. This records the number of occasions on which the consumer price index fell, remained unchanged or rose.

You will see from this that in the developing countries only about 4 per cent of changes in the price index were in a downward direction; in the industrial countries there were no occasions at all when the

---

[2] See Portes, 1977, for a discussion of price stability in the centrally planned economies and its policy implications.

Table 7.2
Direction of Change of Consumer Price Index, 1964–74

	Index fell	No change	Index rose	Total
Industrial Countries:				
No. of observations	0	1	239	240
% of observations	0	0·4	99·6	100·0
Developing Countries:				
No. of observations	31	8	661	700
% of observations	4·4	1·1	94·4	100·0

Source: UN *Statistical Yearbook, 1975,* Table 183.

index fell! In all countries prices are flexible in only one direction – upwards. Prices are 'sticky' downwards so there is little realistic prospect that a price increase will be cancelled out by a subsequent fall. In the face of this downward stickiness of prices *the most that governments can realistically hope for is to prevent further increases*; to actually lower the cost of living is almost certainly beyond their capabilities.

Activity. Study your own country's price indices in order to (1) examine the extent to which the various indices reveal the same trends; (2) compare your country's performance with that of LDCs in general, as given in Table 7.1 and Figure 7.1; and (3) compile figures comparable with those in Table 7.2.

Our next step is to examine the various explanations of inflation that have been offered, as they relate to developing countries.

II. Explanations

One of the points brought out in Chapter 4 was that once population growth becomes rapid, it tends to perpetuate itself. Inflation has a similar characteristic: once it gets under way socio-economic forces are liable to come into play to keep prices moving ever-upwards. It then becomes nearly impossible to disentangle the separate effects of these various forces and to distinguish cause from effect.

So in studying the experiences of a country that moves from a period of price stability to sustained inflation we can ask two questions, which may have different answers. We can ask about the *initiating causes* of the inflation – what started it going in the first place? And we can ask about the *propagating forces* – what factors keep prices rising once the process has commenced? This distinction between initiating and propagating forces is of fundamental importance to an understanding of inflation. The main controversies considered below are about alternative initiating factors but it is important to keep in mind that inflation would be no more than a temporary inconvenience unless there was also a propagation mechanism to keep prices rising.

Since most prices in a mixed economy result from the interaction of supply and demand, we can logically distinguish between explanations of the causes of inflation that stress the demand side of the market (the so-called 'demand-pull' school) and those which emphasize conditions of supply (under which heading we can place the 'cost-push' and 'structuralist' schools).

Demand-oriented explanations

Put in its simplest terms, demand inflation is caused by an excess of aggregate demand for goods and services over available supplies, at a given level of prices. The natural market response to such a situation, of course, is a rise in prices towards a new market-clearing equilibrium in which demand once again equals supply. A new equilibrium may not be achieved, however, because of propagating forces which raise both demand and costs and thus push prices ever higher.

Inflation is not, however, an inevitable outcome of an increase in demand. It all depends on the price elasticity of supply. If the elasticity is large, a small price increase may call forth a large increase in output so that the inflationary impact is slight. In the short run, the main determinants of the supply elasticity will be the extent to which suppliers are operating below productive capacity and the availability of foreign exchange. If there is much surplus capacity, the principal effect of an increase in demand will be to induce greater output, rather than to initiate an inflationary spiral. Similarly, if there is surplus foreign exchange, the effect will be to induce a larger volume of imports. For the economy as a whole, therefore, there is only a large danger of demand inflation if there is a foreign exchange constraint and the economy is already operating near to full capacity. To put it in the language of Chapter 1, the possibility of demand inflation is the greater the nearer the economy is to being on its production-possibility frontier.

The point is illustrated schematically in Figure 7.2. This presents a single aggregate supply curve for the economy as a whole and four aggregate demand curves, with D_1 representing the lowest level of demand and D_4 the highest. With demand held at D_1 the productive system is under-utilized, with levels of real output and utilization at Y_a. This is a situation of deflation, the core concern of Keynes' *General Theory*. His solution was for the state to increase the amount of spending power in the economy, for example by shifting the demand curve from D_1 to D_2 in the diagram. Because of the simplified way in which the supply curve has been drawn the effect of this increase in demand is exclusively on the levels of utilization and output; the price level remains unchanged at P_w. *The principal effect of increasing demand in a deflationary situation is to increase output, employment and real incomes.*

Figure 7.2   *An illustration of demand inflation.*

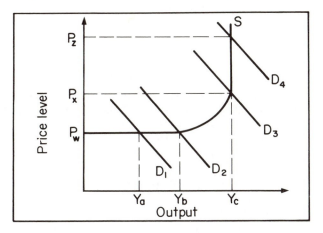

At points to the right of Y_b, however, the elasticity of supply becomes progressively smaller, on the assumption that there is no surplus import capacity and as producers approach the short-run limit of their productive capacity. Therefore, the consequence of further increasing total demand, from D_2 to D_3, is to raise output and capacity utilization from Y_b to Y_c and to raise the price level, from P_w to P_x. Demand inflation is beginning to occur.

Finally, we can take the results of another increase in total demand, from D_3 to D_4. The total supply curve has been drawn as vertical from the point at

which it intersects D_3. What this is intended to convey is that the economy has achieved full capacity utilization at the level of output Y_c. The short-run price elasticity of supply is therefore zero and the only effect of increasing total demand is to raise the price level (from P_x to P_z), leaving real output unchanged at Y_c. *The principal effect of increasing demand in an economy operating at, or near to, full capacity is to raise prices.* This can be called a case of 'pure' demand inflation.

This illustration is a simplification. In practice the aggregate supply curve will rarely be horizontal even at low levels of utilization. Similarly, it will not usually become completely vertical. The concept of 'full utilization' is difficult to apply in practice, especially in developing countries where there is always much unemployment which cannot, however, be cured by increasing total demand. But the essential point made by Figure 7.2 is valid: as total demand is raised to successively higher levels, the impact will more and more be upon prices and less and less on real output.

> **Key concept. Demand inflation** is caused by an excess of aggregate demand for goods and services over available supplies, at a given level of prices. It normally occurs in economies operating at, or near to, full capacity production.

So far the exposition has been silent on the ways in which it is possible to vary the level of total demand in the economy. How might an economy get into a situation of demand inflation? To answer this we have to examine what has become known as the monetarist school of inflation theory.

The essence of the monetarist position has been summed up by Nobel laureate Milton Friedman in the propositions:

[1] Inflation is always and everywhere a monetary phenomenon . . . and [2] can be produced only by a more rapid increase in the quantity of money than in output (1970, p. 24).

The first of these propositions is uncontroversial; the second quite the opposite.

That inflation is a monetary phenomenon is clear if we consider a subsistence economy or an economy where exchange occurs only in the form of direct bartering of one good for another. With subsistence, the family consumes for itself all that it produces. There is no 'price' and thus no question of inflation. With barter, there is a type of price – given by the rate of exchange between one good and another – but there is no possibility of a generalized excess of demand. The amount of good A that has to be exchanged for a unit of good B can go up. This can be thought of as a rise in the price of B, but equally well as a fall in the price of A. There is no possibility of a general excess of demand because demand has to be made effective by purchasing power and, in a barter economy, commodities are the only form of purchasing power: an increase in demand entails an increase in supply.

The practical importance of this point is that people whose economic lives are entirely within the modern, monetized part of the economy will be more strongly affected by inflation than those who still meet many of their own needs for themselves. In times of serious inflation people can, and do, protect themselves from its adverse effects by taking refuge in subsistence production, especially by growing their own food. To put the point differently, inflation is liable to retard the monetization of economic activity which is a normal corollary of modernization.

> **Key concept. Monetization** takes place as the proportion of total economic activity occurring through the intermediation of money increases, with a corresponding decline in the importance of subsistence and barter.

But just because inflation is only possible in a monetized economy does the second part of Friedman's statement follow, that it 'can only be produced by a more rapid increase in the quantity of money than in output'. Many would disagree with this judgement so we must examine it with some care. We start by re-phrasing the statement to read:

> The consequence of an increase in the supply of money greater than an increase in the demand for money will be a rise in the demand for products. With an economy approaching full capacity operation, this will result in demand inflation.

The idea underlying this proposition is that people adjust their spending patterns according to whether or not they are holding the amount of money they wish to hold. They desire the convenience of holding

> **Key concept. The monetarist theory of inflation** emphasizes increases in the supply of money faster than increases in the demand for money as the cause of rising prices. An excess supply of money causes a larger demand for commodities, thus tending to pull prices up.

money balances but if they find themselves with more money than they desire they will spend the surplus on goods and services. Similarly, if they find themselves with smaller balances than they desire, they will replenish their money stocks by cutting expenditures. So *an excess in the supply of money over the demand for it will result in an increase in the demand for products* and hence will tend to cause inflation.

According to the monetary view, then, we have to study the state of demand for, and supply of, money if we are to understand the behaviour of the general price level. The *supply* of money is generally assumed to be under the control of the state (although we will later qualify that assumption), in which case the authorities need only to predict the demand for money in order to achieve a balance between demand and supply. The next step, therefore, is to examine the factors underlying the *demand* for money.

For any given level of prices and set of institutions, the demand for money will principally be a function of three economic variables:

(1) the level of real income (as indicated by constant-price GNP or some similar national accounting aggregate);
(2) the extent of monetization of economic activity (as indicated by the ratio of monetary GNP to non-monetary or subsistence GNP); and
(3) the net utility of holding money.

We can write this symbolically, as follows:

$$MD = f(Y, Z, U)$$

where MD is the demand for money, Y is real GNP, Z is the ratio of monetary to non-monetary activity, and U is the net utility of holding money. Changes in the demand for money will therefore result from changes in any or all of these variables. There will be an increase in demand if real income goes up because there will be a larger 'transactions' demand for money. There will likewise be an increase in transactions demand if economic activities that previously were barter transactions or subsistence production become monetized, i.e. occur by using money as a means of intermediation. Lastly, the demand for money will rise if interest rates on bank deposits go up or if the people expect slower inflation.

The underlying trend in most developing countries is for both Y and Z to gradually increase, so these two variables are likely to result in a gently upward trend in MD. The variable U – the net utility of holding money – is more complex (and difficult to measure) and needs a little more elaboration.

Here too it is convenient to present the matter symbolically:

$$U = f(V, R, X)$$

where V stands for the convenience value of holding money balances, R is the rate of interest payable on bank deposits and X is the expected rate of inflation. U will be a positive function of V and R, and a negative function of X. That is to say, the net utility of holding money will be the larger the greater the convenience value of money (to facilitate everyday spending, to hold as a precaution against unforeseen emergencies, and so on) and the higher is the rate of interest payable on money balances held in bank deposits.

The expected rate of inflation (X) is also liable to affect U and, through it, the demand for money. In this case, we can think of inflation as a cost of holding money, or as a tax on money balances. This is because inflation reduces the purchasing power of money and this loss of spending power is equivalent to paying a tax (often called the inflation tax) proportional to the value of one's money holdings. The higher the expected rate of inflation the greater will be the net utility of money balances.

The net utility of money is thus comprised of its convenience value *plus* any interest payable *less* the expected rate of inflation. If inflation is expected to be rapid, the value of U may be negative – there will be a net disutility – thus reducing the demand for money. Of the variables in the U function, V is likely to be rather stable, R somewhat less so (because the monetary authorities can vary interest rates) and X the most volatile of the three. The *past* rate of inflation is likely to be an important determinant of X.

There is a lot of empirical evidence which bears out the general validity of this description of the demand for money. Of the relevant variables, most studies find Y to be the most important determinant. Only over a long time-span can the value of Z be expected to change very much. Both R and X have been found to be significant determinants of MD but with generally small coefficient values, meaning that large changes in either of them will make only a moderate impact on MD. Most studies also indicate that the demand function for money is fairly stable over time. This makes it much easier to predict MD and hence to manipulate money supply so as to bring it into balance with demand.

> **Activity.** Search for any studies that have been undertaken of the demand for money in your own country and compare their results with the generalizations offered here.

We are now nearer to an understanding of Friedman's second proposition, that inflation can only be caused by a more rapid increase in the quantity of money than in output. He was simplifying by picking output (or income) as the only determinant of the demand for money, but he picked the most important one.

Before reaching a judgement on whether an increase in the supply of money relative to its demand is the only source of inflation we have to review non-monetary theories but it is as well now to draw attention to the fact that monetarist writers do not contend that *any* increase in the supply of money is inflationary: the exposition has throughout been in terms of the relative rates of increase in demand and supply. An economy can increase the quantity of money without inflation to the extent that it is growing in real terms, that economic activity is becoming monetized, and that the net utility of money is going up. Each of these trends will increase the demand for money. In particular, a rapidly developing economy can absorb more non-inflationary money supply increases than a stagnant one. In fact, it is important that money supply be expanded so as to meet additional non-inflationary needs, otherwise monetary stringency may retard the pace of development.

Supply-oriented explanations

It is time now to present the views of those who stress conditions on the supply side of markets as a cause of inflation, concentrating on cost-push and structuralist theories.

In its purest form, the *cost-push* theory ascribes inflation to *increases in cost which are independent of the state of aggregate demand*. The cost of imported goods is continuously rising because of world inflation. This both directly raises the cost of living through higher prices for finished good imports and indirectly through more costly imported materials used by domestic producers. In addition, trade unions may force wages up more rapidly than increases in productivity, raising unit labour costs. Other groups, such as farmers' organizations, may also be strong enough to prevent their own position from being eroded; and the generally low degree of competition in the modern industrial sector (Chapter 10) allows manufacturers to pass cost increases on to the consumer, perhaps adding an enlarged profit margin for themselves.

The essentials of this view are illustrated on the left-hand side of Figure 7.3 (ignore the right-hand side for the time being). The axes are the same as those of Figure 7.2 but this time aggregate demand is held constant at D_1. Because of rising import prices, trade

Figure 7.3   *Cost-push inflation: (a) pure cost-push; (b) cost-push with demand adjustments.*

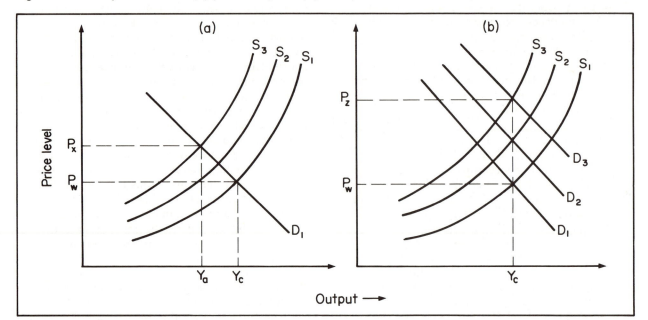

union pressures and so on, unit costs go up and the supply curve shifts to successively higher levels – from S_1 to S_2 to S_3. With demand held at D_1, this results in some loss of output (implying more unemployment), from Y_c to Y_a, and a rise in the price level, from P_w to P_x.

An important feature of this model is that it provides an explanation of the fact noticed from Table 7.2 that there is a ratchet effect at work preventing the general price level from falling. The cost-inflation school explains this by strong union resistances to reductions in wages (the downward 'stickiness' of wages) and cost-plus pricing policies of firms typically selling in monopolistic or oligopolistic markets, whose prices are determined by production costs rather than by the state of demand. With import costs also rising because of similar conditions in the rest of the world, producers mark up their prices to reflect any increases in costs, with each price increase likely to be irreversible. Moreover, their ability to pass increases on to the consuming public makes producers less resistant to wage claims and other cost-raising pressures.

Going back to Figure 7.3, we noted that one of the results of increasing costs with total demand held constant was to reduce output and capacity utilization, lowering living standards and increasing unemployment. Clearly, such a result would be unwelcome to the public and its government alike. The government would find itself under pressure to increase aggregate demand enough to prevent output

and employment from falling. This possibility is illustrated in the right-hand part of the diagram. This assumes that for every upward movement in the supply curve ($S_1 \ldots S_3$) the government will induce a compensating increase in total demand ($D_1 \ldots D_3$) so as to 'validate' the cost increase and prevent output from falling below Y_c. The effect of this response is to increase the rate of inflation, with the price level going up to P_z instead of the P_x in the 'pure' case.

> **Key concept.** In its pure form, the **cost-push theory of inflation** ascribes inflation to increases in costs which are independent of the state of aggregate demand. However, it is often combined with an argument to the effect that governments will seek to avoid losses of output and employment, and 'validate' cost increases, by expanding aggregate demand.

What is suggested here, then, is a trade-off between real incomes and employment on the one hand, and price stability on the other. You may recall that a similar type of trade-off was presented in the Phillips curve of Figure 2.1 on page 34. That illustration and the one in the last paragraph explain inflation by reference to both cost and demand elements. This is also true of the *structuralist* school, to which we now turn.

Structural change is an inseparable companion of economic development. As incomes rise the

Activity. Consider the kind of evidence that would be needed to answer the question, have wage increases been a cause of inflation in your country? This could be made the subject of a class discussion and an assignment to collect the relevant data. Do not neglect the importance of productivity increases, nor of the timing of price and wage increases.

composition of demand changes and so does the structure of output.[3] There is, however, no guarantee that the productive structure will prove sufficiently adaptive to the changing composition of demand to avoid the emergence of disequilibria in product markets, with demand exceeding supply in some cases and supply exceeding demand in others. Even though there may be no overall excess of total demand, the existence of excess demand in some markets, combined with downward inflexibility in prices of products with excess supply, pushes up some prices without compensatory falls elsewhere and thus raises the general price level. It is also likely that the foreign trade sector will be unable to earn enough foreign exchange to meet the growing import needs of the economy, so foreign exchange scarcities will also tend to push up prices.

A common illustration of the type of disequilibria that may occur is provided by the tendency for domestic food production to lag behind demand. Agricultural production is often inelastic with respect to price. Increased demand will have to result in large price rises before output responds much. Food prices thus tend to move ahead of the general price level. This may induce higher prices in the industrial sector too, as trade unions lodge wage claims to protect their workers against the effects of higher food prices and as the cost of agricultural raw material inputs also goes up.

One solution for this state of affairs is to import the goods in short supply, allowing excess demand for particular products to be absorbed by the balance of payments rather than by inflation. However, most LDCs are in no position to import whatever they need and a further important aspect of the structuralist argument concerns the effects of foreign exchange shortages.

Members of this school stress that export earnings are likely to lag behind import needs because of the only slow expansion of world demand for many primary products exported by developing countries. Artificial barriers erected by the industrial nations against industrial exports from LDCs make matters worse, and so do ill-conceived domestic policies towards the export sector. Even if the long-run trend

of export earnings is favourable, some argue that the sharp year-to-year fluctuations characteristic of many world commodity markets may themselves impart an inflationary bias. The ratchet effect will ensure that domestic prices rise when an unexpected shortfall in export earnings reduces the supply of imports, but will not fall back again when export earnings recover. It is also argued that official aid flows fall far short of filling the gap between export earnings and import requirements.

For these reasons, there is liable to be a shortage of imports, so that import prices join agricultural prices in setting the inflationary pace, dragging other prices up behind them. This may happen, for example, if the government attempts to shore up the balance of payments by devaluing the national currency or by imposing import controls. Both policies are likely to cause price rises. Controls are also likely to result in the creation of additional disequilibria, as shown in the next chapter.

Forced-pace import-substituting industrialization behind high protective tariffs is another possible government strategy, either for balance of payments reasons or simply to promote industrialization. Here too the effect on prices will be upward because protective tariffs raise the price of imports and permit the emergence of high-cost domestic producers. So a shift in productive structure towards industry may also create inflationary tendencies, especially if undertaken at the expense of agriculture and expanding food supplies.

In a nutshell, what the structuralists provide is a general model of the relationship between development and the price level, in which under-utilization in some sectors coexists with excess demand in others. If development takes a balanced form, avoiding major disequilibria in product markets and on the balance of payments, the resulting inflation will be mild. But balance may not be feasible: disequilibria and unbalanced growth may be essential in order to stimulate development, with inflation the necessary cost.[4]

Key concept. The **structuralist theory of inflation** postulates that inflation will accompany economic development because of disequilibria created by the structural changes which are necessary to the development process.

[3] See Kuznets, 1966, for an excellent historical exploration of the relationships between economic structure and growth.
[4] Hirschman, 1958, remains an important presentation of this view – see especially his ch. 9.

Figure 7.4 attempts to illustrate this, using a framework similar to Figures 7.2 and 7.3. This displays two alternative supply curves. Curve S_b is

Figure 7.4   *Inflation and economic growth.*

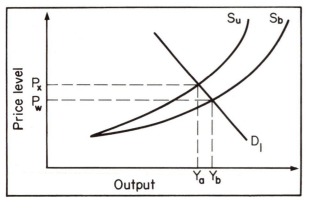

representative of balanced growth, characterized by a relative absence of disequilibria; S_u illustrates the unbalanced growth case, with lagging agriculture, high-cost industrialization and foreign exchange shortages. For any given level of demand, say D_1, balanced growth (if it is feasible) will yield greater output and a lower price level than unbalanced growth (output greater by $Y_a Y_b$, the price level lower by $P_w P_x$). This is because price elasticities of supply are larger with balanced growth, so that greater output is achieved from a smaller price stimulus.

The dynamics of inflation

For price increases to be more than a temporary inconvenience there must be a propagation mechanism within the economy to sustain the inflation, no matter how it is initiated, so we need to understand the propagation forces at work.

Central to such an understanding is the fact that inflation alters the distribution of real incomes. Wages may lag behind prices, causing real earnings to decline; or profit margins may be squeezed by escalating costs, reducing the real incomes of capitalists. It may be landowners who get left behind; it may be the government budget which suffers, with declines in the real value of tax receipts. Faced with declining incomes, the affected groups will try to protect their own interests. Trade unions may defend real wages by becoming more militant; capitalists will seek to raise their profit margins. The government may sustain its spending in the face of declining real revenues by borrowing from the banks, thus pumping more money into the economy;[5] or the same result may occur because inflation reduces financial

discipline and makes the budget harder to control.

The interactions between groups struggling to protect their own positions go a long way towards explaining the dynamics of inflation. For the action of each group will probably cause a further round of price increases, to which others will respond with actions which push prices up again . . . and so on. One example of this type of mechanism is the so-called wage-price spiral, although it is more relevant to industrial countries than to most LDCs. Assume the price level goes up for some reason, say an increase in import prices. If trade unions are strong, organized labour will move to restore the purchasing power of wages by claiming higher wages. If granted, these will cause higher costs which will be passed on to consumers. But in this case the purchasing power of wages will fall again, stimulating new wage claims . . . wages chase prices, prices chase wages.

To the dynamics of this process we can add two other factors which may come into play, especially if inflation becomes chronic. First, people may begin to anticipate inflation, instead of simply reacting defensively to the adverse consequences of past price increases. To go back to the wage-price spiral, say that inflation at 5 per cent has become a normal feature of the economy and that wages are negotiated annually. In the first years of inflation the unions may be content to concentrate on restoring the former purchasing power of wages by settling for 5 per cent wage rises, plus whatever is justified by increased productivity. But after a while, as inflation shows no signs of diminishing, they will realize that they are not fully protecting their members because they are compensating for an erosion of purchasing power that has already occurred. They may, therefore, try to get ahead in the race by anticipating next year's inflation and negotiating for a 10 per cent wage increase – 5 per cent to compensate for last year and another 5 per cent to prevent a decline in real earnings before next year's wage negotiations. If they obtain the 10 per cent this will push costs up more rapidly than formerly, thus pushing the inflation rate above the previous level. If all groups are able to anticipate in this way their expectations become self-fulfilling because each will receive the additional purchasing power that will fuel the price increases that have been anticipated. The stage is then set for a cumulative spiral of accelerating inflation, with incomes chasing prices chasing incomes.

---

[5] In the case of Indonesia's hyperinflation, there is evidence to support the view that government attempts to maintain its expenditure levels while inflation eroded the real value of its tax receipts was an important part of the propagation mechanism in that country. See Aghelvi and Khan, 1977.

This tendency may be exacerbated by a second set of forces, operating from the monetary system. We have seen already that the expectation of inflation diminishes the net utility of holding money (page 163), thus reducing the demand for money and increasing the demand for goods. The larger demand for goods will bid up prices, further accelerating the inflation and perhaps creating a cumulative situation in which there is a flight out of money because of inflation. With the value of money falling, people will try to minimize their money balances in order to buy goods. This money flight, in turn, further aggravates the rate of price increases. Flight from money may also have an adverse effect on real output because money plays an important role in modern economies and a collapse of confidence in money is liable to retard output.[6] Then the flight from money will have a doubly adverse effect on an inflationary excess of demand over supply: increasing total demand for goods while diminishing total supplies.

> **Key concept. Money flight** occurs when rapid inflation so reduces the purchasing power of money that people reduce their money balances as much as possible, preferring instead to hold commodities. The demand for money therefore falls and the demand for goods increases.

These possibilities of a self-fuelled cumulative inflationary spiral, while genuine, are not too alarming, however. In practice cumulative hyperinflation is rare. The demand for money is only moderately sensitive to the rate of inflation, and inflation is only imperfectly anticipated. Only a handful of developing countries have experienced hyperinflation since the 1950s.

On the other hand, few countries have avoided inflation altogether, indicating that there is a propagation mechanism in most economies. And once the process begins, the distinction between demand-induced and supply-induced inflation breaks down, with both demand and supply conditions contributing to the upward price trend. This is an important point to understand: *once inflation is under way demand explanations and supply explanations are not mutually exclusive.* In the discussion of Figure 7.3, for example, we saw how the adjustment of demand to maintain output and employment provided a powerful supplement to the cost-push explanation. Similarly, the structuralist argument does not deny that money plays a role. Rather, it views money supply as expanding in a permissive manner so as to avoid any monetary brake on development, rather than as an actively initiating

cause of inflation. Again, most members of the monetarist school would accept that cost-push forces can help keep prices rising and that structural considerations also contribute. Their position is that the inflation would not have commenced without an excessive growth in the money supply, and that it would soon diminish if the expansion of money supply were restricted to the growth of demand for real money balances.

Our next task is to undertake an overall evaluation of these rival explanations of inflation but the discussion of the last few paragraphs has already signalled a difficulty: the likelihood that both demand and supply forces will be present in any on-going inflation complicates empirical investigation of the initiating forces, because of the problems of establishing a sequence of events and of disentangling the separate effects of the various contributory factors. You are thus forewarned that empirical studies yield rather inconclusive results. You should also keep in mind that there is no reason to expect there to be a single initiating cause of inflation, valid for all circumstances. It is entirely possible for each alternative model to be valid in specific cases.

> **Activity.** Before proceeding further you should review your understanding of the monetarist, cost-push and structuralist explanations described above.

An evaluation of the alternative explanations

Cost-push explanation

We start by assessing the strength of the cost-push explanation. The first thing to note about this is that it was originated to explain the inflations of western industrial countries. At its core is the idea of wage-push inflation, emanating from the strength of organized labour. It is easy to see that this theory is less relevant to many developing countries. Modern sector wage employment is less important relative to total incomes than in industrial countries and trade unions are generally weaker.

Take, for example, the following figures of the average proportion of the labour force engaged in manufacturing and construction, which can be used as a rough proxy for modern sector wage employment (from Mouly and Costa, 1974, Table 2.2):

---

[6] See McKinnon, 1973, ch. 4, for a forcible presentation of this view. He emphasizes the role of money balances as an input into the productive system, so that output is likely to decline if the real value of money balances diminishes.

Underdeveloped countries	15%
Middle income countries	25%
Developed countries	35%

The share of wages in total national income is similarly smaller in LDCs, so that total cost structures are less sensitive to wage movements than in industrial nations. Consider the following shares of wages in national income:[7]

Asia (excluding Japan)	37%
Africa (excluding South Africa)	40%
Latin America	44%
Europe	53%
North America	66%

It is not possible to reduce the statement that trade unions are weaker in developing nations to a statistical demonstration but high levels of unemployment and authoritarian governments, which keep unions under strict control, combine in many LDCs to curb union militancy and to limit their overall impact.

So far as domestic costs are concerned then, the cost-push view provides a less persuasive explanation of inflation in LDCs than for industrialized economies. Moreover, we should recall that the stronger versions of the cost-push argument also make use of demand explanations, as illustrated in the right-hand part of Figure 7.3. Evidence from industrial countries suggests that wage behaviour is not indepdendent of demand conditions, as the pure cost model would have it. Similarly, firms apparently employing mark-up pricing policies in fact adjust their profit margins to changing market conditions, rather than behaving independently of demand.

On the other hand, there is one type of cost inflation which is particularly relevant to many LDCs, resulting from rising import prices. Although there are important exceptions, the typical developing economy is small and its imports are a large proportion of the total supply of goods – often in the range of 20 to 30 per cent of GDP. This dependence on trade makes LDC's price and cost levels highly sensitive to price trends in their industrial trading partners and makes it difficult for them to keep their own inflation rates much below those of the industrial world. But even this does not provide an adequate explanation because it was shown earlier that LDC inflation rates tend to be higher than those of the industrial nations. What is more, LDC import prices have persistently risen less rapidly than consumer prices, as shown by the following statistics:[8]

	Annual % increase in:	
	Consumer prices	Import prices
1950–9	4	1
1960–9	4	1
1967–72	10	2
1972–7	25	15

All in all, then, *the cost-push view does not offer a strong explanation of the initiation of inflation in developing countries.* However, as wage employment grows relative to total incomes and if trade unions become strong, the cost-push theory will become increasingly relevant. It is no coincidence that some of the Latin American countries which have experienced much inflation also have large wage-labour forces organized into strong trade unions, Argentina and Chile being the chief examples.[9]

Structuralist explanation

Does the structuralist model offer a better explanation? One important feature which distinguishes this from the cost-push and monetary models is that it is related explicitly to conditions in developing countries, or at least to the Latin American group of LDCs. We may therefore expect it to be more relevant than the other two. Unfortunately, the structuralist model has the additional feature that it is even more difficult to test empirically than the cost-push and demand-pull models.

One important attempt to do so came to the negative conclusion that structural disequilibria did not appear to be significant in explaining different inflation rates among developing countries, although its author was careful to add that his statistical indicators may not have provided an adequate test of the model.[10] He did, however, find that a tendency for agricultural output to lag behind the rest of the economy had some explanatory power, and food

---

[7] Calculated from International Labour Office, *Year Book of Labour Statistics, 1976* (Geneva, 1976), Table 24. The figures are of total compensation of employees (inclusive of fringe benefits) as a percentage of national income in 1971. They are unweighted means for each continent and the country coverage is only partial, especially for Asia.

[8] 1950–69 data from Heller, 1976, Table 9. 1967–77 data from same sources as for Figure 7.1 (oil-exporting countries excluded).

[9] Glytsos, 1977, has found cost impulses emanating from wages to contribute significantly to inflation in the (mainly Latin American) countries with especially high inflation rates.

[10] See Argy, 1970. See also Glytsos, 1977.

prices do generally go up faster than others in LDCs. Thus, the median overall inflation rate in 1969–74 for the seventy developing countries covered by Table 7.2 was 6·9 per cent annually while the median rate for food prices alone was 8·4 per cent. Assuming that food items make up 40 per cent of total consumption, the overall inflation rate would have been about 5·9 per cent if food prices had kept in line with other prices, or one percentage point less than the actual 6·9 per cent – a significant if not large reduction.

We saw earlier that the existence of a foreign exchange constraint was necessary to the structuralist theory because, if there were ample import capacity, supplies on the markets experiencing excess demand could be augmented with imports, thus avoiding price increases. But for developing countries taken as a whole the evidence for a serious limitation on import capacity is not particularly strong. Even excluding oil-exporting countries, LDCs were able to expand the *volume* of their imports at 6 per cent a year in 1960–70 and at 7·5 per cent in 1970–7. This was admittedly a smaller expansion than achieved by the industrial countries in the 1960s but was actually larger in 1970–7. This feat was, moreover, achieved while increasing foreign exchange reserves, relative to imports, to higher levels than the industrial countries.[11] Of course, specific countries have gone through acute import shortages, and it is likely that they have been especially prone to inflation. It is also likely that the demand for imports in LDCs grew more rapidly than the supply. But the evidence on import capacity does not provide very convincing support for the structuralist view, considered as a *general* theory of inflation in LDCs.

A third feature which receives prominence in structural theory concerns the inflationary effects of import-substituting industrialization. Here too it is difficult to believe that the effects of industrialization could be as large as the structuralist model requires. It is true that many LDCs give their industries high rates of protection but the spread of industrialization is gradual and the weight of manufactured consumer goods in the cost-of-living indices of poor countries is necessarily limited because poor people cannot afford to buy many manufactured goods. Considered on an annual basis, it seems unlikely that import-substitution could contribute more than one percentage point to the inflation rate.[12]

Overall, then, it seems, that the food, import capacity and industrial protection considerations just discussed offer only a rather weak explanation of inflation. *These structural considerations probably do provide an insight into the general tendency for more inflation in LDCs than in industrial countries but they are not powerful enough to explain the widely varying* *inflation experiences among developing countries*, especially as between the Latin American group and the rest. Even within Latin America, for which the structural model was developed, country experiences have differed widely but it does not seem that structural disequilibria could be strong enough to explain more than a small part of these differences, especially the hyperinflations of countries like Brazil and Chile.

Activity. Examine the relative behaviour of price indices for (1) total consumer expenditures, (2) food items only, (3) imports and (4) industrial output in order to obtain a first impression of the strength of structural factors in your own country's inflation. You could take this analysis further if you were able to discover the weight of foods, imports and manufactures in the total consumer price index.

Monetarist explanation

This leaves the monetarist explanation to consider and, in turning to this, we revert again to a model originated primarily as an explanation of inflation in industrial countries. Even though non-monetized, subsistence activity is far more significant in developing countries, the monetary theory has, none the less, been widely applied in studies of LDC inflations, as also in the study of world inflation. Although empirical studies do not provide conclusive results, it does seem that there is somewhat firmer evidence for the validity of the monetary model than of the two alternatives.

The monetarist model has been persuasively applied to explain the international transmission of

---

[11] Industrial country import volumes rose at 9 per cent per annum in 1960–70 and at 5·4 per cent in 1970–7. Foreign exchange reserves of non-oil LDCs in 1977 were equal to 28 per cent of their 1977 imports; the comparable figure for industrial countries was 19 per cent. Figures from IMF *Annual Report, 1976* and International Financial Statistics, May 1978.

[12] From Little, *et al.*, 1970, Table 5.1 it appears that the median rate of tariffs on manufactured goods in developing countries is around 70 per cent. Of this, allow a normal revenue-raising tariff of 20 per cent, leaving the other 50 per cent as 'pure' protection. Now assume that over (A) a twenty-year span or (B) a ten-year span the contribution of the output of the protected industries to consumer spending increases by (1) 15 per cent of total spending or (2) 30 per cent. We then get the following range of estimates of the annual inflation rate attributable to the protection of industry:

	(A)	(B)
(1)	0·375%	0·75%
(2)	0·75%	1·5%

inflation and especially the worldwide acceleration of price increases that occurred in the first half of the 1970s. This acceleration was widely attributed to the escalation of crude oil prices but this did not occur until 1974, by which time world inflation was already increasing (see Figure 7.1). It seems that an important reason for this acceleration was a rapid expansion in world money supply. Changes in market conditions for the currencies of the major trading nations – especially for the American dollar – led to a rapid increase in the world availability of foreign exchange reserves.[13] These, in turn, caused faster increases in domestic money supplies which were followed, as the monetarist model predicts, by accelerated inflation.

A number of studies of inflation in individual developing countries also lend support to the monetarist view. Argy, 1970, while failing to find much statistical support or the structural model, obtained strong results when monetary variables were included. For example, a test to explain differences in LDC inflation rates which included only structural variables yielded a statistical 'explanation' of only 17 per cent of inter-country differences, whereas 93 per cent of the variations were 'explained' when the rate of change of money supply was included.

Detailed studies of two high-inflation LDCs came to broadly similar results. An in-depth examination of the Brazilian case found little support for the structural model but strong evidence in favour of a monetary explanation (Kahil, 1973). A well-known study of the Chilean case agreed on the importance of money supply as a source of inflation (Harberger, 1964). This found that, with a time-lag of about a year, a 1 per cent increase in money supply resulted in a 1 per cent increase in the general price level. (It also found that an extra 1 per cent growth of output meant that prices rose about 1 per cent less than they otherwise would have done, supporting the earlier point that the demand for money is strongly influenced by the real growth of the economy and that a rapidly-expanding economy can absorb a faster growing money supply without inflationary consequences.)[14]

On the basis of these and other studies, we can agree for developing countries with the conclusion of a major survey of the literature on industrial country inflations (Laidler and Parkin, 1975, p. 795), that the evidence on the responsiveness of the inflation rate to excess demand supports the view that sustained expansion of the money supply, faster than the growth of demand for real money balances, is both a necessary and sufficient condition for inflation. Note, though, that to say that excess monetary expansion is necessary and sufficient for inflation is not the same thing as saying that it is the only cause of inflation.

> **Activity.** Try plotting the growth rates of (1) real income, (2) money supply and (3) the price level of your own country on a graph, in an attempt to obtain a rough test of the validity of the monetary explanation of the inflation that has occurred. Allow for time lags between (1) and (2) on the one hand and (3) on the other, of between six months and two years.

Why do governments permit inflation?

Given the universal incidence of inflation, the monetary theory provides only a superficial explanation. Since the money supply is at least partly under the control of the government, the more fundamental question arises, why do so many governments permit the money supply to expand too fast for price stability? Indeed, we will see later that monetary expansion often emanates directly from the government's own budget. Yet inflation is unpopular and governments usually say that price stability is one of their policy objectives. How is this puzzle to be explained?

The answer is probably that effective measures to halt inflation are at least as unpopular as letting it continue at a moderate rate. The existence of large-scale unemployment is one reason for this. In the mid-1970s the western industrial countries found themselves in the uncomfortable and novel position of having both high inflation rates and abnormally high unemployment. A new word was coined to describe this – 'stagflation'. It was a situation which governments found difficult to manage because both the price increases and the shortages of jobs were electorally unpopular and actions to reduce one of these problems tended to make the other worse. *But for the governments of developing countries a combination of inflation and high unemployment is a permanent condition.* Inflation is a characteristic of developing countries (see above) and so is large-scale under-utilization of labour (Chapter 5).

Measures that tackle inflation by cutting back on total demand – reduced government spending, credit

---

[13] This paragraph is based on Heller, 1976. He shows how the world growth rate of international reserves resulted in enlarged increases in domestic money supplies. Annual rates of growth of world international reserves were:

1950–9	2·3%
1960–9	3·1%
1969–74	18.0%

[14] Argy, 1970, also found a 1 per cent growth of real output to be associated with a 1 per cent reduction in inflation.

restrictions, increased taxation – are liable to worsen unemployment, and any government will shrink from anything which does that. Governments, moreover, are expected to play a prominent role in promoting economic development but often find the tax capacities of their countries insufficient to finance desired development projects. So there is a constant temptation to fill the financial gap by borrowing from the banks – an action which increases money supply and thus contributes to inflationary pressures. Most governments spend more than is consistent with a serious effort to halt inflation.

It is also likely that those who gain from inflation, or who would suffer most from attempts to control it, are among the politically most powerful groups in society. The welfare costs of inflation are (1) diffused among the consuming public but (2) tend to be especially concentrated on groups whose economic and political power is relatively slight – the retired, the urban unemployed, the housewives. If this is the case, it seems that inflation has persisted, and will continue to do so, because serious counter-measures are seen by governments as creating larger political problems than those created by inflation itself.

Summary on the causes of inflation

The conclusions of this survey of alternative explanations of inflation can now be summarized as follows:

(1) Both supply and demand factors contribute to an on-going inflation. This makes it difficult to establish the initiating cause.
(2) There is, in any case, no reason for thinking that the initiating force will be the same for all countries, or at different times in a single country.
(3) Although import prices do have an inflationary influence, the cost-push model fails to provide an adequate explanation of the initiation of inflation in most developing countries.
(4) Structural considerations help to explain why LDCs are generally more prone to inflation than industrial countries. But the inflationary effects of structural disequilibria are unlikely to be large in most circumstances and they cannot explain widely varying inflation experiences among developing countries, nor the initiation of rapid inflations experienced in a few of them.
(5) Expansion of the supply of money more rapidly than the growth in demand for it is sufficient to initiate inflation and essential to keep inflation going. This was probably the initiating force in at least some high-inflation countries. However, the impact of rising prices on the general public is limited to the extent that production and consumption still occurs outside the monetized part of the economy.
(6) Governments dislike measures which restrict total demand and money supply because of adverse effects on employment and economic expansion. Anti-inflationary counter-measures may be seen by governments as creating more political problems than allowing moderate inflation to continue.

On the basis of these conclusions, a typical inflationary process might take the following sequence: there will be a persistant upward trend in import prices. An increase in money supply which outstrips the demand for money may be superimposed on this, due perhaps to external forces or a large expansion of domestic credit. The excess money supply spills over into greater demand for goods. This stimulates output in sectors operating below full capacity but, even though there is much unemployment, will bid up prices in other sectors.

Food prices are especially likely to go up and increases in these and other prices, perhaps occurring simultaneously with larger industrial profits, will provoke trade unions into making large wage claims. Employers may not resist these claims very hard because buoyant demand allows them to pass cost increases on to consumers. Rather than cut its own spending and risk a slow-down in the economy, the government allows the money supply to keep moving ahead of demand for money. Demand, cost and structural factors are now interacting in such a way that inflation is likely to continue indefinitely unless the government finally steels itself to adopt effective counter-measures.

The suggestion that governments may believe that the problems and unpopularity of inflation are smaller than anti-inflationary measures brings us to a major issue so far evaded: to what extent and in what circumstances should inflation be regarded as a problem calling for government correction? Does inflation really matter much? It is to this issue that we turn now.

III. Consequences

In order to assess whether inflation matters we must enter into further controversies. There is first a long-standing debate about the effects of inflation on the real growth of an economy, with some arguing that it will promote growth, others taking the weaker position that inflation is an inevitable accompaniment of growth, and yet others urging that inflation will impede growth. A second, related debate concerns the impact of inflation on the distribution of income, with one school urging that this is likely to be beneficial and others taking an opposite stand.

Inflation and economic growth

The pro-inflation case

We have already noted the structuralist position on the relationship between inflation and growth. According to this view, some sectors which are under-utilized and suffering from inadequate demand coexist with others experiencing excess demand and rising prices. Because of poor information flows, various immobilities, shortages of entrepreneurial talent and technological know-how – all tending to reduce supply elasticities – relatively large disequilibria (and the inflation they cause) will be necessary before the economic system responds to break the bottle-necks. A heavy cost would be imposed in terms of reduced output and growth if total demand were held to such low levels that there was no inflation even in the low-elasticity sectors. At moderate rates of inflation – and we concluded earlier that structural disequilibria were only likely to result in modest inflation – there is a trade-off between rising prices and growth. So, it is argued, a society that gives priority to growth must be willing to tolerate the inflation that comes with it.

This view finds wide acceptance among economists but there is another major body of thought which goes further to argue in favour of the deliberate pursuit of inflationary credit creation as a means of accelerating growth. In a nutshell, the argument is that inflation redistributes incomes in such a way as to raise saving and investment, thus accelerating growth.

According to this view, company profits and the government budget are likely to be major beneficiaries from inflation, at the expense of consumers and, especially, the urban wage-labour force. Companies operating in conditions of general excess demand find themselves able to raise prices, initially without any comparable rise in costs. Their profit margins therefore widen. Now, companies often reinvest large proportions of increases in profits, rather than paying them all out to shareholders. Wage workers and many consumers, on the other hand, are likely to consume almost all their incomes, saving little. There has thus been a redistribution of income from low to high savers.

The government budget is another prospective gainer from inflation and the government, too, is likely to have a higher marginal propensity to save than the general public. The chief way in which the budget benefits is through the inflation tax mentioned earlier. Johnson (1967) has explained the concept of the inflation tax as follows:

> In order to maintain its real balances constant in the face of inflation, the public must accumulate money balances at a rate equal to the inflation; this accumulation of money balances in order to preserve real balances is achieved at the cost of sacrificing the consumption of current real income in order to maintain real balances intact, the release of current real income constituting the equivalent of a 'tax' on the holders of real balances; the tax on real balances, in turn, accrues as revenue to the beneficiaries of the inflationary increase in the money supply.

The incidence of this tax, then, falls upon holders of money balances, i.e. virtually everyone. Inflation reduces the purchasing power of a given sum of money. The public has to increase the nominal value of its money stocks in order to maintain their real value, and to achieve this it has to forego expenditures on goods and services. This reduction in spending releases real resources in the economy which can be used for investment. Either the government can tap it all by claiming greater credit from the banks, or it can share the extra credit with the private sector.

> **Key concept.** The **inflation tax** is represented by the sacrifice of goods and services needed in order to maintain the real value of money balances in the face of a rising price level.

The 'revenue' potential of this tax is limited by the initial size of money balances relative to total economic activity, represented by the ratio of money supply to GDP. This ratio is generally in the range of 20 to 30 per cent in LDCs.[15] Assuming the ratio to remain constant at 25 per cent, the revenue-raising and savings effects of the tax are illustrated in Figure 7.5. The speed of inflation (the rate of the inflation tax) is measured on the vertical axis; the resources released by the tax are expressed, as a percentage of GDP, on the horizontal.

Three types of relationships are portrayed by the diagram. The lower of these is called the 'revenue' curve. This tells us the amount of resources (as a percentage of GDP) released by alternative rates of inflation (assuming the money–GDP ratio to remain

---

[15] See McKinnon, 1973, Table 8-4, who gives ratios for eleven LDCs varying (for the latest year shown) between 18 per cent and 30 per cent of GNP, with an unweighted mean of 25·4 per cent.

at 25 per cent). With 10 per cent inflation, the tax will raise a 'revenue' of 2·5 per cent (i.e. the inflation rate multiplied by the money–GDP ratio). With 20 per cent inflation 'revenue' will be 5 per cent of GDP; and so forth.

Figure 7.5   *The inflation tax.*

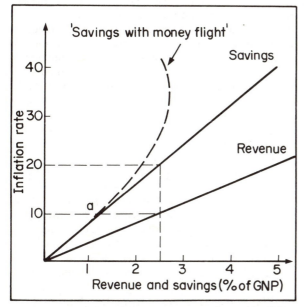

However, it is unrealistic to think that all these revenues will constitute net savings to be invested in development projects. Maybe some of the revenues will come from reduced voluntary savings, rather than reduced consumption. Some of the revenue is liable to spill over into increased commercial bank credit to finance consumption and some is likely to finance increased consumption by the government itself, in forms such as increased spending on general administration. To allow for these factors, the upper unbroken 'savings' curve is drawn on the assumption that only half of the revenues are net savings. In this case 10 per cent inflation raises savings by 1·25 per cent of GDP, 20 per cent inflation by 2·5 per cent of GDP, and so on.

Finally, we can drop the assumption that the ratio of money to GDP will remain unchanged at 25 per cent. The ratio may go down when inflation increases, with the demand for money falling as the net utility of money balances declines. This is illustrated by the dotted 'savings with money flight' curve. It is drawn to show that the power of higher inflation rates to release more resources diminishes sharply at rates above a notional 10 per cent (i.e. at points above 'a' on the dotted curve). The curve eventually bends backwards, because flight from money may become so pronounced at very high inflation rates that revenues

actually diminish as prices soar to ever higher levels. In this respect the inflation tax is like the income tax – levying it at very high rates will induce more tax evasion and may diminish total revenues.

Activity. The notion of the inflation tax is not a simple one and you may like to pause here to review your understanding of the last paragraphs. Use national statistics to calculate the ratio of money supply to GDP and consider the implications of your results for the power of this tax in your own country.

We can complete the pro-inflation case with two further arguments. If we accept that inflation will raise saving, investment and real growth, then this may produce secondary effects which bring further improvements in economic performance. This may occur if the proportion of income voluntarily saved goes up as income rises. If saving is a function of real per capita income, it follows that anything which helps to raise per capita incomes – including an accelerated growth of output resulting from inflation – will also help raise voluntary saving, and hence investment and growth.

Finally, some advocates of growth through inflation have held out the rosy prospect that, after a while, the inflationary process will reverse itself (Lewis, 1955, p. 405):

Inflation for the purpose of capital formation is in due course self-destructive. The inflation has three stages. Prices rise sharply in the first stage while the capital is being created. In the second stage the inflation may peter out of its own accord because the rise in prices has redistributed income in such a way that voluntary saving is rapidly catching up with investment. Then in the third stage prices fall, as the additional output of consumer goods made possible by the capital formation begins to reach the market. It is only the first stage that is dangerous and painful.

However, this seems too optimistic, for we have seen that in practice the general price level almost never falls. To believe in self-destructive inflation we have to believe that prices are not sticky downwards and that for some reason incomes and demand will not go up to the same extent that production goes up. Although more rapid output growth is indeed associated with slower inflation, such optimism would not find much support today. Many would also dispute the idea that, as a result of inflation, voluntary saving would begin to catch up with investment, so we turn now to the views of those who believe that inflation is more likely to hinder growth than promote it.

Anti-inflation arguments

First, the sceptics advance a number of reasons for suspecting that inflation is likely to reduce voluntary saving. Inflation penalizes saving because it reduces the purchasing power of the income that has been set aside. We have already explored this in relation to saving that takes the form of money holdings, suggesting that the higher the expected rate of inflation the smaller will be the real value of money balances that people wish to hold. The case can be broadened to relate to other forms of saving. In most countries there are restrictions on interest rates, with rates on bank deposits generally held down to between 3 and 6 per cent. If it becomes at all rapid, the rate of inflation (the rate of decline in the value of money) will therefore exceed interest rates payable on financial assets. Our saver may put his money in a savings bank but once inflation reaches double figures it is unlikely that the bank will be able to offer him a rate high enough to compensate for the fall in the value of money. When inflation is combined with low interest rates, always borrow, never lend; if you borrow, the real value of what you repay will be less than the real value of what you borrowed in the first instance.

Inflation may also reduce the productivity of investment or distort its composition. If new investments are to have high productivities, those responsible for making investment decisions need to operate in an environment which favours forward planning. But inflation makes forward planning more difficult. It introduces major new elements of uncertainty and makes it more difficult to predict future trends, the state of markets and relative prices.

Inflation may also lure firms into unwise investment decisions because their accounts will probably mislead them about their current profitability. For example, accountants generally calculate depreciation on the basis of what an asset originally cost the firm (as against what its replacement will cost); in times of inflation firms therefore tend to underestimate depreciation – and therefore overestimate profits – because they are not putting enough money into reserves to enable them to replace an asset when it reaches the end of its useful life. Similarly, many of the profits of manufacturing and trading firms in times of rapid inflation are the illusory result of stock appreciation, with production or sales costs failing to fully reflect the amounts that will be needed to make good the supplies used up. It was, for instance, estimated that nearly one-half of the profits of British companies in 1974 were simply the result of stock appreciation. Industrial prices rose by 23 per cent in that year. Because of this, many managements were misled into unwise policies and subsequently found themselves in financial difficulties, leading in some cases to bankruptcy.

Another facet of decision-making with rising prices is that it tends to alter the *composition* of investment in favour of quick-yielding, often speculative projects. Ventures which take some time to be completed, or which yield their benefits only over a long time, are discounted. There is an easy profit to be made out of buying goods, allowing their value to appreciate as prices rise and then selling them off at inflated prices – an activity which has little developmental value. On the other hand, investments, say, in research or heavy industry may be discouraged, with adverse consequences for technological progress and development. Furthermore, almost all governments respond to inflation by imposing price controls. For reasons given later, these are likely to further distort the pattern of investment, discouraging capital formation in industries whose prices can be effectively controlled. Since price controls are especially concentrated on 'essential' goods, this may have a particularly undesirable effect on the pattern of investment and subsequent production.

Quite apart from adverse effects on saving and investment, inflationary pressure may hold back the growth of the economy through its impact on the balance of payments. Assume, for a moment, that the rate of exchange between the domestic currency and foreign currencies is fixed. In this case, excess demand at home will spill over into an increased demand for imports which may be greater than the availability of foreign exchange. Moreover, domestic inflation will raise the cost of producing exports without compensating rises in the world prices at which they are sold. The profitability of exports will decline, the export sector may stagnate and the balance of payments be further undermined. Potential foreign investors may also be discouraged from bringing their finance into a country with high inflation and an over-valued currency, thus further reducing the availability of foreign exchange and the quantity of investment.

A common response to such a situation would be for the government to try to protect the foreign exchange situation by imposing import and exchange restrictions but these will push import prices even higher and have other adverse consequences for economic development, as is shown in the next chapter. With a fixed exchange rate, inflation is likely to hamper economic development by inducing a shortage of foreign exchange. A government can try to escape this consequence by depreciating its currency. But many governments have been reluctant to do this and, in any case, currency depreciation also causes price increases. The price effects of import controls and currency depreciation are discussed further in the next chapter, pages 216–17.

There are, then, arguments to be made for and against the use of inflation as an aid to economic growth. These can be summarized in the following list of the conditions that would have to be satisfied for inflation to accelerate the growth of the economy. *For inflation to result in accelerated growth* **All** *the following conditions have to be satisfied:*

(1) It should result in a net increase in saving. This would result from a redistribution of income from low savers to high savers (including the government) and would have to be sufficient to more than offset the negative effects of inflation on voluntary saving. Note that this condition is unlikely to be satisfied with cost-push inflation, in which profit margins would be squeezed by escalating import and wage costs.

(2) Assuming condition (1) to be met, it would also be necessary that a shortage of savings was the chief factor holding back the growth of the economy (the 'binding constraint'). This may not be the case. Shortages of foreign exchange might be the critical bottle-neck and inflation would make them worse. Or shortages of skills, or knowledge of appropriate technologies might be the binding constraint.

(3) Assuming (2) also to be met, the net increase in investment resulting from greater saving should be more than sufficient to offset the likely negative effects of inflation on the productivity and composition of investment.

(4) Finally, the institutional and political structures of the country should be strong enough to keep inflation sufficiently under control that it does not develop into hyperinflation, causing a flight from money, a retreat into subsistence production, and major economic dislocations.

This is evidently a restrictive set of conditions, not impossible to satisfy but too restrictive to hold in most developing economies.

> **Activity.** As a discussion topic or written assignment, consider whether these conditions are met in your own country.

The evidence

We ought to be able to discover whether inflation assists growth through empirical research. But here too research findings are rather inconclusive.[16] For single-figure inflation rates there is no clear correlation between rising prices and real economic growth. That is to say, inflation of up to about 10 per cent a year seems not to affect growth. There is evidence, however, that more rapid inflation is an obstacle to growth, indicated by statistically significant negative correlations between double-figure, or above-average, inflation and economic growth. This is not unexpected because the negative effects of rising prices on saving, the balance of payments and the efficiency of investment are likely to become rapidly larger as the inflation rate rises, tending increasingly to outweigh the benefits. Latin American examples of rapid inflation further illustrate the damage that rising prices can do to economic expansion.

Inflation and the distribution of income

So far this discussion of the consequences of inflation has been confined to its effects on the growth of the economy. This is appropriate because growth is of critical concern to low-income countries but it contrasts sharply with the approach to this question in high-income countries, where concern with inflation stems mainly from its effects on the distribution of income. Since LDCs are becoming increasingly concerned with distributional questions, we should not neglect this aspect here.

Which groups gain and which lose from inflation depends upon the answers to a number of prior questions. Are local food prices moving ahead of the general price level? Which groups in society are best able to anticipate inflation and protect themselves against it? What kind of inflation is it? (Cost-push and demand-pull inflation have different distributional results.) In line with our earlier conclusions on the causes of inflation, the following discussion will generally assume the existence of demand inflation. We start by looking at the probable *gainers* from inflation.

Who gains from inflation?

To begin with, there is likely to be a general redistribution of resources away from the private sector in favour of the government budget, because of the inflation tax. The budget is also likely to benefit because inflation raises people's money incomes (even though their real incomes may be unchanged), thus putting them into higher income tax brackets and

---

[16] The evidence on which this paragraph is based is in Thirlwall, 1974, ch. 9.

increasing their tax liabilities.* Furthermore, the government is a net debtor and, for the reason given on page 174, inflation will therefore benefit the budget by reducing the real cost of servicing the public debt.

Whether this shift of resources to the government is regarded as desirable will depend on a host of considerations, some of which were touched upon in Chapter 1. Much would depend on how the resulting additions to government spending benefit different social groups. We might note, however, that American studies suggest that the inflation tax is regressive; the income tax effects might also be regressive if the really rich are able to evade their additional tax liabilities, as they often can (see Chapter 6).

In the case of demand-pull inflation, it is also most probable that profits will increase and those who receive them will gain. Indeed, much of the argument that inflation will raise saving *requires* a shift in favour of profits. Prices will rise ahead of costs, giving larger profit margins. Most firms will also be net debtors and will thus benefit from the declining real burden of their debts. Other classes of net debtors will also gain from inflation.

If the government maintains a fixed exchange rate, importers will also benefit. Buoyant demand conditions and limited import capacity will create a scarcity premium on imported goods, enabling importers to raise their domestic prices with no parallel increases in the prices they pay abroad. If food production is relatively inelastic with respect to price – and we have seen this to be probable – then food farmers and distributors may also be among the gainers, enjoying an increase in the prices they receive greater than the inflation of the prices they pay to satisfy their own needs.

And who are the losers?

This description of the groups most likely to gain from inflation goes a long way to define the groups most likely to be the *losers*. If debtors are gainers then creditors and savers must be losers. If, with a fixed exchange rate, importers are gainers, domestic producers of exports and of import substitutes will be

losers. If the food farmers are gainers, those dependent on their crops will suffer.

To put the matter more generally, three broad groups of probable losers can be identified. One is the economically inactive: the unemployed, housewives, children, students, the aged. As consumers they suffer from rising prices and their receipts will not go up to compensate for rising living costs. They will generally be dependent on the incomes of others or on the state. The other major groups of losers are the modern-sector wage-labour force and the urban poor (these two groupings obviously overlap). The wage-labour force is likely to lose through the inflation tax, the income tax and the relative rise in food prices. In many countries the trade union movement will not be strong enough to prevent wages from lagging behind prices. The urban poor who depend on the 'informal sector' (see page 117) for their livelihood will be especially hard hit by rising food prices and by the probability that informal sector earnings will lag even further behind prices than earnings in the modern sector.

We should also consider the effect of inflation on employment. In the 'Phillips curve' illustration in Chapter 2 (page 34), a trade-off was suggested between open unemployment and inflation, with increased unemployment shown as a necessary cost of reduced inflation. Such a trade-off may well exist, at least in the negative sense that policies designed to reduce domestic demand may cause some industrial contraction. On the other hand, the bulk of labour under-utilization in developing countries is not caused by deficiency of aggregate demand so the expansion of demand is not effective in creating employment.

Inflation will also affect the relative prices of labour and capital, probably to the disadvantage of labour. For, while wages may lag behind prices, interest rates are likely to be left even further behind (which is why creditors lose and debtors gain from inflation). So the cost of capital will fall relative to the cost of labour, encouraging the adoption of capital-intensive techniques and discouraging employment creation. But the most important way in which inflation will affect job availabilities will be through its impact on overall economic growth. If it stimulates growth the outcome will be favourable for job creation, but it will hold back the expansion of employment if it retards growth.

Conclusion on distributional effects

It is therefore difficult to generalize about the consequences of inflation for income distribution. These will depend upon the nature of the inflation, the

---

* To illustrate, assume the cut-off point for the income tax is an annual income of $301, below which no tax is payable and above which it is payable at 20 per cent. Now take a worker earning $300 in a country which is experiencing inflation at 15 per cent a year. Because of the existence of a weak trade union, a strong employer and many unemployed he may only receive a partial compensation for the inflation, with a 10 per cent pay rise. His gross income goes up to $330 but he is now liable to pay $6 tax on the extra $30 so that his after-tax income is $324. In real terms this is worth less than his original $300 ($324 \div 1·15 = 282$ which is 6 per cent less than 300), both because of lagging wages and the income tax effect.

behaviour of food prices, exchange-rate policy, the bargaining power of various socio-economic groups, and its impact on the growth rate. However, if it is correct to say that, most inflations are induced by excess demand, that food prices go up more than other consumer prices and that bargaining strength is related to the initial incomes and wealth of each group, then *it is more likely than not that inflation will worsen income inequalities*, with the urban poor being especially vulnerable. There is some empirical evidence to support this conclusion. A study found 'big industrialists, merchants and contractors, together with big landlords' to have been the most probable beneficiaries of inflation in Brazil (Kahil, 1973 p. 332); studies of Ghana and India also suggest that inflation worsened inequalities (Lisk, 1976; and Gupta, 1974).

If this is indeed the general outcome of inflation it is a serious matter. There is already much inequality in most developing countries, as was shown in Chapter 5, and a loss of purchasing power which is merely an inconvenience to the affluent can be a catastrophe for the millions who live on or near the poverty line.

So does inflation matter?

Whether inflation constitutes a problem calling for corrective action depends primarily upon the pace at which the price level is rising. The worldwide nature of inflation makes it practically inevitable that escalating import prices will spill over into the domestic price level. In economies seriously trying to achieve economic growth and development, the structural factors surveyed earlier are also likely to impart an upward movement to the price level. However, in normal conditions these forces will only result in modest price increases and will hence only slightly widen income inequalities. It would retard development efforts to pursue fiscal and monetary policies so restrictive as to prevent even this degree of inflation. Indeed, there is a case for maintaining some pressure of excess demand as a means of keeping the economy operating as near to full capacity as possible. We may thus agree with the quotation from Lord Keynes at the head of the chapter that 'inflation is unjust and deflation is inexpedient'.

Five per cent might be taken as representative of a harmless level of inflation, although, in fact, this would vary according to individual country circumstances. But once inflation begins to rise much above the 5 per cent level, it is much more likely to cause net harm to the economy – worsening inequalities and increasingly holding back economic growth. For most countries, prices rising at 10 per cent or more would be above the harmless level,

especially with inflexible exchange rates. *Double-figure inflation is the enemy*, especially if it climbs above 20 or 30 per cent a year.

Now, referring back to the figures in Table 7.1 (page 158) we see that developing countries as a whole, and each major regional group, experienced double figure inflation in 1972–7, with an overall average of 25 per cent. This is perhaps sufficient to establish that inflation is a serious economic problem for a large proportion of LDCs. The final step, therefore, is to examine policies which governments may employ to keep inflation below dangerous levels.

Activity. You may at this stage wish to review the arguments of this section to see whether you agree with the conclusions arrived at and to consider whether they are valid for your own country.

IV.   Policy Responses

It was suggested earlier that inflation is widespread because governments often believe that serious counter-measures will be politically more unpopular than allowing price rises to continue. If this were generally the case we would have to be pessimistic about the feasibility of effective policy responses. We should not be too sceptical, however. The political costs and benefits will vary according to the pace of inflation and this fact can be used to support the conclusions of the last section.

What was suggested there is that moderate, '5 per cent', inflation calls for no particular policy response other than vigilance: measures so stringent as to prevent this moderate inflation may well damage economic performance – and are also likely to be politically more unpopular than the inflation itself. But if inflation accelerates into the double-figure range the economic case for counter-measures grows stronger – and so does public hostility to rising prices. As the need for counter-measures grows stronger so too does the probability that politicians will see it as in their own interests to do something.

What is signalled by these political-economy considerations, however, is a need to devise policies that at least do not make it more difficult for politicians to act. This involves the selection of measures which are efficient by the criteria developed in Chapter 2, of which perhaps the most important in this context is the need for measures which act directly on the causes of inflation. To try to combat cost inflation by cutting back demand is likely to be both ineffective and politically damaging; the same is true of trying to hold down costs in the face of demand inflation. So, *accurate diagnosis of the initiating cause of inflation is an essential preliminary to sensible policy-making.*

One other preliminary consideration concerns the rate of exchange between domestic and foreign currencies. There have already been several references to the importance of this, stressing the damage that inflation can do to the balance of payments if the rate of exchange is kept fixed. The policy option of exchange rate flexibility, reducing the value of the domestic currency relative to foreign currencies if domestic inflation threatens the competitiveness of the export and import-substituting sectors, is considered in the next chapter, where it is compared with the alternative of exchange controls. However, to keep the exposition here as simple as possible, *we will assume that the government pursues a policy of exchange rate flexibility.*

Depreciation of the currency will, it is true, raise the domestic prices of imported goods, thus adding to inflation. But it will protect the balance of payments and has the additional advantage of improving the government's control over the money supply. Under a fixed exchange rate, the supply of money will be powerfully influenced by what is happening to the balance of payments, with deficits reducing money supply and surpluses increasing it. This will severely restrict the freedom of the government to make independent decisions about monetary policy and aggregate demand, so exchange rate flexibility adds to the effective range of domestic policy options.

Antidotes to cost-push inflation

Since this chapter has doubted the importance of cost-push and structuralist explanations of the initiation of double-figure inflation, we will not spend much space considering policy responses to these two situations, preferring to spend more on methods of managing demand. However, there is no doubt that cost-push and structural elements can be important in particular situations so we must not neglect them altogether.

We saw earlier that at the heart of cost-push explanations of inflation lay the notion of a wage-price spiral (page 167). The type of response which is usually proposed for this case, and has been widely employed in western industrial countries, is a *'prices and incomes' package of policies.* This has been seen as a 'social contract' between the government, as representative of the public interest, and key pressure groups such as trade unions and employers' organizations. The main intention of such a package

is to set limits on collective bargaining so as to hold wage increases to non-inflationary levels, thus weakening the propagation mechanism. To over-simplify a little, this requires wage increases to be held to the rate at which labour productivity is growing, so that increased purchasing power is matched by greater supplies and unit labour costs are stabilized.[17] Governments might attempt to achieve this wage restraint by voluntary agreements, or by inserting government representation into wage bargaining processes, or by legislation. In any case, they are likely to have to offer inducements for trade unionists to accept such a policy, such as restrictions on dividend payments, the subsidization of essential consumer goods and the imposition of price controls. Hence it is best to think of this as a package of measures rather than as a single instrument.

The experience of industrial countries with this type of package has been mixed. In some (West Germany and Sweden are often given as examples) it seems to have worked quite well in helping to contain inflation. In others (Britain being perhaps the most notorious case) incomes policies have created at least as many problems as they have solved and have been unable to prevent above-average inflation for more than brief periods. One difficulty is that prices and incomes policies have sometimes been used to combat demand inflation, not cost inflation. In this situation wages are held down but prices continue to rise because action is not taken to get rid of excess demand. Workers find the purchasing power of their wages falling, trade unions become more militant, there are strikes and the social contract falls into disrepute.

Many developing countries might be said to have a more or less permanent incomes policy, where trade unions are controlled by the state to prevent 'excessive' wage increases. On the other hand, the economic significance of this control is limited by the smallness of the wage bill relative to total incomes in developing countries (page 168). In countries with strong and independent unions, the viability of a prices and incomes package will be especially sensitive to the behaviour of food prices, because of their importance to the cost of living of wage-workers. Rises in the cost of foodstuffs relative to the general price level will reduce the tolerance of unions for wage restraint, in which case adequate agricultural policies will be important in the fight against inflation.

Whether or not the government adopts an incomes policy, it is very likely to impose controls on a wide

---

[17] There is, in fact, a case for holding wage increases a little below the growth of productivity. The issues are well discussed in Bhatt, 1976.

range of consumer-good prices. Indeed, price controls are sometimes presented as a self-sufficient anti-inflationary policy. So it is worth asking, what can price controls do?

There are severe limits on what controls can achieve. Clearly, no government would want to set the control prices so low as to discourage the production and distribution of consumer goods. That would be self-defeating because the object is to protect the living standards of the public, which can scarcely be achieved if supplies are reduced. So control prices have to be high enough to allow 'normal' profits in production and distribution – profits which give enough incentive to producers and distributors to maintain supplies. It follows, then, that controls can only reduce prices to the extent that there were formerly 'abnormal', or monopoly, profits. Even where there were initially large monopoly profits, the price effect of controls will be largely once-and-for-all because after the excess profits have been eliminated the controllers will have to allow prices to rise in line with costs if they are not to discourage supply.

There are other complications. As a practical matter, it is not feasible to impose controls on all goods; the price lists are usually confined to selected 'essential' consumer goods. This introduces a number of distortions. First (and assuming the controls are enforced), the purchasing power that would have been absorbed by the essentials in the absence of controls is now likely to spill over into demand for uncontrolled items, raising their prices and thus the general price level. Secondly, these changes in relative prices will encourage investment in the production of uncontrolled, non-essential goods at the expense of investment in the production of essentials – the opposite of what would be desirable in order to protect the living standards of the poor. Thirdly, the income distribution consequences of controls on essentials are further obscured by uncertainties about how supplies are allocated among customers. Without controls supplies will be rationed by the criterion of ability to pay. Controls remove rationing by price but do not substitute any other allocative mechanism. The price is no longer a market-clearing price, demand will exceed supply and some customers will go unsatisfied. The danger is that the wealthier, more influential consumers will still come out on top. In principle, this difficulty can be removed by introducing a government-administered rationing system but the practical difficulties are formidable and abuses will be inevitable. Except in wartime, most governments are unwilling to introduce rationing.

The potential impact of controls is also limited by other considerations. The most serious is the problem of enforcement. Traders are adept at finding ways of

---

Activity. Use a simple supply and demand diagram to illustrate the excess demand that is created by imposing a control on a commodity at less than a market-clearing price.

---

evading controls and the general public is often unaware of its rights. Sometimes a special corps of price inspectors is employed but it is usually small and has to police a multitude of small shops and market stalls. The inspectors will be tempted by bribes from those exceeding the control limits, and corruption of the law enforcers is one of the main reasons why controls have been ineffective in most countries that have tried them.[18] In fact, it is probably fair to say that in most countries price controls are a facade. They give the appearance that the government is doing something – an appearance boosted by a few well-publicized prosecutions of traders charging excess prices – but in practice make little difference to the cost of living.

Increases in import prices are perhaps the most serious source of cost inflation in many LDCs and the question arises, what should the government do about these? The general answer seems to be that it is better to do nothing other than ensuring that these increases do not spill over into a general inflationary spiral. To try to offset rising import prices by holding down wages or the general level of demand will probably do more harm than good, creating social injustices or retarding the expansion of the economy. The task, then, is to absorb the imported inflation. This was not difficult for most countries until the world price explosion of 1973/74, because import prices were rising only slowly; the large increases in the latter period did, however, cause significant increases in the general price level of many countries, to say nothing of the problems created for the balance of payments.[19] But this was essentially a world problem, best solved by the international co-ordination of national policies; there was little that any developing country could do by itself.

---

[18] For evidence on the effectiveness of controls and a fuller development of the arguments of the last three paragraphs see Killick, 1973.

[19] Assume that imports are equivalent to 25 per cent of GDP and that import prices rise by an average of 8 per cent a year. The direct impact on the general level of domestic prices will be only 2 per cent. In 1960–72 LDC import prices went up at less than 1 per cent a year. However, in 1972–5 they rose at 19 per cent p.a. With an import ratio of 25 per cent, even this rate of import inflation would directly raise the domestic price level by less than 5 per cent per annum.

Minimizing structural inflation

Our earlier consideration of the causes of inflation accepted that structural disequilibria were likely to induce a general tendency for the price level to rise. What, then should governments try to do about this? The position of most structuralists is permissive: structural inflation is a by-product of development and measures to prevent this source of price increase are thus liable to hamper development. Therefore, it is better to accept inflation as a price of development.

This is too fatalistic, however. It overlooks that some of the disequilibria are induced by mistaken government policies rather than being an inevitable out-growth of economic development. We saw, for example, that probably the most important disequilibrium was the tendency for food production to lag behind the expansion of demand, resulting in especially large increases in food prices. It is difficult to believe that lagging agriculture is a desirable or inevitable feature of development. In fact, it is often the result of government policies which discriminate against the agricultural sector (see Chapter 9). Policy changes to eliminate this bias would encourage food production and thus combat structural inflation. The same is true of inflation emanating from shortages of foreign exchange. More often than not, these are caused or aggravated by inadequate government policies towards the external sector and could be alleviated by better policies.

Much the same point can be made about price increases coming from high-cost import-substituting industries. While there is a case for providing a measure of protection to industry at an early stage of development, there is little to be said in favour of indiscriminately high rates of protection. More sensible protection policies would be good both for development and price stability. The same is true of other measures that reduce the exploitation of monopoly power.

So we should not be too permissive about structural inflation. Those disequilibria which result from policy mistakes can and should be rectified. This will, however, leave some inflation emanating from the development process which cannot easily or profitably be prevented by government action.

Controlling aggregate demand

If this chapter is correct in laying stress on excess demand as the most important initiating cause of double-figure inflation, the question arises, what policy instruments are available to governments to avoid excess monetary demand? Both fiscal policy (use of the government's powers of taxation, spending and borrowing) and monetary policy (manipulation of the volume of credit, interest rates and other monetary variables) are valuable in this context. There are also close connections between them.

Fiscal policy

One way of mopping up unwanted purchasing power is to increase *taxation*, while holding government spending as it was. Increases in income taxes have the advantage over commodity (indirect) taxes that they do not raise the prices of goods and their burden is more likely to fall upon those best able to pay. They have the disadvantage, however, of discouraging voluntary saving (some of the new revenue would probably have been saved rather than spent), which limits the amount of spending that is prevented and which may have adverse longer-term effects on investment and growth. Using indirect taxes, on the other hand, will have the initial effect of raising the prices of the goods being taxed, thus seeming to actually aggravate the inflation and possibly provoking defensive reactions from trade unions and others. In theory, an increase in indirect taxation, with government spending held constant, should not raise the general price level. Although the taxes raise the prices of particular goods, by absorbing purchasing power they should lower other prices or prevent them from rising so fast. The reality often appears different, however. There is also a danger that use of this weapon will adversely affect the distribution of income. Much of the extra tax bill may fall upon the poor because we saw in Chapter 6 that indirect taxes are generally more regressive than taxes on incomes (page 137).

How far the government will need to go in raising tax rates to absorb a given amount of purchasing power will partly depend on the existing structure of taxes, and especially on its income elasticity. The income elasticity of taxes is measured by the proportionate increase in revenues generated, with a fixed composition of tax, from a given increase in GDP. An elasticity greater than 1·0 means that the tax structure will claim an increasing share of GDP as GDP increases. If the tax structure has an elasticity greater than unity, then, tax revenues automatically increase by proportionately more than rises in total money incomes, thus reducing the public's spending power. An elastic tax system of this kind operates as a built-in stabilizer – absorbing purchasing power when demand inflation is pushing money incomes up, and augmenting purchasing power if the economy is depressed and money incomes are falling.

The government can also use the *spending* side of its budget to counter demand inflation. The general thrust here, of course, must be to reduce spending. But there are snags. Capital projects are the easiest expenditures to reduce quickly but the projects affected would have contributed to the growth of the economy and the future availability of goods and services. The recurrent budget is the main alternative source of cuts, but what is mainly involved here is the cost of the civil service and the current supplies needed to keep it productive. To make significant short-term reductions in the civil service and its supplies is difficult and unpopular, not least because they will add to a probably already large unemployment problem. Nevertheless, there is always some scope to cut recurrent and capital spending without seriously diminishing the value of government activities in the economy. To the extent that state spending is cut, this will reduce the amount of spending power in the economy.

In weighing the extent to which the Minister of Finance should use his tax and spending powers to limit aggregate demand, the most important magnitude he must study is the expected size of the *budget deficit*. All governments run deficits, in that their total spending exceeds the value of their tax and other current receipts. To some extent this deficit is financed by long-term borrowing, from abroad and from local residents. Borrowing from abroad is unlikely to be inflationary because the foreign exchange brings command over a larger supply of (imported) goods and services. Long-term borrowing from local residents is also unlikely to be inflationary because it will be matched by a reduction in the purchasing power of the general public.

However, it is quite possible that long-term borrowings will only partially cover the excess of state spending over current revenues, leaving a deficit to be financed by other means. Then the government usually fills the gap by short-term borrowing from the central and commerical banks. This government borrowing from the banking system is known as deficit financing and usually has highly expansionary effects on money supply and total demand. To simplify, it increases the money supply by the amount of the deficit but is likely also to result in secondary increases in money supply by increasing the cash base of the banking system and hence its ability to lend more to private borrowers.

> **Key concept.** When governments borrow from the central and commercial banks in order to balance the budget, they are said to be undertaking **deficit financing.**

To say that deficit financing is expansionary does not necessarily mean it is inflationary. We saw

earlier that an expanding money supply is only inflationary when it exceeds the growth in demand for money balances. The expansion in the demand for money sets the limit for non-inflationary increases in money supply and bank credit. In, a mixed economy, we expect some of this increased lending power to be utilized by the private sector, with the remainder representing the non-inflationary maximum of government deficit financing.

The point is illustrated in Figure 7.6, with total bank credit and money supply measured on the vertical axis and time on the horizontal.[20] The MD curve shows how the demand for money can be expected to grow over time in the absence of inflation, as real incomes go up and activity becomes monetized. The increase in MD between two points in time sets the limit to the non-inflationary expansion of bank credit. If V represents private sector demand for bank credit and we assume this demand is always met, then the difference between the expansion of MD and V over a period represents the amount of non-inflationary deficit financing that may be undertaken by the state. Thus, between t_1 and t_2 the demand for money goes up by $m_1 m_2$ and private credit by $v_1 v_2$, leaving $(m_1 m_2) - (v_1 v_2)$ as the non-inflationary limit of deficit financing. (Of course, the V curve could be taken to represent the state's demand for bank credit, in which case $(m_1 m_2) - (v_1 v_2)$ would represent the non-inflationary limit to additional credit for the private sector.)

Figure 7.6 *The non-inflationary limit to deficit financing.*

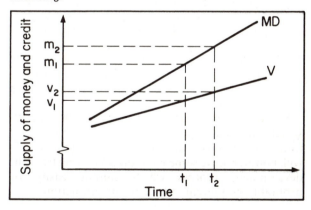

So in putting together his budget proposals for taxation and spending the Finance Minister has to keep in mind the volume of deficit financing they will necessitate. If he is concerned about inflation he has

[20] Money supply is here assumed to increase by the same magnitude as increases in credit, although changes in foreign exchange reserves would cause the two to differ.

to ensure that his proposals will not require state short-term borrowings from the banking system on an inflationary scale. In trying to ensure this, however, he will be faced with difficulties. The amount of deficit financing is a residual item – that part of government current and capital spending which cannot be met by current receipts and long-term borrowings. So any mistakes in budget estimates of the amounts of spending and receipts will change the required level of bank borrowing. Accurate control over deficit financing requires accurate prediction of revenues and expenditures but that is often not feasible. For example, LDC government revenues are dependent on the taxation of imports and exports. But world markets for many LDC exports are volatile, making it extremely difficult to forecast reliably export tax revenues. Moreover, the unpredictability of export proceeds will transmit instability to the country's ability to import, thus also destabilizing receipts from import duties. Often, governments are also unable to estimate accurately their spending needs twelve months in advance, and deviations from these estimates will also alter the deficit financing residual. Lastly, there is commonly a systematic bias in budget estimates – underestimating current spending, overestimating receipts and hence underestimating the financing gap to be filled by bank borrowings.[21] As noted earlier, *most LDC governments undertake more deficit financing than is compatible with the avoidance of inflation.*

Activity. Suggested assignment: make comparisons between your government's original budget estimates of spending, revenue and short-term borrowings, and actual out-turns for the past few fiscal years. How successful was the government in predicting the outcomes? Was there a systematic tendency for the budget estimates to understate deficit financing?

Monetary policy

Deficit financing provides a strong link between fiscal policy and the monetary system so we should turn now to a more explicit consideration of monetary policy. The broad outlines of what is required have already been indicated: measures to prevent the supply of money from moving ahead of demand for it. Changes in money supply can result from any of the following impulses:

(1) A change in the foreign assets of the banking system, of which the country's foreign exchange reserves will be the main component. An increase in these assets results in a parallel rise in domestic money supply. Recall, however, our assumption that the government is maintaining a flexible exchange rate, with the intention of preventing large monetary disturbances emanating from the balance of payments.

(2) A change in bank credit to the central government (already discussed).

(3) A change in bank credit to other public sector institutions, such as public corporations and local government authorities.

(4) A change in bank credit to the private sector.

In each of the last three cases, increased bank lending will result in an enlarged money supply. So if we take (1) to be neutralized by exchange rate flexibility, the task of holding money supply to the level of demand boils down to keeping domestic bank credit within the desired limits.

But this shows up a disadvantage of using monetary policy for anti-inflationary purposes. Much industrial and commercial expansion is financed by bank credit (especially for working capital), so to restrict bank lending is liable to place a brake on new investment and economic expansion. Indeed, it is possible for credit restrictions to be pushed to the extent of forcing a deflation on the economy, with serious avoidable losses of output and employment. Brazil and Chile are among countries which have experienced this.

Is there, then, an unavoidable trade-off between investment and anti-inflationary credit policies? One way of trying to reconcile the two would be to accelerate the growth in demand for money. In this event, credit could be expanded without inflationary consequences, thus helping to maintain the pace of investment. But how to increase the demand for money?

Activity. It would be useful at this point if you recapitulated your understanding of the demand function for money summarized in the equations on pages 162 and 163.

In the short run, there is not much to be done about the rate of growth of real incomes, nor about the rate of monetization of economic activity. Also, the convenience value of holding money is best regarded as a constant. This leaves the rate of interest and the expected rate of inflation as influences on the demand for money which might be manipulated by policy.

---

[21] See Caiden and Wildavsky, 1974, on problems of accurate budgeting in developing countries.

Economists have argued in favour of an *interest rate reform* in this type of situation. This is a euphemism for much higher rates of interest in countries with legal or institutional barriers which hold interest down. The South Korean case is a widely cited example of this type of reform, where the interest payable on one-year bank deposits was pushed up from 15 per cent (already high by LDC standards) in 1964 to 30 per cent two years later. The effect of a move along these lines, of course, is to encourage the holding of larger money balances, reducing the pressure of demand for commodities.

This is illustrated in Figure 7.7. This also presents a demand-for-money function, MD, but this time it is related to the cost of holding money, as determined by the expected rate of inflation less the rate of interest. Holding the expected inflation rate constant, the demand for money increases with the rate of interest. Holding the rate of interest constant, the demand for money goes up as the expected rate of inflation falls.

Assume, for example, that we start from a position in which the interest rate is 5 per cent and the expected rate of inflation is 15 per cent. This gives a net cost of holding money of 10 per cent and a total demand for money balances of q_1. Now assume that interest rate is doubled to 10 per cent p.a., with expected inflation remaining unaffected. This then gives a net cost of holding money of 5 per cent and the demand for money goes up by q_1 to q_2. These increased money balances will withdraw purchasing power from the markets for goods and services, weakening inflationary tendencies. We might therefore take the analysis one step further by assuming that the rate of inflation subsequently declines and that, as a result,

the rate at which people expect prices to rise in the future falls, say, to 10 per cent. In this case both variables are at 10 per cent, leaving a zero net cost of holding money. This results in a further rise in the demand for money, to q_3, diminished inflationary pressures . . . and so on.

A number of reservations can be mentioned to this case for interest rate reform. First, higher interest rates may discourage investment and thus impede the development of the economy. However, this need not happen because when interest rates are held artificially low there will probably be an unsatisfied excess of demand for investment funds, so higher interest rates may not reduce the volume of investment that is undertaken. Moreover, it is likely that higher interest will raise the productivity of new investments because now only projects which promise large returns will be undertaken. So it may well be possible to sustain the overall rate of economic growth even from a reduced volume of investment.

A second danger is that if this type of reform is successful in inducing people to substantially increase their money holdings, this withdrawal of purchasing power from commodity markets could go too far and actually create deflationary losses of output and employment. This is a real danger but against it we can set the possibility that increased real money balances, considered as an input into the productive system, may lead to a more efficient use of resources and hence to greater output and employment.

A third reservation relates to the magnitude of response of the demand for money to a change in the net cost of holding it. Figure 7.7 has been drawn so that the response is substantial but several studies have found the elasticity of demand for money with respect to the cost of holding it to be rather small. If this is the case, it would take a very large rise in interest rates to effect a significant increase in the demand for money.

The size of the elasticity is, of course, an empirical question. Financial reform has achieved major results in a few countries, most notably in South Korea and Taiwan. The Korean interest reform already mentioned was associated with very large increases in real money balances and in the ratio of money supply to GNP. Formerly rapid rates of inflation were held down to single-figure levels, bank lending and investment were sustained at high levels, and the growth of the economy accelerated. Whether a more typical LDC could reproduce these results is unclear, but at least the proponents of financial reform have important precedents to point to.

Whether or not such a reform is carried out, the government will still be faced with the task of keeping the supply of money within the bounds of the demand

Figure 7.7 *The effect of higher interest rates on the demand for money.*

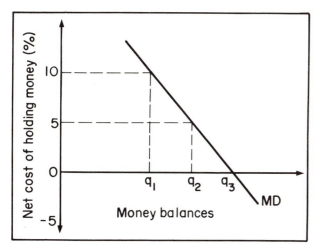

for it, so the question arises, how easily can the government control money supply? In principle, this can be done by manipulating commercial banks' reserve ratios, by issuing them with directives about the volume of lending they may undertake, and by other means. In practice, however, there are large difficulties. We have already indicated one: that the government's own borrowings from the banks can be a major determinant of money supply but that difficulties in predicting budget outcomes make it impossible for the government to control its deficit financing with exactitude.

Empirical studies of bank lending to the parastatal and private sectors suggest that this also can only be regulated within broad limits, partly because commercial banks often react to government intentions sluggishly or unpredictably, and partly because of the political difficulties created by stringent credit restrictions. And while it has been convenient for us to assume away the problems created for monetary control by fluctuating foreign exchange reserves, in practice even countries with a reasonably flexible exchange rate can only partially insulate themselves from this source of monetary instability. The position is obviously much worse for countries maintaining fixed exchange rates. For them, control over money supply does not exist as a policy instrument.[22]

To sum up, it is evident that it would be unwise to expect fiscal and monetary policies to maintain an exact equilibrium in the economy, achieving precisely the required balance between the competing claims of price stability, full capacity utilization and adequate foreign exchange reserves. The difficulties of using both the budget and the money supply are too formidable to permit the 'fine tuning' of most economies. *A rough-and-ready avoidance of the worst extremes of instability is the most that can usually be hoped for* – a conclusion reinforced by the additional consideration that there are substantial, perhaps varying, time-lags between the introduction of policy measures and their economic effects. While waiting for a policy to take effect, some new and unexpected destabilizing force may enter the scene.

Given the difficulties of acting effectively on the causes of inflation, might it not be preferable to abandon the attempt and concentrate instead on preventing the worst effects of rising prices?

Adjusting to inflation

This is an altogether different type of policy response from those so far considered. Let us accept that double-figure inflation is injurious to the financial system, investment, the balance of payments and the

distribution of income. If ways could be found of preventing these injuries, even double-figure inflation would cease to exist as a serious economic problem.

The main type of policy instrument available for this purpose is known as *indexation*. This has been widely employed in Brazil and to a lesser extent elsewhere. It consists of periodic and automatic upward adjustments of incomes, financial assets and certain prices to take account of inflation. For example, wage contracts can be adjusted upwards to compensate workers for past or expected inflation; pensions can be raised in line with the cost of living; even the income tax can be indexed so as to avoid the type of tax effect described on page 176. Financial assets such as savings deposits and government bonds can be regularly revalued so as to avoid the erosion in their real values that would otherwise occur. The exchange rate can be 'indexed' in the sense of being adjusted very frequently, as in Colombia where it is revised daily.

> **Key concept. Indexation** consists of the periodic and automatic revision of incomes, financial asset values, the exchange rate and other variables so as to compensate for the effects of inflation.

So long as it is feasible to cover all major sources of income, debt and other relevant economic variables, indexation provides an attractive escape from the harmful effects of inflation. In Brazil, indexation appears to have revived the size and efficiency of the financial system, strengthened the balance of payments, alleviated some of the adverse income distribution effects (although not as fully as it might have done, because wages have not been effectively indexed and the real incomes of urban workers have been held down), and has been associated with rapid real economic growth.

Brazil, however, is scarcely a typical developing country. It has an average per capita income of well over $1000, a large industrial base and well developed financial and other institutions. To be comprehensive and to avoid major injustices, indexation needs to be applied with sophistication and thus makes heavy demands on administrative capacity. It must be doubted whether many developing countries have this capacity. There are especially large difficulties in protecting the incomes of those working in the rural and informal sectors of the economy. Only partially effective indexation may bring the worst of both

---

[22] Bolnick, 1975, offers a valuable case study of the difficulties referred to in the last two paragraphs.

worlds, providing the illusion that nothing needs to be done about the causes of inflation and yet forcing major distortions on to the economy. Indexation cannot, therefore, be recommended as an appropriate response to inflation in any but a small minority of countries.

Conclusions

The main thrust of this chapter can now be summarized in the following propositions:

(1) Moderate inflation is unlikely to pose any major economic threat and measures to prevent moderate price increases may well do more harm to the progress of the economy than the inflation itself. It is, in any case, politically unlikely that governments will act effectively against moderate inflation.

(2) Rapid, or double-figure, inflation is the enemy, likely to hamper economic growth and worsen income distribution. Policy counter-measures are desirable and may also be politically more feasible.

(3) The formulation of effective policy measures must start with a diagnosis of the initiating causes of the inflation and of the forces keeping it in motion. It is important to choose policies which act upon the causes of the problem.

(4) Cost-push or structural factors may be the causes but excess demand is the most likely culprit.

(5) When confronted with demand inflation, use a combination of fiscal and monetary measures designed to reduce demand while safeguarding the longer-term growth of the economy.

(6) But do not expect too much from these instruments; a rough-and-ready avoidance of the worse extremes of instability is as much as can be hoped for. In the great majority of cases, however, this will be preferable to a retreat into the palliative of indexation.

Suggestions for Revision and Group Discussion

1 Explain and distinguish between the following concepts of inflation:
   (a) Demand inflation.
   (b) Cost inflation.
   (c) Structural inflation.
   (d) Repressed inflation.
   (e) Hyperinflation.
2 Review your understanding of the following:
   (a) Monetization.
   (b) Deflation.

(c) Deficit financing.
(d) Indexation.
(e) The inflation tax.
(f) A wage-price spiral.
(g) Money flight.
(h) Money balances.
(i) The propagation mechanism.

3 Explain the definition of inflation as a persistent fall in the value of money. Since money itself has no price how can its value go up or down?

4 Explain the following equations in your own words:

$$MD = f(Y, Z, U)$$
$$U = f(V, R, X)$$

How does a decline in the demand for money affect the demand for goods?

5 In what circumstances will it be possible to expand money supply faster than the growth of real output without inflationary consequences?

6 Explain the difference between the two cases illustrated in Figure 7.3 (page 164) and the significance of this.

7 Discuss the claim that, for the structuralist model of inflation to be valid, prices have to be sticky in the downward direction and there has to be a foreign exchange constraint.

8 What purposes were served by the assumption in this chapter that the government is maintaining a flexible exchange rate? What changes would have to be made to the presentation if instead a fixed exchange rate were assumed?

9 Review your understanding of the conclusions summarized on this page. If you disagree with any of them write a note stating the grounds of your disagreement.

10 On what grounds has this chapter distinguished between the policy implications of '5 per cent' and 'double-figure' inflation?

11 Review your understanding of Figure 7.5 (page 173) and its bearing upon the use of inflation to promote economic growth.

12 What difficulties is your central bank likely to experience in seeking to control the domestic money supply?

Suggestions for Further Reading

There are two excellent survey articles of the literature on inflation which make a good, but demanding, beginning to further study of this topic. They are by Laidler and Parkin, 1975, and Bronfenbrenner and Holzman, 1965. Unfortunately, neither of these relate to developing countries. A selective review of the literature on inflation in LDCs is offered by Kirkpatrick and Nixson in Parkin and Zis, 1976, although they adopt a different view from that taken in this chapter. Thirlwall, 1974, provides a valuable study of the connections between inflation and growth, and many references to empirical studies. Meier, 1976, Section V.E contains three useful readings.

Most of the literature is strong on analysis but weak on policy. However, Park, 1973, makes a valuable contribution on the role of money in stabilization policy, which is not too technical for the serious student. McKinnon, 1973, while not centrally concerned with inflation, makes a strong case for the type of financial reform discussed in the text and throws much light on the role of money in economic life. Heller, 1976, provides an interesting and clear application of monetarist analysis to the international propagation of inflation. Readers who would like to follow up the topic of indexation should refer to Baer and Beckerman, 1974.

See also the additional references given in the notes to this chapter.

8 Managing the balance of payments

'The optimum condition for any country to enjoy
is that in which prices are steady at a high level
of employment and the balance of payments is
in long- and short-run equilibrium. If heaven is
divided into nation states that is how it will be.
On earth just now it is different.' *W. M. Scammell*

Contents

I. The Balance of Payments and Economic Development

Trade, payments and growth

For all the brave (or foolish?) words about self-reliance and economic independence, the basic condition of the world community is one of mutual interdependence. There is not a country in the world that does not rely for its national well-being on international trade and payments. This truth carries particular force for most developing countries, whose trade and payments magnitudes are particularly large in relation to domestic economic activity.

While there is much scope for argument about whether LDCs benefit as much as they might do, there are three general ways in which participation in the international economy can improve living standards and the rate of economic development:

(1) Trade provides countries with an escape from the confines of the small markets of their own national economies. By opening up the world as a potential market, it creates more profitable investment opportunities (thus accelerating growth) and permits national resources to be employed more productively. This function of trade as expanding the effective size of the market can be very important because the economies of many developing countries are small enough to hold back their efforts to industrialize (see Chapter 10).

(2) By giving access to the products of other nations, it avoids the need to strive for self-sufficiency within national boundaries. A country can transform the products which it makes the most efficiently into other products in which foreign countries have greater efficiency. In the case of developing countries, this pattern of international specialization, or 'comparative advantage', largely boils down to the export of agricultural and mineral products plus an increasingly important volume of consumer-good manufactures, in exchange for capital equipment and a wide range of other industrial goods. Since investment is a crucial component of the development effort and most LDCs do not produce many capital goods other than construction materials, their investments depend upon being able to import capital goods, as well as industrial components and spare parts. Through trade, they can also avail themselves of technologies designed elsewhere.

(3) The capital flows which are an integral feature of world trade and payments give developing countries access to the savings of richer nations, to augment their own savings and raise investment rates. Capital is obtained both from private foreign investors (whose investments often bring with them managerial and technical expertise as well) and as 'aid' from foreign governments and international agencies like the World Bank.

Of course, the system does not work as well as it could, especially from an LDC viewpoint. There is inequality of bargaining power among the world's trading nations and, as a result, the developing nations sometimes get a raw deal. Industrial nations, for instance, impose a variety of restrictions on imports of manufactures from developing countries. They have consistently failed by a large margin to meet the targets for the amount of development aid which they themselves have accepted as an international obligation. They have exerted a

dominance in world monetary arrangements in ways that have failed to meet the needs of the Third World.

But for all these shortcomings, there is little doubt that the benefits flowing from the three sources listed above can be large. Various studies have, for example, shown a positive and significant correlation between the growth of exports and the overall growth of LDC economies. Since exports are part of what we measure when we calculate the growth of an economy, such a correlation is not surprising but even when the tests are applied so as to avoid this problem the relationship still exists, at least for the more prosperous of the LDCs.[1] A dynamic export sector tends to stimulate the expansion of the rest of the economy, partly by ensuring an ample supply of the foreign exchange that is required for its growth.

> **Activity.** How would you rate the export performance of your own country? One way of judging it is to see whether exports have been rising or falling as a proportion of GDP. Study the national accounts for this purpose, looking at both current- and constant-price series. Where the two sets of figures show different trends, try to explain the differences.

It is less easy to be specific about the benefits derived through trade from access to the specializations of other nations. However, this is negatively indicated by attempts to measure the welfare costs of providing protection to domestic industries – costs which arise largely from reducing the gains from trade. Bergsman (1974) shows, for example, that these losses could easily amount to 5 per cent or more of domestic product. Similarly, inflows of capital from the rest of the world do substantially augment the domestic savings of the Third World. In the early 1970s, capital inflows to developing countries (excluding the oil-exporting countries) were equivalent to about a quarter of domestic saving, thus allowing investment to be raised by that proportion. Since investment strongly influences an economy's growth, access to foreigners' savings stimulates economic expansion. Statistical analyses have suggested that foreign private capital (as distinct from public aid) has a particularly potent expansionary effect (Massell, *et al.*, 1972).

Another way of looking at it is to see *foreign exchange as a factor of production*, as an input into the productive system, like labour, capital and natural resources. If we adopt such a perspective, it follows that the performance of an economy will

---

[1] See Michaely, 1977, and the studies cited there. See also Heller and Porter, 1978; and Balassa, 1978.

Table 8.1
Balance of Payments Summary, Major Country Groupings,[a]
1974–7 (in Billions of US Dollars; Averages for 1974–7)

	Industrial countries	Oil exporters	Other LDCs
1. Balance on current account	+7·5	+44·8	−28·8
2. Capital inflows or outflows	−13·1	−20·9	+34·1
3. Net changes in foreign reserves[b]	+5·6	−23·9	−5·3

Notes: (a) This table excludes the more developed primary product exporting countries and countries which are not members of the IMF.
(b) A plus sign indicates an increase in liabilities or a reduction in reserves; a minus sign indicates the opposite.
Source: IMF Annual Report, 1978, Table 6.

depend, among other things, on its ability to earn (or save) foreign exchange. Conversely, shortages of foreign exchange can constrain the growth of the economy. In fact, a large proportion of developing countries have, at one time or another, been hampered by balance of payments difficulties: a Latin American study which compared domestic savings and foreign exchange availabilities found six countries in which foreign exchange was the most serious (the 'binding') constraint, against two in which saving was the chief obstacle.[2] There are many LDCs today with economies held back by foreign exchange scarcities.

Such shortages may be due to policy mistakes which discourage exports and foreign capital. The demand for imports often rises rapidly as output and incomes grow. Unless export earnings are dynamic, this demand for imports may outstrip the availability of foreign exchange to buy them with. But payments difficulties can just as easily arise from conditions in the rest of the world beyond the control of a developing country. The world markets of many primary products are volatile and sensitive to changing economic conditions in industrial countries. The world's demand for some of these products grows only slowly and this places limits on the pace at which producer countries can collectively expand sales without depressing prices. Exports of manufactures, which have gathered momentum in recent years, face many barriers erected against them by the industrial states.

Prior to the quadrupling of petroleum prices in early 1974, there was a clearly established pattern of world payments in which the industrial countries, taken as a group, ran a large current surplus and the developing countries ran a similarly-sized deficit. The jump in oil prices radically altered this pattern and Table 8.1 summarizes the global balance of payments for 1974–7.

What stands out from the table is that the oil exporters earned huge surpluses on current account (line 1), offset by exports of capital of about $21 billion (line 2) and net increases in reserves of about $24 billion (line 3). The industrial countries earned a modest current surplus, remained substantial capital exporters and suffered sizable net reductions in reserves. The 'non-oil' developing countries suffered a very large current deficit but were able to more than offset this by capital imports, so that their net reserves actually rose by over $5 billion per year.

Of course, many individual LDCs fared less well and had to draw down their foreign exchange reserves. Even those who could protect their reserves often did so at the cost of considerable increases in their indebtedness to the rest of the world. The large magnitude of this borrowing is shown in line 2 of Table 8.1, where non-oil LDCs are recorded as having borrowed at an annual rate of $34 billion in 1974–7. This obviously pushed up the amount of foreign exchange that must be used simply in order to meet interest charges and loan repayments, especially because a rising proportion of the finance came from commercial, more expensive, sources.

Figure 8.1 throws further light on this. You will see from the left-hand part of the diagram how the share of LDC debt owed to private creditors went up during the 1970s. The right-hand part of the figure displays debt magnitudes in relation to the value of exports. You can see that these ratios were generally declining in the earlier 1970s but that they began to go up again from 1974. This is true of both total outstanding debt (as a proportion of export earnings) and, especially, of the cost of debt servicing (interest plus repayments).

[2] See the essay by L. Landau in Chenery, 1971. He actually studied eighteen Latin American countries. In ten of them, however, the model he was using was regarded as of doubtful validity or there was no consistent binding constraint.

Figure 8.1 *External debts of non-oil developing countries: (a) sources of credit as percentage of total debt*;
(b) debt and debt-servicing, as percentage of exports†.*

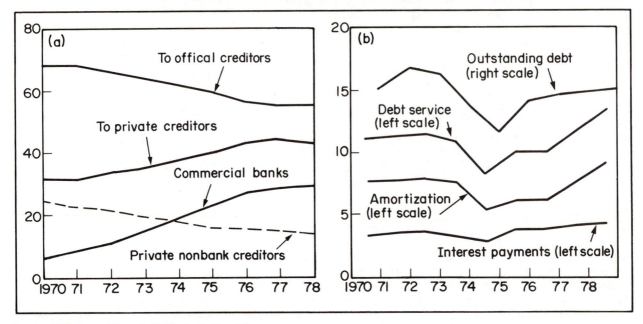

Source: *IMF Annual Report, 1978*, charts 8 and 9
*Public and publicly guaranteed medium-term and long term external debt.
†The debt and debt service ratios plotted in this chart relate only to public and publicly guaranteed medium-term and long-term
external debt.

The non-oil developing countries, then, run a large current deficit and their international indebtedness is growing. Many of them are left with only a thin cushion of international reserves to protect themselves against unforeseen shocks. Few do not have to worry about the state of their external payments.

The management of the balance of payments is thus of great importance to the economic progress of LDCs. It is, moreover, particularly important to scrutinize balance of payments policies because choice of wrong policies can easily compound the original difficulties, perpetuating the problems and introducing additional distortions. There is a wide range of possible policy options available to governments to influence the balance of payments, which we will survey later. However, the policy sections of this chapter focus primarily on the choice between the two principal options, of manipulating the exchange rate or of imposing administrative controls on imports and other foreign exchange payments. In doing this we will employ the criteria developed in Chapter 2 for assessing the efficiency of policy instruments.

The next step, however, is to familiarize you with the structure and interpretation of balance of payments accounts. 'A balance of payments deficit' is

an expression used more often than it is understood, so we first have to make sure we know what we are talking about.

> **Activity**. If your studies have already given you some knowledge of international trade and payments it would be useful to refresh your memory at this point. If this is a new area for you, be not discouraged! Little prior knowledge is assumed.

Understanding balance of payments accounts

> **Key concept**. The **balance of payments** is a systematic record of all economic transactions between residents of the reporting country and residents of the rest of the world.

In order to explain the structure and interpretation of balance of payments accounts, it is convenient to have a specific example in front of us. Since this chapter will use illustrations from the Philippines, we will take that country's accounts as our model. Table 8.2 sets

Table 8.2
Balance of Payments Accounts of the Philippines, 1973 and 1976 (in Millions of Pesos)

	1973		1976	
The Current Account				
A1 Merchandise exports (fob)	12 660		18 751	
A2 Merchandise imports (fob)	−10 794		−27 068	
A3 BALANCE OF TRADE (A1 minus A2)		1 866		−8 317
A4 Exports of services	4 119		6 479	
A5 Imports of services	−4 152		−8 422	
A6 Net receipts of transfer payments	1 555		1 996	
A7 BALANCE ON CURRENT ACCOUNT (net balance of items A1 through A6)		3 388		−8 264
The Capital Account				
B1 Long-term capital receipts by government (net)	494		5 235	
B2 Private and other long-term investments (net)	406		3 388	
B3 THE BASIC BALANCE (A7 plus B1 plus B2)		4 288		359
B4 Short-term, non-monetary capital movements (net)	237		3 470	
B5 Errors and omissions	−7		−1 059	
B6 THE OVERALL BALANCE (B3 plus B4 plus B5)		4 518		2 770
*The Monetary Account**				
C1 Changes in foreign exchange reserves	−4 362		−4 356	
C2 Use of IMF credits and other monetary items	156		1 586	
C3 BALANCE ON MONETARY ACCOUNT (C1 plus C2)		−4 518		−2 770
D Net Total on all Above Items		0		0

Source: Computed from IMF *International Financial Statistics*, September 1977, pp. 294, 297.
Note: * A minus sign indicates an increase in reserves or reduction in liabilities.

out its accounts for 1973 and 1976. Spend a few minutes studying this before proceeding with the text.

First, note that this table is divided into three sub-accounts. The *current account* includes a record of the totals for merchandise trade (the letters 'fob' stand for free on board and indicate that the values exclude the cost of shipping and ocean insurance services). It also includes services, such as payments and receipts for shipping, insurance, tourism and financial services. These services are often called 'invisible' imports and exports, in contrast to visible merchandise trade. The current account is completed by an entry for net receipts (or disbursements) of transfer payments (line A6). Remittances home of incomes earned by nationals working abroad are examples of transfer receipts and so are gifts from foreign governments and charities.

The *capital account* makes a distinction between long-term and short-term investments. The latter but not the former may be shifted between countries at short notice, so that a country receiving short-term capital can rarely depend on retaining it over a period of years. Long-term loans or investments by private multinational companies, on the other hand, cannot

normally be withdrawn at short notice. The 'errors and omissions' item in the capital account will be explained in a moment.

There is finally the *monetary account*. This records changes in the country's official foreign exchange reserves (consisting usually of a mixture of gold and foreign currencies), plus transactions with the International Monetary Fund and certain other monetary items.

A second point to note about the table is that *the net balance of all the items is exactly zero* for both years (see bottom line D). The same is true for each country group in Table 8.1. This is no coincidence. It reflects the fact that balance of payments accounting is based on the double-entry (duality) principle, with each credit entry being matched by a corresponding debit. However, it is not always possible to apply this principle with precision. Many entries in the accounts have to be estimated. Some entries will be inaccurate; others may be omitted altogether. To adjust for these defects and to retain the essential features of double-entry accounting, it is therefore necessary to insert a balancing item called 'errors and omissions' (line B5). We might define this item as having whatever value is necessary to reduce the net balance on the entire account (line D) to zero. With the aid of this adjustment, there is never a surplus or deficit in the accounts taken in their entirety. It is admittedly arbitrary to have placed the errors and omissions item in the capital account but the case of doing so is that the figures for private capital movements (long and short term) are usually the least reliable of all the entries, so that it does not do too much injustice to attribute the net value of all errors and omissions to the capital account, as is done in line B5.

If the net total of the accounts necessarily sums to zero, in what sense is it possible to talk of a deficit or surplus on the balance of payments? Obviously, a deficit or surplus is only possible for some part of the accounts. A third feature to note, then, is that the table offers five different *partial balances* (in lines A3, A7, B3, B6 and C3). Of these, the last two, B6 and C3, are identical but with opposite sign, with the balance on monetary account exactly offsetting the 'overall balance'.

Effectively, then, there are four different balances in Table 8.2. The first of these (in line A3) is not very useful, however, because it refers only to difference between merchandise exports and merchandise imports. Because it excludes so many important items, this *balance of trade* is the least useful of those presented in the table, although it is one that often receives much attention in the newspapers. Too many other important transactions are occurring for this balance to tell us much about the general state of the balance of payments.

The *balance on current account* (line A7) is much more useful, for it encompasses receipts and payments for services as well as goods, and also transfer payments. In fact, when people carelessly refer to 'the' balance of payments they are usually referring to the balance on current account. But even this balance is not generally the most useful for policy-makers in developing countries. If you look at the 1976 figures in Table 8.2 you will see that the Philippines ran a current account deficit of 8264 million pesos in 1976 – a large amount in relation to the total value of her trade. But then look at the capital account. In the same year the country received long-term capital from the rest of the world more than enough to wipe out the current deficit (lines B1 and B2), so that she actually ended with a surplus on the so-called basic balance (line B3).

The *basic balance*, as you can see, gives the net total of current transactions plus long-term capital movements. It is this which is of the most general usefulness when studying the balance of payments of developing countries. The reason for this is that most LDCs can depend on an inflow of long-term capital

each year, as is shown in Table 8.1. They are therefore able to run deficits on current account equivalent in value of the inflow of long-term capital without depleting their foreign exchange reserves. So long as these receipts of capital are consistent with national objectives (are not, for example, regarded as infringing the country's economic independence) and are obtained on reasonable terms, no corrective policies are called for. Referring to Table 8.1 again, the existence of an enormous current deficit for the developing group of countries did not signal a crisis because they were able to attract larger capital inflows than the current deficit and thus added to their foreign reserves. But they did so, as was pointed out, at the cost of increased indebtedness to the rest of the world, although this would only be serious if the debt burdens reached dangerously high levels.

> **Key concept.** The **basic balance** is the net balance on merchandise trade, service transactions, transfers and long-term capital flows. It is important for your understanding of this chapter that you are familiar with this definition.

It is tempting to extend the logic of what has been said to argue in favour of using the *overall balance* (line B6) as the key indicator. If we can include net receipts of long-term capital, why shouldn't we treat short-term capital in the same way? The answer is that this capital is less dependable than long-term flows so that, in most cases, it is injudicious to devise payments policies on an assumed inflow of short-term capital. This money can depart as quickly as it arrives. In periods of temporary shortfall it may well be possible to borrow this type of capital (for example, involuntary credit can be had by not paying import bills!) to tide the country over the crisis but it is undependable (and often expensive) for the purposes of longer-term management.

In the Philippines, the table shows that as well as a small surplus of 359 million pesos on the basic balance in 1976, there was an inflow of short-term capital amounting to 3470 million pesos, partially offset by a negative 'errors and omissions' entry (which might have included an unrecorded outflow of capital). Taking these items together leaves a surplus of 2770 million pesos on the overall balance. At the same time the country obtained credits from the IMF of 1586 million pesos which, when added to the overall surplus, allowed the Philippine government to add to its foreign reserves by the handsome amount of 4356 million pesos (line C1; note that the minus sign indicates an increase in reserves). Whether the country could continue to depend on receipts of short-term credit is uncertain, however; no comparable inflow was recorded in 1973.

We thus conclude in favour of the basic balance as the most generally useful of the partial balances. Unless indicated to the contrary, *references in what follows to balance of payments deficits or surpluses will relate to the basic balance*. However, the other balances all provide useful information and the wise analyst will study the entire accounts rather than rely on a single balance as his policy indicator.

> **Activity.** Utilizing Table 8.2, write a note (1) on the state of the Philippines balance of payments in 1973 and (2) on trends between 1973 and 1976. Reserves increased by similar amounts in both years. Does this mean there was no significant change in the health of the country's balance of payments? What are the most important changes to have occurred?

'Equilibrium' as the balance of payments objective

We have been studying the utility of the various partial balances as policy indicators without so far defining the object of payments policy. For this purpose, we use that economist's favourite, 'equilibrium'. *The task of the policy-makers can be described as the maintenance of equilibrium on the balance of payments*. But what precisely is meant by equilibrium in this context? Having studied the structure of the balance of payments, we are armed to explore this question.

Accepting that the basic balance is the most generally useful of the partial balances, a temptingly simple definition offers itself: in the general case, equilibrium could be said to be established when the basic balance is approximately zero. This definition is intended for those countries where the basic balance is the most useful indicator; it could easily be rewritten for countries in which some other balance is a better guide. For any country, the principle is to keep the most relevant balance at approximately zero – 'approximately' because our control over events is so imperfect that we should be pleased to settle for an outcome which is at least roughly the desired one.

Sadly, the apparent simplicity of defining a payments equilibrium as a zero basic balance falls away on closer examination. Over what time-span should we define this state of affairs? Every month? That would be absurd, for countries' payments are subject to seasonal influences, with some months

showing regular deficits and others regular surpluses. We can overcome the seasonal influences, of course, by taking a twelve-month period, so perhaps equilibrium should be sought for each year's basic balance? But this too is unrealistic. Changes in world market conditions, abnormal weather conditions which affect export crops, discontinuities in capital flows – all these are liable to impose sudden, unpredictable changes upon the payments position which are beyond the power of national governments to correct during a span of twelve months. In fact, it would be undesirable to introduce major policy changes in order to offset some purely temporary problem. It is the principal function of a country's foreign exchange reserves to act as a cushion that will absorb these temporary fluctuations, financing any sudden shortfall in receipts and absorbing any sudden excess.

Our definition of equilibrium should therefore abstract from seasonal and temporary movements. It should refer instead to a period of, say, three or four years, or to a 'normal' year.

But what if the country starts out with a desperately low level of international reserves? Maintaining a zero balance will prevent further deterioration but it will not permit reserves to be rebuilt. Starting with low reserves, it would be better to aim for surpluses. There is also the question of the country's external indebtedness. We saw that in 1976 the Philippines ran a massive current deficit which was, however, slightly more than offset by an inflow of long-term capital, to leave the basic balance approximately zero. What if that country had started 1976 heavily in debt? Its government could hardly be satisfied with further large increases in the debt burden. (In fact, the Philippines' debt ratios were not large, so the example is only hypothetical.)

Again, in clarifying what is meant by a payments equilibrium we should not ignore the circumstances in which it is achieved. What if the government were reluctantly forced to impose stringent import controls in order to avoid a large deficit on basic balance? It would not be helpful to describe that country as enjoying an equilibrium in its payments with the rest of the world, because these restrictions could reduce output, efficiency and welfare at home. Or what if the government instead avoided a large deficit by imposing deflationary policies at home – cutting government spending, raising taxes and interest rates, restricting credit and investment – in order to hold down the demand for imports? The cost would be increased unemployment and reduced growth. Could we describe this as consistent with equilibrium?

The definition of a payments equilibrium is

therefore a *conditional* one, dependent on the simultaneous satisfaction of other conditions. Equilibrium remains the policy objective but we now have to substitute something more complex for the simple definition on page 193.

> **Key concept. Equilibrium** exists in the balance of payments when, in a normal year, the basic balance approximates zero, in conditions where (1) there are no serious unwanted restrictions on trade and payments, (2) external debts and debt servicing are not regarded as too large, (3) foreign exchange reserves are regarded as adequate, and (4) the equilibrium does not depend on the maintenance of unwantedly deflationary domestic policies.

Having now clarified the nature of the balance of payments and the essential task of payments policies, the next step is to explore the connections between transactions with the rest of the world and the domestic economy. Only after we have understood the interactions between 'external' and 'domestic' activities can we grasp the principles of balance of payments management.

> **Activity.** To consolidate your understanding of the last few pages, and accumulate knowledge of your own economy, study its official balance of payments accounts. Calculate the various partial balances over the past few years and try to identify the points of weakness and strength. Is the basic balance the most useful for your country? Would you describe the balance of payments as being in equilibrium?

II. Income Determination in an Open Economy

Starting assumptions

Ignorance of the ways in which international transactions interact with the domestic economy is probably the largest single obstacle to effective payments policies. It is therefore crucial to this chapter to unravel the connections between the balance of payments and the rest of the national economy. This takes us into standard Keynesian theory of income determination. We take first the case of a closed economy – one with no transactions with the rest of the world – but move quickly to the more relevant cases of an open economy.

> **Activity.** You will find the next few pages easier if you have already studied basic Keynesian theory of income determination. This is presented, for example, in Samuelson (1976) ch. 11 and 12; and in Lipsey (1975) ch. 34 and 35.

Some simplifying assumptions will aid the exposition, hopefully without detracting too much from its realism. We assume we are analysing a country whose foreign trade and payments are small in relation to total world trade and payments. This 'small country assumption' is particularly useful for this chapter. Among other things, it enables us to work on the basis that events and policies in 'our' country will have insignificant effects on the rest of the world – effects which can therefore be ignored. It also has the merit of being a realistic assumption for most developing countries.

Besides ignoring foreign repercussions, we shall develop a model of income determination which also ignores the existence of government spending and taxation; the influence of money and interest rates; and the existence of time-lags between a change in one variable and its influence on other variables. Finally, we will for the time being assume that all changes in economic magnitudes are real and that prices remain constant. We will drop this last assumption at a later stage, so as to introduce inflation as an alternative possibility.

The closed economy case

In a closed economy there are two possible types of production of finished goods: consumption goods and capital (investment) goods. Since, in a closed economy, total value-added is the sum of these two, then using Y for national income, C for consumption and I for investment, we can measure the value of national income from the production side as:

$$Y = C + I \qquad (1)$$

Receipts from the sale of these goods accrue as incomes to the factors of production engaged in making them. These incomes can, in turn, be utilized in two ways: they can be spent on consumption or they can be saved for the future. Using S for national saving and Y and C as before, we can therefore write for national income measured from the disposal of incomes:

$$Y = C + S \qquad (2)$$

Now, for the economy to be in equilibrium the intended levels of total supply and total demand should be equal. Thus, planned consumption expenditures should be the same as planned production of consumption goods. If this condition is satisfied, the value of C is the same in both equations. The value of Y is also the same, standing for national income in both cases. With Y and C common to both equations, it follows that for equilibrium to exist planned national saving must equal planned investment:

$$S = I \qquad (3)$$

Unfortunately, the planned values of S and I are not necessarily the same. In fact, there is little reason to think they will normally be so. When they differ, the plans of savers and investors are inconsistent with one another, and one of the tasks of macro-economic management is to try to assist consistency between them. One reason why planned saving and investment may diverge from one another is that they are affected by different considerations. The level of saving, for example, will be strongly influenced by income, with the amount of saving rising with income. Investment plans, on the other hand, will be more sensitive to changing expectations about profits, technological progress and the cost of capital; income may not have much direct impact. Thus, if we draw a diagram with income on the horizontal axis and saving and investment on the vertical, a simplified savings function would slope upwards, whereas a simplified investment function would be horizontal because it does not vary with income – it is exogenous with respect to income. Such functions are shown in the upper part of Figure 8.2.

Figure 8.2 *Saving, investment and the equilibrium level of income.*

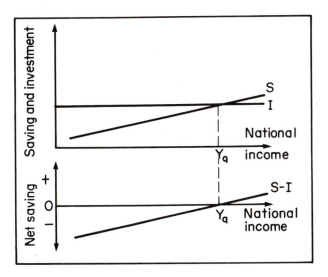

The lower part of the diagram reduces the presentation to a single schedule, showing the net balance of saving minus investment. This is negative at low incomes because there will be little saving, while investment is constant. At income Y_q they are equal (as is also portrayed in the upper section); at incomes above Y_q there is a growing surplus of saving.

Given these functions, there is shown to be a unique level of income, Y_q, at which saving and investment plans are consistent with one another. At points to the left of Y_q investment plans exceed saving plans. Now, investment injects fresh spending power into the economy, while saving is a withdrawal, or leakage, of spending power. So long as investment is greater than saving there is a net injection of purchasing power into the stream of incomes. Total demand will exceed total supply. Output will respond to this unsatisfied demand, more jobs will be created, income will increase and saving plans will therefore be revised upwards. This will continue until any excess of investment over saving is eliminated. The economy will come to rest as Y_q. Investment injections into the income stream will now be exactly matched by saving leakages out of it and, other things being equal, there will be no forces at work to shift income away from Y_q. In short, *the economy is in equilibrium at* Y_q.

> **Activity.** What happens if income is initially at some point to the right of Y_q? Test your understanding of what has been said so far by writing a brief note describing what is likely to happen to the economy and why.

If we go back to the $S = I$ equation we can see that it defines the condition necessary for equilibrium in a closed economy. And if we think of saving as a leakage and investment as an injection, we can rewrite that equation in a general form, also valid for equilibrium in an open economy. *The key condition for the existence of an equilibrium level of income is that leakages equal injections.*

Much has been omitted from this sketch of income determination in a closed economy but for our purposes it is better to proceed without delay to the case of the open economy, rather than elaborating on the closed economy.

Extending the model to the open economy

We now drop the assumption of a closed economy and admit foreign trade into the picture, but keep all the other simplifying assumptions set out on page 194. We start by going back to the definition of national income from the production side. We wrote $Y = C + I$. How does foreign trade fit into this? It introduces a third possible type of output, of goods for export. So for the open economy, and using X to stand for exports, national income from the production side can be written:

$$Y = C + I + X \qquad (4)$$

Looking next at the disposal of national income, foreign trade introduces another possible type of expenditure, on imported goods. So using M for imports, we can rewrite equation (2) on page 194 as:

$$Y = C + S + M \qquad (5)$$

Once again, Y and C are common to both equations, so in conditions of equilibrium it follows that:

$$I + X = S + M \qquad (6)$$

Compare this with equation (3).

This can be verified by asking whether the condition, injections = leakages, is satisfied. Exports, of course, are an injection into the stream of incomes, providing purchasing power to those engaged in the export sector. So the left-hand side of the equation, $I + X$, records the two injections. Spending on imports, by comparison, is a leakage of purchasing power out of the national economy (an injection of income into the rest of the world). So we now have two leakages, S and M, recorded on the right-hand side of equation (6). In other words, $I + X = S + M$ can be rewritten into the general form for national income equilibrium, injections = leakages.

It is unlikely that export earnings will coincide exactly with import demand for the same reason that it was unlikely that investment and saving plans would be the same: they are influenced by different forces. As with saving so with import demand, it will be a rising function of income. As people's purchasing power increases they will want to buy a larger volume of imported goods. The value of exports, on the other hand, will mainly be determined by the state of world commodity markets and supply conditions at home, and will be largely independent of the level of income. We can therefore draw simplified *import and export functions* similar to the saving and investment functions in Figure 8.2. This is done in Figure 8.3.

Here we have an upward-sloping import schedule because the demand for imports is taken to be a function of income. Exports are shown as exogenous with respect to income, being determined instead by such factors as the state of the world economy and domestic weather. In the lower part of the diagram the two elements are combined into a single $X - M$ schedule, showing the balance of payments at different levels of income. This is positive at low levels

Figure 8.3 *Imports, exports and the balance of payments.*

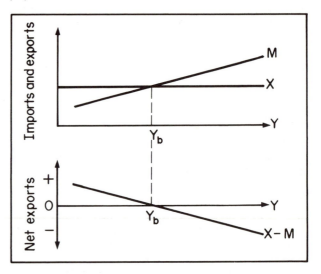

of income, because of limited demand for imports subtracted from constant exports, but as income rises the balance of payments surplus diminishes and is eventually transformed into a deficit, as imports rise with income. As both parts of the diagram show, there is a single level of income, Y_b, at which imports are equal to exports. (A word of caution: the concept of the balance of payments in the theory of income determination is confined to the balance between exports and imports of goods and non-factor services. It is thus approximately the same as the balance on current account, except that transfers and transactions involving wages, interest and profits are excluded.)

It is tempting to think of Y_b as an equilibrium similar to Y_q in Figure 8.2. Y_b does indeed show the unique point at which imports equal exports but it does not necessarily indicate an equilibrium level of income. To establish that we must reintroduce saving and investment. This is done in Figure 8.4, which combines the schedules presented in Figures 8.2 and 8.3. Take first investment and exports (I and X). They are both injections into the stream of incomes and are both exogenous with respect to income. We therefore combine them into a single horizontal *injections schedule*, $I + X$, in the upper part of the diagram. The dotted I schedule is taken from Figure 8.2 and the vertical distance between the I and $I + X$ schedules represents the value of exports presented in Figure 8.3.

This leaves national saving and imports. Both are leakages from the stream of income and both go up as incomes increase. Here too, then, we can combine them into a single *leakages*, or $S + M$, *schedule*, as

Figure 8.4 *Equilibrium in an open economy.*

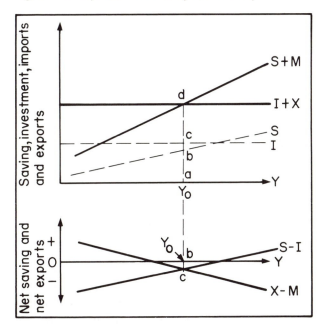

shown in the upper section of the diagram. At any level of income, the vertical distance between the dotted S schedule and the S + M schedule gives the value of imports, derived from Figure 8.3. The gap widens as income increases because the demand for imports goes up.

Now recall the general formula for an equilibrium level of income: injections = leakages. In the upper part of Figure 8.4 this condition is satisfied at the point where the injections schedule intersects the leakages schedule, namely at income Y_0. When we describe Y_0 as an equilibrium level of income this means only that total demand is equal to total supply. At points to the left of Y_0 there would be an excess of demand over supply. This would lead to increases in output, employment and incomes (remember we have assumed away the possibility of inflation), and hence would move income towards Y_0. Similarly, with income to the right of Y_0 there would be an excess of supply over demand, leading to reductions in output and employment until the economy finally came to rest at Y_0.

Activity. To make sure you have understood the analysis so far, satisfy yourself that there is excess demand at points to the left of Y_0 and excess supply at points to the right.

Having established Y_0 as the equilibrium level of national income, what of the import-export balance?

Is that also in equilibrium? It is not. If you look carefully at the upper part of Figure 8.4 you will see that it indicates a deficit on the current account, with imports exceeding exports by the amount cb. At income Y_0 imports are measured by the vertical distance bd, and exports by cd, leaving an excess of imports measured by cb. *The existence of an income equilibrium does not guarantee that imports will equal exports.* There can be a deficit or surplus; only by coincidence, or through government intervention, will national income equilibrium and an equality of imports and exports be achieved simultaneously.

In the case shown, imports are greater than exports. That is, leakages (imports) emanating from the foreign trade sector are greater than injections (exports) from the foreign trade sector. Since for overall equilibrium to exist total injections must equal total leakages, it follows that an excess of imports over exports must be exactly matched by an excess of investment over saving. The upper part of Figure 8.4 confirms that this is so. At income Y_0 saving is measured by the vertical distance ab and investment by ac. There is hence an excess of investment over saving of cb, which is exactly the size of the current account deficit.

This result is confirmed in the lower part of the diagram. This simply reproduces the schedules presented in the lower parts of Figures 8.2 and 8.3 and measures the net balances (positive or negative) of saving minus investment and exports minus imports, at different levels of income. Equilibrium is established where the two schedules intersect, at Y_0. It can be observed that at this income there is both a balance of payments deficit and an excess of investment over saving of cb.

The point can be driven even further home by referring back to equation (6), which expressed the general condition for the equilibrium of an open economy as $I + X = S + M$. Transposing, we can rewrite this as:

$$X - M = S - I \qquad (7)$$

Therefore, any excess of M over X must be exactly matched by an excess of I over S, which is what is shown in Figure 8.4 by the amount cb.

This result can now be generalized into a rule that should be carved on to the hearts of all policy-makers (admittedly a delicate operation): *an excess of imports over exports is necessarily matched by an excess of investment over national saving.* A balance of payments deficit thus has a trade dimension and a domestic dimension. What is the economic logic of this rule?

The essential point is that the existence of foreign trade frees the level of investment from the constraint of national saving. There are now two ways of securing resources for investment: out of domestic saving and by borrowing from the rest of the world. Bear in mind that the balance of payments we are discussing in this context is (approximately) the current account. From the discussion of Table 8.2 we know that the entire balance of payments must sum to zero, so a deficit on the current account must be matched by an offsetting inflow of capital (or loss of reserves). This capital inflow augments national saving and permits a higher level of investment than would otherwise be possible.

The question arises whether Y_o is a viable equilibrium, given that it is associated with an import surplus. The answer depends on the way in which the excess, cb, is financed. If it is financed by a dependable and acceptable inflow of long-term capital, leaving the basic balance approximately zero, it is indeed viable; both national income and the basic balance are in equilibrium and there is no call for fresh government intervention. But if the deficit were financed by expensive short-run commercial credits or by running down the reserves, it is more likely that the government would have to intervene to reduce the current account deficit.

And notice one other implication of this analysis. If income is held constant, a reduction in the current deficit (an increase in exports and/or a reduction in imports) must necessarily be matched by a reduction in the investment surplus (through reduced investment and/or increased saving). *To be effective, balance of payment policies must concern themselves both with the foreign trade sector and with the domestic balance of the economy.* It is because they commonly disregard this fundamental principle that governments often fail to solve their payments difficulties.

Since (holding income constant) reducing an import surplus necessitates reducing the equivalent investment surplus, this can be achieved either by reducing investment or increasing saving, or a mixture of both. Because an increase in saving means a reduction in current consumption, we can say that an improved balance of payments requires reductions in either consumption or investment, or both. Since production for investment and consumption both absorb domestic resources, the essential point can be expressed in the statement that *an improved balance of payments necessitates reductions in the absorption of resources, $C+I$.*

When economists and others set out to explain to the general public why a payments deficit has to be reduced they often express the point by saying that 'the country has been living beyond its means'. We can now see the truth of this statement. If a country incurs an excess of imports over exports, which it finances by borrowing abroad, it is allowing total absorption $(C+I)$ to exceed national income by the amount of the payments deficit. It is augmenting national income by utilizing the savings of foreigners (or by running down reserves accumulated in the past). Eliminating the payments deficit thus involves curtailing $C+I$ to the value of the resources currently available within the domestic economy, ceasing to borrow from the rest of the world.

> **Activity.** Are you sure you understand the statement that, holding income constant, a reduction in an import surplus must be matched by a reduction in domestic absorption? Do not proceed further until you are confident of your understanding of this.

You have probably noticed reference at several points to the fact that the analysis has assumed that national income is held constant. This is a useful simplification but it obscures an important aspect of the situation, namely the monetary effects of the balance of payments.

Recall here the relationship described in Chapter 7 between the balance of payments and the supply of money (see page 182). The payments deficit, cb, in Figure 8.4 will result in a reduction in the domestic money supply, as people use local currency to buy foreign exchange. The reduction in money supply will tend to raise interest rates, reduce investment and consumption. These changes would be equivalent to an upward shift in the $S-I$ schedule and would result in reduced real incomes. Clearly, this result would be most unwelcome to the public and its government. It is likely, therefore, that the government would bring about an increase in domestic credit to neutralize the deflationary monetary effects emanating from the balance of payments. If there is an increase in domestic credit equal to the fall in money supply induced by the payments deficit, then the $S-I$ schedule will remain (approximately) unchanged and national income remains at Y_o. So by holding income constant we are tacitly assuming that the government will act so as to prevent a payments deficit from causing a net reduction in domestic money supply.

A further consequence of assuming an unchanged national income is that it rules out the use of income as a variable to be altered by government policy. For short-run analysis that is sensible, because income is not easily amenable to manipulation except over a period of years. It is worth pointing out, however, that an alternative way of reducing an import surplus is to raise income, holding $C+I$

constant, with accretions to income being saved. The crucial task is to *reduce absorption relative to income*, either by reducing absorption or increasing income, or a mixture of both.

Summary on income determination

The conclusions of the above account of the theory of income determination in an open economy can be summarized in the following propositions.
(1) An economy can be said to be in equilibrium when the total value of planned expenditures is equal to the total planned availability of goods and services. This condition is satisfied when injections into the stream of income are equal to leakages out of it.
(2) In an open economy (and ignoring government spending and taxation) the equality of injections and leakages is achieved when $I + X = S + M$. From this it follows that $X - M = S - I$. An excess of import demand over export earnings is matched by an equal excess of planned investment over national saving.
(3) The existence of an equilibrium level of national income is consistent with a surplus or deficit of exports over imports.
(4) Because an import surplus is matched by an investment surplus, effective balance of payments policies must concern themselves with the savings-investment balance of the economy as well as the foreign trade sector.
(5) An improvement in the export-import balance is contingent upon a reduction of domestic absorption of resources relative to national income. This involves reducing consumption (increasing saving), reducing investment, increasing income, or some combination of these.

> **Activity.** Before proceeding further you should make sure you understand the reasoning underlying these propositions. If your own country produces national accounts from the expenditure side, study these in order to trace the relationship between changes in the export-import and saving-investment balances.

III.   Preliminary Policy Decisions

We have considered the structure and interpretation of the balance of payments accounts. We have also been through the theory of income determination in an open economy. Having studied these two topics we now have a foundation of knowledge upon which to build a discussion of the policies which a country may adopt when faced with a payments deficit on basic balance. The next step is to explore certain broad policy decisions which a national government has to make when confronted with a deficit, proceeding then to a more detailed examination of two of the most important policy instruments in use.

In doing so, however, bear in mind that one of the self-imposed limitations of this book is that it concerns itself solely with national policy. Policies which require international agreement are excluded. In the context of the balance of payments, this is a real restriction because there are constraints on what deficit countries can achieve. The point is that a payments deficit in one part of the world must have counterpart surpluses elsewhere. The fact that the oil-exporting countries collectively run large surpluses necessarily imposes deficits on the rest of the world. In an ideal world, there would be equal obligations on deficit and surplus countries to restore their payments to equilibrium. But in the imperfect world we live in there is little effective pressure on surplus countries. The main burden of adjustment is thrown on those with deficits . . . but it is impossible for them collectively to restore equilibrium so long as other countries remain in surplus.

This consideration came especially to the fore after the 1974 oil price rise but countries like Germany, Japan and Switzerland were already persistently running large surpluses, imposing deficits on the rest of the world. So in the following discussion of national policies we should not lose sight of the need for more effective action at the international level as well.

First decision: should the deficit be financed?

Given the existence of a deficit on basic balance, one possibility is that the government can restrict its policy responses to finding ways of financing the deficit. There are three possibilities:

(1) Obtaining additional long-term capital from the rest of the world.
(2) Attracting additional inflows of short-term capital.
(3) Utilizing the country's foreign exchange reserves.

Unlike the other two, the first option is one that would solve the payments problem by eliminating the deficit. Recall that we are dealing with a deficit on the basic balance – a balance that includes long-term capital flows. Therefore, if sufficient additional long-term capital is obtained the deficit will be eliminated without any need to act on exports, imports and other transactions.

This option is, in fact, a promising one, especially for governments that have hitherto not been trying particularly hard to obtain aid or attract private investments. Table 8.1 (page 189) showed, you may remember, that in 1974–7 the non-oil LDCs were able to offset their large deficits on current account by matching inflows of capital, despite the traumatic effects of the oil price explosion (although there were numerous individual countries which could not weather the storm in this way. Some had already been doing as much as they could, or as they desired, to obtain development aid and to offer inducements to private investors).

It was also shown in the context of Table 8.1 that this 'solution' of the current account deficit was by no means costless, because it involved large increases in external indebtedness and debt servicing outflows. The earlier definition of balance of payments equilibrium (page 194) should be recalled here: an equilibrium could only be said to exist if the external debt and debt-servicing burdens were not considered too large. There are, alas, numerous examples of governments which have borrowed heavily to ease a shortage of foreign exchange but have in consequence run up large debt burdens. These debts themselves became sources of weakness because of the foreign exchange cost of interest and amortization payments. An extreme example is provided by Chile, whose debt service payments in 1977 were equivalent to 32 per cent of export earnings.

If attempts to finance a basic deficit by securing larger inflows of long-term capital are unsuccessful, or if they are rejected as injudicious, there is the alternative of seeking short-term financing. One way of attempting this is to raise interest rates, to attract international short-term investors seeking the highest available yield on their money. Indeed, in industrial countries interest rate policy is strongly influenced by the desire to attract (or discourage) short-term capital. Some developing countries have also employed this instrument successfully but they are the exception rather than the rule. For most, capital receipts may not be elastic with respect to interest rates because there is not a capital market sufficiently developed to handle large short-term capital flows, and because private investors are often not confident enough about the stability of an LDC currency (or of its government) to be willing to risk large sums. This type of capital is a mixed blessing anyway. It may depart as quickly as it enters and is thus an undependable – possibly destabilizing – source of

support. It can also be expensive and thus add to debt problems.

This leaves the third option, of financing the deficit by running down the country's reserves.[3] Always assuming that reserves are large enough for this to be feasible, the crucial question the government's advisers will need to answer is whether or not the deficit is likely to be purely transitory, to be replaced by surpluses or equilibrium after a while. If there are reasons for believing the deficit is temporary, the best policy is to use the reserves to finance the deficit, replenishing them when things improve. This is what reserves are for. More fundamental actions to strengthen the balance of payments, like deflating incomes, depreciating the currency or introducing exchange controls, impose costs on the economy. They destabilize prices, increase uncertainties (which discourages investment), and cause dislocations as resource allocations adjust to the new policies.

It is true that holding a stock of foreign reserves also has a cost. Reserves offer a command over real resources which could otherwise be used for consumption or investment. Nevertheless, there is a strong case for a country to maintain a sufficient cushion of foreign reserves to absorb the temporary deficits that any country can expect to incur from time to time. Admittedly it can be most difficult to diagnose in advance whether a deficit is transitory or persistent, but it is at least sometimes possible to form a judgement.

Of course, many deficits are far from transitory. There may be a non-reversible worsening in the terms of trade, such as occurred for many non-oil exporting countries in 1974. Or domestic pressures to develop and to raise living standards as quickly as possible may cause especially rapid inflation, which we saw in the preceding chapter would adversely affect the balance of payments unless counter-measures were taken. Deficits in such countries will persist over time and a country which tried simply to finance these would sooner or later run out of reserves.

In some countries, the balance of payments is always under too much pressure to permit adequate reserves to be accumulated. The average non-oil developing country has reserves equivalent to about four-and-a-half months of imports but there are usually short-term obligations to set against the reserves. The option of financing deficits out of reserves is thus a limited one for many countries, especially bearing in mind that our earlier definition

---

[3] The next few paragraphs can touch only superficially on the important question of reserve policy. Grubel, 1977 (A) ch. 2 and 3, is especially recommended to the student wishing to delve deeper.

of payments equilibrium included the maintenance of 'adequate' reserves.

The overall conclusion, then, is that, while it is desirable to finance temporary deficits, there will be many circumstances when financing will be unfeasible or injudicious. When this is so, especially when deficits threaten to persist over time, more fundamental policy solutions have to be sought. These are likely to necessitate a further choice: between policies that emphasize action on domestic or on external variables. We examine this choice next.

> **Activity.** A possible assignment: study data on your own country's reserves, aid and other capital receipts to form a judgement about the possibilities of financing future payments deficits.

Second decision: emphasizing domestic or external adjustment?

The earlier presentation of the theory of income determination stressed the close interconnections between the domestic and external balances of the economy, with the corollary that balance of payments policies must concern themselves with changing both. There is, nonetheless, a degree of choice over the extent to which governments design their policies to operate mainly upon domestic variables or upon international transactions. On what grounds may they make such a choice?

Recall the earlier conclusion that an improvement in the current account of the balance of payments requires a reduction in the domestic absorption of resources $(C+I)$ relative to income. The most attractive strategy for adjusting the payments deficit through domestic economic variables would be to follow a growth path that raised income and foreign exchange earnings while holding down domestic consumption. This could take the form of an export drive accompanied by measures to boost domestic saving. This is a particularly attractive strategy for a developing country because it offers a method of strengthening the payments position while simultaneously promoting development. It might be called 'adjustment through growth', by analogy with the strategy of 'redistribution through growth' presented in Chapter 6. Some countries have been highly successful in achieving adjustment through growth, with Taiwan and South Korea among the best-known examples.

But a development strategy is likely to produce major results only after a long time. Adopting a new strategy will not provide quick relief to a government facing a large payments deficit. For the shorter term, the option of raising Y while holding $C+I$ constant may not be practical. As a short-term measure, it is an option best suited to economies suffering from deflation because they can easily increase real incomes by bringing idle productive capacity into use. Most developing countries are not in that situation: their resources are under-utilized but there are deep-seated obstacles in the way of raising utilization. It is not usually possible to do much about the speed with which real incomes are growing in two or three years. Even if it is possible to accelerate the expansion of Y, there is still the difficult task of making sure that the additions to income are not all absorbed by greater consumption and investment.

Only in the longer run, therefore, are measures designed to raise Y likely to bring much relief to the balance of payments. In the shorter term, a policy that emphasizes the manipulation of domestic economic variables is likely to take the more negative form of reducing absorption by cutting consumption and/or investment. This will also reduce the demand for imports and may release resources for the production of exports. But thrusting all the weight of payments adjustment on deflationary domestic policies is likely to impose a heavy cost in foregone investment, employment and growth. For the same reasons, it will also be politically unpopular.

Experiences in the world during the last three decades show that, in fact, governments adhere more resolutely to domestic policy objectives, like full employment and rapid growth, than they do to the maintenance of payments equilibrium. They are reluctant to allow their domestic economic policies to be dictated by the external balance. So, in choosing the degree of emphasis as between policy measures that operate on domestic or external variables, the main emphasis belongs with the latter. The most that can be expected is that domestic policies will back up external measures; reinforcing them, making sure they are not subverted by opposing changes in domestic economic conditions.

The main strategy for dealing with a long-term payments deficit, then, is to deploy policies which act directly upon international transactions, using domestic fiscal and credit policies in a supplementary, reinforcing role. But what are these external measures?

A summary of the chief external policy instruments

There is a spectrum of possibilities here, ranging from the manipulation of exchange rates – an instrument which operates through the price mechanism – to the imposition of administrative controls, which directly regulate current and capital transactions and bypass the price mechanism. The rest of this chapter is taken up with a comparative evaluation of these two alternatives but note also the existence of some halfway houses – instruments which occupy an intermediate position between the polar cases.

Multiple exchange rates

One such is the use of multiple exchange rates, which has been especially popular in Latin America. With this policy, the central bank specifies different rates at which it will exchange local for foreign currency, depending on the nature of the transaction. This enables it to discriminate between different types of transaction, encouraging some (exports, tourism, the importation of essentials) and discouraging others (inessential imports, repatriation of profits, foreign travel). It creates a multi-tiered market for foreign exchange, with the price mechanism still allocating resources but in the context of a multiplicity of administratively determined prices. For this reason, it can be described as a halfway house between the manipulation of a uniform exchange rate and the allocation of foreign exchange by administrative decisions. In fact, one use to which multiple rates have sometimes been put has been to assist a transition from a regime of full controls to a liberalized system with a uniform exchange rate.

Disguised depreciation

Another intermediate case can be called disguised depreciation. When a government devalues its country's currency it raises the local currency price of foreign exchange, to discourage imports and encourage exports. But similar effects can be achieved without altering the rate of exchange. For example, a government can raise the general level of import duties; it can impose a tax on invisible transactions; it can tax profits remitted abroad more heavily than those that remain within the country; it can subsidize exports; it can impose punitive 'fees' on sales of foreign exchange. All these measures have the impact of altering the effective price faced by users and earners of foreign exchange, just as a change in the official exchange rate does. Used singly or in combination, they may sufficiently discourage the use, and encourage the earning or saving, of foreign exchange to get rid of a deficit, always assuming that people respond in the desired manner.

But by comparison with an open depreciation of the currency, it is more cumbersome; more likely to create distortions, anomalies and loop-holes; more difficult to administer. It also reduces the

government's freedom of action to use fiscal policy to promote domestic objectives, since many of its taxes (and some of its spending, if it is subsidizing exports) will be dictated by the payments situation. If there is to be depreciation of the currency, it is preferable in most cases that it should be open, not disguised.

We turn now to consider the relative merits of exchange rate manipulation and direct controls.

> **Activity.** There are certain to be a number of examples of disguised depreciation in the practices of your own government. How many can you identify? Can you specify any favourable and adverse effects they may have?

IV. Explaining the Control and Exchange Rate Options

The first step is to clarify what these options consist of, their characteristics and the factors which determine their effectiveness. Controls are fairly straightforward; the exchange rate option somewhat more involved.

Explaining the controls option

Some writers employ the term 'control' to include the use of multiple exchange rates, and taxes and subsidies on imports and exports. This seems unfortunate, however, because taxes operate through the price system and the outcome will depend upon the responses of consumers and producers rather than being controlled administratively. For present purposes, therefore, we will use the term to refer to an administrative system of what are usually called exchange controls. There are two essential features of such a system: there is a legal obligation on residents to surrender all foreign exchange receipts to the state; and the state must sanction all foreign exchange payments, generally according to some set of allocational priorities. It will usually be the Central Bank to which receipts must be surrendered; and the Bank will generally work with ministries of economic affairs, commerce and trade in allocating foreign exchange among users.

> **Key concept.** A system of **exchange controls** creates a legal obligation on residents to surrender all foreign exchange to the state and creates a legal monopoly in sanctioning foreign exchange expenditures. Allocations among competing uses will usually be made according to a centrally specified set of priorities.

The task of allocating foreign exchange is commonly undertaken through the use of *import licences* and through the exercise of controls on capital transactions. Import licences generally place restrictions upon their users. Licences are likely to be valid only for some specified period, say twelve months; they may only be for a specific commodity or group of commodities; they will specify some upper limit to the value or quantity of the imports in question; they will normally be issued in the name of a specific importer and will not be transferable to others. In the extreme case, a particular item may be banned from importation altogether. As an alternative to licensing, it may be decided to give state corporations a legal monopoly on the importation of specific goods and to use authority over the corporations to limit the amount of imports. Restrictions on capital and related movements most commonly take the form of limitations on the remittances of foreign-owned business, of foreigners working in the country, and of citizens who wish to invest abroad.

All governments employ controls. Many countries, for example, banned trade with the former illegal white government of Rhodesia (Zimbabwe), which was a form of control. Most ban the importation of dirty books and narcotics. Many help local industries by placing restrictions on competing goods from abroad. Because it is the state which decides how foreign exchange should be allocated, it can discriminate among alternative uses in the pursuit of its objectives. And protecting the balance of payments is only one such motive. Ending white domination in Rhodesia or keeping pure the minds of the people have little to do with protecting the foreign exchange reserves.

Controls, then, may be employed to foster a variety of objectives. The case of Ghana can be cited.[4] In the Nkrumah period, until 1965, the import licensing authorities were instructed:

(1) To protect the balance of payments by limiting the value of imports to the estimated foreign exchange available to pay for them.

(2) Within this total, to provide an efficient allocation according to the stated priorities of the government, which included:
  (a) increasing imports from eastern European countries;
  (b) restructuring the composition of imports in favour of capital equipment, at the expense of inessential consumer goods;
  (c) transferring foreign exchange from the private to the public sector; and
  (d) protecting local import-substituting industries.

Later, two other objectives were specified: to allocate licences so as to maximize the use of foreign aid; and to discriminate in favour of indigenous (as distinct from foreign-owned) businesses.

Such use of controls entails establishing priorities for different classes of imports and this is invariably aided by some concept of *essentiality*. Essentiality is usually defined by reference to those consumer goods conventionally considered as necessities, by reference to the availability of locally-made substitutes, by the need to keep local industries supplied with raw materials and spare parts, by the need to maintain investment, and by value judgements about what is luxurious. Sometimes goods classified as essentials are allowed in without hindrance, with restrictions confined to non-essentials.

Activity. The concept of the income elasticity of demand might be used to assist decisions about essentiality. Consider how this might be done but try also to identify the difficulties it might present in practice.

Explaining the use of exchange rates

The exchange rate is a price, expressed as the amount of a foreign currency that can be bought by a unit of domestic currency. Since there is a multitude of foreign currencies there must be a multitude of prices, showing how much of each can be obtained per unit of local currency. These prices are related to each other according to the existing rates of exchange between foreign currencies. Many countries pick one key foreign currency – the US dollar is the most frequent choice – and fix the exchange rate by reference to this. An increasingly common alternative is to express the exchange rate in terms of the so-called SDR. This stands for special drawing right and is issued by the International Monetary Fund (IMF). It is internationally recognized as a monetary unit, and its value is determined by a weighted average of the values of leading world currencies. Your own country probably denominates its exchange rate either in terms of the US dollar or the SDR.

The exchange rate performs the same type of function as other prices in a market or mixed economy. It provides information and incentives to guide decisions about what to produce and what to consume. To be successful as a policy instrument, it should provide sufficient incentive to export and to produce local substitutes for imports (and sufficient

---

[4] This and later references to Ghana are drawn from Killick, 1978, ch. 10.

disincentive to import) to keep the balance of payments in equilibrium. Considered as a price, however, the exchange rate has special qualities. It is probably the single most important price in the economy. It affects numerous other prices and touches the interests of many people. This makes it the centre of much controversy, with major changes in the exchange rate exciting much popular attention.

The exchange rate has the further quality of linking together the general level of prices in the national economy with prices in other countries. If the home country experiences more inflation than its trading partners and competitors but leaves its exchange rate unaltered, its exporting and import-substituting industries will become uncompetitive. Their profits will fall and output will lag. Imports from the rest of the world will become increasingly attractive because their prices will not be rising as fast as of home-produced goods. The country is heading for a payments crisis, with a mounting import bill and stagnant exports. A depreciation of the exchange rate can, however, restore the previous relationship between domestic and foreign price levels. After the depreciation, a unit of domestic currency will buy less foreign currency, which will put up the local prices of imported goods. It will also improve the profitability of exporting because exporters will now be able to convert their foreign exchange earnings at a more favourable rate.

Figure 8.5 gives these abstractions more concrete form. This is a straightforward supply and demand diagram, with quantities of foreign exchange measured along the horizontal axis and its price on the vertical. This price is the exchange rate, expressed as the number of units of home currency (which we will call pesos) per US dollar. As in all conventional supply-demand diagrams, the demand curve has a negative slope. The main component of the demand for foreign exchange will be importers wanting to buy goods from the rest of the world (although you will have realized from the earlier description of the balance of payments that there are a multitude of other uses of foreign exchange besides importing). When the exchange rate is low, the peso price of imported goods will be cheap and we can expect there to be a heavy demand for these goods. With a higher exchange rate, the peso price of imports will also be higher and we expect a smaller volume of imports to be demanded. So the demand curve is drawn with the usual negative slope.

The supply curve is also conventional, with a positive slope, meaning that more foreign exchange will be forthcoming at a higher exchange rate. While capital inflows, transfer payments and the like can be major sources of foreign exchange, the most

Figure 8.5 *A market-determined exchange rate.*

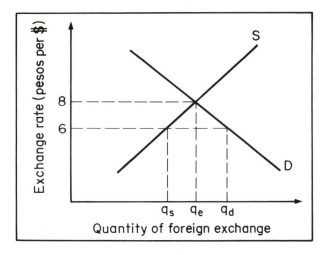

important influence on the supply curve will be export earnings. These can be expected to be a rising function of the exchange rate. For developing countries, the most likely case is that the bulk of its exports are of primary products whose world prices are determined by global supply and demand and will not be influenced by changes in the peso exchange rate. Suppose our country's main export has a world price of US $1000 per tonne. If the exchange rate is, say, 6 pesos per dollar, a tonne of exports will be worth 6000 pesos. Now suppose the exchange rate goes up to 8 pesos per dollar, that there are no taxes on exports and that domestic costs remain as before. A tonne of exports will now fetch 8000 pesos in local currency even though the world price is unaltered. Export producers find their profits larger by 2000 pesos per tonne and, so long as they do not think this is a purely temporary gain, they are likely to respond by increasing output. This, in turn, will increase export earnings and the total supply of foreign exchange. Hence the supply curve is drawn with a positive slope.

> **Activity.** Instead of taking the case of exports with a fixed world price we could have assumed that domestic exporters were free to vary the prices they charge abroad. Would this case make any difference to the use in Figure 8.5 of a positively sloped supply curve?

Figure 8.5 has been drawn so that the supply and demand for foreign exchange are brought into equality at an exchange rate of 8 pesos per dollar. At this price the amount q_e will be demanded and supplied. However, the exchange rates of most LDC currencies are not freely determined by market forces. Within narrow limits (usually within a maximum range of plus or minus 2·25 per cent) they are determined administratively and, for the most part, are changed only infrequently. It is likely that at any one time the rate officially laid down by the government will differ from that rate which would bring supply and demand into equality (the 'market clearing' rate).

Suppose in Figure 8.5 that the official rate was at 6 pesos per dollar. At this rate the demand for foreign exchange would exceed the supply by the amount $q_s q_d$. It would be possible to fill the gap by running down reserves but if the reserves were too small and if the government were not willing to allow the peso to depreciate to 8 pesos per dollar, it would have somehow to ration the uses of foreign exchange to the amount available, q_s. Exchange controls are the most common form of rationing in this situation. If instead the authorities allowed the peso to depreciate to 8 pesos per dollar, equilibrium would be established and foreign exchange would be rationed by market forces.

Since it is a word we will be using a great deal, it is worth pausing here to ask the question, how can an *increase* in the exchange rate be described as a *depreciation* of the currency? The answer is simple: a peso will buy smaller amounts of foreign exchange after the exchange rate has been raised, so it has depreciated in value. Going back to Figure 8.5, at the rate 6 pesos per dollar, one peso would buy one-sixth of a dollar, or about seventeen cents. If the rate is raised to 8 pesos per dollar a peso will buy only one-eighth of a dollar, or twelve-and-a-half cents.

> **Key concept.** A currency can be said to have **depreciated** when it will buy a smaller amount of foreign exchange, by comparison with some earlier point in time.

The discussion so far has been about 'the' exchange rate, as if all buyers and sellers of foreign exchange were faced with the same price. This is a simplification we must now qualify. Purchasers of imports, for example, generally have to pay a local currency price above the landed cost of the imports because the state levies tariffs on them. Moreover, the level of tariff may vary systematically according to the type of import, so that traders will be faced with different effective

prices depending on what they import. Similarly, many countries impose taxes on exports, which means that effectively the exporters receive a lower exchange rate than the official one. There are numerous other devices that drive wedges between the official exchange rate and that actually received or paid by sellers and buyers of foreign exchange. On this basis we can distinguish between the official, or nominal, exchange rate and the 'effective' exchange rate.

> **Key concept.** The **nominal exchange rate** is that rate officially specified by the government and registered with the IMF.* The **effective exchange rate** is the number of units of local currency actually paid or received for an international transaction.*

That this is a distinction of real importance is illustrated by the following estimates of exchange rates in the Philippines in 1971. None of the effective rates was the same as the nominal rate. All but one was above the nominal rate (an example of 'disguised depreciation') and the effective rates were spread between 5·76 and 19·26 pesos per dollar. The rate structure discriminated heavily against imports of what were considered to be non-essentials, whether for consumption or as inputs for the productive system. It also discriminated in favour of non-traditional, and against traditional, exports, to encourage the diversification of the export sector.

Because of the differential impact of taxes and other impositions on foreign transactions, a given change in the nominal exchange rate does not necessarily alter all effective rates in the same way. In the Philippines, the nominal rate went up by 65 per cent in 1966–71 and there were similar rises in the

Table 8.3
Nominal and Selected Effective Exchange Rates in the Philippines, 1971

	Pesos per dollar
Nominal exchange rate	6·44
Effective exchange rates:	
Non-essential consumer imports	19·26
Essential consumer imports	7·04
Non-essential producer imports	12·81
Essential producer imports	7·62
Traditional exports	5·76
Non-traditional exports	7·26

Source: Baldwin, 1975, Table 5–1.

---

*Not all countries have an official rate in this sense. Some allow their currencies to 'float' in accordance with changing market conditions. Others maintain multiple exchange rates. In these cases the definition of the nominal rate could be altered to refer to the market rate or to some average of multiple rates.

effective rates for most categories of imports. The effective rate for essential imported producer goods, however, went up by only 55 per cent; for traditional exports only by 48 per cent; but for non-traditional exports by as much as 74 per cent. So while a change in the nominal rate appears to affect all international transactions equally, we see that in this example the structure of effective rates changed in favour of essential producer goods and non-traditional exports, and to the disfavour of traditional exports.

The practical implication of this discussion is that when we are studying the effects of changes in a nominal rate we must also ask the question, what was the impact of this on effective rates? In general, the impact on effective rates is smaller than the size of a nominal depreciation. A study by Cooper (detailed at the end of the chapter) of twenty-four currency depreciations by LDCs estimated the following average increases in exchange rates:

Nominal	34%
Effective – exports	26%
– imports	28%

> **Activity.** Comb the literature on your own country to see if you can find estimates of effective exchange rates. If you can, study the structure of incentives they provide.

If, for the time being, we make the simplifying assumption that a given proportionate change in the nominal rate will result in the same proportionate change in all effective rates, we can return yet again to Figure 8.5, to consider the conditions that will determine the impact of a change in the nominal rate.

Rather obviously, it will depend on the slope of the supply and demand curves, that is on their *elasticity* with respect to the exchange rate. It is important at this point to remember that we are making a 'small country assumption', i.e. that the home country's exports are small in relation to total world supplies of the commodities in question, and that its demand for imports is small in relation to total world demand. This assumption is convenient because it permits us to disregard the possibility that other countries might retaliate if the home country depreciates its currency. We can also disregard the impact of this action on the income of the rest of the world (but remember that, in practice, industrial states have imposed restrictions on imports of manufactured goods from LDCs, in order to protect incomes and employment at home). Most usefully of all, it allows us to treat our country as a 'price taker' in its international trade. That is, we can infer that changes in the quantity of our country's

exports will have no significant influence on the world prices at which they sell and that changes in home demand for imports will have no influence on the world prices of these goods.

The assumption that our country is a price taker can be expressed more formally by saying that it will face an infinitely elastic world demand curve for its exports (it can sell as much as it wants at the going world price); and it will face an infinitely elastic world supply curve for its imports (it can buy as much as it wants without influencing the foreign exchange prices of its imports). So our small country faces 'external' supply and demand price elasticities that are infinitely large (or at least very big). Given such a situation, *the sizes of the domestic supply elasticity of exports and demand elasticity for imports are the crucial determinants of the impact of a depreciation on the balance of payments.*

The slopes of the supply and demand curves in Figure 8.5 suggest fairly substantial elasticities in both cases.[5] For this reason, an increase in the exchange rate from 6 to 8 pesos per dollar is shown to induce a substantial improvement in the balance of payments, closing the previous foreign exchange gap of $q_s q_d$. There is, however, no assurance that the domestic elasticities will be large. Their likely size is the subject of one of the chief controversies concerning the use of currency depreciation as an instrument of payments policy.

> **Activity.** Draw two supply-demand diagrams similar to Figure 8.5 Starting with a supply-demand gap ($q_s q_d$) of the same size in both cases, draw one diagram with highly elastic supply and demand curves and the other with inelastic curves. Compare the size of depreciation needed to restore equality to the supply and demand for foreign exchange. You will find that a much larger depreciation is needed in the inelastic case.

The chief factors bearing upon the domestic elasticities include:

(1) Whether a depreciation is expected to have lasting real effects. It often happens, for example, that the incentive effects of a depreciation are quickly wiped out by subsequent inflation at home. If that is expected to happen, neither the demand for imports nor the supply of exports is likely to be much affected by a depreciation.

---

[5] If you are not sure about the relationship between the slope of a supply or demand curve and its elasticity see Lipsey, 1975, pp. 104–6; or Samuelson, 1976, pp. 384–6.

(2) The passage of time. Confronted with higher local prices for imports and exports, local consumers have to break out of their old habits; producers have to build new productive capacity for the now more profitable import-substitutes and exports. Unless there already happens to be excess capacity, the adjustment of supply may well take two, three or even more years before it is fully effective. Supply responses of locally made import-substitutes will also influence the elasticity of demand for imports.

(3) The extent to which acceptable import-substitutes can be produced at home. When there is a large import-substitute sector, it will be easier for consumers to switch their spending away from imports in response to an increase in their local currency prices, in favour of domestic goods. The more extensive the availability of substitutes, the larger the price elasticity of demand for imports.

(4) The extent to which exportables are also consumed locally. Say our country is a major exporter of rice, which is also a local staple food. The effect of a currency depreciation will be to raise the local currency price to be obtained from exporting it. Producers will switch supplies from the domestic market in favour of exporting. With a smaller supply, the domestic price will rise and, so long as there is some price elasticity in the domestic demand for rice, this will reduce the quantity demanded at home. Home sales are a reservoir of potential exports which can be tapped if exporting becomes more profitable. Many primary product exports, unfortunately, have little by way of a domestic market and this tells against the existence of large supply elasticities, except as a longer-run response to new capacity creation.

The conditions most favourable to the use of depreciation, then, are when both the domestic elasticities are substantial (always assuming large external elasticities as well). However, we should not take the size of the external elasticities completely for granted, nor ought we to be uncritical of the validity of the small country assumption. It is often true that the demand of any one developing country for a particular import goods is likely to be too small to exert a significant influence on its price, but the same may not be true on the export side. A country may be small yet exert a large influence on total world supplies of its principal export commodity.

Take the export of the spice called cloves by Zanzibar. Zanzibar is a tiny, semi-autonomous island off the east African coast, part of the Republic of Tanzania. By all appearances it is an insignificant member of the world trading community but the fact is that it supplies about a third of total world exports of cloves. A rise or fall in Zanzibar's output can have a major impact on the world clove supply-demand balance. There are other, more important, examples of small countries supplying major proportions of total world supplies of some commodity: Malaysia and rubber, Saudi Arabia and petroleum, Ivory Coast and cocoa, Sri Lanka and tea.

Assume that one of these countries depreciates its currency and that its export supplies go up sharply in response. Since its supplies are large in relation to total world exports, its increased output will significantly affect the world supply-demand balance, depressing the foreign exchange price. In this case, the exporting country will have to set the negative effects of the lowered world price against whatever beneficial effects the depreciation may bring. The point can be put more generally by saying that when the small country assumption is not valid, a currency depreciation may have adverse terms of trade effects to set against the positive effects already discussed, i.e. it may depress export prices relative to import prices.

Activity. Examine the value and composition of your own country's foreign trade to form a judgement about the validity for it of the small country assumption.

Methods of exchange rate adjustment

Although exchange rate adjustment has been referred to above as if it were a single policy option, there are actually various ways in which a country may manage its rate of exchange. With the setting-up of the IMF after the Second World War a system was created which sought to encourage exchange rate stability. Members of the IMF were required to determine an official exchange rate and were expected to change this only when their balance of payments was revealed to be in a condition of 'fundamental disequilibrium'. So an international monetary system (often referred to as the adjustable peg system) was created in which the values of almost all currencies were fixed, subject to only occasional, discontinuous changes. A depreciation under this system is called a devaluation.

Key concept. A devaluation is a substantial and occasional currency depreciation to correct what is regarded as a fundamental disequilibrium in the balance of payments.

Since 1973, however, many countries have opted for greater flexibility. A wider variety of practices has been approved, so much so that the IMF had to amend its Articles of Agreement to accommodate the new practices. There are now three major alternative methods of exchange rate management:

(1) The old *adjustable peg* system of a fixed rate subject to occasional, discontinuous change. Most developing countries still use this method.
(2) *Floating*, i.e. allowing the exchange rate to be determined by the continuous interplay of supply and demand. There is 'clean' floating and 'dirty' floating. With the former, market forces are left entirely free from intervention by the state. Dirty floating is more common, however, in which the Central Bank intervenes to smooth out exchange rate fluctuations and to ensure they are not unduly influenced by purely seasonal or other temporary factors. The Philippines is among the few LDCs which have chosen this method.
(3) Under the *continuous adjustment* method there is an official exchange rate (which is not necessarily the same as the market clearing rate) but this is adjusted frequently, usually by small amounts. Colombia, for example, adjusts its official rate every day; Brazil does so every month.

To go in any depth into which of these alternatives is the better would be beyond the scope of this chapter, although the recommended readings at the end provide references for readers who would like to go into it more fully. The choice will depend on the extent of a country's trade diversification, the geographical pattern of its trade, the nature of the markets on which it is selling its exports, and other factors. In the general case, and always assuming that a country's deficit is not purely temporary, and therefore suitable for financing, *if it is desired to use the exchange rate as an instrument of policy, then the method of continuous adjustment is to be preferred over the other two.*

The reasons, briefly, are that continuous changes are easier to adjust to; less likely to have adverse domestic repercussions; less highly politicized; less likely to permit a payments crisis to develop; provide fewer incentives for destabilizing speculation; and require fewer resources to be locked up in foreign exchange reserves. In principle, floating would also have these advantages but few developing countries have a sufficiently developed foreign exchange market for floating to work effectively.

Controls, depreciations and domestic incomes

The discussion of income determination in an open economy reached the conclusion (page 199) that an improvement in the export-import balance is contingent upon a reduction of domestic absorption of resources (i.e. consumption and investment) relative to income. Having clarified the nature of the controls and depreciation options, we now consider their possible effects on the domestic income-absorption balance. Is either of these measures likely also to bring about the required improvement in the domestic balance?

To answer this it is important to distinguish between economies which are underemployed, in the sense discussed earlier, and economies operating near to full productive capacity. Take first the case of an *underemployed* economy, and assume that the government imposes controls or depreciates the currency sufficiently to effect some given improvement in the export-import balance. The case is illustrated in Figure 8.6, which is based upon the lower part of Figure 8.4.

Figure 8.6 *Real income effects of a reduction in the export-import deficit.*

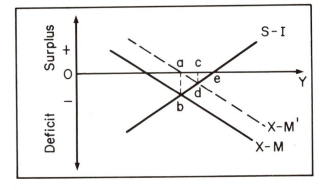

We start with an income equilibrium of a, at which there is an export-import deficit of ab (and, of course, an excess of investment over saving of the same amount). Now suppose one of two possibilities: (1) the government imposes import controls so as to reduce imports by ab below the amount that would be demanded at any level of income; or (2) the government depreciates the currency sufficiently for the combined effect of reduced imports and increased exports to be equal to ab at the original equilibrium income. Both cases are represented by the broken X − M' line. This shows that at the old level of income, a, the payments deficit would be eliminated.

However, the economy would no longer be in equilibrium because the condition X − M = S − I is no longer satisfied. As you can see, it would be satisfied at the income level, c. What has happened is that the reduced deficit has expanded money supply, thus stimulating demand and investment; real incomes have also increased because larger domestic production of import-substitutes has resulted from the switch of purchasing power away from imports and, in the case of depreciation, because of greater production of exports. The increase in income from a to c will increase saving, which is a function of income, and this will improve the domestic income-absorption balance. But the same rise in income will generate additional demand for imports (also a function of income) and this will push the export-import balance into deficit again. So at the new equilibrium income, c, there is still a payments deficit, of cd. The initial impact of the controls or depreciation, improving the export-import balance by ab, is partially undone by the larger import demand induced by higher incomes. Only by import restrictions or a depreciation large enough to shift income all the way to e could the payments deficit be entirely eliminated. Alternatively, the government could introduce supporting fiscal and monetary measures designed to raise saving relative to investment also by the amount ab, in which case the $S-I$ schedule would be shifted to the north-west, leaving national income at a but with the payments deficit eliminated.

The last two paragraphs have been on the assumption of an underemployed economy, so that all increases in income are real and the price level remains constant. This is unrealistic for the circumstances of most LDCs. Their economies will typically behave as if they are operating near to full capacity. Although there may be widespread under-utilization of labour and other resources, there are deep-seated obstacles in the way of raising utilization. The main response to an increase in demand for domestic goods is therefore likely to be inflation rather than increased real output, especially in the shorter term.

If the economy performs as if it were *fully utilized*, we have a more complicated and less favourable case. It is more complicated because the effects on the income-absorption balance will depend on how rising prices affect the distribution of income, people's attitudes to holding money and a variety of other factors. It is less favourable because the increase in domestic demand following the introduction of controls or a depreciation will push up domestic prices, thus again making the prices of imported goods more attractive relative to local goods. Domestic inflation is also likely to raise export production costs, reducing the profitability of exporting. And where an exported commodity also has a significant local market, inflationary pressure at home will raise domestic demand for the exportable, thus tending to reduce exports. However, the magnitude of the inflationary effects will not necessarily be the same for both controls and depreciation and we will make a comparison later.

The case for supplementary fiscal and monetary policies in support of the balance of payments measures is, therefore, even stronger in the case of the fully utilized economy. There will be no automatic tendency for either weapon to induce the required improvement in the income-absorption balance, and the initially beneficial effects on the external balance are liable to be eroded by rising domestic prices unless disinflationary policies are pursued at home.

Our general conclusion, therefore, is that *the use of either controls or exchange depreciation is likely to require the adoption of supporting fiscal and monetary measures to bring about necessary changes in the income-absorption balance and to guard against a further worsening of the balance of payments caused by rising domestic prices.* The desirability of such supporting policies is not, therefore, something which differentiates these instruments from each other.

V. A Comparative Evaluation

Having clarified the nature of the exchange control and currency depreciation options, our final step is to undertake a comparative evaluation of them. For this task we will use the criteria for assessing the efficiency of policy instruments developed in Chapter 2, asking the same questions for both instruments as those listed on page 44:

(1) How large is the likely balance of payments response to the use of these instruments?
(2) With what probability and with what speed will the expected results be achieved?
(3) Do the instruments act upon the causes of the payments deficit?
(4) What are the resource costs of these alternatives?
(5) Are these measures selective in their application and flexible over time?
(6) What will be their indirect economic effects?
(7) What will be their socio-political effects?

We will go through these in the order presented.

> **Activity.** If you have not read Chapter 2 (or have forgotten it!) it would be helpful to consult pages 43–6 before proceeding further.

Magnitude of response

In principle, this is a criterion by which exchange controls should score heavily. Given a payments deficit of a certain size, it is apparently open to the licensing authorities to reduce the value of the import quotas and other foreign exchange outflows by the amount needed in order to eliminate the payments deficit. In practice, however, there are limitations on the magnitude of improvement that can be achieved.

The licensing authorities will normally make their allocations according to some scheme of essentiality. The items they cut first will be things like luxury consumer goods, foreign travel and investments by nationals abroad. This type of cut will be relatively easy to make but if the initial deficit is large it may not be sufficient just to cut these 'luxuries'. Then more difficult decisions will have to be faced whether to reduce imports of more essential consumer goods, whether to cut back on capital goods, whether to limit profit remittances by foreign-owned companies (at the risk of provoking a reduced inflow of foreign capital). The government may be reluctant to make reductions in these areas, in which case it will not be possible to eliminate the deficit.

What the last sentence implies is that it is a mistake to think that just because imports are licensed therefore they are independent of domestic demand. A large excess demand for imports will be reflected in intense pressures (and large offers of bribes) on the licensing authorities and their political bosses to increase licence allocations. This is especially so if the country's payments begin to improve, perhaps because of some temporary increase in world commodity prices. Once it is known that there is extra foreign exchange available there will be a clamour to issue more licences, even though the wiser course may be to rebuild reserves or pay off debts.

A further difficulty of protecting the balance of payments through exchange controls is that these regulate only certain aspects of the balance of payments and leave others – most notably exports – free to find their own levels. Unexpected variations in the uncontrolled transactions may, therefore, prevent the authorities from securing the desired improvement in the payments position. More seriously, an exchange control regime is likely to actually worsen the balance on the uncontrolled items. For the most part, exchange controls are used as an alternative to currency depreciation. This means that they operate in situations where the government is trying to keep the local currency cost of foreign exchange below what the market clearing exchange rate would be. In other words, *exchange controls permit a currency to be over-valued.*

Now, an over-valued currency reduces the profitability of exporting, because the local currency proceeds of foreign exchange earnings are smaller than would be the case with a market-determined exchange rate. It is also liable to discourage tourism, because foreigners get an unfavourable rate of exchange, and other invisible sources of foreign exchange. In short, the circumstances which result in the imposition of exchange controls are likely to be adverse to the earning of foreign exchange. This adverse effect is liable to become stronger over time if there is inflation at home, pushing up export costs with no compensating increases in the local currency incomes earned from exporting. It is therefore quite possible for the exchange control authorities to fail to achieve the desired improvement in the payments position. Although they may be effective in restraining imports and other foreign exchange uses, their efforts can be undermined by adverse trends in earnings.

The sensible conclusion on the magnitude of response to exchange controls is that they are liable to be effective in bringing the desired change if the size of the deficit is small. But if the deficit is large (implying a severely over-valued currency) it may not be possible for controls to bring the payments into balance. It depends on the initial size of the problem and on the success of the government in managing demand at home.

Certainly, there are countries which have sought to correct deficits through exchange controls but failed to get the desired results. In the Philippines, for instance, the introduction and intensification of controls in the first half of the 1950s was unable to prevent the continuation of large payments deficits and losses of reserves; the position improved later but only after steps had been taken to reduce some of the adverse effects of the controls (Baldwin, 1975). The experience of Turkey in 1953–8 was similar: tighter controls were unable to prevent the payments position from worsening, with declining export earnings and mounting external indebtedness (Krueger, 1975). In Ghana, too, controls proved incapable of protecting reserves and avoiding unwanted debts throughout the 1960s and 1970s. The point of these examples is not to suggest that controls are bound to fail – there are other countries whose payments have been improved by controls – but merely to point out that there is no guarantee of achieving the desired magnitude of response. The apparent ability of the authorities to will precisely the result they desire is illusory.

The discussion in Part IV has already clarified the prime determinants of the magnitude of a balance of payments improvement to a currency depreciation. Still retaining a small country assumption, the most important of these are the price elasticity of demand for imports and the price elasticity of supply of exports. There has long been a division among economists about the likely magnitude of these elasticities. There is a large (but perhaps diminishing) school of thought which argues that elasticities will typically be small in LDCs and that depreciation is, therefore, unlikely to be an efficient balance of payments policy. Another school of thought, more influenced by conventional economic theory, takes the opposite view. Both schools tend to dogmatism. This is a pity because the question, whether the elasticities are large enough for depreciation to work, is a factual one which should be settled by empirical research.

Accurate calculation of the elasticities is, however, a difficult task because of the complexities of isolating the response of import demand and export supply to a change in the exchange rate from all the other influences at work in the economy (which may be pulling in a different direction). A more rough-and-ready approach to the effectiveness of depreciations is to examine what has happened to the payments balances of countries which have undertaken currency depreciations.

In a major study already mentioned, Cooper examined the effects of 24 devaluations in 19 developing countries. He found that in 15 of the 24 cases there was an improvement in the current account balance within twelve months of the devaluation; 17 showed an improvement in the balance on monetary account; 21 showed an improvement either on current account or monetary account. In only 3 of the cases was there a worsening on both accounts. He also tried to compare these outcomes with predictions of what would have happened had there been no change in the exchange rate, concluding that devaluation improved the balance of trade in 15 out of the 24 cases. Consistent with our small country assumption, he also found that terms of trade effects of devaluation were negligible for most countries. He added, however, that the magnitude of the balance of payments improvement (as distinct from the direction) was sometimes quite small.

A later study by Bhagwat and Onitsuka (1974) reached more ambivalent conclusions, although it was limited to an examination of the effects of depreciation on the balance of trade only. Their most interesting results relate to a total of 22 devaluations (in 19 countries, 15 of which were LDCs) which were intended to correct a fundamental payments disequilibrium. They found that in almost all cases export performance had significantly improved within three years of the devaluation, compared with

the pre-devaluation situation. However, they also found that imports continued to increase after devaluation, in most cases more rapidly than before.

Both studies just reported simply compare outcomes before and after devaluation, and these are influenced by factors other than the increase in the rate of exchange. A study by Khan (1974), however, sought to isolate specifically the size of the demand elasticities and arrived at important conclusions. He studied import and export demand functions for a sample of fifteen developing countries in 1951–69, with the results summarized in Table 8.4.

Table 8.4
Price Elasticities of Demand for Imports and Exports of 15 Developing Countries, 1951–69

Elasticity size	(Number of countries)	
	Import demand	Export demand
1·0 or larger	10	4
0·75 to 0·99	4	—
0·25 to 0·74	1	5
Smaller than 0·25	—	4
Wrong sign[a]	—	2

Unweighted means of the elasticities:
Import demand   1·44
Export demand   0·68[b]

Source: Khan, 1974.
Notes: (a) In these cases export demand responded perversely to price changes, i.e. declined when prices fell.
(b) Excluding the two 'wrong sign' cases.

We see generally rather large import demand elasticities, with a mean of 1·4 and with only one entry below 0·75. Holding other factors constant, this average means that for every 1 per cent depreciation of the effective exchange rate for imports there will be a 1·4 per cent reduction in the quantity of import demand. The export situation is more mixed. Four countries have large demand elasticities, five are in an intermediate range of 0·25 to 0·74, and six either have small elasticities or demand functions which respond perversely to price changes.

These results generally encourage the view that the magnitude of responses of imports to depreciation may be quite large. But we have to ask how Khan's large import demand elasticities might be reconciled with Bhagwat and Onitsuka's finding of an acceleration in the growth of imports after devaluation? The answer is likely to be found in the fact that the latter study looked at the response of imports to the total economic situation, not just to the higher exchange rate. The devaluation did tend to reduce the demand for imports. But the impact of this was diminished because the change in the effective exchange rate for imports was smaller than the nominal devaluation and because larger incomes from export earnings stimulated demand for imports.

A study by Behrman (1976) of Chile's experiences brings out the same point. While the conventional partial equilibrium elasticities of the type reported in Table 8.4 may be quite large, the ultimate improvement in the balance of payments may be small. When we take into account all the ways in which a depreciation affects prices, incomes, costs and the supply of money, the final 'general equilibrium' elasticities may be quite small, as in the Chilean case. A crucial factor influencing the difference in the values of the partial and general elasticities will be the effectiveness with which the government acts to reduce absorption, so as to avoid the secondary increase in import demand and export costs that are otherwise likely.

The conclusion on the magnitude of the payments improvement resulting from a depreciation is thus similar to the conclusion regarding exchange controls: it all depends. Evidence on partial elasticities encourages us to think that depreciation can be an effective payments policy. But whether a depreciation will achieve the required results will depend heavily (1) upon the extent to which effective exchange rates are allowed to change in line with the official rate; (2) the extent to which complementary policies are enforced on the domestic front; and (3) the particular circumstances of the country in question.

Neither controls nor depreciation emerge as clearly preferable by the 'magnitude of response' criterion. The impact of each is likely to be sensitive to the success of complementary measures in improving the domestic income-absorption balance.

Activity. It is likely that the literature on your own economy includes attempts to estimate import demand elasticities, and supply elasticities for some exports. The experience with exchange controls may also have been written up. Study any such references you can trace in order to form a judgement about the likely magnitude of response to these alternative policies in your country. (See references to country studies at the end of the chapter.)

Speed and certainty of the results

We now come to the question, how probable is it that the expected improvements in the balance of payments will actually be achieved and how quickly will they be achieved?

By this criterion, exchange controls clearly have the advantage. Confidence in achieving some target result through depreciation is diminished by the fact that the government's economists are unlikely to have precise estimates of the size of the relevant elastcities or of the general equilibrium effects of raising the exchange rate. Elasticities will vary for different imports and exports, and with the magnitude of the depreciation itself. The planners are unlikely to have a sufficiently good econometric model of the economy to be able to trace general equilibrium effects more than very approximately. In other words, the government economist who commits himself to a precise forecast of the effect of a depreciation is probably fooling himself or his superiors.

Depreciation similarly does not score well in terms of the quickness with which it produces results. The point was already mentioned on page 207 that the initial domestic supply and demand elasticities may be small. It is only after producers and users have had time to adjust productive capacities and spending patterns that the elasticities will take on maximum values. Depreciation, in short, is a medium-term measure. We should remember, though, that Cooper found generally favourable results from devaluation even within a twelve-month span.

By comparison, the results of exchange controls should be more certain and faster. They should be more certain because at least some of the key balance of payments magnitudes are brought under the direct control of the government, rather than being indirectly manipulated through the influence of price incentives. The results should also be quicker. If the authorities impose a temporary import ban, or severely reduce the approved level of imports, this should begin to reduce arrivals at the ports within a few months.

Some qualifications are in order, however. Enough was said under 'magnitude of response' to indicate that the authorities are not able in practice to exert as much control as it might appear. This increases uncertainties about the effectiveness of controls. There is a common tendency for the actual volume of imports to exceed the planned volume. This may be because of bribery, administrative difficulties, political decisions which countermand the intentions of the controllers, smuggling and other forms of evasion. The scope for evading controls by smuggling varies according to geography and the efficiency of the customs authorities. The Philippines is, no doubt, an extreme case of difficulty, consisting of 7000 islands!

Despite these qualifications, though, the effects of controls are more certain and speedy than with depreciation. Therefore, controls are more suitable in situations of sudden urgent crises in which quick results are essential.

Action upon causes

Our next test is presented in the question, to what extent do these alternative instruments act upon the causes of a payments deficit? One complication in answering this is that the causes of a deficit are liable to differ from one case to the next. A deficit on the basic balance may be caused by a sudden deterioration in the terms of trade, or by an outflow of capital, or by the heavy servicing costs of unwise borrowings in the past. However, for countries experiencing persistent deficits the most likely situation is of deficits resulting from a growth in the domestic demand for imports more rapid than the growth in the volume of exports.

If we take import demand growing faster than export supply as the standard case, it is rather clear how the two instruments fall out by the 'action upon causes' test. Depreciation raises the price of imports relative to domestic goods and increases the profitability of producing import substitutes. It also improves the profitability of exporting and the country's ability to compete in world markets. (It may also stimulate larger inflows of capital, although that is more uncertain. Cooper's study showed fourteen cases in which capital inflows increased after devaluation and ten cases in which they diminished.) Depreciation therefore changes relative prices in directions which will strike at the causes of the deficit, providing disincentives to import and incentives to export. Unless we believe supply and demand to be completely unresponsive to price changes (zero elasticities), or that positive responses will be cancelled out by induced terms of trade effects, we must expect depreciation to weaken the underlying causes of the payments disequilibrium.

The case is different with exchange controls. In themselves, they do nothing to diminish the demand for imports – they merely frustrate this demand from being fully met. They similarly do nothing to stimulate exports; on the contrary, they discriminate against exports, as explained on page 210. In fact, one writer has suggested that exchange controls should be seen essentially as a tax on exports. Being associated with an over-valued currency which holds down the local cost of foreign exchange, controls actually encourage the demand for foreign exchange in a situation in which there is a national scarcity of it. If depreciations encourage capital inflows, over-valued currencies maintained by exchange controls discourage it. This is especially likely if, as is often so, controls are used to limit the repatriation of incomes accruing to foreign investors.

Controls, then, repress deficits rather than curing them. They are like taking an aspirin to get rid of a toothache instead of going to a dentist. Because the causes of the problem are left untouched, the deficit is likely to reappear whenever controls are removed. In fact, it is likely to reappear more severely because, by discriminating against exports and other foreign exchange earnings, controls are liable to worsen the underlying position. This is clearly a serious criticism of controls.

It is possible to employ complementary measures to compensate for these defects, generally by examples of the disguised depreciation described on page 202. For instance, it is possible to offset the discouragement of exports through subsidies. India is a country which found its export performance suffering because of controls and which adopted export subsidies as a corrective. But export subsidies can impose a heavy burden on the government's budget and are liable to introduce distortions of their own. In the Indian case, it is said that the export incentive system resulted in a high-cost pattern of exports which discriminated against the more efficient traditional exports and in which the degree of government assistance was only weakly correlated with the efficiency of the industries being aided.[6]

The 'action on causes' test, then, goes strongly in favour of depreciation.

Resource costs

We can next enquire into the resource costs of using these instruments. There is little to be said that is not obvious. Currency depreciation is essentially self-administering, achieving its effects through the decentralized price mechanism. Little more is required than a notification by the Central Bank to the rest of the financial system and the IMF of the new rates for foreign currencies. However, if a depreciation is achieved by means of dirty floating (see page 208), it will require more administration because of a need for active Central Bank participation in the foreign exchange market to smooth out temporary and destabilizing fluctuations.

Exchange controls require much larger administrative inputs. Senior administrators and

---

[6] See Staelin, 1974: also Frankena, 1975.

clerks will be required to do a large volume of paper work and the cost of these officials to the government budget may be substantial. The information costs of the controls are likely to be an even larger consideration. As pointed out in Chapter 1, centralized allocative systems have enormous appetites for information (see page 21). Data are needed on a firm-by-firm basis on past imports; on requirements for inputs; on plant size and capacity utilization; on production and investment plans; on employment; on a host of other items. But generating, communicating, processing and interpreting that data will impose a significant cost on the economy, in terms of the opportunity cost of the high-level manpower tied up in these tasks. The fact that much of the data gathering will occur in the private sector makes little difference; these are still real resource costs to the economy. It is admittedly possible for the private sector to minimize these costs by inventing figures instead of researching for them, but that brings large problems of its own. We will revert to these, and to the larger question of the costs of reduced efficiency of resource allocation resulting from controls, under the heading of 'indirect economic effects' shortly.

Remember too that controls beget more controls. Example: the government uses licensing to restrict imports of certain consumer goods but wishes to avoid the price inflation that is likely to result from this cut in supply. It therefore imposes price controls as well. To the costs of administering import licences we now have to add the costs of consequential price controls.

The resource cost test is, therefore, another which goes against the exchange control option.

Selectivity and flexibility

The efficiency criterion of selectivity refers to the extent to which the effects of a policy instrument are confined to the problem to which it is addressed; the flexibility of an instrument relates to the ease with which an instrument can be varied or discontinued over time.

Selectivity

As regards selectivity, exchange controls are preferable over depreciation. The controlling authorities can, in principle and subject to qualifications already introduced, tailor their allocations according to the chosen priorities of the government, whereas depreciation affects all foreign exchange transactions (always assuming that effective rates change in line with the official rate).

You will recall the example of the multiple objectives handed down to Ghana's import licensers (page 203), which illustrates the way in which governments can employ controls to discriminate according to their priorities. It is easy to exaggerate the extent of discrimination that can be achieved in practice, however. The more objectives and priorities the controllers are told to follow, the more complex and unmanageable their task becomes. Tinbergen's rule that there must be one instrument for each target (Chapter 2 above) is too rigid, but he is clearly right in warning that we cannot expect a single instrument to simultaneously achieve a multitude of targets. The system is likely to break under the strain if we load it with too many objectives, which is precisely what happened in Ghana.

With depreciation, on the other hand, what happens to the composition of imports, to the geographical pattern of trade, to the import capacity of differently-owned businesses, and so forth, is a by-product of the forces of supply and demand, of the relative strengths of competing forces.

Flexibility

When it comes to the matter of flexibility over time, both instruments have the disadvantage of being difficult to reverse. It is rare for a depreciated currency subsequently to appreciate again, at least in developing countries. Indeed, domestic export production capacity can only be expected to respond much to a depreciation if it is thought to be irreversible. If producers anticipate that in a few months the exchange rate will return to its former level, they will have little incentive to undertake the long-term investments necessary to take advantage of the new profit opportunities created by depreciation. In the upward direction, though, depreciation can be highly flexible in that it can be continuously adjusted by small amounts.

The reason why controls, considered by themselves, are also irreversible has already been stated: they do not cure the causes of the payments weakness and are therefore needed permanently unless good fortune renders them redundant. But even if, through luck or a subsequent depreciation, the controls are no longer needed for balance of payments purposes, country experiences indicate that controls are likely to linger on. Once established, strong vested interests are created to keep them, even after their original purpose is no longer relevant. The officials who administer them will want to keep controls because they may otherwise fear for their jobs, and they enjoy their power (and perhaps access to bribes). Importers who manage to obtain favourable allocations of licences will want to retain the system because, in a situation of shortage, they will earn monopoly profits (see Figure 8.7 below). Perhaps most influential of all, local industries will come to depend on import restrictions to protect them against foreign competition (see Chapter 10, page 259). The Philippines and Turkey are only two of a larger number of countries which imposed controls for balance of payments purposes but then retained them to protect local industry.

In the matter of flexibility, therefore, there are no clear grounds for preferring either alternative. But controls are more discriminating than depreciations.

Indirect economic effects

Both exchange rate manipulations and controls are likely to have widespread implications for the general functioning of the economy, so there is a lot to be said under this heading. We look at their effects on the efficiency of resource allocation; on the structure of investment and production; on the rate of inflation; and on the distribution of income.

Allocation of resources

A comparison of the effects of controls and depreciation on the allocation of resources is essentially an example of the general discussion of the relative merits of market and command economies with respect to static efficiency, set out in Chapter 1 (pages 21–2). You may remember the qualified conclusion there, that the price mechanism would probably achieve greater static efficiency than allocations through central planning. A similar argument can be made in the present context, as follows.

A currency depreciation is likely to improve the allocation of resources and, therefore, their productivity. It will do this by increasing the gains from international trade. Those goods will be imported in which the home country has the largest comparative disadvantage (i.e. can produce only with low efficiency and high costs), in exchange for those goods in which the home country has the greatest comparative advantage, because it is efficient and has low costs. A shift from an over-valued currency to an equilibrium exchange rate will thus attract greater resources into more productive activities and discourage the creation of inefficient industries with costs greatly in excess of world prices. Consumers will benefit from this greater enjoyment of the benefits of trade.

In contrast, controls are unlikely to be as efficient in allocating foreign exchange and domestic resources. One reason mentioned earlier is the information problem. To achieve an efficient allocation, the central planners responsible for administering controls need to obtain, process and interpret a vast volume of information. It is unlikely that this task can be accomplished well, given the shortages of trained manpower and administrative capacity in most developing countries. More seriously, an import licensing system actually creates incentives for the provision of misinformation, as illustrated by the following comment on problems encountered in Ghana (Killick, 1978, p. 285):

> The very existence of import restrictions and an overvalued currency provide a strong incentive for licence applicants to provide false or exaggerated information in the hope of getting large allocations. It was well known that local producers often applied for raw materials greatly in excess of their real needs, naturally presenting supporting 'information' to reinforce their case. This helps to explain why in 1968 approved licences for industrial raw materials averaged a mere 24 per cent of the applications received. Similarly, importers of final goods were constantly striving, by fair means or foul, to increase their own share of the market and thus reap the monopoly profits to be earned from the sale of imports. Far from being a scientific attempt to calculate national needs, licence allocations had to be made on the basis of bluff and counter-bluff.

Where licence allocations are also influenced by the payment of bribes – a common experience – the position is made worse. There is then no question of utilizing foreign exchange in accordance with national priorities and in the promotion of economic efficiency.

It is therefore likely that comprehensive import licensing will result in inefficiencies, such as temporary shortages of consumer goods, imported raw materials, spare parts and items of capital equipment. It is even more likely that it will increase the delay between identifying an import need and actually receiving the goods, because of the time taken to process licence and foreign exchange applications. One comparative study found delays in all cases, ranging from four weeks in Mexico to seven months in India (Little, et al., 1970, p. 209). The effect of these delays is to tie up resources in inventories, to induce temporary shortages and to reduce the average utilization of industrial capacity because of input shortages. Excess capacity (and the under-utilization of scarce capital that it entails) is also likely to be associated with licensing for the additional reason that firms may deliberately build larger plants than they need in order to obtain higher foreign exchange allocations. Pakistan is among the countries which have experienced this (Stern and Falcon, 1970, p. 21).

Structure of investment and production

Controls are also liable to have malign effects on the structure of investment and production. One important aspect of this was already mentioned: controls discriminate against the export sector, whereas an equilibrium exchange rate encourages efficient export industries. The principle of essentiality employed in allocating foreign exchange is also liable to result in distortions.

Refer back, for a moment, to Table 8.3 (page 205) and consider the investment incentives implicit in the Philippines' structure of effective exchange rates for imports. These, we saw, were based on essentiality, with the lowest rates for essential consumer and producer goods and an especially high rate for non-essential consumer goods. The intention, of course, was to allow essentials in at low prices in order to safeguard the real incomes of poorer consumers. The consequence, however, is low levels of protection for local substitutes for essential imports, and high rates of protection for inessentials (Baldwin, 1975, p. 101):

> Exchange controls [in the Philippines] added greatly to the degree of protection provided by explicit fiscal and monetary measures. In 1959, for example, implicit protective rates of 400 per cent were not uncommon for non-essential consumer goods, whereas the average explicit degree of protection in 1956 for this category was around 159 per cent. For the essential consumer-goods group, average implicit and explicit protective rates in the same year were roughly 30 and 5 per cent, respectively.

Foreign exchange allocations according to essentiality are thus likely to pull investment and production towards non-essentials. Low rates of protection for essentials help perpetuate dependence on imports of these goods. This will distort the pattern of industrialization and permit the emergence of inefficient, monopolistic, high-cost industries producing non-essential goods behind high levels of protection. This may be contrasted with allocations resulting from an equilibrium exchange rate, which would not discriminate against the production of essentials but which would offer a safeguard against the growth of highly inefficient industries.

The probability that imported capital equipment will be given a high essentiality status and will be allowed in with few restrictions will, in turn, encourage the development of capital-intensive industries and the use of capital-intensive methods, to the detriment of employment creation.

Numerous countries have discovered precisely the investment and production distortions predicted above. Let the Philippines again be our example (Baldwin, 1975, pp. 131–2):

Resource shifts during the period of exchange control are consistent with those that would be predicted on the basis of knowledge of the protective pattern of the exchange system. The economic subsidies granted on imports of raw materials and capital-goods coupled with the protection given to the final output of previously imported, non-essential goods pulled resources into capital-using and import-dependent industries. The use of capital intensive methods of production was thereby encouraged ... The elasticity of employment with respect to value-added in manufacturing is the lowest of all the productive sectors.

Effects on inflation

The discussion so far has been heavily to the disadvantage of controls. Turning now to the effect of the two instruments on inflation their relative performance is less clear-cut. Two general preliminary points: (1) The way in which either controls or depreciation feeds into domestic inflation will hinge crucially on the strength of the propagation mechanism, discussed in the previous chapter, and on the effectiveness of anti-inflationary policies. (2) The impact of balance of payments instruments on the domestic price level will be strongly influenced by the openness of the economy. The majority of LDCs have small, open economies, whose price levels are thus sensitive to the behaviour of import prices. But in larger countries, such as Brazil or India, external trade is modest relative to total activity, limiting their vulnerability to imported inflation.

Both controls and depreciations will raise prices. Depreciation, of course, is deliberately designed to raise import prices and this effect will be particularly noticeable if it is in the form of a large, discontinuous devaluation rather than one of the more continuous forms of adjustment described earlier. However, a devaluation may not cause the final prices of imported goods to go up by the full extent implied by the rise in the exchange rate if, prior to the change, imports were being limited by controls. In this situation traders would previously have been earning monopoly profits on imported goods, so that a devaluation would act partly by reducing these profit margins.

We should also bear in mind the monetary effects of a devaluation. For the purposes of Chapter 7 on inflation, exchange rate flexibility was assumed on the grounds that a country pursuing such a policy is better able to control the quantity of money and may thus use monetary policy for anti-inflationary purposes. A country maintaining a fixed exchange rate by means of controls is effectively denying itself the use of monetary policy. This creates some presumption that countries with flexible exchange rates may be more successful in limiting inflation.

A second monetary point is that a depreciation (but not controls) raises the amount of local currency that importers have to give up in order to obtain a certain quantity of imports. This increase in the local currency given up to acquire foreign exchange will reduce domestic money supply, thus helping to counteract any general tendency towards inflation. Thus, in the study already referred to, Cooper found a net deflationary effect of this type in fourteen of the twenty-four cases studied.

> **Activity.** If the arguments of the last two paragraphs are not clear, you should refer back to Chapter 7, especially page 182.

Nevertheless, Cooper's research made it clear that devaluations were likely to result in substantial price rises. In the fourteen countries for which he had complete data the average increases were as follows:

Size of the effective devaluation	45%
Index of import prices	34%
Index of wholesale prices	21%
Index of consumer prices	21%

These figures support the idea that final import prices will not rise by the full extent of the devaluation. But we also see an inflation of domestic prices nearly half as large as the effective devaluation. Some of this inflation would have occurred anyway, so to isolate only the effects of the devaluation itself we would need information on how prices would have behaved with an unchanged exchange rate. Cooper used econometric techniques to estimate this, concluding that a 10 per cent devaluation was likely to raise wholesale prices by 3·2 per cent and consumer prices by 4·2 per cent. So the inflationary effects of devaluation are by no means negligible, without being so large as to cancel out the initial balance of payments improvements.

Whether the inflationary effects of depreciation are likely to be bigger or smaller than those of controls is unclear. Controls raise import prices because they reduce supply relative to demand. Their use to maintain a fixed exchange rate will prevent the government from using monetary policy to control inflation. And the fact that controls place most of the burden for securing a balance of payments improvement on reductions in imports, leaving many other foreign transactions uncontrolled, suggests that they may have a more severe impact on final import prices. Similarly, if controls lead to shortages and misallocations, as suggested earlier, they will increase

the incidence of disequilibria and hence strengthen any tendency for structural inflation of the type described on pages 164–6.

There is thus some presumption that controls will be more inflationary than depreciations. But it is only a presumption because there is no hard evidence with which to directly compare the two.

Distribution of income

This discussion of indirect economic effects comes finally to the question, how are the two instruments likely to impinge upon the distribution of income? We will take first the case of currency depreciation.

Expressed in general terms, a depreciation will shift real income in favour of export and efficient import substitution industries and away from consumers of imported goods. How this shift will affect inequality is hard to generalize. It will depend upon the composition of exports and imports, and on the factor proportions employed in the export and import-substitution industries. The circumstances most likely to result in reduced inequality will be where most exports are agricultural and produced by smallholders, where import-substituting industries are relatively labour-intensive, and where most imported consumer goods are items consumed largely by the rich. With such a situation, a depreciation will raise the net incomes of smallholders, generate new industrial employment and reduce the real income of the rich.[7] Urban-rural inequalities are likely to diminish. There is, however, a wide range of alternative economic structures which would produce less favourable results.

> **Activity.** Study the composition of your own country's imports and exports to write a note about the probable distributional effects of a depreciation.

Exchange controls can be used as a means of reducing inequality. Indeed, this is likely to influence the definition of essentiality used in allocating foreign exchange, with attempts made to avoid severe cuts in imported low-income consumer goods. Licence allocations can similarly discriminate in favour of firms operating in underdeveloped regions of a country, as was attempted in Colombia. But while this potential exists, actual experiences have been different.

---

[7] These and related issues are explored at a theoretical level by Knight, 1976.

In general, controls are likely to shift real incomes away from export industries and consumers of non-essential imports in favour of industries producing non-essential import-substitutes. Since the exports of many LDCs are dominated by agricultural products and since we have already argued that the system will favour capital-intensive import-substitution, this shift of real incomes is liable to widen urban-rural and interpersonal inequalities. In practice, licensing usually operates in ways which favour already-established, relatively large firms located in or near the capital city: a result found in countries as diverse as Colombia, Pakistan, Mexico and Ghana.

Perhaps the most distinctive feature of the distributional impact of controls, however, is in the monopoly profits they create for importers. The point can be illustrated by a simple supply-demand diagram, as in Figure 8.7, which we will take to refer to the market for wrist-watches. Assume the government is maintaining an over-valued exchange rate by means of controls. Say this results in a price which has to be paid by traders importing watches (inclusive of taxes, distribution costs and 'normal' profits) of p_1. At price p_1 the public will want to buy q_1 watches but the licensing authorities are unwilling to sanction such a large quantity of imports. Instead they issue licences for a total quantity of q_2. This is represented on the diagram by a vertical supply curve, because the quantity is determined administratively and is not elastic with respect to price.

With supply limited to q_2, the public is willing to pay p_2. Traders are thus able to charge p_2 while their costs are only p_1. The shaded rectangle indicates the excess profits accruing to those fortunate enough to secure licences to import watches. No wonder they are willing to pay bribes! If instead of controls there

was an equilibrium exchange rate, competitive forces would generally eliminate the excess profits, leaving the price and quantity of watches in a position probably intermediate between the two combinations illustrated on the diagram.

In this illustration there is a substantial resdistribution of income in favour of unearned profits by traders, who perhaps share these with officials by paying bribes. Most people would regard this as a socially undesirable change in income distribution, even if those who pay the high final prices may themselves be relatively prosperous. It is, however, possible to avoid this consequence. One common counter-measure is to impose price controls on the restricted items, to prevent traders from exploiting their monopoly powers. But price controls are often ineffective and create substantial problems of their own (see page 179).

An alternative is for the government itself to capture the excess profits by imposing taxes on import licences. They may, for instance, levy a large licensing fee. If they calculate this accurately, the fees will absorb the excess profits, although the consumer is still left paying the higher price. A variant on this would be to offer import licences for public auction. Competition between those wanting foreign exchange should drive up the auction price so as to approximately eliminate excess profits, with the proceeds going to the government budget. Brazil experimented with this method in the early 1950s but practical considerations have made governments reluctant to adopt it.

But although there are ways of avoiding this outcome, the general experience is that import traders generally do well out of licensing systems, with adverse implications for the distribution of income. Bearing this and the earlier discussion in mind, it seems fair to conclude that there is a general presumption that controls are more likely to have adverse effects on income distribution than exchange rate adjustments. However, the precise outcome will depend upon the circumstances of each case and these could be such that controls would operate the more favourably upon income distribution. Nothing stronger than a conclusion mildly favourable to depreciation is warranted in the absence of clear evidence.

To sum up, this discussion of indirect economic effects has concluded that:

(1) Exchange rate flexibility is likely to result in a substantially more efficient allocation of resources than the use of controls.

(2) Controls are likely to introduce undesired

Figure 8.7 *Monopoly profits with import restrictions.*

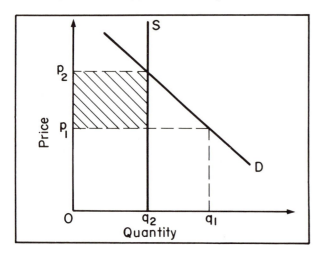

distortions in the structure of investment and production, distortions not present with exchange rate flexibility.

(3) There is a general presumption that depreciation will be associated with less inflation and is less likely to worsen income distribution. However, the evidence is not strong and it is easy to imagine circumstances in which the opposite results would hold.

This brings us to the final criterion of policy efficiency: the socio-political effects.

Socio-political effects

That governments often show great reluctance to devalue, preferring instead to maintain controls, is partly the result of political calculations. Devaluations are unpopular, not only because of their sudden impact on the cost of living and income distribution, but also because the exchange rate is often viewed as a symbol of national prestige. A devaluation may therefore be seen as demeaning to the nation, particularly repugnant to recently-independent states. Whether it is sensible to view the exchange rate in this way is doubtful, but what is important in the political context is that it may be so viewed. A devaluation, moreover, is obviously and explicitly a state decision, so the government cannot avoid incurring the odium created by the change.

Controls do not suffer from the same dis-advantages. Of course, a decision to impose controls is a government one but if these result in shortages, price increases and other ill effects the government can try to shift the blame on to civil servants and on to 'hoarding' by the always unpopular middlemen. This is especially so if the government can say it is trying to protect consumers by using price controls (even though it may know that they are ineffective).

Controls have the additional political attraction that they confer discretionary power upon ministers. The power to approve or disapprove an application for foreign exchange provides a source of patronage which the skilful politician can use to strengthen his own popularity and do down his enemies. Varying the exchange rate confers no equivalent power. Controls are personalized but the exchange rate operates impersonally through the price system.

There is empirical evidence to support the view that devaluations are politically risky. This was among the factors examined by Cooper, who found that in seven out of his twenty-four cases the government had fallen from power within twelve months of devaluing. This was about twice as many as would have been predicted had there been no devaluations, although in

only two cases was the fall from power clearly related to the economic crisis. The risks to the responsible finance ministers were even larger. Fourteen of the twenty-four were out of their jobs within twelve months of the devaluation (including the seven who fell with their governments) – about three times as many as would be predicted without devaluation.

It is significant, though, that Cooper's was a study of devaluations, as compared with floating or continuous adjustment. Major devaluations invariably occur in crisis conditions and are highly political. Weekly or monthly adjustments are more technical, less political, less publicly noticeable. This, in fact, is a major reason for preferring continuous over occasional adjustment.

The seeming political attractions of controls also need to be viewed cautiously. It was suggested earlier that use of controls over a long period is liable to result in a serious weakening of the underlying payments position, as well as creating increasingly large distortions within the domestic economy. In the end, these trends may well create an economic crisis in which a large devaluation, with all its political risks, is unavoidable. If the government devalues and as a result is thrown out of office, are we to blame this on the devaluation or on the controls which made it necessary? The point could be put more broadly: the popularity of a government is likely to be correlated with the performance of the economy. If controls worsen that performance, as they may do, the popularity of the government will be consequently reduced.

The conclusion, then, is that large devaluations are politically risky and that controls commend themselves more to politicians. But this greater attractiveness may rest upon a superficial reading of the political merits of the two alternatives. Strong economic performance aided by continuous (and therefore de-politicized) exchange rate adjustments may offer larger long-term benefits to government ministers.

Conclusions

Having been through the seven criteria of policy efficiency, let us sum up to decide where the overall balance of advantage lies. We found that *controls* were superior in the speed and certainty with which they bring balance of payments relief, that they were more selective and carried smaller short-term political risks for governments. We found exchange rate *depreciation* to act upon the likely causes of a payments deficit while controls did not, that its resource costs were smaller and that its indirect economic effects were considerably more beneficial/less harmful. We found no clear basis to prefer either instrument by the test of magnitude of response.

The choice between these instruments thus accurately reflects the general complexity of economic policy-making: it is rare for one policy to have absolute superiority over feasible alternatives by all relevant criteria. The choice has to be made by weighing the costs and benefits, the strengths and weaknesses. So it is with the case under consideration here. In my view, *the balance of the arguments lies clearly in favour of depreciation*, but that is a judgement you are free to disagree with so long as you can marshall sensible reasons.

Considered as a balance of payments instrument, the fatal flaw of controls is that they fail to correct payments disequilibria, being content instead to repress the symptoms. Unless other things are done as well, this repression eventually ceases to be viable.

One comparative study of six developing countries found that only one had not used controls to manage its balance of payments. Of the other five, it was found that (Little, *et al.*, 1970, p. 330):

Sooner or later, all the countries which experienced balance of payments difficulties . . . ran out of inessential imports which could be restricted. Then they realised that measures to increase exports *must* be used as otherwise 'essential' imports would have to be cut very severely with disastrous effects on domestic output, consumption and investment. Hence, even those countries using import controls had in the end to keep their balance of payments in equilibrium by a combination of devaluation . . . deflation and foreign borrowing. The only major difference between them and other countries was that they had to maintain this balance in a situation in which their economic structures had been distorted by the existence of severe import restrictions . . . this can only have made the task of reconciling growth with balance of payments equilibrium subsequently more difficult.

Activity. The interested student could review this comparative assessment by constructing a table analogous to Table 2.3 (page 49). He should assign his own weights according to the importance he attaches to the various criteria and give scores to the two instruments in a manner similar to that employed for Table 2.3. Do the resulting scores support a conclusion in favour of depreciation?

Four final points. We have throughout treated depreciation and controls as alternatives to each other. However, controls can be used as a temporary

support for depreciation. The strongest advantage of controls is that they achieve results more quickly and certainly, making them better suited for dealing with sudden crises. In crisis situations, then, one possibility is to simultaneously depreciate and temporarily impose controls, allowing the latter to provide enough breathing space for the former to achieve longer-term improvements to the payments situation.

Secondly, however weary he may be by now, the reader must not forget the importance of back-up fiscal and monetary policies to improve the domestic income-absorption balance. Only if this is undertaken with determination can we expect import demand and export supply to respond as needed.

Thirdly, what was said in Chapter 7 of anti-inflation policies can be repeated here: it is unlikely that government action can do more than achieve a rough-and-ready payments equilibrium. The complexities of the problem, the influence of unpredictable external forces, the paucity of information, the imperfection of our understanding of the way economies work, and the problems of effective policy implementation – all these rule out the possibility of maintaining an exact equilibrium at all times.

Finally, remember the earlier caution about the limitations of a purely national approach to payments policy. Many of the difficulties which nation-states labour under could be improved through international action. Some are insoluble without it. There is no doubt that human well-being would be increased if the countries of the world could unite to co-ordinate their national efforts.

Suggestions for Revision and Group Discussion

1 Review your understanding of the following:
  (a) Debt and debt servicing ratios.
  (b) The current account, the basic balance and the monetary account.
  (c) Balance of payments equilibrium.
  (d) Leakages and injections.
  (e) Absorption.
  (f) Depreciation, disguised depreciation and devaluation.
  (g) Exchange controls.
  (h) The principle of essentiality.
2 Why has this chapter picked the basic balance as the single most important indicator of the state of the balance of payments? In what circumstances might the balance on current account or monetary account be preferred?

3 State the meaning and significance of the 'small country assumption'. In what ways would this chapter need modification in the absence of this assumption?

4 What influences the amount of foreign exchange reserves that a country should hold? How might this amount be affected by changes in balance of payment policies?

5 On Figure 8.4 show the points Y_q and Y_b taken from Figures 8.2 and 8.3. Satisfy yourself from the upper part of Figure 8.4 that X = M at Y_b.

6 The exposition of income determination in an open economy deliberately excluded the influence of government spending and taxation. It also excluded explanation of the concept of the 'foreign trade multiplier'. By studying these refinements you would enhance your understanding of the theory in important ways. Consult the textbooks recommended below.

7 Explain in your own words the statement that an excess of imports over exports is necessarily matched by an excess of investment over saving.

8 What is your understanding of the distinction between nominal and effective exchange rates? Suggest how we might explain the differences in depreciation sizes given on page 206.

9 Use Figure 8.7 to illustrate the effect of the imposition by the government of a fee on import licences.

10 Explain the statement on page 209 that the desirability of supporting domestic policies is not a consideration which differentiates exchange controls and depreciation from each other.

11 It is often argued that developing countries stand to gain little from devaluations because the foreign currency prices of their exports are determined by world market conditions and will not be affected by devaluation. Evaluate this argument in the light of the discussion of Parts IV and V above.

Suggestions for Further Reading

(Full publication details of the following recommendations are given in the bibliography at the end of the book.)

General textbooks on international economics are invariably written from an industrial country standpoint – a particularly regrettable narrow-mindedness in authors claiming to write about the international economy. Failing a textbook which gives adequate treatment of the circumstances and problems of LDCs, Grubel, 1977 (B); Sodersten, 1971; and Scammell, 1974 are recommended. Kindleberger, 1973, is another well-established and popular text; the presentation is stimulating but sometimes cryptic.

The Annual Reports of the IMF (Washington) are a valuable source of global data and commentaries on the world payments position. Two other IMF publications are also valuable. Its *Staff Papers* contains many relevant contributions; the monthly *International Financial Statistics* provides information on a wide variety of payments and other economic data, globally and for individual countries.

Of the empirical sources cited in the text utilizing data from large samples of countries, the most outstanding is Richard Cooper's essay in Ranis, 1971. See also Bhagwat and Onitsuka, 1974; and Khan, 1974.

Those who would like to go more thoroughly into the choice of the most appropriate method of exchange rate management for developing countries should consult Crockett and Nsouli, 1977; Cardozo, 1976; and Dreyer, 1978. Part two of Grubel, 1977A, contains an excellent general discussion, although it is not particularly related to developing countries. There are two major series of country studies relevant to this chapter. There is a series of studies published by the National Bureau of Economic Research and distributed by Columbia UP (New York) under the general title *Foreign Trade Regimes and Economic Development*. Country studies under this title have been published (or are pending) on:

Turkey (A. O. Krueger)
Ghana (J. C. Leith)
Israel (M. Michaely)
Egypt (B. Hansen and K. Nashashibi)
Philippines (R. E. Baldwin)
India (J. N. Bhagwati and T. N. Srinivasan)
South Korea (C. R. Frank, K. S. Kim and L. Westphal)
Chile (J. R. Behrman)

The two synthesis volumes of this series, by Bhagwati (1978) and Krueger (1978) respectively, are very valuable contributions, although they appeared too late to be used in the preparation of this chapter.

An earlier series of country studies was published by Oxford UP (London) for OECD under the general heading of *Industry and Trade in Some Developing Countries*. There is a synthesis volume of that title by Little, Scitovsky and Scott, 1970, which is recommended, and the following country studies:

Brazil (J. Bergsman)
India (J. N. Bhagwati and P. Desai)

Taiwan and Philippines (M-H. Hsing, J. H. Power
  and G. P. Sicat)
Mexico (T. King)
Pakistan (S. R. Lewis Jr.)

This chapter has also drawn on materials on
Ghana taken from ch. 10 of Killick, 1978.

See also the additional references given in the notes
to this chapter.

9 Technological backwardness in agriculture

'To innovate is not
to reform.' *Edmund Burke*

Contents

I. Statement of the Problem

The advantage of late-stage development

A great deal has rightly been written about the numerous obstacles which low-income countries confront in trying to develop their economies. Rather less attention has been paid to an important advantage they possess by comparison with the situation faced by the now industrial countries in the eighteenth and nineteenth centuries – the enormously increased stock of useful knowledge which can be drawn upon to raise the productivity of resources. By comparison with the present situation, the development of modern scientific knowledge, its incorporation into productive technology and the increased control over the environment which it permitted were still in their infancy when the European industrial revolutions got under way. Mankind knows so much more today that, without doubt, it is technically feasible to obtain vastly greater output from the resources of Africa, Asia and Latin America than is actually produced.

The potential importance of this has been underlined by attempts to measure the causes of the long-term economic growth of the now industrial countries. These point to a conclusion anticipated by Schumpeter long before, that 'development consists primarily in employing existing resources in a different way, in doing new things with them, irrespective of whether these resources increase or not.' Taken by themselves, increased inputs of capital and labour are found to have contributed only modestly to the growth of output. Overwhelmingly the most important cause was increases in the productivity of resources, in the efficiency with which they were used. Perhaps 80 to 90 per cent of total

Table 9.1
Output per Man in the Agricultural and Non-agricultural Sectors of Developing Countries, 1970

	Value-added per man as % of average for all sectors:		Agriculture as % of non-agriculture
	Agriculture (1)	Non-agriculture (2)	(3)
South Asia	74	155	48
East Asia	53	114	46
Latin America	44	129	34
Africa	46	215	21

Source: Computed from World Bank, *World Tables, 1976*, pp. 416 and 516.

output growth was attributable to this 'fourth factor of production', reflecting more advanced technologies, improved skills, and the economies of scale resulting from these advances. The chief importance of investment in the growth process turns out to have been not so much the resulting increase in the quantity of capital but rather its role as a transmission mechanism, incorporating the latest advances of useful knowledge into production processes.[1]

Pre-scientific methods in a scientific world

But despite the fact that most developing countries have been consciously pursuing development for two or three decades, there remains an enormous gap between actual productivities and what is technically feasible through the application of modern knowledge, especially in agriculture. Indeed, if it were possible to rank all countries according to the extent to which their agricultural systems take advantage of modern know-how we would obtain an order – and a division into 'developed' and 'developing' – similar to a more conventional ranking by per capita income. Millions of the world's cultivators grow their crops and tend their animals with methods essentially unchanged for generations. Their tools may be manufactured rather than handmade but the framework of knowledge within which they operate is scarcely more extensive than that of their great-grandfathers.

Low productivities and poverty are the result. It was shown in Chapter 4 that during the 1960s LDCs were able only to achieve negligible improvements in per capita food production (see page 85). There remain very large gaps in agricultural productivities between the developed and developing countries, as exemplified by the following 1960 figures on wheat production (in tonnes):[2]

	Output per hectare	Output per man employed
Developed countries	2·41	40·9
Developing countries	0·94	8·1

Within developing countries themselves, productivities in agriculture are far below those obtaining in other parts of the economy, as shown by estimates of relative outputs per worker in various regions of the Third World, in Table 9.1.

We see from Table 9.1 that output per man in agriculture is typically only about half of that for the economy as a whole (column 1) and between a fifth and a half of the figure for non-agricultural activities (column 3).

To some extent these figures exaggerate the contrast between agriculture and the rest of the economy because of price distortions and because they do not take account of the larger amounts of capital per worker outside agriculture, raising output per man. What we ideally need is a generalized measure of the productivity of all the factors (not just labour) measured in shadow prices but that is not available. The imperfect evidence that does exist indicates, however, that the capital factor can explain only part of the labour output differentials.[3] And, apart from mining, it is true almost by definition that the agricultural worker has more natural resources at his disposal than his non-agricultural counterpart – a fact tending to raise his output relative to non-agriculture.

Developing countries have, of course, made efforts to take advantage of modern know-how but typically these have only been applied to a fraction of the area

---

[1] See Jones, 1976, pp. 176–8 and 187–9, for a survey of the literature on this topic.
[2] Median values computed from Hayami and Ruttan, 1971, Table 4-1.
[3] See Griffin, 1974, p. 180, for data on investment in agriculture.

which could benefit from it, as in the case of Bangladesh (Chen and Chaudhury, 1975, p. 221):

> The potential of agricultural technology in Bangladesh is reflected by the following figures. In 1969–70, only 350 thousand hectares were irrigated, representing less than 5 per cent of agricultural land ... Altogether only 264 thousand hectares were sown with high-yielding varieties of rice, which was only 3 per cent of total rice acreage cultivated. Yields from these new breeds of rice averaged ... nearly four times the level of local varieties. Had the acreage of high-yielding varieties been increased by only several percentage points and the same concentration of inputs been sustained, Bangladesh would have been completely self-sufficient in foodgrains in 1969–70.

Since in terms of output and employment, agriculture remains the single largest sector in almost all low-income countries, the majority of whose peoples still live in rural communities, the low productivity and relative stagnation of this sector has had serious implications for overall economic performance. It has exerted a brake on the expansion of total output, helped to perpetuate rural poverty, contributed to the under-utilization of labour, and worsened the balance of payments through laggard export performance and the need to import food. It has restrained the growth of the industrial sector, by limiting the rural market for its output, by creating supply bottle-necks for industries processing agricultural output, and its contribution to foreign exchange scarcities. It has also aggravated inflation, as was shown in Chapter 7 (page 169).

Without improved agricultural performance, therefore, the overall progress of the developing countries will continue to be held back. More food is needed, for example, to accommodate growing populations and to raise nutrition to reasonable standards. If the increased output is not forthcoming, either very large amounts of food will have to be imported (with serious, probably unmanageable, balance of payments consequences) or many will remain condemned to substandard, perhaps worsening, diets.[4]

The problem addressed in this chapter is, therefore, of the first importance. The next step is to consider the reasons for the relative backwardness of agriculture and the obstacles to the utilization of modern knowledge in this sector.

> **Activity.** Use national accounting and employment figures for your own country to make estimates comparable with those in Table 9.1. Can you find any other evidence on the relative productivity of the factors of production in agriculture?

II. Causes

The influence of tradition

Since most LDC farmers still use basically traditional methods and live in communities where the values and conventions of the past remain strong, an examination of the influence of tradition provides a natural starting-point in a search for the causes of technological backwardness. There is an influential school of thought which urges that tradition is a major obstacle to technical progress in rural areas and that it is a mistake to apply the western concept of 'economic man' – responding to price incentives to maximize his economic welfare – to the peasants of Africa and Asia. According to this view, social taboos, non-materialistic value systems, the effects of extended family obligations, costly funeral traditions, and the sheer inertia imparted by a history of cultivation methods that have remained essentially unchanged for generations – these and other influences make the 'human factor' perhaps the most serious obstacle to rural modernization.

One, admittedly old-fashioned, example of this type of view was the suggestion that peasants have backward-bending supply curves of output. The idea underlying this was that their values and economic horizons were such that a peasant tended to market just enough to bring him in some target amount of income. He would therefore respond to an increase in the price of his crop by reducing output, because he no longer needed to sell as much to achieve his target income. Conversely, if the price went down he would have to grow more – a supply response the opposite of that postulated in western theory textbooks.

In the face of overwhelming evidence to the contrary, the idea of backward-bending supply curves is rarely put forward today but the view of the peasant as tradition-bound and unresponsive to material incentives remains strong and influential – not least in Ministries of Agriculture. Nobel prizewinner Gunnar Myrdal is among the most distinguished members of this school, whose study of southern Asia emphasizes 'the co-operation of the cultivators' as a limiting factor in the improvement of techniques, and scolds economists for their uncritical application of western norms and for their neglect of institutional factors.[5]

Although this remains an unsettled issue, it is fairly easy to test the validity of the 'tradition-bound' school. For if peasants were indeed different from 'economic man' we would find large inefficiencies in

---

[4] See World Bank, 1978B, for discussion of this issue, and estimates of the magnitudes.
[5] Myrdal, 1968, Vol. II, ch. 26. See also Rogers, 1962.

traditional agriculture. Referring back to the idea of economic efficiency discussed in Chapter 1, we would expect to find output far below the production possibility frontier, with much waste of resources and output poorly suited to the preferences of consumers.

> **Activity.** You may wish at this point to refresh your memory on the discussion of economic efficiency in Chapter 1, Part IV.

As regards static efficiency, most observers of traditional agriculture have not found much fault with it. It is generally a myth that there is a subsistence sector, in the sense of sizeable areas or groups of farmers who produce only for their own families' consumption and nothing for sale. Except when the harvest is particularly poor, almost all farmers produce some surplus for sale and this makes market prices important variables for them. There is wide agreement that they respond to these prices in a 'normal' way, i.e. produce more when prices rise and less when they fall.

Although there is a good deal of under-utilization of rural labour in slack seasons – and this is a symptom of inefficiency – the resources in shortest supply – the constraining resources – tend to be fully utilized. Where population densities are large, land itself will be a constraining resource and is likely to be intensively cultivated; in other situations, capital will be a constraint and what is available is likely to be fully used.

In terms of static efficiency, therefore, actual output is liable to be near to the production possibility frontier and there is not likely to be any major potential for increasing production simply by rearranging the proportions in which the factors of production are combined with each other. Given that rural life is often a hard one, it would be surprising if major possibilities for increasing output within the framework of traditional agriculture had gone unnoticed for generations.

But if traditional agriculture is characterized by static efficiency, how can we explain the low productivities mentioned earlier? Is there not a contradiction here? To answer that we must turn to examine the dynamic aspect of efficiency. This brings us to perhaps the most important fact about traditional agriculture: *it has a low capacity to improve itself over time.* Change does occur, especially in response to growing population pressures, but only slowly and in ways which require a minimal use of modern scientific knowledge.[6] Especially where populations have been static, methods of cultivation today are likely to be similar to those of a hundred years ago.

The technological stagnation of traditional agriculture carries the further implication that, with unchanging methods, returns to investment will be small, which helps to explain the small investments that have often been observed, with consequentially little use of capital. What is often seen as a shortage of capital (leading governments to pin too many hopes on the provision of rural credit) is actually a shortage of the know-how that would make investment attractive.

It may be protested that it is less than just to describe traditional agriculture as dynamically inefficient. After all, there are many examples of major new crops being introduced and successfully adopted by the farming community. A case in point was the introduction of cocoa to Ghana. This crop was brought from abroad by a Ghanaian, rapidly adopted by a multitude of small-scale farmers, against some opposition from the British colonial government, until within a few years it became the country's main export. Certainly, cocoa growing was a major innovation and amply demonstrated the initiative of local farmers. But the key to its rapid adoption was that it could be accommodated within traditional cultivation practices. It did not involve a major incorporation of modern technology and, for all the benefits that Ghana has derived from this industry, it has produced very little by way of dynamic spill-over effects in the rest of the economy.[7] The cocoa farmers today grow their crops by methods similar to those used eighty years ago, and so do Ghana's food farmers.

The question obviously arises, how is the dynamic inefficiency of traditional agriculture to be explained? A number of economic explanations can be given, and they will occupy the next few pages. But those who emphasize the retarding effects of culture and tradition deserve another mention at this point, for it does seem likely that traditionalist societies have inhibited the development of improved methods. One may mention, for example, the low value placed upon non-religious education in some Moslem societies. Economists tend to dismiss this type of explanation and to agree with Schultz that 'since differences in profitability are a strong explanatory variable, it is not necessary to appeal to differences in personality, education and social

---

[6] Chapter 4 (pages 87–8) has already mentioned Boserup's (1965) analysis of the response of traditional agriculture to increasing population pressures.

[7] Readers who would like to follow up this case should refer to Hill, 1963: Szereszewski, 1965: and the essay by Sara Gordon in Pearson and Cownie, 1974.

environment'. Economists, perhaps, have some professional bias towards such judgements but there are certainly economic reasons for the dynamic inefficiency of traditional agriculture, which we will now discuss.

> **Activity.** 'Statically efficient but dynamically inefficient.' Does that description fit traditional agriculture in your own country?

Shortages of appropriate knowledge

One important characteristic of traditional agriculture is that production occurs on small family units. In consequence, the resources available to any one farmer are small. There is no question of a farmer being able to afford the capital and other costs of modern research facilities, which are subject to major economies of scale. In contrast with modern manufacturing, small-scale agriculture is institutionally unsuited to provide itself with research and development. Moreover, a good many of the benefits of successful research are external to those who undertake it, as will be shown later, and this reduces the incentives for farmers to undertake research. Considered commercially, it is also a high-risk activity but farmers are already burdened with quite enough risk. *This unsuitability of traditional agriculture for the creation of research capacities is probably the single most important reason for its relative backwardness.*

What is implied by this is the view that, left to itself, the market mechanism will neglect socially desirable agricultural research; it should, therefore, be a task of the state to remedy this neglect (see page 22 for a general discussion of the role of the state in the face of market neglects of public wants). But few developing country governments have adequately met this need. This has left LDCs dependent on western research, as indicated by the estimate that in 1965 89 per cent of all spending on agricultural research occurred in developed countries (Evenson and Kislev, 1975, Table 5). Such dependence is particularly undesirable for agriculture because most research has related to the crops and conditions of temperate climates and has thus not been relevant to the needs of most developing countries. Quite apart from climatic considerations, much western research has been adapted to the fact of declining agricultural labour forces and hence has tended to be labour-saving, capital-intensive. This too reduces its relevance to conditions in LDCs, with their unemployment and growing rural populations.

We can underline the above by referring to an important feature of agricultural research – that its practical applications are often specific to particular ecological conditions. Findings relating to one zone are often not transferable to others, at least not without local adaptation. This emphasizes the uselessness of much western research for application in LDCs but means also that research in one LDC may not be of direct application in another. For example, in the mid-1960s the Taiwanese provided technical assistance to Sierra Leone in rice cultivation. They established a magnificent demonstration farm showing the enormous yields that could be obtained from the intensive cultivation of wet rice under carefully controlled irrigation. Local farmers were impressed but could learn nothing. For they grew dry rice, low population densities made Sierra Leone suited for extensive, not intensive, cultivation, and irrigation techniques were quite alien.

Because of this location-specific nature of agricultural research and the scarcity of trained manpower, the siting of research stations and choice of the problems they work on is of great importance to the farming community. There are thus likely to be strong vested interests trying to influence decisions on these matters. Colonial governments, for example, were most interested in research that could be of value to their home country and so research in ex-colonies was strongly concentrated on the problems of export commodities. Similarly, in those ex-colonies which had substantial communities of white settler farmers, research efforts were typically focused on their needs. Even where the farming community is wholly indigenous, large landowners are often strong enough to ensure that research is directed to their problems. In general, the smallholder has obtained a raw deal; his special problems, and the crops most important to him, have often received little notice.

In consequence of these forces, the agricultural sector, especially the small food cultivator, has not made much use of modern knowledge, because much past research has been inappropriate to its needs. One common result of this is that extension workers will try to persuade farmers to change to some new practice (such as concentration on a single crop) developed in a different context only for it to be discovered later that this 'improvement' produces worse results than traditional (mixed crop) methods. Meanwhile, farmers' resistances will have been interpreted as evidence that they are tradition-bound conservatives!

Shortages of complementary inputs

It would, of course, be wrong to suggest that all past research has been inappropriate. There are many desirable changes which have not yet been widely applied, so we turn now to look for other causes of technological backwardness.

Since the peasant farmer is responsive to opportunities for profit, we should ask why it may not have been profitable for him to take advantage of useful research results. The essential point is that profitability will depend upon the availability of a range of inputs and on institutional conditions. The most important of these are listed below.

(1) The farmer has to be aware of the possibility of improving his productivity and researchers have to be aware of the farmers problems. This requires the existence of a *channel of communication* between farmers and researchers. Government agricultural extension services are supposed to provide this but are often themselves not well informed about recent advances; or do not enjoy close relationships with the farmers they have to listen to and convince; or only effectively reach a minority of farmers.

(2) New technologies often require *new physical inputs*: improved seed-types, fertilizers, insecticides, perhaps mechanical sprayers, or tractors. The farmers must, therefore, have access to these new inputs, and at reasonable prices – an obvious condition but one that is surprisingly often unsatisfied, perhaps because of an inefficient distribution network.

(3) Sometimes the farmer will have to acquire new skills in order to take full advantage of a new possibility, for example in irrigation methods. This will require the provision of *training facilities*. Adoption of a new technique can thus be frustrated if the government neglects to provide these.

(4) The farmer's profits will also be influenced by the adequacy of the *rural infrastructure*, especially the network of roads, and by the efficiency of the *distributive system*. Availability of storage facilities, the competitiveness and quality of local marketing arrangements, the level of transportation costs – these are all factors likely to make a crucial impact on the price he will receive for his output and hence the profitability of introducing a change. The diffusion of many advances has been held up by the inadequaces of an uncompetitive marketing system.

(5) During peak harvesting and planting seasons there is commonly a shortage of agricultural labour and this, too, may act as a constraint on the adoption of improvements. The shortage can be relieved by a greater use of equipment; for other reasons, too, improved methods often require greater inputs of capital. In these situations, the availability of *credit* to finance the needed investments is an important variable. This was so with the so-called 'green revolution', as will be shown shortly.

(6) *Land tenure systems* can be another important variable. The farmer will be most likely to adopt a new practice if all the benefits will accrue to him and his family. But under many tenurial or sharecropping systems a substantial part of the benefits will go to an absentee landowner, not the farmer (a sharecropper is a person who farms land for the owner in return for a proportion of the crop). In India and Pakistan, for example, half the crop is commonly paid in rent; west African sharecroppers give between a third and two-thirds to the landowner. The cultivator in this situation will obtain only part of the benefits from an improvement but, in many cases, will have to pay the full increase in cost associated with it (although there are some systems in which the owner is expected to contribute to costs). It is easy to see that he will be less likely to take advantage of the improvement than if he owned the land and reaped all the gains.

Summary

It is clear from this discussion that there are many reasons for technological backwardness in agriculture. It is a complex amalgam of shortages of appropriate knowledge and the complementary inputs needed to turn a technical feasibility into a profitable innovation, compounded by the influences of convention and culture. And several points of the analysis imply that governments sometimes worsen the problem, by neglecting the research responsibilities of the state and by the pursuit of policies that discourage technical progress. We will return to this point in Part IV.

Activity. Search for references which discuss agricultural research in your own country and write notes on the extent to which the above analysis is relevant to your case.

III. Nature and Effects of Technological Progress

This chapter has so far been using terms like 'technological progress' in an undefined way. It is time now to look at this more precisely, as a prelude

Figure 9.1 *Technological progress and average costs: (a) the scale-neutral case; (b) the case of a bias to large scale.*

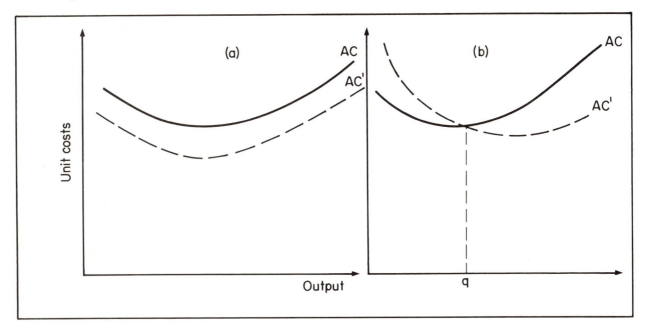

to exploring various features of technological progress, how it may spread through an economy, and the socio-economic ramifications it may have.

The meaning of technological progress

There is surprisingly little standardization of the use of terms in the literature on technical change. Authors define their own meanings, and definitions differ from one writer to the next. We can take advantage of this anarchy to design a description that best fits the case we are studying.

Three different types of technological progress can be identified: (1) advances which allow a greater output of a specified product from a given quantity of inputs; (2) advances which improve the quality of the product; and (3) advances which result in a totally new product. Case (3) is often described as 'product innovation', and we might also put (2) under the same heading. Case (1) is called 'process innovation'. In agriculture most technological progress results from process innovation – lower cost methods of producing familiar crops – so we will concentrate on this case. For present purposes, therefore, the following definition is suitable.

> **Key concept. Technological progress** is the application of an advance in knowledge to the productive system, such that it reduces average unit costs of output, with input prices held constant. These advances may result from the application of improved technologies to production processes, but they may also result from increases in skill and from improvements in economic organization.

Thought of in this way, technological progress can be shown as a downward shift in the average cost curve, always assuming that the prices of inputs remain unchanged. This is illustrated in Figure 9.1 (a) below (ignore the right-hand diagram for the moment).

In Figure 9.1 (a) technological progress is indicated by a lowering of average unit costs from the old AC curve to the new broken AC' curve. Costs are lowered because the productivity of all or some of the inputs has been increased, giving greater output from an unchanged expenditure on inputs. It is the increase in productivities which permits us to talk of this as 'progress'. Not all technological change is progress, as in the case mentioned earlier where 'improved' cultivation methods are promoted by extension workers only for it to be discovered that they lead to higher costs than traditional ways. Progress is *successful* change.

This focus on the effects of progress on costs and productivities means that it can also be illustrated by reference to its effects on production functions. A production function describes the relationship between the quantities of inputs and the resulting quantity of output. Inputs are usually disaggregated into categories such as labour, capital and natural resources. However, a production function of a very general form may be written symbolically as:

$$Q = aI$$

where Q is the quantity of output, I is an aggregated measure of the quantity of inputs and a is a parameter measuring the productivity of the inputs. *Technological progress results in an increase in the value of a.* That is to say, greater output will result from a constant amount of inputs; alternatively, fewer inputs will be needed to produce an unchanged quantity of output.

This latter case, where fewer inputs are needed to produce a given output, can be illustrated by an isoquant map of the type introduced in Chapter 6. We assume there are only two factors of production and that there are constant returns to scale. In Figure 9.2 the isoquant curve PP^1 describes the production function of a producer, showing all possible combinations of labour and capital which would result in a given output, P. The producer chooses that combination which minimizes his costs, so he needs to know the prices of labour and capital before he can decide which production process to choose. The relative prices of the factors is reflected in the slope of the isocost curve AB, and by finding the point of tangency we can determine the least-cost combination for producing quantity P. In Figure 9.2 the producer will minimize costs by choosing ok^1 of capital and ow^1 of labour.

Activity. If you found the last paragraph difficult to follow, refresh your memory on the discussion of Figure 6.1, page 146.

This equilibrium, being an example of static analysis, should be thought of as existing at a point in time. It therefore precludes the possibility of technological progress. But now let us assume some passage of time, during which progress occurs.

We already know that this will alter the production function in such a way that fewer inputs will be needed in order to produce the same quantity of output. This new function is drawn as the isoquant PP^2, which tells us the (reduced) amounts of capital and labour now

needed to *obtain the same output, P.* On the assumptions of constant returns to scale and unchanged factor prices, the diagram has been drawn so that the farmer will reduce his labour inputs by w^1w^2 and his capital inputs by k^1k^2. With this solution, the proportions between the factors are unchanged, so the new equilibrium is on the same ray, ox, as the original one (but this will probably not happen and we will come to other cases soon). (In interpreting Figure 9.2, it is important to understand that isoquant PP^2 is being employed to demonstrate the reduced amounts of inputs needed to obtain an unchanged quantity of output, P. PP^1 and PP^2 do not represent different levels of output.)

Figure 9.2 *Effect of technological progress on production functions.*

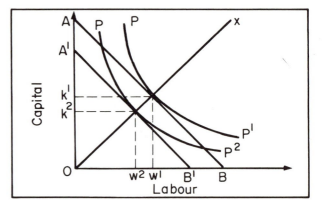

Before passing on, it is worth spending a little time to consider one or two other aspects of our definition of technological progress. Note first that technological progress is described as an application of an *advance in knowledge*. Since there is commonly much ignorance in a country about advances elsewhere, progress can result from the acquisition of knowledge about some possibility which may have been well known in another country for a long time. Progress does not necessarily entail a new invention or idea; improved communication of past ideas can have the same effect.

Secondly, note that the concept of technological progress is wider than innovation, with the latter referring only to the initial applications of an advance in knowledge within an economic system. Innovation is, nonetheless, crucial because it is by this means that progress occurs. The innovators lead the way, establish the potentialities of some new method, and shoulder the risks associated with its first applications. Once the path has been broken and the innovation established as a success, others will follow and the new way will become widely diffused.

> **Key concept.** The earliest applications of a technological advance are called **innovations**, meaning changes made in the established way of doing things.

Thirdly, although it is convenient to talk of 'technological' progress, our definition is not confined to the industrial and mechanical arts. It also includes improvements in *economic organization* – perhaps a change in the time of planting, or a reform of marketing arrangements, or better incentives for extension workers. It further covers improvements in skill, resulting from formal training or from 'learning by doing'. These types of change can also lower average costs, sometimes substantially.

The idea of an 'appropriate' technology

We concluded earlier that the inappropriateness of much past research was one of the chief explanations of technological backwardness in agriculture. You may also recall the statement in Chapter 6 (page 142) that the use of more appropriate technologies is central to the development strategy of redistribution through growth. But 'appropriateness' is vague and we need now to clarify what it means.

The most general feature of an appropriate technology is that it should be related to the development objectives and production problems of the country in question. In particular, the resources needed for the application of such a technology should be matched with relative resource availabilities. We are looking for techniques which will make the heaviest use of the most abundant resources, perhaps land or unskilled labour, and which will economize in the use of scarce resources, such as capital and foreign exchange. Applying this general description specifically to agriculture, four key features can be specified, which are valid for many developing countries.

Agricultural techniques are likely to be appropriate if they are (1) ecologically relevant and versatile; (2) simple; (3) sparing in use of capital relative to labour; (4) applicable to small productive units. (It will be suggested later that a further item could be added to this list: (5) *they should minimize farmers' risks.*) These features can be regarded as criteria to determine whether or not a proposed innovation is likely to be advantageous, and they are sufficiently important to be worth elaborating.

Ecological relevance and versatility

This feature is sufficiently obvious that it needs no more than a mention. It stems from the earlier reference to the fact that the results of agricultural research are often specific to particular ecological conditions. Because of varying soil conditions or rainfall patterns, a crop variety which is superior in one zone may be inferior in another. So for an advance in knowledge to be appropriate it must be capable of successful application in the country or region for which it is being considered – an obvious point but one which carries important implications for research policies.

We can go further to point out that versatility – the applicability, or easy adaptation, of a given advance to a range of different ecological conditions – is a potentially valuable attribute of a technological change, as requiring smaller research and other inputs for an increase in output and as favouring its rapid diffusion among the farming population.

Simplicity

Since we are considering appropriateness to traditional agriculture, technology must be adapted to the basic characteristics of that sector. These include generally low levels of education and modern skills,[8] poor facilities for the maintenance of sophisticated equipment, a probable scarcity of help from extension workers and a possibly indifferent distribution system. Implications: a technological advance will stand a far better chance of successful and widespread adoption if it is simple, in the sense of requiring a minimum of new skills, complementary inputs and institutional changes. Even apparently simple changes, like the introduction of a new seed variety, may actually involve quite complex changes in its use of water and fertilizers, in the spaces between plants, in their need for protection against disease, placing a heavy burden on the extension officers who should instruct farmers in these matters. The position, of course, is far worse with a major piece of farm machinery.

Labour-intensity

The third key feature of a technology appropriate to most developing countries is that it should be sparing in its demand for investible resources. This merits more extensive discussion than the previous two, and can be approached at different levels.

---

[8] Do not make the mistake, however, of considering the traditional farmer to be unskilled. Many a city dweller who thought that farming was simple has learned the contrary to his cost. The point is rather that many farmers have not had the opportunity to acquire the education that would fit them to make the best use of recent technologies. Hence the reference to 'modern' skills.

First, the small farmer is unlikely to be able to afford new methods that require large investments. This might be answered by saying that the state could provide the necessary money through agricultural credit agencies. But, leaving aside the practical difficulties of providing credit to a multitude of small farmers, we can say, secondly, of the state as of the individual farmer: it cannot afford massive investments. Recall a World Bank estimate cited in Chapter 5 (page 128) that available capital resources per new member of the labour force in developing countries are typically only one-twentieth of the per-worker capital available in the industrial world. In an essay listed in the recommended readings at the end of this chapter, Stewart has similarly suggested that the 'appropriate' amount of capital per worker in LDCs is only about one-tenth of levels found in industrial countries. With few exceptions, a shortage of investible resources is one of the defining characteristics of a developing economy. This fact is of particular importance because many of the world's technological advances originated in the capital-rich industrial countries and incorporate large investment requirements – requirements which cannot generally be satisfied in developing countries.

But there is also the question whether, even if feasible, capital-intensity would be desirable. This brings us to a third aspect of the case for labour-intensity and relates to the employment problem explored in Chapters 5 and 6.

The general point is simply put: a capital-intensive method creates few new jobs. This follows from how capital- and labour-intensity are defined. In a simplified two-factor world, capital-intensity refers to a large input of capital per worker (relative to some norm), so that a given innovation will create only a small additional demand for labour. Technological change can be described, therefore, as either capital-saving, labour-saving, or neutral.

If we hold the prices of labour and capital constant, then the amounts employed of each of these factors will be determined by their marginal productivities, as illustrated in Figure 9.3. The price of a factor (the wage paid to labour or the return to capital) and its marginal product are measured on the vertical axis and the quantity of that factor employed is measured on the horizontal.

The MP^1 curve traces the relationship between a factor's marginal product and the quantity of it that is employed. It has a negative slope on the expectation that there will be diminishing returns. Given the MP^1 curve and on conventional (and for present purposes, fairly harmless) assumptions of profit maximization and perfectly competitive markets, when the price of a factor is p^1 the quantity of it employed will be q^1. If a

Figure 9.3 *Factor productivities and employment.*

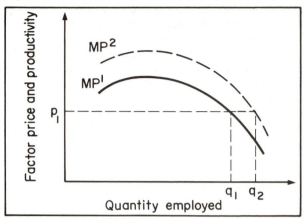

technological advance now raises a factor's marginal productivity in the manner illustrated by the broken MP^2 curve, then (holding the factor price constant) the quantity employed will go up to q^2.

It follows from this that the impact of an innovation on factor proportions will depend on the impact it has on their relative marginal productivities. An innovation can be described as capital-saving (labour-using) if it raises the marginal productivity of labour relative to that of capital because this will increase the demand for labour relative to capital. Conversely, an innovation will be labour-saving (capital-using) if it causes a relative rise in the productivity of (and hence demand for) capital. A neutral innovation is one that leaves relative marginal productivities unchanged. (Note, though, that this is not the only way in which the neutrality of an innovation can be defined. The definition just offered is known as 'Hicks-neutral'. Theorists also employ the concept of a 'Harrod-neutral' innovation, which normally differs from the Hicks-neutral case.[9])

This case illustrated in Figure 9.2 (page 230) was neutral because it left factor proportions unchanged, showing equal percentage reductions in the quantities of labour and capital. But this is a special case. Technological change is, in practice, likely to alter relative factor productivities and hence the proportions in which they are employed. Many believe that the most frequent outcome is for technological advances originating in industrial countries to be labour-saving, raising the marginal

---

[9] Harrod-neutral technological progress is said to occur when, with the capital-output ratio and interest rate held constant, the distribution of income between labour and capital remains unchanged. It is equivalent to Hicks-neutrality only in the special case where the elasticity of substitution between these factors is equal to one. Compare Jones, 1976, pp. 159–68.

productivity of capital relative to labour. The case of a labour-saving (capital-using) innovation is illustrated in Figure 9.4. This incorporates the neutral case of Figure 9.2, where the new equilibrium was on the same factor proportions ray, ox, as the initial one (that is, $ow^2/ok^2 = ow^1/ok^1$). This is contrasted with an alternative new isoquant, PP^3, drawn to illustrate the labour-saving case. With PP^3, nearly as much capital (k^3) is needed to produce output P as with PP^1 (the fall is only from k^1 to k^3) but there is a large proportionate reduction in labour requirements, from w^1 to w^3 (that is, $ow^3/ok^3 < ow^1/ok^1$).

Figure 9.4 *An illustration of a labour-saving innovation.*

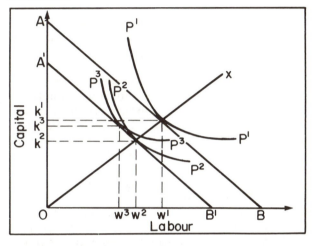

Although it has been convenient for Figures 9.2 and 9.4 to study changes in factor demands *with output held constant*, in real life an innovation would normally be associated with an increase in output, in which case a change could be described as labour-saving if it resulted in a larger proportionate increase in the demand for capital than for labour. Obviously, labour-saving innovations will generate fewer new jobs than capital-saving changes. Given that most LDCs confront large-scale unemployment, a general case is made out for the adoption of capital-saving innovations. However, this assumes (1) that capital-saving methods are known and available, (2) that they do not involve larger social costs than more capital-intensive methods, and (3) that the additional workers they require are unskilled or semi-skilled, rather than scarce skilled workers.

We may link this advocacy of capital-saving technology with another distinction used by writers on technological progress, between embodied and disembodied technological change. Some types of advance take the form of improved equipment – say, the introduction of motor-powered sprayers. They therefore have to be embodied in new investments in machinery. A marketing reform or an improved hybrid seed, on the other hand, does not have to be embodied in new equipment; rather, it raises the productivity of both old and new capital. In general, embodied technological change is more likely to be capital-intensive (labour-saving), and therefore less appropriate, than the disembodied kind.

Subject to the qualifications already introduced, we can now sum up the discussion of labour-intensity by saying that *the innovations most appropriate to developing countries, with large unemployment problems and scarcities of investible resources, are labour-intensive, capital-saving.*

Smallness of scale

The fourth feature of technologies appropriate to LDC conditions is that they should be suited to the needs of small-scale farmers, or smallholders, because most farmers cultivate only small areas. Here too we can draw a contrast with the position in high-income countries, whose farmers typically cultivate far greater areas and whose technologies have been designed with this in mind. There are few farmers in those countries whose farms are too small to efficiently utilize a tractor, whereas individual farms large enough for profitable tractorization are a small minority of total holdings in developing countries.

Thus, many western innovations are of a type illustrated by the right-hand Figure 9.1 (b) on page 229. Farmers producing less than q will actually experience increased costs and the benefits derived by the larger farms from lowered average costs become proportionately greater as scale increases to the right of q. More appropriate technological advance, on the other hand, is of the type illustrated in the left-hand Figure 9.1 (a). In this case all producers stand to enjoy lowered costs, however small their output.

The *divisibility* of a technique is a major determinant of its suitability for small farms. At the one extreme there are highly divisible changes, such as improved seeds or fertilizers or hand tools, which can be used with profit by the most humble smallholder. At the other extreme there are the combine harvesters developed for the cereal farms of North America, which are only profitable when employed on very large areas. Between these extremes there are various implements which are imperfectly divisible but still useful to large numbers of farmers: improved animal-drawn ploughs, mechanical pumps, small threshers.

Notice that here, as in the discussion of labour-intensity, a general presumption is created in favour of disembodied technological change. For techniques that have to be embodied in machinery and other fixed capital are more likely to be biased in favour of the larger producers, whereas most highly divisible advances, such as better seed varieties, are disembodied.

> **Activity.** Investigate important technological changes that have occurred in your country's agriculture and assess their appropriateness by the criteria advanced in this section.

The appropriateness of mechanization

This discussion of appropriate technologies can be used to throw light on an unresolved controversy about the merits of mechanization in LDCs. We can use the four features of appropriateness to assess the suitability of pursuing policies which promote the use of tractors and other agricultural machines.

(1) By the test of *ecological relevance and versatility* mechanization scores fairly well. In most parts of the world, for example, tractor ploughing is technically feasible (although recently wooded countryside which still has tree roots in the soil offers less favourable conditions than obstacle-free fields), and a single model of tractor, equipped with accessories, can be used in quite widely varying conditions, thus possessing the attribute of versatility.

(2) *Simplicity* however, tells against mechanization. It calls for substantial inputs of new skills (properly trained tractor drivers and mechanics) and new institutions (servicing centres). There are many examples of machines which have broken down after a short time and have then been left to rot because they could not be repaired: the complementary skills and institutions necessary for successful mechanization were not in place.

(3) Obviously, mechanization does not possess the attribute of *labour-intensity*. It requires large capital investments and, by substituting for the use of manual labour, reduces the capacity of the rural economy to offer productive employment. Mechanization offers a prime example of embodied technological change, whereas we have found a general case for the promotion of disembodied change. By this criterion, then, mechanization fails badly.

(4) It does the same by the criterion of *smallness of scale* and divisibility, as already implied in the discussion of that topic. With some exceptions, farm machinery is 'lumpy', requiring some minimum level of utilization before it becomes profitable – a minimum frequently well beyond the capacity of the small farmer.

The balance of these considerations is clearly negative: mechanization fails three out of the four tests. We are thus left with a general presumption against policies designed to encourage mechanization. Nor is this a presumption based on merely abstract considerations: many countries have learned this lesson the hard way and in doing so, have imposed new hardships on their peoples. Dumont's (1966) classical study of agricultural policies in Africa cites many examples – Senegal, Morocco, Guinea, Mali, Tanzania and others – of failed attempts at premature mechanization. He concludes (p. 59):[10]

> A whole series of agricultural and general advances must be made before mechanisation can logically be introduced. On the other hand, draught animals, wherever feasible, present only advantages, and can achieve the intermediate stage in agriculture, often the most useful and indispensable.

However, it would be wrong to be wholly negative about mechanization. For one thing, some soil types are almost unworkable with animal-drawn

---

[10] Yudelman, *et al.*, 1971, ch. V, undertake a comparative evaluation of Japanese, Taiwan and Mexican experiences and reach adverse conclusions on Mexico's mechanization policies. Killick, 1978, ch. 8, similarly points to a failure of mechanization in Ghana.

implements. Also, some machines are quite small (sprayers, pumps, hullers), so they may be within the financial reach of low-saving countries, and reduce costs on all except the smallest farms. It is also possible to reduce the bias of tractors and other large machines towards large farms through the provision of tractor ploughing services and through co-operative farming arrangements.

We should also qualify the view presented so far of capital as reducing the number of jobs. There are some circumstances in which capital is better viewed as *complementary*, as offering sufficient advantages that it results in the employment of more people. The illustration most commonly given of this is when the introduction of machinery permits farmers to change from growing a single crop each year to multi-cropping. Boserup (1965) is among those who argue that the introduction of machines to perform peak operations, or break specific labour shortages, or permit irrigation where it was previously impossible, can not only lower costs but also increase the total year-long demand for labour. She cites the example of Japan which is now able to reap three crops even in regions with relatively long cold seasons. The Indian Punjab provides another illustration, as we will observe shortly.

The safest conclusion on mechanization thus seems to be, *judge each case according to its circumstances ... but be careful!* We will see in Part IV that governments are often prejudiced toward mechanization and pursue policies biased in that direction. Even the relatively favourable case of small, divisible machines can produce results which are, at best, ambiguous:[11]

Nowadays [Indonesian] villages are humming with small, Japanese made machines milling paddy; they are called rice hullers. These innovations profit the landowners or the owners of the paddy. The rice is better polished, less broken, and hence fetches a better price. It can also be stored a little longer than the handpounded rice. Yet many female working hours at hand pounding are foregone with consequent distributional effects. The shifts in employment and income distribution will probably never be registered in a census on account of definitions of employment, but they can shake the foundations of a village's life.

Gotsch surveyed the evidence and reported a limited consensus on the following points:[12]

(1) Claims that mechanization has improved yields are questionable because they attribute to mechanization benefits resulting from other causes.

(2) The argument that tractors increase cropping intensity and thereby increase the demand for labour must be seriously qualified. Arid areas with scarce water offer little scope for multi-cropping, and the argument is not very relevant to areas in Africa and Latin America where land remains relatively abundant.

(3) Countries in which rapid mechanization has occurred with socially questionable results have almost always pursued policies that created an artificially profitable economic climate for machines, often with the encouragement of foreign aid donors.

(4) Mechanization has mostly been promoted in pursuit of social objectives, for example the conversion of tenant-farmers into wage-workers, rather than improved agricultural productivities.

In the large areas of Africa and other parts of the Third World where little use is made of animal power, there is often much to be said in favour of introducing animal-drawn ploughs and other implements, as more appropriate than mechanization. Relative to machinery, it does not call for large investments, nor for dependence on purchased inputs; it is simpler and does not make the same demands for modern skills; it is economical on small farms.

The spread of technological change

It has rightly been said that knowledge of what determines the diffusion of an innovation is necessary to any deeper understanding of the process of economic growth. The historical importance of technological progress to the expansion of the now industrial countries was mentioned at the beginning of this chapter, and it is of enormous importance for productivity in agriculture not only that innovations should occur but that they should spread rapidly and extensively throughout the farming population. An improvement confined to just a few farmers can make only a limited impact, to say nothing of its adverse effects on the distribution of income. Fortunately, there is a good deal of evidence on the determinants of technological diffusion, and it emphasizes the importance of economic factors. So we are in a position to offer some fairly firm generalizations, as they relate to LDC agriculture.

---

[11] From the essay by Mohammed Sadli in Edwards, 1974, p. 368.
[12] From the essay by Carl Gotsch in Edwards, 1974, pp. 144–5.

> **Key concept.** The **diffusion** of a technological advance relates to the extent and speed of its adoption by those who can employ it.

Expected *profitability*, on reasonable assumptions about the future behaviour of prices, is one crucial factor that has already been referred to several times. Any rational farmer will need to be convinced that there is a good prospect that he will be able to raise his net income before he will use a new method. Methods which may raise yields but only, say, at the cost of very expensive applications of fertilizer may rightly be rejected, however hard the extension worker may push them.

Exposure to the new method has also been found an important determinant of the rate of adoption. What typically happens is that a few 'progressive' farmers will first introduce some new method – they are the innovators. They will probably have access to better education, more skills, greater financial security, better information and more government help than the majority of their colleagues. They may also have more courage! Since the initial applications are the most risky, others are likely to observe their results closely. If the result is profitable, some of the observers will also adopt the change, increasing the number of points of exposure for non-adopters. So a profitable innovation will spread until eventually most are using it. In other words, the probability that any one farmer will adopt a change will be a rising function of the proportion already using it – a point illustrated in Figure 9.5 shortly. It is, however, possible that the increased output of early innovators will depress prices because of inelastic demand, thus reducing prospective profitability for the late-comers and discouraging diffusion.

The spread of an innovation will also be strongly influenced by its *appropriateness*, already described. That is to say, a high diffusion rate will be most likely with innovations which have the characteristics of ecological relevance and versatility; simplicity; labour intensity; and applicability to the small farmer. If a new technique is highly specific to particular ecological conditions, or demands scarce skills, or involves the farmer in a large investment, or is suited only for the cultivation of large acreages, it is unlikely to be widely employed. Appropriateness encourages diffusion, thus reinforcing the case for the development of such technologies. To some extent, of course, this determinant is linked to that of profitability; to the smallholder the most appropriate technologies are also liable to be the most profitable.

Lastly, there is the factor of *risk*. Most of us prefer to avoid incurring risks but the small farmer especially so. He is likely to be living near the subsistence level; to have few resources in reserve for bad times; to have too small an area of land to be able to diversify his output and spread his risks. He may be at the mercy of an undependable climate. He shoulders risks enough already and risk in his case reduces the probability of survival itself. He is thus unlikely to accept the additional risks of innovation, of trying something new. He is more likely to be among the last to adopt a new practice, needing to be completely convinced of its merits before giving it a try. He will, however, look more eagerly upon a change that would reduce the dangers he faces: new crop varieties more resistant to disease, livestock strains better able to tolerate drought, new methods of storing his produce to reduce wastage. Holding the other factors constant, a high-risk innovation will have a lower diffusion rate than a risk-reducing innovation. Indeed, we might extend the earlier description of appropriate technology to specify that it should also minimize farmers' risks.

We can use diagrams to illustrate this discussion of the determinants of diffusion. Figure 9.5 presents two alternative curves describing the relationship between the probability that an individual farmer will adopt some new advance and the proportion of farmers already using it. Either curve illustrates exposure as a determinant, showing that the probability that the farmer will adopt goes up with the proportion of other farmers who have already done so.

Figure 9.5   *The determinants of diffusion.*

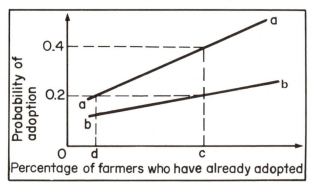

So why are there two curves? These can be used to illustrate the effects of the other determinants. Thus, the contrast between curve aa and curve bb can be used to illustrate any (or a combination) of the following:

(1) an innovation which is less profitable than another;

(2) an innovation which is less appropriate than another;
(3) an innovation which is more risky than another.

The aa curve represents the more profitable/more appropriate/less risky alternative, and the bb curve represents the opposite cases. So, with a given proportion of farmers already using the new method, say at c, the probability that our farmer will also adopt it is only 0·2 in the less favourable case but is 0·4 in the more favourable case, i.e. there is a four-in-ten chance that he will adopt.

If, on the other hand, we take an innovation of *given* profitability, appropriateness and riskiness, we can portray the effects of exposure by reading *along* either one of the curves. For example, Figure 9.5 has been drawn so that, reading along curve aa, the probability of adoption goes up from 0·2 to 0·4 as the percentage of farmers who have already adopted goes up from d per cent to c per cent.

The illustration we have just been considering can be converted into another which, because it includes time, tells us something about the *dynamics* of a typical diffusion path. This is shown in Figure 9.6, which presents an S-shaped diffusion curve. In this case the percentage of farmers who have adopted the new method is measured on the vertical axis, with time on the horizontal.

Figure 9.6 *The S-shaped diffusion curve.*

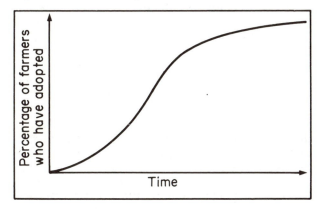

This curve, which has been found to fit historical experiences quite well, postulates the following diffusion process. At first only a few farmers will adopt some new technique. Then as these innovators prove its profitability and familiarize others with it, an increasing number will jump on to the bandwagon, diffusion will accelerate and the curve will gradually assume a steeper slope. But as larger and larger proportions of potential users adopt the improvement, the rate of diffusion necessarily slows

down as saturation point is approached; the curve begins to flatten out and finally becomes horizontal. Note, however, that it is likely to become horizontal below the upper limit of 100 per cent. The change will be less appropriate for some farmers than others, or too risky. Some may be in such remote areas that they do not get the necessary information and exposure; others may be too apathetic, or too wedded to traditional ways, to want to change.

> **Activity.** Assuming that Figure 9.6 illustrates a change that was widely adopted, draw a new curve which represents an innovation only profitable on large farms.

So far, the discussion of this section has been somewhat abstract. It is time to clothe the skeleton with flesh, using the 'green revolution' to illustrate the nature and effects of technological change in agriculture. The following case study is of the Indian Punjab but is believed fairly representative of other regions where similar innovations have occurred.

The case of the green revolution[13]

The green revolution is the popular name given to the new technologies developed since the 1950s for the cultivation of various cereal crops, and widely applied in Asia and other parts of the developing world. These new technologies comprise a package of new inputs but are centred around new high-yielding hybrid seed varieties.

Where it has occurred, the impact of this 'revolution' on output and productivity has been large. In the Indian Punjab, new varieties of maize, wheat, rice and millet were applied; total farm output roughly doubled between 1952 and 1965; and the amount of output that was marketed (as against being used for subsistence consumption) roughly tripled. To some extent, this was a response to greater uses of land, labour and capital. But there were also large increases in the productivities of these factors, as shown by the following figures of average productivities in 1965 as percentages of 1952 levels:

Output per man-day	192%
Output per unit capital outlay	167%
Output per cultivated hectare	147%

What makes the green revolution of particular interest is that it seems an excellent example of a

---

[13] The following paragraphs are largely based on Day and Singh, 1977, with some supplementary use of other sources.

technological advance well suited to developing countries. The new hybrids were developed explicitly for use in LDC conditions and they were applicable (or easily adapted) to a wider range of ecological conditions than is often the case with the results of biological research. Being based essentially upon the use of new seed types, the new technology apparently did not call for radical departures from traditional modes, nor for new modern skills. Being based on new seeds and applications of fertilizers, the new technology did not appear to require large investments, nor to threaten the replacement of labour by capital. Indeed, because they have shorter cropping cycles, the new varieties permit multiple cropping and can thus increase the demand for labour. Seeds and fertilizers being highly divisible inputs, the technology appeared to be as potentially profitable on smallholdings as on large farms.

In short, the green revolution *appeared* to pass all the criteria of 'appropriateness': ecological relevance and versatility; simplicity; labour-intensity; and smallness of scale. As such, it also provided conditions favourable to rapid diffusion. However, when we look more deeply into its actual application a more complex picture emerges, forcing us to qualify some of the judgements in the previous paragraph.

Take first its ecological relevance and versatility. While the new hybrids do have these virtues, it is easy to exaggerate the extent of their applicability and hence their impact on total production. Thus, while marketed output tripled in the Punjab, the impact of the new technologies on output in India as a whole has been less than revolutionary, except perhaps in the case of wheat. It has been confined to a small number of crops and has been largely concentrated in a relatively limited area of northern India, mainly Punjab, Haryana and Western Uttar Pradesh.[14] Since the new varieties mostly require irrigation, they cannot be employed in dry areas and are difficult to introduce where there may be water but where irrigation has not formerly been employed. Because of ecological differences, the new varieties have so far made little impact in Africa and Latin America.

The seeming simplicity of the new technology also gives way to greater complexity on closer examination. At least in the Punjab, *the green revolution did not commence with the introduction of new hybrids; it commenced with mechanization.* The replacement of local seed varieties by hybrids did not become significant until 1962–63, by which time major increases in output and productivities had already been achieved. The mechanization of various tasks was already well under way.[15] By 1961, for example, the use of tractors was about four times the 1952 level; the application of diesel and electric power

to tube wells rose by a similar proportion in the same period; so did the amount of investment per worker.

This meant that the new technology demanded more modern skills, to use and maintain the equipment, than is often believed. Even adopting the new seeds was not straightforward. They yield the biggest improvements when used in conjunction with nitrogenous fertilizers and year-round irrigation, and they tend to be more delicate, less resistant to drought and flooding. They therefore require more intensive care and precisely controlled usage of complementary inputs.

The association of the new technologies with considerable mechanization must also qualify the image of the green revolution as relatively labour-intensive, requiring only modest new investments. For example, outlays per man-day on tractors, mechanized tube wells and threshers were by 1965 more than triple the 1952 level; on fertilizers and other variable inputs outlays were increased more than ten-fold. Machine power per man underwent a $4\frac{1}{2}$-fold expansion. Clearly, therefore, there was a major increase in capital intensity. This also generated greater needs for funds, and in the first half of the period there was an approximately four-fold increase in farmers' indebtedness. However, after 1960 farmers were getting large enough profits to meet their own requirements for funds and to repay their debts. By 1965 their credit needs were small.

Our earlier discussion reached generally rather negative conclusions about the desirability of mechanization. What light does the Punjab case throw on this controversy?

The chief interest here concerns the implications of mechanization for employment. In the Punjab two conflicting forces were at work. On the one hand, demand for labour was reduced due to the adoption of task-specific, labour-saving machines. On the other hand, there were increases in the demand for labour due to more double-cropping, a larger area sown to high-yielding varieties and the application of fertilizers. The net outcome of these forces was that there was less employment in 1954–64 than in the base year of 1952 but that by 1965 total demand for labour was 5 per cent above the 1952 level. This increase was not sufficient to absorb the additional numbers joining the labour force, however, so that, over a complete year, only between 48 and 64 per cent of available man-days were actually utilized. Despite this, there were seasonal shortages of labour, during

---

[14] See Bardhan and Bardhan, 1973, who present data suggesting that, with the exception of wheat, the green revolution has made little difference to overall yields per acre in India (p. 286).

[15] Day and Singh, 1977; see also Ahmed, 1976.

Table 9.2
Characteristics of Innovators, Imitators and Non-adopters in Southern India, 1965

	Innovators	Imitators	Non-adopters
Area cultivated (hectares)	3·2	1·3	1·0
Assets per capita (000' rupees)	22·5	4·3	3·0
Years of education	9	4	2

Source: N. S. Shetty cited by D. Turnham, 1970, p. 148.

the periods when the winter crops were prepared and harvested; it was these seasonal bottle-necks which stimulated the mechanization of land-clearing, irrigation and transportation.

This case does not, therefore, provide any clear-cut pointer on the mechanization issue. There is evidence to support the argument that it can actually increase the demand for labour,[16] but the overall impact was to restrain the absorption of labour. Day and Singh (1977) use their Punjab study to project future developments to 1980. They predict an absolute decline in numbers employed and major increases in the under-utilization of labour, leaving the locally unemployed no alternative but to migrate elsewhere, presumably to the towns.

What can be said about the diffusion process of the green revolution? It appears to conform reasonably well to the model presented in Figures 9.5 and 9.6 above, in that Day and Singh incorporated this type of process into their model and found generally that it fitted the facts. But consider the implications of this. There is evidence from all over the world that it is the largest, most prosperous and best educated farmers who are the innovators and that poor, ill-educated smallholders are among the last to adopt a new practice. In these respects, the statistics from south India in Table 9.2 are characteristic of many countries.

This pattern has unwelcome implications for the distribution of income, which we will take up shortly, but notice that it also forces us to modify the idea that the green revolution was scale-neutral. The larger farmers are seen to be best able to take advantage of new technologies because they are better educated and have larger financial resources (they also receive a disproportionate share of attention from government extension workers and are thus likely to be better informed about new possibilities). It is only a partially valid reply to say that this advantage lies in social factors rather than in the nature of the new technologies. We have seen that mechanization was a major feature of the green revolution in the Punjab; because the new machines were imperfectly divisible

and required sizable investments, they disfavoured small farmers.

To conclude this section, it is apparent that once we depart from neat descriptions of appropriate technology to examine a real-world example, the picture becomes more complex and the outcomes more ambiguous. Even though it appears to offer a favourable example, the green revolution is seen only imperfectly to possess the attributes of appropriateness. It is seen also to carry some rather strong social implications, to which we now turn.

Activity. Enquire about the extent to which the technologies of the green revolution have been adopted in your own country. Write a brief paper summarizing what you can find out about the forms they have taken, and their consequences.

Social and technological interactions

At a number of points we have already alluded to the social implications of technological change and it is well to explore them more systematically before turning to examine policy recommendations. Although the effect of a change on society will depend upon the initial situation – the nature of that society and the direction in which it has been moving – some generalizations can none the less be offered.

Technological change will alter the distribution of income, often in the direction of greater inequality[17]

This will most obviously happen with capital-intensive changes biased towards large scale, or changes involving risks which smallholders cannot afford to take. But even in the case of highly divisible new inputs like seeds and fertilizers, the same trend

---

[16] See also Roy and Blase, 1978, who argue that tractorization in the Punjab stimulated the employment of hired labour by facilitating the more intensive cultivation of land.

[17] See Lipton, 1978, for a useful discussion of this topic.

towards greater inequality within the rural population has been observed. In some cases the poor have been made actually poorer but the more general result has been summed up by Gotsch (op. cit., p. 143) as follows:

> Most of the evidence . . . suggests that the effect of such highly divisible inputs as seeds, fertilisers and pesticides has been to increase the absolute incomes of virtually all classes, although disparities of wealth have continued to increase.

Such a widening of income disparities seems practically inevitable with the type of diffusion process illustrated in Table 9.2, unless deliberate policy measures are taken to avert it. Moreover, increasing inequalities within the rural population will further strengthen the already powerful and may enable them to monopolize the benefits of government research and extension work. There may, moreover, be a tendency for research and technological progress to be especially concentrated in the more fertile zones, with lower-potential areas receiving less attention. In such circumstances, inequalities between rural areas will worsen, with all the consequences that can have for labour migration, ethnic friction and national disunity. Hence the following conclusion of a study of the impact of the green revolution in Bangladesh (Douglas Smith in Stewart, 1975, p. 182):

> The much-heralded seed-water-fertiliser control revolution has the potential to increase dramatically the welfare of nearly all residents of rural Bangladesh. The new technology sets in motion, however, forces of change that will strain current institutional structures to their utmost: inevitable imbalances in class and regional access to scarce inputs will accelerate an on-going process of land agglomeration and add to the vast pool of the landless proletariat.

The last paragraph predicted worsening inequalities within the rural economy. However, technological progress in food production may have a beneficial impact on the real incomes of the urban poor. Take, for instance, the conclusions of a study on the impact of new high-yielding rice varieties in Colombia (Scobie and Pasada, 1977, p. 99):

> Rice prices were much lower than they would have been in the absence of HYV's [high-yielding varieties]; hence Colombian consumers were the beneficiaries of the research program. Both absolutely and relatively, the greatest net benefits went to the lowest income consumers. Fifty percent of Colombian households received 14 percent of the income, but captured 62 per cent of the net benefits from the introduction of HYV's. Producers of rice would have received higher prices and had higher incomes in the absence of the new varieties. Small upland producers were the most severely affected, but numerically they are a minor group (about 6,000 in 1970).

When, as in Colombia, an innovation reduces the final price of an important low-income foodstuff (at the expense of smaller farm incomes), the net effect on the national distribution of real incomes is likely to be complex and difficult to predict.

Technological change is likely to alter the economic status of large numbers of people

First, it accelerates the commercialization of agriculture, shrinking the relative importance of subsistence output and bringing smallholders more and more into contact with the wider economic system. For those with land and ability enough to exploit the new opportunities, technological advance can elevate them from peasants dependent upon subsistence cultivation into commercial farmers. For those not so lucky, the change may be less welcome: from smallholders into landless wage workers or casual labourers. To take India again, census data indicate that the proportion of labourers in the total agricultural labour force rose from 24 to 38 per cent in 1961–71 (although it is not possible to say how much of this increase resulted from technological change). For the least fortunate of all, their new status may be that of semi-permanently unemployed, dependent largely on the generosity of others or forced to join thousands of fellow job-hunters in the cities.

Here too the social ramifications of such trends will be important. Changing production relations will alter traditional systems of obligations, authority and values (it is claimed that the green revolution has blurred the traditional obligations of landlords to tenants in India, for example). A rural proletariat will grow up, more dependent on others than peasants with their own land but less inclined to accept the existing order of things and perhaps better able to organize collectively – a major potentially destabilizing element in rural society. Even family relationships may be altered, as hinted at in the earlier reference to the effects of rice hullers in Indonesia.

Technological change is liable to alter the social organization of production

Especially in the absence of counter-policies, there is likely to be a shift towards larger units of production – either large privately-owned farms, using mainly wage-labour, or some form of collective or co-operative cultivation in which farmers combine together to reap the advantages of large scale. In either case, people will be working together in larger numbers and using different modes of work than in traditional agriculture. And this 'socialization' of labour will alter relationships, attitudes and institutional needs (for example, in patterns of housing and transportation). The collectivization of farming in the People's Republic of China provides an extreme example; a different experiment that has attracted attention is Tanzania's villagization programme, involving the relocation into villages of peasants formerly scattered over large areas, and their organization into co-operative farming units.

This summary has been presented as an account of some ways in which technological change will impinge upon social systems and human relations. But we could reverse the viewpoint to consider ways in which social factors will impinge upon technological modernization. For the capacity and willingness of societies to make the adjustments necessitated by new techniques will go far to determine the pace with which modernization occurs. For this reason, it is wrong to dismiss, as some do, the views of those who see tradition as a barrier to improved cultivation techniques. The successful application of modern knowledge to agriculture demands new skills, new modes of organization, new institutions, new social relationships – painful adjustments, many of them, which are certain to meet resistance. It is partly because of these social dimensions that a change successfully applied in one region may never take root in another, even when technical factors are favourable. In the words of Simon Kuznets (1974, p. 198),

> It is in the interplay of technological and social changes that the key to the process of economic growth lies; and it is this interplay that accounts for the length of time that passes before full integration of a major technological innovation into the productive and social system is attained.

A related point is made in the quotation from Edmund Burke at the beginning of this chapter: 'To innovate is not to reform'. For innovations to yield their maximum advantages and for these advantages to be translated as fully as possible into human welfare, *social* reforms are also needed – to accelerate adaptation to new methods but also to guard against their possible ill effects, on inequality and unemployment.

Modernization thus needs to be set within a framework of policy consciously designed to maximize its benefits to society as a whole. We therefore turn to consider policy responses to the problems identified.

IV. Policy Responses

One of the lessons emerging from this chapter is the wide range of effects that technological progress has on the socio-economic variables that affect the pace and nature of technological progress. It follows from this that agricultural technology policy cannot be a simple matter of using just two or three instruments to maximize the rate of change. Somehow, the policy-makers have to cope with complex interrelations, which means that they need to simultaneously manipulate a rather large number of instruments to induce a subtle combination of outcomes. But not all governments have the ability to do this and so it is useful to go about a discussion of policy responses in two stages: (1) to identify a minimum policy response, which will not be ideal but may at least be manageable; and (2) to proceed to draw attention to additional measures that would be important if policy was to deal adequately with the complexities and interrelations.

A minimum policy response

There are a number of ways in which government actions often retard technological progress in agriculture. *A minimum policy response involves getting rid of these policy aggravations*, which can be classed under three headings:

(1) policies which reduce the profitability of agriculture;
(2) policies which discriminate in favour of large-scale production and capital intensity;
(3) policies which neglect and distort agricultural research.

Policies which reduce the profitability of agriculture

Much stress has been laid throughout this chapter on the importance of profitability: that it is expected to pay is a necessary precondition for the widespread diffusion of any new method. But, wittingly or not, governments often pursue policies which depress profitability in agriculture, reduce investment there and discourage innovations. Pricing policies are a case in point. Through marketing boards and similar agencies, governments commonly determine the prices paid to the farmers and there are many countries in which these arrangements have been used to tax the farmer and subsidize the consumer. In

Nigeria, for instance, marketing boards for export crops have paid to the farmers only a fraction of the crops value on world markets, and in east Africa some produce boards have been used to hold down food prices for the benefit of the urban consumer. One of the justifications given for having boards of this type is that they can stabilize producer prices, thus reducing risks and encouraging investment, but they have frequently been operated in a way which actually destabilizes the farmer's incomes.[18]

Policies of industrial protection can have a like effect in reducing incentives in agriculture, by worsening the 'terms of trade' of the farmers, raising the prices of the industrial inputs and consumer goods which they buy relative to the prices they receive for their produce. Manufacturing industries erected behind high tariff barriers and other forms of protection are liable to be inefficient – otherwise they would not need the protection. So the farmer who, in effect, exchanges his produce for manufactured consumer goods finds himself paying high prices for often inferior articles. If local industry also takes over the production of agricultural implements, pesticides, fertilizers and so forth, the farmer is in danger of seeing his costs pushed up because of industrial inefficiency, his competitiveness on world markets eroded, and his profits reduced. Of course, local industry is not necessarily inefficient but governments have often pursued undiscriminating policies of industrialization which have encouraged the local production of goods selling at prices higher than would obtain if the goods were imported and bore only 'normal' levels of duty (see Chapter 10).

There are various other ways in which policies can discriminate in favour of urban dwellers and against rural communities.[19] The availability and quality of education, health and other social services is almost always superior in the towns, partly because it is cheaper to offer these services where there are large concentrations of population but partly because of a simple pro-urban bias. Much the same could be said of the provision of piped water, electric power and roads. Neglect of roads is particularly serious for the farmer because the quality and proximity of transport makes a great difference to the costs of distributing his produce and hence to the price he receives. Educational policies are frequently discriminatory in an additional way: providing academic and technical skills mainly relevant to the urban economy, and little training which can readily be used in agriculture.

All these types of policy bias have in common that they raise agricultural costs, or reduce agricultural profits, or frustrate the farmer from using his income to raise his living standards in ways he would desire. They all, therefore, discourage investment and

innovation in agriculture; their removal would promote technological progress in that sector.

Policies which discriminate in favour of large-scale production and capital intensity

There is a great deal of evidence from all over the developing world that a disproportionately large share of agricultural extension services and credit goes to the larger-scale and already relatively prosperous farmers. To some extent this results from deliberate manipulation by the powerful in their own interests but there are also strong natural forces tending to produce such a result anyway. Gotsch (op. cit., p. 147) has put the point well:

> With respect to the distribution of extension services . . . little of the available advice goes to those who might need it most . . . From the top there is the desire of the agricultural establishment to be sure that it has the support of influential local citizens in its bureaucratic battles with other sections of the government. Hence the local agent is encouraged to respond quickly and sympathetically to the needs of the well-to-do. Moreover, since he himself is usually poorly paid and without adequate transportation, the availability of a meal and transport when he visits the large farmers is an inducement that he can ill afford to ignore. Lastly, and the importance of this point should not be underestimated, medium and large farmers are prepared to undertake the procedures that are being suggested! To any field worker who sees himself as someone dedicated to creating a more modern agriculture, the self-realisation that accompanies the successful introduction of a new practice is no less rewarding to him than to his counterpart anywhere else in the world. As in the case of credit, it is hard to see how the results could be anything but what they are.

Unless, he might have added, a deliberate and strong attempt is made to overcome these natural forces and to concentrate resources on the smallholder. The introduction of *group* extension methods can be an effective way of countering the natural bias towards large farmers, in which farmers select one or more of their members for training, which he should in turn pass on to his fellows.

A related tendency which also results in a neglect of small farmers is the general preference of governments and foreign aid agencies for big, perhaps grandiose, projects. They are easier to identify and to

---

[18] Those who would like to pursue the marketing board issue should see P. T. Bauer's classic attack on them (1971, ch. 12). Helleiner (1966) offers a more sympathetic view.
[19] For a general discussion of this issue see Lipton, 1977.

manage; they have better publicity value; if successful, they produce satisfyingly large results. Here too a conscious effort is needed if this bias is to be overcome.

The public psychology which favours big projects also spawns a bias in favour of mechanization. It is a bias common in Ministries of Agriculture and public corporations dealing with agriculture – agencies which ought to know better. State farms often abound with machines of various kinds, although their productivities rarely reflect this wealth of resources. Other aspects of government policy also encourage mechanization. Ahmed (1976, p. 92) comments that it is not surprising that tractorization preceded the green revolution in India and Pakistan, because of the incentives that existed:

> These included an overvalued currency, liberal import policies as regards machinery, cheap credit policies ... (biased in favour of large-scale farmers), the rise in farm wages, favourable tax policies, and state-sponsored training and workshop facilities for tractor operators.

Policies which neglect and distort agricultural research

The case was made earlier (page 227) that the market mechanism will result in a neglect of socially desirable agricultural research, which should therefore be undertaken by the state. Traditional agriculture generates limited effective demand for the output of research and development (R & D) activities; many of the benefits from R & D accrue externally; there are large economies of scale and high risks. But governments have often failed adequately to meet this responsibility, resulting in dependence on the R & D work of high-income countries and a dearth of research findings appropriate to LDCs. For instance, in 1965, research expenditures as a proportion of the value of agricultural production in LDCs were less than a third of the developed country average, and the absolute value of research spending per farm was only about one-sixteenth. On any comparative basis, the LDCs were investing less; the productivity of their researchers was lower too.[20]

The ill effects of this neglect have been compounded by the distorted research focus mentioned earlier – in favour of large farmers and export crops, and against the problems of the small food farmer. This is particularly serious because of the ecological specificity of much research; it is rarely the case that the results of research oriented to one type of farm or crop or region can be readily applied to other situations.

Chapter 1 stressed the importance of considering not merely the potential benefits of a government action but also its costs. Only those which promise a net benefit should be undertaken and in this we might look for a defence of the neglect of agricultural R & D. Perhaps it has been held back by costs which are high relative to benefits? This seems unlikely, for there is near unanimity among investigators that agricultural R & D yields very high social rates of return – typically 40 to 50 per cent per year.[21] In short, *there has been a grave underinvestment in agricultural R & D* and there is a clear social case for a greater allocation of resources to this area. Interestingly, high returns are not confined to applied research; they are found also in pure research, partly because applied work builds upon a foundation of basic knowledge generated by pure research.

But if greater resources are to be devoted to research institutions, what policies should they pursue? The following paragraphs offer some suggestions.

Activity. Suggested topic for class research and discussion: do government policies in your own country inhibit technological progress in agriculture? In what ways?

Principles of agricultural research and development policies

First, it is important that the efforts of local agencies be co-ordinated with research going on elsewhere in the world. A number of international centres exist which contribute to the research needs of country groupings and these centres have made major contributions to the discovery of the green revolution technologies. Among the most important of these are the International Centre for the Improvement of Maize and Wheat (CIMMYT) in Mexico, the International Rice Research Institute (IRRI) in the Philippines and the International Institute for Tropical Agriculture (IITA) in Nigeria. Co-ordination with their work is especially important because, although the improvements they produce may be immediately applicable only to limited ecological conditions, the chances are good that their discoveries can be made applicable to a wider range of conditions by local adaptive research. Moreover,

---

[20] See Evenson and Kislev, 1975. As a rough indication of relative research productivities, ten research workers will produce 1.8 scientific publications per year in developed countries against 1.3 in LDCs.

[21] See essay by Evenson in Reynolds, 1975, Tables 8.1 and 8.2.

mobility of research personnel between countries is liable to contribute to the international diffusion of knowledge, for Burns has observed that: 'The mechanism of technological transfer is one of agents, not agencies; of the movement of people among establishments, rather than the routing of information through communications systems'. By implication, a purely national approach to technology policy is subject to limitations; there is a need to utilize and strengthen international efforts as well.

Secondly, however, it is important for local research capabilities to progress from adaptive work to build a capacity for more fundamental research, because of the ecological particularity of cultivation problems and have also mentioned that high returns are obtained from pure as well as applied research. A country may be able to go quite a distance by adapting improvements discovered elsewhere but sooner or later it will find problems unique to itself which cannot be solved in this way. The ecological specificity of agricultural problems does, however, point to a policy dilemma. On the one hand, there are large economies of scale in research, arguing for the creation of one or a few institutions. On the other hand, many problems are local, arguing for the creation of institutions in each major ecological zone. Since resources are limited, a careful balance needs to be struck between these competing considerations. Countries tend to err on the side of spreading small numbers of researchers too thinly across too many research stations.

Thirdly, it is important to define the target groups towards whose problems research is to be directed. If we assume that, on grounds of equity and employment-creation, the government wishes to avoid past biases in favour of large farmers and export crops, it is the small food farmers who should be the target group. Quite apart from the small scale of their operations, calling for highly divisible technologies, this group is particularly oppressed by the riskiness of farming, so research should be directed to ways of reducing risks – by the development of disease- and drought-resistant crops and livestock; by the discovery of quick-yielding varieties which permit multi-cropping (and thus reduce seasonal unemployment); and by methods of crop rotation which permit a risk-spreading diversification into a number of crops even on small acreages.

Fourthly, a potentially large contribution could be made by the development of techniques to bring into profitable use land which is currently too difficult to farm. The UN Food and Agriculture Organization has estimated that in 1962 only 45 per cent of the potential land area suitable for crop production in LDCs was actually being cultivated, although there were large variations in this ratio between different regions and no doubt a good deal of the remainder was productively used as pasture.[22] The almost universal fact of population pressures pushing people on to sub-marginal land – land which receives scant or unreliable rainfall – reinforces the importance of this research priority. In the Near East, north-west Africa and most of Asia, however, almost all potentially cultivable land is already farmed, so research in these regions must concentrate on ways of raising the productivity of existing farm land, rather than means of extending the area. The development of small-scale irrigation and erosion control techniques are especially important examples in this context.

Fifthly, there is the question of product priorities. Here governments should remember the interests of the consumer as well as of the producer. Specifically, research is particularly needed into crops with high nutritional values – cereals, some starchy roots and tubers, some legumes – so as to improve dietary standards. As regards livestock, the development of breeds and methods which would reduce calf mortality (often as high as 50 per cent) and raise the often low cattle fertility rates would be of major importance both to the small farmer and for the improvement of diets.

Lastly, although we have stressed the heavy responsibility of the state in the provision of agricultural R & D, the potential of the private sector should not be forgotten. Private business can help in two areas. When there are potentially profitable commerical opportunities to be exploited, for example in the manufacture of chemical inputs, implements and machines, the private sector's own efforts can provide a valuable supplement to the work of public research agencies. The problem with traditional agriculture is that it does not generate enough effective demand for new inputs to make R & D work commercially attractive, but as productivities and incomes rise demand increases and so do profit opportunities. For example, as knowledge spread and demand increased, commercial seed producers made a major contribution to the diffusion of new hybrid corn (maize) varieties in the USA.

The other area in which the private sector can help is in providing an efficient distribution network for new inputs. The middleman is usually despised and

[22] According to the UN Food and Agriculture Organization's *Provisional Indicative World Plan for Agricultural Development* (1970), the actual area cultivated as a percentage of potential land area suitable for crop production was 50% in Africa south of the Sahara, 84% in Asia and the Far East and 23% in Latin America, with an overall average for these regions of 45%.

government departments are frequently reluctant to distribute inputs through commercial outlets. For the most part, however, this is pure prejudice: despite their faults, private traders generally provide an efficiency of service which few state agencies have been able to match.

The case for a broader policy response

The 'minimum' policy response described above has turned out to be quite demanding! Depending on the number of policy aggravations, it could require an extensive range of changes. Nevertheless, there is a strong case for governments to step beyond the boundaries of the minimum approach and to set their agricultural technology policies in a broader framework.

Recall what was said earlier about the social impact of technological change: it alters the distribution of income, often in an adverse manner; it alters the economic status of large numbers of people; it effects major changes in the social organization of production. In short, it alters the nature of rural society, and the structure of power and authority within it. Recall, too, the emphasis earlier on the need for technology policy to be set in a framework intended to maximize the benefits for society as a whole. The implication is clear: *decisions about technology policy cannot be made in abstraction from higher-order decisions about the kind of society it is desired to create for the future.*

One basic judgement that is required is on whether it is desirable and feasible to achieve sufficient technological progress on the basis of the existing rural socio-economic system or whether a radical restructuring is necessary. This brings us back to the reform versus revolution issue discussed in Chapter 6. Does traditional peasant society possess enough potential for improvement or is a restructuring of that society a prerequisite?

The suggestions made as a minimum policy response were in the reformist tradition but there are more radical alternatives. One that attracted much attention was the 'Maoist' strategy of the People's Republic of China, although China's post-Mao leadership has reversed a good deal of this strategy. No one would advocate a revolution simply in order to accelerate technological progress in agriculture, but a desire for acceleration could be part of a wider case for radical change. Even if we rule revolution out and retain a mixed economy, the societal issue is not one that can be dodged. When we talk of technological change as speeding up the commercialization of agriculture, for example, we imply the emergence of a capitalistic society and a rural proletariat, unless

conscious policy decisions are made to modify that outcome.

If the will and the expertise is there, it is perfectly possible for governments to structure their research efforts in order to anticipate the social consequences of their work and to design the research deliberately in desired social directions. The international bodies mentioned earlier have already sought to respond to past criticisms of the large-farmer bias in their work. Instead of working on optimal insecticide applications, the emphasis has shifted to the breeding of pest-resistant varieties; research resources formerly devoted to work on fertilizer uses have been switched to the development of varieties resistant to disease and drought.

Quite apart from these social issues, the large number of variables which affect the profitability of technological change, and the ability of society to accommodate it, also points in the direction of a broadly conceived technology policy. To repeat the conclusion of Part II: *technological backwardness in agriculture is a result of a complex amalgam of shortages of appropriate knowledge, of complementary inputs needed to turn a technical feasibility into a profitable one, and of the influence of tradition.* It follows that a truly effective technology policy must concern itself not merely with the relatively narrow issues of R & D but with simultaneously creating an environment favourable to innovation and diffusion.

Always assuming benefits to exceed costs, this would ideally involve (1) provision of *training* facilities to provide the skills demanded by new methods; (2) provisions for the systematic communication and dissemination of research results to the farming community, especially through *agricultural extension services*; (3) measures to ensure the availability of needed *material inputs* (fertilizers, seeds, cattle feed, machinery); (4) construction of supporting *infrastructure*, like roads, storage sheds, market-places; (5) the provision of *credit* to meet the likely increase in farmers' needs for working capital and equipment.

> **Activity.** If you are not clear at this point why the items just listed are important to technological progress, you should review your understanding of Part II of this chapter.

What is being advocated here is best described as a *systems approach* to rural technology policy. Cultivation methods are seen as a component of an agricultural 'system' containing a number of other interacting components such as capital inputs and marketing facilities.[23] This system, moreover, interacts with other parts of the national economy, for example, with the manufacturing sector as a provider of inputs and a buyer of agricultural produce for processing. A more familiar title for this type of approach is 'integrated rural development', briefly described in Chapter 6 (see pages 144–5), which involves simultaneous attempts to raise rural productivities and improve rural amenities.

Conclusion

It is sometimes said of economics that it has become too rarified and has little to offer on hard issues of economic policy. There are chapters in this book which reflect this weakness, but this is not one of them. It has been possible here to refer to a large number of policy instruments which can contribute to a solution of technological backwardness in agriculture. But this too can be a sort of weakness. For these instruments will affect other things besides agricultural technology and a government will want to ensure that these other effects are also harmonious with their objectives – no easy task. And in advocating a systems approach we are abstracting from the practical capacity of public administrations to operate at this level of sophistication and to achieve the necessarily advanced levels of co-ordination. In short, there may be an implementation constraint, enforcing a retreat to the type of minimum response outlined a few pages ago.

2 Use Figure 9.2 (page 230) to illustrate the effects of a government subsidy on agricultural machinery.
3 What do you think should be the role of agricultural extension services in the technological modernization of agriculture?
4 Discuss the likely impact of land tenure systems on technological progress in your country's agricultural sector.
5 'The idea that the small farmer is hampered by shortages of credit is a myth; appropriate know-how is the constraint.' Discuss, with reference to your own country.
6 In what ways do the research needs of small farmers in your country differ from those of large farmers? In what ways do their needs coincide?
7 Write a brief note explaining how Figures 9.5 and 9.6 are related to each other.
8 Using Table 9.2 as a frame of reference, search for sources on the characteristics of innovators and non-innovators in your country. Write a note discussing the implications of your findings.
9 Identify and discuss the *three* policy changes which you think would make the greatest contribution to agricultural modernization in your country.
10 Write an essay on the theme, 'To innovate is not to reform', if possible by reference to your own country's agriculture.
11 On what grounds do you think that agricultural R & D should be treated as a public good? What does this imply for the role of the private sector?

Suggestions for Revision and Group Discussion

1 Review your understanding of the following:
   (a) Ecological versatility.
   (b) Technological progress.
   (c) Scale-neutral technological progress.
   (d) Isoquant and isocost curves.
   (e) The distinction between an invention and an innovation.
   (f) The four features of an appropriate technology.
   (g) Labour-saving and capital-saving innovations.
   (h) Embodied and disembodied technological change.
   (i) The relationship between input divisibility and appropriateness.
   (j) Diffusion and its determinants.
   (k) The S-shaped diffusion curve.
   (l) A systems approach to technology policy.

Suggestions for Further Reading

For a general introduction to the concepts and theories of technological change see Mansfield, 1975, ch. 16, although, in common with much of the literature, the focus is more industrial than agricultural. Yotopoulos and Nugent, 1976, ch. 9, also offer a useful introduction and are particularly strong on questions of measurement.

Probably the most useful supplementary reading for this chapter is by Frances Stewart, 1977. This provides in-depth treatment of technology and underdevelopment, explores the notions of

---

[23] To put the matter more formally, a system can be thought of as a complex of interdependent components whose interactions are conditioned by each other and by the influence of the wider environment in which the system exists. A useful introduction to the uses of systems analysis for policy and planning in developing countries is provided by the National Research Council, 1976.

appropriate and inappropriate technologies, and provides case materials. See also the valuable essays by Stewart and Carl Gotsch in Edwards, 1974. Part III of Reynolds, 1975, offers valuable contributions; so do Yudelman, *et al.*, 1971.

Schultz, 1964, offers a brief and easily read study of the transformation of traditional agriculture which has become a classic in its field. Hayami and Ruttan, 1971, study the role of technological progress in agricultural development. Griffin, 1974, provides a trenchant, if sometimes over-argued, study of the political economy of the green revolution.

See also the additional references given in the notes to this chapter.

10 Industrial monopoly

'The greater the power the more
dangerous the abuse.' *Edmund Burke*

Contents

I. Market Structures and Monopoly Power

Monopoly, a forgotten problem

Some pertinent facts:

(1) An international comparison of manufacturing in seven industrial countries and India found output to be more heavily concentrated in a few firms in India than in all but one of the industrial countries.

(2) In 1968, ten Pakistani families controlled nearly one-half of the total assets of privately controlled companies quoted on the Karachi stock exchange; forty-three families controlled two-thirds of the assets.

(3) In Kenya, only 34 per cent of all manufacturing industries were classified as 'competitive' in 1963, a proportion which had fallen to 21 per cent by 1972.

What these facts suggest, and what is borne out by other evidence, is that heavy concentrations of monopoly power are characteristic of the industrial sectors of LDCs.

This is not at all surprising. Industrialization has not yet advanced very far in most of these countries, so there are likely to be only a few firms (perhaps only one) in any given industry. The domestic market is, in any case, too small to support many plants and most LDCs have not yet begun to export industrial goods on a major scale. There are few institutional constraints on the spread and exploitation of monopoly power, and many governments remain indifferent to the existence of such power.

That it threatens a potentially important blemish on the performahce of the economy has long been recognized in western industrial countries. If you look at one of the textbooks of applied economics written for the universities of the industrial world, you are almost certain to find one or more chapters on 'the monopoly problem'. But have you ever read a piece on industrial monopoly in developing countries? Probably not, because monopoly is almost entirely neglected in writings on development. Even though the incidence of monopoly is more severe than in industrial countries, it has been a forgotten problem. This chapter therefore takes us into an under-researched topic.

Monopoly power is not, of course, confined to the markets for manufactured goods. It is to be found in service activities and in agriculture. And it occurs in the markets for labour and capital, as well as in markets for commodities. Nevertheless, it is arguably a more pronounced feature of the industrial sector than of other markets and this chapter will be confined to the case of manufacturing. It will, moreover, be confined to modern industry, leaving to one side the different problems of traditional or 'informal' processing industries. As a final delimitation, we will be concerned here with the issue of monopoly in privately-owned industry, leaving the problems of public enterprise to be handled in the next chapter.

An economic classification of market structures

> **Activity.** You will find this chapter easier if you already have some familiarity with elementary micro-economic theory of market structures as presented, for example, in Lipsey, 1975, Part 4; or Samuelson, 1976, Part 3. You may wish to refresh your memory of this now or as you proceed through the chapter.[1]

Market situations may be classified according to two types of variable: *structural* and *behavioural*. The first relates to the number of firms in the industry, the ease with which new firms may enter it, and the homogeneity of its output. The behavioural variables, on the other hand, are concerned with the properties of these markets when they are in equilibrium: the relationship of price to costs and the resulting level of profits.

The result of employing such criteria has been to identify a range of market types, from the existence of intense competition to its complete absence. Table 10.1 attempts to summarize the characteristics of the chief market types, according to their structural and behavioural characteristics. A comprehension of the monopoly issue requires that you understand the statements summarized in the table, so it is worth going through it with some care.

Perfect competition

The first market type presented there is that theorist's favourite, perfect competition. The word 'perfect' is unfortunate, however, because it is value-loaded (who can criticize anything which is perfect?) and because there are ways in which this market situation may produce an imperfect result. We shall return to this point later and for the time being concentrate on the characteristics of this market form. Structurally, it postulates that in any given industry there will be a large number of producers, no barriers to the entry of additional firms, and that each firm's product will be indistinguishable from the output of the other firms in the industry.

From these structural qualities flow a number of important consequences. First, because there is a very large number of firms in the industry, the actions of any one of them will have no perceptible effect on the rest. In other words, each firm can make its own decisions independently, without worrying about the possibility that its competitors will retaliate in some way. Secondly, the fact that all firms are producing an homogeneous good has the consequence that buyers have no reason to prefer one firm's output over any of the others. If one firm tries to charge more for its product than its competitiors it will lose all its custom, for why should consumers pay more when there are many identical alternatives available at a lower price? To put the matter more technically, the perfectly competitive firm is faced with an infinitely elastic demand schedule. This means that there is no distinction between average revenue (price) and marginal revenue. The third structural feature – freedom of entry for new firms – is also important because it means that abnormal profits cannot be sustained more than briefly. If for some reason existing firms are able to make above-normal profits, new firms will enter the industry, increasing total supplies relative to demand, forcing down price and eliminating excess profits.

---

[1] There is, of course, an enormous literature on market structures and their consequences and the student who wishes to take his understanding beyond the elementary level should consult an intermediate textbook of micro-economic theory. Two such are Mansfield, 1975: and Nicholson, 1975, especially Part IV.

Table 10.1
A Summary of Market Types

	STRUCTURAL VARIABLES			BEHAVIOURAL VARIABLES	
Market type (1)	Number of firms (2)	Product type (3)	Entry conditions (4)	Price–cost relations (5)	Profitability (6)
Perfect competition	Many	Homogeneous	Free	P=MC=minimum AC	'Normal'
Imperfect or monopolistic competition	Many	Differentiated	Free	P=AC > MC. Above minimum AC	'Normal'
Oligopoly	Few	Usually differentiated	Restricted	Indeterminate but generally P > MC and AC	Generally above 'normal'
Monopoly	One or a few acting together	Either	Severely restricted	P > MC and AC	'Super-normal'

This brings us to the behavioural characteristics of perfect competition, recorded in columns (5) and (6) of Table 10.1. Column (6) states that only 'normal' profits are earned in a perfectly competitive equilibrium. By 'normal' is meant that level of profitability which is just, but only just, sufficient to compensate the firm for the cost of its capital and the risks it takes. If the return were less than this it would not be worth staying in business. Firms would leave the industry, reducing total supply, raising prices and hence the profits of those remaining. So profits can be said to be normal when they are just enough to make it worth remaining in business. It is customary to treat this category of profit as a type of cost (the cost of capital and entrepreneurship) and to include it in firms' average cost curves.

From the facts that only normal profits are earned in a perfectly competitive equilibrium and that these are included in average costs, it follows that the price of the product cannot exceed average cost. Remember also that the perfect competitor is faced with an infinitely elastic demand curve, which diagrammatically can be drawn as a horizontal line. *If we now make the conventional assumption that the firm's average cost (AC) curve is U-shaped,* with unit costs first falling as output increases and then rising beyond some optimal level of output, it follows that price is equal to the minimum attainable level of AC. This is illustrated in Figure 10.1, which presents the equilibrium of the firm under perfect competition. Equilibrium is achieved with price at p' and a level of output q'. This is the only combination of price and quantity at which the firm can make profits.

In this model, firms respond passively to competitive pressures with the objective of maximizing profits. You are probably already familiar with the basic condition for profit maximization. This is that, given price, a firm must produce that output at which marginal costs (MC) are equal to marginal revenues (MR). Now, in the perfectly competitive case there is no difference between average and marginal revenues (see the P = AR = MR schedule in the diagram), so profit maximization must occur when price is equal to marginal cost, as is also indicated in the diagram. The MC curve must, of course, lie below the AC curve so long as the latter is falling (only if the cost of producing one more unit is less than the previous average will the average fall further) and above it when AC is rising. Thus, the MC curve cuts through the AC curve at the lowest point on the latter, as shown.

Figure 10.1   *The equilibrium of the perfectly competitive firm.*

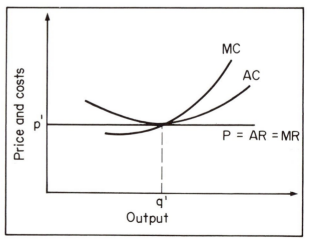

I have elaborated the perfectly competitive model a little because economists have attributed to it considerable importance in the achievement of economic welfare and because it is with this model that monopoly is often compared. We will return to such a comparison later (see pages 263–4) but you should notice how the model depends upon a U-shaped AC curve. *The properties of the perfectly competitive equilibrium would be unattainable if, for example, the AC curve were a continuously falling one.* This is a fact of great significance for an analysis of the economic effects of monopoly, as we will see.

Activity. To test the truth of the italicized sentence in the last paragraph, draw a diagram with a horizontal D = AR = MR curve and a continuously falling AC curve. What is the profit-maximizing level of output and how does this solution contrast with the conditions summarized for perfect competition in columns (5) and (6) of Table 10.1?

Monopolistic competition

The second market type, listed in Table 10.1, is monopolistic competition (sometimes called imperfect competition). We needn't spend much time on this because it does not contribute much to our understanding of the economics of monopoly. It does, however, introduce one interesting feature, that of *product differentiation*. This model drops the assumption that each firm makes an identical product and allows for an important feature of modern competition – that a firm uses advertising, brand names and attractive packaging to persuade buyers that its product is superior to the products of competing firms, even though objectively the differences between them may be trivial. Manufacturers of household detergents, of petrol, of soft drinks and of a multitude of other goods all engage in this form of competition. The intention is to create customer loyalty, which translates in economic theory into a downward-sloping, less than infinitely elastic, demand curve.

Oligopoly

Product differentiation is also a normal feature of the next market type, oligopoly. However, the most important feature of oligopoly is the existence of only a few firms in the industry. As a consequence, an action by one firm will noticeably affect the interests of the others in the industry who, in turn, may modify their own policies in the light of the altered situation. By contrast with perfect competition, then, the relationship between firms in an oligopolistic industry is one of *interdependence*. Each firm must reckon with the likely reactions of the others before deciding on a change of policy. Since its competitiors could react in a variety of ways, there is no unique state of equilibrium for an oligopoly but rather a variety of possible outcomes. These range from the price rivalry associated with perfect competition; to price stability, because each firm is afraid that if it cuts its price its competitors will follow suit and so all would lose; to a kind of follow-my-leadership in which one firm (often the largest) becomes recognized as the leader and tacit agreement grows up that the others will follow it on questions of price; and to more overt types of co-operation in which the firms exchange views and information so as to co-ordinate their policies and avoid 'cut-throat' competition. This latter kind of *collusive* oligopoly is called a cartel, and will be elaborated shortly.

Because of the wide range of possible outcomes resulting from the interdependence of producers, it is impossible to generalize about the behavioural characteristics of oligopoly. In most cases, however, we must expect price to be above marginal cost, because each firm will face a downward-sloping demand curve and the profit maximizing equality of MC and MR will thus be achieved at some value below the ruling price. In most cases, we would also expect price to be above average cost (and profits, therefore, to be above normal) because of collusion within the industry and the existence of obstacles to the entry of new firms into the industry.

So far as industrial products are concerned, oligopoly is the most commonly occurring market form and many argue that the only realistic choice is between different degrees of competition within an oligopolistic framework. Some economists have therefore tried to move away from the idealized and usually impractical notion of perfect competition to define a concept of *workable competition* which would be consistent with the facts of product differentiation and oligopoly. One attempt to define workable competition views it as (Clark, 1940):

Rivalry in selling goods in which each selling unit normally seeks maximum net revenue, under conditions such that the price or prices each seller can charge are effectively limited by the free option of the buyer to buy from a rival seller or sellers of what we think of as the 'same' product, necessitating an effort by each seller to equal or exceed the attractiveness of the others' offerings to a sufficient number of buyers to accomplish the end in view.

Even this more rough-and-ready type of rivalry may not be feasible, however, because oligopolistic firms have strong motives for co-operating instead of competing. If they engage in rivalry they create many uncertainties for themselves because they will only be able to guess at the final outcome. But if they co-operate, they can secure not only more peace of mind but the assurance of larger profits. They can also collaborate to oppose the entry of new firms who might upset their comfort.

We can therefore expect oligopolists to work together, for example to control the supply of raw materials and other inputs, so as to discourage potential new entrants. They may resort to temporary price reductions for the same purpose. They may agree upon collective resale price agreements, in which producers lay down a list of minimum prices below which traders are not allowed to sell. This has the effect of preventing new entrants from demonstrating superior efficiency by lower prices, and of generally reducing price competition. Sometimes oligopolists will agree among themselves on a geographical carve-up of the market. This is merely the beginning of what could be a long list of forms of collaboration; much ingenuity has been displayed in the invention of ways to reduce competition.

Monopoly

By co-ordinating their actions, firms can collectively strive for control over the environment in which they buy and sell, and it is control over market conditions which is the hallmark of monopoly power. This, then, brings us to the last market type listed in Table 10.1, namely monopoly. Many people think of a monopoly as the sole producer in an industry but single-firm monopolies are actually rather rare. It is therefore preferable to define monopoly so as to include the cases of a single firm which is dominant (but not alone) in an industry, and of a group of firms collaborating in a cartel. We also need to recognize the possibility of competition from overseas. Even if a local industry consists only of one firm, that firm will not enjoy monopoly power if it is faced with strong competition from imports from the rest of the world. In other words, *monopoly power in the domestic economy can exist only if the local product sells at a lower price than potentially competing imports or if the state provides local industry with protection against foreign competition.* So long as foreign competition can be eliminated (or much reduced), single-firm monopolies or cartels can exercise independence of action in deciding their policies, rather than responding passively to market forces, as the perfectly competitive firm has to.

Key concept. Monopoly is the concentration of control over price, output and other important market decisions in one firm or a group of firms acting in collaboration.

The single-firm monopoly is the easiest case to analyse because in this case the equilibrium of the firm is identical with the equilibrium of the whole industry. The firm *is* the industry. In this situation the monopoly will, of course, face a downward-sloping demand curve and, given its own cost schedules, will be free to regulate output so as to maximize profits. This case is illustrated in Figure 10.2, which retains the assumption of a U-shaped AC curve.

Figure 10.2 *The equilibrium of the single-firm monopoly with a U-shaped AC curve.*

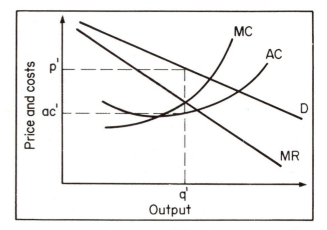

The diagram is drawn so that profits are maximized (MC = MR) at output q'. At this output price (p') exceeds average costs (ac') by ac'p'. The firm therefore earns monopoly, or super-normal, profits of q'(ac'p'), indicated by the shaded rectangle. Price in this case is well above MC, AC and the lowest point of the AC curve.

An important variation on this solution is presented in Figure 10.3. This substitutes a continuously declining AC curve for the conventional U-shape, on the assumption that there are major economies of large-scale production in this industry, with unit costs falling as output is expanded (see page 257 for a definition of economies of scale). In many respects the solution in Figure 10.3 is similar to Figure 10.2: price is above both MC and AC and monopoly profits are again present, as shown by the shaded rectangle. In this case, however, the notion of minimum average costs has no meaning, since AC diminishes over the whole relevant range of output.

Figure 10.3 *The equilibrium of a monopoly with continuously declining average costs.*

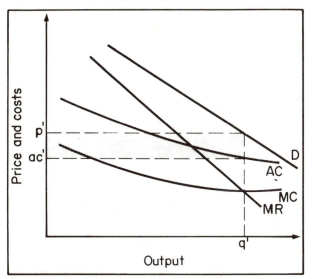

A firm with a cost function similar to that in Figure 10.3 is sometimes called a *natural monopoly*. An industry may begin as a competitive one but, because there are major economies of scale, if one firm manages to capture a larger share of the market than its rivals it will be able to cut its unit costs, thus giving it an even stronger competitive edge, enabling it to expand its market share yet further . . . and so on until it has swallowed the entire market. As we will see, many countries have taken the view that natural monopolies, such as occur in power generation, telecommunications and other public utilities, are most likely to serve the general interest if they are publicly owned rather than left in private hands.

> **Key concept. Natural monopolies** arise in industries subject to major economies of large-scale production. A single firm satisfying an entire market has lower average costs, and can offer lower prices, than would be true if the market were divided between a number of producers.

That a single dominant producer is not necessary for the existence of a monopoly was dramatically shown to the world in 1974, when the members of OPEC (the Organisation of Petroleum Exporting Countries) successfully combined together to enforce a four-fold increase in the world price of crude petroleum. By agreeing collectively not to sell at prices below those they had agreed, and to restrict output to whatever levels were necessary to enforce the prices, this group of governments was able to impose a monopolistic outcome, which it has since been able to consolidate much to the dismay of the rest of the world. But, except in the magnitude and impact of its success, there was nothing new about the collaboration achieved by OPEC. Economics has long had a word for a grouping of firms who co-ordinate their actions to acquire monopoly power. Such groupings are called cartels and as long ago as 1776 provoked a famous remark by Adam Smith:

> People of the same trade seldom meet together, even for merriment and diversion, but the conversation ends in a conspiracy against the public, or in some contrivance to raise prices.

Although the outcome of a cartel can be loosely described as monopolistic, it will not, in fact, normally produce the same result as a single-firm monopoly. Since the object of a cartel is to raise price above competitive levels, the total quantity sold will be smaller. This makes control over output a key task of cartel administration and there is likely to be much hard bargaining among the firms over how much each should produce. The aggregate outcome of such negotiations is unlikely to be identical to the profit-maximizing output of a single-firm monopoly. Conflicts of interest among members and a probably lesser control over the entry of newcomers to the industry impose further constraints on the freedom of a cartel and result in smaller monopoly profits. And in industries subject to major economies of scale, price (and consumer welfare) will be affected by the inability of individual firms to take as much advantage of these economies as a single firm producing the entire output.

Despite these differences, however, it is adequate for most purposes to put dominant firms and cartels together under the general heading of monopolies.

> **Key concept. A cartel** (or collusive oligopoly) is made up of a group of collaborating firms which co-ordinates pricing and other policies in order to minimize competition.

> **Activity.** This completes the elaboration of the market types summarized in Table 10.1. The student should now (1) go over this table again to make sure he understands it; (2) identify examples of each market type from his own country.

II. The Extent of Monopoly Power

To gauge the importance of the monopoly issue in developing countries we need some indications of its extent. This raises the question of how monopoly power may be measured, indeed whether it is measurable at all, so it is to this that we turn next.

Questions of measurement

One choice which poses itself is whether we should seek to measure monopoly power by reference to the structural or the behavioural characteristics discussed in Part I. Since we have defined monopoly as a concentration of control over market decisions, it seems more appropriate to look to behaviour, particularly at price-cost relationships and profits.

One possible measure of this type is that monopoly power can be indicated by the difference between marginal cost and price. We have seen that price in excess of marginal cost is one of the predicted characteristics of monopoly, so the extent of this excess might be used as an indicator of monopoly power. More precisely, this so-called 'Lerner index' would measure monopoly power (M) as:

$$M = \frac{P - MC}{P}$$

where P is price and MC is marginal cost. This is unsatisfactory, however. To a large extent, the excess of P over MC will be determined by the price elasticity of demand, and monopoly power is only one of the factors influencing this. Moreover, the concept of marginal cost is in practice a slippery one (see Chapter 11, page 293) and in most cases the information needed for the Lerner index would not be available.

A simpler, and therefore more attractive, behavioural alternative would be to gauge the extent of monopoly from the difference between the rate of profit earned and an estimate of the 'normal' rate of profit, which might be taken as the rate of interest on industrial loans. But there are also major snags with this measure. First, super-normal profits might be earned because a firm is particularly efficient (or lucky), rather than because it possesses monopoly power. Secondly – and this is an objection that applies also to the Lerner index – a firm may have much monopoly power which is not reflected in excess profits because it has grown inefficient and allowed its costs to rise. British economist John Hicks has remarked that 'the best of all monopoly profits is a quiet life': if firms use their monopolistic advantages to protect themselves against their own high costs, measuring profits will understate the incidence of monopoly.

In despair at finding an adequate behavioural indicator, economists have therefore turned instead to some of the structural characteristics of monopoly. They have focused in particular on the number of firms in the industry and the skewness of output within it. Thus, the most commonly employed measure of monopoly is an *index of concentration*. This measures the percentage contribution of some chosen number of largest firms to total output or employment in an industry. Thus, using a four-firm index, if the four largest firms together produced $120 million-worth of goods out of an industry total of $200 million then the concentration index would be 0·6, or 60 per cent. More generally,

$$C = \frac{XP}{IP} \cdot 100$$

where C = concentration index; XP = the aggregate output (or employment) of the x number of largest firms; and IP = the total output (or employment) of the industry.

It is not difficult to find fault with the concentration index as a measure of monopoly. It fails to handle the case of cartels, where there may be several similarly-sized firms (giving a low index of concentration) who nevertheless work together as a collective monopoly. Also, industries with low concentration ratios may contain firms which are *local* monopolies because high distribution costs prevent firms elsewhere in the country from competing effectively. Again, concentration ratios have to be calculated from official data collected from industrial censuses and these commonly omit an often large number of small-scale establishments. If so, the ratios overstate the degree of concentration. Another disadvantage is that the concentration index tells us nothing about the degree of skewness *within* the x number of largest firms. To go back to the illustration in the last paragraph, it could be that the largest firm had an output of, say, $60 million, with the other $60 million shared equally between the three next-largest firms. In this case, the 30 per cent share of the largest firm is more significant than the 60 per cent of the largest four taken together.

A final drawback to be mentioned – and a highly important one in the typically open economies of developing countries – is that the simple concentration index takes no account of competition from imports. There may be only one firm in a certain industry (giving C = 100 per cent) which, however, is unable to exert much monopoly power because of strong competition from imports. It is, in fact, possible to allow for this in a concentration ratio. This can take the form of a '*hybrid*' index of concentration, which measures the share of the x number of largest firms in the total domestic output of the industry plus competitive imports. This can be written:

$$HC = \frac{XP}{IP + M} \cdot 100$$

where XP and IP are as in the earlier case; HC = the hybrid index of concentration; and M = competitive imports. Even this modification only partly meets the need, however. There may not be a large volume of competitive imports entering the country but the threat of such imports can still be a major constraint on the exercise of monopoly power by a local producer.

Nevertheless, in that it makes some provision for competition from the rest of the world, the hybrid index is preferable to the simple index and we will shortly present the results of a test which uses HC. In the main, however, *a simple index of concentration is the most commonly employed indicator of monopoly power*, so we turn now to consider the results of estimates of C, as they relate to LDCs.

Activity. Suggested (slightly difficult) assignment: one possible indicator of monopoly power not discussed above would be provided by the size of firms' cross-elasticity of demand. The smaller the cross-elasticity, the greater the degree of monopoly power. Study the concept of a firm's cross-elasticity and write a note explaining how this might be used as an indicator of monopoly power. Also mention its drawbacks. Reference: see ch. 4 of Mansfield, 1975.

A review of evidence

As already mentioned, there are good reasons for expecting more industrial monopoly in LDCs than in developed economies. The domestic market of LDCs for manufactures is small, most have been unable to export manufactures on a major scale and industrialization is still at an early stage. So far as modern industry is concerned, then, we must expect only a few modern firms in most industries. This natural tendency to monopoly is likely to be compounded by the often high levels of protection against overseas competition that LDC governments offer their domestic industries.

Since the monopoly issue has been largely ignored in the literature on developing countries, there is not a wealth of evidence to draw upon but there is some which is highly suggestive. One valuable study by Bain (1966), although now rather dated, compared concentration in sixteen manufacturing industries in India in 1960–1 with concentration in the same industries in seven industrial countries: USA, Britain, Japan, France, Italy, Canada and Sweden. The results showed concentration in India to be well above five of the others; only one country (Sweden) had clearly greater concentration than India. This is all the more significant because the Indian economy is much larger (thus able to support more plants per industry), and her industrialization has proceeded further than in the typical LDC.

Among developing countries, Pakistan is the one in which monopoly has been the most thoroughly investigated, and researchers have found considerable degrees of industrial concentration. A major study by White (1974), for example, examined 59 manufacturing industries in West Pakistan (now Pakistan) in 1968. He found that in 15 out of the 59, the four largest firms accounted for the entire productive capacity of these industries. In 33 out of the 59 industries, the four largest firms made up between 80 and 100 per cent of capacity. And in only 5 of the 59 was the share of the four largest less than 30 per cent. Weighting the industries by their contribution to total manufacturing output, he obtained an average concentration ratio of 51 per cent. He compared this with an average for US manufacturing in 1966 of 39 per cent and concluded that industrial concentration in Pakistan was at least as great as, and probably greater than, in the USA – a result similar to the comparison of India and the USA mentioned in the previous paragraph.

A later study of large-scale manufacturing in Pakistan by Sharwani (1976) showed even greater concentration. He also used a simple concentration index but measured the share of only the two largest firms, as compared with White's four. He obtained average ratios of 56 per cent for 1967, 59 per cent in 1970 and 62 per cent for 1973. All his coefficients were well above White's, even though he was using only two-firm ratios. And note the rising trend over time.

A further dimension of industrial concentration in Pakistan is added by the fact that a small group of families controls a large proportion of all industry. Thus, White found that a mere ten families controlled 44 per cent of the total assets of privately-controlled companies listed on the Karachi stock exchange and that forty-three families controlled 65 per cent of the assets. Foreign ownership was of rather slight importance: only about 10 per cent of manufacturing was foreign-owned. A similar situation existed in India, where a small number of families and partnerships operated through 'management agencies' to exercise control over a large proportion of all privately-owned industry, achieving an only slightly lesser concentration of ownership than in Pakistan.

All the ratios reported so far have been of the simple type defined on page 254. In a study of industrial structure in Kenya, however, House (1973 and 1976) employed a refinement similar to the hybrid ratio defined on page 255 and obtained revealing results. He measured the share of the three largest firms in total employment in each industry, adjusting the results for the proportion of total sales satisfied by imports. This procedure has the effect of incorporating competing imports, which is much to be preferred in an open economy like Kenya's, and gives lower ratios than the simple ratio which ignores imports.*

He nevertheless obtained an unweighted average ratio of 44 per cent for manufacturing industry in Kenya in 1963 and evidence that this was rising over time. Using data on concentration and on the number of firms within each industry, House then presented a schematic classification of market types in Kenyan manufacturing, using categories similar to those discussed in Part I. His results, and comparable data for the UK in 1951, are summarized in Table 10.2.

We see that 43 to 51 per cent of total Kenyan manufacturing was classified under 'monopoly and concentrated oligopoly', a much larger proportion than in Britain. A sharply rising share was described as 'unconcentrated oligopoly', although in 1972 the proportion was well below the 1951 British estimate. The share of 'competitive' industries in Kenya fell and by 1972 was the same as in 1951 Britain. In other words, the Kenyan incidence of monopolistic situations was more severe than in Britain; and the relative importance of competitive industries was falling.

There are thus good grounds for believing the incidence of industrial monopoly to be quite severe in developing countries. Having established this, the next step is to examine its causes.

Activity. Search for references on industrial concentration and market structure in your own country. If you cannot find any, examine industrial statistics to see if you can glean from these any indirect indicators of industrial concentration.

III. The Sources of Monopoly Power

In large degree, *the extent of monopoly power is determined by the size of the domestic market, techniques of production and industrial protection.* These factors combine to determine how many plants can be sustained in an industry, how easy or difficult it will be for new firms to enter, and the extent to which domestic monopoly power will be limited by competition from the outside world. Of course, there are other influences too. Exporting can offer an escape from the confines of the domestic market. Product differentiation can erect additional barriers to entry to potential newcomers. So can advantages possessed by multinational corporations. We will return to these factors later but first examine market size, technology and protection as sources of monopoly power.

The size of the domestic market

If we take production techniques and imports as given, the number of efficient-sized plants an industry can support will largely depend upon the magnitude of the local market for its output. Now, the size of the market for manufactured goods in most LDCs is

---

Table 10.2
Classification of Kenyan and British Manufacturing by Market Type

| Market type | (Percentages) Kenya | | | UK |
	1963	1967	1972	1951
Monopoly and concentrated oligopoly	49	51	43	30
Unconcentrated oligopoly	16	25	36	49
Competitive	35	24	21	21
Total	100	100	100	100

Sources: House, 1976, explains and discusses the results for 1963 and 1967. The table, and unpublished data for 1972, were kindly supplied by the author. I have reworked his figures to exclude unclassified industries. UK figures from Utton, 1970, p. 79.

---

* Go back again to the numerical example provided on page 254. If in addition to the $200 million of domestic output there were competitive imports worth $100 million then the four-firm ratio would fall to 40 per cent ($120 \div (200 + 100) = 0.4$).

much smaller than in even the smaller industrial countries. This means they can support smaller numbers of efficient-sized plants because of the widespread existence of economies of scale. The contrast between developing and developed country markets can be demonstrated by referring to the economy of Ghana (Killick, 1978, p. 200):

> The point can be demonstrated . . . strikingly by referring to the conclusions of an International Economic Association conference that, 'it seemed to be our general impression that most of the major industrial economies of scale could be achieved by a relatively high-income nation of 50 million; that nations of 10–15 million were probably too small to get all the technical economies available . . .' Now reduce this to values. We take $1400 as a representative per capita income of high-income countries . . . This means that countries with gross products of about $14,000 million to $21,000 million were considered too small to get all available scale economies. Now compare with Ghana's GDP in 1965, of about $1,500 million at the official exchange rate, or, say, $1,000 million after adjusting for the over-valuation of the cedi. Ghana's economy measured in this way, was only one-fourteenth of the countries identified at the lower end of the range of those too small to obtain full economies of scale. This understates the comparison, moreover, for, with relatively high income elasticities of demand for manufactured consumer goods, the relevant market size is proportionately greater in a high-income country than is indicated simply by comparing GDP values.

It may be objected that it is misleading to use Ghana for the comparison because it is a small country (although, in fact, its total GDP is above the LDC average). But if one goes through the statistics of countries classified by the World Bank as 'developing' (excluding oil exporters) one finds that even in 1974 only 12 out of 98 had GDPs of more than $14 000 million and this number fell to 8 out of 98 if one took $21 000 million as the cut-off figure.

To some extent, the possibility of exporting releases some industries from the limitations of the domestic market. It is misleading to think of developing countries as exporting only primary products; manufactured goods actually account for up to a quarter of their export earnings,[2] and countries such as Taiwan, Singapore and Pakistan have been very successful in expanding industrial exports. There remain, on the other hand, formidable obstacles to the expansion of industrial exports in many LDCs, and this helps to explain why in 1968 export sales only contributed about 6 per cent of total LDC industrial output.[3]

As a generalization, then, it is safe to conclude that the size of the market for manufactured goods made

in developing countries is much smaller than for industrial nations. This results in strong tendencies towards industrial concentration and monopoly power. It does so because of the pervasiveness of economies of scale, which is the next factor to be considered.

Activity. Make an estimate of the size of the domestic market similar to the one for Ghana quoted above. Use the official exchange rate to convert into dollars and also make a downward adjustment if you think your currency is over-valued.

Production techniques and scale economies

When we refer to a firm enjoying economies of large-scale production (sometimes called 'increasing returns to scale'), we are describing a situation in which unit costs diminish as output increases over a wide range of output. This is the situation portrayed in Figure 10.3 on page 253. Scale economies are one of the most important features of modern industry, occurring importantly in a wide variety of manufacturing.

Key concept. Economies of scale exist when increases in output cause total costs to rise less than proportionately and average unit costs fall.

Economies of scale can arise because of advantages of running a large organization: it is feasible to hire more specialized staff; research activities are often not economical for small firms; large firms can often get raw materials and bank loans more cheaply than small ones. Most evidence suggests, however, that these organizational economies are not very important and that there are offsetting diseconomies as well. From an organizational point of view, the small firm is not generally at a major disadvantage.

This brings us to a fact of great importance to this chapter: *most large economies of scale are technological.*[4] They arise, firstly, from the application of mass production techniques, where

---

[2] The World Bank, 1976, p. 449, shows 'manufactures and other' exports (i.e. excluding food, other agricultural products and minerals) as comprising 24 per cent of developing country exports. If the oil-exporting countries are excluded, this proportion goes up to about 35 per cent.

[3] Calculated from data on thirty-seven developing countries in Appendix Table 5.2 of Rahman, 1973.

[4] For substantiating evidence see Bain, 1956, pp. 83–93; Williamson, 1967; Pratten and Dean, 1970, p. 103.

output is a continuous flow rather than a succession of batches. The use of assembly lines, conveyor belts and the like results in higher productivities because workers become skilled from constant repetition of the same task, and because there is no need for frequent changes of tools and resetting of machines. They arise, secondly, because of indivisibilities in the use of specific pieces of equipment. For specialized tasks it may only be feasible to buy a machine with a large productive capacity. A small firm may have to buy a bigger machine than it needs, obtaining only a fraction of the output the equipment is capable of. The large firm, on the other hand, will be able to keep the machine fully employed and be able to spread its cost over a large volume of output.

A third source of scale economies has been called the 'economies of massed resources'. This refers to savings that are possible because a large firm does not need to keep as many stocks or as much reserve capacity, relative to its output, as the small firm does. However, most major economies are of the two types mentioned in the previous paragraph.

The relevance of scale economies to a study of monopoly power is that, when there are important economies over a range of output large relative to the size of the market, this gives rise to a natural monopoly of the type described on page 253. With a small market and important scale economies, the economy will not support more than one or a few efficient plants. Once one or two firms have become established and captured a major share of the market, it is difficult for new firms to compete effectively. To get their costs down to the level of their rivals they need large-scale production but most of the demand is already satisfied and it will be difficult to persuade large numbers of buyers to switch to the new brand. Even if they thought they could sell on a sufficient scale, they are likely to find it difficult to muster enough financing to establish an efficient-sized plant. In other words, scale economies are a barrier to the entry of new firms.

Since most scale economies are technological, their importance varies according to the product being manufactured. For example, there are major economies in most heavy industries – the production of steel and other metals, motor vehicles, chemical products – which is a reason why heavy industry is especially liable to be inefficient in LDCs and prone to monopolization. At the other end of the spectrum, there is a variety of manufactured consumer goods for which scale economies are unimportant – clothing, food processing, concrete products, jewellery and toy-making are examples. Taking manufacturing as a whole, however, scale economies are large and it is worth quoting the conclusion of a thorough survey of

the importance of this in LDCs (Sutcliffe, 1971, p. 226):

> There is a large number of industries ... in which economies of scale can be obtained up to levels of output greatly in excess of those in most underdeveloped countries, and also greatly in excess of current consumption of those commodities in the same countries ...

One consequence of this is high industrial concentration, but even with output concentrated heavily on a small number of plants they may still be too small to achieve minimum unit costs. For example, the study by Bain which showed India's industrial concentration to be above that of the USA nevertheless found that the average size of an Indian factory was only about a quarter of the US average, with the probable implication that much of Indian industry was too small to be cost-efficient.

But this brings us to an important part of the argument: *the existence and size of scale economies are largely a consequence of the techniques of production employed.* Industrial technology has almost exclusively been developed in Europe, North America and Japan. This technology has been designed to fit the resources available in these capital-rich, labour-scarce economies with their large domestic markets. It is inappropriate to most capital-scarce LDCs with small domestic markets but, by and large, little use has yet been made of more appropriate methods. Industry in developing countries remains dependent on western technology and this dependence is a major cause of monopoly in LDCs.

> **Activity**. Students may find it helpful at this point to refresh their memories on the notion of 'appropriate' technology discussed in Chapter 9, pages 231–5.

The connection between scale economies and production techniques is illustrated in Figure 10.4. This shows three alternative average cost curves, labelled 'traditional', 'western' and 'appropriate'. Assume that this refers to some industry for which there is a traditional, pre-scientific method of manufacture, maybe the production of footwear. The diagram shows that the incorporation of modern scientific knowledge (and probably capital-intensive techniques) into shoe production results in a 'western' AC curve with lower than 'traditional' unit costs at all outputs greater than q^1. Unit costs are much lower at the bottom of the 'western' AC curve because there are scale economies up to output q^3.

Figure 10.4 *Technologies and average costs.*

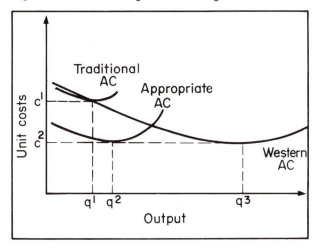

The 'appropriate' AC curve envisages the development of new production methods which take advantage of modern knowledge but in a manner suited to LDC conditions. It will be more labour-intensive, will use fewer capital resources, will be simpler and will be efficient at smaller levels of output. This has been drawn so that at its lowest point unit costs are the same as the lowest point on the 'western' curve (c^2) but its minimum is achieved at a smaller output, q^2.

To illustrate the relevance of this to the monopoly issue, assume that the total market for footwear is twice times q^3 and there are no imports. This means that when western techniques are used the market will only sustain two firms operating at minimum average costs, resulting in a concentration of monopoly power. If an appropriate technology is developed, however, the market will be large enough to sustain $2(q^3/q^2)$ firms and, since the diagram has been drawn so that q^3 is about three times as great as q^2, this means that the market could sustain six efficient firms using 'appropriate' production methods.

The conclusion offers itself that the monopoly issue will remain a major one so long as manufacturing in developing countries remains technologically dependent on the west. Until low-cost techniques have been discovered for small-scale manufacturing, developing countries will often find themselves faced with a trade-off between the avoidance of monopoly and the achievement of efficient, low-cost production. Preventing monopoly may also prevent the enjoyment of economies of scale. The existence of this trade-off poses a difficult choice for policy-makers and perhaps helps to explain why few LDCs have adopted strong anti-monopoly measures.

Industrial protection was the third major source of

monopoly power mentioned earlier, so we now examine that.

> **Activity.** One of the implications of the curves drawn in Figure 10.4 is that western-style industries will often force traditional processing out of business. Can you provide examples of this from your own country? Can you provide any counter-examples of traditionally processed goods that have remained competitive?

Monopoly power and industrial protection

The connection between monopoly power and protection from overseas competition is quite simple. Most manufacturing industries in developing countries produce goods that formerly were imported. Providing protection to these domestic manufacturers shields them from foreign competition and erects another barrier to entry – this time a barrier to the entry of goods made abroad, rather than to the entry of a new firm into the local industry.

Protection can take a number of forms. The most common is the imposition of *tariffs* on competing imports. Thus, an imported good which can be delivered to the local port for, say, $10 a unit may have a 50 per cent tariff imposed upon it giving an after-tax price of $15. This means that domestic producers can have costs of up to 50 per cent more than the landed costs of the foreign-made goods and still be able to sell their products (assuming the quality is as good). Take as an example the production of student note-pads like the one you have in front of you. There may be only one local producer but he will not wield much monopoly power if he faces strong competition from imported pads. But let him persuade the government to impose a stiff tariff on the imports: he is then in a position to exploit his local monopoly and earn larger profits, while still holding his price below the after-tax cost of the imports.

The use of licensing to impose *import quotas* is another form of protection, as we saw in Chapter 8 (page 216). In this case the government simply decrees that no more than a certain number of pads can be imported in the year and, so long as this number is less than the size of local demand, the domestic producer can exploit this to raise the price of his own goods and earn monopoly profits. In fact, quotas give greater opportunities for domestic firms to exploit their market power than do tariffs.[5]

---

[5] For a demonstration of this point, see Yotopoulos and Nugent, 1976, pp. 119–20.

It was because of the influence of protection on the exercise of local monopoly power that it was suggested earlier that a hybrid index of concentration, which makes provision for competitive imports, was preferable to a simple index which ignores them. In fact, the work on Kenya cited earlier produced stronger results when a hybrid index was used, compared with a simple index. Studies of the relation between profitability and industrial concentration have also attested to the importance of protection, finding profitability to be positively correlated with concentration and negatively correlated with imports – the greater the extent to which imports are allowed to compete with local industry the smaller the local profits. Some of this evidence will be reviewed shortly.

The influence of protection is all the greater because developing countries are heavy protectors. Consider the following examples of average tariff levels on manufactures in 1962:[6]

Industrial countries	%
European common market	11
Japan	16
Sweden	7
United States	12
Unweighted average	11
Developing countries	
Argentina	141
Brazil	99
Mexico	22
Pakistan	93
Philippines	46
Taiwan	30
Unweighted average	72

So in the typical developing country there is a combination of much concentration within locally-based industry plus high levels of protection against competition from imports. It is a combination that invites the use of monopoly power to exploit consumers.

> **Activity.** In the literature on the economy of your own country there may be a study of industrial protection. If you can find one, refer to it to gauge whether your country is a high protector and in this way contributes to the incidence of monopoly power.

Because of high protection in LDCs, many western firms who formerly sold their output to these countries have moved inside the protective wall by setting up subsidiary companies in the local economies. The importance of direct investments by these 'multinational corporations' adds a further dimension to the monopoly issue.

Multinationals and monopoly power

During the last two or three decades there has been a tremendous growth in business conducted by multinational corporations (MNCs), so that production controlled by MNCs is now actually greater than the total value of world trade.[7] There have always been large international movements of private capital. What is new is that, while most of it took the form of loan finance in the nineteenth and early part of the twentieth centuries, three-quarters of it now takes the form of direct investments by already established firms in overseas subsidiaries. There has, moreover, been an accelerating trend and the share of MNCs in developing country manufacturing has risen during the last two decades.

We should keep the MNC dimension in proportion, however. About two-thirds of MNC investments are in industrial countries and much of their investment in the Third World is concentrated in a few of its most developed members, such as Brazil, Argentina, Mexico and Venezuela. In some developing countries, a high proportion of manufacturing is controlled but in others (Pakistan is a case already mentioned) it is of secondary importance.

A multinational corporation can be defined as an enterprise controlling productive assets in two or more countries. The key word here is 'control'. Usually, this is achieved by the creation of wholly-owned subsidiaries but there is a growing trend towards the creation of mixed enterprises, with some government or other local shareholding but with control retained by the parent company. Assuming that its activities beyond the home country are substantial, one of the key characteristics of an MNC is that it is likely to use control over its subsidiaries to

---

[6] From Little, Scitovsky and Scott, 1970, Table 5.1. For readers who are familiar with the distinction between nominal and effective protection, the figures given above are of nominal protection. An unweighted average of effective protection for the same group of developing countries was 139 per cent (effective rates not available for the industrial countries).

[7] This and other information provided in the next few paragraphs is taken from the valuable United Nations study, *Multinational Corporations in World Development* (1973).

pursue its *global* ambitions. This tendency for the interests of subsidiaries to be subordinated to the worldwide objectives of the parent company is liable to create a conflict of interest between the MNC and the countries in which it locates its subsidiaries.

For our purposes, the interesting question is whether MNCs are a source of monopoly power over and above those already discussed. Do they increase or reduce competition within the manufacturing sectors of developing countries?

For the most part, MNCs operate in markets which are oligopolistic, both in their home country and internationally (Vernon, 1974, p. 276):

> Multinational enterprises appear mostly in industries dominated by comparatively large firms and characterised by high entry barriers . . . The problems of competition policy associated with multinational enterprises, therefore, are mainly the familiar ones associated with oligopoly behaviour. Two features, however, are distinctive. First, the oligopoly's leadership generally includes firms operating from quite different national bases. Second, the interaction of the leaders typically spreads over many national jurisdictions.

Direct investment in subsidiaries can thus be seen as an instrument in the manoeuvres of giant companies for the maximum share of world-wide oligopolistic markets. And some of them are giants indeed. In 1971, for example, the value-added of each of the ten largest MNCs was greater than $10 billion – a sum larger than the GNP of more than eighty countries.

But the fact that many of them command enormous resources and operate in global oligopolies does not necessarily mean that their subsidiaries possess large monopoly powers within any particular country. The entry of an MNC subsidiary into an industry may inject an element of competition formerly lacking. Or the existence of one subsidiary may provoke other MNCs to move into the same market rather than let their rival take it over by default. Much depends on whether the world oligopoly is collusive or competitive.

To illustrate, in most former British colonies the commercial banking system has been dominated by two or three British-based banks. In the tradition of British banking, these have generally co-operated to avoid competing with one another. More recently, however, some large and aggressive American banks have entered the scene and, by refusing to play the collusive game, have created a more competitive banking industry. Moreover, foreign dominance of banking has sometimes led governments to set up their own commerical banks, although they have

often played the collusive game instead of breaking it up.

So MNC investments can actually increase competition, creating 'miniature replicas' of the industrial structures of their home countries, even though the LDC markets are much smaller.[8] Indeed, some writers are afraid this has gone too far (Parry, 1973, p. 1213):

> The oligopolistic nature of the international firm, especially in the context of the desire to maintain market position, together with national barriers to trade [e.g. protection] . . . has resulted in a number of countries in a proliferation of small-scale, foreign-owned units with little prospect of rationalisation or consolidation . . . This situation results in a perpetuation of market imperfections reflected in considerable excess capacity and inefficiency in resource utilisation.

It is equally possible, however, for one subsidiary to dominate an industry within a developing country to such an extent that its international rivals do not see it as in their interests to move in and compete. This tendency is strengthened by decisions from the parent company which restrict the freedom of its subsidiaries to export their output. Such restrictions force subsidiaries to rely on sales in the domestic economy and thus intensify their desire to dominate that market (not to mention the other objectionable consequences of restrictions on exports).

It is therefore difficult to generalize about the impact of MNCs on competition. If it involves creating a new enterprise (as distinct from buying up an existing one), it may create more competition, as also if it stimulates investments by rivals. But if it is able to destroy or prevent rivals and achieve protection from competing imports, it may wield large monopoly powers. We have little evidence on what the typical net effect is. There is evidence from Latin America and Pakistan showing significantly more concentration in industries dominated by MNCs. Research on Uganda, on the other hand, failed to find any significant difference between foreign- and locally-owned firms with respect to industrial concentration. And a study of the pharmaceutical industry in Brazil suggested that MNCs were associated with smaller degrees of concentration.[9]

---

[8] See Evans, 1977, for an interesting exposition of the idea that MNCs create 'miniature replicas' through their investments in subsidiaries and for an empirical test of it.

[9] The country studies referred to in this paragraph are by Khilji, 1975 (Pakistan); Gershenberg and Ryan, 1978 (Uganda); and Evans, 1977 (Brazil). See also references cited by Lall, 1978.

Even where MNCs are associated with much concentration, the interpretation of this correlation is not straightforward. Is concentration higher because MNCs are attracted to naturally monopolistic industries, or does their entry into these industries create concentration where there was formerly competition? Lall (1978, p. 229) surveyed the literature on this topic and reached the following conclusion:

The general upshot of the work done seems to confirm *a priori* expectations that TNCs [MNCs] are a significant and growing force in the manufacturing sectors of most LDCs, that they are present in industries with high degrees of concentration, and that they are generally larger than domestic private firms. We are, however, unable to say confidently from the evidence whether or not TNCs *cause* higher levels of concentration. TNCs certainly flourish in sectors that are marked by high levels of oligopoly, but the causes of oligopolisation may well lie elsewhere, in scale economies of production, R and D, marketing, finance, or some other factor . . .

One conclusion that can safely be drawn is that the MNC question is closely related to the technological dependence mentioned earlier. MNCs flourish in industries with advanced technologies. It is superior access to these technologies (often buttressed by patent laws which give a legal monopoly over a technique for a period of time) which give them an advantage over local entrepreneurs. Again, we are led to the conclusion that the use of technologies appropriate to LDC conditions would stimulate competition and diminish monopoly power.

Activity. Search for data on the incidence of foreign ownership in your own country's manufacturing sector, for example in the industrial statistics. Are there any studies of the impact of this on market structure? Can you find examples of MNC subsidiaries which are monopolies in the domestic market, and of others which have led to greater competition?

Constraints on monopoly power

Small market size, technological dependence, protection and maybe foreign ownership are the chief sources identified above. But lest the reader gets an exaggerated idea of the magnitude of monopoly power, it is well to point out that there are constraints which limit firms' freedom of action in exploiting control over price and output.

This is most obvious with cartels. One of the great difficulties of administering a cartel is that, although the arrangement may be in the *collective* interests of all its members, it will be in the interests of any one of them to cheat the others so long as the cheater can get away with it. The cartel sets a price higher than the competitive price and restricts output to the quantity demanded at that price. Each member of the cartel thus finds itself producing less than it can, so a single firm could benefit by secretly cutting its price a little and selling a substantially larger volume. If the others do not find out, it is gaining at their expense. The higher the cartel price is above the competitive level (and the greater, therefore, the restriction of output), the greater is the incentive for a member to cheat.

This consideration helps to explain why cartels are often rather unstable. But even if all members are scrupulous in adhering to a collective pact, large difficulties arise because of the danger of entry by new firms outside the cartel. If the law forbids cartels they will be forced underground, making them more difficult to administer. And while firms may agree to co-operate for short-term gains, they are less likely to go so far as to co-ordinate long-term plans.

Single-firm monopolies are free of these problems but this does not mean they are entirely unconstrained. Even if they are the only producer and enjoy high protection from imports, they still have to be careful not to exploit their position so blatantly as to attract a competitor or to provoke the government to act against them. In this respect, MNC subsidiaries may be particularly vulnerable. Because they are foreign they will be unpopular anyway; they will also be visible; and the threat of nationalization will have to be taken seriously (as will be seen at the beginning of the next chapter).

Given these constraints on the exploitation of monopoly power, the question arises whether monopoly does much harm. This brings us to the next stage, of studying the costs and benefits of monopoly.

IV. The Costs and Benefits of Monopoly

It is convenient to consider the various effects of monopoly according to its impact on static, distributional and dynamic efficiency, as defined in Chapter 1. We will start with static efficiency, which has been the traditional concern of writings on monopoly.

Activity. If necessary, refresh your memory on the meaning of static efficiency, by referring back to pages 14–15.

Impact on static efficiency

The discussion of Table 10.1 already provided some indications of the static effects of monopoly. When discussing their behavioural characteristics, we suggested that monopolies would earn super-normal profits and that price would be greater than MC and AC. If we are willing to assume the existence of identical cost conditions for competitive and monopolistic firms (thus ruling out the existence of scale economies, among other things) we can go further to offer the generalization that *under monopoly, prices and profits will be higher and output will be smaller than under perfect competition.*

This result will have adverse implications for the efficiency of resource allocation. The composition of output will not be what consumers would choose if prices accurately reflected the resource costs of production: too little will be produced of the monopolized goods, with a consequential distortion in the allocation of the nation's productive resources. In addition, there will be a reallocation of welfare from consumers to monopoly-capitalists.

Figure 10.5 illustrates these allocative and distributional effects for an industry. Remember we are assuming cost conditions to be the same for competitive and monopolistic producers, so the MC curve represents the marginal costs of the single-firm monopolist or the sum of the marginal costs of

competitive producers (to keep the diagram simple I have omitted the AC curve).

Assume we start with a competitive situation and then move to monopoly. The perfectly competitive solution for the industry is at price p^1, output q^1. At this point, price is equal to marginal cost and each competitive producer is maximizing his profits. (Recall from Figure 10.1 that the individual competitive producer is faced with a perfectly elastic demand curve so that P = MR. If P = MR and P = MC then MC = MR and profits are being maximized. The difference between Figures 10.1 and 10.5 is that 10.1 relates to a single firm whereas 10.5 refers to the entire industry.)

The monopolistic equilibrium, on the other hand, is at p^2, q^2. In the case of the single-firm monopoly, there is no distinction between the firm and the industry, and it is at this combination of price and output that the monopolist is maximizing his profits (MC = MR). Price is above both MC and the competitive price, p^1. Output is less by q^2q^1.

The *distributional* impact of monopoly is illustrated by the cross-hatched rectangle, p^1p^2ab. This represents a transfer of welfare from consumers to the monopolist. Buyers lose what is known as 'consumers surplus' by the amount of the price increase times the quantity bought at the new price. There is an exactly matching gain by the monopolist, which is why this is called a transfer.

But in addition there are 'deadweight' losses resulting from the decline in output from q^1 to q^2. First, there is a secondary loss of consumers surplus indicated by the dotted triangle abd. This is the consumers surplus that would have been enjoyed on the extra output q^2q^1 at price p^1. Secondly, there is a loss of 'producers surplus' shown by the shaded area bcd, which is the difference between the marginal costs of producing q^2q^1 and the revenue received at price p^1. The sum of these deadweight losses is known as the loss of *allocative efficiency* resulting from monopoly. Their total is indicated by the area acd.

Attempts have been made to measure the allocative efficiency costs of monopoly in the USA and other industrial countries. Despite large estimation problems and differences in the assumptions made by various researchers, most agree that allocative losses are rather trivial. Most results indicate annual losses equivalent to less than 1 per cent of GNP. A similar study of the costs of protection, which included four LDCs in its sample of six countries, also found trivial losses resulting from allocative inefficiency.[10]

Figure 10.5 *A comparison of industry equilibria under competitive and monopolistic conditions.*

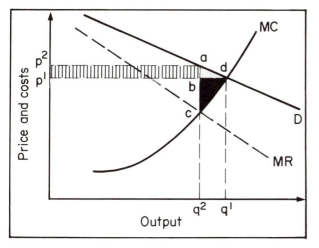

---

[10] Readers interested in these attempts to measure efficiency losses should consult Harberger, 1959; Kammerschen, 1966; Worcester, 1973; and Bergsman, 1974. Kammerschen's is the only study to find large allocative losses (6 per cent of GNP).

But if that is the case, what is all the fuss about? Why should I inflict a chapter on monopoly on you if its negative effects are so small relative to total economic activity? Well, we should not forget the distributional effects indicated in the diagram and there is an additional kind of cost attributable to monopoly which has so far been neglected. This relates to the notion of *X-inefficiency*.

In terms of the analysis of Chapter 1, the rather small losses of allocative efficiency just described could be thought of as a movement along a production-possibility frontier from a sub-optimal to an optimal position, i.e. from a to q in Figure 10.6.

Figure 10.6 *Allocative efficiency and X-efficiency.*

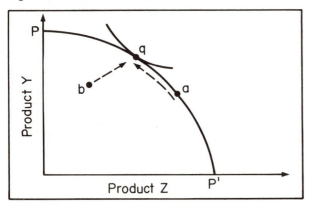

X-inefficiency, on the other hand, refers to a failure to reach that frontier; firms remain inside it because they are not getting as much output as they could from the resources they employ. Thus, the removal of X-inefficiency is illustrated by a movement from b to q in Figure 10.6.

There are reasons for believing that monopoly leads to substantially reduced X-efficiency. With perfect competition, the firm must maximize profits; if it does not it goes out of business. But the possession of monopoly power gives a firm latitude in deciding its objectives – a latitude facilitated by the separation in the modern firm of managers from owners, with shareholders rarely exerting genuine control over the enterprises that formally belong to them. Instead of profit maximization, managements may pursue maximum size or maximum growth. Or managements may agree with Hicks that a quiet life is the best of all monopoly profits. Perhaps they will fail to articulate any precise objectives at all.

Monopoly power – control over market decisions – protects a firm against its own inefficiency and allows the pursuit of non-profit goals. It takes the pressure off managements to seek and achieve least-cost methods of production. It allows them to be less

responsive to changing market conditions. It permits the existence of 'organizational slack' and an escape from the discomfort of having to work as hard as possible all the time. So the adverse effects of monopoly are not merely measured by the larger profits, and losses of consumers and producers surplus; resources will also be less productive and production costs higher. This undermines the assumption of Figure 10.5 of identical cost conditions in competitive and monopolistic industries.

> **Key concept. X-inefficiency** is denoted by the existence of avoidably high costs of production (low levels of productivity) resulting from organizational slack and the pursuit of objectives other than profit maximization.

Although here too there are major measurement problems, there is evidence from industrial countries that the X-inefficiency factor is more significant than the loss of allocative efficiency mentioned earlier. That there is ample scope for improved efficiency in much modern industry is suggested by the discovery by many researchers of a wide spread of productivities among firms within a single industry. It is suggested by the fact that when, in 1974, a power strike forced the British government to introduce a compulsory three-day working week, this 40 per cent cut in working time was only accompanied by a 20 to 30 per cent reduction in output. It is suggested also by detailed studies that have sought specifically to measure the incidence of allocative and X-inefficiency.[11]

Scale economies reconsidered

X-inefficiency, of course, raises monopoly cost structures above competitive levels, while economies of scale pull in the opposite direction. We earlier drew attention to the importance of scale economies as a barrier to entry and a major source of monopoly power. Most scale economies, it was suggested, are technical and derived from the characteristics of industrial technologies developed in western countries and Japan. Given LDC dependence on these technologies, we suggested the existence of a trade-off between the existence of monopoly and the enjoyment of scale economies.

The severity of this trade-off should not be exaggerated, however. Since most economies are

---

[11] For a review of this evidence and a general exposition of the notion of 'X-inefficiency' see Leibenstein, 1976, especially ch. 3 and 12.

technical rather than organizational, scale provides little defence for the formation of powerful conglomerates (firms diversified into many different industries), or of mergers of existing firms within an industry. Still less do they offer a justification for cartels, because this type of collusive grouping does little or nothing to enable individual firms to reap the benefits of large-scale production.

Even in the case of single-plant monopolies, scale economies by no means always provide an offset against the possible ill-effects of industrial concentration. The magnitude of scale economies varies from one industry to the next and this helps to explain why small firms continue to play an important role in industrial countries. Even in the giant economy of the USA, 203 000 out of a total recorded 313 000 manufacturing establishments in 1972 had a labour force of under 20 people, and in the same year establishments with under 100 workers accounted for 21 per cent of total manufacturing value-added.

That it is an over-simplification to equate bigness with superior efficiency is also suggested by the fact that British companies are generally a good deal larger than their continental European counterparts but British performance is notoriously poor. A similar conclusion is suggested by the results of research which show the performance of MNCs (as indicated by growth of sales) to be negatively correlated with size.[12]

The fact remains that there can be major trade-offs between large numbers of firms and the enjoyment of scale economies. From the point of view of the consumer, however, *scale economies only offer a justification of monopoly if a significant part of the cost reductions permitted by large size are passed on in the form of lower prices*. The point is illustrated in Figure 10.7.

Let p^1 be the price that would obtain in competitive conditions, with each firm producing q^1 output. The ACE curve portrays the *minimum attainable* unit cost at each level of output. A single-plant monopoly could produce at q^2 and would hence be capable of attaining unit costs indicated by the vertical distance q^2a. For simplicity, we assume completely inelastic demand between prices p^1 and p^2, so the firm can continue to sell output q^2 at either price. In the absence of monopoly profits, a single firm operating on the ACE curve would charge a price of p^2 and buyers would obviously gain heavily from this.

However, the management of a single firm is not likely to pass up the chance to exploit its monopoly power. It could do this by charging a price that would bring it super-normal profits. Or it could use its power for the sake of a quiet life, by relaxing effort and allowing costs to rise above minimum attainable levels, i.e. by relaxing X-efficiency. Or it could opt for some combination of super-normal profits and X-inefficiency. In Figure 10.7 the ACX curve introduces the idea of X-inefficiency as a consequence of monopoly power. The greater the firm's output, the greater its monopoly power is assumed to be and hence the greater its freedom to allow costs to rise above minimum attainable levels. Thus the vertical distance between the ACE and ACX curves provides a measure of the degree of X-inefficiency at any level of output.

If we assume our monopolist to be operating on the ACX curve, his actual unit costs will be q^2b. That there are still scale economies is shown by the downward slope of the curve but whether the consumer benefits from these now depends crucially on the level of super-normal profits. If, for example, the firm takes super-normal profits of bc per unit of output, then it will charge the price p^1 (which is the same as the competitive price). In this case all the potential gains to the consumer of scale economies have been absorbed by X-inefficiency and super-normal profits. If the management receives monopoly profits per unit of less than bc, the consumer will gain by paying a price below that which would obtain in competitive conditions.

Figure 10.7 *Scale economies, X-inefficiency and monopoly profits.*

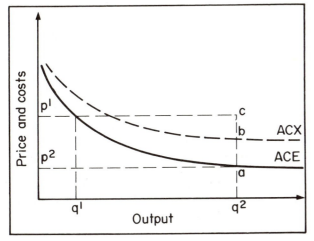

Activity. The above discussion of Figure 10.7 proceeded on the simplifying assumption of a completely inelastic demand curve. In what ways would the analysis need modification if the price elasticity of demand were greater than zero?

---

[12] See the essay by Hymer and Rowthorn in Kindleberger, 1970.

What conclusions can we draw from this discussion? It is essentially a matter of setting the allocative and X-efficiency costs of monopoly against the possible cost savings through scale economies. By making alternative assumptions about the price elasticity of demand, it is possible to use econometric methods to make illustrative estimates of the magnitude of cost savings necessary to offset the probable increase in price resulting from monopoly. The results indicate fairly clearly that improbably large cost savings would have to result from monopolization in order to offset the adverse effects of higher prices and reduced output (Yotopoulos and Nugent, 1976, pp. 120–3).

For example, with a demand elasticity of 2·0 there would have to be a cost reduction of over 20 per cent to offset the effects of the probable price rise. With an elasticity of 1·5, the necessary cost reduction would have to be over 40 per cent. With an elasticity of 1·1, the cost saving would have to be over 70 per cent. Such large savings are unlikely to be achieved in many cases, especially if we expect monopoly power to be associated with declining X-efficiency.

We are now in a position to summarize this discussion of the static efficiency effects of monopoly, with the following conclusion. *Monopoly is likely to reduce static efficiency* (1) *through the misallocation of productive resources, leading to losses of consumers and producers surpluses, and* (2) *through reduced X-efficiency. To set against these losses there may be enhanced productivity and lowered unit costs resulting from economies of large-scale production. In most, but not all, cases cost savings are unlikely to be large enough to offset the adverse effects. Because of their limited power to achieve scale economies, cartels and mergers are especially likely to worsen static efficiency.*

Monopoly and the distribution of income

The chief effect of monopoly on the distribution of income has already been considered in the discussion of Figure 10.5 (page 263) and we need not use much more space on it. As was shown there, when monopolies earn super-normal profits by raising price above competitive levels, there is a transfer of welfare from consumers to monopoly-capitalists. That is to say, the higher price results in a loss of consumers surplus matched exactly by a gain in producers surplus. The extent of this is illustrated in Figure 10.5 by the cross-hatched rectangle p^1p^2ab.

This type of transfer can generally be expected to be regressive, a shift of real income to the rich from the not-so-rich. In most countries such a redistribution is likely to be judged socially undesirable, a movement away from a just distribution of income. In the language of Chapter 1, therefore, monopoly is liable to reduce distributional efficiency. The gains in producers surplus are not likely to be regarded as offsetting the losses of consumers surplus.

> **Activity.** You may like at this point to refresh your memory on the description of distributional efficiency (page 15).

There is, moreover, good reason for thinking that monopoly is associated with extra-normal profits and hence with the regressive effects just mentioned. There have been many investigations of the association between industrial concentration (taken as a proxy for monopoly power) and profitability in western countries, and these almost invariably find a significant positive correlation: the greater the concentration the larger the profit margin. Investigations of the Pakistan case are unanimous in discovering a similar correlation. This was also found in Kenya, where industries with concentration ratios greater than 40 per cent had an excess of price over cost twice as large as industries with ratios of less than 40 per cent.

One last point. We are here confining ourselves to the industrial sector. Now, it is the relatively well-to-do who spend the largest proportions of their income on manufactured goods; the poor spend most on basic foodstuffs and have little left over for such 'luxuries'. The incidence of monopoly profits will thus in itself tend to be progressive (with the rich relatively harder hit than the poor). However, the net effect of the transfer to the owners of monopolies is still likely to be regressive. On balance, we are on fairly safe ground in reaching the conclusion that in most cases *monopoly will reduce distributional efficiency.*

Two views of the dynamics of monopoly

Since our concern is with developing countries, it is of more than ordinary importance to enquire about the possible impact of monopoly on the dynamics of development. We can do this by contrasting two radically different schools of thought, personified in the names of Karl Marx and Joseph Schumpeter. Both agreed that the spread of monopoly was an inevitable feature of the development of capitalism but they drew entirely different conclusions about the consequences of this.

Marxian school of thought

Take first the Marxian position. Observing the capitalism of nineteenth-century Europe, Marx foresaw an inevitable concentration of productive capital in the hands of an ever-diminishing number of monopoly-capitalists. In his view, monopolies were inevitable because of economies of scale, mergers and the superior access of big business to credit. Once established, monopoly perpetuates and strengthens itself – it earns larger profits which can be reinvested in further expansion. Monopolies, he said, employ more capital relative to labour, compared with smaller, more competitive firms. So he saw the spread of monopoly as reducing the demand for labour, a tendency reinforced by a labour-saving bias in technical progress.

He thus envisaged a diminishing demand for labour, resulting in mass unemployment and reducing the purchasing power for the products of industry. Profits – the life-blood of the capitalist system – would be forced down because of inadequate demand, while unemployment would lead to mounting social strife. These forces would eventually lead to stagnation, revolt and the collapse of monopoly-capitalism. The growth of monopoly was thus seen by Marx as transitional, leading in the longer-run to stagnation and collapse.

A similar general outlook has been applied to the situation of developing countries in a study by Merhav (1969). Because of their technological dependence on the west and the small size of their domestic markets, he argues that it is inevitable that LDC industry will be dominated by monopolies. These will have few linkages with the rest of the economy and thus do little to expand the size of the market. Once established, monopoly structures will be perpetuated by natural and contrived barriers to the entry of new competitors. Despite these barriers, however, profits will be constrained by the narrowness of the domestic market and by the threat of competition from imports. He therefore predicts that industrial expansion, which should 'set the pace and pattern of development', will run out of steam, leading eventually to a stagnation similar to that predicted by Marx.

Schumpeterian school of thought

Big issues are thrown up by these analyses but let us turn now to the alternative Schumpeterian view. Writing in the earlier decades of this century, Schumpeter was much more positive about the effects of monopoly. We should not worry too much about market structure, he said: the main problem of capitalism is not how it manages existing structures but how it destroys and creates them. If the growth of a monopoly reduces price competition for some commodity that doesn't matter too much. The competition that matters is (Schumpeter, 1943, p. 84):

> The competition from the new commodity, the new technology, the new source of supply, the new type of organisation ... competition which commands a decisive cost or quality advantage and which strikes not at the margins of the profits and the outputs of the existing firms but at their foundations and their very lives.

Competition for Scumpeter was 'creative destruction', in which he saw monopoly as playing an active role. Monopoly-capitalists, in his view, are more likely to be dynamic innovators, for two reasons. Their larger profits provide resources which can be reinvested in research and development (R & D). And the greater security provided by their control over market conditions encourages them to incur the high risks often associated with innovation. Galbraith (1967) has given this argument a more modern twist: monopoly power facilitates long-term business planning, which also encourages innovation and growth.

An evaluation

How are we to judge between these views of monopoly as leading either to stagnation or to innovative growth? We could proceed by examining the logic of both arguments, and there is certainly enough to get one's teeth into. But in essence we are confronted by two alternative historical predictions, so it may be preferable to test them primarily against evidence on what has actually happened.

To point out that predictions of capitalist stagnation and collapse have not stood the test of time must, of course, infuriate Marxists. They might reply that I have presented only the barest bones of their critique, have failed to do justice to the full range of their arguments ... and that, in any case, the collapse is on its way. The bare facts are, nevertheless, that in western industrial countries the general trend is for the share of wages in national income to rise rather than fall, in exact contradiction of Marx's prediction. Social critics in these countries today are more concerned with the evils of over-consumption, or 'affluence', than with the danger of under-consumption. And, while the size of firms does grow larger, there is no unambiguous evidence of a long-term trend towards increasing industrial concentration in these countries. Indeed, at the international level, there has arguably been increase in competition, with some retreat from protectionism and the emergence of the European Economic Community.

The mature economies of the industrial west have thus not slipped into stagnation as they were predicted to do. But what of Merhav's similar predictions for LDCs? Appeal to facts is less persuasive in this case because the time-span is not long enough to provide a strong test. However, there is at least some information for testing his prediction of decelerating industrial expansion, summarized in Table 10.3.

Table 10.3
Average Annual Growth Rates of Manufacturing Production in Developing Countries, 1960–73

	(Per cent per annum)		
	1960–5	1965–70	1965–73
Higher-income LDCs	7·7	8·5	8·7
Middle-income LDCs	11·2	9·2	8·3
Lower-income LDCs	9·5	4·0	3·7
Oil producing LDCs	5·1	7·4	8·4
All developing countries	8·3	7·2	7·3

Source: World Bank, 1976, p. 393.

Taking all developing countries together, no clear trend emerges. The fast expansion of the early 1960s was not sustained but growth since 1965 has continued to be rapid – considerably faster than in industrial countries. However, much of this strong performance is attributable to high-income and oil-producing LDCs. The table shows that lower- and middle-income LDCs have indeed experienced decelerating industrialization, as Merhav predicts. On the other hand, this deceleration may be due to causes that have little to do with monopoly.

Merhav's analysis is, in fact, based on a thoroughly pessimistic set of judgements which others would not necessarily share. He is pessimistic about the role of non-industrial sectors in development; about the possibilities of utilizing more appropriate, labour-intensive technologies; about the prospects for exporting as an escape from the confines of the domestic market. Merhav may in the end be proved right but he is too reluctant to consider more favourable possibilities for his argument to be fully convincing.

When we turn to test the Schumpeterian case, here too much evidence contradicts his predictions. Note

first the emphasis we have put on X-inefficiency as a cost of monopoly. It was a cost he did not consider, indeed would have been bound to deny. The monopolist who opts for the quiet life, who uses monopoly power as a protection against his own high costs, is hardly likely to be the dynamic innovator of Schumpeter's vision.

On the other hand, we have noted a positive correlation between industrial concentration and profitability. While we saw this to have adverse distributional consequences, it might at least assist economic growth. With larger profits there can be more reinvestment and faster expansion. But there is little evidence to show that monopoly undertakes more R & D and is more innovative than competitive firms. The results of an authoritative survey of research findings on this, while stressing the difficulties of such research, nevertheless concluded that (Kamien and Schwartz, 1975):

(1) R & D activity increases with firm size up to a point, beyond which it levels off or declines. The threshold for efficient R & D work may be a barrier to entry but not a formidable one.
(2) There is little evidence that R & D increases with monopoly power. A market structure somewhere between perfect competition and monopoly promotes the highest rate of innovation.
(3) The largest firms generally appear to be far less efficient innovators than smaller rivals, and they do not employ the best innovative talent.

Perhaps these results should not surprise us. Quite apart from X-inefficiency, monopolies have a vested interest in *existing* products and processes. It is the new up-and-coming firm which stands to gain most from introducing fresh methods and products.

Having cast doubt upon both the Marxian and Schumpeterian analyses we cannot, unfortunately, reach any firm conclusion about the probable effect of monopolies on long-term growth. Their larger profits may be reinvested to fuel faster expansion. But their vested interest in the *status quo*, their attempts to frustrate the entry of would-be competitors, and their insulation from the stimulus of competition pull in the opposite direction. Such an indecisive conclusion is unsatisfactory but more evidence is needed before we can be more definite.

> **Activity.** If (as was discovered in Pakistan) MNC subsidiaries exercise more monopoly power than locally owned firms, how might this affect the impact of monopoly on domestic economic growth?

A summing-up

Taking the discussion overall, what can we say about the net balance of the static, distributional and dynamic effects of monopoly?

As regards static effects, we reached the negative conclusion that, in general, the costs of monopoly were likely to outweigh the benefits (although there could be situations in which the opposite was true). Secondly, we concluded that monopoly would reduce distributional efficiency but were, thirdly, unable to reach any firm conclusion about the impact of monopoly on economic growth. Taking the analysis as a whole, however, it seems reasonable to conclude that, in general, the disadvantages of monopoly outweigh the advantages.

This conclusion is reinforced by a further consideration, where economics merges into politics. Many monopolies command large resources which will be deployed to further the objectives of the firm – objectives which are unlikely to coincide with social priorities. The economic power possessed by a large firm will influence the development of new technology, the tastes of the consuming public, the creation of jobs, the distribution of incomes. Its decisions whether and when to invest will have a sizeable impact on total economic activity, perhaps in ways which pull against the government's preferences.

This economic power is likely to be regarded as especially problematic if it is wielded by MNCs. In such cases, major decisions will not only be taken according to commerical, as distinct from social, criteria; they may also be taken in some other country and clash with the national interest. One of the costs of private foreign investment is loss of control over national resources.

We should, however, resist the temptation to exaggerate the force of monopoly power. We noted earlier (page 262) that there are constraints on the exercise of this power. Some researches in industrial countries suggest that monopoly prices are not usually very far above competitive levels. And although there is a clearly established correlation between industrial concentration and profitability, the coefficient expressing the relationship between these variables is often not large, implying that it takes a big increase in concentration to effect a modest rise in profitability.

One difficulty is that most evaluations of monopoly compare it with the perfectly competitive model. Perfect competition is not, however, a practical alternative in most cases. It would be preferable to compare monopoly with the outcome of 'workable competition' (page 251) but that concept is too loose to lead to predictable results. So by contrasting monopoly with an impractical ideal we tend to overstate its disadvantages.

Despite this qualification, however, we may conclude that *there are good grounds for believing that monopoly usually has socially undesirable effects. It is therefore a proper object of public concern and of government policy.* The stage is thus set for a consideration of alternative policy approaches to this problem.

Activity. This would be a good point at which to review your understanding of the above analysis of the costs and benefits of monopoly. Is it possible to identify any evidence on the effects of monopoly in your own country? If so, is it consistent with the conclusion just stated?

The political economy of anti-monopoly

In proceeding to consider measures that governments can take against concentrations of monopoly power we should not underestimate the political barriers that may exist against effective action. A number of powerful interests will have a stake in monopoly: most obviously the owners and managers, but also the workers and their trade unions, who are also liable to benefit from monopoly power. Monopolies have the resources with which to offer bribes and other inducements so as to ensure a 'sympathetic' hearing from government ministers and officials. The situation is, of course, worse if these vested interests are also strong within the ruling party, clique or military council. In Pakistan, for example, it was found that (White, 1974, pp. 155–6):

> The leading industrial families and groups were not passive recipients of the benefits of government policies. A number of them had an active hand in formulating and even administering these policies. A number of the family members were ministers in the central government and ambassadors abroad at various times. They were frequently appointed by the government as members of special committees to study problems and recommend policies concerning industrial matters ... The manufacturing interests ... were generally able to control the field on crucial questions like the duties and taxes that would affect the internal terms of trade for agricultural and manufactured products ...

Even in the absence of this type of political influence, the growing tendency for governments to take a part-ownership in industrial ventures makes them more sympathetic to claims for protection against competition, and more reluctant to act against the market power of concerns of which they themselves are part-owners.

The prospects of effective anti-monopoly measures are further dimmed by the weakness of political advantage to be derived from them. An explanation of why the USA has strong anti-trust laws is that protection of the small man against the big has been a continuous thread of concern in American politics. There are votes to be won by taking an anti-trust stance in America but the same is generally not true in developing countries, where electorates are rarely allowed meaningful votes anyway, and where there is unlikely to be much public awareness of the extent and effects of monopoly.

We should not be too pessimistic, however. Monopoly is one of the few issues that unites the political right and left. The right dislike it because it undermines the virtues of a free-enterprise economy; the left dislike it because of its adverse effects on income distribution and the diffusion of economic power. Perhaps Pakistan is, after all, an encouraging case. Despite the political power of the leading industrial families, that country has enacted fairly strong anti-monopoly legislation.

We will, therefore, proceed on the assumption that monopoly is seen as having socially undesirable effects and that those interested in maintaining monopolistic privileges are not strong enough to prevent the adoption of anti-trust measures.

> **Key concept.** In US terminology, a trust is a firm (or group of firms) exercising monopoly power. **Anti-trust** therefore refers to measures designed to prevent or limit the emergence of monopolies. 'Anti-trust' will be used below as shorthand for anti-monopoly measures.

V. Alternative Policy Responses

Principles of policy: rules versus pragmatism

There is a standing controversy in the literature about whether the best way of handling monopoly is to create a set of legislative *rules* outlawing certain types of monopolistic structure (such as the formation of cartels) or whether it is preferable to take a more pragmatic view by creating certain *discretionary powers* to be exercised only after a practice has been established contrary to the public interest. In general, the rules approach focuses on structural variables of the type presented in Table 10.1. For example, it

could be decreed that it is illegal for any company (or cartel) to command more than a certain percentage of the total market. The pragmatic approach, by contrast, focuses more on behavioural variables, seeking to establish whether or not the consequences of a certain market situation are against the public interest.

The best-known example of a country that has adopted a rules approach is the USA. There, for example, a famous Supreme Court judgement laid it down that:

> A combination formed for the purpose and with the effect of raising, depressing, fixing, pegging or stabilising the price of a commodity in interstate commerce is illegal *per se.*

Most other governments have been more pragmatic, passing laws and creating institutions which must establish the net effects of a monopolistic practice before deciding whether to take action against it. A developing country following this type of approach is Pakistan, whose legislation will be described shortly.

> **Activity.** Has your own country enacted anti-trust legislation? If so, does it follow a 'rules' or 'pragmatic' approach? Summarize the provisions of the law.

From our earlier analysis of the costs and benefits of monopoly, it is fairly obvious that, in principle, a pragmatic approach is to be preferred. Indeed, once it is acknowledged that a monopoly might confer net benefits upon society, a blanket ban on monopolies is ruled out as an optimal policy response. This is particularly so in LDCs, where economies of scale are likely to bulk especially large. It would seem essential to undertake case-by-case evaluations of the net balance of costs and benefits before deciding whether state action is socially desirable.

This point is reinforced by the second-best considerations introduced in Chapter 1 (see pages 18–20). Second-best theory shows that in the real world of many market imperfections, we can have no confidence that applying some universal rule will always bring increases in social welfare. On the contrary, it points to the desirability of careful, case-by-case study in order to determine the best policy response to a given problem. So logic seems firmly in favour of a pragmatic response to the monopoly problem. But, as is so often the case, logic does not end the argument. There are, in fact, major doubts about whether the pragmatic approach provides a superior *practical* substitute for the enactment of general anti-trust prohibitions.

There are a number of difficulties. First, case-by-case evaluation requires the public interest to be defined in a meaningfully precise way. How else can public officials determine whether such-and-such ought to be stopped? But we saw in Chapter 1 (pages 9 and 27) that it is probably impossible to give the public interest any precise definition. Secondly there are enormous difficulties in the way of measuring the costs and benefits of a market practice with any accuracy. It may be possible to obtain a measurement of economies of scale but how do we establish the impact on X-efficiency, or on technological progress, or on the size distribution of income? And how do we sum these effects into a single figure of net cost or benefit? Attempts to make such calculations will involve substantial manpower and informational costs but are likely to produce only inconclusive results.

Such, at least, has been the experience in Britain, a country which has pursued pragmatic anti-trust policies but where one authority has concluded (Oliver and Webster, 1977, pp. 259–60):

> In the United Kingdom any decision involves the weighing of advantages and disadvantages which may not be subject to accurate measurement, against a criterion of public interest which is not always clear. In addition the factual information ... has to be used to provide a basis for predictions about what could happen if the agreement or monopoly were removed. How can predictions be made when an unrestricted industry has not operated for many years? ... it is clear that the British solution involves inconsistencies over time as the variables are weighed in a different way.

Moreover, the difficulties and costs of a pragmatic approach will likely be greater in developing-country conditions. Precise information will be harder to get; the government will have less expertise available to it and this expertise will have a higher opportunity-cost; there may be fewer social sanctions against corruption, so decisions may be influenced by bribes rather than by the merits of the case. Providing public authorities with discretionary powers may have the further disadvantage of deciding difficult cases on political grounds, whereas a set of legislative rules is administered by the courts, which will help to keep decisions out of the political arena. Rules also evade difficult decisions about the public interest; the question becomes whether a certain action is within the law, notwithstanding its broader social effects.

An obvious conclusion at this point, then, is that there is no chance of an optimal policy response to the monopoly problem. Both the rules and the pragmatic approaches are subject to severe difficulties, so the most we can hope for is a solution which is practical and offers reasonable prospects, on balance, of bringing improvement.

One possible approach would make use of the distinction emerging at a number of points in this chapter, between the effects of a single-plant monopoly and of monopolistic collusion between a group of nominally independent firms. The basis of this distinction is that most scale economies are technical and relate to the productive capacity of the plant. There is little evidence of net organizational economies resulting from the creation of large multi-plant conglomerates.

Given these facts, it seems sensible to try to prevent the emergence of multi-plant monopolistic structures by acting against the creation of mergers of large firms, of cartels and of other collusive restrictions of competition. This has been the main thrust of US efforts in recent years, where it has been found much more difficult to dismantle monopolies once established than to nip them in the bud by forbidding mergers, cartels and the like.

Single-plant monopolies, with their superior ability to achieve scale economies, are a tougher problem for the policy-maker because of the trade-off they present between the avoidance of industrial concentration and the advantages of large-scale production. In such cases it does not seem advisable to legislate a general rule to the effect that no single firm should command more than, say, a third of the market. A case-by-case approach seems unavoidable in these cases.

To sum up, the following might provide a sensible set of policy principles

(1) *Prevention is better than correction.* It is easier and more effective to act against the formation of collusive agreements and monopolies than to break them up once formed.

(2) *Some types of monopolistic action are most appropriately dealt with by the application of laws forbidding or restraining them.* Multi-plant mergers, cartels and collusive agreements between oligopolistic firms are cases in point.

(3) *Single-plant monopolies are best dealt with pragmatically*, through investigation by some quasi-judicial body. This should have discretionary powers to break up or regulate monopolies, which may only be used, however, when it has been shown that a monopoly has been contrary to the public interest.

These principles do not, of course, dispose of all the

difficulties mentioned earlier. To repeat, there is no possibility of an optimal response. One of their advantages, however, is that they would limit the number of cases that would need investigation in detail and would thus concentrate scarce expertise on a restricted number of the most difficult cases.

> **Activity.** Write a note analysing what you think are the chief weaknesses of the three principles just set out. On balance, do you accept them; could you suggest ways in which they could be improved; could you suggest any alternative principles?

Implementing the principles

The principles suggested above are a blend of the rules and pragmatic approaches and we have to consider how they might be put into practice. Instead of trying the impossible task of designing a blueprint applicable to all countries, it is better to provide some clues by describing how other countries have gone about these tasks.

The *USA* has probably taken the rules approach further than any other major country. Laws exist prohibiting or restraining take-overs, mergers, cartels, price discrimination, and a variety of other practices liable to reduce competition. Public prosecutions under these laws are initiated either by the Antitrust Division of the Deparatment (i.e. Ministry) of Justice or by a Federal Trade Commission. Since these are prosecutions under the ordinary laws of the land, they are handled by normal judicial processes through regularly appointed courts, with rights of appeal going up to the Supreme Court.

In *Britain*, where the general approach to the problem is more pragmatic, there are two principal institutions concerned with the implementation of anti-trust legislation. First, there is a Monopolies and Mergers Commission. This reviews the practices of 'dominant' firms (i.e. firms having at least a one-third share of the market) and of potentially collusive oligopolies; it also investigates the desirability of planned mergers between firms. The commission is not powerful, since it cannot initiate investigations, nor does it have legal powers to enforce its findings.

Secondly, there is a Registrar of Restrictive Practices, whose task is to maintain a record of all restrictive practices (whose definition has been widened to include resale price maintenance, and information agreements among oligopolists) and to bring prosecutions before a specially created but judicial Restrictive Practices Court. In these cases

there is a presumption that a restrictive practice is against the public interest. However, the law defines a variety of defences by which a practice may be justified, so the administration of the law consists essentially of a case-by-case study of the pros and cons of the practice under examination.

We may also mention the example of *Pakistan*, whose legislation was clearly influenced by the British model but is by no means a carbon copy of it. Pakistan's anti-trust legislation created a Monopoly Control Authority (MCA) charged with the responsibility of maintaining a register of companies and practices which may come within the purview of the law, and of investigating these to see whether they are in the public interest. The MCA has jurisdiction over situations of 'undue economic power', having the right to investigate single-firm monopolies, groups of companies controlling more than 20 per cent of a market and mergers that would create monopoly power. It also has power over 'unreasonably restrictive trade practices' which include price-fixing, market-sharing and resale price maintenance.

Although the presumption in Pakistan is that monopoly power and restrictive practices are contrary to the general interest, it is open to defendants to justify themselves on the grounds that their practices yield superior efficiency, technological progress or the promotion of exports. In these cases, they have to show that the beneficial results cannot be obtained by means less restrictive of competition and that benefits more than outweigh costs. Unlike the British Monopolies Commission, the MCA has powers to enforce its decisions, for example by ordering the dissolution of an offending company or changes in its ownership.

There is no clear consensus about the effectiveness of these countries' efforts. Pakistan's MCA only started work in 1972 and it is too early to form a judgement about its impact. It is known to have experienced difficulties in securing the intentions of the law; but the fact that it exists, has powers of investigation and can attract publicity on the news media is believed to have exerted a restraining influence over those who possess monopoly power.

Although US anti-trust legislation dates back to 1890, the argument can also be made for this country that it is too early to pass judgement on its efficacy! Despite the long history, a variety of circumstances prevented the active implementation of anti-trust measures until after the Second World War. Even now, the legal processes involved are enormously lengthy. Some observers are optimistic about the effectiveness of the US legislation, others more sceptical. There seems to be some agreement, both in the USA and Britain, that anti-trust measures can have a strong impact in the prevention of mergers and take-overs, and in inhibiting various forms of restrictive practice. British legislation has, for example, virtually put an end to formal resale price maintenance. But the law has found it much more difficult to cope with the problems created by giant, single-firm monopolies, and tight-knit oligopolies dominated by a small number of major concerns. And businessmen have not been slow to forge informal 'gentlemen's agreements' to replace more openly collusive arrangements.

It will probably never be possible to form a definitive judgement because, in order to evaluate the potency of anti-trust, we need to compare its results with what would have existed without the legislation. That we can never do because it is probable that the mere existence of anti-trust laws has deterred some restraints of competition (just as the absence of anti-trust laws in many LDCs encourages monopolistic practices). What the case materials do show, however, is that there is a wide range of legal forms a country may adopt, depending on its intentions and circumstances. One area which particularly merits the concern of LDC governments and is not adequately dealt with in most industrial country legislation, is the desirability of enacting safeguards against restrictions imposed by MNCs on their subsidiaries in such matters as export policy and the purchase of supplies. This type of restraint is particularly likely to be against the interests of the 'host' country.

The centrality of technology and protection

Recall from page 256 the statement that 'the extent of monopoly power is determined by the size of the domestic market, techniques of production and industrial protection'. That suggests, of course, that if we want policies to go to the root of the problem they have to address themselves to these three factors.

Unfortunately, there is little that can be done about the size of the domestic market except in the long run. By and large, the size of this is determined by the stage of development and the distribution of income. The stage of development is a given because even in the most dynamic economies development is a long-term process. The distribution of income may be more amenable to medium-term policy manipulation (see Chapter 6) but the difficulty is that policies to reduce income inequalities are likely to *narrow* the market for manufactured consumer goods. This is because these goods generally have large income elasticities of demand, with the rich spending proportionately more of their incomes on them than the poor.

Redistributing income from the rich to the poor will thus shift the composition of demand away from manufactures, at least in the medium term. For present purposes, then, it seems sensible to treat the enlargement of the domestic market as a goal not amenable to medium-term policy manipulation.

That leaves us with technology and protection as the two other sources of monopoly power. Fortunately, both are easier to influence by policy. Economies of scale have emerged in this chapter as the major potential benefit to be derived from industrial monopoly but we have argued that the existence of such economies is a function of LDC dependence on western technologies. *The development of more appropriate industrial technologies, efficient at small volumes of production, would weaken the natural tendency towards monopoly and lessen the difficulties of dealing with monopolies which already exist.* Since MNCs usually possess technological advantages, the development of efficient techniques appropriate for indigenous businesses would help reduce dependence on foreign expertise and any concentrations of monopoly power possessed by MNCs.

Technology policy, albeit agricultural technology, receives extensive coverage in Chapter 9 and it would be repetitive to go over the same ground here. Having thus noted the central importance of technology policy as a means of dealing with monopoly, we will leave it there. The reader is invited to refresh his memory on the treatment of this topic in Chapter 9. Additional references, relating specially to industrial techniques, are given at the end of this chapter.

> **Activity.** Since Chapter 9 relates to agriculture, a possible exercise would be for students to write an essay outlining ways in which the discussion there would need to be modified to deal with the industrial case.

Coming now to industrial protection policy, we enter another large controversy whose boundaries lie well outside the confines of the monopoly issue. Although we cannot go into them here, various arguments have been presented in favour of protecting manufacturing in developing countries. The best known of these is the 'infant industry' case, which argues in favour of temporary protection until the 'infants' have learned to stand on their own feet, become internationally competitive and no longer need state support. Another influential set of arguments is that industry should be protected because it is penalized by a failure of market prices to reflect social values (especially a tendency for money wage rates to exceed the opportunity cost of labour – see page 35) and because industry generates external benefits not reflected in its selling prices.

It is not necessary here to go into the question whether manufacturing in general merits protection. There would presumably be little quarrel with the principle that the benefits derived from protection should bear some reasonable relation to the costs it imposes on the consumer and the efficiency of the productive system. There will be disagreements as to what the ceiling is, but we could all agree that there is *some* cost which it would not be worth paying for the benefits of enhanced industrialization. What level of protection might be economically justified varies from case to case but Little, *et al.* (1970, pp. 158–9) suggest that an average for all industries of 20 per cent would be the maximum justifiable, with 50 per cent as the upper limit for any single industry. This upper limit for the average of 20 per cent can be compared with the figures on page 260 showing an unweighted average for six developing countries of 72 per cent. It seems likely that consumers in many developing countries are paying an unduly high price for industrialization.

More pertinent to the monopoly issue, however, is the formulation of protection policies that would avoid domestic exploitation of monopoly power created by protection. Protection allows domestic producers to charge above international prices and these higher prices may be attributable to any of the following reasons:

(1) The domestic producer, however hard he tries, cannot get his costs down to internationally competitive levels. In the language of international trade theory, this would be a case of comparative disadvantage. In the language used when analysing the economic effects of monopoly, it would be a case of allocative inefficiency.
(2) Prices are above internationally competitive levels because of X-inefficiency, i.e. avoidably high costs. Because of protection, the domestic producer can permit high costs and inefficient management while still making a profit.
(3) Prices are above internationally competitive levels because the domestic producer is exploiting his monopoly power to obtain extra-normal profits.

Of these, only (1) can provide an economic justification of protection. To the extent that government protection results in X-inefficiency or monopoly profits, it should be eliminated. This would leave comparative disadvantage as the only admissible

economic argument for protection. In this case, the question is whether the costs of the protection needed can be justified by the expected benefits.

Since it seems likely that many countries offer excessive protection, resulting in X-inefficiency and/or monopoly profits, the general policy conclusion is a recommendation for governments to overhaul their protective systems to ensure that only socially justifiable levels of protection are provided. While carrying out such an overhaul, they should also consider the point that budget subsidies can be designed to afford the same degree of protection as a tariff or quota but will not result in any rise in price to the consumer. There will thus be no loss of consumers surplus of the type illustrated in Figure 10.5. The burden falls on the general taxpayer, whereas a tariff imposes a loss on consumers which contributes nothing to domestic output.

The disadvantage of changing to budget subsidies as an instrument of protection is its cost to government revenues, although there are a variety of ways of minimizing this burden. And the burden at least has the positive aspect that governments are likely to be more discriminating in the protection they provide if it creates a claim on the budget. High-protection countries would be less common if the burden of protection fell on the government's budget rather than on the general consumer.

It would be a logical extension of a shift to less protection to try to negotiate a free trade area or customs union with neighbouring countries (like the Latin American Free Trade Area or the European Economic Community). The arguments in favour of regional integration among developing countries are strong and wide-ranging. In particular, the creation of such groupings can greatly increase the size of the market for industrial goods, lessening the trade-off between scale economies and competition, and increasing competition within the region. Whether the political conditions yet exist for the meaningful economic integration of major groupings of LDCs must, however, remain doubtful for some time.

Licensing and nationalization

To a greater or lesser degree, all governments possess licensing powers which could be used to provide safeguards against monopoly power. *Import quotas*, although they reduce competition from the rest of the world, could be administered so as to encourage the spread of competition within the domestic economy, by giving newcomers preference over large established firms in the allocation of foreign exchange. Similarly, it is customary in most countries to require new investors to obtain an *industrial licence* before they may proceed with their projects. Here, too, the system could be used to foster competition, for example by giving preference to the creation of new firms over the expansion of those already in existence. India is a country whose government has sought to use its licensing powers to discriminate against large concerns. There, small firms are subject to fewer licensing restrictions and certain activities are reserved exclusively for small-scale production.

More often than not, however, licensing laws are administered without reference to monopoly (an aspect of the general neglect mentioned at the beginning of this chapter). In some cases they actually encourage it. This is most common with import licensing. Licensing authorities generally make foreign exchange allocations on the basis of firms' historical import needs, which has the effect of favouring the *status quo*, with new firms finding it more difficult to obtain enough foreign exchange. Industrial licensing can also be used to discourage competition, as it was in Ghana, where the authorities were anxious to ensure that no more plants were established than could be justified by the existing size of the market.

Activity. Does your government operate a system of industrial licensing? If so, look for public statements on the criteria according to which licences will be granted. Do they include any reference to the avoidance of monopoly or encouragement of competition?

Another way of protecting the consumer against exploitation by monopolies is through the use of price *controls*. In principle, these can be used to keep prices down to competitive levels, thus suppressing the consequences of industrial concentration. The practice is a different matter, however. Control prices are invariably established on a cost-plus basis, with producers permitted to charge a price which covers their full cost plus a 'reasonable' rate of return. Such an approach offers little protection against X-inefficiency. The monopolist may allow his costs to rise (or dress profits up in the form of costs) in the knowledge that the price controllers are unlikely to have sufficient information to be able to challenge the reported cost levels. Price controls create other problems too, as we saw in Chapter 7 (see page 179), and it would be unwise to pin strong hopes on this instrument.

Another potentially important anti-trust instrument is the use of *nationalization:* the (usually compulsory) acquisition by the state of industries formerly privately owned. As we will see in the next chapter, LDC governments have made extensive use of nationalization during the last two decades, although mostly against foreign-owned concerns.[13]

As an anti-monopoly device, nationalization has most commonly been employed in the context of public utilities such as power, transport and telecommunications. These are generally regarded as natural monopolies best operated in the general interest by bringing them under public ownership. Not all countries have followed this course, however. The USA provides an exception, where most public utilities are still privately owned but controlled by specially-created regulatory bodies with powers over pricing and production. As with price controls, such bodies have found it difficult to deal with the problem of X-inefficiency, concentrating on the avoidance of extra-normal profits but less well equipped to hold costs down to minimum feasible levels.

Nationalization is, then, a serious anti-trust policy option. But public enterprises have their own problems and the next chapter is taken up with some of these. It seems preferable, therefore, to defer judgement on the merits of public ownership until you have studied the next chapter.

Suggestions for Revision and Group Discussions

1 Review your understanding of the following:
   (a) The distinction between structural and behavioural market variables.
   (b) Normal and super-normal profits.
   (c) Oligopoly.
   (d) Workable competition.
   (e) Monopoly power.
   (f) Industrial concentration.
   (g) Economies of scale (increasing returns to scale).
   (h) Natural monopolies.
   (i) Cartels.
   (j) Allocative efficiency and X-efficiency.
   (k) A multinational corporation.
   (l) The distinction between the rules approach and the pragmatic approach to anti-trust policy.
2 Explain the statement that control over market conditions is the hallmark of monopoly.

---

[13] An apparent exception to this was an announcement by the Pakistan government early in 1972 that it had 'nationalized' thirty-one large firms in heavy industries. This was a misnomer, however, because the firms remained under their original ownership. The government confined itself to appointing its own managers to run these companies.

3 Describe the conditions that will affect the ability of a cartel to provide its members with monopoly profits.

4 Discuss the meaning and limitations of a hybrid index of industrial concentration as a measure of the degree of monopoly. In what ways will the index be affected by the level of protection against competition from imports?

5 Would you expect to find a greater or lesser incidence of industrial monopoly in India than in, say, Liberia, or Burma, or Honduras? Justify your answer.

6 Describe in your own words the relationship between the use of western industrial technologies and the incidence of monopoly in developing countries.

7 It is stated on page 257 that most important scale economies are technological and that there is little evidence for the existence of net organizational economies of scale. In what ways would the policy conclusions of this chapter need to be modified if there were large net organizational economies?

8 According to the quote from Vernon on page 261 MNCs 'appear mostly in industries dominated by comparatively large firms and characterised by high entry barriers ...' Do you see any contradiction between this and the conclusion on page 261 that it is difficult to generalize about the impact of MNCs on competition in developing countries?

9 To obtain a fuller understanding of the dynamic effects of monopoly, write a review of the book by Merhav detailed in the bibliography. Pay particular attention to the assumptions underlying his analysis.

10 What policy conclusion would you draw from empirical findings that profitability is positively correlated with the level of industrial protection?

11 What problems does X-inefficiency create for the regulation of monopolies in the public interest?

12 Roger Opie has argued that monopoly policy 'becomes important and valuable only in conditions of full employment. There is little point in getting excited about a possible misallocation of resources if resources are unemployed on a national scale anyway' (in Kaser and Portes, 1971, p. 212). Consider and discuss this statement

carefully. You may find it helpful to bear in mind the three forms of economic efficiency discussed in Chapter 1, especially as summarized on page 17.

Suggestions for Further Reading

(Full publication details of the following recommendations are given in the bibliography at the end of the book.)

There is no satisfactory general treatment of the monopoly problem in developing countries; further study of this subject therefore involves consulting a variety of sources. For the theoretical foundations, see the suggestions made on page 249 and in footnote 1. You should also see Rowley, 1972, especially the essay in it by Comanor and Leibenstein.

The Marxian critique of monopoly capitalism is usefully summarized in Freedman, 1961; Merhav, 1969, applies a similar critique to conditions in developing countries. Schumpeter's views are presented in Part II of his *Capitalism, Socialism and Democracy* (1947); Galbraith, 1967, provides a more modern presentation of a somewhat similar viewpoint.

As regards developing country materials, Bain, 1966, provides comparisons between India and several industrial countries. For Pakistani materials see White, 1974; Khilji, 1975; Sharwani, 1976; and Amjad, 1977. The Kenyan materials are in two articles by House, 1973 and 1976.

On the various aspects of policy, Sharp, 1973, ch. 5, provides a useful summary of British policy experiences. Lipsey and Steiner, 1975 ch. 18, include a brief but authoritative account of American experiences. On protection policy, see Bergsman, 1974; and Little, Scitovsky and Scott, 1970, especially ch. 4 and 5. References on technology policy are given at the end of ch. 9 but for discussions relating more to industrial matters see Stewart, 1977; the essays by Stewart and Khan in Edwards, 1974; and essays by Marsden and 'the Sussex Group' in Jolly, *et al.*, 1973.

See also the additional references given in the footnotes to this chapter.

11 The performance of public enterprise

'The great thing is indeed that
the muddled state too is one of
the sharpest realities . . .' *Henry James*

Contents

I. Introduction

The spread of public enterprise

Direct participation by the state in production has an ancient history and has played an important role in countries now highly industrialized. It was also an important feature of the colonial histories of many recently independent states. Nevertheless, the recent spread of public enterprise (abbreviated to PE hereafter) is one of the most fundamental changes occurring both in the industrial west and in developing countries.

One feature of the spread of PE has been the extensive use since the mid-1950s of the policy weapon of *nationalization:* the acquisition by the state, if necessary by compulsion, of property formerly owned by private interests. In developing countries, nationalization has generally been concentrated on foreign-owned concerns, and it has been estimated that between 1956 and 1972 forty LDCs used this weapon to take over assets worth $10 billion, or about a quarter of the total value of foreign investment in those countries at the end of 1972 (Williams, 1975). Over this period the number of acts of nationalization increased, with an average of only about three a year in 1956–59 rising to fourteen a year in 1969–72, and with the value of assets involved more than doubling over the same years.

These state acquisitions have, moreover, been amplified by government initiatives to set up new publicly owned enterprises where none existed before.

Table 11.1
The Growth of Public Enterprise in India

	1951	1956	1961	1966	1973
No. of enterprises	5	21	42	74	113
Cumulative investments in these (Rs. crores*)	29	81	956	2 415	5 571
No. of employees (thousands)	n.a.	n.a.	185	471	805
Employees as % of private modern sector employment	n.a.	n.a.	15	19	36

Source: *Statistical Outline of India*, 1975, Tata Services, Bombay, 1974.
Note: * A crore is 10 million rupees, equal at end–1976 to roughly US $1·1 million.

India is a case in point. She has made little use of nationalization (assets nationalised in 1956–72 were only equal to about 3 per cent of the value of foreign investments there) and yet has a large and growing PE sector, as indicated in Table 11.1.

Data on South Korea – another country which has made limited use of nationalization – reveal a similar story, with the number of PEs rising from 36 in 1960 to 104 in 1973, and with a roughly $3\frac{1}{2}$-fold increase in the real output of public enterprises during 1963–72 (Jones, 1975). In the absence of comparable figures for other developing countries we cannot assess how representative these cases are, but they are important and there is no doubt that a growing PE sector is typical of a large number of LDCs.

The most universally occurring PEs run public utilities of various kinds. The provision of electricity, piped water, postal and telecommunication services, and railway services is almost everywhere entrusted to state-owned bodies. Agricultural marketing boards are also common; so are general-purpose development corporations and investment banks. Enterprises directly involved in the production of commodities are only a little less prevalent: state manufacturing and mining concerns, state farms. These typically have some form of semi-autonomous status in law (but not necessarily in practice). The British concept of the public corporation has been widely adopted. This type of organization has an independent legal status in the sense that it can sue and be sued, is supposed to be autonomous in the everyday conduct of its business, but is accountable to a minister and, through him, to the general public. Many nationalized and other PEs, however, have the legal status of joint-stock (or limited liability) companies, like most private firms, even though they are government-owned. A smaller number of PEs are run directly as central government departments – as is often the case with postal services – or by local government bodies.

What is generally called the mixed enterprise is another category which deserves special mention. It is increasingly common for governments to enter into partnership arrangements with private (usually foreign) investors in which ownership is divided between the two partners, with the private investor providing the management. Often, but not always, the government will take a formally controlling share of 51 per cent or more.

> **Key concept.** Most public enterprises are either **public corporations** (which have independent legal status but are answerable to parliament through a minister), or **joint-stock companies** (like most private enterprises), or are **government departments** (integrated into the regular civil service). Although they usually take the legal form of joint-stock companies, **mixed enterprises** (with ownership shared between the state and a private partner who provides managerial services) deserve separate mention because they are becoming increasingly common.

Whether these differences in legal form matter is a question we will take up later. What is clear is that the expansion of public enterprises in the economy means that the efficiency with which they conduct their affairs is of much importance to overall economic performance. It is with this question of PE performance that this chapter is concerned and by choosing this topic we step into an arena hot with public controversy. Many people strongly advocate more public ownership as essential to further economic progress. But at least as many others see public ownership as synonymous with inefficiency and the waste of public resources.

Judgements about efficiency presuppose agreed criteria by which performance may be gauged. The success of an enterprise should be assessed by its ability to do the job it was created to do, and this requires us to ask about the reasons for creating PEs in the first place. The next step, then, is to survey the arguments most commonly advanced by politicians and economists in favour of public ownership, so as to be in a better position to decide the criteria relevant to the assessment of PE performance.

> **Activity.** Try to assemble data for a table similar to Table 11.1 for your own country, showing the current importance of the public sector and trends over time. If such data are not available, draw up a list of all the major PEs and use this to make a qualitative assessment of their importance in the economy.

II. Arguments and Pressures for Public Ownership

For this purpose it is convenient, if rather arbitrary, to group the arguments under three headings: (1) ideological and political, (2) developmental, and (3) a miscellaneous group of other arguments.

Ideological and political reasons

Most people would regard public enterprise as a means to achieve specified ends: as a policy instrument rather than as an objective. Nevertheless, a strong influence on the rapid expansion of the state sector has been a socialist ideology in which public ownership of the means of production has at least some of the attributes of being an end in itself, an ultimate goal. Many socialists have difficulty in deciding whether public ownership is best regarded as a means or an end, but the thorough-going Marxist would dismiss the distinction as a meaningless one – public ownership is an essential ingredient of his conception of a socialist society.

Ideology has thus provided the rationale for the near-complete public ownership of the means of production in centrally planned countries such as the Soviet Union, China, Cuba and Vietnam, and has been achieved by means of extensive nationalization. A weaker, but still influential, ideological thrust can be observed in LDC mixed economies ruled by non-revolutionary socialists. The growth of Indian public enterprise illustrated in Table 11.1 can, for example, be directly related to various industrial policy resolutions of the Congress Party;[1] similar influences have been strong in countries as far apart as Tanzania, Guinea, Burma and Egypt. Very often in this type of country socialist theory has been strongly reinforced by economic nationalism, by a desire to reduce dependence on private foreign capital and to ensure that the 'commanding heights' of economic activity are under domestic control.

In mixed-economy LDCs, nationalization has thus been largely confined to the state acquisition of foreign-owned concerns, with indigenous capital left largely undisturbed in private hands. A socialist strategy in this type of economy looks for a gradual socialization of production through a public sector growing more rapidly than private capitalism – capitalism is not to be expropriated but is to be outpaced. So there is an important difference between revolutionary and reformist solutions. To the revolutionary solution, based upon the wholesale nationalization of both foreign and local capital, the subsequent performance of PEs is not so crucial to the achievement of the ideological objective; the economy has already been socialized. But PE performance is of critical importance to the reformist solution, which depends upon the public sector being more dynamic, being able to surpass the expansion of local capitalism.

The important influence of socialist and nationalist philosophies should not leave the impression that this has been the sole, or even the most important, influence on the growth of PE. It is probably true to say that, outside the communist countries, most PEs have been created in response to pragmatic, non-ideological considerations, rather than as part of a strategy of socialization. Indeed, in countries like Japan and Turkey state participation was designed as a stimulant to private investment, and Japanese PEs were subsequently sold off to the private sector. South Korea is another essentially capitalist country which has nonetheless made extensive use of PE as a pragmatic response to felt problems. Public ownership can be part of a capitalist strategy too!

It would also be a mistake to think of ideology as being the only important way in which politics affects the growth of the public sector. There is another set of political arguments, not at all philosophical and rarely given much public ventilation, which has also been influential. Politicians frequently favour PE because they see it as a source of political power: giving them the ability to place friends and supporters in jobs or to provide them with contracts; giving the appearance of determined action and providing the publicity attached to the opening of a new project; perhaps opening up new illicit sources of income for themselves and their parties. It is impossible to measure the influence of this type of consideration but there are too many known examples to dismiss it as trivial. There are also cases in which industries have been brought under public ownership on grounds of state security. The manufacture of armaments is an obvious case in point.

---

[1] See Bhagwati and Desai, 1970, for an account of ideological influences on the expansion of the Indian PE sector.

Developmental arguments

Not many would dispute that the public sector has a major role to play in the development process, in providing or augmenting the infrastructural basis of economic growth. Economic development will expand the needs for electrical power and treated water, for transport and communications, for improved marketing and distribution systems. If these needs are not met development will be frustrated, and most would agree that in a mixed economy it is primarily the responsibility of the state to meet these needs. Thus, most controversy about the role of PEs in development centres around the extent to which the state should become involved in directly productive activities, such as manufacturing, mining and farming.

A variety of arguments have been made in favour of directly productive state participation, which can be summarized as follows. First PE has been seen as a device for *raising aggregate saving and investment*, and thus as mobilizing greater resources for development. This can be achieved in a number of ways. We can consider as one of the features of capitalism that a substantial part of the national product accrues in the form of property incomes, a good deal of which are either consumed by the well-to-do or remitted abroad by foreigners. Either way, these incomes are not available for reinvestment in the future expansion of the economy, whereas they could all be reinvested if they were to accrue in the public sector. Even if PEs turned out to be less efficient and profitable than their private equivalents, there is still liable to be a net increase in the volume of investment.[2] We should note, though, that, as it relates to the nationalization of existing assets, this argument is only strong when these assets are confiscated without payment of compensation. For otherwise the incomes generated by the compensation payments will themselves be a leakage into the consumption of the rich, or abroad, comparable in magnitude to pre-nationalization property incomes.

A rather different way in which state participation might raise the volume of investment is where there exist an *entrepreneurial gap* which can be filled by PEs. In many societies there is a limited supply of indigenous entrepreneurial ability. Because of the small size of the domestic economy, or for other reasons, foreign investors may be reluctant to fill this vacuum; even if foreign investors are willing, the government may be reluctant to accept the high degree of dependence on foreign capital which would result. Thus, the argument runs, there is little

alternative but for the state itself to fill this gap by setting up PEs.

This need is likely to be especially acute when the government is trying to develop heavy industry, for this involves large risks and massive investments. At an early stage of development heavy industry is unlikely to be attractive to private investors. This has been another contributory factor to the growth of the PE sector in India, for a large proportion of investments in that sector have occurred in the steel and engineering industries. As at March 1973, 66 per cent of total investments in PEs in India were concentrated in the steel (33 per cent), engineering and chemical industries. The task of the state, then, is to use its fiscal powers and its ability to attract international aid to muster resources and to venture in where private investors hold back. (These arguments about using PEs in order to raise investment ratios, it might be added, fit very well with a reformist-socialist strategy of achieving a socialization of production by having the public sector growing more rapidly than the private.)

To these arguments about the quantity of investment can be added another, that PEs can be used to *accelerate technological progress*. To some extent, this follows from the expectation that PEs will lead to a higher investment ratio: since much technological change is embodied in new capital formation (see Chapter 9), more investment is likely to result in accelerated technological change. However, the case can be made broader by suggesting that the managements of PEs will be less likely to share the capital-intensity biases of multinational investors and can, in any case, be instructed to search for, and develop, more appropriate technologies than would otherwise be used. Moreover, there will be no case for industrial secrets within the PE sector and this openness will encourage the more rapid diffusion of improved techniques.

Yet another argument can be added by suggesting that an enlarged PE sector can *improve the composition of investment*. Because a larger proportion of total investment will be under the direct control of the government, it should be easier to ensure that new capital formation occurs in the sectors with the highest development priorities, rather than in the manufacture of luxury consumer goods.

---

[2] Bronfenbrenner (1955) develops a simple model showing how nationalization can significantly raise the development investment ratio, and thus future incomes, even though he makes generous allowance for possible lower efficiency in PEs. However, his model is based upon the confiscation of private property, without payment of compensation, whereas compensation has been paid in most postwar acts of nationalization outside the centrally planned economies.

PE investment can also be used to promote regional development, through industrial location policies and the creation of special agencies charged with the development of a particular area. The creation of river valley authorities is an illustration of this use of PE which has been tried in a number of developing countries. These have generally been modelled on the American Tennessee Valley Authority, a multi-purpose agency set up in 1933 to conserve and develop an area of about 66,000 square kilometres (about the same area as Guatemala, Benin or South Korea) and generally regarded as having been highly successful.

A final developmental argument is that a large and growing public sector will increase the amenability of the national economy to effective *development planning*. It is difficult to effectively include the private sector in the planning process, and unanticipated actions by the private sector can undermine the targets of a development plan. So the larger the share of economic activity that occurs within the public sector the easier it should be to plan for the whole economy.

These, then, are the chief developmental arguments commonly made in favour of public ownership. They can, moreover, be reinforced by *historical examples* in which PE has played a crucial role in national economic development. The Soviet Union provides one of these, of course, but the difficulty with this case is that it is impossible to disentangle the direct contribution of public ownership from the many other changes that occurred in Soviet economic life and policies after the 1917 revolution. We know that the economy has achieved impressive growth since the revolution – a growth combined with a relatively equal distribution of income and the absence of large-scale unemployment – but we cannot tell what results might be obtained from copying only some features of post-revolutionary policies without adopting the rest. We should also bear in mind that in 1917 the Russian economy was very much larger and wealthier than almost all today's developing countries, again raising the question whether the Soviet experience could be easily transplanted into LDC conditions. In these respects, the Cuban experience has not been encouraging, for the Castro government has so far failed in its attempts to achieve accelerated growth.[3]

Within an entirely different social context, Japan provides an earlier example of how PE can be used to plant the seeds of modernization. Especially after the Meiji restoration in 1868, but even before that, the state established a large number of industrial concerns – in textiles, cement, mining, chemicals, machine tools and a host of other industries – which most historians agree had an important impact on subsequent industrialization. They were created from a mixture of motives: to provide jobs for unemployed members of the military class, to protect the balance of payments, and to introduce modern western technology to backward industries. Although at their peak PEs only accounted for about 10 per cent of factory employment, they were nevertheless of great importance in heavy industry, and an authority on Japan's economic history has asserted that 'there was scarcely any important Japanese industry of the Western type during the later decades of the nineteenth century which did not owe its establishment to State initiative'.[4] Most of these state industries were eventually sold to private investors and one of the features of the Japanese case is that PE was not seen as an alternative to private enterprise but as a stimulant. There was, in fact, a particularly close degree of co-operation between government and private enterprise after the Meiji restoration.

South Korea provides a more recent illustration. According to Jones (1975, pp. 202–3):

> Public enterprises clearly constituted a leading sector during the period of rapid Korean growth. The evidence supporting this conclusion may be briefly recapitulated as follows.
> (1) From 1963 to 1972 the sector grew at a real average annual rate of 14·5 per cent, while the whole economy grew at 9·5 per cent and the non-agricultural economy at 12·2 per cent . . .
> (2) During the same period, the sector absorbed roughly 30 per cent of the economy's investment, and performed more than 40 per cent of all financial intermediation . . .
> (3) The sector as a whole has extremely high forward linkages, but modest backward linkages relative to the entire non-agricultural economy. Much of the growth during the period, however, came from 'new' industries which had very high linkages in both directions . . .

Other arguments for public enterprise

We come now to a miscellaneous collection of 'other' arguments, which it is convenient to place under three headings: (1) arguments for protecting consumers; (2) arguments for protecting employment; (3) arguments for improving the distribution of income.

Protecting the consumer

A large share of the output of state enterprises takes

---

[3] On the Cuban case see the essay by Dudley Seers in Chenery, *et al.*, 1974.
[4] Allen, 1962, p. 24. The interested reader should also consult ch. IV of Hirschmeier, 1964.

the form of *public goods* of the types described in Chapter 1 (see page 22). Since the case in favour of state intervention to protect the consumer against the market neglect of public wants has already been outlined there, it will not be repeated here. This is a widely accepted argument in favour of PE and an important one, virtually necessitating a large role for the state in mixed economies.

A desire to protect consumers from *monopolistic exploitation* provides another motive for PE. First, there are the natural monopolies considered in Chapter 10 (see page 253). These most commonly occur in the provision of public utilities – power, telecommunications, transport – but in the small economies of many LDCs they exist also in manufacturing. We have already mentioned the developmental case for placing public utilities in the public sector. Thus, the developmental and consumer-protection cases seem to coincide on this point, except that the two motives conflict when it comes to pricing policies. Even where a private monopoly is not a 'natural' one, in the sense defined in Chapter 10, nationalization provides one of the means the state can employ to protect the consumer against excessive prices and to safeguard against undesirable concentrations of private economic power.

Protecting employment

Some PEs are set up principally to protect or create employment. One common sequence is for a private concern to run into financial difficulties and for the state to take it over to protect the jobs that would be lost if it were to close down. This has been called the 'lame duck' argument for PE. An example of this type, which we will refer to again, was the decision by the Government of Ghana to nationalize a number of gold mines rather than see 15 000 miners thrown out of work. There are other cases where PEs have been established specifically to create new jobs. The Japanese example has already been cited; Ghana provides another, where a Workers Brigade was established to provide productive jobs for the unemployed. In other cases, the employment-creation motive shows up in the deliberate over-manning of PEs ostensibly established for other motives.

Improving the distribution of income

Nationalization and the creation of PEs can be used to improve the distribution of income in a number of circumstances: (1) where PE can be expected to provide an important item of low-income

consumption at a lower cost than a private concern; (2) where large agricultural estates being farmed by capital-intensive methods are taken over for collective cultivation by large numbers of landless people; (3) where PEs can reduce the element of monopoly profit in the distribution of the national income.

Rather obviously, the effectiveness of nationalization to reduce inequality will greatly depend upon whether compensation is paid to the former owners and how much they receive. There are cases where compensation has seemed excessively generous. In the case of foreign investments, the government is likely to come under strong international pressure to pay full compensation, against the threat of a withdrawal of aid and the discouragement of further private investments. In fact, compensation was paid on about two-thirds of the foreign assets nationalized in mixed-economy LDCs in 1956–72 (Williams, 1975).

Quite apart from compensation, there is also the danger that the benefits of PE may be concentrated on small privileged groups, such as the managements and workers of the enterprises, rather than on the generality of the poor. For example, the distributional effects of the nationalization of Ghana's gold mines were ambiguous: it protected the jobs of several thousand mine workers, but at a heavy cost to the Ghanaian taxpayer who typically earns only a small income.

This completes our review of the main arguments for PE. Of course, the motivation for the creation of any particular PE will vary from case to case. It is therefore impossible to generalize about the relative importance of the various arguments outlined above. The main purpose of this survey has been to clarify the criteria by which the performance of PEs can be assessed. Thus armed, we turn now to survey PE performance.

Activity. This would be an appropriate point at which to review your understanding of the arguments summarized above and to consider the implications they have for the criteria to be used in assessing PE performance. Do you think any important arguments have been left out?

III. Assessing the Efficiency of Public Enterprise

The problem of conflicting objectives

Expressed in its most general form, the purpose of public enterprise might be described by the instructions, 'promote the public interest' or, a little more precisely, 'maximize net social benefits'. The trouble is that such generalities are so lacking in content as to be little more than slogans. It was suggested in Chapter 1 (page 9) that concepts like 'the public interest' are not very useful, but we run into major problems when we try to be more precise about PE objectives. What is clear from Part II is that there are a number of different motives for public ownership and therefore a variety of tests that might be applied in appraising their performance.

More serious still, there are liable to be severe tensions between some of the objectives. We saw that the principal developmental argument for PE was that it would raise the quantity of saving and investment. This implies that prices will be set high enough to permit substantial profits to be earned. But we also saw that a desire to protect consumers against high prices was another important motive. Take another example. Both the developmental and the consumer-protection cases require that PEs operate efficiently, in the sense of keeping costs down; but the party-political motives, which value PEs for the patronage and publicity they generate, and which thus tend to be grandiose, are likely to result in high-cost projects. Or again, the over-manning of PEs in the name of employment creation clearly conflicts both with the desire for profitability and cost-efficiency.

Of course, these trade-offs could be resolved if governments were willing to be precise and consistent in the priorities they attach to the various objectives. But governments are rarely willing or able to meet that condition, as was shown in the first two chapters. So a problem is signalled: the absence of agreed criteria for assessing the efficiency of PEs; the absence even of agreement that they are primarily to be judged on *economic* grounds. Nevertheless, it is convenient for the time being to proceed *as if* PEs should be tested by economic criteria, returning later to take up non-economic considerations.

Activity. Find out what you can about the reasons given by the government for the creation of PEs in your own country. Can you identify any potential conflicts between these reasons?

The profitability test

In private and public sectors alike, an enterprise's profitability is the most widely used indicator of efficiency. For an enterprise selling in competitive conditions, its ability to earn profits proves a measure of its market strength, its ability to keep down costs.

Profitability will also affect the amount of investment, for much industrial investment is financed out of reinvested profits, and hence the contribution of the firm to the overall growth of the economy. Since much new technology is embodied in capital equipment, the profitable firm is also more likely to be an innovator, an agent of technological progress. We have seen that much of the developmental case for PE is based on this type of consideration.

But while profitability has these virtues as an efficiency criterion, it also has major drawbacks when applied to PEs. First, it is only a reasonable indicator of cost-efficiency when the enterprise is selling on competitive markets, whereas many state enterprises are monopolies or large in relation to the markets they sell on. For instance, at the beginning of the 1960s, PEs in India had 100 per cent monopolies in the shipbuilding, penicillin, aircraft, newsprint, telephones and cable industries, and were powerfully represented in other industries with large monopoly concentrations (Bain, 1966, pp. 110–11). Similarly, Jones (1975, p. 190) noted that Korean PEs overwhelmingly sell in highly imperfect markets.

PEs may also be given special treatment in the allocation of import licences, government contracts and so on, which again would undermine the significance of their profitability. On the other side of the coin, the profitability test tacitly accepts the economist's model of the firm as a profit-maximizer, or at least as giving profit a high priority in the pecking order of its objectives. But it has already been shown that PEs are liable to be given other objectives which may conflict with commercial profit maximization.

In any case, the developmental argument that PEs can earn surpluses for reinvestment and innovation should not be overrated. It accepts too readily the premise that development is a function of the rate of investment and pays insufficient attention to the importance of the *productivity* of new investment. Investment by PEs will not promote growth if it is in ill-conceived projects. The developmental argument also overlooks the danger that PE surpluses may be appropriated by the government as a general source of revenue and be spent for non-developmental purposes. In other words, we should not take for granted that the public sector has a higher marginal propensity to save than private capitalists. Lastly, *current* profitability may be a poor guide to the long-term developmental contribution of a project, because temporary factors may distort profitability (in either direction) and because the project may generate external costs and benefits which do not show up in profit-and-loss accounts. The state enterprises of Meiji Japan, which were described earlier as having played an important role in building a modern industrial sector, were complete failures by the profit criterion and a considerable drain on government revenues.

Clearly, then, profitability is a most imperfect guide to PE performance. Yet it remains the almost universally applied test and this fact requires us to take it seriously. For if the general public, government ministers and enterprise managers all accept this as the most pertinent yardstick, it is more likely that enterprises will be allowed to operate in a profit-maximizing manner and their success or failure by this criterion will have a strong impact on management morale.

What, then, is the observed record on the profitability of PEs in developing countries? Generally poor. The most comprehensive study available, although it is now out of date, took a sample of sixty-four government-owned corporations in twenty-six developing countries, using data for each relating to an average of seven years (Gantt and Dutto, 1968). The authors used what they called the flow of funds as their basic measure of performance, which was defined as the difference between current enterprise revenues and current expenditures (i.e. before depreciation and new investment). This was expressed as a percentage of 'activity', defined as the means of the value of current revenues plus current expenditures.* They then compared the flow of funds with gross investment by the corporations to measure the extent to which they had been able to finance their own investment. The results are summarized in Table 11.2.

Table 11.2
The Financial Performance of Public Corporations

	Flow of funds*	Deficit after gross investment*
Europe	0·7	−80·0
Latin America	2·1	−56·3
Africa	19·5	−61·1
Asia	16·4	−74·8
All countries	8·0	−66·3

Source: Gantt and Dutto, 1968, Table 8.
Note: *These figures are expressed as a percentage of 'activity', as defined in the text.

What we see is that most corporations only barely managed to earn surpluses on current account, averaging only 8 per cent of activity, although the African and Asian enterprises did better. The net result of this low level of profitability was that most

corporations could cover only a small proportion of their capital needs, leaving a large overall deficit to be financed externally. In fact, the flow of funds was only sufficient to cover about a third of replacement investment (although the African and Asian corporations again had a better achievement), leaving nothing at all to finance net *additions* to fixed capital. Almost 90 per cent of total investment needs had to be financed externally; much of this came from the parent governments and represented a significant burden on budget revenues.

A variety of country examples can be cited to reinforce the results just summarized and to suggest that the problem remains a real one.[5] In India, directly productive PEs made large overall losses in 1971–3; enterprises rendering services showed a surplus, however; and all PEs taken together averaged a total annual surplus of Rs 2·25 crores, against a total public investment in 1972 of Rs 5052 crores – a return of 0·04 per cent (Rs 1 crore = $1·25 million). In Ghana state enterprises made large losses throughout the 1960s, although there was an improving trend during the latter part of the decade. Nigerian development corporations similarly invested in many unprofitable subsidiaries and their record has been described as 'hardly short of disastrous'. A government study of public corporations in Tanzania showed that in 1969–73 net cumulative losses were equivalent to 91 per cent of their capital. Performance in Korea was better but, even so, gross PE savings were only sufficient to finance 37 per cent of gross PE investment in 1963–73. Of course, there were some profit-earning enterprises in each of these countries but when the results are consolidated, the overall financial position is weak.

Alternative criteria
Technical efficiency

Given the various disadvantages of relying on the profitability test, we should supplement this by applying other standards. One supplementary line of approach is to employ various tests of technical

---

* Expressed algebraically, let f = flow of funds, r = current revenue, x = current expenditures, then f is given by:

$$f = 2\left(\frac{r-x}{r+x}\right)$$

---

[5] The sources consulted for the following examples included. Bhagwati and Desai, 1970 (India); Killick, 1978, ch. 9 (Ghana); Jones, 1975 (Korea); C. R. Frank in Ranis, 1971 (Nigeria); and *The Standard* (Nairobi) 14 December 1976 (Tanzania).

efficiency. These generally rely on the comparative use of ratios of inputs to output, or on measures of productivity. Examples of this type of test include the following:

(1) Comparisons of ratios of material inputs to output, used to assess the efficiency with which an enterprise is utilizing its raw materials.
(2) Comparisons of gross output per man employed, or per unit of capital employed. An alternative, and generally preferable, test is to use value-added instead of gross output, i.e. gross output less the cost of material and service inputs. Either test provides a measure of gross labour or capital productivity.
(3) Comparisons of the extent of capacity utilization, taken as a proxy for the productivity of capital and as a test of management calibre.
(4) Comparisons of average unit costs, used as a test of cost-efficiency.
(5) Comparisons of the efficiency with which firms earn or save foreign exchange, usually expressed in terms of the cost of domestic resources used per unit of foreign exchange earned or saved.

These criteria of technical efficiency are certainly relevant to our task, partly because they are likely to be correlated with profitability and partly because the development and consumer-protection arguments for PE imply a need for these types of efficiency. They can all be used to make comparisons between firms and to observe trends over time.

It is, unfortunately, impossible to present any general results for PEs in developing countries because researchers have not yet attempted international comparisons of these types of variable. By way of illustration, therefore, the results of a study of Ghana are summarized below (taken from Killick, 1978, ch. 9).

First, *value-added per man*. In 1969–70 this measure of productivity was found in state manufacturing enterprises to average only 55 per cent of the comparable level in the private sector. This was an aggregated result for all manufacturing, but the same picture emerged when the study was confined only to those industries in which there were both state and private concerns. A similar finding was discovered in the gold mining industry, with labour productivity high and rising in the private mine and lower and falling in state mines. The record of state farms was even worse, with average output per man only about a fifth of that achieved on private smallholdings; it was said in fact, that state farm workers and their families consumed practically all they produced, leaving little surplus output to be marketed.

Secondly, *capacity utilization*. Industrial capacity utilization was generally low in Ghana in the 1960s but especially so in PEs. It was estimated for 1963–4, for example, that actual output was only 29 per cent of rated capacity. Conditions were particularly bad then and probably improved later but the study being summarized provides many examples of continuing gross under-utilization, implying low productivities of capital and, probably, weak managements.

Thirdly, *unit production costs*. The evidence here is not strong but unit labour costs were higher in state manufacturing concerns than in the private sector and this probably resulted in higher overall unit costs. Unit costs in state gold mines were well over three times as great as on the private mine, although this is a somewhat unfair comparison because the private mine was milling richer ore. Unit costs on state farms were far in excess of those on peasant smallholdings.

Finally, *efficiency of foreign exchange saving*. A study of the domestic resource costs of earning or saving a unit of foreign exchange found Ghanaian PEs to be generally inefficient, although not more so than the manufacturing sector taken as a whole. About 43 per cent of Ghanaian manufacturing earned or saved foreign exchange only at an excessively high domestic cost and a further 24 per cent were net losers of foreign exchange. Most of the state gold-mines were reasonably efficient foreign exchange earners (although much less so than the private mine), except for one of the largest which was actually a net foreign exchange loser.

Technologies employed

Moving from these measures of technical efficiency, it is also pertinent to enquire into the technologies employed by PEs, for we saw that proponents of PE have argued that it can be used to accelerate technological progress and to develop more appropriate technologies. Unfortunately, there is little hard information on this aspect of PE performance. There are, however, a number of impressionistic grounds for doubting whether PEs have fulfilled their promise in this area. First, the generally poor financial record shown above is liable to have inhibited their rate of innovation. Secondly, that PEs are commonly frustrated by bureaucratic red tape from diversifying by product-innovations is one of the most frequenty recurring complaints of those who have written on this subject. Thirdly, that PEs tend to be too grandiose and to have a bias towards capital-intensity is another common complaint and implies that they have not utilized more appropriate technologies, as defined in Chapter 9. The Ghana study provides a number of illustrations of this point and Jones (1975, p. 124) found Korean PEs to have an average capital–labour ratio about three times as great as the non-agricultural private sector.

Development planning

As a last test, we can ask whether experience with PEs has justified the claim that they are easier to bring within the framework of national development planning than their counterparts in the private sector. Although there is no definitive evidence, it does seem likely that PEs have been more amenable to national planning than private firms, but that the extent of their integration into planning has left much to be desired. Development plans are often hazy about the future of the PE sector and even about their past record. It is equally commonplace to find PEs without meaningful medium-term plans, or with plans covering a different period from the national plan. In the Ghana case, it proved extremely difficult for the planners to obtain the statistics they needed from state enterprises and to establish sufficiently good communications with PE managements for their intentions to be integrated into the national plan. One difficulty in this connection is that most PEs have semi-autonomous legal status and thus cannot simply be treated in the manner of government departments.

Summing-up on performance

Multiple policy objectives call for multiple performance criteria and this creates the possibility that an enterprise may do poorly by some tests but well by others. If, for example, it is government policy to hold down the price of an enterprise's product, that enterprise is unlikely to be profitable but may achieve high technical efficiency. This possibility of conflicting performance indicators practically rules out any overall generalization about PE performance in developing countries. The Ghanaian case was rather exceptional in this respect because in that country most indicators pointed in the same direction. It was possible to conclude that study (Killick, 1978, p. 227):

> In the end, it has proved harder to use a single criterion of comparative economic performance, which is analytically satisfying and amenable to empirical testing, than it has been to characterise the general standard of economic performance of Ghana's public sector. Despite measurement problems, the spotty nature of the evidence and substantial variations between specific enterprises, it may fairly be concluded that the comparative performance of the public sector was poor in the sixties.

However, the Ghanaian experience was an especially negative one and by no means all country studies have come to such negative conclusions. PE performance in Turkey, for instance, has been given a fairly high rating[6] and Jones concluded his study of Korean PE with the judgement that (pp. 205–6):

> I believe that by world standards for public enterprise the Korean sector does extremely well. At the crudest levels, this follows from the fact that when an economy is growing at a real rate of 10 per cent annually, a sector which takes 30 per cent of investment cannot be using its resources too inefficiently. At a less aggregate level, it is simply not possible to find in Korea any prolonged examples of the sorts of egregious inefficiency which characterise many public enterprise sectors ... It is, however, widely believed that Korean public enterprises are less cost-efficient than their private counterparts. I would certainly agree with this view, but would also ague strongly that the public/private gap is much smaller in Korea than in most LDCs.

Nevertheless and as Jones implies, it is a good deal easier to find examples of negative conclusions than positive ones. Thus Bhagwati and Desai's study of the Indian case (1970, p. 167) concluded that, 'The overall dissatisfaction with the public sector's performance so far is ... not entirely unjustified; and the prospects for its future performance are fairly dim ...' Similarly, Gantt and Dutto's study of financial performance quoted earlier ends by pointing out that (1968, p. 128):

> the simple fact that subsidies from the central government budget are widespread and may represent a not inconsiderable proportion of government expenditures is sufficient to raise the question of the social opportunity costs of continuing to subsidise government-owned corporations.

So while it would be wrong to issue a blanket condemnation of PEs as inefficient, complaints of poor economic results are sufficiently numerous and important to justify treating sub-standard performance as a common problem. The next step, therefore, is to investigate some of the more serious causes of this. Although this discussion will again be illustrated mainly by Ghanaian and Korean experiences, studies of other countries throw up broadly similar explanations of poor PE performance, so that the forces at work in Ghana and

---

[6] See the essay by Land and the comment by Rockwell in Ranis, 1971.

Korea may fairly be taken as typical of many other countries.[7]

Activity. Can you discover any study of PE performance in your own country? If so, compare its results with those summarized above. If not, a suggested class assignment would be to undertake an analysis of the annual reports of leading PEs for the purpose of gauging their performance. Rockley, 1972 especially ch. 7, provides an excellent introduction to the evaluative interpretation of financial statements. (See also the suggested extension of this exercise on page 290.)

IV. Causes of Poor Performance

Inadequate project planning

So far as newly created PEs are concerned, the care with which they are initially planned will obviously have an important bearing on subsequent performance, and one of the burdens under which many PEs struggle is that they were poorly planned. A variety of weaknesses have been observed. Some enterprises are set up without any prior feasibility study; in such cases it is largely a matter of luck whether the project has any prospect of subsequent success. In most cases, though, some feasibility study is undertaken but often of poor quality. Scarcely less frequently, the study is undertaken by people who have a strong interest in making sure that the study shows the project to be a 'good' one. This is most notoriously the case with feasibility studies undertaken by firms who will build the project, or provide supplies for it, if it is undertaken. That consultants should have no financial interest in the outcome of their investigations seems an elementary safeguard but it is rarely applied and governments have been amazingly willing to entrust project studies to those who stand to gain from producing a favourable report. This is partly because the associated ministries or development corporations tend themselves to be interested parties, identifying themselves with 'their' projects and only too happy to uncritically accept positive feasibility reports.

A further type of planning weakness which has been widely observed is a tendency for project designs to be grandiose and biased towards capital-intensity. Capacities are built in excess of any realistic estimate of the size of the market; lavish staff housing is provided; the latest, most expensive equipment is imported. The effect is to create projects burdened with large capital costs, whose technologies are inappropriate to the economies they serve, and which provide few jobs.

They may also be poorly located. The siting of a factory may be more powerfully influenced by where a certain minister or general comes from than by economic considerations. A sugar factory may be placed where sugar will grow only poorly or a glass factory may have to ship its output many kilometres over rough roads to reach its principal market, suffering large losses through breakage. More defensibly, the government may decide that industry should be spread throughout the country rather than being concentrated in a few industrial centres – possibly a desirable social policy but one liable to impose large economic handicaps on projects. A case in point was the decision by the Indian government that a government-owned fertilizer plant should be set up in each state.

Even well-designed and suitably located projects that have been found viable after disinterested appraisals are liable to suffer from another frequently occurring defect: a chronic tendency for the actual cost of plant and equipment to be far above the original estimates used in the evaluation. A common cause of this, apart from the obvious one of inflation, is that the construction period turns out to be longer than anticipated, pushing up costs and deferring the time when the project begins to earn revenues. Even more frequently, the escalation of costs is due to over-optimism in the original estimates, either unconscious or deliberate.

Finance and manpower

PE managements commonly complain that they are hamstrung by shortages of funds, that they cannot afford the investments they would like to undertake and even that they do not have enough working capital to keep their enterprises operating efficiently on a day-to-day basis. There were several instances of this in Ghana, the most severe being the state gold-mines, whose managing director spent much of his time dashing between his headquarters and the Ministry of Finance, several hours drive away, trying to raise enough money to pay current bills so that supplies of fuel, explosives and other materials would not dry up. A corporation in such dire straits clearly cannot run its operations efficiently.

But the question arises whether shortages of funds

---

[7] See the references in note 5 and also Shirokov, 1973, ch. 2. Similar sources of difficulty continue to be experienced even in the Soviet economy – see Nove, 1973, ch. 3, and 1977, ch. 4.

are not as much a symptom of inefficiency as they are a cause of it. First, there is the tendency referred to a moment ago for many projects to be over-designed, capital-intensive. This tendency can burden an enterprise with large interest and loan repayment obligations and keep enterprises short of liquid resources. Shortages of working capital (to finance inventories of materials, work-in-progress and finished products, to facilitate the provision of trade credit, to meet unexpected commitments and to maintain adequate bank balances) are probably the most commonly occurring financial constraints in PEs. These may arise because working capital needs are underestimated at the planning stage, but they most commonly occur because the projects are not profitable and because their losses absorb the funds needed for efficient day-to-day operation. You will recall the results summarized in Table 11.2 (page 284) and the finding that public corporations are generally dependent on outside sources to finance most of their gross investment needs. This is in contrast with private firms, who maintain their working capital, and finance much of their fixed investment, out of reinvested profits.

There are also PEs whose balance sheets show large current assets but who nevertheless find themselves short of funds because much of this is locked up in excessively large inventories. Indian data suggest, for example, that public industrial concerns typically hold unsold inventories of final products equal to nearly a year's total output.[8] This is another case where it is probably more sensible to think of the resulting lack of liquidity more as a symptom of poor performance (unsaleable products or poor marketing) than as a cause of it.

But once this situation becomes established, it results in a vicious circle. Poor financial results lead to shortages of funds and these shortages cause results to deteriorate even further. Management and worker morale suffers. Frequent requests for public subsidies undermine the government's confidence in the enterprise and make it more inclined to meddle in day-to-day management, which usually makes matters even worse.

Shortages of skilled workers, especially of managerial skills, can provide another aggravation. It is, after all, a characteristic of most LDCs that they have too few experienced skilled workers and this affects PEs no less than other producers – more so if they cannot afford, or are not allowed, to offer competitive salaries. Shortages of engineering and other technical skills have adverse consequences for the efficiency of many public concerns, but that their managements are of poor calibre is an even more frequent complaint.

Quite apart from a general shortage of managerial skills, there are some circumstances peculiar to PEs which accentuate the problem. It is, for instance, not uncommon for senior managers to be appointed from the ranks of the regular civil service. Jones (1975, p. 179) quotes a study of the social backgrounds of PE executives which found that nearly half had been appointed from the regular civil service or from the armed forces. He notes that critics of Korean PE consider this appointment system to represent a political retirement programme, which saddles enterprises with managements untrained in business skills. Rather obviously, the qualities that make a good soldier or civil servant are different from the qualities of a good manager, who needs not only to be an administrator but also an incisive decision-maker, an aggressive innovator, a willing risk-taker. Sometimes managers are appointed as a reward for their services to the ruling political party or to some powerful minister; in these cases their qualifications for the job are liable to be especially dubious. Even when managers are recruited on the open market, ideological or bureaucratic reluctance to pay high salaries may prevent PEs from offering terms good enough to attract good-quality applicants.

The employment of management agents from overseas offers an escape from domestic shortages of skill. When they are carefully selected on thoroughly prepared contractual terms, such agents can provide sound managements, who can also provide training to local people to take over in the future. But nationalistic considerations often stand in the way of such a solution. In any case, by no means all expatriate managers are interested in training others to take their places and they are sometimes recruited under contractual terms which give them little incentive for maximum effort. The Ghana study cites as a typical example an agreement with a foreign firm to provide a management team for a glass factory. The agents were paid a fixed percentage of total sales, irrespective of the number of personnel they supplied, and there was no firm provision for the training of Ghanaian counterparts. While the agreement gave the agents an incentive to maximize sales, it did not link rewards to cost reductions or profitability. Recourse to expatriates offers no assurance of improved performance unless sensible terms are agreed with reputable agencies.

But at the very time when they are suffering from these shortages of skilled manpower, PEs are often

---

[8] Bhagwati and Desai, 1970, p. 167, show inventories averaging just under twelve months' output held by Indian public industrial concerns in 1960–6, with a few enterprises holding unsold stocks equal to up to three years' output.

under pressure to carry a larger number of unskilled or semi-skilled workers than they need. This raises costs (especially when the enterprises are forced by government also to pay above-average wages to their unskilled workers) and is also liable to have adverse effects on industrial relations, thus compounding the difficulties. The Ghanaian, Korean and Indian cases all provide examples of this situation. PE workforces are often bottom-heavy: too many labourers, too few skills.

The operating environment

An unfavourable economic environment is another common source of poor performance. There are two aspects to this: (1) general economic conditions which tell against efficiency in both the public and private sectors; and (2) difficulties peculiar to PEs, arising from their relationships with the civil service.

As regards the general economic environment, many LDC economies are prone to recurring balance of payments crises, domestic inflation, and unpredictable variations in the levels of investment and economic activity. Such an environment, with all its uncertainties, makes it difficult for managements to plan ahead. These problems are often compounded by frequent changes in governments, or their policies, which add further elements of uncertainty. So managements find themselves forced to operate almost on a month-by-month basis, with meaningful medium-term planning almost impossible.

Maladministration of exchange control systems also creates headaches for managements (see Chapter 8). Civil service delays in processing licence applications, the unpredictable and often arbitrary size of foreign exchange allocations, their occasional inadequacy even to meet current requirements for imported materials and spare parts, and delays between the issuance of licences and actual receipt of the imports – all these factors operate powerfully against economic efficiency throughout the economy and result in below-capacity levels of operation. It might be thought that the public sector would be given specially favourable treatment in this regard but the evidence suggests the contrary.

One of the special features of a PE is that it is accountable to the general public through Parliament (assuming there is one). This means in practice that most PEs are answerable to a minister for the general conduct of their business, and they will therefore depend in some degree upon his department's officials. While it is desirable that PEs should be publicly accountable, the resulting dependence on the civil service puts further obstacles in the way of efficiency. First, because a minister is

typically in charge of any one department for only two or three years, he cannot be expected to achieve a thorough familiarity with all the PEs which report to his ministry. He therefore relies on the advice of his officials who, for reasons already given, may not have the training or temperament to understand the complex demands of running a business. Secondly, civil service procedures are usually slow moving, whereas many business decisions have to be made quickly to take advantage of some new opportunity or to meet a crisis. Managements may thus suffer the frustrations of seeing opportunities slip away while they await a ruling from their ministry.

A third and related point concerns the inappropriateness of government budgetary procedures for business purposes. We have seen that many PEs depend on government financial support. They therefore have to conform to budgetary routines, but these can be very time-consuming and may have unsatisfactory outcomes because Treasury officials do not understand the needs of the enterprise. Even when adequate sums are voted in the budget, the management may still experience delays in getting the money released – delays that can make all the difference between profit and loss. To quote the Korean example again, Jones (1975, p. 178) noted that:

> In practice the [government] control structure allows lower-level bureaucrats to exercise control for the sake of control, rather than to insure achievement of goals dictated by intervention motives. The result is inflexibility arising from being locked into a year-old budget in a dynamic environment. This in turn produces the many unintended deviations which are at the root of public enterprise inefficiency.

The trivialization of political control

The reference in the above quotation to 'control for the sake of control' brings us to the troubled relationships which often exist between the government and its PEs. The general principle laid down in the statutes of most PEs is that they should be accountable to the government on overall policy but that they should enjoy autonomy in their day-to-day operations. This rather sharp distinction between policy and everyday management creates difficulties, for management practices may have strong policy implications, and general policies have to be translated into everday implementation. It is not surprising, therefore, that a major comparative study of state enterprise concluded that, 'The most important of the many problems with which every country under study struggles, mostly with indifferent success, is that of the proper balance of managerial autonomy and political responsibility' (Friedmann and Garner, 1970, p. 335). Even if everyone did their best to strike a good balance between these competing claims, it would be a difficult thing to achieve.

How much more difficult, then, when governments and their ministers do not even try? The experience in a wide variety of countries, developing and industrial, is that governments have shown little eagerness to provide unambiguous statements of their PE policy objectives. In consequence, they have rarely given clear guidance to management on what the main lines of policy should be. They have also been reluctant to formally commit themselves in such matters, preferring that such guidance as they do give should be off-the-record 'lunch table directives' (for which, of course, they cannot be held accountable in Parliament).

But this reluctance to specify policy has rarely been matched by an equal reticence when it comes to everyday management. An official report on Ghana's state gold-mines gave expression to a point that could be extended to enterprises in many other countries:

> Governments have made poor use of their control over the policies of the SGMC. In principle, governments should exercise overall control over the general lines of policy of public corporations and leave the corporations free to take the day-to-day decisions necessary to implement these policies. In the case of the SGMC it has been the other way round: a good deal of detailed interference and very little by way of general policy guidance.

Enterprise managements find themselves told who they should hire; they find their disciplinary procedures shortcircuited by (usually off-the-record) ministerial directives; they find themselves subject to detailed treasury control over minor spending decisions; they are told to whom they must award contracts and to whom they must extend credit. Some state airlines have even been under ministerial instructions as to which ladies they must employ as air hostesses, for reasons best left to the imagination.

Not all PEs are equally vulnerable to this type of detailed intervention. To some extent it will depend on their financial viability and on whether they are regarded as successful. The popular, financially independent concern is likely to suffer less from detailed intervention; the less successful loss-makers, dependent on government subventions, will be most vulnerable – and this will further lessen their chances of achieving financial strength.

So, while there are exceptions, the general experience is what can be called a *trivialization of*

political control – a general disinterest by ministers in policy combined with frequent, often ill-judged and sometimes self-seeking, interferences with everyday operations. The potentially damaging effect of this on PE performance needs no elaborating and the importance of this factor has led a number of observers to place upon it most of the blame for substandard PE performance. Thus, a comparative study of Ghana, Nigeria and Uganda found PEs in the latter to have a superior record because they had not at that time been a politicized as they had in the west African countries (Frank, op. cit., p. 117). It concluded that the 'political milieu' was far the most important determinant of efficiency.

Activity. If you undertook the exercise suggested on page 287, you could now extend it by examining the causes of any substandard performance you found, using the points presented above for guidance.

Since substandard performance is frequent among public concerns, what might be done to improve the situation, given the causes summarized in this section? One answer to this question would be to urge that the sources of weakness should be corrected: project planning should be improved, manpower constraints removed, the operating environment should be reformed to aid greater efficiency, politicians should attend more to the determination of broad policies and avoid detailed interference. But this is mere exhortation – and exhortation is one of the least effective policy instruments.

A more promising approach is to search for an *incentive system* which will provide material and other inducements for PEs to raise their efficiency. Parts V and VI, dealing with policy responses to PE inefficiency, take such an approach and consider alternative incentive systems. Part V takes up the possibilities of improving performance by utilizing the discipline of market forces; Part VI looks at non-market alternatives.

V. Policy Responses: Using Market Disciplines

Solution 1: profit maximization

The most full-blooded market solution would be for governments to instruct their PEs to operate on fully commercial lines and maximize profits. Some objections to such an approach have already been mentioned. PEs might abuse their market powers to exploit consumers and take other socially undesirable actions in pursuit of the largest possible surpluses. There may also be ideological objections from socialists to the idea that PEs should behave as if they were capitalist concerns. However, the Marxist position is that the difference between capitalist and socialist enterprises is not whether they earn surpluses but in who expropriates these and how they are used. In the Soviet Union and eastern European socialist countries, enterprise profitability is used as a performance indicator and as a determinant of the size of incentive bonuses paid to workforces.

The merits of the profit-maximizing solution should not be dismissed out of hand. The pursuit of profits provides a strong incentive to keep down costs; it will generate reinvestible surpluses to raise the pace of growth and innovation in the economy; it provides a more-or-less objective test of performance; and the morale of managements and labour forces is likely to be higher in concerns which achieve profitability.

This solution does, however, have some strong implications. There is the point made earlier that profitability serves as a tolerably good indicator of efficiency only when the enterprise is selling in a competitive market. That consideration immediately raises major problems with regard to natural monopolies such as power generation, water supply, railways and postal services. Because of the essentiality of the commodity they are supplying and the cheapness of the raw material (untreated water), many water supply agencies could earn themselves large profits if they set their prices to do so, but few of us would regard that as desirable. The same is probably true of electricity and postal services.

In general, the profit-maximizing solution would only be appropriate for enterprises actually or potentially operating in competitive markets. This carries the further implication that governments interested in such a policy must be willing to allow PEs to compete with each other, and also to allow private firms to compete fairly with the public sector. Governments would thus have to eschew discriminating in favour of (or against) PEs in matters such as the awarding of government contracts, the granting of import licences and tax waivers. Governments would also have to be willing to allow PEs to diversify their output in response to changing market opportunities. One of the disadvantages under which some PEs labour is that they are saddled with specialization in a product which no longer offers many profit opportunities.

Allowing PEs to diversify is, of course, strongly consonant with a social-democratic strategy of expanding the public sector relative to the private sector. By the same logic, a crisis is likely to arise in the competitive, profit-maximizing solution if PEs prove unable to compete with private enterprise. The crunch comes when the government has to decide whether to allow an inefficient state enterprise to go out of existence because it cannot compete. There are few examples of that being permitted.

A potentially more serious drawback of the profit-maximizing solution concerns the extent to which it might conflict with social objectives for which PEs were established. It is natural to think of PEs as intended to promote the public interest, however that might be defined, but there may be a poor correlation between the public interest and commercial profitability. Discrepancies can arise because of interest conflicts between profitability and the welfare of consumers; because market prices do not reflect true scarcity values in the economy (for reasons mentioned in the appendix to Chapter 2); because of external economies and diseconomies (Chapter 1); and because of the effects of profitability on the distribution of income.

To take up the last point, a PE which is making a profit is, in effect, imposing a tax on its customers equal to the average amount of profit per unit of sales. These customers are unlikely to be a representative cross-section of the whole population. They will be drawn from some groups more than others and the 'tax' they pay will have a differential effect on income distribution – regressive if the item in question is an important low-income consumption good, progressive if it is bought mainly by the rich. But that is not the end of the matter because we also have to ask, what happens to the profits? They may be reinvested by the enterprise, in which case we need to study the distributional effects of its new investments; they may be expropriated by the government and added to general revenues, in which case we would need to study the distributional impact of additional government spending.

A poor correlation between private and social profitability also means that a PE should not be disbanded simply because it cannot earn a commercial surplus. It may generate compensating social benefits not reflected in its cash flow. Thus, a railway may show large financial losses but provide an important social service by linking remote areas with the rest of the country and, by offering access to markets, stimulating rural production. A loss-making PE also has distributional implications because it means that the generality of taxpayers are subsidizing the particular groups who are its customers. Here too the effect could be either progressive or regressive.

One potentially attractive way of reconciling the profit criterion with the maintenance of socially desirable but loss-making services is for the government to provide 'social subsidies' to PEs. British Rail, for example, is required to run certain unprofitable routes which the government regards as socially necessary, and the government pays a subsidy to cover the deficits of these routes. This principle of providing government subsidies to cover the losses of socially desirable services has the advantages of permitting the profit criterion to continue to be employed in the non-subsidized aspects of an enterprise's operations, and of identifying the precise monetary cost of a socially motivated policy. This would facilitate judgements about whether the social benefits were worth the cost involved. It is also more appropriate that the cost of running an activity for social reasons should be borne by the general taxpayer rather than by the users of some other, profitable, activity.

It would, however, be difficult to apply this principle in all cases. It is easy to find out the deficit caused by keeping open a certain railway line; in other cases it would be much less easy to establish the facts. There is a danger that PEs would manipulate their accounts so as to obtain a larger subsidy than would be strictly justified, or that they would allow the costs of the subsidized operations to rise because these would be covered by the government in any case. Governments should state the maximum subsidy they are willing to provide and instruct PEs to maximize profits on their overall operations, thus providing an incentive to keep costs down.

> **Key concept.** According to the **social subsidy principle** PEs are instructed to maximize profits, subject to the continued provision of socially desirable but loss-making operations, for which the government provides a predetermined subsidy from its general revenues.

Summing up on profit-maximizing, we have seen that there are robust practical arguments in favour of this solution. But we have also seen there to be theoretical and practical objections to it. At most, it could only be given limited application and offers no general solution.

Solution 2: a rate-of-return approach

An alternative approach, which retains some of the virtues of the profit-maximization solution but tries to avoid the social abuses it might create, is to instruct PEs to pursue pricing and other policies that will earn some target rate of return on their capital employed. This rate of return should reflect the opportunity cost of capital, i.e. the returns that could be expected from investment elsewhere in the economy, and, therefore, the target rate should be uniform for all PEs. The rate could be specified either in market prices, as a commercial return, or in shadow prices, as a social return (see page 56).

> **Activity.** Write a note sketching the economic objections that could be raised against specifying different target rates of return for different PEs.

When specified in market prices, this solution is open to some of the objections mentioned in the context of profit maximization. Their ability to earn the target rate would not tell us much about the efficiency of natural monopolies. The inability of other PEs to achieve the target because they had been given costly social responsibilities would likewise not necessarily indicate inefficiency, although the payment of a social subsidy could overcome this snag.

In principle, it would be more appropriate to specify the target rate in shadow prices than in commercial terms but this too is open to objection. For one thing, the real-world estimation of shadow prices is a rough-and-ready approximation of the theoretical solutions. The usefulness of these prices is thus not always clear; they can be strongly influenced by subjective considerations and hence be rather arbitrary. There is a loss of objectivity when utilizing shadow prices and a shrewd management may be able to manipulate its social accounting so that its capital appears to yield whatever rate of return its minister might lay down.

Whether specified in shadow or market prices, the rate of return approach is open to the further objection that it includes in the denominator all past investments of an enterprise, whereas what is most important is the return to current and future investments. For instance, some PEs come into existence as 'lame ducks' in distress, taken over from the private sector (see page 282). By virtue of the fact that they got into difficulties, it is probable that their former private managements made some mistaken investments and it may be unreasonable to ask the new public managements to turn these old investments into paying propositions. It could be argued generally for past investment mistakes that these should be written off as 'sunk costs': whether or not these assets pay for themselves does not matter because nothing would be saved by not using them.[9]

---

[9] Glenn Jenkins has pointed out, however, that not all the original investment values should be written off because they have a liquidation value which is part of the resource cost of keeping an enterprise going.

Moreover, PEs would be affected by past investment mistakes in differing degrees, so that it would not be appropriate to try to enforce a uniform return upon each of them.

The alternative is to concentrate on the prospective returns to *new* investments, for which a uniform rate (in combination with social subsidies) might well be feasible. This would still impose a financial discipline on PE managements, giving them incentives to select high-yielding investments and to minimize costs. It would focus particular attention on the importance of maintaining a high standard of present and future decision-making, which might be a more realistic strategy than an alternative which also requires past mistakes somehow to be remedied.

What is usually proposed in this connection is that PE investment decisions should be taken on the basis of cost-benefit analysis, of the type introduced in the appendix to Chapter 2. Always assuming that shadow price estimation is not too difficult or open to manipulation, most economists would argue for the use of social cost-benefit analysis, employing shadow prices instead of market prices. In this solution, then, PEs are instructed to earn some target *social* rate of return on new investments, this rate representing the social opportunity cost of capital.

Solution 3: marginal cost pricing

The two solutions considered so far focus on the return to capital as providing an incentive for economic efficiency. In these solutions, PE managements would set their prices in such a way as either to maximize profits or achieve a target rate of return. A third alternative differs in that it seeks to establish a *pricing* rule which would raise economic efficiency. PE profitability would then be a residual outcome of applying the pricing rule and, as will be shown, the rule could lead either to losses or profits.

Simply stated, the rule is that *PEs should price their output at the marginal cost of producing it*. For shorthand this will be summarized as P = MC. This rule is derived directly from standard price theory. It is presented in most micro-economic textbooks and the reader who wishes to delve more deeply into this topic should consult one of these works (e.g. Samuelson, 1976, ch. 23) because we can do no more here than offer a brief explanation. The essential points are that static economic efficiency, outlined in Chapter 1, requires that, at the margin, the price of each product should be equal to the real resource cost of producing it and that the price should also be equal to the satisfaction derived from it by the purchaser. If price is in excess of marginal cost, the welfare derived from the economy's resources can be increased by

expanding output and lowering price until P = MC. Winch (1971, pp. 104–5) provides a succinct formal statement of the underlying theory:

> The conditions of optimality require the equation of the marginal rate of substitution with the marginal rate of transformation for any two goods. Rational consumers equate the marginal rate of substitution to the price ratio while the marginal rate of transformation emerges in a monetary system as a ratio of marginal costs. If the ratio of the prices of the two goods is equated to the ratio of their marginal costs, the marginal rate of substitution will be equated to the marginal rate of transformation. Clearly this condition will be satisfied if price is everywhere equated to marginal cost.

If this condition is met simultaneously in all markets, it can be shown that the outcome will be 'Pareto-optimal' because it would be impossible to make any consumer better off without making another worse off. Hence it is argued that PEs would contribute to the achievement of this optimality by observing the marginal cost pricing rule.

The apparent simplicity of P = MC is, however, misleading. For one thing, we should not take for granted that enterprises know what their marginal costs are, or even that the concept is a precise one. One can, for example, distinguish between short-run marginal costs (SRMC) and long-run marginal costs (LRMC). It is a distinction with important implications for profitability. SRMC relates to the cost of those inputs – mainly materials and some categories of labour – which need to be increased in order to expand output from a given plant size. Application of P = SRMC would thus confine price to the cost of those variable inputs directly associated with the 'last' unit of output. LRMC, on the other hand, relates to a change in total costs associated with a permanent increase in output, i.e. an *expansion* of plant size. This is a broader concept of cost because, unlike SRMC, it includes provision for overheads and capital costs, both of which will usually go up with a permanent increase in output. So prices with the LRMC rule will be higher than with the SRMC rule; profits in the former case will thus be larger (or losses smaller) than with P = SRMC.

There is also the question, what unit of output should we take in trying to measure MC? Take the case of an electricity supply corporation. It is likely to operate various types of generating plant, powered by diesel fuel, or coal, or water (hydro-electricity). It will be serving families in crowded cities and in rural communities; it will also be serving industrial users. Its marginal costs will vary both with regard to the type of plant and the type of customer. It will be vastly more expensive to serve one more rural family with power coming from a local diesel generator than to supply an increase in output to an industrial consumer from a large hydro-electric dam. How, then, are we to interpret $P = MC$? A different price for each marginal cost? That would (1) be very complicated to apply and (2) raise complaints about the social injustice of charging rural consumers more than city dwellers. Or perhaps a uniform price should be charged which is some average of the various marginal costs? That too could be complicated to compute and, by requiring industry to subsidize domestic users, could retard the pace of industrialization.

Again, there is the question whether commercial calculations of marginal costs provide an accurate measure of the social value of the resources used in production. For reasons that should be familiar to you by now, there are a number of reasons why market prices may diverge from social values. The answer, no doubt, is to calculate marginal costs in shadow prices, but as a practical solution that is open to objections mentioned earlier (see page 292).

Quite apart from the complexities of the MC concept, there are a number of other practical obstacles to the application of $P = MC$. Consider first its implications for enterprise profitability. *The $P = MC$ rule will result in losses for enterprises with falling average costs, and profits for enterprises with rising average costs.* This is illustrated in Figure 11.1, which should be interpreted as referring to the short run.

Figure 11.1 *Profitability and marginal cost pricing.*

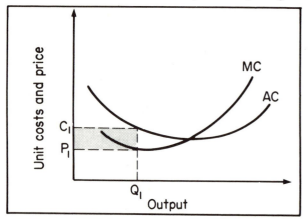

This shows a shallow U-shaped average cost curve. Marginal costs must be below the average so long as AC is falling and above it when AC is rising; an MC curve has been drawn to show this familiar relationship. MC equals AC only at the bottom of the

AC curve. Now consider an enterprise which is producing Q_1 of output. With $P = MC$ it sets its price at P_1. However, the average unit cost of production at output Q_1 is C_1, which is well above P_1. In following the $P = MC$ rule, therefore, it will not be covering its total costs; in fact it will make the deficit represented by the shaded rectangle in the diagram. We can generalize from this: the $P = MC$ rule will cause all industries with falling average costs to make losses. The opposite is the case with enterprises operating on the rising portion of the AC curve.

Activity. Use Figure 11.1 to illustrate the truth of the last sentence.

It follows that application of this pricing rule enormously reduces the significance of profitability as an indicator of efficiency. For whether an enterprise is operating with falling or rising ACs will depend largely upon the size of the market on which it is selling and upon the importance of technical economies of large-scale production. Management influence over both of these variables is likely to be weak, in which case profitability will be determined by factors largely beyond their control. This is of particular importance for natural monopolies included in the public sector because, by definition, they are industries subject to major scale economies (see page 253), so application of $P = MC$ will cause them to make losses. This, in turn, will have important implications for the government's budget, which will have to subsidize these industries. It will also affect the distribution of income, because the general taxpayer will be subsidizing the users of loss-making PEs.

In an otherwise commendable attempt to lay down general principles of policy for its PEs, the British government tried to escape from the unwelcome budgetary implications of the $P = MC$ rule by publishing a White Paper which required PEs (1) generally to price according to LRMC, (2) to use cost-benefit methods in evaluating new investments and (3) to earn certain target rates of return on total capital employed. This attempt was not successful and one reason for its failure was the tension in both laying down a pricing rule and specifying a target rate of return.

Another practical limitation of $P = MC$ is that it does not (in the way that profit maximization does) provide an incentive to minimize costs; it merely says, 'charge according to your MCs, at whatever level they may happen to be'. Competitive markets would provide a spur to cost-minimization but many PEs possess monopoly power and thus do not have to worry much about competition.

In addition to the practical snags just outlined, the $P = MC$ rule is subject to some rather strong theoretical objections. One of these concerns the limited welfare significance of Pareto optimality, which the rule is intended to promote. Even assuming that the $P = MC$ rule would move the economy nearer the Pareto optimum, the resulting allocation of resources (and the pattern of profits, losses, taxes and subsidies it implies) would result in a distribution of income different from that which would result, say, if the profit maximization solution were applied. It is impossible to judge which of the distributions would maximize welfare except on the basis of subject value-judgements, so it depends on what our judgement happens to be as to whether we think a movement towards Pareto-optimality is 'a good thing' or not.

Similarly, we should not forget the dynamic aspect of efficiency, set out in Chapter 1. We have seen that the $P = MC$ rule may result in PEs making deficits. But one of the main arguments in favour of PE is that it can, by earning profits, raise investment and accelerate technological progress. In the case of enterprises with declining average costs, then, a conflict is revealed between the desire for static efficiency and for long-term economic development.

A further theoretical objection relates to the *problem of the second best*, also outlined in Chapter 1.

Activity. You may at this point wish to refresh your memory on the problem of the second best by referring to pages 18–20.

You will recall that the theory of the second best has shown that, when there exist a number of constraints on the achievement of Pareto optimality (i.e. always), to remove any one of these will not necessarily lead to an increase in efficiency and may do the reverse. Applying this to the problem in hand, in an economic system where many private producers sell at prices which differ from marginal costs, to instruct the public sector to follow the $P = MC$ rule may not lead to any overall increase in static efficiency. It might instead bias the economy towards the allocation of too many or too few resources to the public sector.

The same logic holds for the situation *within* the public sector. To illustrate: postal and telephone services are to some extent substitutes for each other. Imagine now that the postal service is subsidized by the state, and that the price (postage) charged for delivering a letter is below marginal cost. The consequence in this case of telling the telephone service to follow $P = MC$ would be to place it at a competitive disadvantage *vis-à-vis* letters. This would tend to result in too many resources being devoted to the postal services, not enough to the telephones. With postal prices below MC, we might get a more productive allocation of resources by also allowing the telephone service to charge below MC, perhaps in the same ratio to MC as the postal authorities.

One should not, however, exaggerate the power of the second-best argument. The practical outcome of it is that there can be no universally valid pricing rule. It does not say that $P = MC$ is always wrong, merely that there is no assurance that it is right. Pricing policy thus has to be determined by examination of the circumstances of each enterprise, and it could well be that application of $P = MC$ would often represent an improvement over existing practices. We might even invoke the moral philosophy of Immanuel Kant in favour of $P = MC$: behave so that each of your actions is capable of being made into a universal rule.

These considerations suggest a tentative conclusion on $P = MC$. *There is a case for the pragmatic application of this rule if it is interpreted as referring to social, long-term marginal costs, and if it is combined with complementary measures that give enterprises strong incentives to keep their cost schedules as low as possible.* Long-run marginal costs should be used because they would result in less unprofitability than the SRMC case and thus conflict less with the developmental case of PE. The costs in question should, so far as practicable, be measured in social terms because of discrepancies between market prices and social valuations. The rule should be pragmatically applied in recognition that there will be cases in which it is not appropriate, for second-best, distributional or developmental reasons.

Each of the 'market solutions' presented above has been shown to be fraught with difficulties and of limited validity. There must therefore remain a good deal of doubt about the ability of any of them to achieve adequate improvements in the economic performance of the public sector. There may also be ideological objections to the use of market incentives. So the question arises whether non-market measures might be more effective. It is to this question that we now turn.

Activity. Review your understanding of the three solutions presented above. Write notes on the enterprise circumstances which would be favourable to the application of each of these.

VI. Policy Responses: Non-market Solutions

Targets and bonuses

The centrally planned economies of Eastern Europe, where most of the productive system is publicly owned, have made extensive use of non-market incentives to raise the efficiency of their PEs, so we should examine what can be learned from their experiences. The main type of incentive in these economies is the setting of various plan *targets*, fulfillment of which is linked to the payment of monetary *bonuses* to the workforce and management.

Most of the targets relate to some aspect of technical efficiency, as summarized on page 285. The most common of these are:

(1) targets for the volume or value of output or sales;
(2) targets for reductions in unit costs;
(3) targets for output per worker.

Of these, the most important are *output targets* because the success of the national plan depends upon meeting these. They may be expressed either in terms of physical output (number of units produced) or of the value of output. In both cases, difficulties have been encountered. Since the targets are set by reference to productive capacity and availability of raw materials (as well as to past levels of output), an incentive is created for managements to understate their capacity and to hoard materials. With quantity targets, enterprises producing a mix of products may be induced to concentrate on that type of production which makes it easiest to meet the target. A factory producing sheet glass (to take an actual Soviet example) may have its target expressed in terms of square metres of glass, in which case management will have an incentive to concentrate on making thin glass. Or the target could be in tonnes of glass, in which case there will be an incentive to switch to thick glass. (The Russian satirical magazine *Krokodil* once published a cartoon in which a nail factory had over-fulfilled its target for tonnes of output by making one giant nail that stretched from one end of the factory to the other.)

In principle, such problems can be met by specifying very detailed targets but the administrative demands are forbidding and the central planners are unlikely to have sufficient information to be able to get down to such detail in a realistic way. Even where an enterprise is producing an homogeneous output there is still scope for manipulation. Former Soviet Premier Nikita Kruschev gave the example of a target

for the production of chandeliers expressed in tonnes of output, to which the manufacturers responded by producing very heavy chandeliers!

Some of these distortions can be overcome by expressing targets in value terms rather than quantity, but this resort has problems of its own. For an enterprise with a mix of products, a target value of output will give its management an incentive to switch to that line with the highest price, whether or not there is a demand for it. More generally, this type of target tends to distort the system towards products incorporating high-value materials and with high unit prices. This problem might be met by setting the target for the value of sales rather than output. But this, too, may bring unintended results. Setting targets for Russian restaurants in terms of the value of sales, for instance, induced them to avoid serving cheap meals. Targets set in monetary values also tend to magnify the distorting effects of pricing policy mistakes. There was in the USSR a tendency to under-price spare parts, relative to finished products. This predictably led to an under-supply of spares and thus to much inefficiency in the use of machinery.

Whether expressed in quantity or value, output targets have the further disadvantage of tempting managements to achieve targets at the expense of quality. Again, it would in principle be possible to avoid this by specifying both quantity and quality but here too it must be doubted whether the planners have sufficient data and expertise to do this realistically, especially in LDC conditions. One aspect of the problem of quality is that output targets result in what is known in the centrally planned economies as 'storming' – a mad rush at the end of the plan period to raise output and meet the target, inevitably at the expense of quality. Since targets are usually set monthly, it is a standing joke that consumers should avoid buying items that were produced at the end of the month.

Snags arising from the other types of target mentioned earlier can be dealt with more summarily. As regards targets for *cost reductions*, these again tend to operate at the expense of quality, in favour of cheaper inputs, and perhaps at the expense of adequate maintenance and depreciation. In any case, costs will be strongly influenced by input prices, which will largely be beyond the control of the user-managements, so that unit costs may be a poor performance indicator. This type of target also raises the question whether the central planners can have enough reliable data (and capacity to handle it) with which to set meaningful cost targets; managements are probably in a strong position to manipulate cost statistics to their own advantage, especially in LDC conditions.

Setting targets for *output per worker* also introduces distortions. Here too there is an incentive to skimp on quality and to concentrate on those product lines which will maximize the quantity or value of output. Productivity targets will create a disincentive to the expansion of employment. They will instead encourage the use of capital-intensive methods because output per worker is closely correlated with the amount of capital per worker. In fact, this type of target would be particularly inappropriate for a developing country facing a scarcity of investible resources and an unemployment problem.

A final danger to be mentioned under this heading is the tendency to set multiple targets – on output, costs, profits, productivity – which are likely to conflict with one another. This is one of the greatest headaches of Soviet enterprise managers, although the Polish planners have sought to solve it by paying bonuses on the basis of a weighted average of specific target performances.

Activity. Imagine yourself a PE manager in a developing country who has been told to raise the level of his plant's capacity utilization by a certain target percentage. You and your workforce will be paid a bonus if you successfully meet this target. Discuss the advantages and disadvantages of this type of incentive for management and for the national economy.

To sum up, we see that the payment of bonuses on the basis of target fulfilment provides no panacea for the problem of PE inefficiency. One western authority has summarized some of the principal results of the Soviet incentive system in the following terms:[10]

The principal managerial incentive in Soviet industry is the bonus paid for overfulfilment of plan targets. The incentive system is successful in the sense that it elicits a high level of managerial effort and performance. But it has the unintended consequence of causing managers to engage in a wide variety of practices that are contrary to the interests of the state. Managers systematically conceal their true production capacity from the planners, produce unplanned types of products, and falsify the quantity and quality of production. In the procurement of materials and supplies they tend to order larger quantities than they need, hoard scarce materials, and employ unauthorised special agents who use influence and gifts to ease the management's procurement problems. The incentive system causes managers to shy away from innovations that upset the smooth working of the firm.

One particular problem that has only been hinted at in the foregoing is that the output resulting from incentive systems of the type mentioned may bear little relation to consumer preferences, both as regards the composition of output and its quality.

But it would be wrong to suggest that targets create only problems and have no positive benefits. Eastern European industry has progressed greatly during the last thirty years. I have personally been able to observe large improvements in the range and quality of consumer goods available in East German shops. It is impossible to measure the extent to which targets and bonuses have contributed, but it is unlikely that such progress could have occurred unless the incentive system had made a contribution. As with market solutions, we are dealing in advantages and disadvantages, not in absolute 'goods' or 'bads'.

Legal and institutional reforms

Reference was made earlier to the strong influence in LDC legislation of the British concept of the public corporation – a legal form which generally requires the corporations to be run on commercial lines, free from governmental interference in day-to-day operations, but makes them answerable to a minister for the general conduct of their affairs. The minister is seen as the arbiter of the public interest and is empowered to 'give directives of a general nature as to the performance of the corporations in relation to matters appearing to the minister to affect the national interest'.

However, prominence was given in Part IV to the 'trivialization of political control' as a reason for substandard economic performance by PEs. The implication is that the British formula has failed to strike a reasonable balance between public accountability and managerial autonomy. There is a school of thought which attributes this failure to the inappropriateness of the British model to LDC conditions and which therefore looks to the development of more indigenous legal forms to overcome the failings and secure improved performance.[11] If the British-style public corporation has failed to strike the balance we are seeking, it is tempting to look to legal reform for a solution. Perhaps the joint-stock company is a legal model which might better protect managements against political meddling, or some as yet undiscovered legal status?

---

[10] G. Grossman in Holzman, 1962, p. 349.
[11] The next few paragraphs are largely based on Pozen, 1976, who provides a pioneering study of the influence of legal forms on LDC public enterprise performance, and their relationships with government.

As a test of this possibility we may refer to Pozen's (1976) study of PEs in Ghana, which came to the following conclusions:

(1) Ghana did not simply copy the British public corporation model. Numerous adaptations were made to suit PE statutes to local circumstances. It would thus be an over-simplification to describe this as an example of an inappropriate legal transfer from a different socio-political milieu.

(2) Public corporations in Ghana did retain certain core characteristics in common with the British model. That they failed in practice to strike a good balance between public accountability and managerial autonomy cannot, however, be attributed to the inappropriateness of these characteristics to the Ghanaian situation because *there has been a similar failure to strike the desired balance in the UK*. This suggests that the basic concept of the public corporation may be fatally flawed, irrespective of where it is applied.

(3) Various other legal forms were tried in Ghana. Did these offer improved frameworks for PE efficiency? Apparently not. Indeed, legal forms may be of little significance, because Ghanaian PEs whose legal status underwent various changes – from government department to public corporation to joint-stock company – continued with similar operating practices and performances. The extent of governmental control over operations altered with varying *political* circumstances but was little affected by changes in legal status.

(4) Pozen is therefore sceptical about the view of lawyers as 'policy-makers who can profoundly influence the performance of the state sector by imaginative reforms'. Political realities, and the often covert nature of governmental objectives, are likely to be much more powerful influences than statutory forms: 'Despite the noble speeches, the actual objectives of particular interest groups, like political patronage, regularly took precedence over societal goals like corporate surpluses to finance development'. The objectives of legal reformers are therefore likely to differ from those of government ministers and it is the latter who really determine what happens.

In reaching this rather gloomy conclusion, Pozen is by no means alone. Jones' Korean study (1975, p. 210) concluded that:

The formal legal distinction between autonomous departmental agency and public corporation has only limited impact on functional control. Public corporations are generally as tightly controlled as the departmental agencies . . . What is needed here is not so much a new legal form, but a conscious delineation of the intended deviations, specification of relevant target variables, association of managerial incentives with the degree of attainment of those targets, and the granting of real managerial discretion in all other matters.

Industrial country studies have reached similar judgements.[12] On the other hand, we may still hope that a well-designed legal framework might at least make it *easier* to achieve the desired balance between accountability and operational autonomy, while conceding that legal reform by itself offers only an incomplete solution. For example, there is a consensus that the joint-stock company status is well suited to mixed enterprises, jointly owned by state and private investors, because the proportions of shares and directorships held by the two partners can be varied within that legal structure. If it is possible to identify an appropriate legal form for one type of PE, we should not entirely despair of making similar discoveries for others.

One radically different institutional form which can be mentioned is *workers' control*. By this is meant an enterprise in which the workers form a co-operative arrangement to manage an enterprise themselves. Most arguments in favour of this type of organization are concerned with ideology rather than with economic efficiency. Workers control is seen as extending the democratic ideal into the work-place and as avoiding the inequalities and elitism associated with capitalistic forms. However, it is also argued that greater efficiency may result because workers will identify themselves more with the interests of the firm and thus put in a greater effort.

Against this, it has been found that conflicts are likely to arise between the interests of worker-managements and the general public, with the managements no less tempted to engage in monopolistic restrictions of output and employment in pursuit of maximum bonus payments than the private capitalist seeking maximum profits.[13] There is also a danger of diminished labour discipline under this type of management, of reduced rates of investment and innovation (because a high proportion of profits may be distributed as bonuses), and of difficulties in fitting this decentralized decision-making unit into the framework of national economic planning.

Without passing a judgement on the *social* case for

---

[12] See, for example, Coombes, 1971, p. 210.
[13] The interested reader should see Vanek, 1970, and Meade, 1972.

worker's control, therefore, we can infer that there is not a very strong *efficiency* case for it.

In addition to the possibilities already considered, there are two other institutional reforms which might provide useful spurs to greater efficiency. One is the device of using a specialized *parliamentary committee* to act as a watch-dog of the public interest; increasing the openness of the system; forcing ministers to be more specific about their objectives and to defend their actions; bringing publicity to facts which may otherwise be suppressed; raising the standard of public discussion of the performance and problems of the public sector. It is generally held that the Select Committee on Nationalized Industries of the British House of Commons has performed valuably in these ways and has helped to keep all concerned on their toes. Whether this device is easily transferable to the political systems of many LDCs is doubtful, however. Some have no parliaments; in others the parliaments are rubber stamps, not encouraged to take on tasks of this kind. Even where parliamentary democracy functions reasonably well, there may not be the information, expertise or inclination for parliamentary committees of this type to be effective. Nevertheless, it is an instrument worth trying when conditions permit.

A second possibility, which may more readily take root in a variety of soils, is to set up agencies especially responsible for the *efficiency auditing* of public enterprises. Efficiency auditing is concerned not so much with the accuracy of book-keeping and financial control as with the diagnostic analysis of past performance, to assess the extent to which enterprise objectives have been secured, to locate points of weakness and suggest remedies. An agency exclusively dealing with the public sector could, over the years, build up sufficient knowledge and expertise to be able to set meaningful norms of efficiency and make practical suggestions for improvements. This function might, perhaps, be combined with conventional financial auditing, and a number of countries have created a special independent body responsible for auditing PE accounts.

Activity. What legal forms have been most commonly established for public enterprises in your own country? Is it possible to identify any link between their legal status and the relationships they have established with the government? Have either of the devices mentioned in the last two paragraphs been employed? If not, would they be feasible in your country?

VII. Conclusions: The Primacy of Politics

Given our earlier conclusion that substandard economic performance by PEs is rather widespread, how much impact are the policy instruments reviewed in Parts V and VI likely to make? It must be admitted that they may not, in fact, be adequate to solve the problem of PE inefficiency. Working on the tacit assumption that governments attach priority to raising efficiency, we have seen each alternative policy response to be subject to severe limitations and that they may sometimes have undesired consequences. Wherever possible, their various advantages, and the circumstances in which they may be most effective, have been highlighted, but it has been easier to identify snags than to generate optimism.

The real pitfall, however, lies with the assumption that economic efficiency has a high priority among governments' objectives for the public sector. In many cases the reality may be otherwise. Part II showed that there is a wide variety of motives for setting up PEs. There are ideological impulses, in which public ownership is often seen as an end in itself rather than as a means to other (economic) ends; there are desires to use PEs as a way of protecting jobs or of reducing consumer prices; and there are the (usually unstated) objectives of using the public sector for party and personal advantage. *This multiplicity of potentially conflicting objectives is the largest single difficulty under which PEs labour.*

Indeed, to talk of a pecking order of objectives at all may be misleading. The general case is that ministers are unable or unwilling to be specific about their objectives and priorities. The management of a public concern can expect to have to operate with vaguely expressed, contradictory and changing terms of reference – not an environment that encourages efficiency, by whatever criterion we may use.

Some would go further than this, as does Pozen, to suggest that, despite protestations to the contrary, politicians' true objectives for PEs have little to do with the public interest. Party, sectional and personal advantage may be the dominant goals. The large uncertainties of political life often give ministers short time-horizons, so that they are more interested in quick returns and short-term advantages than with the longer-term developmental effects of their policies. At the crux of the problem is the fact that, while the beneficiaries of non-developmental actions tend to be easily identified, organized and vocal, the losers of the economic benefits foregone are diffused, inarticulate, unorganized. If party activists are not rewarded with jobs they will soon make their presence felt, but it is the general consumer and taxpayer who shoulders the burden of having unqualified people in senior positions, and the weight and cause of this additional burden may not be easily identified by the public.

This line of argument raises the question whether the economist has much role to play in working for PE efficiency. We should not be too pessimistic. Not every government subordinates the public interest to sectional advantage; some seriously give priority to economic efficiency. In these situations the economist clearly has a part to play. Even in less favourable conditions, the economists can help to draw attention to the economic costs involved in the pursuit of non-economic objectives. To cite Ghana's state gold-mines for the last time, it was possible to say of the government's policy of keeping open a mine that had run out of ore (Killick, 1978, p. 239):

> It can be estimated that the per-worker cost of keeping the mine 'open' was well in excess of ₡800 annually, which figure may be compared with a statutory minimum wage worth less than ₡200 a year in the first half of the sixties, rising to about ₡230 by the end of the sixties. It would have been financially possible to close the mine and pay about four times as many unemployed the minimum wage with no net cost to the budget. More positively, it would have been possible to invest money spent on the mine in new activities providing jobs on a permanent basis and contributing to the development of the economy . . . only on the most short-term or parochial political grounds might these costs have been worthwhile; even as a social policy to alleviate unemployment overmanning the public sector was probably an unnecessarily costly policy. If so, it was also inequitable, for the devotion of large resources to a small number of workers absorbed finances which could have provided relief to a far larger number of people.

By drawing attention to facts of this type, by insisting that governments should consider the opportunity costs of their actions, and by questioning whether poor nations can afford the luxury of providing high-cost benefits to a few at the expense of the many, economists can hope to persuade governments against policies which fly in the face of economic rationality. Failing this, they may at least force governments to offer some public justification for what they are doing.

Nevertheless, the generally negative tenor of this conclusion, and of much that precedes it, does raise a question of fundamental importance. If governments are rarely clear and consistent in their objectives; if the public sector is frequently used to benefit special interests rather than the general public; if inefficiency is pervasive and the policy instruments available for improving performance are not strong – don't these conditions seriously weaken the case in favour of public enterprise?

Activity. A class discussion is suggested on the question raised in the last sentence.

Suggestions for Revision and Group Discussions

1 Review your understanding of the following:
  (a) Nationalization.
  (b) A public corporation.
  (c) A joint-stock company.
  (d) A natural monopoly.
  (e) The social subsidy principle.
  (f) The trivialization of political control.
  (g) Marginal costs.
  (h) A mixed enterprise.
  (i) Workers' control.

2 It was suggested in the text that potential conflicts between governments' objectives for PEs could be reduced if these objectives were precisely specified. Make sure you understand this point, if necessary by referring back to Chapter 2, Part II.

3 Discuss the view that PEs will make the greatest contribution to economic development if they are allowed to maximize profits.

4 Summarize the main economic consequences of decisions whether or not to pay full compensation to the private owners of firms that are being nationalized.

5 Summarize the chief factors which may reduce the usefulness of each of the following as indicators of PE efficiency:
  (a) The ratio of material inputs to output.
  (b) Gross output per man.
  (c) Gross output per unit of capital employed.
  (d) Average unit costs of production.

6 Give your understanding of the statement, 'The P = MC rule will result in losses for enterprises with falling average costs and profits for enterprises with rising average costs'. Relate this to the case of natural monopolies.

7 State your understanding of the P = SRMC and P = LRMC rules, and the difference between them.

8 Evaluate the conclusion on page 299 that the policy instruments available for improving performance may not be adequate to solve the problem of PE inefficiency.

9 Read the essay by Bronfenbrenner detailed in the bibliography below. This was first published in 1955; suggest ways in which it might need to be revised in the light of subsequent LDC experiences.

10 Chapter 10 concluded with a reference to the potential use of nationalization as an anti-trust policy but deferred any assessment. In the light of the discussions of this chapter, write an evaluation of the merits of using nationalization for anti-trust purposes, by comparison with the alternatives set out in Chapter 10.

Suggestions for Further Reading

The literature on public enterprise in developing countries is not very satisfactory. Hanson, 1965, still provides the best general survey of the role of public enterprise in economic development, although it is now seriously out of date. Jones, 1975, provides a valuable study of the role of Korea's public enterprise sector in that country's development. The Ghanaian materials used in this chapter are from ch. 9 of Killick, 1978. Bhagwati and Desai, 1970, contains useful information on India's public sector.

There is a large, erudite but somewhat inconclusive literature on the theory of PE price and investment decisions. Turvey, 1968, provides a useful collection of readings, although with an industrial-country orientation; see also Turvey, 1971; and ch. 6 of Winch, 1971.

Bronfenbrenner's 1955 essay remains a stimulating discussion of the case of confiscation of private businesses as an instrument of economic development. Chapter 4 of Nove, 1977, provides many illustrations and insights into the problems of state enterprises in the Soviet Union, which are also relevant to developing countries.

See also the additional references given in the notes to this chapter.

Bibliography

Adelman, Irma and Morris, Cynthia Taft, *Economic Growth and Social Equity in Developing Countries* (Stanford UP, 1973).

Agarwala, A. N. and Singh, S. P. (eds), *Economics of Underdevelopment* (Bombay, OUP, 1958).

Aghelvi, Bijan B. and Khan, Mohsin S., 'Inflationary finance and the dynamics of inflation: Indonesia, 1951–72', *American Economic Review* (June 1977).

Ahluwalia, Montek S., 'Inequality, poverty and development', *Journal of Development Economics* (December 1976).

Ahmed, Iftikhar, 'The green revolution and tractorisation', *International Labour Review* (July–August 1976).

Allen, G. C., *A Short Economic History of Modern Japan* (London, Allen & Unwin, 1962).

Amjad, R., 'Profitability and industrial concentration in Pakistan', *Journal of Development Studies* (April 1977).

Anand, Sudhir, 'Aspects of poverty in Malaysia', *Review of Income and Wealth* (March, 1977).

Argy, Victor, 'Structural inflation in developing countries', *Oxford Economic Papers* (March 1970).

Atkinson, A. B., *The Economics of Inequality* (London, OUP, 1975).

Baer, W. and Beckerman P., 'Indexing in Brazil', *World Development* (October–December 1974).

—— and Kerstenetzkey, I. (eds), *Inflation and Growth in Latin America* (New Haven, Yale UP, 1964).

Bain, J. S., *Barriers to New Competition* (Cambridge, Harvard UP, 1956).

—— *International Differences in Industrial Structure* (New Haven, Yale UP, 1966).

Balakrishnan, T. R., 'A cost benefit analysis of the Barbados family planning programme', *Population Studies* (July 1973).

Balassa, Bela, 'Exports and economic growth: further evidence', *Journal of Development Economics* (June 1978).

Baldwin, R. E., *Foreign Trade Regimes and Economic Development: Philippines* (New York, Columbia UP, 1975).

Ballentine, J. Gregory and Soligo, Ronald, 'Consumption and earnings patterns and income distribution', *Economic Development and Cultural Change* (July 1978).

Bardhan, K. and Bardhan, P., 'The green revolution and socio-economic tension: the case of India', *International Social Science Journal* no. 3 (1973).

Baster, Nancy (ed), *Measuring Development* (London, Cass, 1974).

Bauer, P. T., *Dissent on Development* (London, Weidenfeld & Nicolson, 1971).

Bauer, R. A. and Gergen, K. J. (eds) *The Study of Policy Formation* (New York, Free Press, 1968).

Beckerman, Wilfred, 'Some reflections on redistribution with growth', *World Development* (August 1977).

Behrman, J. R., *Foreign Trade Regimes and Economic Development: Chile* (New York, Columbia UP, 1976).

Berelson, B., *et al.*, *Family Planning and Population Programmes* (Chicago UP, 1966).

Bergsman, Joel, *Brazil: Industrialization and Trade Policies* (London, OUP, 1970).

—— 'Commercial policy, allocative and X-efficiency', *Quarterly Journal of Economics* (August 1974).

Bhagwat, A. and Onitsuka, Y., 'Export-import responses to devaluation: experience of the non-industrial countries in the 1960s', *IMF Staff Papers* (July 1974).

Bhagwati, Jagdish, *Anatomy and Consequences of Exchange Control Regimes* (Cambridge, Mass., Ballinger Co., 1978).

—— and Desai, Padma, *India: Planning for Industrialisation* (London, OUP, 1970).

—— and Srinivasan, T. N., *Foreign Trade Regimes and Economic Development: India* (New York, Columbia UP, 1976).

Bhatt, V. V., 'Incomes policy and development planning', *Finance and Development* (December 1976).

Bierman, H. and Smidt, S., *Capital Budgeting Decision* (New York, Macmillan, 1971).

Birdsall, Nancy, 'Analytical approaches to the relationship of population growth and development', *Population and Development Review* (March–June 1977).

Birgegard, Lars-Erik, *The Project Selection Process in Developing Countries* (Stockholm School of Economics, Economic Research Institute, 1975).

Blandy, Richard, 'The welfare analysis of fertility reduction', *Economic Journal* (March 1974).

Blinder, Alan S., *et al.*, *Economics of Public Finance* (Washington, Brookings Institute, 1974).

Blitzer, C. R., Clark, P. B. and Taylor, L. (eds), *Economy-Wide Models and Development Planning* (London, OUP, 1975).

Bolnick, R. B., 'Behaviour of the determinants of money supply in Kenya', *Eastern Africa Economic Review* (June 1975).

Bos, H. C., Linemann, H. and de Wolff, P. (eds), *Economic Structure and Development* (Amsterdam, North-Holland, 1973).

Boserup, Esther, *Conditions of Agricultural Growth* (London, Allen & Unwin, 1965).

Braybrooke, D. and Lindblom, C. E., *A Strategy of Decision* (New York, Free Press, 1963).

Bronfenbrenner, M., 'The appeal of confiscation in economic development', *Economic Development and Cultural Change* (April 1955). (Reproduced in Agarwala and Singh, 1958.)

—— and Holzman, F. D., 'A survey of inflation theory', in American Economic Association and Royal Economic Society, *Surveys of Economic Theory*, vol. I. (London, Macmillan, 1965).

Burkhead, J. and Miner, J., *Public Expenditure* (London, Macmillan, 1971).

Caiden, N. and Wildavsky, A., *Planning and Budgeting in Poor Countries* (New York, Wiley, 1974).

Cardozo, O. C., 'Flexible exchange rates, inflation and economic development', *World Development* (July 1976).

Cassen, Robert H., 'Population and development: a survey', *World Development* (October–November 1976).

Chelliah, R. J., 'Trends in taxation in developing countries', *IMF Staff Papers* (July 1971).

Chen, Lincoln and Chaudhury, Rafiqul Huda, 'Demographic change and food production in Bangladesh, 1960–74', *Population and Development Review* (December 1975).

Chen, Pi-Chao, 'China's birth control action programme, 1956–64', *Population Studies* (July 1970).

Chenery, H. B. (ed), *Studies in Development Planning* (Cambridge, Mass., Harvard UP, 1971).

—— Ahluwalia, M. S., Bell, C. L. G., Duloy, J. H. and Jolly, R. (eds), *Redistribution with Growth* (London, OUP, 1974).

Clark, Colin and Haswell M. R., *The Economics of Subsistence Agriculture* (London, Macmillan, 1964).

Clark, J. H., 'Towards a concept of workable competition', *American Economic Review* (June 1940).

Coombes, David, *State Enterprise: Business or Politics?* (London, Allen & Unwin, 1971).

Crockett, A. D. and Nsouli, S. M., 'Exchange rate policies for developing countries', *Journal of Development Studies* (January 1977).

Dahl, Robert A., *Modern Political Analysis* (New Jersey, Prentice-Hall, 1970).

Day, R. H. and Singh, I., *Economic Development as an Adaptive Process: The Green Revolution in the Indian Punjab* (CUP, 1977).

Dean, Edwin, *Plan Implementation in Nigeria: 1962–1966* (Ibadan, OUP, 1972).

Deane, Phyllis, *The First Industrial Revolution* (CUP, 1965).

Drewnowski, Jan, 'The economic theory of socialism: a suggestion for reconsideration', *Journal of Political Economy* (August 1961).

Dreyer, Jacob S. V., 'Determinants of exchange rate regimes for currencies of developing countries: some preliminary results', *World Development* (April 1978).

Dumont, Rene, *False Start in Africa* (London, Andre Deutsch, 1966).

Eckstein, Alexander (ed), *Comparison of Economic Systems* (Berkeley, California UP, 1971).

Edwards, E. O. (ed), *Employment in Developing Countries* (New York, Columbia UP, 1974).

Elliot, John E., 'Economic planning reconsidered', *Quarterly Journal of Economics* (February 1958).

Evans, Peter B., 'Direct investment and industrial concentration', *Journal of Development Studies* (July 1977).

Evenson, R. E. and Kislev, Y., 'Investment in agricultural research and extension: a survey of international data', *Economic Development and Cultural Change* (April 1975).

Faber, M. and Seers, D. (eds), *The Crisis in Planning* (two volumes) (London, Chatto & Windus, 1972).

Fishlow, Albert, 'Brazilian size distribution of income', *American Economic Review* (May 1972).

Fleming, J. M., 'Targets and instruments', *IMF Staff Papers* (November 1968).

Foster, C. D., *Politics, Finance and the Role of Economics* (London, Allen & Unwin, 1971).

Fox, K. A., Sengupta, J. K. and Thorbecke, E., *The Theory of Quantitative Economic Policy* (Amsterdam, North-Holland, 1973).

Frank, C. R., Kim, K. S. and Westphal, L., *Foreign Trade Regimes and Economic Development: South Korea* (New York, Columbia UP, 1975).

Frankena, M., 'Devaluation, recession and nontraditional manufactured exports from India', *Economic Development and Cultural Change* (October 1975).

Freedman, R. (ed), *Marx on Economics* (London, Penguin, 1961).

Frejka, Tomas, *The Future of Population Growth* (New York, Wiley, 1973).

Friedman, David, *Laissez-Faire in Population: The Least-bad Solution* (New York, The Population Council, 1972).

Friedman, Milton, *The Counter-Revolution in Monetary Theory* (London, Institute of Economic Affairs, 1970).

Friedmann, W. G. and Garner, J. F. (eds), *Government Enterprise: A Comparative Study* (New York, Columbia UP, 1970).

Fromm, G. and Taubman, P., *Public Economic Theory and Policy* (New York, Macmillan, 1973).

Galbraith, J. K., *The Affluent Society* (London, Penguin, 1962).

—— *The New Industrial State* (Boston, Houghton Mifflin, 1967).

Gantt, A. H. and Dutto, G., 'Financial performance of government-owned corporations in less developed countries', *IMF Staff Papers* (March 1968).

Gershenberg, I. and Ryan, T. C. I., 'Does parentage matter? An analysis of transnational and other firms: an East African case', *Journal of Developing Areas* (Fall, 1978).

Glytsos, Nicholas P., 'Determinants of wage and price changes in less developed countries', *Journal of Development Economics* (December 1977).

Gray, H. P. and Tangri, S. S. (eds), *Economic Development and Population Growth* (Lexington, Heath, 1970).

Griffin, Keith, *The Political Economy of Agrarian Change* (London, Macmillan, 1974).

—— and Enos, J. L., *Planning Development* (London, Addison-Wesley, 1970).

Grossman, Gregory, *Economic Systems* (Englewood Cliffs, Prentice Hall, 1974).

Grubel, Herbert G., *International Monetary System* (London, Penguin, 1977 (A)).

—— *International Economics* (Homewood, Ill, Irwins, 1977 (B)).

Gupta, A. P., 'Inflation, income distribution and industrial relations in India', *International Labour Review* (August 1974).

Hansen, B. and Nashashibi, K., *Foreign Trade Regimes and Economic Development: Egypt* (New York, Columbia UP, 1975).

Hanson, A. H., *Public Enterprise and Economic Development* (London, Routledge and Kegan Paul, 1965).

Harberger, A. C., 'Using the resources at hand more effectively', *American Economic Review* (May 1959).

—— 'Some notes on inflation', in Baer and Kerstenetzkey (1964).

Hart, Keith, 'Informal income opportunities and urban employment in Ghana', *Journal of Modern African Studies*, no. 1 (1973).

Haveman, R. H. and Margolis, J., *Public Expenditures and Policy Analysis* (Chicago, Markham, 1970).

Hayami, Yujiro and Ruttan, Vernon W., *Agricultural Development: An International Perspective* (Baltimore, Johns Hopkins, 1971).

Hayek, Friedrich A., *The Road to Serfdom* (Chicago UP, 1944).

Healey, Derek T., 'Development policy: new thinking about an interpretation', *Journal of Economic Literature* (September 1972).

Helleiner, G. K., *Peasant Agriculture, Government and Economic Growth in Nigeria* (New York, Irwins, 1966).

Heller, H. R., 'International reserves and world-wide inflation', *IMF Staff Papers* (March 1976).

Heller, Peter S. and Porter, Richard C., 'Exports and growth: an empirical re-investigation', *Journal of Development Economics* (June 1978).

Hill, Polly, *The Migrant Cocoa Farmers of Southern Ghana* (London, CUP, 1963).

Hirschman, Albert O., *Strategy of Economic Development* (New Haven, Yale UP, 1958).

—— *Journeys Towards Progress* (New York, Twentieth Century Fund, 1963).

Hirschmeier, J., *The Origins of Entrepreneurship in Meiji, Japan* (Cambridge, Mass., Harvard UP, 1964).

Holzman, F. D. (ed), *Readings on the Soviet Economy* (Chicago, Rand McNally, 1962).

House, William J., 'Market structure and industry performance: the case of Kenya', *Oxford Economic Papers* (November 1973).

—— 'Market structure and industry performance: the case of Kenya revisited', *Journal of Economic Studies* (November 1976).

Hsing, Mo-huan, Power, J. H. and Sicat, G. P., *Taiwan and the Philippines: Industrialization and Trade Policies* (London, OUP, 1971).

Huang, Y., 'Distribution of the tax burden in Tanzania', *Economic Journal* (March 1976).

Hunt, E. K. and Schwartz, J. G. (eds), *A Critique of Economic Theory* (London, Penguin, 1972).

International Labour Office, *Towards Full Employment: A Programme for Colombia* (Geneva, ILO, 1970).

—— *Employment, Incomes and Equality: A Strategy for Increasing Productive Employment in Kenya* (Geneva, ILO, 1972).

—— *Employment, Growth and Basic Needs* (Geneva, ILO, 1976).

International Monetary Fund, *Annual Report, 1975* (Washington, 1975).

—— *Annual Report 1976* (Washington, 1976).

—— *Annual Report 1977* (Washington, 1977).

—— *International Financial Statistics* (Washington (Monthly)).

Islam, Nurul, *Development Planning in Bangladesh: A Study*

in Political Economy (London, Hurst, 1977).

Johansen, L., *Public Economics* (Amsterdam, North-Holland, 1971).

Johnson, H. G., *Essays in Monetary Economics* (London, Allen & Unwin, 1967).

Johnston, Bruce F., 'Food, health and population in development', *Journal of Economic Literature* (September 1977).

—— and Kilby, P., *Agriculture and Structural Transformation* (New York, OUP, 1975).

Jolly, R., de Kadt, E., Singer H. and Wilson, F. (eds), *Third World Employment* (London, Penguin, 1973).

Jones, Hywell G., *An Introduction to Modern Theories of Economic Growth* (New York, McGraw-Hill, 1976).

Jones, Leroy P., *Public Enterprise and Economic Development: the Korean Case* (Box 113, Cheongryang, Seoul, Korea Development Institute, 1975).

Kahil, Raouf, *Inflation and Economic Development in Brazil, 1946–63* (London, OUP, 1973).

Kamien, M. I. and Schwartz, N. L., 'Market, structure and innovation: a survey', *Journal of Economic Literature* (March 1975).

Kammerschen, D., *Western Economic Journal* (Summer 1966).

Kaser, M. C. and Portes, R. (eds), *Planning and Market Relations* (London, Macmillan, 1971).

Keeley, Michael C. (ed), *Population, Public Policy, and Economic Development* (New York, Praeger, 1976).

Kelley, Allen C., 'Savings, demographic change, and economic development', *Economic Development and Cultural Change* (July 1976).

—— Williamson, J. G. and Cheetham, R. J., *Dualistic Economic Development* (University of Chicago Press, 1972).

Khan, M. S., 'Import and export demand in developing countries', *IMF Staff Papers* (November 1974).

Khilji, F., 'Multinational corporations and restrictive business practices: the case of Pakistan', *Pakistan Development Review* (Winter 1975).

Killick, Tony, 'Unemployment as an indicator of prosperity: a statistical curiosity', *Economic Bulletin of Ghana*, no. 3, (1972).

—— 'Price controls in Africa', *Journal of Modern African Studies* (September 1973).

—— 'The possibilities of development planning', *Oxford Economic Papers* (July 1976).

—— *Development Economics in Action: A Study of Economic Policies in Ghana* (London, Heinemann, 1978).

—— (ed), *The Kenyan Economy* (Nairobi and London, Heinemann, 1980 (forthcoming)).

Kindleberger, C. P. (ed), *The International Corporation* (Cambridge, Mass., MIT Press, 1970).

—— *International Economics* (Homewood, Irwins, 1973).

King, Timothy, *Mexico: Industrialization and Trade Policies since 1940* (London, OUP, 1970).

Knight, J. B., 'Devaluation and income distribution in less-developed countries', *Oxford Economic Papers* (July 1976).

Krishna, Raj, *Rural Unemployment – A Survey of Concepts and Estimates for India* (Washington, World Bank Staff Working Paper No. 234, April 1976).

Kritz, E. and Ramos J., 'The measurement of urban underemployment', *International Labour Review* (January–February 1976).

Krueger, Anne O., *Foreign Trade Regimes and Economic Development: Turkey* (New York, Columbia UP, 1975).

—— *Liberalization Attempts and Consequences* (Cambridge, Mass., Ballinger Co., 1978).

Kuznets, Simon, *Economic Growth and Structure* (London, Heinemann, 1965).

——*Modern Economic Growth: Rate, Structure and Spread* (New Haven, Yale UP, 1966).

——*Population, Capital and Growth* (London, Heinemann, 1974).

—— 'Fertility differentials between less developed and developed regions: components and implications', *Proceedings of the American Philosophical Society* (October 1975).

—— 'Demographic aspects of size distribution of income: an exploratory essay', *Economic Development and Cultural Change* (October 1976).

Laidler, D. E. W. and Parkin, J. M., 'Inflation – a survey', *Economic Journal* (December 1975).

Lal, Deepak, 'Supply price and surplus labour: some Indian evidence', *World Development*, October/November 1976.

Lall, Sanjaya, 'Transnationals, domestic enterprises and industrial structure in host LDCs: a survey', *Oxford Economic Papers* (July 1978).

Layard, R. (ed), *Cost-Benefit Analysis* (London, Penguin, 1972).

Leff, N. H., 'Dependency rates and saving rates', *American Economic Review* (December 1969).

Leibenstein, Harvey, 'Allocative efficiency Vs "X-efficiency"', *American Economic Review* (June 1966).

—— *Beyond Economic Man* (Cambridge, Mass, Harvard UP, 1976).

Leith, J. C., *Foreign Trade Regimes and Economic Development: Ghana* (New York, Columbia UP, 1975).

Lerner, Abba P., *Economics of Control: Principles of Welfare Economics* (New York, Macmillan, 1944).

Levi, John F. S., 'Population pressure and agricultural change in the land-intensive economy', *Journal of Development Studies* (October 1976).

Levy, Haim and Sarnat, Marshall, 'Investment incentives and the allocation of resources', *Economic Development and Cultural Change* (April 1975).

Lewis, S. R. Jr., *Pakistan: Industrialization and Trade Policies* (London, OUP, 1970).

Lewis, W. A., *The Theory of Economic Growth* (London, Allen & Unwin, 1955).

—— *Development Planning: The Essentials of Economic Policy* (London, Allen & Unwin, 1966).

Lindblom, Charles E., *The Policy-making Process* (Englewood, Prentice Hall, 1968).

Lipsey, Richard G., *An Introduction to Positive Economics* (London, Weidenfeld and Nicolson, 1975).

—— and Lancaster, Kelvin, 'The general theory of the second best', *Review of Economic Studies*, no. 1, (1957).

—— and Steiner, P. O., *Economics* (New York, Harper and Row, 1975).

Lipton, Michael, *Why Poor People Stay Poor* (London, M. T. Smith, 1977).

—— 'Inter-farm, inter-regional and farm/non-farm income distribution: the impact of new cereal varieties', *World Development* (March 1978).

Lisk, F., 'Inflation in Ghana, 1964–75', *International Labour Review* (May–June 1976).

Little, I. M. D. and Mirrlees, J. A., *Project Appraisal and Planning in Developing Countries* (London, Heinemann, 1974).

—— Scitovsky, T. and Scott, M., *Industry and Trade in Some Developing Countries: A Comparative Study* (London, OUP, 1970).

Manove, Michael, 'A model of Soviet-type economic planning', *American Economic Review* (June 1971).

Mansfield, Edwin, *Microeconomics: Theory and Applications* (New York, Norton, 1975).

Massell, B., Pearson, S. R. and Fitch, J. B., 'Foreign exchange and economic development: an empirical study of selected Latin American countries', *Review of Economics and Statistics* (May 1972).

McKinnon, Ronald I., *Money and Capital in Economic Development* (Washington, Brookings Institute, 1973).

Meade, J. E., *The Theory of Indicative Planning* (Manchester UP, 1970).

—— 'The theory of labour-managed firms and of profit sharing', *Economic Journal* (March 1972 (special issue)).

Meir, G. M. (ed), *Leading Issues in Economic Development* (New York, OUP, 1976).

Merhav, Meir, *Technological Dependence, Monopoly and Growth* (Oxford, Pergamon Press, 1969).

Michaely, M., *Foreign Trade Regimes and Economic Development: Israel* (New York, Columbia UP, 1975).

—— 'Exports and growth: an empirical investigation', *Journal of Development Economics* (March 1977).

Mikesell, R. F. and Zinser, J. E., 'The nature of the savings function in developing countries: a survey of the theoretical and empirical literature', *Journal of Economic Literature* (March 1973).

Mishan, E. J., 'Second thoughts on second best', *Oxford Economic Papers* (October 1962).

Morawetz, D., 'Employment implications of industrialisation in developing countries', *Economic Journal* (September 1974).

Mosley, Paul, 'Towards a "satisficing" theory of economic policy', *Economic Journal* (March 1976).

Mouly, J. and Costa, E., *Employment Policies in Developing Countries* (London, Allen & Unwin, 1974).

Musgrave, R. A. and Musgrave, P. B., *Public Finance in Theory and Practice* (New York, McGraw-Hill, 1976).

Myint, H., *The Economics of the Developing Countries* (London, Hutchinson, 1967).

—— *Southeast Asia's Economy* (London, Penguin, 1972).

Myrdal, Gunnar, *Asian Drama* (3 vols.) (New York, Twentieth Century Fund, 1968).

Nash, Manning (ed), *Essays on Economic Development and Cultural Change* (Chicago UP, 1977).

National Research Council, *Systems Analysis and Operations Research* (Washington, NRC, 1976).

Nicholson, Walter, *Intermediate Microeconomics and its Applications* (Hinsdale, Dryden Press, 1975).

Nkrumah, Kwame, *Africa Must Unite* (New York, International Publishers, 1972).

Nortman, Dorothy, 'Status of national family planning programmes of developing countries in relation to demographic targets', *Population Studies* (March 1972).

Nove, Alec, *Efficiency Criteria for Nationalised Industries* (London, Allen & Unwin, 1973).

—— *The Soviet Economic System* (London, Allen & Unwin, 1977).

O'Connor, R. and Henry, E. W., *Input-Output Analysis and its Applications* (London, Griffin, 1975).

Oliver, J. M. and Webster, G. H., *Public Policy and Economic Theory* (London, Hutchinson, 1970).

Orleans, L. A., 'China's experience in population control: the elusive model', *World Development* (July–August 1975).

Pack, Howard, 'The employment-output trade-off in LDCs: a microeconomic approach', *Oxford Economic Papers* (November 1974).

—— 'The substitution of labour for capital in Kenyan manufacturing', *Economic Journal* (March 1976).

Park, Yung Chul, 'The role of money in stabilisation policy in developing countries', *IMF Staff Papers* (July 1973).

Parkin, M. and Zis, G. (eds), *Inflation in the Open Economy* (Manchester UP, 1976).

Parry, T. G., 'The international firm and national economic policy', *Economic Journal* (December 1973).

Pearson, Scott R. and Cownie, John, *Commodity Exports and African Economic Development* (Massachusetts, Lexington Books, 1974).

Pechman, J. A. and Okner, B. A., *Who Bears the Tax Burden?* (Washington, Brookings Institute, 1975).

Portes, Richard, 'The control of inflation: lessons from East European experience', *Economica* (May 1977).

Pozen, Robert, *Legal Choices for State Enterprise in the Third World* (New York UP, 1976).

Pratten, C. and Dean, R., *Economies of Large-scale Production in British Industry* (CUP, 1970).

Pressman, J. L. and Wildavsky, A., *Implementation* (Berkely, California UP, 1973).

Rahman, A. H. M. M., *Exports of Manufactures from Developing Countries*, Rotterdam UP, 1973.

Ranis, G. (ed), *Government and Economic Development* (New Haven, Yale UP, 1971).

Rawls, John, *A Theory of Justice* (Cambridge, Mass., Harvard UP, 1971).

Reutlinger, Shlomo and Selowsky, Marcelo, *Malnutrition and Poverty: Magnitude and Policy Options*, World Bank Staff Occasional Papers No. 23, (Baltimore, Johns Hopkins, 1976).

Reynolds, L. G. (ed), *Agriculture in Development Theory* (New Haven, Yale UP, 1975).

Robinson, Warren C. (ed), *Population and Development Planning* (New York, Population Council, 1975).

Rockley, L. E. *The Non-accountant's Guide to Finance* (London, Business Books, 1972).

Roemer, M. and Stern J. J., *Appraisal of Development Projects* (New York, Praeger, 1975).

Rogers, Everett, *Diffusion of Innovations* (New York, Free Press, 1962).

Rowley, C. K. (ed), *Readings in Industrial Economics*, Vol. 2 (London, Macmillan, 1972).

Roy, Shymalal and Blase, Melvin G., 'Farm tractorisation, productivity and labour employment: a case study of Indian Punjab', *Journal of Development Studies* (January 1978).

Sabot, R. H., 'The meaning and measurement of urban surplus labour', *Oxford Economic Papers* (November 1977).

Samuelson, Paul A., *Economics* (New York, McGraw-Hill, 1976).

Scammell, W. M., *International Trade and Payments* (London, Macmillan, 1974).

Schultz, T. W., *Transforming Traditional Agriculture* (New Haven, Yale UP, 1964).

Schumpeter, Joseph, *Capitalism, Socialism and Democracy* (London, Allen & Unwin, 1947).

Scitovsky, Tibor, 'Two concepts of external economies', *Journal of Political Economy* (April 1954) (reproduced in Agarwala and Singh, 1958).

—— *Welfare and Competition* (London, Allen & Unwin, 1970).

Scobie, Grant M. and Posada, Rafael, *The Impact of High-yielding Rice Varieties in Latin America* (Colombia, Centro Internacional de Agricultura Tropical, 1977).

Sharp, Margaret, *The State, the Enterprise and the Individual* (New York, Wiley, 1973).

Sharwani, K., 'Some new evidence on concentration and profitability in Pakistan's large scale manufacturing industries', *Pakistan Development Review* (Autumn 1976).

Shen, T. Y., 'Sectoral development planning in tropical Africa', *Eastern Africa Economic Review* (June 1975).

—— 'Macro development planning in tropical Africa', *Journal of Development Studies* (July 1977).

Shirokov, G. K., *Industrialisation of India* (Moscow, Progress Publishers, 1973).

Shonfield, Andrew, *Modern Capitalism* (London, OUP, 1969).

Simon, Herbert A., *Models of Man* (New York, Wiley, 1957).

Sodersten, Bo, *International Economics* (London, Macmillan, 1971).

Spulber, N. and Horowitz, I., *Quantitative Economic Policy and Planning* (New York, Norton, 1976).

Squire, Lyn and Tak, H. G. van der, *Economic Analysis of Projects* (Baltimore, Johns Hopkins UP, 1975).

Staelin, C. P., 'The cost and composition of Indian exports', *Journal of Development Economics* (September 1974).

Stamper, B. Maxwell, *Population and Planning in Developing Nations* (New York, Population Council, 1977).

Stern, J. J. and Falcon, W. P., *Growth and Development in Pakistan, 1955–69* (Harvard University, Center for International Affairs, 1970).

Stewart, Frances (ed), *Employment, Income Distribution and Development* (London, Cass, 1975).

—— *Technology and Underdevelopment* (London, Macmillan, 1977).

—— and Streeten, Paul, 'New strategies for development: poverty, income distribution and growth', *Oxford Economic Papers* (November 1976).

Stolper, W. F., *Planning Without Facts* (Cambridge, Mass., Harvard UP, 1966).

Sutcliffe, R. B., *Industry and Development* (London, Addison-Wesley, 1971).

Sweezy, Paul M., *The Theory of Capitalist Development* (New York, Monthly Review Press, 1942).

Szereszewski, R., *Structural Changes in the Economy of Ghana, 1891–1911* (London, Weidenfeld & Nicolson, 1965).

Theil, H., *Economic Forecasts and Policy* (Amsterdam, North-Holland, 1961).

Thirlwall, A. P., *Inflation, Saving and Growth in Developing Countries* (London, Macmillan, 1974).

Tien, H. Y., *China's Population Struggle* (Columbus, Ohio State UP, 1973).

Tinbergen, Jan, *On the Theory of Economic Policy* (Amsterdam, North-Holland, 1955).

—— *Central Planning* (New Haven, Yale UP, 1964).

—— *Development Planning* (London, Weidenfeld & Nicolson, 1967 (A)).

—— *Economic Policy: Principles and Design* (Amsterdam, North-Holland, 1967 (B)).

—— *Income Distribution: Analysis and Policies* (Amsterdam, North-Holland, 1975).

Todaro, Michael P., 'A model of labour migration and urban unemployment in less developed countries', *American Economic Review* (March 1969).

—— 'Income expectations, rural-urban migration and employment in Africa', *International Labour Review* (November 1971).

—— *Economics for a Developing World* (London, Longman, 1977).

Townsend, P., *The Concept of Poverty* (London, Heinemann, 1970).

Trewartha, G. T., *A Geography of Population: World Patterns* (New York, Wiley, 1969).

Turnham, David (assisted by Jaeger, I.), *The Employment Problem in Less Developed Countries* (Paris, Organisation for Economic Co-operation and Development (OECD), 1971).

Turvey, R. (ed), *Public Enterprise* (London, Penguin, 1968).

—— *Economic Analysis and Public Enterprises* (London, Allen & Unwin, 1971).

Tyler, William G., 'Labour absorption with import-substituting industrialisation: an examination of elasticities of substitution in the Brazilian manufacturing sector', *Oxford Economic Papers* (March, 1974).

United Nations, *Multinational Corporations in World Development* (New York, United Nations (ref. ST/ECA/190), 1973).

—— Industrial Development Organisation (UNIDO), *Guidelines for Project Evaluation* (New York, United Nations (ref. E. 72.II.B. 11), 1972).

US National Academy of Sciences, *Rapid Population Growth*, Vol. II (Baltimore, Johns Hopkins UP, 1971).

Utton, M. A., *Industrial Concentration* (London, Penguin, 1970).

Vanek, J., *General Theory of Labour Managed Economies* (Ithaca, Cornell UP, 1970).

Vernon, Raymond, 'Competition policy towards multinational corporations', *American Economic Review* (May 1974).

Wall, D. (ed), *Chicago Essays in Economic Development* (Chicago UP, 1972).

Wasay, Abdul, 'An urban poverty-line estimate', *Pakistan Development Review* (Spring 1977).

Waterstone, Albert, *Development Planning: The Lessons of Experience* (London, OUP, 1966).

Westlake, M. J., 'Tax evasion, tax incidence and the distribution of income in Kenya', *Eastern Africa Economic Review* (December 1973).

White, L. J., *Industrial Concentration and Economic Power in Pakistan* (Princeton UP, 1974).

Wildavsky, Aaron, *The Politics of the Budgetary Process* (Boston, Little Brown, 1974).

Williams, M. L., 'The extent and significance of the nationalization of foreign-owned assets in developing countries, 1956–72', *Oxford Economic Papers* (July 1975).

Williamson, O. E., 'Hierarchical control and optimum firm size', *Journal of Political Economy* (April 1967).

Winch, D. M., *Analytical Welfare Economics* (London, Penguin, 1971).

Winston, Gordon C., 'Factor substitution, ex ante and ex post', *Journal of Development Economics* (September 1974).

Worcester, D., *Southern Economic Journal* (October 1973).

World Bank, *Population Policies and Economic Development* (Baltimore, Johns Hopkins UP, 1974).

—— *The Assault on World Poverty* (Baltimore, Johns Hopkins UP, 1975).

—— *World Tables, 1976* (Baltimore, Johns Hopkins UP, 1976).

—— *Annual Report, 1978* (Washington, 1978 (A)).

—— *World Development Report, 1978* (Washington, 1978 (B)).

Yamane, T., *Statistics: An Introductory Analysis* (New York, Harper and Row, 1967).

Yotopoulos, P. A. and Nugent, J. F., *Economics of Development: Empirical Investigations* (New York, Harper and Row, 1976).

Yudelman, M., Butler, G. and Banerji, R., *Technological Change in Agriculture and Employment* (Paris, OECD, 1971).

Author Index

(Does not include references in the bibliography on pages 302–7)

Subject Index